Interdisciplinary perspectives on modern history

Editors
Robert Fogel and Stephan Thernstrom

The emergence of the middle class

Other books in this series

Eric H. Monkkonen: *Police in urban America, 1860–1920*

Mary P. Ryan: *Cradle of the middle class: the family in Oneida County, New York, 1790–1865*

Ann Kussmaul: *Servants in husbandry in early modern England*

Tamara K. Hareven: *Family time and industrial time: the relationship between the family and work in a New England industrial community*

David Rosner: *A once charitable enterprise: hospitals and health care in Brooklyn and New York, 1885–1915*

Arnold R. Hirsch: *Making the second ghetto: race and housing in Chicago, 1940–1960*

Roy Rosenzweig: *Eight hours for what we will: workers and leisure in an industrial city, 1870–1920*

Hal S. Barron: *Those who stayed behind: rural society in nineteenth-century New England*

Jon Gjerde: *From peasants to farmers: the migration from Balestrand, Norway, to the Upper Middle West*

Ewa Morawska: *For bread with butter: the life-worlds of East Central Europeans in Johnstown, Pennsylvania, 1890–1940*

Alexander Keyssar: *Out of work: the first century of unemployment in Massachusetts*

Lance E. Davis and Robert A. Huttenback: *Mammon and the pursuit of Empire: the political economy of British imperialism, 1860–1912* (abridged edition also published)

Reed Ueda: *Avenues to adulthood: the origins of the high school and social mobility in an American suburb*

Allan G. Bogue: *The congressman's Civil War*

Joel Perlmann: *Ethnic differences: schooling and social structure among the Irish, Italians, Jews, and blacks in an American city, 1880–1935*

The emergence of
the middle class

*Social experience in
the American city, 1760–1900*

STUART M. BLUMIN
Cornell University

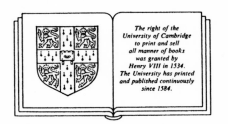

*The right of the
University of Cambridge
to print and sell
all manner of books
was granted by
Henry VIII in 1534.
The University has printed
and published continuously
since 1584.*

CAMBRIDGE UNIVERSITY PRESS
Cambridge
New York   Port Chester   Melbourne   Sydney

Published by the Press Syndicate of the University of Cambridge
The Pitt Building, Trumpington Street, Cambridge CB2 1RP
40 West 20th Street, New York, NY 10011, USA
10 Stamford Road, Oakleigh, Melbourne 3166, Australia

© Cambridge University Press 1989

First published 1989

Library of Congress Cataloging-in-Publication Data
Blumin, Stuart M.
The emergence of the middle class: social experience in the
American city, 1760–1900 / Stuart M. Blumin.
    p. cm. – (Interdisciplinary perspectives on modern history)
Bibliography: p.
Includes index.
ISBN 0-521-25075-7. – ISBN 0-521-37612-2 (pbk.)
1. Middle classes – United States – History – 18th century.
2. Middle classes – United States – History – 19th century. I. Title.
II. Series
HT690.U6B58   1989
305.5'5'0973 – dc19   88–32975
                                                                   CIP

British Library Cataloguing in Publication Data
Blumin, Stuart M. (Stuart Mack)
The emergence of the middle class: social
experience in the American city, 1760–1900
– (Interdisciplinary perspectives on modern
history)
1. United States. Middle classes, 1760–1900
I. Title II. Series
305.5'5'0973

ISBN 0-521-25075-7 hard covers
ISBN 0-521-37612-2 paperback

Transferred to digital printing 2002

This is Deborah's book

Contents

List of tables and figures   *page* viii

Preface   xi

1   The elusive middle class   1

2   "Middling sorts" in the eighteenth-century city   17

3   Toward white collar: nonmanual work in Jacksonian
    America   66

4   Republican prejudice: work, well-being, and social
    definition   108

5   "Things are in the saddle": consumption, urban
    space, and the middle-class home   138

6   Coming to order: voluntary associations and the
    organization of social life and consciousness   192

7   Experience and consciousness in the antebellum city   230

8   White-collar worlds: the postbellum middle class   258

Epilogue: City, town, village, farm – the geography
             of class in nineteenth-century America   298

Notes   311

Bibliography   389

Index   424

Tables and figures

Tables

2.1 Floor space in dwelling by occupational category, Philadelphia, 1798   *page* 44

2.2 Zone of residence by occupational category, Philadelphia, 1798   47

2.3 Median floor space in dwelling by occupational category and zone of residence, Philadelphia, 1798   47

2.4 Assessed value of dwelling by occupational category, Philadelphia, 1798   51

3.1 Selected nonmanual employees by age, American-born white males, Philadelphia, 1860   77

4.1 Occupational category by reported value of real and personal property, males aged 18 and older, Philadelphia, 1860   118

5.1 School attendance by age of child and occupational category of father, American-born white children, Philadelphia, 1860   190

8.1 Male householders in a three-block portion of the northwestern periphery of Philadelphia, 1880, by age and occupational category   283

Figures

2.1 Southeast corner of Third and Market Streets, Philadelphia ("Cooke's Folly")   24

2.2 Map of Philadelphia, 1796   25

2.3 Mean tax assessment by ward, Philadelphia, 1798   43

2.4 Selected characteristics of street and alley dwellings, High Street Ward, Philadelphia, 1798   49

3.1 South Boston Iron Company advertisement, 1851   72

3.2 Tailor shop interior, from Edward Hazen, *The Panorama of Professions and Trades*, 1836   85

3.3 D. D. Badger & Co., Architectural Iron Works, New York, ca. 1860   87

3.4   Interior, L. S. Drigg's lace and bonnet store, Boston, 1852   88
3.5   Plan of the Novelty Works, New York, 1851   90
3.6   Entrance, Novelty Works, New York, 1851   91
3.7   William Strickland, *Christ Church* (with retail stores in
      foreground), Philadelphia, 1811   92
3.8   E. M. Blunt, print shop and store, New York, 1811   94
3.9   J. C. Booth & Co., clothing store, New York, 1845   96
3.10 Chestnut Street, Philadelphia, 1860   97
3.11 John H. Pray & Sons, carpet store, Boston, 1855   99
3.12 Lord & Taylor, dry goods emporium, New York, ca. 1860   100
3.13 Jayne's Granite Buildings, Philadelphia, 1850   101
3.14 Interior, Ball, Black & Co., jewelry store, New York, ca.
      1855   102
3.15 Interior, D. Appleton & Co., bookstore, New York, 1854   103
3.16 Interior, I. M. Singer & Co., sewing machine salesroom,
      New York, 1857   104
3.17 Interior, Charles Oakford's hat store, Philadelphia, ca.
      1855   104
3.18 Interior, Ball's Great Daguerrian Gallery of the West,
      Cincinnati, 1854   105
3.19 Interior, Canfield, Brother & Co.'s jewelry store,
      Baltimore, 1854   106
3.20 Interior, A. Rankin & Co., hosiery store, New York, 1852   106
5.1   Bookbinder, 1845   142
5.2   Bookbindery interior, 1845   143
5.3   Drinker's Court, Philadelphia   148
5.4   27 Vandam Street, New York   152
5.5   328 and 330 South Third Street, Philadelphia   154
5.6   Elevation of a design for a moderately priced city house,
      from Gervase Wheeler, *Homes for the People*, ca. 1855   156
5.7   Selected areal grid-units, Philadelphia, 1860   167
5.8   South side of Pine Street, below Third, Philadelphia   171
5.9   Stampers Street, Philadelphia   172
5.10 Master Charlie's sidewalk acquaintances, 1857   181
5.11 Master Charley in the parlor, 1860   182
8.1   Factory production in the 1880s: sugar making   263
8.2   Felt makers, 1876   264
8.3   Prang's Aids for Object Teaching: Trades &
      Occupations – Shoemaker   265
8.4   Prang's Aids for Object Teaching: Trades &
      Occupations – Tailor   266
8.5   Houses on the Philadelphia nonsuburban periphery   282
8.6   Schlicht & Field Co. catalogue, 1886   294

Preface

Nathaniel Booth must bear part of the responsibility for this book. Some years ago, when I was in the early stages of research for a book set in Kingston, New York, I came across a long and detailed diary that Booth had maintained while living in Kingston during the 1840s and 1850s. Reading the diary helped me immeasurably to come to grips with the central concerns of my book – the changing patterns of local life and the changing meanings of communal identity in an emerging nineteenth-century American city. At that time, Booth was interesting to me primarily as a participant in this quieter side of the nineteenth-century urban revolution – the crossing of what I called the urban threshold. But as I finished my book I began to think about Booth in a somewhat different way. Stimulated by what were then novel historical accounts of increasingly distinct working-class cultures in both England and America, and by new works framed in the somewhat older tradition of elite urban studies, I began to look upon my old friend Booth as a neglected American of a most important kind. Booth, who made his living as a grocer, an occasional freelance bookkeeper, and an increasingly busy shipper of Kingston bluestone, was neither a manual laborer nor a member of any sort of upper class. To call him "middle class," however, was to place him in an ambiguous, largely unexamined social category to which I and many other historians had made frequent but only casual reference. There was no longer anything casual about the terms "working class" and "upper class" in American historical writing; on the contrary, they were coming to refer to specific social patterns and identities, and to specific persons whose lives were very different from the one recorded in Booth's diary. Perhaps, I speculated, "middle class," too, could be made to shed its seemingly harmless ambiguity to take on specific and useful new meanings. Perhaps the experiences, values, and social identities of Nathaniel Booth and a large number of other Americans like him could be better understood in this way. Nathaniel Booth, in short, made me inquire into the meaning of "middle class" as a specific aspect of American social development. The present book, which wanders far from the pages of Booth's diary, is a result of that inquiry.

Booth's contribution to these pages was entirely involuntary. I owe a heartier acknowledgment, therefore, to those individuals and institutions who knowingly and willingly assisted me in my work. In this project, as in all others since I joined the faculty of Cornell University, virtually all of my research expenses were defrayed by the Return Jonathan Meigs research fund, administered by the Department of History. The still more precious resource of free time was provided by a sabbatical leave from Cornell, and by a Fellowship for University Teachers awarded by the National Endowment for the Humanities for the academic year 1987–8. Expert assistance and access to collections were willingly offered by the archivists and librarians of the Historical Society of Pennsylvania, the Library Company of Philadelphia, the Presbyterian Historical Society, the Philadelphia City Archives, the Philadelphia Register of Wills, the Philadelphia Social History Project, the Grand Lodge of Free and Accepted Masons of Pennsylvania, the New-York Historical Society, the New York Public Library, the Massachusetts Historical Society, Baker Library of the Harvard University Graduate School of Business Administration, the National Museum of American History of the Smithsonian Institution, the Library of Congress, the British Library, the Institute of Historical Research (London), the University of London Library, the Guildhall Library (London), and, most frequently of all, the John M. Olin Graduate Research Library of Cornell University. Undoubtedly there is a measure of institutional pride as well as gratitude in my wishing to single out Caroline Spicer and the rest of the staff of Olin's Reference Department for special praise. They help to make Olin Library the most satisfying of homes for scholarly research. Several Cornell students willingly endured the grim labor of coding census schedules and probate inventories, searching through city directories, and feeding Revolutionary-age information into Bicentennial-age computers. Robert F. Berkhofer III, Janet Glass, Jenny Nusbaum, and David Futrelle made the largest contributions of this sort. A large portion of the first draft was typed by Connie Kindig, Jackie Hubble, Marianne Christofferson, and Cathy Hendley. The maps and bar charts were drawn by the Syracuse University Cartographic Laboratory, under the supervision of Michael Kirchoff. The editors of *The American Historical Review* and *The Journal of Urban History* kindly permitted me to reprint portions of my articles "The Hypothesis of Middle-Class Formation in Nineteenth-Century America: A Critique and Some Proposals," *American Historical Review* 90 (1985): 299–338, and "Explaining the New Metropolis: Perception, Depiction, and Analysis in Mid-Nineteenth Century New York City," *Journal of Urban History* 11 (1984): 9–38.

Several colleagues and friends took time and energy from their own work to read and criticize mine. I am grateful to Clyde Griffen and Joel H. Silbey for their incisive criticisms of parts of the first draft of this book, and to Glenn Altschuler, who read and carefully criticized, to my great profit, the entire first draft. Richard Stott usefully criticized a later draft, but his most important contributions, and the ones I most enjoyed, were the insights he offered during countless conversations we have held during the past several years to discuss both of our projects. I can only hope that Richard's work benefited as much as mine did from these invariably lively and delightful talks. Stephan Thernstrom, as co-editor of these Interdisciplinary Perspectives on Modern History, supported my work from beginning to end, always in the strongest terms, and with a scholarly authority that often helped me find the courage to continue. I shall never cease to be grateful for his generosity. Frank Smith, my editor at the Cambridge University Press, was no less supportive, and a pleasure to work with, as was everyone else with whom I had contact at the Press.

A much older and more profound debt, never adequately acknowledged, is to Thomas C. Cochran, whose career and character are best expressed by the nearly forgotten phrase "a gentleman and a scholar." The help he gave me many years ago reflected both of these qualities, and it is the gentleman as much as the scholar whom I remember with such fondness today. Finally, there is Deborah, who has helped in ways beyond counting, and with a meaning beyond expressing. It is with the deepest pleasure that I dedicate this book to her.

Ithaca, New York   STUART M. BLUMIN

1 *The elusive middle class*

"The most valuable class in any community," wrote Walt Whitman from his editorial desk in 1858, "is the middle class, the men of moderate means, living at the rate of a thousand dollars a year or thereabouts."[1] A strange statement from a man who wrote so lovingly and so often of "blacksmiths with grimed and hairy chests," of "the builders and steerers of ships and the wielders of axes and mauls, and the drivers of horses," of "laborers seated at noon-time with their open dinner-kettles." Whitman found little poetry in the lives of the salaried suburbanites his editorial goes on to describe, and, considering the whole of his work, we may doubt considerably the depth of his own belief in this fleeting editorial judgment.[2] Yet, his statement is significant for the very nature of its phrasing, and for the seemingly casual association it makes between social class and a particular level of income. A generation or two earlier the term "middle class" seldom appeared on the printed page in America, and probably was seldom uttered in either the city or the country. Rather, a variety of less precise, less concise, and usually plural phrases expressed the idea of social intermediacy – "people of middling rank," the "middling sorts," the "middle condition of mankind," occasionally the "middle (or middling) classes."[3] Although these phrases increasingly were joined to claims of social respectability, an older tradition associated them with very modest levels of social and economic aspiration, closer to the bottom of society than to the top. The term "most valuable" was, therefore, freshly linked to the term "middle class." And finally, the specification of $1,000 as the defining income of the middle class is particularly significant, as this was a level of income denied to nearly all who worked at the manual trades and less skilled jobs that Whitman so often celebrated in his poetry, and who asserted respectability only by setting themselves apart – as society's bone and sinew, as the real producers of wealth – from those who asserted superiority by means of wealth and manners. Whitman, minstrel of the hard-muscled, suntanned common man, momentarily gave voice to a very

1

different kind of adulation that, in fact, was becoming characteristic of the American culture to which he was so deeply committed. For that one moment Whitman celebrated, in the clearest possible terms, the emergence in America of the white-collar, suburbanizing middle class.

It is the purpose of this book to expand upon that moment, not by celebrating, but by examining at close range the various processes that gave meaning to Whitman's statement. Put another way, I seek to analyze here what can be called the development, or formation, and the elevation, or rise, of the American middle class. All of these phrases, and particularly the last, are weary clichés and signifiers of much abused concepts pertaining to the nature of American social development. To invoke them at all, much less to base an entire study on them, is to court serious risks that range from ambiguity to irrelevance, and to confront continuously the paradox that the concept of the middle class, historically and in the present, is both pervasive and elusive; indeed, that it is elusive precisely because it is pervasive. Americans use the term with remarkable imprecision; yet, we seem to represent something very important about our culture and society by doing so. It is here that ambiguity is joined to irrelevance, within the powerful historiographical tradition invoked by the term "consensus." America, according to this tradition (or these traditions – one can speak here of both the "consensual" and the "ethnocultural" points of view), has had no middle class, but rather a pervasive middle-class culture, and a society in which the most serious conflicts have revolved around differences of race, ethnicity, religion, and region rather than the diverging interests and ideologies of economic classes. In this sense, the term "middle class" is a misnomer and is best understood as a somewhat inappropriate linguistic import from England, where a genuinely intermediate social group, located between a formally aristocratic upper class and a decidedly plebeian lower class, struggled on behalf of those bourgeois values that here so easily won acceptance that they became nearly synonymous with the national culture. "Americans," wrote Louis Hartz more than thirty years ago, "a kind of national embodiment of the concept of the bourgeoisie, have . . . rarely used that concept in their social thought," for "a triumphant middle class . . . can take itself for granted."[4]

Hartz, like Alexis de Tocqueville before him, attempted to define the modalities of national character and political culture in America.[5] This book is rooted in a somewhat different tradition, one that emphasizes the variations that spring from specific social contexts, and that focuses upon the ways in which unequal distributions of wealth, income, opportunity, workplace tasks and authority, political power,

legal status, and social prestige have organized the lives and consciousness of specific groups of Americans. This tradition has enjoyed
an impressive resurgence in recent years, most notably in numerous
studies of working-class culture, social life, and protest that have done
much to define the lower limit of the bourgeois consensus, and to
place a substantial number of working-class men and women beyond
that limit. To be sure, some of these studies have identified groups
or types of workers whose ambitions, life-styles, and political values
were resolutely "middle class" (Paul Faler's "loyalists" and Bruce
Laurie's "revivalists" come most readily to mind), but each of these
studies (and others) points to workers – "traditionalists," "radicals,"
or simply unlabeled toilers and strikers – who inhabited a social,
moral, and ideological world that was different from and even antagonistic to that of the professionals and businessmen who came to
be called the middle class. These workers were, and knew they were,
of another social order.[6] Meanwhile, other scholars have delineated
urban upper classes that formed not merely an *haute bourgeoisie* of
extremely wealthy professionals, merchants, bankers, manufacturers,
and speculators but also an aspiring aristocracy, at least in the me-
taphoric sense of an ascriptive upper class that succeeded to varying
degrees and for varying lengths of time in denying its bourgeois
origins.[7] And finally, underscoring these studies of distinctive working-class and patrician cultures are several recent analyses of the dimensions of economic inequality in nineteenth-century America,
which point to striking increases in inequality in the antebellum era
and to the maintenance of high levels of inequality throughout the
nineteenth century.[8] It is becoming increasingly clear, in short, that
Americans diverged widely in their economic circumstances, and that
they translated their economic differences into significant differences
in life-style, outlook, and aspiration. However broad the bourgeois
consensus may have been in comparison to European societies, it did
not preclude the formation of distinct classes within American society.
The all-encompassing American bourgeoisie, then, may well have
been a class after all – the power of its values serving to reinforce
rather than to destroy social class boundaries.[9]

But does all this necessarily lead to the concept of an emerging
middle class? The discovery of definable social classes at the top and
bottom of society lends plausibility to the proposition that such a class
or classes also may be found in its middle, and accentuates the relative
neglect of middling folk by the very historians who have advanced
our understanding of the nineteenth-century urban and industrial
revolutions by focusing upon urban elites and industrial workers as
distinct historical groups. But this discovery does little or nothing to

establish the character or significance of an emerging intermediate class, which, if it is to be understood as a distinct social formation, must be examined directly and in appropriate theoretical terms. A few years before Louis Hartz described the "triumphant middle class" that really was no class, the Marxist sociologist C. Wright Mills wrote, "The early history of the middle classes in America is a history of how the small entrepreneur, the free man of the old middle classes, came into his time of daylight, of how he fought against enemies he could see, and of the world he built."[10] At first glance an anticipation of E. P. Thompson's insistence on the historicity of class, and on the formation of classes as concrete, discrete, and significant historical events,[11] Mills's statement actually introduced a discussion of the "old middle classes" of the nineteenth century that differed little from Hartz's conception of a bourgeois society. "Here the middle class was so broad a stratum and of such economic weight," Mills continued, "that even by the standards of the statistician the society as a whole was a middle-class society."[12] Apparently, the consensual interpretation of at least the pre-industrial and early industrial American past ran broad and deep in the 1950s, when Mills wrote these lines. Neither Mills nor anyone else of his generation saw any need to pursue further the suggestion that the "old" middle class was a definable and significant social formation of a specific historical era, or that the "small entrepreneur" shaped a new social identity through his struggle against "enemies he could see."

Historians writing after Mills and Hartz occasionally used the term "middle class" to refer to some specific, intermediate stratum within American society – as did Sam Bass Warner, Jr., for example, when he described as "middle class" that segment of Boston's population that moved to the streetcar suburbs during the last three decades of the nineteenth century.[13] But it was not until twenty-five years after Mills wrote in *White Collar* of how the "old middle classes" came into their "time of daylight" that American historians began to translate this vivid expression into propositions concerning the formation of a distinct and even self-conscious middle class during the nineteenth century. In 1976 Burton Bledstein purported to find within an emerging nineteenth-century "culture of professionalism" "a cultural process by which the middle class in America matured and defined itself." "The middle class in America," Bledstein wrote, "appeared as a new class with an unprecedented enthusiasm for its own forms of self-discipline."[14] Bledstein did not pursue this idea as far as he might have, but his suggestion that the middle class was a new and maturing entity within a larger society was something rather new in American historical literature, as was the language he used to express it. Two years later, in his book on religious revivals and social change in Rochester, Paul E. Johnson stated the case for middle-class formation even more forcefully. To Johnson, the efforts of "whig politicians, industrial moralizers, temperance advocates, missionaries, and family reformers" to "build a world that replaced force, barbarism, and unrestrained passion with Christian self-control" constituted "the moral imperative around which the northern middle class *became a class.*"[15] Also in 1978, Paul Boyer wrote, somewhat more temperately, that these efforts at moral and social reform helped "an embryonic urban middle class define itself," and he described a century-long struggle by the middle class to "achieve a greater degree of internal order and cohesion."[16] And in 1981, Mary P. Ryan framed her stimulating analysis of family life, evangelical reform, and urban-industrial development in Utica, New York, as "a chronicle of the formation of a new American middle class," complaining as she did so that the middle class "is largely a residual category in American historiography, the assumed, but largely unexamined, context for much of the writing about popular culture and reform movements." "Historians," wrote Ryan, "have hardly begun to analyze middle Americans as a class unto themselves."[17]

Despite the subsequent appearance of several studies that make more or less serious reference to an emerging middle class, Ryan's complaint remains apt.[18] How, then, shall we respond to the challenge "to analyze middle Americans as a class unto themselves"? What are the most promising theoretical foundations for constructing a solid substantive narrative of the formation and ascendancy of an American middle class? Historians are ordinarily predisposed to dispense with this kind of question, and to proceed at once to organizing a narrative that explains and justifies itself in the telling. In the present instance, however, it is precisely the kind of question that ought to be considered – and answered – in some detail before turning to the details of time and place.

The most obvious theoretical foundation for the study of an emerging social class is Marxism. However, for this study it is also one of the most problematic, for the equally obvious reason that in its most common forms Marxism denies the significance of intermediate classes as social groups, save for the temporarily intermediate (and ultimately dominant) class that represents a new and ascending mode of production. Other intermediate groups, according to this central train of Marxist thought, are both temporary and illusory, consisting of mere appendages of the dominant class or of transitional classes that represent the remains of former modes of production.[19] Thus, although Marxists generally recognize (as did Marx himself) the existence of intermediate groups in any given society at any given time,[20] many also insist that the concept of "middle class" obscures the fundamental two-class structure of capitalist (or feudal) society, and distorts the concept of class by creating an artificial social group that bears no definable and essential relation to the means of production, and contains within it no potential for genuine coherence and consciousness. Even the new and apparently robust intermediate formations of mature capitalist society are dismissed in this way. Several contemporary Marxists, eager to demonstrate that the "new middle class" does not threaten Marxism as a general theory of historical development, have devoted considerable attention to theoretical demonstrations of the essential differences between intermediate groups and "the two basic classes of a capitalist formation," or the "contradictory class locations" (and hence the classlessness) of intermediate strata, or, most recently, the idea that "middle-class formation is an expression of the class polarization process"; indeed, that the middle class, far from being "the harbinger of a new order," is "gradually disintegrating as a class."[21] In sum, "There is no fixed place for the middle class, no determined role, no necessary direction or certainty of outcome when the class asserts itself. The historical existence, the place in the social division of labor, the class situation of the middle are expressions of a larger set of class relations."[22]

The would-be historian of the middle class need not be discouraged by this onslaught. The Marxist objection to the concept of middle-class formation rests ultimately on the distinction between the essential classes – classes that are generated by the capitalist mode of production – and the inessential intermediate groups that bear no significant or consistent relation to the means of production. It can be countered, however, that the distinction between essential and inessential classes is derived not from observed differences in social, cultural, or ideological coherence at any given time but from the predictive aspects of what is, at bottom, an epochal theory of past and future capitalist development.[23] Marxists predict – on the basis of the logical structure of this theory – that intermediate classes will simply dissolve and be absorbed into the two essential classes as capitalism becomes more fully developed. In the meantime, having no essential role to play (at best the middle class "mediates the capital/labor social relation"), intermediate classes are simply and safely dismissed, and the basic two-class model confirmed, even with respect to earlier stages of capitalist development. Marxists do recognize the deductive character of this argument and sometimes employ the distinction between "class" and "stratification" to give voice to the superiority of theory over mere observation: "Class is an analytic

category with which the social structure is defined. Stratification describes divisions within the class structure."[24] But is it not correct to
insist that at some point this distinction between essential classes and
inessential classes or strata be subjected to empirical rather than logical
proof? In his recent attempt to reconcile Marxist theory with the persistence of intermediate classes, Dale L. Johnson writes that "histor-
ical/empirical research must be carried out within the premise that
middle-class formation is an expression of the class polarization process." *Must* it indeed? Is it necessarily the case that class polarization
is the essence of capitalist development and that any evidence of the
formation or continuing vitality of intermediate classes must be sub-
ordinated to that deeper reality? Marxists can, I believe, fairly propose
a long developmental perspective that will permit observation of the
eventual disappearance of transitional and inessential classes, but in
the meantime they can only assert that a two-class model for describing past and present capitalist society is something more than a necessity for their own theoretical consistency. And perhaps we might
note that if Johnson is deprived of his premise, there remains in his
discussion the interesting proposition that the American "petty
bourgeoisie," "formed . . . in premonopoly stages of capitalist development," was "a social class of major social weight" throughout the
nineteenth century.[25]

Rejecting this rather schematic brand of Marxism does not require
that we reject as well the fundamental insights of Marx and his followers concerning the relevance of classes to our understanding of
the history of capitalist society. What ought to be resisted is, to use
J. H. Hexter's terms, Marx's "complete and coherent theory of social
change," his "package deal" for the interpretation of history.[26] Any
"framework" for the study of real societies, writes Hexter, ought to
be a "temporary scaffolding," not "a prefabricated theory of social
change for which historians will forever thereafter be called upon to
supply proofs. [It] must take social and economic groupings as it finds
them."[27] A middle class that was something more than an "expression
of the class polarization process" may well have been one of those
social and economic groupings in the nineteenth century, and I would
observe that there are scholars who have worked wholly or partly
within the Marxist tradition who have done other than merely argue
the middle class out of existence. Even Dale Johnson, who insists on
the transitory character of the middle class, does after all describe it
as a class, not as a stratum or a collection of "contradictory class
locations," and concedes its importance as a class in the nineteenth
century. Others follow a similar line of thought: Nicos Poulantzas
more abstractly in *Classes in Contemporary Capitalism*, C. Wright Mills

more concretely in *White Collar*.[28] And there are still others who, beginning with Marxist categories, define intermediate classes without bothering either to subordinate them to more basic classes or to predict their eventual dissolution. Stanislaw Ossowski, for example, has found within the basic structure of Marxist theory the necessity of at least one intermediate class, for Marx specified two basic dichotomous relations – ownership or nonownership of the means of production and employment or nonemployment of hired labor. The "overlapping of two mutually incompatible dichotomic divisions leads to the establishment of at least a third category, and thus a three-term scheme emerges." More specifically, from the very architecture of Marxist theory there emerges an intermediate class consisting "of those who own the means of production but do not employ hired labour."[29] What is notable is not Ossowski's discovery of independent producers – all Marxists are aware of them – but his discussion of a class of such producers no less clearly linked to the means of production than are the bourgeoisie or the proletariat and, so long as the dual dichotomies remain unaligned, no more likely than they to disappear.

Ossowski's interpretation of Marx is singularly static and, as we will see, yields an intermediate group that does not accord with nineteenth-century American documents. More dynamic, and of greater use to the empirically minded historian of the middle class, are Anthony Giddens's attempts to leaven Marxist theories of class development with a Weberian yeast.[30] In *The Class Structure of the Advanced Societies*, Giddens maintains the Marxist insistence on "the explanatory salience of class as central to the notion of class society." "A class society," he writes, "is not one in which there simply exist classes, but one in which class relationships are of primary significance to the explanatory interpretation of large areas of social conduct." At the same time, he recognizes the crucial problem of implementing this fundamental proposition in the analysis of specific societies, of identifying in specific ways "*the modes in which* 'economic' relationships become translated into 'non-economic' social structures." Marxism by itself seems inadequate to the task, and Giddens offers instead a broader method for making the transition from the abstract theory of class to concrete descriptions and analyses of what he calls "the *structuration* of class relationships" in the real world. Giddens first distinguishes between "mediate structuration," by which he means the degree of "mobility closure" that provides for – or, in the case of highly mobile, "open" societies, fails to provide for – "the reproduction of common life experience over the generations," and three forms of "proximate structuration" that "condition or shape class formation" in more immediate ways. These three are the division of labor within productive enterprises; authority relationships within those enterprises (here Giddens seems to be thinking of large, multitiered corporations and of Ralf Dahrendorf's objection to the Marxist focus on legal ownership of, rather than effective authority over, the means of production in a corporate economy); and class relations originating in the sphere of consumption, in particular those identifiable "distributive groupings" that arise from common patterns of consumption. To Giddens, it is the degree to which these sources of "proximate structuration" converge or diverge within a more or less mobile society that determines both the clarity and the salience of class in a given society. Where there is an inconsistent relation among type of work, authority, and levels and patterns of consumption, and at the same time a high degree of vertical mobility, the class principle will be weak. Where these relations are consistent within a setting of "mobility closure," they reinforce each other and reaffirm the significance of class. To Giddens, in short, class is an empirical question – a principle of social organization that can vary in shape and in strength between one society and another. It is not a necessary adjunct to a theory of capitalist development. Even more than Ossowski, Giddens suggests the probability of discovering in any society more than two classes and even proposes that *"a threefold class structure is generic to capitalist society,"* for this is the consistent pattern of relations between the sources of structuration that Giddens purports to find in the capitalist world, at least in the advanced capitalist world of the twentieth century.[31]

The real usefulness of Giddens's theory to the historian of the nineteenth-century middle class, however, may lie not so much in his overlapping categories of class-forming experience as in his adjoining discussion of class consciousness. The issue of middle-class consciousness is a difficult one, for the favorable position of middling folk in American society and politics, in combination with the individualism that lies at the heart of the middle-class system of values, would seem to preclude the development of the kind of class-based solidarity that Marxists call class consciousness.[32] And as ethnocultural political historians point out, political movements based explicitly on the grievances or aspirations of intermediate social classes are indeed rare in American history.[33] But is this because middle-class consciousness does not exist or because it is built around values that reduce the likelihood of its manifestation in politics? This question brings us face-to-face with a central paradox in the concept of middle-class formation, the building of a class that binds itself together as a social group in part through the common embrace of an ideology of social atomism. Giddens speaks directly to this paradox by distinguishing between class consciousness and what he calls "class awareness":

> We may say that, in so far as class is a structured phenomenon, there will tend to exist a common awareness and acceptance of similar attitudes and beliefs, linked to a common style of life, among the members of the class. "Class awareness," as I use the term here, does not involve a recognition [admission?] that these attitudes and beliefs signify a particular class affiliation, or the recognition [admission?] that there exist other classes, characterized by different attitudes, beliefs, and styles of life; "class consciousness," by contrast, . . . does imply both of these. The difference between class awareness and class consciousness is a fundamental one, because class awareness may take the form of *a denial of the existence or reality of classes*. Thus the class awareness of the middle class, in so far as it involves beliefs which place a premium upon individual responsibility and achievement, is of this order.[34]

I have taken the liberty to suggest a slight emendation of terms in this statement, because it does not seem possible that the members of a class can be aware of the "similar attitudes and beliefs" associated with their "common style of life" without recognizing "that there exist other classes, characterized by different attitudes, beliefs, and styles of life." But this change of meaning, though not trivial, does not alter the larger purpose of Giddens's distinction between "consciousness" and "awareness," which suggests that different types of class perception – including those that do not posit classes as "conflict groups," as antagonistic interest groups, or even as significant groups of any kind – can grow out of situations in which class is a social and cultural reality.[35] Moreover, certain kinds of consciousness or awareness may be expected from certain classes, the middle class in particular being the one most likely to express awareness of its common attitudes and beliefs as a denial of the significance of class.

Giddens, in sum, provides the historian of the middle class with a theory that no longer subordinates the middle to the polar extremes and no longer requires that a class manifest itself in an aggressive and self-conscious ideology – in what is usually called class consciousness. This theory creates the opportunity for reformulating the hypothesis of middle-class formation in terms of the "structuration" of certain types of social and cultural experience, to which expressions of class consciousness or awareness are related as a matter of secondary importance. But is it persuasive? I believe it is, insofar as it enables us to look for patterns of experience (patterns that might reasonably be called "middle class") that we would not discover if we thought only of different kinds of social strata or if we focused only on how class manifests itself in consciousness. This is, admittedly, a theoretical approach to class and class formation that is significantly more modest and less assertive than that of the Marxists. But for this very reason, and because it is more genuinely exploratory, it is, I believe, a more workable and ultimately more satisfactory response to Ryan's call for analysis of "middle Americans as a class unto themselves."

I would, indeed, state the central questions that will guide this study even more broadly than Giddens suggests, for the specific experiences (or forms of "structuration") that he describes may be questioned, and others added, without disturbing the essential idea that classes are formed through the convergence of relevant experience. Did significant aspects of the daily lives of middling folk change during the nineteenth century in ways that indicate the formation of a new, relatively coherent, and relatively clearly bounded (if not self-conscious) social group, located in an intermediate position within a hierarchically organized social structure? More simply put, can we identify an emerging middle-class way of life in the nineteenth century? What were the specific components of that way of life? And assuming that such a convergence of relevant experience did occur, how did it affect the social identification of middling folk? Did they become conscious or aware of themselves as a middle class?

To frame questions this broadly is to risk losing contact with Marx's crucial insights into the ways classes are formed through economic relations and the conflicts arising out of them. In an earlier discussion I identified five substantive types or areas of personal and social experience – work, consumption, residential location, formal and informal voluntary association, and family organization and strategy – that would seem to encompass nearly all relevant aspects of an emerging middle-class "way of life."[36] These categories of experience still seem useful to me as ways of adding flesh to the theoretical skeleton I have described, but in the chapters that follow I will, in Marxian fashion, accord primacy to changes in work, to the economic and social relations of the workplace, and to the social identities that arose from, and were most generally framed in terms of, economic activity. On the other hand, I will examine other dimensions of social life, including those "originating in the sphere of consumption," and, like Giddens (but not like either Marx or Weber), will describe them as aspects of class and class formation. As I have already suggested, I will not feel obliged to discuss intermediate classes as inessential or transitory, or to subordinate middle-class formation to the purportedly more profound and enduring process of class polarization. And finally, I will further distance myself from the epochal (one might say millenarian) Marx,[37] by embracing E. P. Thompson's suggestion that classes are formed in the variable, historically specific, day-to-day experiences of ordinary people – that class is "something which in fact happens (and can be shown to have happened) in human relationships" – even though Thompson himself might object to the application of this idea to intermediate classes, and to experiences that express social differentiation but not overt conflict.[38]

This book, then, is a study of middling folk, and of the proposition that Americans (or at least urban Americans) of middling economic and social position were formed and formed themselves into a relatively coherent and ascending middle class during the middle decades of the nineteenth century. It should be noted that this is not one subject but three. The ascendancy, or elevation, of the nineteenth-century middle class to a level of affluence, prestige, and power distinctly higher than that of eighteenth-century "middling sorts" is at once interconnected with and separate from the formation of a more distinct middle class. Class formation could, after all, have occurred without any visible shift in the location of its members within economic, social, or political hierarchies. That it did involve such a shift adds a dimension to the story of the emerging middle class that is not anticipated in the foregoing theoretical discussion. The history of middling Americans, moreover, is worth examining even without reference to the emergence and elevation of a coherent middle class. As I have already observed, our understanding of the urban and industrial revolutions of the nineteenth century has been enhanced by many recent studies of urban elites and of industrial workers, but only a beginning has been made toward fitting into this story of economic development and social transformation the experiences of large numbers of men and women who were neither elites nor manual workers. Their story too deserves to be told, whether or not it is the story of increasing class coherence. It must also be understood that class and class formation are abstractions that acquire meaning only when they do describe the patterns inherent in vast numbers of individual experiences and habits of mind. Put another way, if this is a study of middle-class formation in the contexts of urbanization and capitalist industrial development in America, it is also a study of Joseph Graisbury, an eighteenth-century Philadelphia tailor who recorded in his business records the time he lost to bouts of drunkenness; of Jane Hewett, a tavernkeeper listed at just above the median assessment on the 1783 Annapolis tax list; of Nathan Webb, a Boston schoolteacher who in 1788 became indignant when a young clerk refused to attend a dancing school in the company of a master saddler;

of William Gowans, who fought off smallpox and other discouragements to become a retail bookseller in New York City in the early 1830s; of William Hoffman, who left his parents' farm in 1848 to work as a clerk in an Albany dry goods store; and of Elizabeth Ginna, who in 1855 purchased a moderately priced piano from J. E. Gould's Great Piano and Melodeon Emporium in Philadelphia. The social transformation and elevation of the American middle class are, at the same time, the stories of Joseph Graisbury, Jane Hewett, Nathan Webb, William Gowans, William Hoffman, and Elizabeth Ginna.

The temporal focus of this study is on the three or four decades preceding the Civil War, which a number of historians have already identified as the period in which classes began to take shape in American cities, but its boundaries extend beyond the antebellum period – backward to the final third of the eighteenth century, and forward into the final third of the nineteenth century. The look forward into the post–Civil War period is suggested by my judgment, which will emerge in due course, that a middle class was *not* fully formed before the war, and that developments of the postwar period – most notably, widening differences between the worlds of nonmanual and manual work, the expansion of middle-class suburbanization, and the resumption and expansion of social and economic conflict that was phrased in class terms – contributed to the further articulation of the American middle class.[39] Looking backward into the eighteenth century responds to the judgment by several historians that the "middling sort" of that era "did not form a class,"[40] and, more generally, that we must "recognize the problems in employing the concept of class in eighteenth-century society, for the historical stage of a mature class formation had not yet been reached."[41] It seems particularly important to be able to understand and evaluate these statements – to ascertain that the middle class had not already emerged by the end of the eighteenth century – before we conclude that middle-class formation was specific to the nineteenth century, or that it could have occurred only in the contexts of large-scale industrialization and urbanization.[42] A close analysis of the social circumstances and identities of preindustrial "middling sorts" is, therefore, an indispensable prologue to the examination of the nineteenth-century middle class.

Class formation is ordinarily assumed to be an urban phenomenon, for it is in cities that people perceive and behave toward one another categorically, and in which occupational and social classification is least often mitigated by personal relationships that cross the lines between social categories. In the city, writes Louis Wirth, "Our physical contacts are close, but our social contacts are distant. . . . We see the uniform which denotes the role of the functionaries, and are oblivious to the personal eccentricities hidden behind the uniform."[43] Cities, too, are generally thought to be centers of social innovation, "crucibles" of social change, to use Gary Nash's image, "electric transformers," "the accelerators of all historical time," to use Fernand Braudel's.[44] The few existing studies of middle-class formation (or that make more than a passing reference to this idea) are set in cities, albeit fairly small ones – Utica, early Rochester, Providence[45] – and the present study is also addressed to urban populations and places. It is not a case study of a single city or set of specific cities, however, for I wanted to be able to distinguish between local particularities and general patterns; to avoid the limits and lacunae of information that are invariably encountered in any specific locality; to utilize data that are not strictly local and that are difficult to integrate into local studies (national magazines, for example); and to call upon the data and discussions of other scholars who have addressed relevant questions in a wide variety of places.[46] This is, indeed, a work of synthesis as well as a work of original research, although it is by no means free of regional and other forms of locational bias – to the Northeast, for example, and even to the large cities of the Northeast. I do not apologize for this bias, but merely call the reader's attention to it, as well as to my attempt to address (and to some extent redress) it in the epilogue.

My own research has been conducted mainly in the Northeast's (and the nation's) largest cities, especially Philadelphia and New York. Indeed, it is possible to discover a case study of Philadelphia imbedded within the chapters that follow, and perhaps another of New York, while Boston and a few other major cities make appearances of greater and lesser significance. This focus upon the larger city in a study of the middle class may seem somewhat perverse and even self-defeating, in light of the tendency of certain social observers of the nineteenth century to portray the big city as a two-class society, consisting only of the very rich and the very poor. Junius Henri Browne, for example, claimed in 1869 that in New York City "there are two great and distinct classes of people – those who pass their days in trying to make enough money to live; and those who, having more than enough, are troubled about the manner of spending it."[47] Many others wrote in the same vein, perhaps none more directly than James Dabney McCabe, who wrote of New York in 1868 that "there are but two classes in the city – the poor and the rich."[48] Historians have recently returned to contemporary descriptions of this sort, and to other documents that appear to confirm the view of the big city as increasingly bifurcated into *haut bourgeois* and working-class cultures and social worlds. For example, Peter Buckley's recent attempt to understand New York's Astor Place riot of 1849 in these terms traces the development of "two cultural axes, . . . two distinct idioms," and even two physical courses of cultural divergence: "one course followed Chatham Street and then up the Bowery; . . . the other followed the uptown march of fashion along Broadway to the luxury of the Fifteenth Ward."[49] Of any middle course, or of any cultural or social lines of divergence within the bourgeoisie or anywhere else in urban society, there is no mention. Similarly, Michael Katz, Michael Doucet, and Mark Stern offer statements similar to those of Browne and McCabe as evidence supporting a more general two-class model of urban society in industrializing North America: "On that the evidence appears unequivocal. A two-class model describes not only the objective relations of early industrial cities but the perception of their principal interpreters as well."[50] Can we contradict this "unequivocal" testimony, and examine a phenomenon that some contemporaries claimed did not exist?

Indeed we can. The principal observers of mid-nineteenth-century social and cultural bifurcation in the big city were seizing upon the most dramatic aspects of a new phenomenon, the emergence of distinct urban quarters, the elaboration of distinct styles of living within these quarters, and the visible association of these quarters and styles with particular types of work and levels of income and wealth. The most dramatic aspects of this tangible change in city life were those that affected and extended the city's extremes, and it was to these extremes that contemporary writers almost invariably turned to heighten the impact of their story. It is significant, too, that they now had at their disposal the relatively new literary genres of the sensationalist urban sketch and *roman-feuilleton*, bred in London and Paris in the preceding decades to give voice to the drama and mystery of life in the nineteenth-century metropolis. These genres, imported with little alteration, further impelled the American city writers to portray the big city as a shockingly abnormal collection of the very rich and the very poor, and to emphasize the difference between the big city and more traditional communities by exaggerating the polarization of urban society. It is not inappropriate to point out that there was money to be made this way (Adrienne Siegel has recently estimated that through the 1860s three times as many novels were written about the city than were written about the trans-Appalachian West), and that writers such as Charles F. Briggs, E. Z. C. Judson, George G. Foster, and Joseph Holt Ingraham responded to the opportunity with unseemly glee.[51] "What a task we have undertaken!" exclaimed "Gaslight" Foster in 1850: "To penetrate beneath the thick veil of night and lay bare the fearful mysteries of darkness in the metropolis."[52] Most of the "mysteries" involved the dissipations of the rich and the miseries of the poor, and it is hardly surprising that the daily routines of ordinary middling folk are seldom recognized in these books. But did these authors really believe that the big city contained no middle class? In the sentence immediately following his description of New York as a city of "the poor and the rich," McCabe wrote, "The middle class, which is so numerous in other cities, hardly exists at all here." However, a closer look reveals that what McCabe really meant was that high housing costs had driven the middle class to the suburbs, not that the metropolis as a whole contained no middle class.[53] And it can be noted that McCabe was able to use the term "middle class" in a popular text with neither quotation marks nor accompanying definition, and was willing to concede the presence of a middle class in cities other than the one whose "secrets" he had set out to betray. To be sure, McCabe and the other observers of the big city had reason to be genuinely impressed by the extremes of wealth and poverty they found there, but their dismissal of middling folk should itself be dismissed as little more than adherence to the themes and styles of urban sensationalism.

Perhaps, too, the city writers of the nineteenth century ignored middling folk because they did not know how to deal with them.[54] To these writers, no less than to historians of later generations, the middle class was elusive. What I have sought in this introductory chapter is a means for making this segment of the urban population comprehensible, perhaps as a social class but at the very least as a large group of people whose historical role in the industrial and urban revolutions (as contributors to events, and as recipients, whose lives are altered by events) is not yet well understood. "A triumphant middle class," Hartz observes, "can take itself for granted." We who would understand that triumph cannot.

2 "Middling sorts" in the eighteenth-century city

On December 6, 1765, in the midst of the Stamp Act crisis, former Lieutenant-Governor Cadwallader Colden of New York undertook to explain to the British Secretary of State and to the Board of Trade how the crisis reflected basic divisions within the society of the province. "The People of New York," Colden wrote, "are properly distinguished into different Ranks." In the first rank Colden placed "The Proprietors of the Large Tracts of Land who include within their claims from 100,000 to above one million acres under one Grant." Second were "The Gentlemen of the Law," while "The Merchants make the third class." In the fourth and "last Rank," Colden concluded, "may be placed the Farmers & Mechanics. . . . This last Rank comprehends the bulk of the People and in them consists the strength of the Province. They are the most usefull and the most moral, but alwise made the Dupes of the former, and often are ignorantly made their Tools for the worst purposes."[1]

Colden's description is a peculiar one to the twentieth-century reader, who would not divide his own society into three sets of rich men followed by everyone else. It would have seemed strange to Walt Whitman's generation, too, even allowing for the thin thread that connects the "most usefull" and "most moral" farmers and mechanics of colonial New York (identified by Colden some years earlier as "middling people," and as "the middling rank of mankind")[2] with Whitman's "most valuable . . . middle class" of salaried suburbanites. Yet, Colden's statement accords in a fundamental way with what recent scholars have written about the structure of eighteenth-century society on both sides of the Atlantic – that society was organized primarily into vertically arranged interests (religious and political as well as economic) rather than into horizontally layered, antagonistic classes; that "ranks" identified the flow of influence, patronage, and deference within this system of interests, rather than the experiences and consciousness of separate classes; and that society as a whole was profoundly elitist in its recruitment of political leadership and in

its assignment of social prestige.[3] Within this aristocratic and preindustrial world there was, to be sure, a recognizable "middling rank"
that was not yet, however, a "middle class." If, for example, Colden's
"Farmers & Mechanics" were the most useful and moral of New
York's citizens, they were also the "Tools" (perhaps the "clients") of
their betters. And there were "meaner sorts" of whom Colden took
no note – incipient proletarians whose day-to-day struggles against
their own poverty and other people's privilege did not yet resemble
the more fully articulated class conflict of the nineteenth century.[4]

The language Colden used was understood at both the center and
the outposts of the eighteenth-century Atlantic world. There are a
number of reasons, however, why his "pre-class" view of vertical
interests may apply with greater force to European than to American
society. In New England, and in other provinces where landowning
was very widespread, patronage and clientage were weaker and less
extensive than they were in Europe, while cities of all regions in the
new world lacked the hierarchy of greater and lesser guilds, the formal
connection between guilds and the governance of the city, and a
variety of customs and beliefs that in many parts of the old world
underscored the corporate but hierarchical character of each trade and
of the city as a whole.[5] Higher wage rates and living standards may
have imparted at least a feeling of greater independence among American urban workers, while free market and other liberal ideals were
penetrating various levels of colonial society.[6] The major political conflict of the era, moreover, eventuated in a republic whose strength,
according to many contemporaries, rested on the simple virtues, plain
habits, and, above all, the independence, of its ordinary citizens.[7]
Colden's analysis, indeed, may have been somewhat peculiar and
old-fashioned in 1765, though it was not unique.[8] In most contemporary American documents, ranks refer to horizontally defined levels, almost always within a three-tiered social structure, and seldom
to vertical interests that cut through those levels. Thirty years and
one revolution after Colden divided New York society into ranks that
were also interests, the Philadelphia *Aurora*, in a brief essay warning
of the evil effects of luxury and social ambition, described republican
America in quite different terms: "Those in *high life* ape the fashions
and manners of the English, French and other nations; the *middle class*
those of the higher or more affluent, . . . and *the poor* copy the example
of the class above them."[9]

But if Colden was a little behind the times in 1765, the *Aurora*, in
its use of the quite modern term "middle class," was somewhat ahead
of the times in 1796. "Class," including variants of "middle class,"
was by then appearing with somewhat greater frequency, especially

in the pages of the more radical newspapers, but even at the end of the century it was still far more common to express social levels in terms of ranks, sorts, stations, conditions, orders, or even estates.[10] It is sometimes suggested that these linguistic conventions reflect in their own way the pre-class character of preindustrial American society, and in particular the resilience of personalized, deferential relations within a changing social order. Terms such as "the better sort" and "people of middling rank," according to this argument, reveal the imprint of aristocratic Europe, despite the absence or attenuation in America of clearly bounded "interests" and the "detailed and intricate network of patronage and connection" that still prevailed in the old world.[11]

Demonstrating the connection between social taxonomy and the structure of day-to-day social relations is no simple matter, but there is a logical correspondence between customary eighteenth-century terms and pre-class relations that does encourage this line of inquiry. Terms such as "rank" and "station" refer directly to individuals within a hierarchical relationship, and only indirectly, or secondarily, to the category of individuals that share that rank or station. Category, indeed, is not necessarily implied by these terms, as there can be a rank or station occupied by only one person – the commanding general of an army, for example – but even where it is implied the primary reference is to the individual and the hierarchical relation. A term such as "sorts" is primarily categorical but also suggests a looseness of categorical definition – a category of somewhat ambiguous meaning, perhaps, or of indistinct boundaries. "Class," on the other hand, is primarily and distinctly categorical and, once stripped of the overlays of meaning applied later by observers of industrial society, suggests neither an individual's relation to individuals of other classes, nor a necessary relation, hierarchical or otherwise, between one class and another. Its essential specification is of a homogeneous group, set off in a particular way from other groups. It is worth noting that in eighteenth-century America "class" was used to specify a wide variety of such groups – sexes, races, age groups, political factions, types of personal temperament, even, on occasion, levels of society.[12] But does the relative rarity of the latter usage, and the far more abundant social taxonomy of ranks, conditions, sorts, orders, and estates, truly bring into focus the deferential character of social relations in the preindustrial American city? If so, does the modest tendency toward the use of "class" after the Revolution (and the first appearance of the term "middle class" in the *Aurora* and a few other places in the late 1780s and 1790s) signal, as Gary Nash has claimed, the beginnings of a major shift in the social landscape, and a dawning consciousness of class among those who lived in the "urban crucibles" of changing economic and social relations?[13] The purpose of this chapter is to understand the meaning of "middling ranks," "middling sorts," "people of the middle condition," and even the late-appearing "middle class," both in the context of eighteenth-century urban society and in frank anticipation of the very different social world that would succeed it.

The pedestrian city and the culture of rank

Consider first some of the things that shaped day-to-day social life in eighteenth-century American cities. These cities have been described many times as small but cosmopolitan centers of maritime commerce and artisanal production – "pedestrian" or "walking" cities in which merchants, artisans, and laborers of all sorts worked in close proximity to one another, to their own and other people's families, and to streets that bustled with a variety of activities. John Lambert, an Englishman who arrived in America just after the end of the century, described the New York City waterfront this way:

> The carters were driving in every direction; and the sailors and labourers upon the wharfs, and on board the vessels, were moving their ponderous burthens from place to place. The merchants and their clerks were busily engaged in their counting-houses, or upon the piers. The Tontine coffee-house was filled with underwriters, brokers, merchants, traders, and politicians. . . . The steps and balcony of the coffee-house were crowded with people bidding, or listening to the several auctioneers, who had elevated themselves upon a hogshead of sugar, a puncheon of rum, or a bale of cotton; and with Stentorian voices were exclaiming, "Once, twice. Once, twice." "Another cent." "Thank ye, gentlemen. . . . " The coffee-house slip, and the corners of Wall and Pearl-streets were jammed up with carts, drays, and wheelbarrows; horses and men were huddled promiscuously together, leaving little or no room for passengers to pass. . . . Everything was in motion; all was life, bustle, and activity.[14]

Merchants, auctioneers, brokers, and clerks work close to or on the streets and wharves in this scene, controlling the flow of goods being brought into and out of the port by the sailors, laborers, carters, and draymen. Lambert could have added other characters: ship chandlers and provisioners, coopers, riggers, and other artisans serving commerce and shipping, ships' passengers such as himself, and women and children living nearby, some of them above the counting houses, stores, and artisans' shops that lined the wharves. Abraham Ritter's recollection of the Philadelphia waterfront at the end of the eighteenth century was in part that of a child's playground – "Sleds flew rapidly from the summit [of the hill rising from Market Street Wharf] to its base, at the expense of our heels and the profit of the shoemaker, whilst our hearts did not return from their beat until the wharf's level checked the impetus."[15] In warmer weather boys swam off of the collapsed pier at Clifford's Wharf above Market Street, and bought watermelons for a penny as they were unloaded a few wharves farther south. The playground could even extend indoors, into the Water Street grocery of Job Butcher, for example, where Ritter and his young friends "had the freedom of the store from front to rear. [Butcher had] one or two pet Raccoons, with which, between school-hours, we were allowed to play to our heart's content."[16]

The merchants of Water Street, or Coffee House Slip, or Long Wharf in Boston, were among the wealthiest and most powerful men of their communities. They were not, however, shut off from less exalted citizens in office towers and suburbs. Their work carried them often into the streets, and sometimes even carried the streets into their homes. In 1798 the Philadelphia merchant William Davy testified in a complicated court case that a secret messenger, who was to sail in one of Davy's ships, "a hardy, lusty, brawny, weather beaten man," was "conducted from the counting house to the parlour" for refreshment.[17] Even the wealthiest merchants lived quite close to their wharf-side warehouses and counting rooms, and in many cases lived on the same premises as the latter, as Davy obviously did. Philadelphia's Stephen Girard owned a compound of docks and stores that stretched from the river through to Water Street, and from Water Street through to his provision store on Front Street. Girard lived in the center of this complex, on Water Street, behind and above his ground-floor counting room. Next door was another counting room, below a second story used for storing books and papers.[18] The merchant moved frequently between these domestic and work spaces, as well as outward to the streets, wharves, and other places. The hours of business for merchants, it should be noted, were variable and seldom long. Arthur H. Cole established some years ago that the tempo of mercantile life in the late colonial era was generally slow, and that merchants could and did engage in a number of nonbusiness activities that took them away from their counting house.[19] The Duc de la Rochefoucault Liancourt observed in the 1790s that Charleston's merchants worked no later than four o'clock, and spent the rest of the day at tea parties and dinners, and at the city's two gaming houses.[20] Merchants' clerks worked longer hours, but they were not always at their desks, or even at the store. When Robert Hunter, the son of a

London merchant, called on an old friend now clerking for a Philadelphia merchant (the year was 1785), he noted that the latter, one
Millson, rose at seven, went (downstairs) to the countinghouse, and
worked all day. Yet Millson was able to receive his friend, joined him
on a business hours walk to the State House on Wednesday, and on
a longer walk around the city on Friday. This occurred in early November, still a fairly busy time in the mercantile calendar.[21]

Artisans of the waterfront and elsewhere in the city lived and
worked in still smaller quarters, equally close to the street, to family
members, customers, members of their own and other trades, to other
shops, and to taverns and the other customers of taverns. Most lived
above street-level shops (which were not, however, as open to the
street as the illustrations in Carl Bridenbaugh's widely consulted *Colonial Craftsman* imply – Bridenbaugh extracted these illustrations from
Diderot's *Encyclopédie*, not from American sources),[22] and worked at
tasks and hours variable enough to permit a good deal of personal
contact with people other than those who worked in the shop.[23] The
exact configuration of home, shop, and street depended in part on
the trade, the prosperity of the artisan, and the extent to which production was geared to retail rather than custom sales. Silversmiths,
for example, generally maintained a front-room "show shop" in their
homes, while confining production (and their journeymen and apprentices) to a separate workshop in a back building, or even in a
larger manufactory at a separate address.[24] Joseph Anthony of Philadelphia had a particularly elegant show shop in his home at 94 High
Street during and after the 1790s. An insurance survey of 1793 lists
paneled display cases with mahogany counters, glass-enclosed mahogany shelves, large circular windows, and a "Frontispiece" with
fluted pilasters.[25] Other tradesmen may have separated production
from sales in this way, but the practice was probably most often found
among prosperous artisans who sold high-priced consumer goods on
major streets in the center of the city. The Philadelphia hatter Isaac
Parrish, for example, whose house and store was in a large, three-
story brick house on Second Street a few doors above Market, maintained a two-story brick workshop in nearby Pewter Platter Alley.[26]

We should observe here that very few of the city's countinghouses
or retail stores were designed to dignify or set apart these nonmanual
workplaces from those of humbler folk. Merchants and other elites
built homes of increasing size and elegance during this era but generally showed little interest in elevating the style and appearance of
either the exteriors or the interiors of their countinghouses, stores,
and offices. Most retail stores were merely the front rooms of ordinary
houses, and larger businesses that occupied entire buildings ordi-

narily clung to common residential styles. For example, the first office of the Insurance Company of North America, which was founded in Philadelphia in 1792, merely joined together two houses of quite ordinary design.[27] Two banks were built in Philadelphia during this decade, but as Elizabeth Spera notes in her study of late-eighteenth-century commercial architecture, these were "the sole Philadelphia examples of successful commercial buildings of an assertive size, scale, and style." The two banks, Spera concludes, "do not define a class of commercial building that was yet of importance in 1800."[28] Nor was there a distinctive retail style. The exception that proves the rule here is the spectacular failure of "Cooke's Folly," completed in 1794 at the behest of Joseph Cooke, an English-born goldsmith, jeweler, and real estate investor, at the corner of Third and Market streets in Philadelphia. The elegant retail shop was by this time well established in London, and Cooke ventured to import the idea to the metropolis of the new world. His building was a large one by contemporary standards – 81 feet along Third Street, 26 feet along Market Street, and seven stories high, including two underground levels and one of garrets – and was of unprecedented elegance for a commercial structure (Figure 2.1). Cooke spared no expense, even promising an eight-dollar pair of silver buckles "as a premium, or token of friendship," to each workman who stayed on the job until the building was completed.[29] Most interesting from an architectural point of view were the full-story display windows that encased the entire ground floor, which Cooke intended to use in part as his own show shop. Other stores were to join him on the ground floor, while upper stories were intended for coffeehouses, public rooms, and lodgings. The effect, however, was all too spectacular. As Spera notes, "The building was an oddity of perhaps frightening scale and display which served not to attract and serve the marketplace but rather to disorient and repel."[30] A year before it was built a Boston almanac advised shopkeepers, "Aim not at making a great figure in your shop, in unnecessary ornaments, but let it be neat and useful: too great an appearance may rather prevent than encourage customers."[31] Neither Philadelphians nor Bostonians, it seems, were quite ready for the elegant shops of London's West End, and Cooke's building was a decided failure. Cooke was unable to raise further funds when construction was completed, could not sell the building, and could not even sell lottery tickets with the building offered as a prize. Cooke failed, and the building was eventually demolished.[32]

The city that turned its back on Joseph Cooke's adventure in modern commercial architecture was the largest in the new nation; yet, it was still very small and preserved many of the characteristics of a

Figure 2.1. Southeast corner of Third and Market Streets, Philadelphia ("Cooke's Folly") (courtesy of the Library Company of Philadelphia)

preindustrial provincial town, whose streets and markets reflected its proximity to the rural hinterland no less tangibly than the wharves, warehouses, and tall ships beyond Water Street reflected its status as a major port. Philadelphia was densely populated at its center, and along and just behind its waterfront for perhaps a mile and a half during the last years of the eighteenth century, but a westward walk of only eight or nine blocks, even along its most central streets, carried one from the waterfront to the edge of the city (Figure 2.2). Just beyond the edge were not commuter suburbs but empty blocks, farms, grain and cattle markets, and a few country estates – the country seat of dry goods merchant Solomon White, for example, stood at Eleventh and Callowhill Streets, well out in the countryside (Callowhill, indeed, was very sparsely settled west of Fourth Street), but less than a mile from Water Street.[33] Within the built-up part of the city there were no distinct and homogeneous quarters of housing for the wealthy, or for the poor, although the peripheral districts, Southwark and the outer parts of Northern Liberties, were largely populated by artisans of the humbler trades and by less skilled workers. Closer to the center the homes of the wealthy, the middling sort, and the poor stood in close proximity to one another – distinguished from

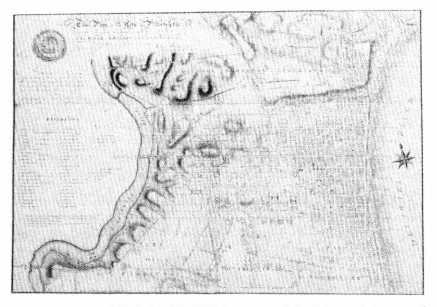

Figure 2.2. Map of Philadelphia, 1796 (courtesy of the Library Company of Philadelphia)

each other, to be sure, by size, architecture, and type of frontage – and to the stores, workshops, markets, taverns, and other institutions that scattered across the city. The city, in short, was small in scale, small in the scale of its enterprises, and largely lacking in the specialized areal homogeneity that would later come to characterize large parts of the modern metropolis. Work took most people only a short distance from their homes, to proprietorships and small partnerships almost invariably identified on store- and shop-front signs by the names of their owners. Within their homes and workplaces people were close to the streets, and often on them, and the streets themselves reflected the variety of homes, stores, and workshops that rose only two or three stories above them. Adding to this variety, we might note, were large numbers of people who conducted their business *in* the streets – peddlers of all kinds of urban wares and country goods, operating from carts and stationary stands. In William and Thomas Birch's engraving of the corner of Third and Market, "Cooke's Folly" rises above a city busy with the kind of everyday commerce it knew very well and evidently still preferred.[34] The scale and intimate character of the city stand out in many ways, indeed, not least in Article 6 of the constitution of the Taylors Company of Philadelphia. This item directed each monthly meeting of the company to appoint two members to inform the membership of the next meeting, not by advertising in the newspapers or even by posting broadsides, but by calling upon each member at his house at least an hour before the meeting was scheduled to begin.[35]

This preindustrial scale and organization of work and urban form have been summarized accurately by Gary Nash and others as a "face-to-face" society – a simple but essential idea, but also one that is easily misunderstood.[36] The term suggests a highly personalized society, in which people of different social conditions frequently interacted within an environment small enough so that they could recognize each other as individuals, understand something of each other's personalities and character, and in many cases know and use each other's names. It does not necessarily suggest, however, a society of egalitarian familiarity. On the contrary, face-to-face interactions between individuals in a highly stratified society can take on a decidedly inegalitarian form, in which inferiors defer to betters, and betters command and patronize inferiors, even in highly ritualized ways. "Virtually everyone of wealth or position in the port towns," writes Nash, "adhered to the axiom that rank and status must be carefully preserved and social roles clearly differentiated if society was to retain its equilibrium."[37] How were rank and status to be preserved, and to what extent did less exalted folk perceive the axiomatic connection between hierarchy and social equilibrium?

The fundamental divisions within urban society were to some extent maintained through institutions and practices that had little to do with deferential relations between people of different ranks. The private dinner parties, exclusive dancing assemblies, and other social institutions of the "better sort" helped to define and reinforce the urban elite by establishing spaces from which social inferiors were simply excluded. To be sure, the small size and spatial integration of the cities invested in some of these institutions and events a degree of public theatricality, an open and more or less ritualized display of superior and inferior status. In 1782, for example, about 750 "gentlemen and ladies" attended a supper and ball at the State House in Philadelphia to celebrate the birth of the Dauphin, while, according to one newspaper's account, some 12,000 more ordinary *citoyens* watched their arrival and a fireworks display that had been provided for them outdoors.[38] Occupancy of an expensive pew in a fashionable church was also in some measure a public display of personal status, and one of a more regular kind.[39] Other exclusive institutions, however, remained outside the public view – the Philadelphia fishing clubs, for example, were located on the Schuylkill River outside the city, where "the best and most respectable company in Philadelphia" could "divert themselves with walking, fishing, going up the water, dancing, singing, conversing, or just as they please," without being observed (or acknowledged) by those of middling or inferior rank.[40] The various formal organizations that had accumulated in the city by the latter years of the eighteenth century probably did more to homogenize interactions than to provide opportunities for patronage and deference.[41] A few even brought people of different ranks together in what appear to have been egalitarian settings – Masonic lodges, for example, combined merchants and professionals with moderately prosperous artisans and others of middling rank, and many of the latter served as lodge officers.[42]

The formal institution that involved the greatest range of individuals in questions of rank and privilege was, of course, government. Historians have long stressed the consistent recruitment of political leaders and major public officials from the "better sorts" in every city, despite significant differences in each city's political structure, through at least the first two-thirds of the eighteenth century. In Philadelphia a virtually self-perpetuating municipal Corporation fell easily into the hands of a small number of wealthy families. The power of this aristocratic body was actually quite limited, and the business of the city passed increasingly into the hands of specialized boards and commissions created by the provincial Assembly. But these men too were drawn almost entirely from the city's elite.[43] James Henretta observes that in Boston, where political affairs were conducted within a structurally more democratic town meeting, "the assumption of a graded social, economic, and political scale neatly calibrated so as to indicate the relation of each individual to the whole was the basic principle upon which the functioning of town-meeting 'democracy' depended."[44] As in Philadelphia, this neat calibration placed only wealthy men in higher offices, and men of middling rank only in the lower offices through which policies generated at higher levels were carried out. Even in New York, where a greater degree of areal segregation, representation by ward on the Common Council, and a broad franchise created a tradition of artisanal officeholding in the municipal legislature, mechanics and other middling sorts were found mainly in the lower, non-policy offices.[45] New York, indeed, seat of the intense political rivalry between the wealthy Livingston and DeLancey families, was in some respects the most elitist city of all. Edward Countryman observes that "middling people" were "neither in nor out" of the larger political community that revolved around elections for and service within the provincial Assembly. They could vote, but elite office seekers courted their votes cynically, and paid little attention to their interests or opinions except at election time, in part because no widely held democratic theory of representation compelled it.[46] The character of New York's political culture is nicely conveyed by an attack on the DeLanceys published in the pro-Livingston *New-York Journal* in 1770. Recounting an attempt by James DeLancey to gain support among the increasingly influential "middle rank of people" who had formed themselves into Sons of Liberty, the *Journal* noted: "The expediency of this conduct was strongly enforced by a consideration that generally promised success, viz. the ascendency gained by the people of figure over their inferiors, by mixing with them."[47]

These particular inferiors – radical activists in the emerging Revolution – may have been less than grateful for the condescending attentions of a James DeLancey. Nash has argued, in fact, that each of the port cities experienced challenges to elitist political assumptions and institutions at various times during the eighteenth century, and that these challenges coalesced even before the Revolution in a "popular" politics that significantly altered the terms according to which middling and poor people acquiesced in rule by the wealthy.[48] This new political sensitivity among non-elites, joined to new and more vigorous forms of electioneering, may have caused the terms of deference to be renegotiated, as Nash suggests. But renegotiation did not go so far as to undermine the traditional foundations of elite rule. Wealthy merchants and professionals continued to occupy the policy-making positions of municipal government, and to represent the city in provincial legislatures. More importantly, there is little evidence that they did so in the face of active opposition by middling and poor people, or on behalf of new theories that subjected public servants to the will of their constituents. Non-elites continued to acquiesce in the political leadership of wealthy men who claimed the right to rule as a prerogative of their superior position in society, and who continued, without apparent political risk, to scorn the political abilities of the "unthinking multitude."[49] "Popular" politics, in other words, was still contained within a fundamentally deferential system on the eve of the Revolution, and, as I argue in the final section of this chapter, the challenge of the Revolution itself was mounted only with considerable difficulty. Nash's splendid narrative of the ascending popular politics of the eighteenth century city could as well have focused on the resilience of political deference as on its retreat.[50]

Relations between people of different ranks, however, was less frequently mediated through formal institutions than through informal rules and customs governing face-to-face conduct. Were these as finely calibrated as the rules and customs governing the filling of public offices? One correspondent to the *Pennsylvania Packet* obviously thought so: "If men in a midling station in life are not capable of shewing great examples," he wrote, "they may shew or follow good examples."[51] In truth, it is very difficult to say whether most people "in a midling station in life" perceived themselves in this fashion, and even more difficult to say whether this kind of belief influenced their behavior toward people of higher and lower ranks. The ordinary people of eighteenth-century America left behind them few records that disclose their social attitudes or behavior, and the newspapers of the cities, which survive in abundance, give us only an occasional glimpse (such as the above) of actual or expected social relations in the shops, markets, streets, and other public spaces.[52] Perhaps the most revealing surviving sources of the social attitudes and mores of ordinary folk are almanacs, which were produced in large numbers and competed intensely for the shillings of plain people as repositories of practical information and sound advice.[53] *The Pennsylvania Town and Country-man's Almanack, for . . . 1773* offers this guide to social behavior before persons of higher and lower social rank:

> Apply to Persons of Quality with an Air of Regard, rather than Softness, by few Words, fewer Repetitions, and the most important Truths; being humble, and not fawning; with Superiors, courteous and fair spoken; not over familiar, not surly, with Inferiors.
>
> In the Presence of great Men, neither demonstrate thyself melancholy nor musing; it implies the Absence of thy Mind in the Presence of thy Body, which they impute to thy Disregard of them; be not overfree nor too forward.[54]

How suggestive this passage is of the forms and rituals of a society based on rank, patronage, and deference. Note that it advises middling people, who had both superiors and inferiors to address. The same advice could still be given two decades later, as in *The Federal Almanack, for . . . 1794*, which told its readers to show "a due respect to superiors, modest affability to equals, and generous compassion to inferiors."[55] Against it, to be sure, we may place other statements urging ordinary people to adopt a bearing of manly independence, and still others that ridicule the fawning sycophant and arrogant aristocrat.[56] Yet these, in their own way, only confirm how difficult it was to erase deferential social relations from the face-to-face society of the new republic. So too does the following tale of mischievous social leveling, which must have delighted readers impatient with the social claims of local gentlemen:

> A Cobler was sitting in his shop singing merrily; his song was this, *"Tamilarne* was, and he was," and continued so singing, and nothing else, many times together; which a gentleman that passed

by, took notice of, and said to the Cobler, prithee, friend, what was he? Why, said the Cobler, as great a fool as yourself, for aught I know. Sirrah says the gentleman, you are a rascal, come out, and I'll kick you. No sir, says he, 'tis no matter, I thank you for your love as much as if I had it, for I don't want kicking. Sirrah, says the gentleman again, come out, and I will give you a kick. No Sir, says he, you need not trouble yourself, I wont come out if you'd give me two.[57]

As the designations "gentleman" and "Cobler" in this tale suggest, the culture of rank was not purely personal, but was also categorical, as it was even in societies with much stronger and more extensive bonds of personal patronage and clientage. The basic categories were, of course, derived largely from attitudes associating different levels of social worth with different kinds of work. In the port cities of British North America, attitudes toward work were not very different from those found in English cities. Respect accrued to the genteel *rentier*, but no less dignified (in America, at least) than large-scale landlording and the traditional professions of aristocratic or genteel younger sons (the military, law, and the clergy) was the pursuit of long-distance trade. Nonmanual work on a smaller scale, such as keeping a retail store (often called "dealing," "trading," or "mongering"), was significantly less respectable, while work with one's hands, even in a skilled and valuable craft, was distinctly degrading. The cobbler in the above sketch was a "rascal" not only because he was cleverly insulting, or even because he was poor, but in large part because he was a mender of shoes. It would be difficult to overstate the significance of this prejudice to our understanding of the social meaning of middling rank, for the vast majority of those deemed to be middling sorts were in fact handworking artisans. According to the best estimates, some 20% of the adult male work force of the port cities consisted of nonmanual proprietors and workers who were not among the urban elite. But at least 50% were artisans, two and a half times the number of middling storekeepers and clerks, and a proportion quite sufficient to establish a close identification of middling status with skilled manual work.[58] The difficulty of probing the character of actual day-to-day interactions in the city remains. But in the light of these proportions it is worth looking more closely at this categorical dimension of the culture of rank.

Manual work and middling rank

"In the colonies as in London," writes Stephen Botein, "printers had to face the hard, discouraging fact that in the eyes of their neighbors they were by training mechanics, without full legitimacy as men of intellect and creed." The printer, "however prominent, . . . was still a 'meer mechanic.' "[59] The term "mechanic" was indeed used in eighteenth-century America to specify the limits of legitimate social aspiration for men who worked at manual trades. It could be used scornfully (as in the protest, by an opponent of nonimportation, "of the Impropriety of Men of liberal Education, being dictated to by illeterate Mechanicks"),[60] or offhandedly, or playfully, or even in vigorous defense of the mechanic's worth. But even in the latter instances the implication is clear that the degradation of those who performed manual work was a major part of the social landscape, and a major determinant of the social meaning of middling rank. The *Aurora* was Philadelphia's most radical newspaper, and considered itself the defender of the interests of mechanics and other middling folk.[61] In 1796 it published a fable in which a hardworking bee, obviously an artisan, reproached a wealthy and arrogant beetle for confiscating a grain of corn that a poor ant had left in a public passage (the reference here is to a city ordinance, very unpopular with shop owners, forbidding the blocking of sidewalks with merchandise). The beetle replies: "Insolent mechanic, . . . whilst thou art proud of thy riches, consider the dirty channels through which they have flowed, and thou wilt blush if thou hast a spark of sensibility left."[62]

The *Aurora's* attack on social prejudice is unambiguous (even the prosperous artisan is regarded as an inferior by the aristocratic beetle), and is unusually direct. Responses in public print to the degradation of mechanics were usually more subtle, as in the tale of the gentleman and the cobbler, or in a still more interesting inversion contained in a pamphlet, published in Philadelphia in 1772, satirizing the use of fashionable and expensive clothing to support claims of social respectability. "Since then to our clothes we owe the decision of our merits," writes the narrator, "I frankly confess, that there are but few persons in the world for whom I have so much veneration as I have for my Taylor." The narrator visits his tailor's shop, and stands in silent admiration while he observes how clothes, and the tailor himself, quite literally make the man: "He has just cut out a dean. . . . Over the chair hung two excellencies without sleeves. One of his journeymen was giving existence to a landed gentleman. . . . On the bench lay a great many young beaux."[63] The elevation of the tailor here is unnatural and ironic, a social relation turned upside down as a result of the moral inversion caused by the veneration of exterior appearance rather than inner worth. The social inversion is offered as *evidence* of the moral inversion and underscores the real status of the tailor as an inferior. We will see this same motif again in the

Jacksonian era, used in a direct assault on the social degradation of the manual worker.

A few personal records, too, speak to this prejudice in interesting ways. On November 11, 1788, a Boston schoolteacher named Nathan Webb made this entry in his diary:

> In this day's paper came out a piece which gave me much plea-
> sure which was to burlesque a certain character who assumes to
> himself the character of Gentleman when in fact he is only a
> Stockjobber's lackey & to support his mightiness has only 7 dol-
> lars p[er] month yet thinks it beneath his dignified person to be in
> the company or even taught in the same school to dance where
> reputable Mechanicks attend – He has made his dissatisfaction
> known to Mr. G____th his Instructor & is a youngster of about 20
> – An upstart [illeg.] is the best I can say of him – Mr W[illia]m
> L[eac]h a worthy Saddler is the person whom he so much
> undervalues.[64]

William Leach was an established and probably fairly prosperous master saddler with a shop on one of Boston's major streets, and was Webb's friend. What is notable here is not that Webb and at least one other person defended Leach, but that a twenty-year-old clerk could object so strongly to attending dancing school with even an established master mechanic. The "Stockjobber's lackey" clearly overstepped the bounds of social custom, and his public chastisement was probably widely approved. (Leach, incidentally, added what might have been a characteristic mechanic's chastisement – Webb's next diary entry notes that Leach beat up the upstart clerk, an event at which the schoolteacher confesses satisfaction, despite his disapproval of fighting.)[65] But if the young clerk misread the rules by which proper social relations were maintained, the customary hierarchical distinction between nonmanual and manual work comes through this episode fairly clearly. If the clerk had been older, or a partner in his firm, or if Leach had been less well established, the event might have come to a very different conclusion.

A similar pattern of social prejudice emerges from the memoirs of Alexander Graydon, first published in 1811, which recall their author's somewhat raucous youth in Philadelphia in the years just preceding the Revolution. Graydon had been sent from Bristol, Pennsylvania, to study at a Philadelphia academy. After a brief period of study, Graydon and some of his friends contemplated leaving the academy: "We cheerfully renounced the learned professions for the sake of the supposed liberty that would be the consequence. We were all, therefore, to be merchants, as to be mechanics was too humiliating."[66]

Graydon actually did leave the academy, fell out with his school friends, and found new ones:

> ... whose education and habits had been wholly different from my own. They were chiefly designed for the sea, or engaged in the less humiliating mechanical employments, and were but the more to my taste for affecting a sort of rough independence of manners, which appeared to me manly. They were not, however, worthless; and such of them as were destined to become men and citizens, have, with few exceptions, filled their parts in society with reputation and respectability.[67]

Although it might be argued here that Graydon and his school friends considered an artisanal career at least plausible enough to mention, that Graydon describes some mechanical trades as "less humiliating" than others, that he made friends with artisans, and that most of his artisan friends became respectable citizens, the tenor of his remarks suggests that Graydon embraced the same hierarchical distinction that later caused the Boston clerk to refuse companionship with the saddler William Leach. The mechanic, to Graydon, was not merely inferior but "humiliated," and his friends among the "less humiliating" trades were "rough." Graydon has to state that they were "not worthless" and their ultimate respectability (which he also has to state, and with more than a hint of condescension) derived from the fact that they "filled their parts." Perhaps most importantly, they were the temporary friends of an adolescent binge of emancipation, and are not even named in the memoir. Graydon, it is clear, was slumming.

Historians have sometimes puzzled over the precise meaning of the term "mechanic," and have not always appreciated the importance of its ambiguity. Elites, who understood perfectly well the distinction between skilled artisans and unskilled workers, often expressed their indifference to it by referring to "mechanics" as all those who worked at manual occupations. In statements such as Cadwallader Colden's description of New York society, the important hierarchial distinction was the one that set off the several elites from everyone else – differences between artisans and laborers were of no real consequence. The effect, needless to say, was to identify middling people much more closely with the bottom of society than with the top. Elites who did note the difference between middling and poor people, moreover, often did so only as a secondary matter while lumping both together, as in discussions of "the middling and poorer sort."[68] It is interesting that both middling and poor people could make the same association, often in the offhanded manner that implied common usage. When the First Company of Philadelphia Militia Artillery petitioned the Supreme Executive Council in 1779 for fairer regulations concerning evasion of service, they observed that it is "the middling and poor" who bear the burden and risk for those who do not serve.[69] A letter to the *New-York Journal* in 1768, signed "A CITIZEN," complained that a new building law would raise home construction costs beyond the reach of "the Poor and Middling People."[70] "How many poor men, common men, and mechanics have been made happy within this fortnight," asked an anonymous critic of cynical electioneering in 1776, "by a shake of the hand, a pleasing smile and a little familiar chat with gentlemen, who have not for these seven years past condescended to look at them. Blessed state that brings all so nearly on a level!"[71] In Baltimore in 1794, a coalition that included the Mechanical Society and several Republican Societies objected to *viva voce* voting in the proposed city charter, "because this method very much impedes the freedom of elections, and lays the poor and middling class of people too open to influence from the rich and the great."[72]

A particularly valuable expression of the relative proximity of middling sorts to those above and below them is contained in a letter, signed "A TRADESMAN," printed in the *New-York Journal* in 1767. It is well worth quoting at length:

> Though I am a Tradesman, and depend upon my daily labour for the Support of myself and Family, Yet, I commonly read your Paper; and my neighbours and I have been more amused and instructed by the useful Pieces in it, than with the Articles about the Poles or Corsicans: But I cannot help observing that you have lately had fewer Pieces than formerly on our distressed Situation. – Are our Circumstances altered? Is Money grown more plenty? Have our Tradesmen full Employment? Are we more Frugal? Is Grain cheaper? Are our Importations less? – not to mention the Play-House and Equipages, which it is hoped none but People of Fortune frequent, or use.... [W]hat a dismal Prospect is before us! a long Winter, and no Work; many unprovided with Firewood, or Money to buy it; House-rent, and Taxes high; our Neighbours daily breaking, their Furniture at Vendue in every Corner. Surely it is high Time for the middling People to abstain from *every Superfluity*, in *Dress*, *Furniture*, and *Living*: And I will venture to say, they will be as well esteemed by their Neighbours, – for at present they are only envied at, talked of, and if unfortunate severly reflected on; mere Conveniences will give the most lasting Satisfaction; Show and Finery will soon or late give Pain. If by good Management we can save a little, How loudly will the

Distresses of our Neighbours call for it? Some former able House-keepers starving, yet ashamed to beg: some Families starving for want of work; some dragged to Gaol. . . . The very mention of these, raises every tender Emotion in the human Breast: How must *we* feel that too frequently see them?[73]

"TRADESMAN" clearly identifies himself in this letter with a "middling People" who are vulnerable to economic distress, who "too frequently see" the actual distress of poorer folk who are their neighbors, and who threaten to bring on their own ruin by their aspiration to exceed a frugal life. He does not identify with "People of Fortune," who are alone justified in attending theaters and driving carriages, and to whom the suffering of the poor offers no lessons in self-conduct. The view of urban society we are offered here is one that emphasizes (and accepts) the gap between the rich and everyone else, and that recognizes "middling People" as both prosperous (in good times) and vulnerable, and as people who share the latter condition with the poor.

Middling status, then, especially as it was embodied in the image of the handworking, leather-aproned mechanic, would appear to have been quite humble, not much above that of the poor, and well below that of the rich. Yet, as many historians have noted, artisans were able to assert claims for a higher degree of respectability, both as the producers of essential goods and as independent businessmen. "Mechanic" to them meant possession of a skill that distinguished artisans from laborers and other unskilled workers, and some artisans, unlike the "TRADESMAN" quoted above, took pains to disassociate themselves from the poor on this and other grounds.[74] Even fairly small craftsmen, moreover, were men of business, serving a variety of customers, organizing their own daily affairs, keeping their own accounts, and doing so in a culture dominated not by aristocratic *rentiers* but by other businessmen. Most masters were teachers and (theoretically, at least) moral guardians of apprenticed youth, many were employers of one or more journeymen, and a small number were in actuality manufacturers, builders, designers, and publishers who provided the materials for and supervised the production of their employees.[75] A few trades – most notably, silversmithing and others that involved working in precious metals – were lucrative enough to attract the sons of merchants, and in Philadelphia one silversmith was the son of a German count.[76] In a number of other trades, too, especially those producing high-priced or fashionable goods – carriages, hats, fine clothes, for example – there were always a few quite successful men who stood out above the rest.[77]

There was, in short, a fundamental, unresolved contradiction in

the social standing of the majority of middling folk. The social degradation of manual work circumscribed the status of all artisans, but
the independence of many, and the prosperity of a few, strained the
very idea of a clearly differentiated set of social levels – more, no
doubt, than did the vertical communities of interest that supposedly
bound specific elites and non-elites through a chain of patronage and
deference. The contradiction, it should be emphasized, was not
merely in the criteria by which the "better sort" assumed the social
worth of those they saw below them, but was internal to the culture
of middling folk. "Philadelphia's artisan culture," writes Eric Foner,
"was pervaded by ambiguities and tensions, beginning with the inherent dualism of the artisan's role, on the one hand, as a small
entrepreneur and employer and, on the other, as a laborer and
craftsman."[78]

Artisans did address these tensions, and came closest to resolving
them when they portrayed themselves as independent enterprisers
who, however, were content to live frugally on the modest incomes
that traditionally fell to the manual trades. The almanacs, most of
which appear to have been written by printers and other artisans, are
filled with advice that balanced industry and diligence with frugality
and simplicity, and with invocations of the superiority of plain living
over ostentation:

> Want you to know what keeps the Mind
> In ev'ry Sense of Life resign'd?
> These are the Things: a little Wealth,
> A little Bus'ness just for Health;
> A little House, and Fire Nose-high;
> One spare Bed where a Friend may lie ...[79]

There is, to be sure, a hint of cynicism in the phrase "A little
Bus'ness just for Health," but the almanacs, even at their most mischievous, invariably limited the proper ambition of ordinary people
to a life of simple comfort. To artisans specifically, the advice "Keep
thy shop, and thy shop will keep thee"[80] encapsulated the modest
meaning of independence in business.

So too, in a far more revealing way, did the collective response of
Philadelphia's master tanners, curriers, and shoemakers to price controls imposed on their goods by an extralegal committee during the
wartime inflation of 1779:

> For many years preceding the issuing of the present currency, the
> prices of skins, leather, and shoes were so proportional to each
> other as to leave the tradesmen a bare living profit; this is evi-
> dently proved by the circumstance well known to every body,
> that no person of either of these trades, however industrious and

attentive to his business, however frugal in his manner of living, has been able to raise a fortune rapidly, and the far greater part of us have been contented to live decently without acquiring wealth, nor are the few among us who rank as men of property, possessed of more than moderate estates. Our professions rendered us useful and necessary members of the community; proud of that rank, we aspired no higher, and should never have troubled the public by drawing their attention to us as a body, had not an attempt been made which (however well intended) must necessarily, if persisted in, end in the impoverishment and ruin of ourselves and our families.[81]

The manner in which the leatherworking artisans began their protest is most interesting. They portrayed themselves not as poor men but as useful citizens content to live within the boundaries of what was often called a "decent competency" (the leatherworkers' own phrase is "to live decently without acquiring wealth"). There were "men of property" among them, but these possessed no more than "moderate estates." Proud of being "useful and necessary members of the community," they "aspired no higher." The first words of this broadside invoke traditional relations of price and profit, and the opening passage as a whole is clearly grounded in traditional notions of a "moral economy." Yet these were businessmen, and their protest was phrased also in the far newer language of free market economics. Using a phrase that merchants had used in their own remonstrance, the leatherworking artisans concluded their broadside by opposing all price controls on the ground that "trade should be free as air."[82]

Other ambiguities arise when we consider that not all middling folk were artisans. Retail shopkeepers, small-scale importers, innkeepers, public officials of various kinds, clerks, and even a number of professionals and semiprofessionals – schoolteachers, doctors and lawyers with small practices, ministers to congregations of ordinary people – also stood outside and below the urban elite on the social scale. I know of no attempt by a contemporary commentator on eighteenth-century urban society to isolate this group of nonmanual middling folk as a social category separate from the skilled mechanics. John Lambert, writing of New York in the first decade of the nineteenth century, describes a "second class" consisting of "small merchants, retail dealers, clerks, subordinate officers of the government, and members of the professions," which he distinguishes from a "third class" consisting of "the inferior orders of the people."[83] But Lambert's classification scheme was unique. No one else writing up to this time pushed artisans into the bottom rank, and none focused on shopkeepers, officials, clerks, and small professionals as the substance and

core of the middling sort. (Very few, we may recall, used the term
"class.") Nonmanual middling folk, indeed, received very little attention, but were generally assigned, explicitly or implicitly, to a large
middle category that was dominated in numbers and in character by
skilled mechanics.

The contradictions and ambiguities of middling status were to some
extent irreducible. Yet, even considering the socially elevating effects
of business proprietorship and essential skill, the social standing of
the artisan-dominated middle category was a modest one. "Middling
rank" did refer, on balance, to a rather humble position in society,
one easily conflated with that of "inferior" sorts by elites who stood
so far above both.

The material lives of middling folk

Underscoring the differing social implications of nonmanual and manual work of various kinds, were the differing economic rewards that
flowed to merchants, retailers, artisans, and laborers, and the material
life-styles that accompanied particular ways of making a living. In the
previous section I referred briefly to the dignity that artisans attached
to living simply, within bounds of their "decent competency," avoiding the ostentation and dissipation that could bring only ruin to men
of limited means. Other historians have made more of this elevation
of the simple life, noting that artisans used it to assert moral superiority over both the rich and poor, and, in the years following the
Revolution, to associate their own way of life with the strength and
even the survival of the republic.[84] Plain-living artisans may indeed
have prided themselves on their simple virtues, and there was no
lack of encouragement to them from serious political writers, most of
whom stood above the artisans in the social order. But in the face-
to-face society of the eighteenth-century city this kind of moral superiority existed parallel to, not within, what I have been calling the
culture of rank. Within the latter, wealth conferred prestige and influence, and ostentation was its badge. In the presence of this badge,
simplicity compelled humility rather than pride. It is essential, therefore, that we consider the ways in which differences of wealth and
life-style intersected with socially distinctive categories of work.

Historians who in recent years have analyzed local tax assessment
lists and probate records in an attempt to measure inequalities in the
distribution of wealth have found that in the largest cities the wealthiest 5% of taxpayers or decedents owned upward of half of the community's assessed or inventoried wealth in the Revolutionary era.[85]
The difficulties of translating these documents into accurate descrip-

tions of the actual distribution of wealth are immense and, I believe, unresolved,[86] but the quantitative analyses of inequality do lend support to the long-established view that the urban merchant elite, especially in the second half of the eighteenth century, developed an opulent style of living that differed greatly from that of their less affluent neighbors. It was in these years, as Carl Bridenbaugh somewhat acidly observes, that "Boston's quality grew accustomed to a gay and expensive existence and took on the cosmopolitan outlook, hauteur, insistence on privilege, and elaborate ritualism of a free-spending, pleasure-loving, Anglican coterie."[87] Describing her analysis of Philadelphia estate inventories from 1774, Alice Hanson Jones writes, "I had the feeling that I could almost literally see the emergence of wealth in the city, analogous to the rise of town wealth in Europe in the late Middle Ages."[88] New and expensively furnished town houses and country mansions, carriages attended by liveried servants, expensive and fashionable clothes, private dinner parties and formally organized dancing assemblies were the foundations of a life-style that often impressed even European aristocrats. "The profusion and luxury of Philadelphia on great days," observed the Duc de la Rochefoucault Liancourt at the end of the century, "at the tables of the wealthy, in their equipages, and in the dresses of their wives and daughters, are . . . extreme. I have seen balls on the President's birth-day where the splendor of the rooms, and the variety and richness of the dresses, did not suffer in comparison with Europe."[89] The English gentleman John Lambert, who found that "the style of living in New York is fashionable and splendid," attended a dancing assembly at the City Hotel and "did not perceive any thing different from an Engish assembly."[90]

It was, to be sure, a bourgeois upper class that these Europeans were describing, and a recently established one at that. Isaac Weld, who liked practically nothing about the United States, noted of "the uppermost circles in Philadelphia" that "nothing could make them happier than that an order of nobility should be established, by which they might be exalted above their fellow-citizens, as much as they are in their own conceit."[91] The parvenu character of the Philadelphia elite was obvious, especially to a European aristocrat such as Rochefoucault.[92] Still, it was also obvious that Philadelphia and other cities had acquired an affluent upper stratum that rather successfully emulated the opulent life-styles of the European upper class.[93]

But what of the material lives of less exalted folk, and in particular those of middling rank? Analysts of the distribution of wealth have observed a reduction in the proportion of wealth owned by middle-decile taxpayers and decedents,[94] but this reflects mainly the increasing fortunes of the rich, and says nothing of the actual resources and life-styles of middling people. Other scholars have come closer to the mark by analyzing (or making educated guesses at) artisanal incomes. Contemporaries frequently observed how much better off manual workmen were in America than they were in Europe,[95] but the emphasis in most recent research has been on the limited incomes and economic insecurities against which artisans and other workers struggled. Noting the increasing numbers of people excused from paying taxes in Boston and Philadelphia, Nash writes of "crumbling economic security within the lower middle class,"[96] and his statement receives surprising support from historians who are better known for stressing the prosperity and entrepreneurial spirit of the artisan class. Jackson T. Main, for example, in *The Social Structure of Revolutionary America*, clouds a sunny picture of well-fed, well-clothed, well-warmed, home-owning craftsmen by adding that "most artisans lived near the margin, were vulnerable to depressions, and could purchase few luxuries." Married journeymen craftsmen "just about broke even," while most masters earned "little more than journeymen."[97] Or as Charles Olton puts it, "most mechanics lived dangerously close to bankruptcy most of the time."[98] The most careful analysis of artisanal incomes thus far is Billy G. Smith's tabulations of the profits, wages, and living costs of shoemakers and tailors (as well as of mariners and laborers) in Philadelphia before and after the Revolution. Smith found that fully employed journeymen in these two trades earned wages that barely covered minimum costs of rent, food, firewood, and clothing, while in shoemaking, fully engaged masters earned about 22% more than bare subsistence on their own labor, and another 25% or so on the labor of each fully employed journeyman.[99] Tailors made slightly more.[100] Few if any artisans could expect full employment even in the best of years, however, and most masters worked either alone or with only occasional help from journeymen, so Smith's estimates must be regarded as exceeding any realistic maximum for the ordinary artisans of these two crafts. Even at their maximum they suggest how little the margin of comfort and safety was in Philadelphia, at least for those who worked in the less lucrative trades.

It is actually rather difficult to reconstruct artisanal incomes, even for those few artisans whose account books survive to our own day, for these books appear to have been kept primarily or entirely to maintain an accurate record of debts and payments on debts rather than to serve the calculation of profits or losses. Almanacs occasionally advised small shopkeepers to "often state your accounts, and examine whether you gain or lose," but artisans appear not to have done so.[101] In this and other ways, however, artisans' account books suggest a way of life – or at the least an approach to business and personal affairs – rather different from that of the merchants. Merchants (or rather their clerks) kept neat and orderly books that conformed to and sometimes went beyond standard accounting practices. For example, Joshua Haines, a Philadelphia importer, kept an elaborate and extremely orderly set of books, with an indexed ledger, a coding scheme for interpreting entries, and account and book headings executed in a flowery, calligraphic hand. William Forbes, also of Philadelphia, left behind an account book devoted entirely to transactions with his cooper, implying a very specialized set of books for his business as a whole. Garret Abeel, a New York City retailer and occasional wholesaler, kept a very neat and detailed daybook, with a separate column to indicate payment next to specific entries. Artisans, who did not employ clerks trained in bookkeeping and penmanship, kept cruder and simpler account books that, moreover, almost invariably mixed business with personal transactions, and even with entries that were not transactions at all. David Evans, for example, a Philadelphia cabinetmaker whose customers included George Washington and John Adams, kept a detailed but somewhat disorganized daybook that included a number of personal transactions and events. In November, 1780, he entered in solemn tones the death of his father-in-law. The hatter William Lawrence's daybook was neater than Evans's, but it too mixed personal with business affairs, as did the daybook of A. Howell, a hatter, who entered personal loans and rentals, family deaths, and a twelve-year diary of the weather. Most interesting, however, is the very primitive ledger of Joseph Graisbury, a Philadelphia tailor. Graisbury seems to have used only this ledger, entering daily transactions directly into individual accounts in a tiny hand, and crossing out accounts when they were settled. The ledger is devoted entirely to business, except for an extraordinary account entitled "Michael Higgins My Sergeant," which records lost time for being "Laid out Drunk" with Ned and Harry for two days and nights, "1 Day Lost being on Monday in Bad Company Drunk," and "1½ Days Lost at the horse Race." Stitched into the ledger at this page is a smaller sheet detailing, in a confessional tone, the two-day binge recorded in the sergeant's account.[102]

To look at the artisans' account books in this way is to gain a glimpse, through a very narrow window, of men in pursuit of a "decent competency" for themselves and their families. What that competency meant in terms of actual material resources, however, and how those resources compared to the material goods available to families above and below the artisans in the social structure, must be established through other documents. One such resource – perhaps the most fundamental of all – was the quantity and quality of living space, and one exceptionally pertinent and surprisingly neglected document is the surviving set of tax assessment lists that served as the basis for the Federal Direct Tax of 1798. Unlike most local tax assessment lists, these unique federal lists (representing the first and only time the federal government ventured to tax local property) describe individual dwellings in great detail, recording, for example, the width, depth, and number of stories of each dwelling, the materials of which it was built, the number and size of its windows, and the number and types of its outbuildings. As the name of the occupant of each rented dwelling was listed separately from that of its owner, and as the location of each property was specified as precisely as possible (by address where addresses existed), one can associate specific kinds and amounts of housing space with specific occupational groups, providing only that a large enough number of occupants can be traced to other records (city directories, for example) that list occupations. The detailed lists appear to survive for only a few places, but fortunately these include three central wards of the City of Philadelphia, and all of the Northern Liberties that formed a significant portion of that city's periphery and semiperiphery. I recorded all of the listings from the three central wards (High Street, Walnut, and South, the last actually stretching from the center to the western edge of the city), all of the listings from the inner section of Northern Liberties East, and a sufficient number of cases from the inner portion of Northern Liberties West to give adequate weight to the urban periphery. The resulting file of 1,256 cases appears, on the basis of the mean assessments and populations of each ward and district, to represent quite well the metropolis as a whole (see Figure 2.3).[103] I then searched for the occupants of the 1,256 dwellings in the city directories of 1797, 1798, and 1799 (two in the latter year), and found 892 (71% of the entire file) listed there by occupation, or designated as gentlemen or gentlewomen. This somewhat smaller file of nearly nine hundred men and women identified by occupation, address, and a number of housing characteristics, is not quite as representative as the larger file, for city directories were less inclusive of poorer artisans, journeymen, unskilled workers, and the residents of the urban periphery than they were of more prosperous and centrally located residents of the city.[104] Still, just over half of the smaller file consists of manual proprietors and workers, 10% unskilled and 40.5% skilled. About two-thirds consists of artisans, shopkeepers, tavernkeepers, and others whom contemporaries regarded as middling folk.

Table 2.1, based on this file of Philadelphia householders, summarizes the distribution among them of one very basic aspect of urban

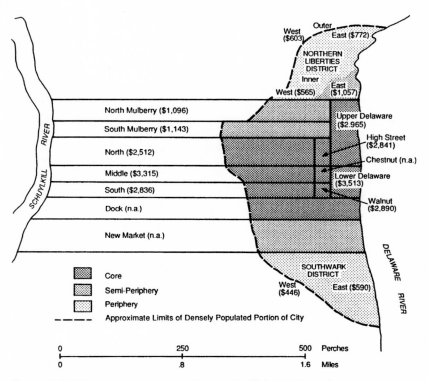

Figure 2.3. Mean tax assessment by ward, Philadelphia, 1798

living – the amount of floor space within dwelling houses – according to broad categories of occupation.[105] The median floor space for each occupational group reveals, first of all, a striking difference between the merchants, professionals, and high-ranking public officials that constitute the first category (1,566 square feet) and the middling and poorer sorts that make up the other three. Differences among the latter three groups are smaller in magnitude, and it is particularly interesting to note that the median for artisans is only 136 square feet higher than the median for carters, sailors, laborers, and other un-skilled workers. Storekeepers, grocers, and other nonmanual mid-dling folk enjoyed somewhat more living space than the artisans, but 900 square feet, the median for that group, is not very large, in fact not much more than half the median for the merchants and profes-sionals. The median artisan lived in only 648 square feet, somewhat less than the 800 square feet that Sam Bass Warner, in *The Private City*, attributed to the ordinary artisans and storekeepers of Phila-delphia when he described their "cramped" and modest way of life.[106]

Table 2.1. *Floor space in dwelling by occupational category, Philadelphia, 1798*

	Occupational category			
	High nonmanual	Low nonmanual	High manual	Low manual
Median floor space (in sq. ft.)	1,566	900	648	512
Categories of floor space (in percentages)				
Over 2,000 (10th decile)	33.5	8.6	4.2	1.1
1,601–2,000 (9th decile)	16.2	15.6	7.5	2.2
901–1,600 (4th quintile)	34.0	24.6	20.3	3.4
601–900 (3d quintile)	10.2	25.8	25.8	21.3
451–600 (2d quintile)	4.1	14.8	21.4	30.3
Under 451 (1st quintile)	2.0	10.7	20.8	41.6
Total	100.0	100.1	100.0	99.9
n	197	244	360	89

Note: The high nonmanual category includes merchants of various kinds, brokers, professionals, and high-ranking public officials. It includes gentlemen and gentlewomen as well. The low nonmanual category includes storekeepers of all kinds, grocers, innkeepers, real estate agents, sea captains, manufacturers, clerks, accountants, and minor public officials. The high manual category includes all artisans, and the low manual category includes laborers, sailors, carters, stevedores, and a variety of other unskilled manual occupations.

Source: Manuscript assessment lists, Particular List A, Federal Direct Tax of 1798; city directories of 1797, 1798, and 1799.

Not all artisans lived in houses of 648 square feet, and not all storekeepers in houses of 900. Table 2.1 displays the distribution of dwelling sizes for each occupational category, within approximate quintiles (and the highest two deciles) of the city's houses arranged by size. The "high nonmanuals" were clustered in the upper two quintiles, and fully a third were in the highest decile, which consisted of dwellings larger than 2,000 square feet. "Low manuals" mirrored this distribution by locating mainly in the bottom two quintiles, representing houses of 600 square feet or less. Middling folk, however, were spread much more evenly – storekeepers and other "low nonmanuals" were actually overrepresented in the ninth decile, while artisans were spread almost evenly across all the quintiles except the highest. To some extent this wide variation in artisanal housing reflects the differences among trades – hatters (84.6%) and precious metals craftsmen (71.4%) were clustered in the highest two quintiles, while butchers (78.6%), cabinetmakers (66.7%), blacksmiths (63.2%), shipwrights (61.1%), and coopers (57.9%) were concentrated in the lowest two. But other trades – tailors, tanners, carpenters, and bakers, for example – were spread fairly evenly, reflecting the significant differences of economic well-being among their greater and lesser practitioners.

How shall we understand life in 648 square feet, or 900 square feet, of Philadelphia housing at the end of the eighteenth century? First we must note, as many others have before, that it usually included work as well as domestic life. Only 10% of the artisans in the file maintained a workshop outside of and on the same premises as their dwelling, and only 124 workshops are identified separately from any dwelling by the assessors for the 1798 tax, in the lists of commercial buildings that survive for 11 of the 17 wards and districts that constituted urban Philadelphia.[107] These figures support the traditional view that most artisans maintained workshops within the walls of their dwellings, often in the front room of the ground floor, sometimes on the entire ground floor, sometimes in a garret. Some trades may have permitted putting tools and materials away at the end of the day and using the workshop as family living space in the evening, but most clearly did not. For many artisans, therefore, and probably the large majority who were not in the construction trades, actual living quarters constituted but a portion of the interior space enumerated in Table 2.1 – two rooms or three, two-thirds or perhaps only half of the 600, 700, or 800 square feet contained within the dwelling as a whole. Even some of the artisans who lived in large buildings may have been quite cramped, for some required larger workshops, while others added a front-room "show shop" that forced the workshop into other spaces. John McAllister, a whip and cane maker at 48 Chestnut Street, lived in a three-story house of 1,728 square feet, one of the larger artisanal dwellings. McAllister was one of the few Philadelphia artisans who advertised in the newspapers in 1798 (this alone suggests that his was a particularly large shop), and in his ad he refers to the large assortment of whips and canes on hand in his shop, which was at the same address as, and (judging from the absence of a separate shop on the assessment list) within the walls of, his home.[108] McAllister probably devoted at least the entire ground floor to his business, reducing by a significant amount the space in which he and his family lived. In his fairly extreme case a larger than average area was left for domestic affairs, but it is clear that most artisans, including even some of those that appear in the upper quintiles of Table 2.1, lived in very small homes. Laborers who owned or rented houses in Philadelphia, and who did not have to share space with a workshop, probably lived under conditions no more cramped than those of most skilled tradesmen.

The workshops that squeezed artisan families into such small spaces also compelled them to live in close proximity to the noises, smells, and other distractions of work itself, a fact that must often have influenced the character of artisans' homes. Even more influential, perhaps, was work *within* the few rooms that middling folk (non-manual as well as artisanal) had left for domestic life. Cooking and other forms of household production were much more difficult to isolate from dining, visiting, and other leisure activities within a two- or three-room home than they were within a home of six or seven rooms. Approximately half of Philadelphia's houses, we should note, had exterior kitchens, usually behind the house in a separate building and sometimes connected to the house by a covered walkway that Philadelphians called a piazza.[109] These kitchens permitted the removal of cooking, washing, and a few other heavy household chores from living spaces, and increased the possibility that some of these spaces could be nicely furnished as parlors or dining rooms. However, the exterior kitchen was more commonly found behind large houses than behind small ones. Approximately two-thirds of the dwellings larger than 900 square feet had kitchens beyond their walls, a proportion that dropped to under half for homes of from 600 to 900 square feet, and to only one-fourth for homes smaller than 600 square feet. Hence, the inequalities of living space were even greater than they appear to be in Table 2.1.[110] Philadelphians who owned or rented large houses had the opportunity to live very differently (they would have said more graciously) than those who lived in small and even average-sized houses, where the tools and the chores of both the workshop and the home were always close at hand.

Householders owned or rented city space as well as dwelling space, and this, too, varied significantly by occupational category. City dwellers of all types mingled in the central wards of Philadelphia and, as we have observed, no section of the city was set aside as an exclusive quarter for the rich. (The latter, incidentally, was less true in New York, where lower Broadway and the streets extending westward from it toward the Hudson River constituted a fairly distinct upper-class district.)[111] But as Figure 2.3 suggests, and Tables 2.2 and 2.3 confirm, the distribution of homes and families in urban space was far from random in Philadelphia. The vast majority of merchants and professionals lived in the central wards, and those that lived outside of these wards occupied much smaller houses (see Table 2.3). It is reasonable to assume that the latter were, in the main, those less

Table 2.2. *Zone of residence by occupational category, Philadelphia, 1798*

| | Occupational category | | | |
	High nonmanual	Low nonmanual	High manual	Low manual
Zone of residence (in percentages):				
Core	69.0	39.3	35.3	12.4
Semiperiphery	27.4	38.5	35.0	38.2
Periphery	3.6	22.2	29.7	49.4
Total	100.0	100.0	100.0	100.0

| | Zone of residence | | |
	Core	Semiperiphery	Periphery
Occupational category (in percentages):			
High nonmanual	36.8	17.5	3.3
Low nonmanual	25.9	30.5	25.5
High manual	34.3	40.9	50.5
Low manual	3.0	11.1	20.7
Total	100.0	100.0	100.0

Source: See Table 2.1.

Table 2.3. *Median floor space in dwelling by occupational category and zone of residence, Philadelphia, 1798*

| | Occupational category | | | | |
	High nonmanual	Low nonmanual	High manual	Low manual	(All cases)
Zone of residence (in square feet):					
Core	1,812	1,335	900	720	(1,200)
Semiperiphery	1,188	900	644	544	(684)
Periphery	1,000	720	544	504	(560)
Entire city	(1,566)	(900)	(648)	(512)	(720)

Note: Includes entire file of 1,256 cases.
Source: See Table 2.1.

prosperous and less prominent "high nonmanuals" who were not (or not yet) among the urban elite.[112] Fairly large numbers of "low nonmanuals" and artisans lived among the wealthy in the central wards, but most did not, and many lived well beyond – again in significantly smaller houses – in areas of the city where there were very few merchants and professionals, and very large numbers of unskilled workers.[113] These were the least attractive and least convenient parts of the city, where two-story houses outnumbered three-story houses, where wooden construction was more common than brick (58% of the houses in Northern Liberties West, as compared with 4% in Walnut Ward, were built of wood), and where municipal services were most poorly performed.[114] In the setting of their homes, no less perhaps than in their size and character, middling folk were more clearly distinguished from the rich than from the poor.

Moreover, some of the homes of shopkeepers and artisans who did live in the center of the city were distinguished from those of the better sort, though in a somewhat different way. Virtually all of the blocks within the core of the city were crisscrossed with alleys and courts, along which stood houses that were smaller and humbler than those that lined the nearby streets. The few unskilled householders who lived in the central wards resided almost exclusively on these narrow lanes (9 of 11 in High Street, Walnut, and South wards), and so did nearly a third of the "low nonmanuals" and artisans. By contrast, only 7 of 136 (about 5%) of the merchants and professionals of High Street, Walnut, and South wards lived in alleys. It hardly needs stating that the alleys of the central wards were dominated by and easily associated with the middling and poor of those wards. In the three central wards detailed in the 1798 tax assessment lists, more than 90% of the identifiable residents of alleys pursued middling or unskilled occupations, and nearly 60% performed skilled or unskilled manual work. This was in a section of the city in which nearly three of every eight householders were merchants, professionals or other "high nonmanuals."[115] To be sure, the segregation of ranks within the urban core was far from perfect, for the homes of the more prosperous shopkeepers and artisans intermingled with those of the better sorts along the major streets. The single city block that constituted High Street Ward displays both the pattern of segregation by residential frontage and its imperfections (see Figure 2.4). Along Market (or High) Street, between Front Street and Second, stood a row of some of the most expensive dwellings in the city, ranging in assessed value from $3,500 to $8,000. Living in the $8,000 house was William Ball, a retired merchant and planter, and the First Provincial Grand Master of the Ancient (York) Order of Masons.[116] Most of Ball's neighbors were wealthy merchants, but three were hatters (including his immediate neighbor to the west), and four more were shopkeepers of different kinds (though at least two of these may well have been importers or wholesalers as well as retailers). Second and Front Streets

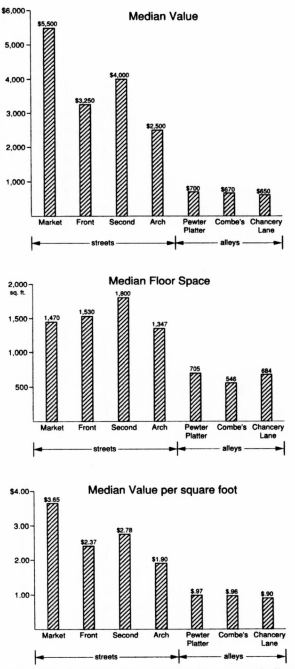

Figure 2.4. Selected characteristics of street and alley dwellings, High Street Ward, Philadelphia, 1798

were two of Philadelphia's most important downtown streets, and were dominated by wealthy merchants. Like Market Street, however, the merchants shared this valuable frontage with some of the city's most prosperous tradesmen, most of whom were hatters, silversmiths, and goldsmiths. William Cobbett published *Porcupine's Gazette* at 25 North Second, and at 14 North Front lived and worked Thomas Wishart, whom Abraham Ritter recalled as an "eminent tallow chandler."[117] Arch (or Mulberry) Street was more genuinely heterogeneous (and its houses significantly less valuable), perhaps because it constituted a boundary of sorts between the core of the city and the less affluent neighborhood to the north. Arch had its merchants and gentlemen, but there were larger numbers of middling folk, and its tradesmen included a rigger, a tailor, a bricklayer, and a bleeder.

Three alleys lay behind these major streets in High Street Ward. On Pewter Platter Alley, a 16-foot-wide lane running just behind Market Street, resided 28 householders, in homes averaging only $670 in assessed value. Only one resident of this alley, a physician, pursued a "high nonmanual" occupation; 3 were "low nonmanuals" (a grocer, a shopkeeper, and a minor official), 13 were artisans, 5 were unskilled, and 6 were not listed in any of the city directories (5 of these were women). Combe's Alley, like Pewter Platter, was filled with middling and poor folk – two grocers, two boardinghouse keepers, a schoolteacher, 8 artisans, a carter, a wool comber, and 4 others who cannot be identified by occupation. On Chancery Lane were only 10 households, including one headed by a merchant and another by a "gentleman," both living in houses somewhat above the average in size and value. Their neighbors, however, were shopkeepers and artisans, the latter including a block and pump maker, a ship joiner, and a shoemaker. The streets and alleys of this central ward were obviously very different kinds of urban spaces, even though they were separated by only a few feet. No doubt, living on one or the other carried with it very different and very clear social implications. It may be significant, indeed, that residents of the alleys were far more transient in their places of residence than were the residents of the streets – 14 of 18 Market Street residents, but only 8 of 28 householders of Pewter Platter Alley, for example, can be traced back from the 1798 tax list to a street directory published in 1795.[118]

The assessors summarized all of these variations in housing size, character, and location in arriving at their final evaluations, which are themselves summarized in Table 2.4. Not surprisingly, there is an even greater disparity here than there is in the distribution of housing sizes between the "high nonmanuals" and all the other occupational groups (compare Tables 2.1 and 2.4). The median valuation

Table 2.4. *Assessed value of dwelling by occupational category,*
Philadelphia, 1798

		Occupational category		
		High nonmanual	Low nonmanual	High manual	Low manual
Median assessed value		$2,963	$1,200	$800	$500
Categories of assessed value (in percentages):					
Over $3,800	(10th decile)	36.7	9.4	4.2	1.1
$2,301–3,800	(9th decile)	23.0	14.7	9.2	—
$1,151–2,300	(4th quintile)	25.0	28.6	20.6	3.4
$701–1,150	(3d quintile)	10.7	21.2	19.2	19.1
$401–700	(2d quintile)	4.1	16.3	25.1	31.5
Under $401	(1st quintile)	.5	9.8	21.7	44.9
Total		100.0	100.0	100.0	100.0
	n	196	245	359	89

Source: See Table 2.1.

for merchants and professionals was nearly $3,000, approximately 2.5 times the median for storekeepers and other "low nonmanuals," and 3.7 times the median for artisans. The storekeepers' median, meanwhile, was 50% higher than the artisans', and the artisans' 60% higher than the unskilled workers' – noticeable differences, to be sure, but not nearly as great as the gap between the better sort and everyone else. In the decile and quintile distributions, the only significant difference between Table 2.1 and Table 2.4 is the greater concentration in the latter of "high nonmanuals" in the highest two deciles. Moreover, these figures almost certainly understate the actual disparity between the housing values of the merchant elite and those of the rest of urban society, not only because the poorest shopkeepers, artisans, and laborers are underrepresented in the data, but also because in Philadelphia no less than in other places the homes of the wealthy were undervalued to a greater extent than were the homes of the middling and poor.[119] Even at face value, however, all of the patterns that emerge from the Federal Direct Tax assessment lists suggest highly visible differences between the material lives of the merchant and professional elite, and those of the city's middling and poorer folk.

Housing was not the only consumer good that defined urban ways of life. What of the furnishings and other personal goods that filled these domestic spaces, the food that was eaten there, and the clothing that was stored there and worn on the city's streets? In her meticulous study of late colonial estate inventories, Alice Hanson Jones tabulates differences in the household furnishings and other consumer goods belonging to merchants, shopkeepers, and artisans that are quite consistent with the differences of living space and housing values just described. In the Mid-Atlantic colonies, according to Jones, merchants averaged £69.8 (sterling) in consumer goods, while shopkeepers (£25.8) and artisans (£16.4) owned smaller and fairly similar amounts.[120] "Laborers and mariners" owned slightly more than the artisans (£18.9), but this category in Jones's tables is probably distorted somewhat because sea captains, and even former captains engaged in commerce or farming, sometimes referred to themselves as "mariners" in their wills. In Philadelphia, where the wealthiest and most free-spending of the region's merchants, retailers, and tradesmen lived, the differences between the merchants and the middling sorts were significantly greater. Jones's sample includes 8 inventories of Philadelphia merchants, 8 of shopkeepers and other nonmanual middling businessmen (including an innkeeper, a livery stable keeper, a tobacconist, a druggist, and a brewer), and 19 inventories of artisans.[121] The merchants of Philadelphia averaged £212.2 in consumer goods, while the shopkeepers and the artisans averaged £45.4 and £37.2 respectively.

What these values meant in terms of actual living conditions can be understood only by turning to the inventories themselves. The merchants' inventories ranged a great deal from the average, from the £22.2 in consumer goods of Joseph Dempsey (who lived well outside the core of the city in Southwark, and was apparently single), to the £509.8 of Samuel Neave. Neave was an extremely rich man, whose net worth was more than £6,600 sterling at the time of his death, and whose large city house was filled with mahogany and walnut furniture, china, carpeting, and silver, and who maintained as well a less opulently furnished "Country Seat."[122] But the five merchants whose consumer goods were much closer to and even somewhat below the average lived quite well too. Thomas Gilbert's £157 of consumer goods included about three dozen silver spoons, tankards, and other pieces (valued at £33.3), a mahogany tea chest, a good deal of walnut furniture, damask bottomed chairs, carpeting, thirty-three bottles of wine, and a riding chair.[123] Edmund Kearney, whose goods were valued at almost exactly the same amount (£155), had somewhat less silver but more china and carpeting.[124] The details vary from case to case, but the picture is a clear one. Six of the eight Philadelphia merchants in Jones's sample lived in large, expensively furnished houses, in which all of these highly valued goods, and others, provided a domestic setting of comfort and even opulence.

Middling folk enjoyed comforts too, but on an entirely different plane. Of the 19 artisans and 8 "low nonmanuals" among Jones's Philadelphia decedents only 7 owned consumer goods valued in excess of £60. None of these 7 approached any of the 6 wealthy merchants in the opulence of their homes. Joseph Frazer, for example, was a well-to-do baker whose net worth was over £800 sterling and whose consumer goods were valued at £93.8, third highest among the 27 shopkeepers and tradesmen. Frazer's house included front and back parlors as well as rooms upstairs, but these were furnished much differently from the parlors and chambers of the merchants. In the baker's front parlor were a desk, a covered table, a breakfast table, three rushbottom chairs, a bookcase, and a few ornaments, valued together at approximately £6. Curiously, they shared space with two casks of nails, which at £7.6 were by far the most valuable objects in the room. The back parlor did contain an eight-day clock and a mahogany dining table, but the rest of its contents also contrasted with the furnishings of merchants' parlors – a pine breakfast table, two kegs of rum and brandy, china bowls that were "broken & whole," and about £5 worth of silver. Upstairs was one more mahogany piece (a chest of drawers) and the only carpet in the house, described as three-quarters worn.[125] This was the home of a quite prosperous artisan, but it was by no means a place of opulence or style.

Frazer lived in a manner fairly similar to that of several less wealthy artisans. The painter Enoch Hughes, for example, lived with his family above and behind his shop on Front Street, in three rooms, a kitchen, and a garret that contained one small bed. Hughes's net worth was only £107.5, but nearly a third of it (£37.6, almost exactly the mean for artisans) was invested in consumer goods that filled two of his three domestic rooms. In a room behind the shop were several walnut pieces (two tables, six leather-bottomed chairs, a desk, and a cradle), a pine table and stand, a small amount of Delft and china, a Bible, and a law book. Upstairs in front were two beds and bedsteads, one with curtains, a chest, table, and armchair made of pine, a £4 silver watch, and £2 worth of other silver pieces. The back room upstairs, like the garret, contained only a bed.[126] Hughes's parlor (it is not identified as such on the inventory) was actually more nicely furnished than Frazer's, but the rest of his small home was furnished more sparsely, and entirely in inexpensive woods. No room in the painter's house was carpeted.

If Hughes's consumer goods were almost exactly average for the inventoried artisans, William Goetting's, at £45.1, were almost exactly average for the shopkeepers and other "low nonmanuals." His home, which appears to have been limited to three rooms over his shop in

Northern Liberties, had a little more furniture than Hughes's, but all
of it was plain and cheap, and the inventory lists "a parcel of old
rubbish in the yard."[127] Christopher Stevenson, an innkeeper who
died at forty (Goetting died at forty-nine), owned goods worth a little
less (£40.8), but in one room, a parlor, they were somewhat nicer –
a clock worth £5, a walnut dining table, a mahogany-framed mirror,
and a few pieces of Queen's ware and Delft on the mantel, along with
plainer items.[128] In only one or two cases, indeed, did the families of
either artisans or "low nonmanual" businessmen live in homes that
contained more than one attractively furnished room. John Philip
Stein, a brewer, invested more in consumer goods than did Goetting,
Stevenson, or any of the other nonmanual middling sorts, and it is
possible to find in his list of chattels (valued at £82.6, but undiffer-
entiated as to room), the makings of one parlor and one bedchamber
furnished entirely in walnut. But even Stein's home lacked the opulence of the merchants'. Pine mixes with walnut on his inventory,
there is little silver or expensive china, and there is neither uphol-
stered furniture nor carpeting anywhere on the list.[129]

Of the 27 middling cases in the sample, 10 lived in homes that
lacked even the modest comforts enjoyed by Enoch Hughes and
Christopher Stevenson. A few were poor, and one or two appear to
have been bachelors or widowers, but several were family men of at
least moderate wealth whose homes, like that of Joseph Frazer, did
not reflect their means. James Stoops, for example, was a brickmaker
worth £400 sterling, mostly in real estate. His consumer goods were
worth only £15.5, and his house contained only a few inexpensive
beds, tables, chairs, and desks, some bedding and pewter, "sundry
old books," and a good clock worth £4.[130] Joseph Janvier, a shipwright,
had a net worth of £330 (again mostly in real estate), but his furnishings and other personal goods were valued only at £16.2. Janvier
owned two walnut tables and two bedsteads of average value, but
very little else of value, and very little other furniture – two chests,
a pine table, eight chairs, and two mirrors.[131] The inventory of Robert
Walker, a Southwark joiner worth £90, includes a few beds, a (mahogany) cradle, and "a lot of household & kitchen furniture," the
latter evaluated at all of ten shillings.[132] Walker, in particular, was the
sort of artisan who was probably underrepresented in the probate
records. We may wish to conclude that extremely modest homes such
as his were as common among ordinary middling folk as were the
somewhat more comfortable homes described in the previous
paragraphs.

The dining rooms and tableware of the merchants and their less
wealthy neighbors were very different, but the food they ate may

have been less so. Good food was plentiful and inexpensive in Philadelphia's markets, and European visitors to this and other American cities often commented on the well-fed workmen they saw about them. "There is not a family" among the "inferior classes of workmen," observed Rochefoucault, "who does not eat meat twice a day at least, and drink tea and coffee; . . . the proverbial wish of *having a chicken in the pot*, is more than accomplished in America."[133] Rochefoucault, we can be sure, did not make a systematic study of artisans' and other manual workers' tables, and it is interesting to note that the two trades he goes on to mention in this discussion, tailors and hairdressers, were among those whose *leading* practitioners would have been in a position to serve a visiting French duke. Indeed, it is reasonable to assume that most Europeans who commented on the well-being of American mechanics were unduly influenced by the more prosperous artisans they saw around them, and remained ignorant of the larger numbers of poorer artisans and less skilled workers who lived on narrow alleys and in peripheral neighborhoods, and who did not enjoy the custom of the rich and well connected. Did these men and their families eat meat twice a day and drink tea and coffee? Enduring evidence of these perishable goods, particularly from the homes of ordinary people, is hard to find, although the estate inventories do offer some clues. They confirm, for example, by the nearly universal listing of tea and coffee pots, coffee mills, and various other implements, that tea and coffee were in fact consumed by people of all ranks (even the porter in Jones's Philadelphia sample, who owned only £4.6 of household goods, had two teakettles and a coffeepot).[134] The rich, to be sure, had more elaborate kitchens than middling and poor folk, and with one exception it was only the merchants who kept on hand supplies of Madeira and other wines. The exception was the prosperous baker Joseph Frazer, a thirsty man, who also laid in ample stores of brandy, gin, and rum. Nearly all the merchants, but apparently only about a third of the shopkeepers and artisans, owned table knives, but this may reflect a difference in table manners, or in the value of each group's small implements, rather than in the incidence of meat eating. William Douty, a clockmaker in Northern Liberties, seemingly owned no knives, but he did own three hogs, and John Fisher, a brickmaker, owned some salt pork.[135] Merchants, no doubt, occasionally enjoyed sumptuous dinners that middling folk could not afford. But the everyday fare of the middling and upper ranks of urban society may well have been much the same.

Clothing was certainly different, in part because of differences in wealth, in part because of the demands of different kinds of work, and in part because of traditional constraints against dressing above or below one's station. But the differences can be exaggerated. The Philadelphia antiquarian John Fanning Watson, whose 1845 *Annals of Philadelphia and Pennsylvania in the Olden Time* is a widely consulted source concerning urban life in the Revolutionary era, describes tradesmen's dress in humble terms, emphasizing the leather apron as the emblem as well as the necessary protective outer garment of a less proud generation of artisans who "did not then ... present the appearance in dress of gentlemen." Under the leather apron, continues Watson, were "dingy buckskin breeches, once yellow, and check shirts and a red flannel jacket," while the wives of tradesmen wore equally distinctive "shortgowns of green baize."[136] However, Watson's nostalgic descriptions of a pre-Jacksonian city in which people lived plainly, and in which inferiors knew and happily kept their places, cannot always be relied upon. A more recent description of urban mechanics' dress emphasizes "hair curled at the side in emulation of the upper class," and "cocked hats, stocks, ruffled shirts, buckled shoes, and coats," in addition to the necessary leather aprons.[137] Almanacs of the period complained of excess in dress, and advised tradesmen and others against it, sometimes as a practical matter (don't dress better than your creditors, advised one almanac),[138] and sometimes in service to sumptuary tradition and the culture of rank. "Let your apparel be such as becomes your station," *Father Tammany's Almanac* told shopkeepers and tradesmen in 1786, "and seek not to imitate those who are in better circumstances than yourself."[139] Whether this was practical advice or moral injunction is difficult to say, but in Nathaniel Ames's *Astrological Diary* dressing above one's station was explicitly condemned as a threat to the maintenance of proper social relations: "The middle sort strive to equal those of quality. ... The lowest rank of men would pass for a middle sort. ... Thus a whole nation falls to ruin; all conditions and ranks of men are confounded."[140]

Complaints such as these reflect both the strength and the weakness of sumptuary traditions – the continuing belief that middling sorts should dress more plainly than better sorts, and defiance of that belief by those who would dress above their station. But they do not tell us how observance and defiance were balanced in the actual dress of ordinary people. Again, the estate inventories provide the most solid clues. The clothing listed in the merchants' inventories in Jones's Philadelphia sample averaged £13.3 in value, more than three times the average value for artisans (£3.9) and shopkeepers (£4.0). These figures exclude the gold and silver watches and gold-headed canes that appear on a number of inventories (the latter only on those of the merchants). If watches and canes are included, the merchants' average increases to £19.3 sterling, while the shopkeepers' and artisans' averages increase by much smaller amounts, to £4.9 and £5.7, respectively. The inventories generally do not describe clothing in detail, but they suggest that some middling folk did carry silver watches, and that a larger number wore silver knee or shoe buckles. The latter were not expensive items, however, and it is perhaps more significant that the few middling wardrobes described in the inventories consisted mainly of old and apparently plain clothes of no great quantity. The only exception in the sample is Jacob Chrystler, who owned five tight-bodied coats, one greatcoat, seven jackets, five pairs of breeches, five shirts, two black neckcloths, four pairs of stockings, two pairs of boots and two pairs of shoes, one pair each of silver knee and shoe buckles, and a number of mohair and silk-covered coat and jacket buttons.[141] Not surprisingly, Chrystler was a prosperous tailor.

One other item on the estate inventories distinguished the merchants from middling and poorer folk. Seven of the eight merchants in Jones's sample, but only five of twenty-seven shopkeepers and artisans, owned some kind of personal conveyance. Among the latter, moreover, all five owned only riding chairs, while three of the merchants owned more imposing vehicles – a chariot, a coach, and a riding chaise. Samuel Neave's chariot was valued at more than £40 sterling (his three coach horses were worth another £77), and appears on the list of carriages that Pierre Du Simitière drew up in Philadelphia in 1772, two years before Neave's death. Du Simitière (an artist who may have prepared his list as a way of identifying potential patrons) found 84 carriages of various kinds in the city, including 10 coaches, 47 chariots or post-chaises, and 27 coach-wagons or phaetons. Of the 84 carriage owners, 27 were merchants, professionals, high-ranking public officials, or other members of the urban elite; 5 were artisans or manufacturers – 2 carpenters, a tanner, a glass and button maker, and a brewer – all of whom owned coach-wagons, the least expensive vehicles on the list. A sea captain and a grocer each owned a chariot.[142] The expensive carriage was perhaps the foremost emblem of mercantile opulence in the Revolutionary era. It is obvious that only a handful of those who were not among the city's elite could ever aspire to own one.

What all of these details tell us is that there was a material foundation for the culture of rank in late-eighteenth-century American cities – a fairly close correspondence between the day-to-day life-styles and the perceived social worth of merchants, shopkeepers, artisans, and laborers.[143] America in this era was not a land of scarcity, but neither was it yet a land of abundance for large numbers of its city dwellers. The limits of abundance in this "best poor man's country," indeed, were reflected most clearly in the cramped and modestly furnished homes of the middle stratum of the urban population – homes that resembled those of the poor more closely than those of the rich. People of middling rank lived in small, inexpensively furnished houses, in which domestic activities were accommodated to those of the workshop or store. To be sure, middling folk ate well, and probably dressed fairly well too, but their decent competency did not buy them the life of comfort that the urban middle classes of subsequent generations would enjoy. A few shopkeepers and artisans of the eighteenth century were men of wealth, and an unknown fraction of the middling sort did live in comfort, but the material lives of most were simple enough, and hard enough, to underscore the humble connotation of middling rank. The beetle thought the bee insolent (in the Philadelphia *Aurora*'s fable of 1796) because his riches flowed through the "dirty channels" that provided most of his fellow bees with only a trickle. Had the channels flowed more freely for all, the beetle would no doubt have thought them clean.

The mechanics' revolution – and after

The character of the culture of rank, and the meaning of middling status within that culture, are probably best revealed in the politics of the Revolutionary era, when mechanics and other ordinary citizens found the best opportunity for asserting themselves against the institutions and assumptions that had so circumscribed their role in public affairs. Large numbers of the "middling and poor" did in fact assert themselves in very striking ways as the imperial crisis developed, protesting British policy in increasingly autonomous crowds, routing suspected Tories and punishing violators of nonimportation as members of sanctioned or unsanctioned "committees of safety," democratically electing officers and petitioning for fairer laws within Revolutionary militia units.[144] These were, however, distinctly plebeian modes of exerting pressure on the political system, and some had a long history of containment within the deferential political order.[145] Whatever they may say about the ascending political consciousness and influence of the common citizen, they speak first and foremost of the inferior position of the mechanic, the seaman, and the laborer within the political system as a whole, and in particular of their traditional exclusion from the political bodies in which public policy was deliberated and made. The formation of mechanics' committees, on the other hand, and the increasing representation of artisans (but not of seamen, laborers, or other "inferior sorts") on the extralegal deliberative bodies that appeared in each city to direct the course of colonial resistance, may have been another matter. Here, seemingly, was a genuine breakthrough for men of middling condition, and an apparently irreversible reorganization of political roles in eighteenth-century American society – in Richard Alan Ryerson's terms a "mechanics' revolution" that "destroyed forever the old mercantile and Quaker elites of both city and province, and transformed the greater part of both official and effective power to an aggressive, rising, pluralistic middle class."[146] It is to this "mechanics' revolution" – the one in the committee room – that we must turn to find the most telling test of the changing or persisting meaning of middling status in the late-eighteenth-century city.

The clearest story of increasing artisanal participation in the decision-making apparatus of resistance and revolution is set in Philadelphia (as Ryerson's reference to Quakers suggests). Extralegal committees appeared early and openly in Philadelphia, in the absence of leadership from conservative-dominated official bodies of municipal and provincial government. Despite the vacuum that this situation implies, the leaders of the early committees were drawn almost exclusively from the wealthiest men in the city. Nearly all were merchants, professionals, and manufacturers, with only 5 of 138 committee positions (through June of 1774) occupied by mechanics. However, leadership of the protest movement broadened as the movement itself moved toward the more radical goal of national independence. According to Ryerson, the selection of a "mechanics' ticket" over a "conservative ticket" to form a Committee of 66 in November 1774 "gave every occupational group and every class above the level of unskilled labor a direct and significant voice in political affairs for the first time in Philadelphia's history." In truth, only 17 of the 66 members of the committee were mechanics, and only one-quarter of those eligible to vote in the committee election took the trouble to do so. But artisan representation increased sharply thereafter, reaching 40% on the Committee of 100 selected in February 1776. It was between 1774 and 1776, as Ryerson concludes, that the mechanics' revolution fundamentally altered "the social location of political power" in America's most important city.[147]

In other cities, too, artisans sought new avenues of political participation, mainly through extralegal committees but occasionally within provincial or state legislatures. In 1774 in New York City, artisans formed a General Committee of Mechanics, which met as often as once a week to formulate and communicate artisan opinion, and which challenged a merchant-led Committee of 50 that rejected nonimportation in response to Boston's appeal for help in the wake of the Intolerable Acts. In 1777, the city's first delegation of the new state legislature included three artisans, the baker Abraham P. Lott, the cooper Daniel Dunscomb, and Abraham Brasher, a silversmith.[148] Artisans were numerically dominant in Charleston's Sons of Liberty, and were apparently numerous in some of the caucuses and clubs that operated behind the scenes in the Boston resistance.[149] In nearly all of the major port cities (Baltimore appears to have been an exception)[150] mechanics had significantly increased their role in political decision making during the course of the imperial crisis.

No doubt the Revolution did change "the social location of political power" in ways that suggest something other than continuing deference by middling folk to merchant leadership and an elitist view of the mechanic's place in the social structure. In Philadelphia and in other cities it was clearly a catalyst for the crystallization of new attitudes, and for a new, more assertive public posture on the part of artisans and other ordinary citizens of middling rank. But there are other, less radical implications in several aspects of this story of ascending popular politics. One, seldom noticed by historians, is the lateness of the artisan upsurge. Despite the obvious opportunity provided by the rapid expansion of political roles within an increasingly revolutionary setting, it was only as the resistance movement entered its second decade that artisans began to find a significant voice in many of the extralegal committees or in legal bodies of government. Mechanics were well represented in organizations formed to direct and control public protest, but only in 1774 and after did they appear on the various committees emerging as alternative governments within the Revolutionary city. Why were the artisans not more assertive at an earlier stage of the escalating protest? Or, to phrase the question a different way, why were their assertions not focused on the gaining of political authority for representatives of their own kind?

The most reasonable answer is that through much of the crisis – until resistance began to turn into revolution – artisans continued to view their proper political role in traditionally circumscribed terms, as a popular resistance exerting pressure from below, but not as a source of political leadership. In this connection we might note that in New York, which did send artisans to the state legislature in 1777, the one attempt to nominate an artisan for the provincial Assembly during an earlier stage of the imperial crisis failed miserably. Amos Dodge, a carpenter, was put forward in 1768, but finished last in the voting, and apparently received no more than 12% of the votes of his fellow artisans. "Dodge," writes Patricia U. Bonomi, "lacked the sort of finish that was regarded in that day as more or less indispensable for holding high public office, and his candidacy seems not to have been taken very seriously by the others."[151] In New York, indeed,

the signs of continuing deference are as impressive as the signs of
ascending participatory democracy. In 1774, when the merchant-dominated Committee of 50 rejected nonimportation, the General Committee of Mechanics responded by forming a rival Committee of 25.
Despite the clear collision of interests on this issue between importing
merchants and local producers, this "mechanics'" committee consisted largely, if not entirely, of merchants and "gentlemen."[152] Mechanics served in very small numbers in the committees that
coordinated even the last stages of resistance in New York, and it
may be significant that the three recognized leaders of New York's
radical mechanics – Isaac Sears, John Lamb, and Alexander McDougall
– were rising merchants.[153] These three men appear to have lost touch
with their humbler followers at various phases of the imperial crisis
– after the passing of the Stamp Act crisis, for example, and especially
after 1774 – but when they did they were not replaced by new leaders,
either from the ranks of mechanics or from among the rest of New
York's parvenu merchants. Pressure from the middling and lower
sorts seems to have relied heavily on the personal leadership of these
three radical merchants, and to have been sporadic through the decade preceding independence, waning when the leaders failed to give
it voice.

There are indications, moreover, that the mechanics' revolution was
to some extent engineered from above, even in cities where greater
numbers of mechanics served in leadership roles. Ryerson himself
suggests that the increasing presence of mechanics on the extralegal
committees in Philadelphia was in large part a deliberate tactic
adopted by wealthier, nonartisanal leaders in order to strengthen the
popular appeal of the resistance movement. "Philadelphia's committees were balanced and inclusive," he writes, "because those who
composed the election tickets and led the new boards willed it so."[154]
Alan and Katherine Day arrive at a similar conclusion after discovering
some twenty artisans among the sixty known members of the North
End Caucus in Boston.[155] This need to mobilize public support behind
one rather than another set of traditional leaders may also help explain
why some merchants and professionals were willing to run for committee membership on "mechanics' tickets." The naming of such tickets, and the incorporation of artisans into decision-making bodies,
were real concessions to a more popular form of government. They
were, however, concessions to the exigencies of mobilization in a time
of crisis. The extent to which they were also necessary responses to
a vigorous new claim by the artisans to a share in the exercise of
authority remains unclear.

Third, the mechanics that did join extralegal committees and state legislatures were invariably selected from the most prosperous and ambitious artisans in the city. All were masters, nearly all were owners of significant amounts of property, and some were wealthy.[156] Olton describes them as "manufacturing entrepreneurs with continuing and accelerating upward social, economic, and political aspirations."[157] These were the artisans who were most like the merchants in life-style and outlook, and though their inclusion in policy-making bodies was a significant departure from the old system, the "mechanics' revolution" was less significant than it would have been if more or-dinary mechanics had been included as well. In adhering to the radical agenda of the resistance and revolution, artisan committeemen pur-ported to speak for all mechanics, large and small, but they do not appear to have pressed the issues of local political leadership and participation. "Nowhere in the sources of this history," writes Olton, "is there evidence that they wished to displace the leadership of the merchants; the mechanics' political activity represented an attempt by a secure but rising class of entrepreneurs with special needs to join others in the exercise of political power."[158]

Finally, we must recognize the importance of the "special needs" and particular interests of the artisans in shaping their participation in the resistance movement. The centerpiece of colonial resistance was nonimportation, a policy that helped local producers as much as it inconvenienced or endangered many importers. In terms of eco-nomic interests, therefore, mechanics were the natural allies of radical merchants and professionals, and, when given the opportunity, could be counted on to help overcome more conservative merchants reluc-tant to vote for or comply with nonimportation as a policy of resis-tance. In the committees, artisan leaders represented this "mechanics' interest" (a vertically defined "interest" of the traditional sort) as well as the aspirations of a previously excluded social stratum, and it should be clear that these aspirations were to a considerable extent legitimized by the fact that the artisans' economic interests had quite suddenly become politically significant. That it was so significant was not the artisans' doing; rather, it reflected the broader patterns of imperial economic and political relations, and the policy options those patterns made available to resistance leaders. Would artisan partici-pation have been so acceptable to radical merchants and professionals, had those patterns and policy options been different? Could artisans have asserted themselves as an unjustly excluded social group (even as "a rising class of entrepreneurs") if they were not so relevant as an economically defined "interest"? There was, in short, a fortuitous element in the political ascendancy of the artisanal leaders.

The mechanics' revolution, though, was by no means an accident.

It must be recognized that artisans and other middling folk fought for and gained political recognition during the Revolutionary era. Yet the most important point that emerges from these political events of the 1760s and 1770s is that a rare combination of circumstances and notable changes was required before middling folk of any kind could exert even a modest influence over political affairs, even in the context of a larger revolution in which political roles were rapidly expanding in number, and in which the mobilization of popular support was an unprecedented necessity. Given this context, the very rise of a mechanics' interest, the obstacles it had to overcome, and the length of time it took to overcome these obstacles, express most clearly the humble position that middling folk occupied in urban society and politics. Moreover, the downward shift in the "social location of political power" that Ryerson describes, and the successful assault on deference politics that constitutes the central theme of Gary Nash's more general study, may have been less profound and less enduring than either claims. After the Revolution old assumptions and political relations reasserted themselves in striking ways. Prosperous masters in several cities formed permanent associations, and through them continued to press the mechanics' interest in politics, but rarely did this effort translate into artisan officeholding at any but the lowest levels. In Baltimore, for example, the Association of Tradesmen and Manufacturers was founded in 1785 and nominated its first candidate for the state Assembly in 1787. He was a physician.[159] Not until 1805 was a mechanic, one Robert Steuart, put forward for the Assembly. Steuart was a "stone cutter" who was in reality a wealthy quarry owner, contractor, and builder; yet he was criticized "for overstepping the bounds of a mechanic."[160] We have already seen that in 1794, when Baltimoreans were considering a proposed city charter, mechanics objected to *viva voce* voting because the "rich and the great" would exert too much influence over the "poor and middling." As late as 1808 a Baltimore editor could use very similar language to explain why mechanics were still excluded from the city council: "The fact is this, (with the exception of some worthy characters) that the great ones of the earth cannot bear to be put on a level with the middling classes of mankind."[161]

Baltimore was perhaps the most conservative of cities with respect to artisanal political participation. But even in Philadelphia, where artisans had been most visibly active in the politics of the resistance and the Revolution, old patterns of political recruitment and influence returned soon after the Revolution ended. "By the 1790s," writes Robert F. Oaks, "Philadelphia was again a merchant-dominated society."[162] Merchants and professionals did indeed fill most important public offices in the 1790s, to the extent that nominations of humbler people were occasions for comment. In October 1796 a letter in the *Aurora* praised a nomination meeting for choosing Common Council candidates "from the different trades and mechanic arts," an action that, he claimed, "removes" the obviously still extant opinion that such people ought not to hold this kind of public office.[163] An interesting glimpse of this return to merchant-dominated politics in Philadelphia is obtained by comparing two committees of this decade that dealt with outbreaks of yellow fever. The first, formed during the worst days of the terrible epidemic of 1793, consisted, in Mathew Carey's description, of "men taken from the middle walks of life, and of the moderate pitch of abilities."[164] The mayor and three or four merchants were on the committee (the mayor and two merchants held the highest three offices), but so too were larger numbers of middling folk – coopers, painters, carpenters, schoolteachers, innkeepers, and others.[165] However, what must be added to this apparent incident of democratic mobilization is the observation that most of the city's prominent citizens had fled the city, and were still absent when the committee was formed. A year later the crisis loomed again in the form of an outbreak in Baltimore, impelling Philadelphians to form a new committee charged with preventing trade and travel between the two cities. This time the merchants were in town, and they dominated the committee. Of 16 identifiable members, 10 or 11 were merchants, 1 was listed in the directory as a gentleman, and 1 was a justice of the peace. They were joined by an apothecary and a bookseller, and 1 artisan, a clock and watch maker. A final position was held by either a merchant tailor or his son, who was a merchant.[166]

In sum, it is the strength of the culture of rank, not its weakness, that stands out in the political and social history of the American port cities during and after the Revolution. Artisans asserted themselves, especially during the Revolution, in ways they had not done before, but they did not succeed in elevating themselves much above the modest rank that separated them from the better sort, and "middling rank" and its equivalents remained terms suggestive of the limits of prestige that could attach to a social stratum numerically dominated and largely defined by handworking mechanics. At most the Revolution heightened the contradiction that simultaneously recognized independent businessmen as the essential figures in urban society, and degraded those independent businessmen who happened to work with their hands. As long as this contradiction remained unresolved, the most significant boundary in urban society would be the one that separated the merchant and professional elite from everyone else. Eventually it would be resolved, or nearly so, not by the removal of the prejudice against manual work but by new economic relations in a new urban setting that refocused that prejudice on those who were not men of business. In the urban-industrial revolution of the Jacksonian era and beyond, middling folk would redefine themselves, and elevate themselves, in ways that were not possible in the craft economies and little urban worlds of the eighteenth century.

3 Toward white collar: nonmanual work in Jacksonian America

It is a commonly accepted view among historians that the Jacksonian era, and the years immediately after it, witnessed many fundamental changes in American life. Indeed, the existence of various interconnected revolutions in political, economic, and social life during the two, three, or four decades preceding the Civil War appears to be one of the staples of American historical thought. The various "new" histories of recent years, however novel they may have been in subject and technique, have served mainly to reinforce this old idea, and in some instances to extend it into new areas. This seems particularly true of the "new working class history," whose practitioners have made vigorous claims for the importance of changes in the structure of industrial production, in the institutional and ideological responses of workers to these changes, and in new configurations of class and class consciousness that reflected the impact of new experiences on traditional ways of life and thought. Our understanding of the Jacksonian revolution must now, it seems, include the notion of an emerging working class.[1]

Must it include as well the notion of an emerging middle class? We have already noted the attempts of several recent historians to chronicle "the formation of a new American middle class"[2] during this period, and I attempted to show in the preceding chapter that such a class had not already formed by the end of the eighteenth century. In what ways might we expect to find evidence of the formation and ascendancy of a relatively distinct middle class in the rapidly growing and industrializing (and already much larger and more complex) "urban crucibles" of the nineteenth century? The working-class historians themselves provide the most obvious clues, most generally by suggesting the increasing salience of class in Jacksonian America, and more specifically by noting the reciprocal influence that emerging classes are likely to have upon one another. In one of the most insightful of the recent working-class histories, Sean Wilentz observes that "the history of the crafts leads directly to what might be called the problem of the middle class." Not only the workers, but also the employers and independent small producers, set the "terms of confrontation" by which both the working class and the middle class came to recognize and define themselves. "To make sense of the emerging middle class in this context," writes Wilentz, "is to begin to comprehend the dialectics of power and social change."[3] Classes develop simultaneously, and in the context of each other's increasing presence – the process that creates one class includes the creation of others.

Wilentz's discussion is directed in part to the overt conflicts and diverging ideologies that give meaning to the phrase "terms of confrontation." But it refers as well to more basic developments, changes in modes of production and distribution that, even in the absence of specific episodes of confrontation, altered the relations between workers and their employers. Put another way, Wilentz's propositions concerning class consciousness and ideology are grounded in the history of work. In this he is far from alone, and his excellent discussion of changes in work and workplace relations within the core of the industrializing metropolis only makes more complete what is by now a well-told tale of the effects of early industrialization on the training, the skills, the work experiences, and the opportunities of manual workers.[4] But what is still missing, glaringly so in the light of Wilentz's comments on the reciprocity of working-class and middle-class formation, is any sustained effort to uncover and understand the history of nonmanual work in the same era.

Was there a revolution in work in the nonmanual sector, parallel to and perhaps interconnected with the revolution in work in the manual sector, during the Jacksonian era? If so, was it associated with changes in economic well-being and perceived social worth in ways that suggest the emergence of a new middle class? In the next two chapters I attempt to answer both of these questions (the first one here, the second in Chapter 4), and in both cases my answer is in the affirmative. Furthermore, I argue that even if the consideration of other aspects of social life and thought later compels us to set limits on the idea of middle-class formation, changes in nonmanual work and workplace relations constituted a significant though hitherto largely unchronicled component of that broad revolution that historians have located in American society (perhaps I should say American urban society) during the second quarter or middle third of the nineteenth century.

In an important sense, the phraseology I am using here may misrepresent the kinds of changes I wish to discuss. Work, defined as a set of specific tasks performed in specific ways, did not change in the nonmanual sector to the degree that it did for many who toiled at increasingly specialized, routinized, and even mechanized manual jobs. As Alfred Chandler has pointed out, merchants and clerks of the 1840s (and most who worked beyond into the 1850s and 1860s) conducted their affairs and carried out their tasks with essentially the same techniques and implements, and according to the same principles, as those who preceded them by many decades. The same transactions, the same accounting systems, the same letter books and writing desks, occupied the workdays and workplaces of men of commerce in both the Jacksonian and the colonial eras.[5] Changes in commercial work did occur, and we will take note of them, but the most significant elements of change lay not in the structure or technology of specific tasks, but in a number of somewhat broader relations: first, in the increasing alignment of nonmanual work with entrepreneurship and salaried (as opposed to wage-earning) employment, and, to cite the well-known reverse of the coin, the increasing alignment of manual work with employment for wages; second, in the increasing specialization of firms in the nonmanual sector; and third, in the increasing physical separation of manual from nonmanual work, the increasing distinctiveness of manual and nonmanual work environments, and the rapid elevation of nonmanual work environments by means of architecture, interior design, and the location of firms within urban space. Let us consider each in turn.

Business and work: a new alignment

"The occupations of Philadelphia in 1860," writes Sam Bass Warner, Jr., "remained much as they had in 1774. The city was still an agglomeration of old trades – laborers, clerks, carpenters, tailors, weavers, shoemakers, grocers, liquor dealers, butchers, tobacco dealers, cordwainers, blacksmiths, and cabinetmakers."[6] A mere glance at the city directories of the late-eighteenth and mid-nineteenth centuries lends credence to this statement. Save for peruke makers, machinists, and a few other trades that had disappeared or arisen in the intervening years, the occupations listed in the directories of the two eras are much the same. But what Warner does not sufficiently acknowledge, and what the city directories do not reveal, is how much the meanings of many of those unchanging occupational designations had been transformed. Some, indeed, had nearly lost their meaning, as they continued to describe with a single, traditional term – "tailor," say, or "shoemaker" – men whose work experiences were becoming steadily more divergent. Under the disguise of old labels, the "agglomeration of old trades" had in fact become something quite new, not only in Philadelphia but in all the cities of antebellum America.

Consider first the furniture industry, and the memoir of Ernest Hagen, a German-born cabinetmaker who worked in New York during the middle decades of the nineteenth century. Cabinetmaking was one of the industrializing trades of the antebellum era, evolving slowly at first, and then rather quickly after the introduction around 1840 of circular saws for cutting veneers, from the traditional collection of small, independent, handworking, custom shops of the preindustrial era, to a more complicated arrangement of interdependent factories, dealers, auction houses, sawmills, and specialized small workshops.[7] Hagen describes some of these institutions in New York during the 1850s. At or near the top of the industry was Charles O. Baudouine's Broadway furniture emporium and factory, which employed two hundred cabinetmakers, upholsterers, clerks, and others, for the manufacture, importation, and sale of furniture in the French style. Henry Weil operated a different sort of large-scale enterprise, manufacturing goods in an East Side factory for shipment to New Orleans and other distant markets. Near Weil's factory was a large collection of very small, unmechanized shops, producing not the expensive custom goods of earlier small shops, but inexpensive goods for the new retail furniture stores. Most of these shops were clustered around riverfront sawmills, from which they obtained the materials for the specialized production of cheap sofas, bedsteads, bureaus, bookcases, card tables, or other pieces, usually in a single pattern or style. Hagen does not discuss the furniture dealers, or indicate how many men who came to be involved only in the distribution or sale of furniture once had been cabinetmakers. Besides Baudouine and Weil he identifies by name only two other men, A. Dohrmann, master of a small East Side workshop, and J. Mathew Maier, who in 1850 was a fellow journeyman with Hagen in Dohrmann's shop. All four of these men were listed in *Doggett's New York City Directory, for 1850–51* as cabinetmakers; yet it is clear that only Dohrmann and Maier continued to produce goods with their own hands. Dohrmann was in fact a handworking master, and in this sense at least – though certainly not in the kind of work he produced or in his relationship with his customers – he was a throwback to the preindustrial era. But Baudouine and Weil were wealthy manufacturers. The work they performed was not sawing, gluing, carving, or veneering, but buying, selling, shipping, and the managing of other people's production.[8]

Gotlieb Vollmer of Philadelphia was also a former cabinetmaker who, by the late 1850s, had become a furniture manufacturer. His business, however, which employed from two dozen to three dozen hands, was smaller than Baudouine's or Weil's. (In *McElroy's Philadelphia Directory* of 1860, Vollmer is included under "cabinet makers" in the listing of businesses. In the main body of the directory his occupation is listed as "furniture.")[9] Vollmer's ledger from the years 1860 and 1861 survives, and provides an interesting insight into the significance of the transition from handworking artisan to industrial manager. The ledger is much more "businesslike" than the financial records of David Evans and other producing artisans of the eighteenth century. Vollmer used traditional bookkeeping methods, but he improved on the basic system by posting frequently to his ledger, and by calculating weekly summaries of purchases, sales, wages, and other expenses. The ledger is very orderly, and reflects quite clearly the business manager's interest in the frequent generation of accurate information concerning the flow and profitability of business.[10] This contrasts markedly with older artisanal records that focused on personal accounts receivable and payable – that is, on who owed how much to whom – rather than on profitability and the contributions to profit or loss of different categories of revenue and expense. A larger manufacturing firm such as Brewster & Co., New York carriagemakers (if I may switch industries for a moment), could go further than Vollmer, recording transactions by invoice number in a separate sales journal.[11] But it is apparent from Vollmer's ledger that even fairly small manufacturers were capable of conducting their business affairs more like contemporary merchant capitalists than like the artisans of the preindustrial era.

Similar examples of artisans turned nonmanual businessmen can be drawn from other industries. Even more rapidly than in cabinet-making, the production of clothing evolved from custom tailoring in small shops into a complex industry, producing and selling vast quantities of ready-to-wear clothing through networks of sweated outworkers, contractors, central shops, jobbers, wholesalers, and large and small retailers.[12] The clothiers who ran this industry were often former tailors who now supervised and coordinated the work of hundreds, sometimes even thousands, of other people. J. C. Booth and H. L. Foster, "Fashionable Clothiers" in New York City, noted in their 1850 directory advertisement that "one of the members of the firm attends exclusively to selecting goods for the establishment, the other superintends in person the manufacturing department." Edward Fox, too, boasted of the internal arrangements of his large and modern clothing business, which included a custom department, a cutting department (employing "none but the most experienced artisans" and "none but the most thorough workmen"), a ready-made clothing department, and a furnishings department. Booth, Foster, and Fox are all listed as tailors in the directories in which these advertisements appeared, but the advertisements themselves demonstrate that these were businessmen who no longer worked with a needle or shears.[13]

It is clear from these few examples from the furniture and clothing industries that the traditional taxonomy of occupations, developed in the context of an artisanal economy, was changing too slowly to reflect the new nonmanual roles that were being generated by early industrial development. Censuses and city directories listed some men as manufacturers, and others by the names of the products they sold in their wholesale or retail stores. But numerous emerging manufacturers, wholesalers, and retailers continued to be listed as artisans, and even a few manufacturers were designated as skilled manual workers without ever having been artisans in the first place – the "founder" Cyrus Alger, for example, who was in reality a wealthy industrial capitalist who operated the sprawling South Boston Iron Company from his office on Central Wharf in downtown Boston (see Figure 3.1).[14] These were early days in the transformation of occupations and work roles, and it is not surprising that traditional occupational labels should have been applied in a misleadingly uniform way to men whose actual work experiences were rapidly diverging. In any case, where before there were only artisans, there were now manufacturers, contractors, subcontractors, supervisors, retailers, wholesalers – men who withdrew from direct participation in production in order to supervise or coordinate the manual work of others, or to sell or distribute goods they did not make themselves. Not all of these new men withdrew entirely from production – Lorin Brooks, a New York bootmaker, may have made some of the boots he sold from the modern retail store depicted in his 1842 directory ad[15] – and many antebellum manufacturers and retailers had not been artisans in the first place. Many traditional artisans remained, especially in the neighborhood service trades. But in every city there were numerous men, ostensibly members of manual trades, who simply no longer worked with their hands. These men were now nonmanual businessmen and managers, and, as we will see later, even those who continued to identify with their old trades, or with the "mechanics' interest" in general, were transforming those identities and that interest in ways that diverged sharply from those of their manual employees.[16] "The master cordwainers were no longer craftsmen in the classical sense," writes Ian Quimby; "they were merchant capitalists."[17]

My point is that even those who were not quite "merchant capitalists" were now performing new kinds of tasks that were giving new shape and significance to what I have been calling the "non-

SOUTH BOSTON IRON COMPANY.

CYRUS ALGER, and others, PROPRIETORS,

IRON CASTINGS

Of all descriptions, on hand and made to order at the shortest notice

IRON AND BRONZE CANNON

OF ALL SIZES, AND

HEAVY BRASS CASTINGS

MADE TO ORDER.

FORGE.

LOCOMOTIVE CRANKS, ANCHORS, SHAFTS, and SHAPES
of all kinds, made at the shortest notice, and of the best
quality, both as to material and workmanship

WORKS,
AT SOUTH BOSTON.

OFFICE,
No. 2 CENTRAL WHARF.

Figure 3.1. South Boston Iron Company advertisement, 1851 (courtesy of Cornell University Libraries)

manual sector." How many were there, and how should our recognition of their numbers affect our understanding of the nonmanual
sector as a whole? It is impossible to identify all those improperly
listed in manual trades, but the manuscript population census schedules of 1860 provide a useful clue by listing the value of each person's
real and personal property holdings. Presumably, it was the wealthiest of the "artisans" who, in the main, were clothiers rather than
tailors, or foundry owners rather than founders. Of course, the property listings are not perfectly reliable, and it is by no means clear how
one can draw a line that most effectively separates the two groups.
In Philadelphia, among twenty-two major trades representing more
than half of the city's listed artisans, approximately 2% reported more
than $7,500 in real and personal property, a level of wealth that placed
them close to the wealthiest decile of heads of household, and within
the wealthiest 5% of the adult male population. Another 9% reported
between $1,000 and $7,500, which placed them in the wealthiest 30%
of household heads, and in the wealthiest 15% of the adult male
population.[18] No doubt there were manual artisans among them, but
these were surely more than offset by nonmanual "artisans" who,
for one reason or another, and along with more than a third of the
city's merchants and lawyers, reported no property at all. It is reasonable to conclude that more than the 11% observed above – perhaps
15% would be a better estimate – should be recognized as members
of the nonmanual work force.

That work force, it is worth noting, was growing even from other
sources, and expanding in relation to skilled and unskilled manual
work. In 1860 approximately 25% of Philadelphia's male inhabitants
above the age of seventeen were listed on the census in explicitly
nonmanual occupations.[19] This appears to be a modestly higher proportion than equivalent occupations bore to the total work force of
Philadelphia on the eve of the Revolution. If 15% of those listed as
artisans in 1860 are transferred to the nonmanual sector, however,
the proportion of nonmanual workers rises to approximately one-
third. Philadelphia, moreover, which did contain very large numbers
of wage-earning manual workers in its vast industrial sector, probably
had a somewhat smaller nonmanual sector than most cities. The
younger industrial center of Milwaukee had a nonmanual sector of
almost exactly the same relative size as Philadelphia's, but the less
industrialized city of Boston had as many as 40% of its household
heads listed in explicitly nonmanual occupations.[20] (Heads of household are more likely to have a somewhat higher representation in the
nonmanual sector, but the proportion for Philadelphia's household
heads was just under 30%, still significantly below Boston's.)[21] The

booming new city of San Francisco had a "white collar" sector of 36%, according to Peter Decker's tabulations of the California state census of 1852, and a nearly identical proportion was obtained by Mary Ryan from the 1855 New York State census for Utica. In the more heavily industrialized small city of Poughkeepsie it was 29%.[22] None of these proportions is adjusted to include nonmanual businessmen who were listed as artisans. Perhaps, then, it is reasonable to conclude that the proportion of nonmanual businessmen and employees in American cities that were not unusually heavily industrialized reached or exceeded 40% of the total work force. But it was high, and apparently growing, even in industrial cities such as Philadelphia. Industrialization itself had contributed to the robust expansion of commercial life and to the generation of many new roles beyond the workshop floor.

More important than the growth of the nonmanual sector, however, was the increasing realignment of the relationship between work and business proprietorship. In the eighteenth century, many business proprietors were men who performed manual work, and a significant proportion of the city's manual workers were shop-owning masters. That this was rapidly changing in the Jacksonian era was demonstrated many years ago by the earliest labor historians, who, when attempting to explain the economic forces underlying the first phases of the American labor movement, focused much of their attention on the "crisis of the artisan" and on the steadily diminishing presence in most industries of the once independent, handworking master craftsman. According to this well-known view the craftsman, unable to compete with the heavily capitalized and commercially skilled merchant capitalist in the exploitation of rapidly developing distant markets, gradually fell under the merchant's control, eventually working as a factory foreman or garret boss if he was lucky, or as a wage-earning journeyman or factory hand if he was not.[23] More recent research has modified this argument somewhat, in part by finding instances where craftsmen did rise within their trades to become large or small manufacturers. Particularly prevalent in industrial satellite towns such as Paterson, Newark, or Lynn, where few merchants resided, and in industries such as machine building, where technical skill was as important as marketing, successful artisan-entrepreneurs could be found as well in the less technologically advanced, demand-driven industries of the major cities.[24] Charles Oakford of Philadelphia, to cite one example, began filling orders for hats in 1827, his capital consisting of youth, a few dollars, a good deal of skill and ambition, and a personality that quickly won customers and financial backers. This was not an unfavorable combination, and as Oakford's business grew it evolved through a number of shops into a fashionable and profitable retail store supplied by an off-premises manufactory.[25] But Oakford's experience, as a hatter turned retailer and manufacturer, and the experiences of "tailors" such as Edward Fox and "cabinetmakers" such as Henry Weil only reinforce the argument that the ownership of productive enterprises was falling increasingly into the hands of men who did not work, or no longer worked, alongside their employees on the workshop floor. To an unprecedented degree, employees produced and owners managed – and herein lay a new alignment of economic relations, familiar enough to a mature industrial society but revolutionary in its implications for a society still so close to the world of small artisan shops and leather-aproned masters.

Of course, there was still a large number of handworking master craftsmen, and their continuing presence in the urban economy reminds us that the alignment of work-type and proprietorship was not complete by 1860. In Philadelphia there were more than 3,600 artisan shops with fewer than six employees in 1860, and these accounted for some 58% of the city's industrial firms.[26] Perhaps not all of them were genuine proprietorships with handworking masters, but it is clear that shops that did conform to these criteria were far more numerous in Philadelphia on the eve of the Civil War than they had been on the eve of the Revolution. However, it is also clear that other kinds of businesses had multiplied at a much more rapid rate, and that even 3,600 artisan shops in this city of more than half a million people constituted a shrinking proportion of the city's businesses. Two or three generations earlier not 58% but nearly all of the city's industrial workshops were operated by handworking masters, and the producing sector was itself numerically larger in the overall mix of business firms. Just how much smaller the industrial proportion (and more specifically the artisanal proportion) had become is impossible to specify, as we lack reliable tabulations of nonindustrial businesses. Edwin T. Freedley, in his classic contemporary account of Philadelphia manufacturing just before the Civil War, claims that there were 7,404 stores in the city, although he cites no sources and fails to say whether he means to include other than retail stores in that number.[27] The New York State census of 1855 counted 9,617 retail stores in the somewhat larger city of New York, plus a slightly larger number of wholesale businesses, groceries, hotels, and inns, the total of 19,074 amounting to three commercial business firms for every one hundred inhabitants.[28] Applying this ratio to Philadelphia in 1860 yields approximately 17,000 commercial firms, but whether one uses this or Freedley's smaller number the fact emerges that the proportion of manual proprietorships had diminished markedly within the urban economy, to no more than one-quarter, and probably as few as one-sixth or one-seventh of the total number of businesses in the city.[29]

Many of these workshops, moreover, may not have been regarded as businesses in the same way that their predecessors (or their larger contemporaries) were. The eighteenth-century master craftsman was an independent business proprietor who maintained accounts with a wide variety of customers, and whose own taste and skill did much to set the terms and pace of his shop's activity. "But what," asks Wilentz, "was the independence of the small garret master, scrambling to meet the demands of the slopshops or the wholesalers?"[30] The question applies equally as well to the small East Side cabinetmakers, and to other small masters who produced cheap goods of one or two types or styles for sale, not to the general public but to a wholesaler, an auction house, or a Chatham Street retailer. To what extent was the general public even aware of the existence of these small businesses?[31] (The Boston furniture auctions, and no doubt most others who sold the output of these small shops, put their own labels on their goods.)[32] Far more visible were the bakers, blacksmiths, and a few others who worked in the neighborhood service trades, and the butchers, who often continued to provide their services from central markets. But these were precisely the trades least affected by new technologies and new methods of business organization, and were easily perceived as exceptions, even as archaic exceptions, to the increasingly evident alignment between business ownership and nonmanual work.

It may be argued that the growing number of clerks and other nonmanual employees disturbed this alignment from an entirely different direction, for now, in addition to proprietors who worked with their hands, there were significant numbers of employees who worked with their heads. It is true that the new nonmanual work roles generated by antebellum industrial and commercial development were not all proprietary ones, and that there was a general expansion in the cities of nonmanual employment. But quite beside the fact that clerks, salesmen, bookkeepers, and other nonmanual employees still constituted a rather small proportion of the male work force (the 10% that Ryan found in Utica was probably higher than in most cities),[33] we must note that most clerical employees were young men who, like their eighteenth-century predecessors, continued to be regarded and to regard themselves as businessmen-in-training rather than as permanent employees. In this and in other ways, not the least significant of which was that they were paid a salary rather than a wage, nonmanual employees were distinguished from manual workers. Actually, the work clerks performed was not always cleaner

Table 3.1. *Selected nonmanual employees by age, American-born white males, Philadelphia, 1860*

	Age				
	18–29	30–39	40 and older	Total	*n*
Occupation (in percentages):					
Clerk	68.8	17.6	13.6	100.0	816
Salesman	65.4	18.0	16.6	100.0	156
Bookkeeper	63.2	26.5	10.3	100.0	68
Accountant	30.0	45.0	25.0	100.0	20
Collector	—	33.3	66.7	100.0	12

Source: U.S. Census of Population, manuscript schedules (Philadelphia Social History Project file).

or more "mental" than the work performed by skilled manual workers, although sweeping the shop, stocking shelves, delivering merchandise to customers, and distributing handbills in the streets were chores reserved mainly for the youngest and most junior clerks. And there were signs even in this era of the emergence of a more permanent "white collar" work force. In Philadelphia more than 30% of the native white males listed on the 1860 census as clerks, salesmen, or bookkeepers were thirty or older, and a significant number were in their forties, fifties, and sixties. Accountants and collectors, whose responsibilities were somewhat heavier, were generally middle-aged (see Table 3.1). Still, most clerks were young, and the assumption remained that most would one day be businessmen on their own. When eighteen-year-old William Hoffman began his clerkship in an Albany dry goods store in the spring of 1848 he was given all of the mindless, physically exhausting chores noted above. Yet within a month he was being reassured by his employer that perseverance and good work would result in Hoffman's "becoming a Business Man," just as they had for so many who had come before him.[34] As Hoffman and others like him matured and gained experience they were given greater responsibilities – making sales, collecting from customers (including other businessmen) on outstanding accounts, writing letters, even operating the store in the proprietors' absence – and in time many did become proprietors themselves. Samuel G. Damon was only nineteen when he managed a Lowell, Massachusetts, shoe store for its absentee owner in 1840. Damon appears to have had a nearly free rein in running the store, and within a few years was in business for himself in Boston.[35] Charles A. Grinnell was obviously unsupervised when he traveled on horseback across rural

Maryland and Virginia in 1837, collecting on accounts for his employer, Tiffany, Fite & Co. of Baltimore.[36] By 1845 the firm's name had been changed to Tiffany, Fite, & Grinnell,[37] but employees such as Damon and Grinnell did not have to wait until their names were painted on the front of the store before they were taken seriously as business managers. The merchant's clerk, wrote *Hunt's Merchants' Magazine* in 1855, "is to business what the wife is to the order and success of the home – the genius that gives form and fashion to the materials for prosperity which are furnished by another."[38] We will continue to take note of the various ways in which salaried nonmanual employees, along with their employers, were increasingly distinguished – in their experience and in the minds of their contemporaries – from wage-earning manual workers and the surviving small master craftsmen.

Specialization in the nonmanual sector

Some of the institutional rearrangements in the Jacksonian economy were the result of early industrialization, and reflected changing relations within and between industrial and commercial forms. Others were more purely commercial in origin, and reflected the rising volume of trade, improvements in transportation, the growth of cities and their hinterlands, and other developments relating to the movement of goods no less than to their production. The principal result of these changes, according to most historians, was the creation of a new and more complex array of far more specialized commercial firms, whose activities constituted a major part of what Thomas Cochran has called "The Business Revolution" of the period 1790 to 1840, and what Glenn Porter and Harold Livesay have identified as the transition (around 1815) from "The Age of the All-Purpose Merchant" to "The Age of the Wholesaler."[39] Alfred Chandler, even while dissenting from Cochran's use of the term "revolution" for the period preceding 1840, describes the transition most succinctly:

> In the 1790s the general merchant, the businessman who had dominated the economy of the colonial period, was still the grand distributor. He bought and sold all types of products and carried out all the basic commercial functions. He was an exporter, wholesaler, importer, retailer, shipowner, banker, and insurer. By the 1840s, however, such tasks were being carried out by different types of specialized enterprises. Banks, insurance companies, and common carriers had appeared. Merchants had begun to specialize in one or two lines of goods: cotton, provisions, wheat, dry

goods, hardware, or drugs. They concentrated more and more on
a single function: retailing, wholesaling, importing, or exporting.[40]
In developing the history of increasing commercial specialization
scholars have thus far focused mainly on wholesaling. The rising
volume of long-distance trade, first in American cotton, then in British
cotton goods, later in many imported and domestic products, made
it feasible for once general merchants to concentrate on the importation, exportation, or domestic distribution of a single line of goods.
Having simplified both their source of goods and their market, these
specialists could then realize further efficiencies, avoiding warehous-
ing and the risks of ownership by serving only as brokers or manufacturers' agents, or they could combine brokerage with traditional
market activity as commission merchants.[41] A few, especially in New
York City, responded to the increased pace of trade by becoming
auctioneers, and apparently further stimulated trade by doing so.[42]
The specialized brokers, agents, and commission merchants, along
with the more or less specialized auctioneers, in turn called into existence a new type of wholesale merchant, the jobber, who assembled
an array of goods for generalized country storekeepers who could not
make the rounds of specialized wholesalers, wait around in the city
for the right auction, or get credit from the auctioneers.[43] In the meantime, as Chandler notes and Cochran emphasizes, all of these new
wholesale specialists availed themselves of new, equally specialized
firms – railroad and packet lines, freight forwarders, banks, insurance
companies, credit reporting agencies, commercial newspapers and
magazines – which could concentrate on providing one service because of both the rising volume of trade and the demand for services
from wholesale firms that no longer performed those services for
themselves.[44]

Less well told is the history of specialization at the retail level, and
of the emergence of retailing as a distinct and significant component
of the urban economy. Most retailing in the preindustrial cities had
been performed by men whose primary function lay elsewhere, either
in importing and exporting or in artisanal production, and by men
and women of modest means who sold goods from very small shops
or peddled them in the streets. But in the nineteenth century, as
artisans became increasingly confined to production, supervision, and
subcontracting on behalf of merchant capitalists and other manufacturers, and as importers and other large-scale merchants withdrew
from retailing to focus on one or another type of wholesaling, a vacuum was created at the retail level that was filled in part by independent retailers – men who had little or nothing to do with
production, shipping, or wholesaling. To be sure, some were former

artisans who did not entirely banish production or repair work from their shops, and a number of new retail stores were really outlets for manufacturing firms whose workshops were located on other premises. Some retailers seem also to have expanded into importing and wholesaling, and some importers and wholesalers continued to sell at the retail level. The retail sector, in short, was not entirely distinct. But it was growing increasingly so, and its progress was noted by contemporaries, who more and more frequently dignified the retailer with the term "retail merchant" – a term that does not seem to have existed in America in the eighteenth century. By the Jacksonian era, writers were using it to identify the new sort of retailer, and to distinguish him from the petty traders of a former era. "Dealers in a small way, in cities and large towns," explained Edward Hazen in 1836, "are frequently denominated shop-keepers; but those who do an extensive retail business, are usually called merchants or grocers, according as they deal in dry goods or groceries."[45]

The increasing visibility and respectability of the retailer can be traced in an interesting way through the pages of *Hunt's Merchants' Magazine*, which first appeared in 1839, and which quickly established itself as the unofficial but authentic voice of the mercantile community. In the first issues no notice was taken of the retailer, and in essays such as Charles Edwards's "What Constitutes a Merchant" it is clear that the mercantile community was assumed to include only the large importers and wholesalers.[46] Within a year or so, however, *Hunt's* was beginning to expand its notion of "the commercial class" to include "all those who stand between the producer and the consumer,"[47] and by 1841 the term "retail merchant" was applied to country storekeepers.[48] By the following year the city retailer began to appear, and was treated more and more seriously as a man of commerce.[49] By the latter 1840s, *Hunt's* was running numerous articles, under headings such as "Method in Trade Carried to Perfection," "A Model Store in Philadelphia," "System of Neatness in the Salesroom," and "A Model Warehouse for Fancy Goods" ("warehouse" in those days meant a place where goods were displayed and sold), either extolling the modern commercial methods of a specific retail merchant or advising retailers on the proper conduct of business.[50] The latter was offered not condescendingly but in the same voice as that which offered advice to importers and wholesalers. By 1850, the retailer was well established, within Freeman Hunt's mind at least, as a full-fledged member of the mercantile community.

To some extent the increasing visibility and respectability of the retailer rested on a few spectacular examples, the first and most prominent of which was New York's A. T. Stewart, who worked himself up from a small, one-man dry goods store through a succession of larger stores, including his "Marble Palace," built in 1846 as New York's first large and elegant dry goods emporium (and greatly expanded in the following fifteen years), and culminating in his Astor Place store, built between 1859 and 1862 on the entire block stretching from Broadway to Fourth Avenue, and from Ninth Street to Tenth Street. Stewart was a wholesaler, and eventually a manufacturer too, but his considerable fame was earned as a retailer, and there is some truth in the claim that through his innovations in retailing Stewart "raised his status, and that of his followers, from 'monger' to 'merchant.' "[51] But this overstates Stewart's influence. Others (including some notable firms that survive today, such as Lord & Taylor and Brooks Brothers) were about to build large, elegant retail stores, and no doubt would have done so even without Stewart's example. More importantly, even before the Marble Palace, though on a much smaller scale, large numbers of retailers were making their own contributions to the emergence of a distinctive retail sector. They did so in part by defining and shaping a new physical environment for selling goods (a subject discussed in the next section), and in part by pursuing the same strategy of specialization that had already reshaped the institutions of long-distance trade.

Product specialization in antebellum retailing was, in one sense, a sign not of the maturation of the retail sector but of its continuing dependence on specialized manufacturers and wholesalers. Some retailers specialized in one line of goods because they were former artisans who had made those goods themselves and had become retail merchants only by gradually – and in many cases not completely – transforming their workshops into stores. Others operated retail outlets for specialized manufacturers, or established regularized relationships with manufacturers whose output in a single item – books, for example – was large enough to keep their stores fully supplied.[52] Still others operated the retail branches of firms that were also importers or domestic wholesalers of specific types of goods. Given these interconnections, it is hardly surprising that city retailers should reflect the same kind of specialization that was advancing within the urban economy as a whole. Newspaper advertisements of city firms that appear to have been devoted entirely or primarily to retailing reveal something of the pace of increasing specialization in retailing between the Revolutionary era and the Civil War. In Philadelphia specialists in a single line of goods increased from 37% of the retail advertisers to 81% between 1792 and 1855. In New York the increase was from 36% to 90% between 1772 and 1855, while in the somewhat smaller port of Charleston it was from 29% to 79% over the same

period. In the small inland city of Hartford, Connecticut, the proportion of specialists among advertising retailers rose from 24% to
60% between 1792 and 1845.[53] These figures are similar to those obtained by analyzing the advertisements of all commercial firms, including wholesalers and those whose functions were either mixed or
impossible to specify.[54] One should be careful not to generalize too
broadly from the activities of business firms that went to the trouble
and expense of advertising in the newspaper, but the striking increase
in specializing retail advertisers does demonstrate that product
specialization was by no means limited to manufacturers and
wholesalers.[55]

The significance of specialization, particularly among retailers, lies
partly in the way contemporaries connected it to the modernization
of business practices. Increasingly in the Jacksonian era, commentators applauded the efficiencies of specialized firms, condemned attempts by businessmen already established as wholesalers or retailers
to expand vertically to other market levels (though some firms that
were able to do this efficiently were greatly admired), and ridiculed
general merchants and storekeepers as quaint survivals from a day
gone by.[56] The truly impressive businesses were those that had mas-
tered some specific function within an ever more complex and risky
business world. They need not be large; indeed, Porter and Livesay
as well as Chandler emphasize the fact that many businesses, especially in the commercial sector, deliberately remained small so that
operations could proceed smoothly under the direction of only two
or three partners, and so that some of the complexities of distribution
could remain outside the firm in the marketplace.[57] Whether a store
was large or small, wholesale or retail, what was admired was systematic management of the routine tasks that made up the business
day of a specialized firm. *Hunt's* delighted in the smallest details of
a well-run retail business:

> The shelves and rows of goods in each department are numbered,
> and upon the tag attached to the goods is marked the letter of the
> department, the number of the shelf and row on that shelf to
> which such piece of goods belongs. . . . Books are kept, in which
> the sales of each clerk are entered for the day, and the salary of
> the clerk cast, as a per centage on each day, week, and year, and,
> at the foot of the page, the aggregate of the sales appear, and the
> per centage that it has cost to effect these sales, is easily calculated
> for each day, month or year. The counters are designated by an
> imaginary color, as the blue, green, brown, etc., counter. The
> yard-sticks and counter-brush belong to it, are painted to corre-
> spond with the imaginary color of the counter; so, by a very sim-

> ple arrangement, each of these necessaries is kept where it
> belongs; and should any be missing, the faulty clerks are easily
> known.[58]

The stores that were described this way in *Hunt's*, or that boasted
of systematic merchandising practices in their own advertisements,
were in fact larger than most.[59] But if smaller retailers had no need
for color-coded sales counters or other techniques for managing a
large staff of clerks and the flow of masses of merchandise, they, too,
as nonartisanal experts in a particular product or line of products,
had become specialized businessmen of a new sort. Porter and Livesay
note that the general merchant and storekeeper of the eighteenth
century thrived not only because the volume of trade was too small
to support specialists, but also because goods tended to be simpler,
less likely to change according to advancing technologies, and more
likely to be familiar to nonspecialists on both sides of the sales
counter.[60] All of this had changed by the mid-nineteenth century.
Smaller retailers, no less than their larger competitors, now required
a skill that preindustrial shopkeepers did not – they needed to know
more about the goods they were selling than did the customers they
were selling them to. This kind of specialized knowledge formerly
had been found mainly in the artisan shops, but now customers found
it increasingly in retail stores, among manufacturers' sales managers,
independent retailers, and retail clerks and salesmen. Artisans such
as the Philadelphia cabinetmaker George Henkels could complain that
retailers and clerks did not really know enough to advise and instruct
customers properly. Writing just after the Civil War, Henkels complained that "manufacturing is fast getting to be a separate business
from the selling, and the responsibility for quality is so divided that
the purchaser must rely more on his own judgment than he does on
the representation of the dealer."[61] But Henkels himself, now a manufacturer rather than a producing artisan, maintained a large retail
"warehouse," and it is highly unlikely that it was staffed by cabinetmakers rather than by clerks.[62] In Henkels's business and in countless others, the age of specialization had created a new type of expert,
whose skill was manifested on the salesroom rather than the workshop floor. It was a skill that helped find a place for "retail merchants"
and their clerks within the mercantile community.

The changing environments of nonmanual work

That place was finally secured, however, by a set of developments
that historians have almost entirely neglected – the differentiation of
nonmanual from manual work environments, and the unmistakable

elevation of nonmanual workplaces, partly as an unintended side effect of increasing functional specialization, and partly as a deliberate attempt to give shape and style to a business world of managers, merchandisers, financiers, and others who conducted and facilitated trade. These are developments that cannot be measured in a precise way, but whose progress can be traced clearly enough through documents that give us more than an occasional glimpse of the places where people in a variety of circumstances spent their working days.

The physical separation of nonmanual from manual work is easily understood as a concomitant of increasing economic specialization in the Jacksonian era. The traditional artisan shop was a place where goods were both made and sold within narrow physical confines that hardly admitted of the separation of sales and record keeping from production, even when these were performed by different people. Indeed, in the execution of certain kinds of preindustrial custom work, tailoring, for instance, it is difficult to draw a precise boundary between sales and production as separate functions, much less to place them in separate spaces. In the illustration heading the chapter on tailoring in Edward Hazen's *Panorama of Professions and Trades*, first published in 1836 (and apparently the first book to include workshop illustrations by an American artist),[63] a customer and his companion stand in the midst of all of the functions the artist needed to portray (Figure 3.2). The master measures the customer and calls off the measurements to an apprentice. The cutting shears that the master will use later lie on the counter between them. On another counter, sitting in the traditional cross-legged position of the tailor, are two journeymen or apprentices, one sewing, the other pressing. All face inward to the center of the room, while a half-opened door leads to an undefined space, possibly only to a staircase to living quarters. Although it was published as late as 1836, when tailoring and many other trades were changing very rapidly away from this kind of setting, Hazen's book was like most other "books of trades" published before the Civil War in presenting a misleadingly antiquated view of occupational life to young readers.[64] Hence, we see in his illustration not a typical tailor's shop of the 1830s but a somewhat stylized image of tailoring before the age of sweatshops, garret bosses, and clothiers. In it a central motif is the integration of tasks in a single space, and in this sense, at least, the image is an accurate representation of preindustrial artisanal production.

Industrialization pulled apart these tasks, consigning most manual work to one set of places and most nonmanual work to another. This was most obvious where production and retailing, once combined in countless artisan shops, split into separate businesses, but it was no

Figure 3.2. Tailor shop interior, from Edward Hazen, *The Panorama of Professions and Trades*, 1836 (courtesy of Cornell University Libraries)

less significant within large numbers of producing firms that continued to sell on the retail level. Particularly in those industries where workshops grew into large manufactories or where water power was needed to run machinery – but also in smaller-scale and sweated industries – the spatial and physical requirements for the efficient performance of manual and nonmanual tasks diverged rapidly. Large-scale and mechanized production required cheap land, and migrated to the urban periphery and beyond to mill sites in emerging factory towns; less mechanized and highly seasonal production that could be decentralized required access to cheap labor, and was diffused among the sweatshops of the poorer inner-city neighborhoods.[65] But the sale of goods from these diverse workshops, especially on the retail level, required an attractive location in those quarters and on those streets that were emerging within each growing city as specialized zones for shopping. The city had always separated economic functions to some degree, but industrialization, commercial specialization, and the growth of the city itself gave this spatial separation a new shape and significance in the Jacksonian era. By 1833 a guide to New York could locate the specialized commercial firms of the emerging metropolis with remarkable precision: "Pearl-street . . . is the principal seat of the [wholesale] dry goods and hardware business. . . . South-street, running along the East River, contains the warehouses and offices of most of the principal shipping merchants. Wallstreet . . . is occupied by the Banks, Insurance Companies, Merchants' Exchange, Newspapers, and Brokers' offices. . . . Canal-street . . . is a spacious street, principally occupied by retail stores."[66] New York's most famous retail street, identified here only as "the principal thoroughfare, and most fashionable promenade,"[67] was, of course, Broadway. Long before A. T. Stewart dignified the "shilling side" with his Marble Palace, Broadway was the center of wealth and fashion in New York. And as wealthy residents began to abandon lower Broadway for new homes on Fifth Avenue and other streets north of the old city center (and near, but not on, Broadway itself), the whole length of Broadway was transformed into a nerve center of shopping and display – "the most showy, the most crowded, and the richest fashionable thoroughfare on the continent. The shops," continues this 1849 description, "are more numerous, more extensive, and filled with more expensive and rarer assortments of goods than those of any other street in America."[68] This was certainly true, but every city had its more modest analogue to Broadway – Washington Street in Boston, Chestnut Street in Philadelphia, for example – and these and lesser streets, along with the Wall Streets and Pearl Streets that housed each city's bankers and wholesalers, constituted increasingly distinct centers of nonmanual work.

Contemporary depictions and discussions of all types of industrial firms give substance to this separation of manual from nonmanual work in the antebellum city. From at least the mid–1840s manufacturers' city directory advertisements frequently noted or depicted a factory on or beyond the city periphery and a separate store or office downtown. The Paterson Machine Company, for example, maintained an office on Pine Street in New York as early as 1845, while the People's Stove Works of Peekskill sold goods from their "warerooms" on New York's Water Street in 1854.[69] Janeway and Company's wallpaper factory was in New Brunswick, New Jersey, but their store was on Dey Street in New York.[70] A. W. Gray & Co., New York pump manufacturers, did not bother to identify the location of their factory, but they prominently displayed on its side their "sales room" location at 118 Maiden Lane.[71] D. D. Badger & Co.'s architectural iron works, foundry, and machine shop was on the East River above 13th Street, but their office was in the expanding downtown

Figure 3.3. D. D. Badger & Co., Architectural Iron Works, New York, ca. 1860 (courtesy of the Library of Congress)

at 42 Duane Street (Figure 3.3).[72] These examples are all from New York, but manufacturers from other cities can be cited just as easily. At least three peripheral iron foundries (two in South Boston and one in East Boston) were run from offices in the heart of downtown Boston, while Henry Pettes & Company sold carpets woven in its Roxbury factory from its store on Washington Street.[73] Companies manufacturing glass, twine, sugar, and varnish all advertised factories outside of the city (in East Cambridge, Andover, East Boston, and Brighton) and stores or offices in downtown Boston.[74] In Philadelphia, Cornelius & Baker sold lamps and chandeliers from a handsome store on Chestnut Street, but made these goods in two factories, one a few blocks to the north on Cherry Street, the other well beyond the city limits in Kensington.[75] Charles Cumming's glue and whip factory was also north of the city in Northern Liberties, but his store was in the heart of the downtown on the corner of Third and Market.[76] William D. Rogers manufactured coaches and carriages in a factory in Penn Township and sold them from an elegant "carriage repository" on Chestnut Street.[77]

Even more striking is the physical separation of nonmanual from manual work in firms that combined manufacturing and selling on the same premises. In the clothing industry, for example, it was common practice to "put out" the less skilled stages of production through

Figure 3.4. Interior, L. S. Drigg's lace and bonnet store, Boston, 1852 (courtesy of Cornell University Libraries)

garret bosses and other contractors, but to keep the skilled cutters under immediate supervision in a central shop on the same premises as the retail outlet. Unlike in the old tailor's shop, however, the cutters and most other central shop workers (all but the fitters) were segregated from the sales areas and were entirely out of sight to both customers and clerks. The twenty-five cutters employed in Brooks Brothers' new Broadway clothing emporium in 1859, for example, worked in one of several upstairs "apartments" devoted to custom production, while two hundred clerks and salesmen worked on the sales floors below.[78] L. S. Drigg's Boston lace and bonnet store confined its manual workers to a "manufacturing room" adjacent to, but distinctly separated from, the sales area (Figure 3.4).[79] Even quite small merchant tailors could separate workers in this fashion. Josselyn and Churchill received customers in their second-story shop on Boston's Washington Street in 1852, but their workshop was in a garret on the fifth floor of the same building.[80]

Office work, too, was often combined on the same premises with manufacturing, even in firms that maintained their principal offices downtown. For as production expanded and grew more complex, on-site supervisory and record-keeping roles multiplied. Some firms, moreover, did keep their main offices at the factory. But office workers were separated from factory workers, and in numerous advertisements and other illustrations of antebellum factories, manufactories, and mills there appear separate buildings or distinct sections or entrances labeled as the office. As early as 1820, the New-York Sugar Refining Company identified its office on the corner of Church and Leonard Streets, in a separate building on the same grounds as the mill,[81] but such illustrations are far more common after 1840. Usually the office was tiny in comparison with the rest of the works, as this was not yet the age when industrial firms would require large corps of officers and office workers. Yet the office was beginning to appear as a distinct work environment, not merely in the banks, insurance companies, railroad companies, and wholesale warehouses (where the word "countinghouse" was giving way to "office"),[82] and not only in the downtown headquarters of industrial firms but also in the little rooms and buildings attached to the nation's new workshops. An interesting illustration of this embryonic industrial office may be found in a *Harper's New Monthly Magazine* article of 1851, describing the Novelty Works, a large New York foundry noted for the manufacture of marine steam engines.[83] The ground-floor plan of the works (Figure 3.5) reveals a small office just below the entrance to the works, separated from the various workshops and internally subdivided into an "office" and a "clerk's office." The size and subdivisions of the

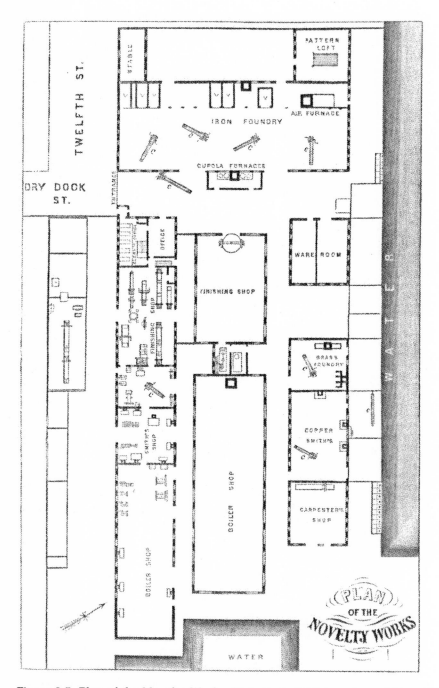

Figure 3.5. Plan of the Novelty Works, New York, 1851 (courtesy of Cornell University Libraries)

Figure 3.6. Entrance, Novelty Works, New York, 1851 (courtesy of Cornell University Libraries)

office were actually greater than they appear here, for unlike the workshops, which were mainly single-story structures, the office was a four-story building, with four times the floor space indicated on the plan. What is perhaps most interesting about it, however, is its entrance, which appears on the plan and in an accompanying illustration (Figure 3.6) as a separate (and rather attractive) doorway next to the gateway through which the manual employees entered and left the works. From their very first step on company property, in other words, the manual and nonmanual employees of the Novelty Works were separated into different spaces.

As manual and nonmanual workplaces became more separated in space, they diverged in attractiveness and style. Manual workers continued to toil amidst the dirt, noise, heat, smells, and other discomforts that seemed inseparable from the rough business of getting things built, but increasing numbers of nonmanual proprietors and

Figure 3.7. William Strickland, *Christ Church* (with retail stores in foreground), Philadelphia, 1811 (courtesy of The Historical Society of Pennsylvania)

workers found themselves in stores, offices, and even whole districts of stores and offices, that were cleaner, brighter, and more elegant than ever before, and that in many cases were deliberately designed to be so. The elevation of nonmanual work milieux was most significant in retailing, as the new "retail merchants" of the Jacksonian era reshaped their businesses to enhance both their profits and their prestige. But it is found as well in the stores and offices of wholesalers, manufacturers, insurance companies, and banks, and in the nation's earliest office buildings, which even before the Civil War would begin to raise the city's skyline above the steeples of the eighteenth-century churches.

Only a little of this is evident in the paintings, engravings, and occasional illustrated advertisements of the first two decades of the nineteenth century. In the foreground of William Strickland's 1811 oil painting of Philadelphia's Christ Church (Figure 3.7), for example, are representations of the exteriors of two stores, one a dry goods store very much like those of the eighteenth century, the other a new book and stationery store that went perhaps a step beyond its predecessors in the size and attractiveness of its window display and sign.[84] A few illustrated advertisements in the Philadelphia city directory of 1818 (for stores selling silver plate, umbrellas, saddles, and hats) depict well-articulated and attractive storefronts,[85] but there is little else to indicate that Philadelphia's retail stores were becoming more distinct or more elaborate during these years. Philadelphia, moreover, probably was ahead of other cities in this respect. The few illustrations from the first two decades of the nineteenth century suggest that New Yorkers remained indifferent to the design of commercial buildings. The first storefront depicted in a New York City directory appeared on behalf of E. M. Blunt, a printer of navigators' charts who sold a variety of navigational aids (including quadrants, spyglasses, and other goods he obviously did not make) from a store on Water Street (Figure 3.8). Yet, beneath the third-story sign there is nothing on the face of this Georgian building to indicate that it contained a store of a particular kind, or indeed a store of any kind, rather than a workshop or even a residence. As this and a few other such views suggest, New Yorkers even more than Philadelphians continued to make and sell goods, and to make their homes, behind building fronts that did little to proclaim any of these as a separate activity.[86]

Distinct architectural idioms for commercial buildings developed rapidly, however, during and after the 1820s, just as specialization was beginning to take hold in all sectors of the urban economy. The building of Quincy Market in Boston in 1825, of a two-story arcade of shops on Chestnut Street in Philadelphia in 1827, and of several Greek Revival warehouses on Pearl Street and Coenties Slip in New York in 1829, signaled not only a "new counting house style" but also a new attentiveness to style among both wholesalers and retailers.[87] The new warehouses of New York, beginning with one designed for Arthur and Lewis Tappan by Ithiel Town, seem to have been particularly influential in the diffusion of elements of the Greek Revival as the most common style for designing and redesigning retail storefronts.[88] This style was in fact well suited to the retailers' needs. Doric pilasters applied to each end of the storefront, and perhaps also to the door frame in its center, clearly set off the store from adjacent buildings, and framed and gave prominence to the display windows. The lintel above the pilasters helped unify the storefront, distinguished it and the store as a whole from whatever occupied the upper

Figure 3.8. E. M. Blunt, print shop and store, New York, 1811 (courtesy of Cornell University Libraries)

stories, and carried the store's sign. Though suggestive of more mon-
umental applications of classical motifs, it was a simple design that
could be executed inexpensively and effectively without the use of a
professional architect. In Minard Lafever's *Modern Builder's Guide*, an
1833 revision of his very popular and influential handbook to Greek
Revival design first published in 1829, no notice is taken of storefronts,
and all of the illustrations and discussions are pitched to more complex designs and more imposing buildings.[89] Lafever's own practice,
though still a young and small one, seems to have included no commissions for retail storefronts.[90] Almost certainly, these early Greek
Revival retail storefronts, along with others that were increasingly
elaborated in older styles, were the work of master carpenters and
masons, who were finding a new market for their services in the
retailers of the 1830s, and a vernacular particularly well suited to that
market in the simpler elements of the Greek Revival.

Contemporary street scenes reveal that Greek Revival storefronts
proliferated during the 1830s, but it was not until the 1840s, aided no
doubt by new economies in the publication of illustrations, that significant numbers of retailers began incorporating pictures of their
storefronts in their advertisements. J. C. Booth & Co. (predecessor
to the larger firm of Booth and Foster mentioned earlier) provided a
typical illustration in 1845, complete with well-designed window displays and a well-attired customer (or is it the proprietor?) standing
in the doorway (Figure 3.9). By this time such storefronts were common, and (along with other elements such as the awning supports
and sign boards that ran along the curb in front of rows of adjacent
stores), gave a distinct character to emerging retail districts. Illustrations of street scenes in these districts were more common after 1830,[91]
and these were eventually systematized by city directory publishers
into pictorial directories of principal shopping streets, showing (sometimes in "snakeskin" fashion) block after block of retail and wholesale
stores (Figure 3.10).[92] Some of these blocks displayed rows of uniform
storefronts, and by the late 1850s there were a number of architect-
designed blocks of stores, all with handsome, identical facades.[93] By
the 1850s the design of individual storefronts, too, had entered a new
phase, characterized by more elaborate ornamentation in a greater
variety of styles, and by the integration of ground-floor and upper-
story facades, the latter reflective of the growth of many stores to a
point where they required entire buildings to themselves. In 1853, E.
A. Brooks's "Metropolitan Boot and Shoe Emporium" required (despite its grandiose name) only the ground floor of 575 Broadway, but
its enormous display window was crowned by an ornate sign that
contrasted markedly with the plain building front above it. Francis

Figure 3.9. J. C. Booth & Co., clothing store, New York, 1845 (courtesy of Cornell University Libraries)

Figure 3.10. Chestnut Street, Philadelphia, 1860 (courtesy of The Historical Society of Pennsylvania)

Tomes and Sons' gun, cutlery, jewelry, and "fancy hardware" store on Maiden Lane was obviously larger, for the ornamentation on the delicately arched ground-floor facade was repeated above the windows of all four of the upper stories. Edward H. Newman's Broadway ribbon, lace, veil, and mourning goods store was even more elaborately designed, and its upper stories even more carefully integrated with the ground floor facade.[94] A somewhat more restrained example that still conveys the distance retail stores had traveled since the early days of the ground-floor Greek Revival facade, is the carpet store designed by Nathan A. Bradley for the Boston firm of John H. Pray & Sons (Figure 3.11). On this facade three arches spring from the capitals of four Doric columns that frame the large windows and doorway. Above the sign four three-story piers rise toward arches that echo the ground floor arches, and toward a heavy, bracketed cornice. The uninterrupted flow of the piers gives the four-story facade a striking verticality, while the overall effect is one of dignity and stability. Yet Pray's was not a very large store according to the new standards of the 1850s. During this decade other retailers, particularly the large, departmentalized dry goods firms (they were not quite "department stores" as yet) were building huge emporia, sometimes absorbing whole city blocks and providing block-long rows of plate glass window displays of fashionable goods (Figure 3.12). These were some of the city's largest, most elegantly designed, and best-known buildings, American "palaces" to which prosperous residents and tourists flocked. And they were matched by other large structures that housed workers of the nonmanual sector – office buildings built by insurance companies, banks, and others, in one very striking case by a Philadelphia manufacturer and wholesale druggist named David Jayne. The office building constructed by Dr. Jayne on Chestnut Street was an eight-story skyscraper in a bold Venetian design, and was topped by a Gothic tower that brought the total height of the building to 130 feet (Figure 3.13).[95] Finally, while Jayne, Lord & Taylor, and numerous others were embellishing the facades of downtown business buildings, the very idea of the business facade was becoming systematized by James Bogardus, who applied the first cast-iron storefront to a New York drugstore in 1848. Within a few years Bogardus and a few others were shipping cast-iron store and office facades, in the styles that had been developed by big-city businessmen in stone and marble over the previous twenty or thirty years, to smaller downtowns all across America.[96]

As retailers and other nonmanual businessmen embellished the exteriors of their buildings, they transformed the interiors as well, and in the process created work environments of unprecedented el-

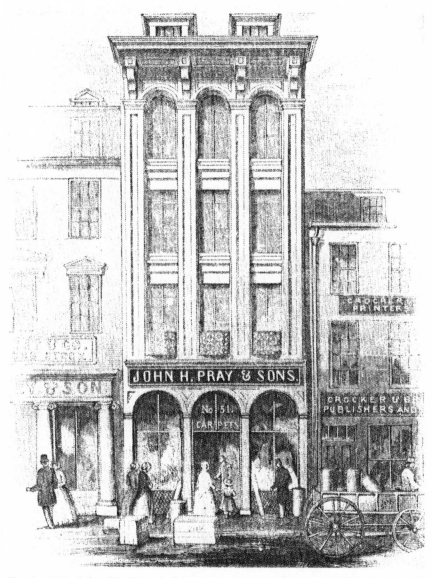

Figure 3.11. John H. Pray & Sons, carpet store, Boston, 1855 (courtesy of Cornell University Libraries)

Figure 3.12. Lord & Taylor, dry goods emporium, New York, ca. 1860 (courtesy of the Collection of Advertising History, Archives Center, National Museum of American History, Smithsonian Institution)

egance and dignity for themselves and their clerks. Whether there were significant changes in store interiors during the era of the Greek Revival is difficult to say, but by the 1850s it was becoming increasingly common for retailers to include illustrations of store interiors in their advertising, and for parlor magazines such as *Gleason's* (later *Ballou's*) *Pictorial Drawing-Room Companion* to run illustrated articles on new and notable stores in the major cities.[97] The common motif in these illustrations is the elegance of the store itself. Whether the establishment was a jewelry store such as Ball, Black & Co. of New

Figure 3.13. Jayne's Granite Buildings, Philadelphia, 1850 (courtesy of Cornell University Libraries)

Figure 3.14. Interior, Ball, Black & Co., jewelry store, New York, ca. 1855 (courtesy of the Collection of Advertising History, Archives Center, National Museum of American History, Smithsonian Institution)

York (Figure 3.14), a bookstore such as D. Appleton & Co. (Figure 3.15), the showroom of I. M. Singer's sewing machine company (Figure 3.16), Charles Oakford's Philadelphia hat store (Figure 3.17), or even a Cincinnati "daguerrian gallery" (Figure 3.18), far greater care was taken by the artist to depict the richly ornamented interior of the store than to show the variety or attractiveness of the goods being sold there. In some illustrations the clothing, refined bearing, and physical attractiveness of the patrons and the clerks (the latter invariably the equal of the former) receive as much emphasis as the furnishings. In the illustrated magazine articles the text, too, ordinarily focuses on the store rather than the merchandise. "As you enter the spacious doorway," writes *Gleason's* of Canfield, Brother & Co.'s Baltimore jewelry store (Figure 3.19), "the view presented by the interior is of the most magnificent description; the sales-room extends the whole length of the building, and the goods are displayed in a way that at once shows to the greatest advantage, and strikes the beholder with the belief the whole has been the work of a master-mind." The long descriptions that follow are of the ceiling, counters, display cases, and the stained-glass window at the rear of the store. Only near the

Figure 3.15. Interior, D. Appleton & Co., bookstore, New York, 1854 (courtesy of Cornell University Libraries)

end of the article is there a sentence about the goods for sale at Canfield's. This is followed by a final, quite discordant sentence acknowledging the company's factory: "This establishment is propelled by steam-power, with a full force of foreign and native workmen."[98] There is no picture of the factory or its workmen.

All of these examples are of fairly large establishments that catered to a prosperous clientele. Occasionally, a somewhat more modest firm such as the Bowery hosiery store of A. Rankin & Co. (Figure 3.20) presented an interior view of a store that was clean, orderly, and attractive, and where salesclerks wore suits, white collars, and cravats, but that lacked the opulence of the jewelers and the dry goods palaces. But still smaller retailers did not advertise in this fashion – indeed, most did not advertise at all – and surely some large though unspecifiable share of the retail sales transacted in antebellum American cities continued to take place in humble, perhaps even dingy environments, quite unlike those of the Canfields or even the Rankins.[99] Still, an important development had occurred in many of the environments in which retailers, store managers, and salesclerks worked, and an ideal had been articulated that was intended to apply more generally to the business of selling goods to customers. The

Figure 3.16. Interior, I. M. Singer & Co., sewing machine salesroom, New York, 1857 (courtesy of the Library of Congress)

Figure 3.17. Interior, Charles Oakford's hat store, Philadelphia, ca. 1855 (courtesy of the Library Company of Philadelphia)

Figure 3.18. Interior, Ball's Great Daguerrian Gallery of the West, Cincinnati, 1854 (courtesy of Cornell University Libraries)

articles in *Gleason's Pictorial Drawing-Room Companion* express this ideal quite clearly, as do the nonillustrated articles in *Hunt's Merchants' Magazine* that praised and described just as vividly one or another "model store." *Hunt's* once criticized American retail merchants for tying up too much capital in "costly palaces,"[100] but Freeman Hunt and others whose opinions appeared in the magazine clearly approved of the trend toward a more distinct and imposing business environment, and associated this trend with the prestige of the business community. Charles Sumner, whose speech before the Boston Mercantile Library Association of November 13, 1854, was printed in *Hunt's*, linked Boston's new "warehouses which outdo the baronial castle, and salesrooms which outdo the ducal palace," to an elaborate and enthusiastically embraced image of the merchant as a modern "feudal chief." "With these magnificent appliances [i.e., the warehouses and salesrooms], the relations of dependence and protection, which marked the early feudalism, are reproduced in the more comprehensive feudalism of trade."[101] Many Americans would no doubt have recoiled from the idea of a benevolent mercantile feudalism, but Sumner was using a common metaphor, the palace, to associate the merchant's worth and prestige with the appearance of his salesrooms.

Figure 3.19. Interior, Canfield, Brother & Co.'s jewelry store, Baltimore, 1854 (courtesy of Cornell University Libraries)

Figure 3.20. Interior, A. Rankin & Co., hosiery store, New York, 1852 (courtesy of the Collection of Advertising History, Archives Center, National Museum of American History, Smithsonian Institution)

From the more relaxed perspective of the "Editor's Easy Chair," *Harper's* expressed this secular worshipfulness in a more playful way, by comparing the succession of store windows on Broadway to "the three-miles-long nave of a Crystal Palace, for admittance to which no charge is made. These are windows which regularly beguile us of a quarter of an hour on our morning's walk officeward."[102] To be beguiled is not necessarily to pay homage, but it is safe to say, without multiplying examples, that many Americans (and some Europeans as well) were impressed by what had happened to the once very ordinary business of keeping a store.[103]

All these changes suggest a significant divergence of experience between manual and nonmanual workers in the cities of the Jacksonian era, and a clarification of the contribution that the manual-nonmanual dichotomy made to the ways in which antebellum Americans defined their society and assumed individual identities within it. More specifically, they suggest that large numbers of previously humble or ambiguously placed "middling folk" were elevated by the redrawing of society's most critical boundary below, rather than above, the smaller businessmen, now that so many of them no longer shared the social stigma of manual labor with wage-earning mechanics. Does this mean that the enlarged, more distinctly commercial and managerial sector of wholesalers, manufacturers, downtown retailers, and other specialized businessmen who "worked with their heads" in increasingly distinctive business milieux, had become a "business class?" Is the elevation into this class of previously degraded middling folk the fundamental reality that underlies some historians' perceptions of a new and ascending middle class in this era? If it is, should we speak of the resolution of vaguely defined urban strata into two distinctive (and antagonistic?) classes, rather than of an *intermediate* social formation that is properly termed a "middle class?" These are questions of central significance to our understanding of the character of the Jacksonian social revolution. The ways in which the changes in work and the structure of occupations that we have reviewed here helped modify urban society are the subject of the next chapter.

4 *Republican prejudice: work, well-being, and social definition*

"Manual labor has a position with us," wrote Nathan Appleton in 1844, "which it has never possessed in any period of the world. . . . The high reward of labor in all its branches, is the great, important distinction which diffuses comfort, intelligence, and self-respect through the whole mass of the community, in a degree unknown in the previous history of civilization." High wages, unlimited opportunities for self-advancement, and the respect conferred by Americans on all forms of honest labor, Appleton argued, have nearly erased the distinction between capital and labor, and have created, for the first time in history, a society ruled by merit rather than birth: "The labor of a single year gives to every laborer, if he choose to save his earnings, a very considerable capital. He takes at his pleasure a place in society."[1]

Appleton's remarks were far from unusual. In all the forums of public discussion – books, magazines, newspapers, lyceums, the political stump – prominent Americans celebrated the comforts, opportunities, and dignity of the working man, and offered these as emblems of the superiority of American republican institutions and values over those of aristocratic Europe. The celebration was general enough to transcend the intense political combat of the antebellum era. In his study of the political writings of forty-two major political figures from Massachusetts, Carl Siracusa notes that "the image of the respectable worker" was cultivated by the leaders of all the major parties, who, despite the sharpness of partisan debate over many of the issues that accompanied industrialization, "disagreed hardly at all about the role and value of the worker."[2] And it was advanced by men outside politics (and outside Massachusetts) – by Edwin Freedley, for example, who explained Philadelphia's success as a "centre of Wealth and Population" by referring first to the "social position of the Mechanic and the Artisan," and to the good sense of the citizens of Philadelphia, who "are far too clear-headed and practical in their views to do any thing to degrade labor and check useful enterprise."[3]

Yet, as Siracusa correctly points out, there was an enormous disjuncture between public rhetoric of this sort and the actual economic, social, and cultural circumstances surrounding manual work. Inequalities were increasing rapidly in the egalitarian republic, skills were degraded and opportunities foreclosed for most workers by the factory and putting-out systems of production, and workers struggled not to save a "very considerable capital" but to cover living costs. Culturally, too, "the respectable worker was a myth." "By countless subtle (and not so subtle) snubs, insults, and condescensions, the message was conveyed to the worker that he was a lesser sort of being." In short, the nearly universal tendency to emphasize only the positive aspects of industrial and social development constituted, in Siracusa's words, "nothing less than a massive failure of social awareness and imagination." Perhaps it would be more accurate to speak here of too much imagination rather than too little, but Siracusa demonstrates clearly enough the need to look beyond the celebratory rhetoric to social conditions and attitudes that may have differed significantly from those proclaimed on the political stump and the lyceum platform.[4]

The question of how early industrialization affected the incomes, wealth, and opportunities of artisans and other manual workers is actually a complex one that would, if fully pursued, take us well beyond our subject. What is of primary interest here is the extent to which the economic circumstances of wage earners and small master craftsmen diverged from those of nonmanual workers and proprietors, and the ways in which Americans of various ranks and conditions made sense of this divergence in social terms. This does nothing to reduce, but rather compounds, the complexities and documentary lacunae that make generalizations about these everyday matters so difficult. Still, on the subjects of manual and nonmanual income, wealth, and opportunity, we can make comparisons that at least suggest a significant divergence of experience. On the subject of attitudes the evidence is perhaps more compelling that, among those who did not work with their hands, the "respectable worker" was indeed a myth.

Work and well-being

Recent studies of the incomes of skilled manual workers in major cities have tended to confirm long-standing impressions that married workers usually could not support their families without additional contributions from other family members. In New York in 1850, according to Wilentz, the average annual income for male workers in the skilled trades was approximately $300, while minimal living costs for an average-sized family exceeded $500.[5] Wilentz's income estimates are very similar to those provided for Philadelphia by Bruce Laurie, Theodore Hershberg, and George Alter. Yearly wages paid to males in fourteen major industries in Philadelphia averaged $288 in 1850, considerably below the $500 to $600 estimated by both contemporaries and recent scholars as the amount needed to sustain a family in modest circumstances.[6] The wages of skilled workers in both cities were undoubtedly somewhat higher than these figures suggest, as in each case the overall average is reduced by the lower wages paid to less skilled male workers within the workshops listed on the census of manufactures. *The British Mechanic's and Labourer's Handbook and True Guide to the United States*, published in 1840, advised prospective emigrants that a full year's work in most skilled trades in America would yield an income of $500 to $600, and it appears that real wage rates for both skilled and unskilled workers were rising, not falling, during this period of declining prices.[7] Perhaps, too, we should question the meaning of minimal living costs in a budget that, for example, allocates two pounds of meat per day and four pounds of sugar per week to a family of five.[8] Still, it is clear that married skilled workers struggled to make ends meet. Even in better times, few could count on the full year's work on which the emigrant guide's figures were predicated (it is interesting that economic historians' time series show relatively high nominal and real wage rates during the depression of the late 1830s, when few workers could have expected to be paid for anything approaching a full year's work), and the additional income contributed in good or bad times by working wives and children, or by wives who took in and cared for boarders, could not have lifted very many skilled workers' families above a modest style of living.[9] Moreover, as Laurie, Hershberg, and Alter note, the circumstances of small master craftsmen may not have been much better. The average gross profit of small artisan shops in Philadelphia (those reporting capital of $500 or less on the 1850 census of manufactures) amounted to $482.[10] Reducing this average for shop rent and other operating expenses (including, perhaps, the wages of an occasional journeyman) yields a net income to Philadelphia's small handworking masters that could not have been significantly higher than the wages paid to skilled workers.

Foreign visitors, it is true, invariably marveled at the apparent prosperity of American workers. Not merely the genteel visitors, but also the working-class authors of emigrant guidebooks, noted that "the American mechanic is rarely found without money in his pocket, and in store, for all his purposes."[11] The abundance of food on the tables of workingmen's boardinghouses was a common theme in the *British Mechanic's and Labourer's Handbook*, while nearly everyone agreed that "the American mechanic almost invariably dresses well. . . . There is very little difference, if indeed any, in point of appearance, between the young men of most trades and their employers, or, in fact, the first tradesmen and merchants of the city."[12] These foreign commentators had no interest in inflating the workingman's condition to the greater glory of American republican institutions. Why should they have been nearly as insensitive as Nathan Appleton to the apparent realities of workers' incomes and living costs? Or, to reverse the question, how can we reconcile the grim calculations of the working-class historians with the observations of these disinterested observers? The most obvious answer is that the visitors were comparing American workers to the much poorer workers of Europe. Sympathetic Americans who submitted budgets to newspapers may have insisted on the right of workers to eat meat every day, but in England and Ireland workers ate very little meat (the English ate less than half as much as American workers, and the Irish ate virtually no meat at all, according to Richard Stott's recent estimate), and they dressed and were housed more poorly too.[13] Workers in the new world struggled against a different standard of comfort and decency, a fact that forgives the foreign observers if not the Americans. But there is a less obvious explanation that may pertain to the perceptions of both groups. Unusually large numbers of the men and women who worked at manual jobs in the antebellum American city were young and single. These young, unattached workers, many of whom were recent migrants from the countryside and from abroad, spent large proportions of their wages on their own food and clothing, and even on small incomes were able to eat well and dress "high."[14] They were also the most visible of American workers. It is no mere coincidence that this was the era of Mose the Bowery B'hoy, who quickly emerged from Benjamin Baker's play *A Glance at New York in 1848* as America's semifictional urban folk hero. Mose was young, single, fast with his fists, and equally fast with his feet on his way to help fight a fire. Above all, he was a swaggering, cocksure working-class dandy. His girl friend, Lize, was his female counterpart who, in George G. Foster's characterization, walked with "a swing of mischief and defiance," and dressed "high," in "startling contrasts which Lize considers 'some pumpkins' and Mose swears is 'gallus!' "[15] Undoubtedly there were large numbers of real Moses and Lizes – young, single workers who ate well, dressed extravagantly, and had a good deal of conspicuous fun. To observers from outside the working class they were tangible evidence that American workers were paid enough to live far above the level of mere subsistence. The evidence was, however, misleading. Most of the b'hoys and g'hals of the Bowery and elsewhere would marry, bear children, and settle down to a much less extravagant life – comfortable in comparison to the workers of Europe, but modest and difficult by American standards. Few indeed would have enough to lay by "a very considerable capital."

Nonmanual incomes are less well documented than the incomes of manual workers, but it is clear that most of those who "worked with their heads" earned significantly more than the $500 or $600 toward which artisans and other mechanics strove. To be sure, it is often noted that many clerks worked for very low salaries – when William Hoffman began his clerkship in Albany in 1848 his salary was only $50 per annum, plus room, board, and laundry[16] – but what is not always understood is that the supply of applicants for clerkships was always very high, and that young, would-be men of commerce were willing to accept a very low salary as the price one paid for gaining the training, experience, and contacts that could lead to a lucrative business career. It is, indeed, more accurate to consider most young clerks as apprentices rather than as employees during their first two or three years on the job. When Edward Tailer complained to his employer (a New York dry goods importer) that a $50 salary for his first year of employment and $100 for his second was too low, the latter replied that there were young men willing to work until they were twenty-one for no salary at all. Tailer actually won his point, and his salary was increased to $150. But what is more important is that as he gained experience the young clerk's salary rapidly rose beyond the pay levels of skilled manual workers – to $450 when Tailer was still twenty-one, and to $1,000 the following year at a different firm. Two years later Tailer signed on with yet another firm as a traveling salesman, at $1,200 for the first year and $1,500 for the second and third. Tailer never collected the latter sum, however, for by the beginning of the second year, at twenty-five years of age, he was in business for himself.[17]

The rapidity of Tailer's rise may not have been typical, but it does illustrate the important point that the salaries paid to clerks, accountants, and other nonmanual employees were much more elastic than skilled workers' wages. At any given moment there were large numbers of young clerks (or "apprentice merchants") who made less money than most skilled workers. But the clerks, unlike the manual workers, had good reason to believe that their incomes would soon rise, and that even as employees they would earn enough money to support themselves and their families. Those who worked for import-export merchants and other long-distance traders might even find the opportunity to enhance their incomes by trading on their own. In 1848, eighteen-year-old Robert McCoskry Graham and three of his fellow clerks were rewarded by their employer with $400 for the purchase of goods to be sent out on their own account on the firm's new California steamer.[18] As commerce became more specialized, and the retail sector expanded and became more distinct, increasing numbers of clerks were denied this opportunity, and it is possible that even before the Civil War the largest dry goods palaces were beginning to develop the more permanently low-paid (and increasingly female) sales forces more properly associated with the postwar department stores.[19] But most antebellum clerks, including even those very young men who worked for practically nothing, continued to enjoy at least the prospect of a good income.

The incomes of nonmanual businessmen are more elusive than those of their clerks, for they depended upon the highly variable profits of firms of different sizes and types, upon swings in the business cycle, and upon individual skill and good luck. Obviously, under ordinary circumstances most businessmen earned more money than their employees, and the larger businessmen whose careers have been traced by contemporaries and by historians earned a great deal more.[20] But what of the smallest nonartisanal proprietors? Did they earn more than small master artisans, skilled wage earners, or experienced clerks? Consider first the well-documented case of William Gowans, a young bookseller who later became a prosperous auctioneer and retailer of antique books. Gowans was approximately twenty when he left his father's house in Fredonia, Indiana, in the autumn of 1825, first for Louisville, where he speculated unsuccessfully in a flour shipment to New Orleans, and then for New Orleans, Natchez, and finally New York, where his luck at first failed to improve. Lacking capital or connections, Gowans found work in New York in a series of low-paying manual jobs – gardener, stone polisher, stevedore, newspaper folder – and during his first winter nearly apprenticed himself to a cabinetmaker. During his second winter in New York a friend found him a job in a theater, and then another in a bookstore. This job he lost after two months when he came down with smallpox, which left him unable to work for four months. Gowans spent the next winter without a job, but he attended book auctions, bought books that he sold to friends and peddled from a basket, and in this way supported himself through the winter. In the spring of 1828, Gowans hired a carpenter to build a bookcase that could be attached to the outside of a building, and paid one dollar a week to a storekeeper for the right to attach it to his store. From this humble stand, which he soon moved to a busier street, the previously discouraged entrepreneur (who had contemplated suicide) began to gain both profits and heart. "The first few books that I sold," he wrote his father four years later, "gave me a sensation of Joy not in my power to describe." Gowans's excitement was not misplaced. His profit after the first year at his stand was exactly $735.70, a sum significantly in excess of the wages of a skilled worker, and probably of the income of a small master artisan. In the second year, still at his outdoor stand, Gowans earned $1,050. By the following year Gowans had rented a small store and moved indoors. Despite his paying $600 in rent, his net profit during his first full year as a genuine retail storekeeper was $1,953.[21] Gowans's business would continue to grow, and when he died in 1870 his obituary would repeat what was by then the standard encomium to the self-made businessman.[22] What is notable about his career, however, is not how far the determined and resourceful entrepreneur could rise, but how much of an income could be gained from even a very small and fledgling retail business.

The experiences of William Gowans, and to some extent those of the clerks William Hoffman, Edward Tailer, and Robert McCoskry Graham, can be set in a larger context by examining representative entries in the records of R. G. Dun & Co., the nation's first important credit-reporting agency. The R. G. Dun credit reports make occasional direct references to annual incomes. Thus, we learn that before buying his employer's Chatham Street furniture store in 1852, Charles Peck was paid a salary of only $500, but that other former New York City clerks had been paid as much as $1,500 and $2,000 before going into business for themselves.[23] We learn also that B. F. Horn of Boston, a dry goods retailer, was making $3,000 to $4,000 per annum in the mid–1850s, while Aaron R. Gay, who owned a "small and safe" stationery store a few blocks away was earning $2,000 to $3,000.[24] In New York City, at roughly the same time, Edwin A. Brooks (nephew of the shoe retailer Lorin Brooks, whom we met in the preceding chapter), William H. Lee, Oscar Cheesman, and the partnerships of Bigelow & Mead and Jones & Shepard each cleared approximately $6,000 per year selling shoes, furniture, and china from small- to medium-sized retail stores.[25] Were these typical incomes for ordinary nonmanual businesses in the larger cities? The vast majority of R. G. Dun & Co. credit reports do not specify incomes, but a close examination of detailed reports on 135 nonmanual businesses and businessmen in New York and Boston (mostly retailers, but including also a few wholesalers, manufacturers, and agents) suggests that 113, or 84%, produced profits in the range of those just noted. Typical in most respects was Frederick A. Gould, a Boston dry goods retailer who in 1847 was, in the words of the credit investigator, merely "making a living" from the store he had opened a year or two earlier. In 1850, Gould was still "not worth much," but by 1853 he had accumulated a surplus of $6,000, and was estimated to be worth $10,000 a year later. By 1858 Gould had a reputation as "a judicious and hitherto successful retailer" who was in "no danger unless spiritualism carries him off. It is said he has this disease." The "disease," a rather fashionable one in Boston, evidently was fatal to neither Gould nor his business. On the eve of the Civil War he was described as "a gentlemanly tradesman," and before the war had ended, his wealth was estimated at $25,000.[26] For a while, William Rowe, Jr., enjoyed similar success in his New York City carpet store. Starting out with a capital of $1,000 saved from his salary as a clerk, Rowe improved his capital to $5,000 within two years, even while "making a comfortable living." Yet his store is also described as small, and we soon learn from his credit report that it was vulnerable to swings in the business cycle. After the panic in 1857, Rowe lost ground, and in 1858 his business failed.[27]

Rowe's failure reminds us that all of these incomes must be understood in the context of the precariousness of small-scale business enterprise in antebellum America. Business failure afflicted about one-fifth of the 113 nonmanual businessmen in my sample who appear to have made a good living for at least a few years. On the other hand, most such failures occurred during a particularly acute downswing in the business cycle, and many of the money-making men who failed, including William Rowe, were able to continue their businesses or start new ones, reestablishing both their incomes and their credit within a brief period of time.[28] Businessmen's way of life, in other words, was probably not as precarious as their particular business enterprises. Moreover, the failure rate of these ordinary retailers, wholesalers, manufacturers, and agents was significantly lower than those of the minority of nonmanual businessmen who never made a good income, and of master craftsmen. Of the 22 sampled storekeepers who did not thrive even in good times, 13 failed. So too did 21 of 52 sampled handworking master craftsmen in the two cities.

The high failure rate among artisans reflects the significantly smaller incomes that accrued to most of those who remained in the manual sector. Only 6 of the 52 credit reports on handworking craftsmen suggest incomes comparable to those gained by small but successful retailers, and 2 of these 6 failed. Another was a bachelor who lived economically, saved money, and invested in real estate.[29] Success of the latter sort was not foreclosed even to artisans who had families to support, but far more characteristic were the struggles of the New

York shoemaker William Scorgie, a "good mechanic" who produced "the best kind of work," but who accumulated nothing beyond the small capital tied up in his shop, and who lost even that to pay off small liabilities when he failed in 1857.[30] Typical of those who survived the panic was one H. McGrath, an "industrious, capable, and economical" cabinetmaker who never gained more than a small living in good times or bad. McGrath was estimated to be worth no more than $800 after more than twenty years in business for himself.[31] The experiences of nonmanual and manual proprietors in both of these industries were, according to the credit reports, very different indeed. In New York, only 3 of 22 sampled cabinetmakers earned more than a very small income from their trades, while 21 of 27 furniture dealers, wholesalers, and manufacturers gained incomes that permitted them to live better than the artisans, even while increasing their personal and business capital. And 32 of 37 retailers, wholesalers, and manufacturers of shoes, but none of 8 shoemakers, enjoyed the same sort of income.

The R. G. Dun & Co. credit reports, and other surviving documents that allude to the earnings of small retailers, clerks, and independent artisans, strongly suggest that even modestly placed proprietors and workers within the *non*manual sector usually escaped the limits of income faced year after year by manual workers and their families. It is interesting, though not conclusive, that *Hunt's Merchants' Magazine*, in a brief article comparing the cost of living in London and New York in 1858, estimated the annual expenses of a "frugal family of four persons" living in New York at $1,329.91, a figure more than double that of the highest workingman's family budget published in the same decade.[32] *Hunt's*, as we have seen, addressed itself to small-scale as well as large-scale men of commerce, and this article would seem to refer to men such as Edward Tailer, William Gowans, and Aaron Gay – the $1,500 it specifies as the annual income of its hypothetical "plain living" family was exactly the sum Tailer had contracted to receive in his second year as a traveling salesman, and a somewhat smaller income than Gowans and Gay each had earned from a small retail store. Salesmen, retailers, and other modest men of the nonmanual sector may or may not have lived much above the mass of skilled manual workers and independent artisans, but there were at least a few observers of the 1850s who assumed that they did, and some compelling documents to suggest that they were probably right.[33]

Examining the relative wealth of manual and nonmanual workers and proprietors would appear to be a good deal simpler and potentially more fruitful than examining relative incomes. Particularly for the close of the antebellum period, when the enumerators of the Eighth Census were instructed to record the value of the real and personal property owned by each individual, a comprehensive data file exists that seems to permit a penetrating analysis of the relationship between work-type and economic well-being. However, quite apart from the assumption that well-being can be measured in durable goods and investments without reference to expenditures for food, entertainment, and other pleasant ephemera, there are weaknesses in the census data that must cloud even the most careful analysis. I have already discussed the fact that many occupational titles disguise variations ranging from wage-earning worker to industrial capitalist. I have also suggested that the property entries are also somewhat unreliable, particularly in that too large a proportion of the enumerated inhabitants, and even of those listed in the most remunerative occupations, listed no property at all. In Philadelphia, at least, fully 61% of the adult males listing occupations reported no property, as did more than 31% of the men listed as merchants, 39% of those listed as attorneys, and 50% of those who were bankers.[34] The property entries that do exist may well approximate the actual levels of wealth of those who reported them,[35] but clearly many individuals either did not answer the census enumerator's question or falsely replied that they owned no property.[36]

Despite these rather severe limitations it is possible to discern instructive patterns in the relationship between listed occupations and reported wealth. Table 4.1 divides the working adult male population of Philadelphia into high and low categories of nonmanual and manual work, based on the occupational listings in the census. In the high nonmanual category are merchants, bankers, professionals, and a few other occupations generally associated with very high income and prestige. The low nonmanual category includes all other explicitly nonmanual proprietors and workers, while the skilled manual category includes all those listed in the skilled trades. The final category includes those listing manual jobs that demanded little or no skill.[37] Whether one includes or excludes those respondents who reported no property (as in Table 4.1a and Table 4.1b, respectively), there are striking differences in property holding between the various occupational categories. All of these differences reinforce the hierarchy of occupations implied in the categorization scheme, and it is unlikely that more significant differences would be obtained by rearranging the occupations in any other way. The specific patterns in Table 4.1 need not be discussed in any detail. Perhaps they are most effectively summarized by noting that there is a strong relationship between occupational category and the absence of reported property, and that

Table 4.1. *Occupational category by reported value of real and personal property, males aged 18 and older, Philadelphia, 1860 (in percentages of occupational categories)*

a. Inclusive of respondents reporting no property

				Total real and personal property					Percentage Total	Number
	$0	$1–499	$500–999	$1,000–1,999	$2,000–4,999	$5,000–9,999	$10,000–19,999	$20,000+		
High nonmanual	37.2	4.2	4.8	7.1	8.6	10.0	11.0	17.2	100.1	5,471
Low nonmanual	49.5	13.6	8.3	7.3	8.8	5.5	3.7	3.3	100.0	26,338
Skilled manual	62.2	20.6	4.5	4.2	4.4	2.0	1.2	.9	100.0	59,840
Unskilled manual	72.3	20.1	2.5	2.3	2.0	.5	.2	.1	100.0	34,075
										125,724

b. Exclusive of respondents reporting no property

			Total real and personal property					Percentage Total	Number
	$1–499	$500–999	$1,000–1,999	$2,000–4,999	$5,000–9,999	$10,000–19,999	$20,000+		
High nonmanual	6.6	7.7	11.3	13.6	16.0	17.5	27.4	100.1	3,435
Low nonmanual	27.0	16.4	14.5	17.4	10.9	7.4	6.4	100.0	13,308
Skilled manual	54.4	12.0	11.0	11.8	5.4	3.3	2.3	100.2	22,591
Unskilled manual	72.4	8.9	8.3	7.4	1.8	.8	.5	100.1	9,438
									48,772

Note: "Number" reflects weighting of 6 for sampled American-born whites.

Source: U.S. Census of Population, 1860, manuscript schedules (Philadelphia Social History Project file).

those in each occupational category who did report property (Table 4.1b) cluster at distinctly different levels of wealth: More than 60% of the merchants and professionals reported more than $5,000; just under half of the "low" nonmanual proprietors and workers reported between $500 and $5,000; and a majority of both skilled and unskilled manual proprietors and workers reported less than $500. Yet striking as these differences may be, they underestimate the actual differences between the nonmanual and manual sectors. Many of the wealthier manual workers, as suggested in the preceding chapter, were in reality manufacturers, retailers, and other nonmanual businessmen who retained artisanal occupational labels. Moving them from the manual to the nonmanual categories would sharpen the differences between the low nonmanual and both manual categories, and reduce the differences between the remaining skilled and unskilled manual workers. Resolving the question of which of the respondents who reported no property were truly propertyless would have a similar effect. As it stands, Table 4.1a understates the differences between the occupational categories by including in each category large but unknown numbers of false entries in the propertyless column, while Table 4.1b understates the differences by eliminating the truly propertyless who were, in fact, mainly in the manual sector. The striking pattern of Table 4.1, in short, is only suggestive of what must have been a still more pronounced divergence between the fortunes of men who worked in the nonmanual and manual sectors in Philadelphia.[38]

The politicians and other prominent Americans who boasted of the superior condition of American workers wrote and spoke not merely of higher wages and better living conditions but also of the seemingly unlimited opportunities for workers to rise out of the working class to become entrepreneurs and even wealthy capitalists. It is not clear how many workers subscribed to the success ethic, or saw themselves as fully qualified citizens of the "democracy of expectant capitalists."[39] Certainly, the idea of an open, expanding, opportunistic society was central to the way in which many nonworkers perceived and defined American society in the Jacksonian era. Unfortunately, tracing the careers of representative antebellum Americans, and gaining a clear sense from these careers of the opportunities actually open to Americans of all sorts, are tasks even more problematic than the comprehensive and reliable tabulation of incomes and wealth.[40] To the troublesome issue of occupational taxonomy we must add here the difficulties of reliably identifying specific individuals in sequential historical records, and of properly interpreting rates of mobility derived from the experiences of that possibly unrepresentative minority who remained in one city (and in that city's records) long enough to be located two or more times.[41] These issues have been faced and resolved most effectively by Clyde and Sally Griffen in their fine study of mobility in Poughkeepsie between 1850 and 1880. In this smaller city an apparently comprehensive directory of businesses allowed the Griffens to sort out wage earners from master artisans, so that the transition from employment to proprietorship among manual workers could be tabulated with reasonable accuracy.[42] (The Griffens did not, however, attempt to separate the small, handworking masters from large, nonmanual businessmen listed with artisanal occupational titles in their sources.) During the 1850s nearly a quarter of Poughkeepsie's nontransient skilled workers moved out of wage employment, 1% to become professionals, another 1% to become clerical workers, and 22% to become proprietors. Most of the last appear to have become masters in their trades, but some opened small neighborhood groceries, taverns, or tobacco shops.[43] However, over a thirty-year period (the Griffens take us well beyond the antebellum era) only a slightly higher proportion moved up from skilled employment – 28% for white, American-born workers of native parentage, and 30% for the cohort as a whole (the latter figure is brought up by the remarkable 49% upward career mobility rate of German immigrants).[44] Interestingly, many of these upwardly mobile workers were the children of nonmanual workers and proprietors. The thirty-year upward mobility rate for skilled workers who were the children of skilled workers was only 22%.[45] All these figures suggest that upward mobility among skilled workers was neither very widespread nor very dramatic. Most of Poughkeepsie's skilled workers remained in manual jobs, and the minority that did not moved mostly into small proprietorships. Far more impressive was the mobility of clerical workers. During the 1850s alone some 37% of Poughkeepsie's clerks became proprietors or professionals.[46]

The Griffens write of the declining opportunities of the skilled manual workers during the latter part of the nineteenth century, and of the homogenization of working-class experience in the context of skill dilution and reduced artisan mobility. Skilled and less skilled workers, they claim, "increasingly . . . came to occupy a common working-class world."[47] Could the workers of the larger cities have experienced somewhat earlier this working-class world of diminishing range and opportunity? There is no antebellum study of mobility in a major city that grapples with the difficulties of this topic as successfully as the Griffens, and there is none that matches the detail with which their results are presented. Peter Knights has tabulated occupational mobility within very small samples of Boston heads of household during each of the three decades preceding the Civil War, using occupational categories that appear to separate skilled wage earners from large and small artisanal proprietors. During the 1830s, according to Knights, only 1 of 28 nontransient skilled workers moved into a higher ranking occupation, while in the 1840s 2 of 31 became small proprietors. During the 1850s 8 of 45 moved into clerical or proprietary positions. The handful of clerks in Knights's samples were more mobile – 5 of 13 became proprietors within the decade.[48] My own samples of the male work force in Philadelphia during each of the four decades preceding the Civil War are much larger than Knights's, and include men who were not heads of household. According to these city directory samples the upward mobility of clerical workers ranged from 25% to 38% per decade between 1820 and 1860, while the upward mobility of craftsmen ranged from 5% to 10%.[49] Interpreting the latter figures is made more difficult, however, by the fact that the directories did not provide any means for distinguishing between skilled workers and large and small artisanal proprietors. Neither my results nor Knights's are definitive. At best, they suggest that the patterns of modest mobility between the manual and nonmanual sectors that the Griffens discovered in Poughkeepsie during the period 1850–80 may well have been present in larger American cities during the three or four decades before the Civil War.

What is perhaps most significant about these brief inquiries into the incomes, wealth, and mobility patterns of workers and proprietors in the nonmanual and manual sectors of antebellum cities is that they all point in the same direction – to a divergence of economic circumstances between men who "worked with their heads" and men who "worked with their hands." Small nonmanual businessmen and experienced clerks appear to have made more money than skilled workers and handworking masters, enough to support their families without calling upon wives and children to work. They accumulated more property, too, while clerical workers seem to have moved much more frequently into income- and wealth-enhancing business proprietorships. This apparent divergence of economic well-being and opportunity underscores a similar bifurcation of work experiences and environments described in the preceding chapter, and leads to the important question of how the values and attitudes of antebellum Americans – their "culture," broadly understood – may have mitigated or further reinforced what thus far looks very much like a hardening of class boundaries along the manual-nonmanual fault line.

The respectable worker reconsidered

Appleton and the other celebrants of the American republic vigorously denied that classes existed in America, or that manual workers were treated with anything other than the respect due to productive members of society. But if this were an accurate description of prevailing American social values, it meant that these values had changed a good deal since the eighteenth century, when the social degradation of manual labor was pervasive. I will argue here that American values had not changed in this respect – that Americans who did not work with their hands did, despite the currency of the "image of the respectable worker," continue to consider as socially inferior those who performed manual work. Indeed, the emerging structures of work and well-being almost certainly revitalized this old prejudice by making it more reasonable in the light of underlying economic realities. In any case, it is visible in many different kinds of documents from the Jacksonian era, including even some of those that purport to uphold the dignity of the manual worker. Not surprisingly, it is particularly well expressed by those spokesmen for working men and women who, while asserting that all value is created by labor and that all labor is honorable, bitterly complained of the humiliation of workers.

The Mechanic's Free Press, edited by a committee of the Mechanic's Library Company of Philadelphia (and principally by William Heighton, an English-born cordwainer), was probably the first American journal published by and for journeymen craftsmen.[50] Begun as early as 1828, this voice of the promoters of America's first citywide trade association remains one of the most authentic documents of the early labor movement, and of the values and sentiments of the more disaffected of the journeymen who experienced the first phases of industrialization. *The Mechanic's Free Press* was an excellent forum for the presentation and discussion of practical programs for the restoration of journeymen's rights, and its pages are filled with proposals issuing from both editors and readers – free public schools, a mechanics' lien law, a labor-for-labor cooperative association, the ten-hour day, and perhaps above all, the organization and support of workingmen's political tickets that would destroy the hegemony of the unresponsive, lawyer-led, major political parties. Supporting these proposals were occasional discussions of Ricardian economic theory and American republican values, but even more basic and more pervasive was the recurring complaint against the social degradation of mechanics by those who defined themselves as "good society."[51] "The Mechanics are a class men," wrote "Peter Single" in an early issue, "who compose that proportion of the population of our country, on whom depends its present and future welfare; from them emanates her glory, her greatness, and her power." Yet men who "rose from nothing" to wealth "despise the mechanic because he is so – Crush the poor man by the iron hand of despotism, and

when they drain all that they can from his labours, despise him."[52]
"We have more than once had our indignation roused against a certain
class of the community," wrote one of the editors a year later, "who
affect to despise that portion of their neighbours who obtain an honest
livelihood in mechanical employments."[53]

These were very typical expressions of the workingman's grievance,
not against his economic exploitation by means of low wages and
long hours, but against the humiliation he was made to suffer because
he performed manual labor. Other letters and editorials expressed
the same grievance in the context of more specific complaints and
proposals. A successful workingmen's ticket, argued the editors,
would provide an opportunity "to disprove the notion that men of
mechanical pursuits are unfitted for political and civil stations by
reason of their inability to perform the duties, which would in such
cases devolve upon them."[54] A correspondent agreed that a workingmen's ticket was necessary, but emphasized instead that workers'
rights were safer in the hands of a man "with but a moderate share
of school learning," than with "one who has been taught from his
cradle that there is something servile in human labour."[55] "Hamden"
(perhaps one of the editors) defended and drummed up support for
the paper itself in similar terms. Why, he asked, had the rest of the
"editorial fraternity" of Philadelphia ignored *The Mechanic's Free Press*?
"Is it because . . . the working part of the community, (upon whom
they are dependent for their bread,) are too degraded and contempt-
ible an order of men, to be entitled to their notice?" "Hamden" called
upon workers to reject "the predictions of those useless animals,"
who

> . . . declare that the operative part of the community, particularly
> mechanics, are not capable of supporting or conducting a newspa-
> per; that they are fit for nothing but manual and mechanical la-
> bour, having little more intellect than the brute creation and little
> else to distinguish them from the latter, than the circumstance of
> their possessing human form.[56]

There were various other ways of keeping this complaint before
the paper's readers. One rather fanciful article reports "from the aged
tongue of a veteran of the Revolution" that "it was originally contemplated to establish certain rules in 'good society, having for their
object the expulsion of Mechanics, and a visible line of distinction
drawn between them.' " These "rules" would have excluded mechanics from the public market before nine o'clock, so that the "rich
and opulent, consequently the respectable," could have the first
choice of goods; required apprentices to wear "trio coloured cockades,
to distinguish them from the sons of gentlemen, and members of

'good society' "; and excluded those not "so entitled by birth and fortune" from the lower boxes of the theater.[57] Another article reported a scene that "took place in Chesnut Street a short time since," in which the writer discussed with "a good natured mechanic" the latter's claim of friendship with "*Lawyer* Flash." The mechanic objected to any suggestion that the lawyer's friendliness was mere electioneering, but the writer's skepticism was confirmed when the lawyer appeared and brushed past the mechanic's outstretched hand, "and nearly knocked him down by his eagerness to escape from him."[58]

More interesting are articles in which mechanics gain at least a measure of revenge for the snubs of "good society." The following item is worth quoting at length, in part because its author does not quite succeed in turning the world upside down, his tone of triumph giving way at the very end to the more customary lamentation:

> Inveterate as I profess to be, against the distinction dress makes between a lawyer and a mechanic, I cannot at the same time refrain from pitying that lawyer, who, having no credit with an honest mechanic, creeps into court, or steals to his garret with a pair of soleless shoes or boots, and stockingless feet, added to a half worn coat and rusty hat – indeed such an one is to be pitied, yet he looks upon the mechanic as his *inferior*!! I knew such an one – he was the gayest among the gay, while his credit lasted; but as soon as his *bilking* days were over, my gentleman became a forsaken member of "good society." The tailor refused him a coat; a client passed his door because his dress was shabby; the bootmaker refused him boots; the land-surveyor was apprehensive of his qualifications in consequence thereof; the hatter refused him a hat; a landed proprietor took him for a mechanic, and passed his office! Here, gentle reader, is a proof that we make lawyers. . . .
> Yes, we manufacture them wholesale and retail, and give them diplomas to pass muster in "good society," to which, alas! we are not admitted.[59]

That the villains in these articles were often lawyers reflects the editors' commitment to the idea of a workingmen's ticket, and their political strategy of discrediting lawyers as the cynical and self-serving leaders of the two major parties. But the editors and their readers also identified more immediate enemies in the merchants and manufacturers who deprived journeymen of the rewards of their labor, and who treated mechanics with as much disdain as did the lawyers. Included among these "accumulators of wealth and popularity" (the term "popularity" is significant here, I believe) were the master mechanics, whose interests in employment-related issues such as the ten-hour day stood in obvious contrast to those of the journeymen, and who were already identifiable as nonproducers.[60] Small producing masters were rarely mentioned, and then only to contrast them with the larger proprietors. The shoe business in Philadelphia, wrote "Crispin," is "conducted by two distinct classes of men, that is, the laboring manufacturer and the capitalist or merchant." The first "occupies perhaps as low a situation in the scale of social existence, if not lower, than any other class of mechanics," while the latter two take all of the wealth, "consequence and credit."[61] Large masters and merchant capitalists were opposed both as employers and as nonproducers, but it was the latter complaint that dominated. William Heighton's Ricardian point of view certainly gave focus to this complaint, but so, too, did the sting of social degradation that he, his colleagues, and his correspondents expressed so clearly. Resentment toward the humiliations imposed upon the manual worker by "good society" is perhaps the dominant theme in The Mechanic's Free Press.

It is less dominant in the later "agrarian" journal of George Henry Evans, published during the mid–1840s as a "New Series" of Evans's earlier radical paper, The Working Man's Advocate.[62] But it is by no means absent there, despite Evans's single-minded promotion of an idea – the free distribution of public lands in farm-sized parcels to actual settlers – that would seem to be, and no doubt was, far from the daily concerns of ordinary urban working men and women.[63] Evans did not see it that way. Land reform was to him the ultimate answer to the urban labor surplus that lay at the heart of working-class distress. Evans's interest in what he was sure was the underlying mechanism of class exploitation distracted him somewhat from the more obvious day-to-day grievances of workers, and his solution was, as he emphasized, a fairly conservative one that would preserve existing property rights while transforming urban wage slaves into yeoman farmers.[64] The most culpable enemies he identified were not the industrialists who drove those slaves but "monopolistic" real estate speculators – including the ultimate in aristocratic, absentee landlords, the British investor in American land – who prevented urban workers from acquiring their own farms. Evans occasionally conceded that merchants (but not bankers, brokers, lawyers, doctors, or clergymen) performed a useful role in society, and in an early issue his colleague John Commerford sympathetically addressed the problem of labor surplus among nonmanual workers.[65] Still, The Working Man's Advocate found ample room for complaining about merchants, clerks, and others who disdained manual work and those who performed it. A letter from "Huge Paw," for example, complained that the "few who labor not, are placed far above us in the scale of respectability, of wealth, and of influence." (Huge Paw turned to the Bible for the image that would best express his indignation: "They eat no bread ... in the sweat of their face.")[66] The "present system of labor ... crowns the [capitalist] with honor, the [producer] with disgrace," wrote another contributor (actually a speaker at the 1844 New England Convention of Workingmen). The capitalist is granted respectability, but the worker is "despised."[67]

Evans himself turned occasionally to the subject of social prejudice among nonworkers, especially when the latter were Whigs. In an editorial entitled "Who are 'Common People'?" Evans contrasted the "whig nobility" and "codfish aristocracy" with "those who work for a living; those who wield the hammer and guide the plow." "Take off your hats, farmers and mechanics!" he continued, "the embodiment of cologne water, soft soap, and silk gloves will condescend to address such of you as have the votes to bestow."[68] Another editorial on a Whig mass meeting commented on the elaborately constructed and decorated speakers' platform:

> ... telling the poor working man, as plainly as do the elegant portico of Astor House, the bronze lions on either side of the Bank steps, or the beautiful balconies of Lafayette Place, *this is no place for you: after you have put art's finishing stroke on these productions of your toil they are no longer to be polluted by your proximity.*[69]

The political context of many of these statements in both *The Mechanic's Free Press* and *The Working Man's Advocate* suggests how deeply some mechanics must have resented the way politicians pandered to the "respectable worker" during election campaigns. "Politicians may fawn around the *respectable* mechanic and farmer," wrote the *Social Reformer* in an editorial reprinted by Evans, and "Moralists prate of the *esteem* in which the faithful working man should be held," but "hypocrites, or worse, are they all. They consider Labor a disgrace, and those who perform it, servile and mean."[70] But while this last statement seems quite sincere, we may detect in many of the editorial complaints against hypocritical politicians a language that seems hardly less inflated or rhetorical than that of the political lawyers themselves. If the latter did cynically cultivate the image of the respectable worker to their own political advantage, the workingmen's editors promoted their own political programs (though seldom their own political careers) by constructing what might be called the counterimage of the despised worker. There was, I believe, a good deal of real social prejudice to justify that counterimage, but it is clear that political advocacy exerted its own influence on the language of the editorial spokesmen for the working class. To gain a firmer grasp on

prevailing attitudes toward manual workers, it is necessary to consider other sorts of documents, including those produced by men and
women who had no political stake in the counterimage of the despised
worker.

Magazines written for a prosperous or specifically mercantile readership had no such stake. On the contrary, it is in the leading journals
of this type that we find existing institutions defended by the most
restrained and responsible adherence to the opposite image of the
respectable worker. Yet, even in the promotion of that image there
is a consistent note of condescension that would seem to confirm,
rather than deny, the complaints of the working-class editors and
correspondents. "Looking beyond the external attitude of the working-man," wrote *Harper's Monthly* of the literature of the mid-
nineteenth century, "it has found beneath the bronzed face and soiled
garments the true image of manhood."[71] Sun-darkened skin and dirty
and tattered clothes, along with rough hands, mental sluggishness,
and even an apelike or otherwise bestial character or carriage were
fairly common elements in the depiction of manual workers at mid-
century, and it is apparent from this statement that the editors of
Harper's were not above using some of them to invoke a "manhood"
that they obviously felt was ironic. But why, William Heighton or
"Huge Paw" might ask, must one look *beneath* the external appearance
of the worker to find a contradictory, redeeming truth? In its discussions of recent and projected future improvements in the well-being
and social standing of the worker, *Harper's* revealed more than it
perhaps intended about its own and more general attitudes toward
the manual worker:

> Industry has too generally been synonymous with beast-like
> drudgery. But this degradation can not continue. Labor has not
> been as promptly affected by the spirit of the age as other social
> interests. Nor is this surprising. It was isolated from the great
> controlling forces of the world. It stood apart by itself, and partici-
> pated no more than machinery in the ongoings of society. It was
> not a living part of the determinative will of the public mind. Prej-
> udices scowled on it. Selfishness abused it, and rejoiced in the
> abuse.[72]

It should be emphasized that, quite apart from the prejudices attached to it, the view of the urban class structure articulated in *Harper's*
was organized quite clearly along manual-nonmanual lines. "If our
bankers lodge in palaces, then our bankers' bakers ought to keep
phaetons, and a seat in Grace Church," reasoned the editor in a
lighthearted jab at the opulence of the city's upper class. "If bankers

will dress their walls in fresco, their daughters in Mechlin, their lap-
dogs in ribbons, and their religion in purple velvet, there is no reason
in the world why their carpenters should not strike for silver bell-
pulls, and an occasional seat at the opera."[73] This play upon the
manual-nonmanual dichotomy for humorous effect is mirrored in the
more serious discussions in *Hunt's Merchants' Magazine* of the contributions and relative worth of the manual and nonmanual sectors.
"While the labor of the mechanic moulders or decays after him, the
title of merchant is sounded for ages," wrote Charles Edwards in one
of the first issues.[74] The contrast was seldom so crudely put, but it
appears in a variety of forms throughout the magazine's many issues
– as advice to mechanics not to try to become merchants, for example,
as emphasis on the differences between commercial and mechanical
skill, or as rebuttal of Ricardian economics and the articulation of
what might be called a "commercial theory of value."[75] Value, argued
Edward Everett, is created not by the production of goods but by
their movement to the market, and by their exchange for money or
for other goods that the producer presently lacks. Until such movements and transactions occur the producer's goods (save for the few
he can use himself) are of no value to him or to anyone else; hence,
it is the merchant, not the producer, who creates value.[76] In another
publication one of *Hunt's* occasional contributors, the Reverend Jonathan F. Stearns, expressed this idea by co-opting and extending one
of the radical mechanics' favorite images: The merchant class "forms
the very sinews, ligaments, and conducting arteries of all social organization."[77]

The manual-nonmanual dichotomy was, indeed, central to the
thought and language of Freeman Hunt and nearly all of his contributing authors, and although few directly addressed its social implications in this business journal, the assumption of the inferiority of
the mechanic peeks through even where it was not intended. Extolling
the completion of a new steamship, Philip Hone commented: "The
science and skill of the architect will be suitably compensated, the
intelligent merchants will receive their well-earned commissions, and
a hundred worthy artisans will have supported their families during
the winter."[78] Science, intelligence, and even skill belong here only
to professionals and merchants, who justifiably pocket ample commissions while "worthy" artisans get through the winter. Even Nathan Appleton, in the very essay (reprinted in *Hunt's*) that I quoted
at the beginning of this chapter, finally conceded that the "respectable
worker" was an ideal toward which society should strive, rather than
a present reality. "It is our mission," concluded Appleton, "to amal-
gamate, equalize and improve the whole mass of population, by el-

evating the lower portions from their usual abject state, and depressing the higher, in dispensing with a privileged aristocracy."[79] His fellow Bostonian, Theodore Parker, agreed: "Producers seem more noble than the distributors. . . . This may not be the popular judgment now, but must one day become so."[80]

The "lower portions," toiling in "their usual abject state," did not include clerks, who were, after all, "distributors" rather than "producers." The pages of *Hunt's* are sprinkled with references to the "business qualities" of clerks, as well as to their "gentlemanly appearance," "exterior polish," and, at times, their excessive pride. "Most of them are too proud to be tailors, or carpenters, or builders, or printers," complained the editor of another journal in an item reprinted approvingly by Hunt.[81] But this pride, though invariably disparaged, was continually reinforced by *Hunt's* celebration of the worth and dignity of the man of commerce: "It is not stating the truth too strongly to say that America is proud of her merchants. In fact it is another name for gentleman among us."[82] The clerk, too, basked in that celebration, and in the always present implication (or explication) of his superiority, as a young man of commerce, over the mechanic.

The actual social distance between young clerks and mechanics may have been small in many instances, especially when the former were country boys not yet secure on the ladder to higher salaries and future independence. It is all the more interesting, therefore, that the didactic literature aimed at young people magnified the manual-nonmanual divide, though it often did so in covert ways, even while claiming to do the very opposite. According to Rex Burns, children's magazines such as Lydia Maria Child's *Juvenile Miscellany* and Samuel Griswold Goodrich's *Parley's Magazine* consistently attached "more prestige to business or the professions than to the so-called 'true producers' of wealth" and wrote of the manual trades with an equally consistent condescension.[83] One story in Goodrich's *Merry's Museum*, which demonstrated how, "By perseverance, industry, honesty, and a thirst for knowledge, 'The despised apprentice became an able and profound lawyer and was esteemed for real talent and moral worth,' "[84] mirrors perfectly the contrast between despised manual workers and pretentious lawyers that pervades the workingmen's newspapers. Burns, in effect, suggests that instruction in the social superiority of nonmanual occupations was the "hidden agenda" of much of this literature. He could have made the same observation about nonfictional advice books written for young clerks and mechanics. Although few advice books were addressed specifically to young manual workers during this era, I have located two pairs of publications, one written by John Frost, an author of school texts, the other by the clergyman James W. Alexander, that offer advice to clerks and mechanics as separate groups. The difference in content, form, and even tone within each pair conveys quite clearly how each author based his understanding of social worth on the manual-nonmanual dichotomy, despite his occasional assertion that any occupation was as honorable as any other.

Frost's *Young Merchant*, published in 1839, is a long, detailed, but unexceptional review of the personal qualities necessary for success in business, the specific strategies that an aspiring businessman can adopt to improve the likelihood of his success, and the duties that devolve upon the businessman once success has been achieved. Like much of the advice offered in *Hunt's Merchants' Magazine* and in other publications, Frost's specific suggestions are predicated on the assumption that merchants and other nonmanual businessmen are likely to grow rich and acquire a high position in society. Hence, clerks are advised, when choosing a companion, to "seek that of the respectable in character and station," while young merchants are reminded of their paternalistic duties toward clerks and "other dependents." Established merchants (and manufacturers) are advised to become patrons of the arts.[85] The conscientious discharge of the various duties described in *The Young Merchant* will "realize large and rich rewards": wealth, the "power of rewarding merit by giving employment, patronage and good advice," "the distinction and consideration among men, which results from respectability of station and character," domestic comfort and felicity in a "well-ordered home," and the opportunity of "taking a leading part" in public affairs. All of these the successful businessman "realizes towards the close of his career in 'large amounts.' "[86]

It would hardly be worth taking note of this quite conventional recitation of virtues, strategies, duties, and rewards, had Frost not written another book four years later, addressed this time to *The Young Mechanic*. In the early pages of this second book, Frost explicitly denies that any intrinsic connection exists between manual work and social worth, and asserts that usefulness, happiness, respectability, and wealth await the successful American mechanic.[87] For these reasons, the young mechanic, no less than the young merchant, deserves advice for the shaping of a successful career. But the falsity of this attempt to minimize the differences between the audiences of Frost's two books soon becomes apparent. For one thing, Frost admits that Americans do generally disdain manual labor. Such prejudice, however untenable, "is constantly assigned by purse-proud fathers and silly mothers as a reason for determining their children's pursuits in life. There is a very general impression that a merchant, a clergyman, doctor or lawyer stands higher, and should stand higher, in the social scale than a mechanic or farmer."[88] More importantly, Frost himself, once he is beyond the introductory affirmation of the mechanic's potential worth, slips into the same prejudice, to a degree that betrays his introductory remarks as a ritualistic gesture to the "respectable worker." Taste in the fine arts, for example, is denied to the "lower orders of society," not only because they have not been sufficiently educated, but also because of the effects of labor upon body and mind:

> Labour requires strained, forced, and violent motions. This race of men walk not for pleasure, but to perform journeys of necessity. They take advantage therefore of bending the body forward, and assisting their motion by a sling with their arms. Their low station, their wants, and their drudgeries, give them a sordidness and ungenerosity of disposition, together with a coarseness and nakedness of expression; whence their motions and address are equally rude and ungraceful.[89]

That Frost could write these lines in a book that purports to advise manual workers as to the best means for advancing their careers would seem nothing less than astonishing. Actually, by the time the reader reaches these lines it is already clear that Frost has little knowledge of or interest in manual work or the lives of artisans and other manual workers. Increasingly, his advice (for example, to study music, drawing, horsemanship and dancing, and to acquire polite manners and good taste)[90] is directed to "boys" rather than to mechanics, and it is evident that the boys to whom he refers are the sons of prosperous families rather than apprentices or the sons of mechanics. Why, then, the title and the early discussion of the worthy mechanic? I can only surmise that Frost either attempted and then retreated from a subject he did not understand, or merely tacked on the title and a few justifying remarks once it occurred to him to sell the book as a sequel to *The Young Merchant*. For whatever reason, *The Young Mechanic* offers advice that few young mechanics could have found relevant to their lives, and the contempt its author expresses toward manual labor in his description of apelike workers is, in the final analysis, quite consistent with the book as a whole.

James W. Alexander's parallel publications for mechanics and clerks display even more clearly the importance of the manual-nonmanual dichotomy in shaping social perceptions and values. Alexander's *American Mechanic and Working-Man* was published in two volumes in 1847 as an expanded edition of his one-volume *The American Mechanic*, which first appeared in 1838 under the pseudonym Charles Quill. Like Frost's *Young Mechanic*, Alexander's volumes attempt to deny the significance of the distinction between manual and nonmanual work, and end up achieving the very opposite. The term "workingman," he concedes, "as usually employed, . . . designates the artisan, the mechanic, the operative, or the labourer; all, in a word, who work with their hands."[91] Alexander proposes instead to apply the term to "every man who honestly supports himself by industrious application to useful business."[92] For that purpose he compares bookkeepers to carters, mill directors to operatives, and architects to hod carriers, and in the process succeeds only in underscoring the differences between them. Bookkeepers, mill directors, and architects, moreover, make no further appearances in these volumes, which quickly revert to the intended readership announced at the outset, the "apprentice, the journeyman, and the master-mechanic."[93] That the latter were not only a distinct but also a socially inferior group in Alexander's mind is driven home by the very language he uses to define their respectability. "Ours is not a country where one may sneer at the 'mechanic'," he boasts, while "the day is past" when the idea of a program of study for mechanics "is strange or ludicrous."[94] "Let no one be surprised," he rather self-consciously warns, "at my quoting choice poetry to mechanics."[95]

It is, however, in the content and tone of the advice he dispenses to manual workers, and to clerks in his later essay, "The Merchant's Clerk Cheered and Counselled,"[96] that Alexander best conveys the significance he attaches to the difference "between head-work and hand-work."[97] Unlike Frost, Alexander does adhere to the task of providing advice to artisans and other manual workers. But the advice itself is no less condescending than Frost's neglect. Alexander's principal message to the mechanic is that he content himself with a humble life of manual work and simple domestic pleasures. He should avoid working too hard, for "he who overtasks his days has no evenings," and the ambition for worldly wealth is destructive and illusory.[98] Take heed of the old shoemaker, Alexander counsels, whose motto, "be honest and industrious," earned him only a lonely and wretched old age, for he had worked too hard and neglected his domestic pleasures.[99] Avoid unions and ignore theories of equal rights, which breed only discontent, and read for self-improvement and pleasure rather than to rise in the world.[100] Spend summer evenings in your cottage garden.[101] Alexander, in sum, advises the mechanic to make the best of, but also to know, be content with, and keep, his rather humble place.

Even more condescending than the message itself is the form and tone with which it is conveyed. Much of *The American Mechanic* is written in homey, playful, even childish little sketches, in which wise mechanics, speaking mainly in proverbs, display a humble philosophy of simple contentment and virtue. "There is something in the homespun philosophy of *Uncle Benjamin* which always secures my attention," explains the author. "Rude as it is, it has that strength which is often wanting in schools and books. Uncle Benjamin has never read Lord Chesterfield, and, therefore, has not learned how exceedingly vulgar it is to use a common proverb." More candidly, "In the belief that the common mind in every age is best reached by parables, I have sometimes indulged in a little fiction."[102] (Apparently, the mechanic could appreciate "choice poetry" but not plain didactic prose.) This condescension to "the common mind" is not found in Alexander's essay addressed to clerks. The advice there, moreover, is very different. As a prospective businessman, the clerk should work hard and prepare himself not only for business but also for a high position in society. He should grow rich in learning, in part so that he can converse with a "brilliant wife."[103] He will come to occupy, in short, a social world entirely separate from that of the humble mechanic. Indeed, he already does. In a Scottish edition of his essay, Alexander explains in a footnote the American use of the word "clerk" to his readers in the British Isles: "In America it is customary to denominate as 'clerk' all young men engaged in commercial pursuits. . . . Of course, the term is not applied to those engaged in mechanical trades."[104]

Simple images and complex realities

All of these commentators, from "Huge Paw" to "Charles Quill" (the pseudonyms are themselves instructive), founded their social perceptions and identities on the distinction between manual and nonmanual work, and suggest from a wide enough variety of perspectives how profound this simple distinction was in the shaping of antebellum American society. But could it have been definitive in a place as varied and complex as the large antebellum city? There were indeed other figures in this impossibly simple carpet – exceptions of economic circumstance and social identity that did not conform to the manual-nonmanual dichotomy. We must consider how their presence may have affected the relationship between work and prestige. For example, there were the small shop- and tavernkeepers in working-class neighborhoods, many of whom, as Clyde and Sally Griffen point out, were former manual workers who moved from the workroom to the barroom or grocery when they became too old to keep up with the pace of younger workers. Some no doubt moved up to higher levels of income and prestige by crossing into the nonmanual sector, but others merely moved along (or, in terms of income, even down) into another phase of the working-class life cycle.[105] These men had become nonmanual proprietors, but their tobacco shops, groceries, newsstands, and taverns were not vehicles for the journey out of the working class. Their mobility was lateral rather than upward, and in their life-styles and personal associations, and presumably their sentiments as well, they remained unexceptional figures in the working-class community, even though they no longer worked with their hands.

And just as there were nonmanual proprietors who remained in the working class, there were mechanics who did not. In two recent studies, Gary John Kornblith and John S. Gilkeson, Jr., have explained how the members of mechanics' associations in Providence, Boston, and Salem reformulated an artisan ideology into a newer, "middle-class view of society" that, in Gilkeson's estimation, included a belief in the harmony of interests among producers, a suspicion of great wealth, and a claim by economically successful artisans for greater social and political recognition.[106] Kornblith's emphasis is on the latter, and on the development of a liberal, pro-capitalist view of economic relations,[107] but both emphasize that these were mechanics, not merchants or clerks, who were articulating an explicitly middle-class social ideology. They did so, moreover, *as* mechanics. Both Gilkeson and Kornblith quote a select committee of the Providence Association of Mechanics and Manufacturers, which concluded in 1852: "It is the influence . . . which is exerted by the middling class, that is most felt in the community. It is this class to which, as mechanics, we belong."[108]

Too much should not be made of these exceptions. The small shopkeepers in working-class neighborhoods may be said to have remained in the working class precisely because they remained among their old neighbors and friends, and because they had no contact with and remained invisible to middle- and upper-class residents of the city. Working-class neighborhoods were generally on or near the periphery of the city, and even when they were physically close to the emerging downtown wholesale, retail, and financial districts, they formed a world apart from them. New York's working-class East Side began only three blocks from Broadway, but business commuters and well-to-do shoppers never entered it, and knew of it mainly through the rather sensationalized accounts of poverty, prostitution, and violent crime that filled the print media of the day. Even the most sober and responsible of these accounts rarely mentioned the small shops and shopkeepers of the East Side (tavernkeepers, of course, received a good deal of attention), and we may safely assert that these nonmanual proprietors impinged but little on the consciousness of those who lived, worked, and shopped in more prosperous parts of the city.[109]

The mechanics who proclaimed their middle-class status and promoted liberal economic ideas through such agencies as the Providence Association of Mechanics and Manufacturers were much more visible, but not necessarily as mechanics. As Kornblith points out, most of the members of the mechanics' societies, and nearly all of their important spokesmen, were large- and medium-sized masters who no longer worked with their hands.[110] In other words, they were the very men I have been describing as manufacturers and other nonmanual businessmen, not as mechanics, despite their adherence to traditional artisanal labels. Kornblith and Gilkeson demonstrate (as does Sean Wilentz in his discussion of the larger New York masters who did not necessarily belong to that city's General Society of Mechanics and Tradesmen)[111] that at least some of these larger masters continued to identify themselves as artisans, and to associate themselves in a serious way with their trades and with the "mechanics' interest." However, they also show how different the masters' reformulation of that identity and that interest was from the emerging ideology of the journeymen's trades union movement. As journeymen emphasized the split between nonproducing masters and the genuine but exploited and despised producers who were their employees, the masters were impelled to distance themselves from wealthy merchant-capitalists, and to emphasize the harmony of interests among all who belonged to the trade. And as journeymen accused the masters of destroying the trade and its skills by introducing machines, green hands, and other skill-degrading innovations in a relentless search for higher profits, the masters responded by portraying themselves as progressive businessmen who improved the trade and increased its value to society by making it more productive and, in many instances, more scientific. The appeal to science (embodied in the prominent role played by prosperous masters in the founding of the Franklin Institute and other organizations devoted to the practical applications of science)[112] was especially important, as it helped the masters to transcend the stigma associated with manual work even while it legitimized their position as productive members of their trades.[113] It was a subtle response to those who would denigrate them as mechanics, as well as to those who would criticize them for ceasing to be so. In this and in other ways, the point of view developed within the mechanics' societies was that of the employing manufacturer rather than that of the handworking artisan. It may be significant that the masters who joined, led, and addressed these organizations continued to call themselves "mechanics" (most of the societies were founded and named in the late eighteenth century), but it is no less significant that this usage was shaped by an increasingly sharp debate in which both nonmanual masters and manual workers sought justification in aspects of a more harmonious past. Those outside this increasingly attenuated community of "mechanics" were not fooled. When the Reverend Jonathan F. Stearns set out to define the "business class," he included "not the merchant or the trader only" but "all those whose vocation it is to organize and direct the industrial forces of the community – the manufacturer, the master mechanic, the contractor, or the superintendent, in the various enterprises of production, accommodation or improvement."[114] The Reverend John Todd also identified "master mechanics," along with bankers, merchants, and others as "men of business," and left little room for wondering whether they belonged in the workshop or the office:

> The man who carries on any business must have others to carry out his plans. He must contrive, others must execute. The general must plan the battle, the soldiers must carry his plan into execution. It is mind using matter; the brain employing muscle and sinew. It was estimated that the mind of Bonaparte was equal in battle to forty thousand men. The skill and mind of the manufacturer or the merchant are often worth more than the labor of all whom he employs. He must take the responsibility, and do all the planning. Hence he advertises for *hands*, not heads – for manual labor, and not mental.[115]

Todd's description glosses over those master craftsmen who combined management, sales, and other nonmanual business tasks with continuing or occasional turns at the workbench. Not all of these men were in the neighborhood service trades, and not all of the larger artisan-manufacturers ceased to see themselves, or to be seen, as mechanics. More generally, no single scheme could sort several hundred thousand workers and proprietors, working in several thousand occupations, into two or three distinct and inclusive categories of social worth. But to John Todd and many others, the manual-nonmanual dichotomy was the most compelling way to make sense of all this variety. Moreover, it made *increasing* sense. As never before, men who worked with their heads and men who worked with their hands differed in other ways too – in their income, wealth, and economic opportunity, and, as we saw in the preceding chapter, in the circumstances surrounding work itself. The shrinking proportion of handworking master craftsmen and the elevation of storekeepers and their clerks by means of specialization and the creation of more distinct and more dignified work environments, no less than the association between work-type and economic well-being, reinforced the ancient prejudice against manual work. For all these reasons, social definition had become easier, not more difficult, in the large, industrializing cities of the antebellum era.

But why should historians who have sensed this clarification speak in terms of *middle*-class formation? Many contemporaries spoke of a "business class" and a "working class," and the manual-nonmanual dichotomy suggests two classes rather than three. In what ways can we find in the new occupational alignments of the Jacksonian era the emergence of a more visible and more clearly defined intermediate category in the urban social structure? The simplest answer to this question is that the "business class," once so clearly associated with large-scale, wealthy, and socially prominent merchants, could not incorporate without considerable strain all of the new men I have described in these chapters. Retailers behind their Greek Revival storefronts, small and medium-sized manufacturers in their down-town offices or warerooms, clerks, salesmen, and accountants who were being groomed for ordinary proprietorships – none of these could be spoken of in the same breath with the poor and "inferior" inhabitants of the city, as were the mainly artisanal "middling sorts" of the eighteenth century. But neither were they members of the mercantile elite, although the economic world they inhabited was much closer to the elite's in function, style, and urban space. This stretching of the business class, in conjunction with the increasing clarification of the boundary between manual and nonmanual worlds of work, made the idea of a new and ascending middle class plausible, and we will see that contemporary observers other than Walt Whitman did attempt to define such a class, some, but not all, pointing as Whitman did to the lower levels of the expanded and more complex nonmanual sector. Before we consider these taxonomic experiments, however, we must examine other dimensions of the social experience of middling city folk. We must ask how this broader range of experience related to changes we have already observed in the structure and rewards of work, and whether in this relationship we can identify and describe an emerging middle-class way of life.

5 "Things are in the saddle": consumption, urban space, and the middle-class home

Things are in the saddle,
And ride mankind

— R. W. Emerson, "Ode Inscribed
to W. H. Channing," 1847

Emerson's complaint was not a new one among thoughtful Americans, but it had acquired a new urgency in the Jacksonian era, when rising personal incomes and an expanding array of consumer goods (and of attractive downtown retail shops) produced striking changes in the habits and life-styles of large numbers of urban Americans, unleashing what one recent historian of New York City has called "a revolution of expectations regarding luxuries and comforts."[1] Some city people forthrightly pursued an extravagant way of life during these years, pushing aside the once influential doctrine that associated virtue with plain living. A larger number, no doubt, retained that doctrine (which survived, according to David Shi, "as a conservative moral idiom, . . . an expression of fears and ambivalence about the pace and nature of social change"),[2] even while redefining the meanings of simplicity and comfort in accordance with new conditions. In the words of one contemporary:

> Time was when it was sufficient for a comfortable liver to have
> half a house, or to have one spare front-room for company: now,
> the same man must have a whole house, and the first story must
> be thrown into parlors. Not *very* long since, one servant, for gen-
> eral purposes, was all that was deemed necessary: now, the re-
> quirement is extended to two certainly, with special aid for extra
> occasions, and a nurse for the little ones. . . . It is not many years
> since the class spoken of were only occasionally favored with a
> piano: now, that instrument must be set down as a requisite to
> parlor equipment. The same is true of the dietetic department, of
> our social entertainments and modes of dressing – great changes
> have occurred with our so-called advancing civilization.[3]

Recent historians have made it clear that "the class spoken of" was the urban middle class, whose members experienced a domestic revolution during these years that went beyond the acquisition and furnishing of a larger and more elegant home (completely separated, we might add, from the male household head's place of business) to the sanctification of the home and of domestic affairs, the redefinition of gender roles within the home, and the reformulation of strategies of child nurturance and education, the whole constituting, to Mary Ryan especially, not merely a middle-class phenomenon but a phenomenon critical to the formation and perpetuation of the middle class.[4] Ryan's arguments, and those of the numerous other recent scholars of the middle-class domestic revolution, are persuasive; yet they bear reconsideration, especially at that point where new patterns of consumption are associated specifically with the middle class. Contemporaries wrote often of *general* improvements in American living standards, and some alleged that new patterns of consumption were reducing, not increasing, the differences between social classes. Frederick B. Perkins, for example, wrote in 1861 that "the increase in the supply of money, the decrease of any distinction between classes of society, and the general diffusion of wealth and comfort, render the difference between the furniture of the rich, and that of the poor, much less at the present day than formerly. Comparatively few luxuries of any kind are now accessible to the rich, which are not so to the farmer and the mechanic."[5] Perkins and many others agreed with the author of *The British Mechanic's and Labourer's Handbook* that American mechanics dressed nearly as well as merchants,[6] while the author of the introduction to the statistical compilation of the 1860 census of manufactures claimed that the piano was often to be found "in the cottage of the humbler class of artisans and laborers in our cities" and helped extend the domestic revolution beyond the middle class: "It beguiles the hours of sorrow and alleviates the cares of business, while it diffuses through all classes an increasing taste for the enjoyments of the social and domestic circle, harmonized and elevated under the influence of music."[7]

Statements of this sort rarely were backed up by evidence, and many may be dismissed as mere embellishments on the theme of the respectable worker. Few urban artisans or laborers, for example, owned pianos.[8] Few, for that matter, lived in "cottages," though the term seems to have been used fairly often (recall James W. Alexander's discussions of the urban worker's "cottage garden") as a way of softening the realities of urban working-class housing. I have already suggested that the incomes of manual workers and small master mechanics were much more restricted than those generated within the nonmanual sector and that, very young clerks and small shop- and tavernkeepers of working-class neighborhoods aside, there was probably significantly less overlap than there is today between the incomes and the assets of men who worked with their heads and those of men who worked with their hands. Still, there are good reasons for questioning whether consumption patterns in the ante- bellum era obscured or reinforced class distinctions. One, just noted, is that manual workers may have participated to some degree in a general improvement of living standards. Another is that workers and their families, despite lower incomes, may have purchased cloth- ing and other goods that were similar in style to those purchased by somewhat wealthier people – that the design of goods, and the ways in which they were purchased and used, may have tended to ho- mogenize appearances rather than to create visible emblems of class. Contemporary observers who wrote of "the general diffusion of wealth and comfort," and of the "decrease of any distinction between classes of people," may have been justified in focusing not on a middle-class consumer revolution but on a general rise in living stan- dards, and on new styles that made "common men" out of all but the very rich and the very poor.

The plain dark democracy of broadcloth

Did consumption contribute to class distinctions in this era, or did it tend to dissolve the boundaries that were taking shape in the ur- ban workplace? The most dramatic changes in the production of consumer goods were those that made ordinary goods cheaper. Hence, those mechanics who were able to find work fairly often, and who maintained their skill levels in the face of industrializa- tion, were able to take advantage of significant price reductions in cloth, clothing, and a number of household goods that previously had been available only to people with larger incomes. Workers in the new furniture factories and specialized cheap furniture shops, for example, may have experienced new limitations of income and opportunity, but they and other workers benefited from the low prices of mass-produced furniture. One English traveler, Isabella Lucy Bird Bishop, reported in 1856 that a Cincinnati furniture fac- tory she visited turned out common chairs at $5 to $25 per dozen, and bedsteads at $5 to $25 apiece.[9] Carpets, too, once restricted to the well-to-do, plummeted in price after the introduction of power- loom weaving, and became accessible to all classes.[10] In 1860 sev- eral Philadelphia carpet stores advertised all-wool ingrain carpets at 45¢ to 75¢ per yard, and cheaper carpets for as little as 20¢ per yard.[11] By 1860, reports Edgar W. Martin, "as good an eight-day clock could be obtained for $3.00 or $4.00 as would have sold for $20.00 before 1837, and a one-day clock could be sold at a fair profit for 75 cents."[12] Willowware and other transfer printed ceramics had sold for three or four times the price of ordinary cream-color earthenware at the beginning of the century, but by the 1850s they were generally less than twice as expensive as cream color.[13] Perhaps the most significant price changes were those introduced by the new ready-to-wear clothing industry. Clothiers usually did not advertise their prices during this era, but a few of the less expensive ready-to-wear clothing stores, such as Philadelphia's Phoenix Clothing Bazaar, listed prices for business coats ($4.25 to $8.00), vests ($1.00 to $3.00), and other items of respectable dress that were within range for a number of manual workers.[14] In the same year (1860) Dickerson's hat store of Philadelphia advertised "fine dress hats" at $2.50, while an unnamed competitor offered the "cheapest silk hats" from a "one-price store" that was in the midst of a working-class neighborhood.[15]

These final items suggest that workers may have emulated (or duplicated without seeking to emulate) middle-class styles of consumption, especially in clothing, which was certainly one of the most visible and status-relevant types of consumer goods. But the question of class-related styles of clothing in antebellum urban America is a difficult one to resolve. Edgar Martin simply assumed that "shirt sleeves, heavy brogan boots and shoes, and rough wool hats were, of course, the rule" for manual workers during the workday, but neither he nor anyone else has been able to prove the existence of a distinctive working-class mode of dressing either on or off the job.[16] Contemporary commentators, as we have seen, were more likely to argue the opposite point, at least with respect to workers they saw in the streets. Illustrations of workplaces and street scenes offer an interesting but limited and sometimes contradictory view of contemporary perceptions. Some views of factories and smaller workshops portray working men and women in plain and sometimes rough clothes, usually covered by an apron. Men's shirts are often white (or at any rate are light and uniform in color), but sleeves are usually rolled and shirt collars are absent or open. Men work hatless, or wear soft caps or hats, or the paper hats traditional to a few trades. Women wear plain, unadorned dresses, sometimes with an apron.[17] Other views, however, depict workers who are better dressed, with closed collars, cravats, and vests for men, and lace-trimmed dresses for women. The illustration accompanying an article on bookbinding in the April 26, 1845,

Figure 5.1. Bookbinder, 1845 (courtesy of Cornell University Libraries)

issue of *The American Penny Magazine*, for example, portrays a skilled workman who might easily be imagined exchanging his apron for a business-style coat and hat at the end of the day, and blending into a sidewalk crowd of retailers and clerks (Figure 5.1).[18] A broader view of the bindery in the May 10 issue confirms this suggestion, at least for the half-dozen or so workmen whose hats and coats hang on the workshop wall (Figure 5.2).[19] These workers may have been fully qualified citizens of what *The Illus-*

Figure 5.2. Bookbindery interior, 1845 (courtesy of Cornell University Libraries)

trated News would call, a few years later, the "plain dark democracy of broadcloth."[20]

It is probable, however, that most contemporaries perceived differences where we can see only similarities. Inexpensive clothes, clothes purchased in secondhand shops, and clothes worn for too long a time created visible differences within the broadcloth democracy, even in the absence of differences in style. Moreover, depictions of businessmen, clerks, prosperous shoppers, and pedestrians in downtown retail districts convey a greater opulence of dress than appears in any of the workshop views (see, for example, Figures 3.10, 3.12, 3.14, and 3.18). Bowery b'hoys and other working-class dandies may have tried to match this opulence, but the effect was very different. Mose and the b'hoys wore black frock coats, tall beaver hats, and silk cravats, but greased and curled "soap locks" sticking down out of their hats, and black cigars sticking out of their teeth, gave the b'hoys anything but a respectable appearance. Lize dressed "high" but, in George Foster's estimation, not well, in bright, clashing colors "gotten together in utter defiance of those conventional laws of harmony and taste imposed by Madame Lawson and the French mantua-makers of Broadway."[21] There is a suggestion here not only of defiance but of parody as well – Mose and Lize may have deliberately combined some of the elements of middle- and upper-class dress to create a counterstyle that expressed contempt for bloodless gentility. In any case, it certainly expressed the high spirits of the young people of the "Republic of the Bowery," and just as certainly did not express any desire on their part to emulate the dress and mien of the middle class.[22] In this they succeeded, and in the very act of utilizing elements of middle-class dress came closer than anyone else to developing a distinctively working-class style.

The b'hoys and g'hals of the Bowery were the most visible but not the most typical or numerous of city workers. And they bought their defiance dearly, as did other workers who sought to dress either "high" or well. James Dawson Burn, an English journeyman hatter who wrote of his experiences in American workshops, chided American workers for paying too much attention to, and too much money on, their clothes (the "Middle and upper ranks of society" were criticized too, but separately), while the British Mechanic's and Labourer's Handbook noted that workers sacrificed other things to dress well.[23] Contemporaries estimated that clothing accounted for approximately 20% of workers' annual living expenses, an especially high percentage given their very high outlays (estimated at 40% to 45% of total expenses) for food.[24] According to these estimates, more than a third of what was not spent on food was spent on clothing. Some of what was left was spent on leisure activity (though the published budgets do not admit that workers drank or sought other amusement), and it is important to note that if the clothing of the middle and working classes grew more alike, the places in which that clothing was displayed, after as well as during working hours, grew physically more separate.

Partly because of the changing physical structure and increasing scale of the big city, but also, I would suggest, owing to changing sensibilities and social identities, institutions of leisure and entertainment served increasingly specialized clienteles or audiences during this era. Some, such as the German beer gardens, were organized along ethnic lines, but others served to separate further classes already being sorted into more distinct physical spaces for work and residence. Theaters traditionally had brought all classes of city people together for an evening's entertainment, although once inside the house patrons had divided themselves by income and sensibility into boxes, the gallery, and the pit. During the 1830s and 1840s, however, entire theaters became associated with specific classes.[25] In New York the Park became a fashionable theater, while the Chatham served a distinctly working-class audience.

The Bowery was superior to the Chatham, but by the 1840s was, according to George Foster,

> . . . representative of that immense and important class of our
> population, inhabiting the Sahara of the East, and living – some-
> how – from day to day and week to week – upon the labor of
> their hands. The butcher-boy, the mechanic with his boisterous
> family – the b'hoy in red flannel shirt-sleeves and cone-shaped
> trousers – the shop-woman, the sewing and folding and press-
> room girl, the straw-braider, the type-rubber, the map-colorer, the
> paper-box and flower maker, the g'hal, in short, in all her various
> aspects and phases – with a liberal sprinkling of under-crust
> blacklegs and fancy men – these make up the great staple of Bow-
> ery audiences.[26]

The Bowery Theater had become a raucous center of working-class entertainment, just as the Bowery itself had become, in Sean Wilentz's terms, "New York's plebeian boulevard, the workingman's counterpart to fashionable Broadway."[27] Meanwhile, theaters closer to Broadway drew a more respectable audience, and a new interest in Italian opera among the "upper ten thousand" (or, as many critics claimed, an intensified interest in showing off expensive clothes at the opera) led to the completion of the Astor Place Opera House in 1847, a few months before Francis Chanfrau unveiled his Mose the Bowery B'hoy at the Olympic Theater.[28] It was in front of this elegant new opera house, and in response to the appearance on its stage of the English actor William Macready (bitter foe of the American actor Edwin Forrest, who was very popular in the Bowery), that the bloody Astor Place riot of 1849 pitted, in one well-to-do contemporary's terms, a "mob" of "the baser sort" against five hundred police and militiamen who represented "the better class of the community."[29] Separate theaters and theatrical styles had come to symbolize, and even to exacerbate, class tensions in the industrializing city. The Astor Place riot may have been, as Wilentz claims, only a "nebulous form of class conflict," but it did express in clear enough terms the increasing social gulf between the Bowery and Broadway.[30]

In truth, it is difficult if not impossible to document the extent of the separation of classes in the theater, as well as in the barrooms, oyster cellars, restaurants, pleasure gardens, ice-cream saloons, and all the other respectable and illicit places of public amusement and refreshment in the growing city. In cities like New York, which were developing fairly distinct districts of working-class, middle-class, and upper-class residence, it is certainly plausible that neighborhood restaurants and saloons, and even certain theaters, were patronized by a homogeneous clientele. But in cities like Philadelphia, where, as we shall see, districts were generally not so distinct, local institutions of leisure were equally accessible to a wider range of social types. There were, in addition, institutions that were not associated with any neighborhood and that presumably drew patrons from across the city. Were these patrons similar or dissimilar in their social characteristics? The price of a ticket to Sanford's minstrel theater on Eleventh Street near Chestnut in Philadelphia was only 25¢ in 1858 (minstrels were, by this time, reputed to be a form of working-class theater),[31] but the same 25¢ would buy a ticket to the amphitheater of the new Academy of Music for a production of Verdi's *Ernani*.[32] Were the inexpensive opera seats intended for and actually purchased by underpaid young clerks? How many clerks went to Sanford's instead, and how many mechanics, dressed in four-dollar frock coats, attended the opera? Contemporary commentators do not answer these questions, but they do write convincingly of an accelerating separation of classes in places of public amusement, in Philadelphia as well as in New York – George Foster's discussions of such eating places as Delmonico's, Sweeney's, and Butter Cake Dick's constitutes, indeed, a kind of guided tour through the class structure of the metropolis.[33] The direction of change, if not its extent, is unmistakable. The city had acquired a variety of new institutions that clearly expressed the styles and ambitions of specific and very different clienteles. In the evening as well as during the workday, the city was sorting its classes of people into increasingly distinct institutions and spaces.

The home and its interior

Workers who spent large portions of their income on food and clothes (and unknown additional amounts on drink and entertainment) had less money left over for renting and furnishing the kind of household that, increasingly in this era, signified respectability. *The British Mechanic's and Labourer's Handbook* advised potential emigrants to New York City that they would pay $150 per annum for a two-story wooden house or $200 for a brick house in one of the outer wards, and $50 more for equivalent accommodations in one of the lower wards (where most of the manual jobs were located).[34] The *Handbook*, it should be noted, was published in 1840, and could not have anticipated the enormous additional pressure that would be placed upon the housing market in New York by the massive upsurge in foreign immigration and domestic in-migration of the next two decades. In 1840, New York City contained a little more than 300,000 inhabitants; by 1860 it had added another half million, most of whom were forced to squeeze into increasingly crowded working-class districts along the East and Hudson rivers.[35] Boardinghouses absorbed many of the unmarried male workers of the lower wards, and tenements – in former single-family dwellings, in cellars, in back-lot and courtyard buildings, and, increasingly, in new buildings built specifically as multiple-household dwellings – absorbed most of those workers who had families.[36] By 1864, according to a careful and well-known survey of the city's housing and sanitary conditions, more than half a million New Yorkers lived in tenements.[37] Most were poor immigrants, and most tenements were appallingly squalid, but some tenement dwellers were skilled, American-born mechanics who were making the best of life in an overcrowded city. Indeed, if the sanitary inspectors counted accurately, the bulk of the skilled native working class must have lived in tenements, although there were surely significant numbers, particularly in the outer wards, who continued to share or even occupy as single-family dwellings the small frame and brick houses described by the *British Mechanic's and Labourer's Handbook* in 1840.[38]

Mechanics' tenements were not necessarily squalid. Several of the sanitary inspectors noted tenement buildings or even groups of buildings in which living conditions were healthy and clean, and even in some of the worst districts of the city, where the inhabitants were "of the laboring class, poor, imperfectly nourished, . . . uncleanly in their persons and habits, and grossly addicted to intemperance," and where the houses were "the usual three to six-story tenements, generally out of repair," there were also "many families of mechanics of more temperate habits, whose comforts are consequently greater."[39] Moreover, in other cities, where the pressure on real estate was not as acute as it was in New York, fewer workers lived in tenement houses or in such densely crowded districts. In 1845, only one-quarter of Boston's families lived in buildings containing more than three families, while nearly a third lived in single-family dwellings. The 42% who shared a building with one or two other families probably included the major portion of the skilled work force.[40] Philadelphia and Baltimore both accommodated to rapid growth by building row houses rather than tenements and by increasing the numbers of small houses and tenements in back alleys and courtyards.[41] New York's widespread use of the three- to six-story tenement house was, indeed, unique. In 1870 the federal census recorded nearly fifteen persons and three families per dwelling in New York City (the more precise

Figure 5.3. Drinker's Court, Philadelphia (photo by the author)

figures are 14.72 and 2.90, respectively), while only some of the industrial cities around New York and Boston even approached ten persons or two families per dwelling. Most cities had still smaller ratios: Baltimore and Philadelphia, each in its own eyes a "City of Homes," averaged only 6.6 and 6.0 persons and 1.24 and 1.14 families per dwelling, respectively.[42]

The better tenements of New York, and the workingmen's houses of Boston, Philadelphia, Baltimore, and other cities, provided skilled mechanics and their families with housing that may have been adequate in many respects, but that was neither spacious, attractive, nor very comfortable. The little back-alley houses of Philadelphia ordinarily contained only one room per story, and most were only two stories tall (see Figure 5.3).[43] Many mechanics lived in three-room tenements or houses, or in three rooms of a subdivided house, but there probably were few (except for carpenters and other construction tradesmen who built houses for themselves on cheaper land beyond the inner city) who could afford more than three rooms.[44] These rooms were furnished with bedsteads, chairs, tables, and other articles from the inexpensive furniture stores, and their floors were often covered with carpets – an improvement, perhaps, over the sanded floors and sparsely furnished living quarters of most eighteenth-century mechanics.

James Dawson Burn, the English hatter, noted that even the "poorer classes of the people" had "bits of carpet," while the furniture was "generally good" in the homes of "people of prudent habits."[45] This is hardly a catalogue of opulence, however, and even suggests that workers may have had to choose between a decently furnished home and evenings spent at the Bowery Theater. Few workers, moreover, enjoyed the comforts of indoor toilets or running water, although some of the newer New York tenements did, apparently, have a water spigot on each floor.[46] And finally, the buildings that workers lived in, save for those that had been converted into tenements from former homes of the well-to-do, were architecturally unembellished, and were located in the city's least attractive surroundings – narrow alleys, dingy courtyards, or whole districts of tenement houses, usually hard by the factories, foundries, tanneries, breweries, shipyards, gashouses, and other workplaces that manual workers sought to be near, and that everyone else avoided. When Samuel Gompers's family emigrated from London to New York they improved their living quarters from a two-room flat in Spitalfields to a four-room tenement on the East Side. They did not, however, improve their surroundings. Behind the New York tenement was a brewery, and across the street was a slaughterhouse, which filled the air of the neighborhood with the sickening odor and sounds of dead and dying animals.[47]

Middling folk of the nonmanual sector lived much better than the mechanics, not only because more money bought more and better goods, but also because these men could afford to commute to work each day on the city's omnibuses, street railways, and ferries, and hence could rent or purchase larger and more attractive homes in the less congested and less expensive parts of the city.[48] When Walt Whitman wrote of the "most valuable" middle class in 1858, it was to promote the construction of inexpensive houses in Brooklyn, and to observe as well as to encourage the flight of salaried New Yorkers across the river to both better and cheaper homes.[49] Frank Leslie's Illustrated Newspaper made the same observation around the same time in a humorous sketch, "On the Inconvenience of Living in a Very Friendly Neighborhood." The narrator of the sketch is a "young clerk in a wholesale, down-town store, on a rising salary of – well, no matter what per annum." He rents a small house with a large backyard in Brooklyn for $200, where he lives with his wife and baby, happily, except for a too friendly neighbor who wants to borrow one thing after another, including at one point the couple's baby. The neighbor is also a nonmanual worker, a "drummer" for a New York dry goods establishment, and the two commute together each day.[50] Edward

Spann notes that there were large numbers of real clerks and "drum-mers" who, along with many of their employers, found good homes in Brooklyn and in other peripheral areas within and beyond the borders of New York City – Mott Haven, Morrisania, and Fordham in what is now the Bronx, Yorkville on the upper East Side, and several less distant sections separating the wealthy area around Fifth Avenue from the working-class districts along the rivers.[51] In one of these sections, stretching from Thirtieth to Forty-fifth street on the East Side, "handsome dwellings" rented for $300 to $400 per annum, beyond the means of the Brooklyn clerk, perhaps, but well within the budget of the "frugal family of four" described in *Hunt's Merchants' Magazine*.[52]

But even those nonmanual businessmen and workers who did not leave the inner city lived significantly better than the skilled mechan-ics. Some lived in hotels, which began to appear in greater numbers in the 1830s in the downtown retail districts of the larger cities. The new hotels were considerably larger and more opulent than their predecessors (one popular history notes that Holt's Hotel in New York, one of the first of the new era, "was as roughly comparable to the old City Hotel as Scheherazade to Harriet Beecher Stowe"),[53] and anticipated the dry goods palaces as major tourist attractions of the developing downtowns.[54] They anticipated the post–Civil War upper- and middle-class apartment houses, too, for the hotels devoted much of their room to permanent residents, nearly all of whom, as we shall see, were businessmen, professionals, and nonmanual employees. Spann observes that the hotels introduced many Americans to mod-ern domestic comforts, including gas lighting, indoor plumbing, and steam heat.[55] Some of the permanent residents may already have known these or equivalent comforts, but the fact remains that all who lived in the new downtown hotels were living according to a high contemporary standard of comfort.

Other businessmen and clerks lived in boardinghouses, which in itself did not distinguish them from even the poorest workers. But as in earlier eras there were boardinghouses to suit various tastes and incomes, and the better ones catered specifically to the business class. When William Gowans finally established himself as a retail bookseller he moved to a better boardinghouse, where he paid $3.00 rather than $1.75 per week, where there were "generally 4 or 5 kinds of meat on the table," and, perhaps most importantly, where most of the other boarders were merchants. Gowans, who had worked at several back-breaking manual jobs after he arrived in New York, retained an honest sympathy for the workingman. Still, when he could afford to live among merchants, he did so, explaining to his father in a somewhat rambling fashion: "I prefer to live among the society that I live among to those that I formerly lived among not that I despise those that [I] lived among but that I find the Clas of merch[ants] much more intelligent and consequently the[y] suit my taste better."[56] Not all of the downtown boardinghouses catered to so homogeneous a clientele, and some men of the nonmanual sector – young clerks especially – could not afford to "suit their tastes" by boarding only with merchants in comfortable houses. But as Thomas Butler Gunn pointed out in his humorous "physiology" of New York boardinghouses, the greater incomes of men of commerce bought greater comforts. "If 'money be no object,' " wrote Gunn, the potential boarder "will not have to seek far, or fare badly. But the researches of him whose aspirations are circumscribed by a shallow purse will produce different results."[57]

Businessmen, professionals, and even some clerical employees who were married and had children often succeeded in finding attractive private homes not far from their downtown offices and stores. In New York, at least, these "second-rate, genteel houses," as James Fenimore Cooper called them, seem to have conformed fairly closely to a standard type that was far above the level of working-class housing.[58] A surviving row of five homes on Vandam Street between McDougal and Varick illustrates the type (Figure 5.4).[59] These houses, built between 1828 and 1834, are twenty feet across, two rooms deep, and two and a half stories tall, supplemented by a half-basement that usually contained the kitchen and family dining room. The first floor was devoted to formal parlors – the chapels, we are told, of the new middle-class domestic religion – while the second story contained two or three bedrooms. The attic story could be used for storage, additional family bedrooms, or servants' quarters. As Figure 5.4 illustrates, these were substantially built, even fairly impressive homes, although their relatively unornamented exteriors reflect the fact that they were intended for moderately prosperous families and not the very rich (Cooper called the occupants of homes of this type "chiefly merchants, or professional men, in moderate circumstances, who pay rents of from 300 to 500 dollars a year").[60] The occupants in 1835 were as follows: Edgar Harriott, a Broadway tailor; Ichabod Hoit, a merchant with a store on Ann Street (Benjamin Brady, a currier, also lived in this house, apparently as a boarder); Alfred Thomas, who listed no occupation in any of the city directories of this era; James Brooks, whose china store was on Canal Street; and Henry Elsworth, a merchant with a store on West Street.[61] None of these men appears to have been rich, and Vandam Street itself was not fashionable, especially at this early date in the evolution of the city's neighborhoods.

Figure 5.4. 27 Vandam Street, New York (photo by the author)

Some of the other residents of this block in 1835 were merchants, professionals, and officials, but there were also shoemakers, cabinetmakers, and even carters. The other two blocks of Vandam Street, stretching west toward the Hudson River, contained even fewer men of the nonmanual sector, and greater numbers of carters, artisans, and other workers, most of whom shared more humble houses with one or more others.[62] The merchant householders of Vandam Street, in short, were able to buy comfort and proximity to their work, but not exclusivity.

Other cities provided other types of homes for middling folk. In Philadelphia, somewhat smaller two-and-a-half-story or three-story houses, many built a generation or two earlier, still existed in fairly large numbers near the downtown. These houses provided single-family living to clerks and smaller businessmen who probably would not have been able to afford to rent entire houses in or near the downtown in New York. The late colonial brick house at 330 South Third Street, for example, is sixteen feet wide, twenty feet deep, two and a half stories tall, and, at least originally, was attached to a two-story kitchen (Figure 5.5).[63] In 1860 it was occupied by Dennis Murphy, who operated a hosiery and trimmings store in the adjoining house. Murphy reported $1,000 in personal property to the census enumerator, and seems to have rented his dwelling from Edward Stiles, a grocer worth $3,000 who lived among somewhat better-off neighbors near his grocery at Eleventh and Spring Garden.[64] Murphy and his immediate neighbors illustrate some of the variations in downtown living space in mid-nineteenth-century Philadelphia, and suggest how these variations were associated with work and wealth. Dr. Arnold Kinkelein lived just north of Murphy's store, in the somewhat larger house on the corner of Third and Union Streets. Murphy's neighbor to the south was Andrew J. Galbraith, a gilder and fabricator of mirror and picture frames. Unlike Murphy, Galbraith (who reported no property on the census) combined shop and dwelling on the same premises. Three doors farther south, a truss and bandage maker named Benjamin W. Stratton did the same. Still farther south, near the corner of Pine Street, was the tailoring shop (or clothing store) of John Tack, and the millinery store of his wife (or daughter) Elizabeth. Tack was well-to-do (he reported $11,000 on the census) and lived in an attractive house on the corner of Third and Pine. Four grown sons, all clerks, lived with him. The doctor and the well-to-do tailor, in other words, lived in good, medium-sized, corner houses on pleasant streets. The small retailer lived in a smaller house, but by renting a second building for his store was able to use his dwelling entirely for domestic purposes. The two ordinary self-employed ar-

Figure 5.5. 328 and 330 South Third Street, Philadelphia (photo by the author)

tisans shared a pleasant street-front location with their more prosperous neighbors but were compelled to devote some of the space in
their homes to their workshops. They lived, therefore, in spaces probably no larger than those available to fellow artisans who lived in
alleys or courtyards.[65]

The removal of work from the homes of middling folk permitted
the multiplication of parlors, bedrooms, and other purely domestic
spaces, even in smaller houses inherited from the eighteenth century.
Newer houses, moreover, were often larger, and it is clear that businessmen and salaried workers who complained about rising urban
housing costs, and who fled to Brooklyn and other less central districts
in search of more satisfactory homes, were pursuing a rapidly changing standard of middle-class space and comfort. This changing standard is reflected in Gervase Wheeler's *Homes for the People*, one of
several architectural books written during this era in response to the
enormous demand for new home designs that accompanied urban
growth and new concepts of domesticity. Wheeler offered plans for
all levels of the urban and suburban market, including tenements and
cottages for "those who have to calculate every item of house-keeping
cost, and who, living by mechanical labor, have need of frugal employment of their means to bring up a family in respectability and
comfort."[66] His tenement design, the only realistic plan in the book
for housing urban workers, specifies individual apartments of four
rooms plus a water closet – a quite conventional allocation for a model
tenement intended to upgrade the housing of urban workers, and
one that totals 646 square feet of interior space, almost exactly the
median of the estimated actual living space of Philadelphia artisans
in 1798.[67] In striking contrast to this continuity of perceived standards
for city people "living by mechanical labor" are Wheeler's designs for
the urban middle class. His city or suburban home "for those of
moderate means" is a house of three stories and a basement, richly
ornamented in a Gothic style, and totaling no less than 3,375 square
feet on the three stories of living space (Figure 5.6).[68] Costing from
$3,000 to $3,500 to build in 1855, according to the author, this model
home was clearly beyond the means of artisans earning $500 or $600
per year (or even of those who earned somewhat more) but was
affordable to any of the small nonmanual businessmen whose incomes were reviewed in Chapter 4. So, too, were several other suburban villas Wheeler designed of a similar size.[69] These were much
larger homes than those of late-eighteenth-century middling folk.
They were, of course, models, not actual homes, but they are offered
as practical, not visionary schemes, and are priced, sized, and related

Figure 5.6. Elevation of a design for a moderately priced city house, from Gervase Wheeler, *Homes for the People*, ca. 1855 (courtesy of Cornell University Libraries)

to specific clientele in a manner that could not have varied much from prevailing standards.

Historians have described the filling of these larger domestic spaces with increasingly elaborate and expensive furnishings. Sam Bass Warner, Jr., effectively summarizes a view of the emerging middle-class home that is by now very familiar:

> In the years between 1827 and 1860 the new middle class enjoyed a number of important advances in everyday consumption. The bare floors, whitewashed walls, and scant furniture of middle-income eighteenth-century homes gave way to wool carpeting, wallpaper, and all manner of furnishings. The houses themselves became relatively cheaper and grew in size from three rooms to four-to-six rooms in row houses or flats in row houses. The children slept one to a bed, and indoor toilets became common in their homes. In contrast to the eighteenth century when the middle-income house generally included the shop, the husband now commonly worked in an office, store or shop outside his home, and the first-floor, front room became a parlor instead of a work room. Mid-nineteenth-century families of the new middle class did not need to put their children to work in the family trade or shop; they could take full advantage of the new public grammar school education. Finally, they had grown prosperous enough to attend the increasing variety of offerings of commercial downtown entertainment.
>
> Almost every item on this list of middle-class consumption gains lay beyond the reach of Philadelphia's artisan population.[70]

The "new middle class" to which Warner refers included "downtown businessmen, downtown retailers, [and] owners and superintendents of manufacturing establishments,"[71] all men of the nonmanual sector. Is his description of their domestically oriented "consumption gains" accurate? If so, does it point to a specifically middle-class domestic revolution? A number of historians have made similar claims for such a revolution in this era, but for evidence they seldom have gone beyond more or less reliable contemporary descriptions, advice books (which may suggest what was regarded as a realistic aspiration more accurately than they describe a widespread day-to-day reality), and quantitative evidence pertaining to such matters as indoor plumbing. As to the last, the evidence may be read in different ways. By 1848, notes Spann, 14,507 New York City homes had been connected to the new Croton water system, a development that "brought a revolution in urban living standards" for "the middle class in particular."[72] In Philadelphia, some 15,000 homes had water closets and 3,500 had baths by 1850. "Clearly," writes Warner, "the middle class of Philadelphia had adopted modern plumbing as an essential in its standard of living."[73] Indoor plumbing was not only a personal amenity but, as Faye Dudden points out in her excellent study of household service in the nineteenth century, greatly eased the task of cleaning the house and contributed to rising middle-class standards of domestic cleanliness.[74] But the numbers themselves suggest something of the limits of this revolution in convenience and hygiene. If 15,000 or so middle-class (and upper-class) homes were supplied with running water in 1850 in Philadelphia and New York, another 10,000 to 20,000 were not. To use an appropriate metaphor, the glass was still half empty.[75]

Is it possible to collect and examine more telling evidence as to the character and extent of the antebellum revolution in domestic living arrangements? Estate inventories, a rich resource for the eighteenth century, were compiled through much of the nineteenth century as well, although not for as high a proportion of decedents and generally not in as much detail as in the earlier period. In Philadelphia there are probate records for only 465 decedents of the year 1861, a tiny fraction of the approximately 5,000 adult Philadelphians who died in that year.[76] Fewer than a quarter of these records (109 in all) contain reasonably detailed inventories of individuals whose occupations, or whose husbands' occupations, were either indicated in the probate records or could be located in the city directories.[77] This is a small number of records, whose representativeness may be questioned; yet they do provide a closer and in some respects less problematic view of the realities of domestic arrangements than can be gained from other sources. A surprising number, moreover, pertain to middling and poorer folk – forty-five of the inventories describe the homes of mechanics, laborers, and modestly situated farmers and tavernkeepers, and most of the remainder list the furnishings of businessmen and professionals who were not wealthy. The latter should provide an accurate enough view of the homes of those men and women Warner has called Philadelphia's "new middle class."

The inventories substantiate Warner's description, as well as his assertion that the domestic revolution was limited to the nonmanual middle class. Of the thirty-eight inventories that describe the homes of nonwealthy businessmen, professionals, and clerks (three pertain to the widows of such men), only five suggest living arrangements that were not distinctly superior both to middling folk of earlier generations and to contemporary artisans. Four of these five were storekeepers who lived over their stores (the fifth was a country grocer who lived well beyond the built-up portion of the city), and three of the four did own goods that were worth somewhat more than even the most prosperous artisans.[78] More characteristic of middling businessmen, however, are inventories suggestive of much more spacious living quarters, and much more comfortable living conditions. Perhaps most typical are those that describe expensively furnished parlors, fairly well-stocked dining rooms and well-equipped kitchens, and somewhat more plainly furnished upstairs bedrooms. The home of Joseph K. Bacon, a manufacturer of paper boxes, provides a good example. The entry to Bacon's house on North Ninth Street contained only a hat stand and some tapestry carpet (there was oilcloth on the floor of the vestibule and behind the stairs), but his parlor was full of good furniture, including a piano valued at $150. The parlor floor was covered with Brussels carpet, and its walls were hung with engravings, a mirror, and an oil painting. Two alabaster and two terra-cotta vases stood on the mantel or on tables, and the windows were hung with corniced draperies. The parlor shared first-floor space with a dining room and apparently a kitchen, neither of which was heavily furnished. Upstairs were two stories consisting of four bedrooms and what appears to have been a child's playroom. All of these rooms were fully furnished, but only the second-story front, which was clearly the master bedroom, contained furniture of much value. This room also contained an oil painting and an engraving, and had curtains on the windows. In the stable of this three-story house were a horse evaluated at $100, a wagon worth $65, and some harness.[79]

Bacon was a moderately prosperous manufacturer with an estate worth just under $7,000. William Campbell, a partner in a lumberyard, was worth a little more than twice that sum, and his house, which was not far from Bacon's on Eleventh and Callowhill, was a little more heavily furnished. Campbell's parlor was quite similar to Bacon's (both had on their walls engravings of Benjamin Franklin, patron saint of the Philadelphia bourgeoisie), but in Campbell's house there was also a sitting room containing a sofa, marble-top center table, rocking chair, bookcase, mahogany work stand (for Mrs. Campbell's needlework), and various ornaments and pictures (the portrait of Garibaldi complementing or perhaps qualifying the icon that hung in the parlor). Upstairs were five bedrooms, and again only the front room of the second story contained furniture and other items of note (here the engraving is unidentified – was it Kossuth or Adam Smith?). Unlike Bacon's house, the Campbell house is specifically mentioned as having a bathroom.[80]

A few of the houses of these nonwealthy businessmen were somewhat more elaborately furnished than Bacon's or Campbell's. William B. Potts, a produce merchant, left an estate smaller than Campbell's, but more of it was invested in furnishings, which included two pianos (one in the parlor, the other in the dining room, which served as a second parlor), no fewer than four sofas and ten chairs in the front parlor, and a good deal of furniture in the four bedrooms below the garret.[81] A somewhat larger number of these homes, however, were less rather than more elaborate, and a few were rented flats or rooms, where retailers, clerks, retired merchants, and merchants' widows lived in small but well-furnished spaces, some no doubt amid the relics of former full-sized homes. Lewis A. Clark, a salesman in a bookstore, lived with his family in furnished rooms (his only furniture consisted of two child's chairs and a small iron bedstead), which were nicely embellished with pictures, various silver and silver-plated sets and pieces, and a large number of books, including 15 volumes of Irving's works and 21 bound volumes of *Harper's New Monthly Magazine*. Clark also left a fairly extensive wardrobe (one of the few detailed in the Philadelphia inventories) that included two black frock coats evaluated at $25 (much more expensive than the coats offered for sale in the cheap clothing stores), six shirts, four vests (one made of black silk), twelve linen collars, and a number of other items that call to mind the well-dressed clerks of the illustrated retail interiors.[82] James A. Lehman, a partner in a Market Street dry goods store, also boarded in or rented furnished rooms, which he decorated with numerous pictures and ornaments, including a music box evaluated at $10. Lehman also found quarters for a horse and carriage, worth $135.[83] Samuel C. Mott, an accountant, Jonah Thompson, a merchant, and Sarah Smith, a merchant's widow, all owned the furnishings of their flats or rooms, and all lived comfortably among pianos, books, oil paintings, and other embellishments.[84]

All of these men and women (except the five first noted) lived quite well, but their domestic arrangements are clearly distinguishable from those of the rich. Thirteen of the inventories describe the homes and household possessions of wealthy businessmen and their widows, and in nearly every case these homes were distinctly more sumptuous than the comfortable homes of prosperous but nonwealthy businessmen. The Walnut Street home of retired broker George W. Edwards, to cite just one example, consisted of a parlor, dining room, hall, kitchen, pantry, bathroom, several cellars, and at least seven bedrooms. In the parlor were three expensive sofas, thirteen chairs, a piano, three marble busts and stands (evaluated at $150), and a $40 étagère. Gas fixtures and a radiator tell us how the house was illuminated and heated. The dining room contained, in addition to the dining table, chairs, and sideboard, two sofas, a desk, a bookcase, and books valued at $200. In the hall was a very expensive sofa, along with a variety of chairs and tables, several large chests, two more marble busts and stands, gas chandeliers, and twenty-nine oil paintings and engravings (evaluated at $1,000). Upstairs, the Edwards house was far more expensively furnished than any of the middle-class homes, where luxury was largely confined to the more public first-floor rooms. The master bedroom contained a French bedstead, two expensive wardrobes, chairs, ottomans, tables, nine engravings and other pictures, and a silver chest containing $1,000 worth of silver. Two other bedrooms were more expensively furnished than the master bedroom of Joseph Bacon's house. The furnishings of Edwards's home were evaluated at more than $5,000, four times the amount assigned to the household goods of William Campbell, whose house was one of the most expensively furnished of the nonwealthy businessmen.[85]

Equally striking are the differences between the homes of middling nonmanual businessmen (and clerks) and those of artisans and less skilled manual workers. Of the inventoried decedents of 1861, 27 were listed in the city directories or described in the probate records as artisans, and 2 more could be identified as the widows of artisans. Of these 29 men and women, only 2 maintained households that were comparable to some of the more modest of the homes already described. It is probable, moreover, that neither of these two was a handworking artisan at the time of his death. One, Isaac Lukens, was listed in the city directory as a stonemason, but his will identifies him as a stonemason and builder.[86] The other was a plumber named Presley B. Forsyth, whose business on Seventh Street between Market and Chestnut earned him an estate of nearly $5,000 – easily the largest estate of the artisans and artisans' widows in my list of decedents.[87] Forsyth may have molded pipe and installed fixtures all of his working days, but it is much more likely that he spent his last years managing the work of others. The R. G. Dun & Co. records describe the firm of Forsyth & Bro. as "a very thriving concern [of] large and growing means," and Presley himself as a man of extravagant personal tastes.[88] *The Philadelphia Shopping Guide & Housekeeper's Companion for 1859* lists Forsyth's business in capital letters, a practice that was intended to identify, according to the guide's compiler, "very showy stores and desirable goods."[89]

Seven other artisans (including one artisan's widow) lived in homes that were somewhat larger or more nicely furnished than the three-room mechanics' tenements and houses described by James Dawson Burn and other contemporaries. But all seven of these homes – which included an eight-room house and a six-room house on the city's periphery – were less expensively furnished than even the most modest of middle-class homes. All but one of the valuations of household goods among this group totaled between $200 and $300, and the exception, the inventory of a hatter named Charles Hinckle, was only $304.50.[90] Hinckle, incidentally, was one of only 3 artisans of the 29 who owned pianos. The other 2, not surprisingly, were Isaac Lukens and Presley B. Forsyth.

Twenty artisans (and sixteen less skilled workers, tavernkeepers, and farmers) lived in small, very plainly furnished – in some cases, very poorly furnished – homes. Felix Campbell, a machinist, owned only $62.48 worth of furnishings and utensils, including a dozen "common chairs," some inexpensive bedsteads and tables, an unspecified amount of rag, oilcloth, and other cheap carpet, one picture, a few books, and a bird and birdcage valued at 50¢.[91] Charles Geisler, a butcher in the Northern Liberties market, lived in three very plain rooms containing only $40 worth of furnishings and other goods, while Simeon B. Hannold, a shipwright, had a desk, a bureau, a sofa, thirteen old chairs, assorted bedding, a few tables, some carpeting, and a few other items, all of which were valued at just under $70.[92] Somewhat better off, and perhaps more typical, were Peter Rodgers, a locksmith whose home above his shop contained parlor furniture, beds, and kitchen equipment valued at $132, and William Sheaff, a mason, who furnished his two-story house in West Philadelphia with $112 worth of chairs, tables, beds, bureaus, carpeting, and other goods.[93] Some of these plain-living artisans owned other property and cannot be considered poor. The cabinetmaker George Stites, for example, owned only $70 worth of household furnishings, but his inventory included two mortgages totaling $850, and nearly $240 in cash.[94] William Silvers, a carpenter whose furniture was valued at $99, owned his house in Germantown, four lots in New Jersey, and some woodland in Cumberland County, Pennsylvania.[95] These men and a few others left estates that were as large as those of some members of the nonmanual middle class. Why, then, did they not spend as much money on their homes?

Part of the answer to this question lies in differing market capacities, obscured by the total valuations of a few overlapping artisanal and commercial estates. Artisans were more vulnerable to year-to-year and seasonal variations in income and, especially in those trades requiring heavy physical labor, could be less certain of performing any manual work at all past middle age. The more farsighted among them were acutely aware of the need to save, or to invest whatever surplus funds they came by in appreciating or income-producing assets rather than in Brussels carpets, pianos, or overstuffed parlor sofas. Successful artisans, therefore, were likely to attend first to these matters of old-age security, and only then to the present comforts of a well-furnished home. But the estate inventories point as well to a broader divergence of experience between artisans and nonmanual businessmen, and to deeper cultural divisions revolving around the proper character and even the significance of the physical home. Most artisans, it appears, were largely indifferent (we shall see later that they could even be hostile) to the kinds of domestic furnishings and spaces that businessmen were coming to value so highly, and were less interested in using the well-furnished parlor as a private (and status-enhancing) meeting place for the family and acceptable visitors. These differences, in turn, almost certainly were connected, as Richard Stott argues, with the much greater influence of middle-class women, compared to their working-class counterparts, in the shaping of their own families' domestic affairs.[96] I return to some of these issues in the final section of this chapter and consider class-related experiences of domestic visiting and more formally organized types of voluntary association, inside and outside of the home, in Chapter 6. Here I would only reemphasize the categorical nature of variation in the domestic arrangements of nonmanual businessmen and artisans. What emerges quite clearly from the Philadelphia estate inventories is that the antebellum domestic revolution was, as Warner and other historians have claimed, restricted to the nonmanual middle class.

Locating homes in urban space

City householders purchased not only living space and furnishings, but location as well. And in the Jacksonian era city people made these purchases within a rapidly enlarging urban world of developing and shifting districts and neighborhoods, a city undergoing the first stages of that long process of growth, deconcentration, and spatial reorganization that would eventually produce the class- and function-segregated metropolis. By the eve of the Civil War the walking city had already begun to give way to new patterns. The wealthy were abandoning their old homes in the center of the city for new elite neighborhoods outside the old center, and in many instances beyond the city itself in emerging suburbs. Their places were taken by proliferating wholesale, retail, industrial, and financial institutions, and by some of the immigrant and native-born workers who took up a variety of industrial jobs in and near the downtown. Other workers sought jobs and homes on the expanding industrial periphery, in and near the mills, foundries, and factories that were too large to squeeze into a crowded and expensive central city. Middling folk are somewhat more difficult to locate on this rapidly shifting map, but we have already seen some of them taking up jobs in the new downtown, and homes or rooms nearby, in more distant urban districts, and in the suburbs. The suburbs were, of course, the most interesting and portentous additions to the urban map. Traditionally, the periphery of the city was one of its least attractive areas, and even as late as 1850 George Foster could evoke the image of "suburbs, surrounded by open lots, rubbish-heaps, lumber-yards, and the other offal with which a large city surrounds itself as with a rampart, thrown up out of its own grave."[97] This image was already giving way to a new reality of spacious semirural homes gathered into pleasant and prestigious communities of city commuters and their families. In 1846, according to Henry Binford, approximately 1,500 of the listings in the Boston city directory were of suburban residents who worked in the city. By 1860 this commuter population had expanded beyond 10,000, and former fringe areas such as mainland Charlestown, Cambridge, Cambridgeport, and East Cambridge had evolved into attractive commuter suburbs.[98] It hardly needs stating that Boston's experience was not unique.[99]

Had the households of the city, then, become more decisively segregated by class in this era? Was the emerging metropolis developing distinct and homogeneous residential neighborhoods on a significant scale? Were any of these middle-class neighborhoods? Had the house in the suburbs, or in some less distant but equally homogeneous neighborhood, become a characteristic middle-class consumer good? These are significant questions, for identifiable neighborhoods can confer and shape social identities in at least two very different ways – through the "shared symbolization" of urban space that derives from and expresses membership in specific "social worlds," and through the daily social interactions that, in a homogeneous milieu, serve to build up and reinforce the substance and the boundaries of the social group.[100] Could middle-class neighborhoods have performed these functions in the antebellum city? Can it be said that middling folk deliberately located their dwellings, either in homogeneous middle-class neighborhoods or in some other way, with these objectives in mind? If so, do we find in these locational strategies further evidence of a fundamental shift away from the heterogeneous face-to-face society of the eighteenth-century city?

Most historians have argued that the cities of this era had not yet developed such homogeneous neighborhoods, especially for their middle classes.[101] Indeed, the most recent, detailed, and technically advanced analysis, a study of residential homogeneity in mid-nineteenth-century Philadelphia by Janet Rothenberg Pack, concludes that this City of Homes may have become somewhat *less* segregated by class during the last decade before the Civil War. Pack utilized the data of the Philadelphia Social History Project, which locates the adult males listed on the census within a grid of rectangular areal units a little larger than an average-sized city block. Calculating an index of homogeneity (according to the project's vertical occupational classifications) for each of these very small grid-units, Pack finds that only 7% of the city's adult male population of 1850 lived in very homogeneous grid-units (where at least 65% to 70%, but more typically 85% to 90%, of the grid-unit's adult males were in the same occupational category), while a little more than 60% lived in grid-units that were moderately homogeneous (where at least half of the men were in the same occupational category).[102] Both of these proportions declined by 1860 (to approximately 3% and 52%, respectively), probably because the very rapid growth during this decade of the more crowded and heterogeneous districts surrounding the city center outweighed the expansion of the more homogeneous urban periphery.[103] Suburban neighborhoods were indeed more homogeneous, but only a small minority of the nonmanual work force lived in them, and fewer than 10% of the men in nonmanual occupations (fewer than 7% in 1860) lived in moderately or very homogeneous grid-units anywhere in the city.[104] During the next twenty years an increasing proportion of Philadelphia's nonmanual businessmen and workers would move to homogeneous neighborhoods, but it is clear that before the Civil War such neighborhoods played a very small role in shaping middle-class life.[105]

Pack's argument does not preclude the existence of visibly different patterns in the spatial distribution of Philadelphia's households, and for several reasons, some of them technical, her analysis overstates their physical integration. Her file of adult males does not distinguish between heads of household, adult sons and other resident family members, boarders, and domestic servants; hence, among other things, it cannot reveal how many workers who were the apparent neighbors of wealthy businessmen and professionals were in fact servants in their households.[106] Nor do her homogeneity indices distinguish between handworking artisans and artisan-businessmen who managed substantial firms.[107] More important than these technical matters, however, is the insensitivity of the grid-unit to the historic Philadelphia pattern of differentiating residential spaces by type of frontage (that is, by placement on major streets, minor streets, alleys, or courts) rather than by area. This practice of placing large and expensive houses on major streets, and much smaller and cheaper houses and tenements on the alleys and courts behind them, continued into the nineteenth century. Alan Burstein, in his study of immigrants in Philadelphia, notes that "the prevalence of alley dwellings was particularly important in distributing Irish immigrants throughout the old city,"[108] while Roger Miller and Joseph Siry have found that the street-alley distinction was carried across the Schuylkill River to the emerging suburb of West Philadelphia. "A typical building scheme of the 1840s and 1850s," write Miller and Siry, "was the simultaneous construction of a magnificent townhouse on one of the city's primary east-west streets and provision of worker rows in the mews, fronting on alleys cut through the interior of the block."[109] The effect, as in the eighteenth century, was to segregate the city's classes into visibly and comprehensively distinct residential spaces according to a system that not even the most microcosmic areal analysis can recapture. Businessmen and workers occupied the same areal grid-units, but were they really neighbors? It is obvious that to answer this question we must attempt to locate the city's residents as precisely as possible, not merely in very small areas but on specific types of frontage and even at specific addresses. Indeed, we must go even farther and ascertain whether particular families shared dwellings with other families, and whether particular workers occupied residential space as householders, boarders, or even as household servants. Finally, we should attempt, wherever possible, to probe beneath occupational labels, which, as already seen, are sometimes misleading.

To reconstitute the entire city in this fashion is neither feasible nor necessary. Instead, I have selected for closer examination five grid-units from different parts of the city, each of which contained within it a relatively heterogeneous mixture of manual and nonmanual workers and proprietors (Figure 5.7). The 1860 census data pertaining to each grid-unit were then re-collected, household and family relationships were imputed, and all adult males and all female household heads were traced to the city directory. Addresses found in the directory were recorded, and additional addresses were imputed for some of those individuals not listed in the directory, according to their placement within the census (i.e., in the same households as, or in households between and proximate to, those located in the directory). The latter procedure was performed cautiously and conservatively; hence, some cases were sacrificed to the need to be certain of accuracy in the assignment of addresses.[110]

The first grid-unit I selected is in the heart of the downtown retail district and extends from below Sixth Street on the east to

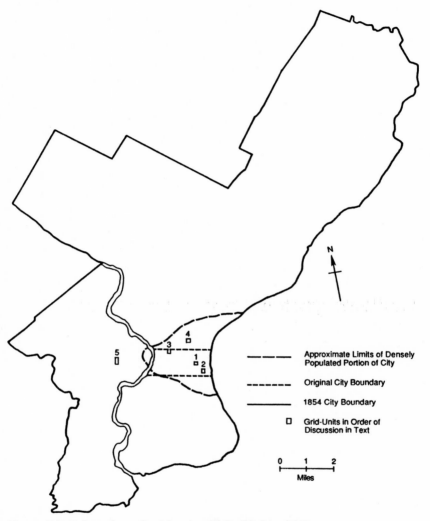

Figure 5.7. Selected areal grid-units, Philadelphia, 1860

above Seventh on the west, and from above Chestnut Street on
the north to below Walnut on the south. It is quite unlike the
other grid-units I discuss in that it was in the middle of an area in
which private houses were rapidly disappearing in the face of commercial expansion. I selected it mainly because it provides an excellent view of one variant of mid-nineteenth-century city living,
namely, boarding in downtown hotels and boardinghouses. There
were three fairly large hotels in this tiny section of the downtown:

the American across from Independence Hall on Chestnut Street, the Jones a block farther west on the south side of Chestnut, and the Commercial on Sixth between Chestnut and Market. All three catered to permanent residents and nearly all of these residents were professionals, businessmen, and clerks. Living at the American Hotel, for example, in addition to the two hotelkeepers, were 10 merchants, 2 agents, a grocer, a druggist, a coal dealer, a broker, a manufacturer, an attorney, an architect, an artist, 8 men who identified themselves as "gentlemen," 2 salesmen, and 13 clerks. Only 2 men – one who appears to have been in the navy and another whose occupation was listed as "mariner"– might have performed manual work.[111] The other two hotels differed only in having a larger proportion of clerks and salesmen among their residents – 17 of 28 at the Commercial, and 21 of 32 at the Jones. Each had only one resident (other than cooks, waiters, and other hotel service workers) who might have performed manual work – a turner at the Commercial (who reported $1,000 in personal property on the census, and who appears to have been the hotelkeeper's son), and a glass stainer at the Jones. All three of the hotels, as is suggested by the large number of clerks and salesmen, served a permanent clientele that was predominantly young and single, but there were many older men as well (31 of 47 residents of the American were thirty or older, and 12 were at least forty), and significant numbers at each hotel were men of at least middling wealth. A few were wealthy. Clearly, these hotels were, in effect, large boardinghouses for the business class.

There were four boardinghouses and one smaller residential hotel in this grid-unit, all on major streets (Sixth, Seventh, and Walnut), and all catering primarily or entirely to businessmen, professionals, and clerks. In the boardinghouse at 522 Walnut Street lived three merchants, three salesmen, five clerks, a lamp maker (who reported $2,000 on the census and was probably not a handworking artisan), and a waiter who probably lived there as a servant. The smaller scale of these boardinghouses made it possible, and perhaps urgent, to construct very homogeneous residential groups. The five boarders at 123 South Seventh Street consisted of a fairly wealthy iron maker, a quite wealthy agent, and three naval officers. The small hotel at 110 South Sixth was home to two liquor dealers, a clerk, a bookkeeper, and five railroad agents. The waiter and barkeeper who lived there were almost certainly hotel employees.

The hotels and boardinghouses of this grid-unit, in sum, combined in close quarters men ranging from well-to-do merchants and professionals to propertyless clerks, but all but excluded mechanics of any kind. A number of unskilled male workers also lived at these addresses, but only as service workers, not as fellow residents or neighbors. These men were, in effect, household servants, and we can be sure that they appeared before the other residents only in that capacity. The presence of these workers in the hotels and boarding-houses (at the Jones Hotel there were twenty-four such workers, and thirty-two paying residents) would, of course, cause any analysis based only on the mix of occupations within the areal grid-unit to miss entirely what was a very striking form of residential segregation in this part of the city.[112]

Society Hill, a neighborhood in which private homes predominated, adjoined the commercial downtown on the south. This was an area from which downtown businessmen could easily walk to work, and it appears that the blocks lying between Walnut Street and Spruce (and extending westward along the expanding downtown all the way to and beyond Rittenhouse Square) constituted a fairly homogeneous upper- and middle-class district. Below Spruce, however, resided a more varied mixture of professionals, businessmen, shopkeeping artisans, and workers of all sorts, and we may regard the grid-unit extending from just south of Spruce to Lombard Street, and from west of Second Street to Fourth, as representative of a large and heavily populated area above and below the downtown that would seem to confirm the proposition that the physical segregation of classes had not proceeded very far in the antebellum city. Yet even here we can find a class pattern in the distribution of homes, a pattern that on some streets was more clearly etched than the one we discovered in the townscape of the late eighteenth century.

I have already described a quite varied collection of householders along one side of Third Street in this grid-unit, and in fact the greatest variety of neighbors was to be found along the numbered, north-south streets. These were the commercial streets of this section, where shops and stores of various kinds served the city as well as the nearby east-west streets and interior alleys that were more completely residential in character. Along Fourth Street, between Spruce and Pine, were 38 households, some sharing dwellings with other households, some living above street-front shops and stores, others living in individual, street-front houses.[113] Of these households, 14 were headed by nonmanual businessmen and employees, mainly retailers who sold dry goods, shoes, tobacco, dress trimmings, liquor, and other goods, but also including a sea captain and a collector. Another 14 were headed by artisans (bakers, barbers, printers, a shoemaker, a tailor, and others), 3 were headed by unskilled workers, and 7 were headed by men and women for whom I could find no occupation. Of the artisans 3 reported enough property on the census ($1,000, $2,000, and $21,000) to suggest they might have been retailers, contractors, or managers; but even if these men are excluded or reclassified, there remains an impressive mix of residents on this block of Fourth Street, from a dry goods merchant reporting $10,000 on the census to a shoemaker reporting $500, to a propertyless laborer. Nor do clusters of merchants or manual workers on one side of the street or at one end of the block suggest we have happened upon a boundary between two homogeneous neighborhoods; rather, storekeepers, artisans, and workers were intermingled throughout according to no visible pattern. Indeed, the only evidence of class segregation lies within a few of the households. Of the private householders, 9 (7 manual, 2 non-manual) took in boarders, in each case from their own side of the manual-nonmanual divide, while the two boardinghouses on the block were homogeneous as to the type of work their residents performed. One contained three agents, while the other provided room and board to three cabinetmakers, two upholsterers, a painter, a varnisher, and a coachmaker.

It is on the east-west streets and the alleys that we find evidence of class segregation within this heterogeneous area. Pine Street, for example, was a street of substantial homes for the business class (Figure 5.8). From 222 Pine to Pine and Fourth streets I have identified 11 householders. Of these, 5 were wealthy or at least prosperous merchants; 1 was a physician (who took in a moderately wealthy actuary as a boarder); 1 was a clerk (whose boarder was a salesman); and 1 was a woman who reported no occupation but did report property totaling $20,000 to the census enumerator. The other 3 households were headed by well-to-do artisan-businessmen. John Tack has already been described as a tailor or clothier worth $11,000 (with four resident sons, all clerks), while Joseph H. Campion and Thomas H. Moore, neighbors on Pine Street below Third, were partners in one of the city's largest and best-known furniture businesses.[114] We might note in passing how well Campion and Moore illustrate the pitfalls of even the most careful categorical analysis of the census data. Both men are listed on the census as master cabinetmakers, and neither reported any property to the census enumerator. Yet both were wealthy manufacturers and dealers, not master workmen whose presence added variety to a street otherwise filled with nonmanual businessmen.

Stampers Street, a narrow alley that ran behind the south side of Pine Street between Second and Third, resembled Pine only in its uniformity (Figure 5.9). At least 22 households were located on Stampers (only half a dozen or so within the boundaries of the grid-unit,

Figure 5.8. South side of Pine Street, below Third, Philadelphia (photo by the author)

Figure 5.9. Stampers Street, Philadelphia (photo by the author)

but I shall describe the whole street), and of these only 5 were headed by men or women who were not artisans or other manual workers: a tavernkeeper (whose 2 boarders were a laborer and a mariner), a clerk, 2 unspecified dealers, and a female shopkeeper who shared a dwelling with a shoemaker. A baker, who is listed at $500, was the only resident of this alley who reported any property at all to the census enumerator in 1860. Of the 22 households 16 were headed by propertyless artisans and unskilled workers. Stampers Street lay only a few yards from Pine, but it is no doubt safe to assume that the residents of the two streets inhabited very different social worlds. Pine and Stampers, indeed, provide a nearly perfect illustration of how major streets and narrow alleys served to sort out the city's heterogeneous social elements into relatively homogeneous urban spaces.

Two other east-west streets and alleys in this grid-unit (Union and Cypress) conformed to this pattern of residential differentiation, while Lombard, which lay only one block from the old city's boundary with the predominantly working-class district of Southwark, was more heterogeneous. Lombard appears to have been evolving from a middle-class to a working-class street, and reveals most dramatically the variety of forces being exerted on the neighborhoods immediately surrounding the central business district. Still, above Lombard, it was the Pine Street–Stampers Street dichotomy that was no doubt more characteristic of this part of the city. What is surprising here, in fact, is not that a single residential street could be so varied in character, but that so heterogeneous a district near the downtown could still arrange many of its households into spatial patterns that reflected and reinforced class differences.

Neighborhoods more distant from the immense variety of downtown institutions and employment opportunities took shape in response to fewer and simpler forces – location along omnibus or street railway lines, for example, or proximity to a single large factory or cluster of factories. We have noted that as New York "moved uptown" its classes split into increasingly distinct areas, the wealthy occupying the central spine of Manhattan above Washington Square and commuting down the broad avenues each day to work and shop in Wall Street and lower Broadway, the working class expanding eastward into the increasingly crowded and increasingly distinct district of tenement houses and workshops beyond Five Points. But, as Pack has demonstrated, in Philadelphia even areas well removed from the downtown were often heterogeneous. Only the most distant new neighborhoods were built on land not already occupied by people who were often different from those who were pushing out from the downtown (workers in formerly peripheral industries, for example, or drovers in cattle markets), and who did not give way at once to upper- or middle-class residential development. Most new or rapidly growing districts, moreover, were not entirely residential, and developed around or in proximity to a variety of industrial and commercial activities, many of which were demanded by residential development itself. Hence, there were few if any upper- or middle-class districts beyond the downtown, and even in the distant suburbs, that did not contain a fairly wide range of artisans, service workers, and others who worked with their hands. How was this heterogeneity organized in urban space?

Two grid-units more distant from the downtown than the one just examined, and another in the suburbs, demonstrate how clearly the business and working classes were separated in the expanding city. There were fairly large numbers of manual workers' households in the grid-unit just east of Logan Square, in an area dominated by middle-class residences. A dozen or so of these artisans', service workers', and laborers' households were intermingled with those of the storekeepers inhabiting Sixteenth Street (a commercial north-south street running through the middle of the grid-unit), and three were in the 1500 block of Race Street, an east-west street on which middle-class homes predominated. All but one or two of the rest were squeezed into three narrow alleys that wended through the interior of the block north of Race and east of Sixteenth, and on Gebhard Street a somewhat wider alley running from Cherry to Race. A few householders of Gebhard Street reported property worth $1,000 or so on the census, and two of these (a clerk reporting $1,300 and an engineer reporting $5,000) were not manual workers. All the rest, and all of the householders of the other three alleys (Path, Graydon, and Cowslip), were artisans and laborers who reported little or no property to the census enumerator. On Graydon, for example, lived a carter worth $500, a brickmaker worth $150 (and two propertyless artisans, a painter and a carpenter, boarding with him), and five propertyless householders: two shoemakers, a bricklayer, a hostler, and a washerwoman.

The broad residential streets that ran through this grid-unit (Cherry, Race, Summer, and one slightly narrower street, Palmetto) were just as uniform as the narrow alleys. On Cherry Street there were 7 identifiable households, headed by a broker, a merchant (whose boarders were a lawyer and a clerk), a druggist, an accountant, a surgeon, a woman reporting $5,000 on the census, and a household head reporting no occupation and $10,000 in property. Race Street, as I have noted, had 3 artisan households mixed in with those of nonmanual businessmen on the 1500 block, but on the 1600 block there were no such intruders. Actually, a number of the householders of Race Street were identified with artisanal occupational titles, but all of these men owned enough property to make their real status as nonmanual businessmen unambiguous – the master printer, for example, was worth $39,000, the master cooper reported $38,000, and the two jewelers were worth $9,000 and $80,000. Most of these "artisans" were wealthier, according to the census entries, than their merchant neighbors. On Summer Street there was only one such artisan, the tailor John Sarmiento, who reported $30,000 and was one of Philadelphia's most fashionable Chestnut Street clothiers. Palmetto Street, finally, was both narrower and less prosperous than the other east-west streets, but was still distinctly middle class. (The correlation between street width and prosperity is perfect in this grid-unit. Recall that Gebhard, the widest of the alleys, contained the least poor of the alley-dwelling householders.)

North of the old city limit, in what was once the district of Spring Garden, were a number of grid-units that contained concentrations of both manual and nonmanual workers. One of these lay south and west of the intersection of Mt. Vernon and Tenth Streets. There were only two narrow alleys in this grid-unit, one a tiny court containing 3 working-class households, the other a block-long alley, Nectarine Street, lined with 26 households, one of which was headed by a grocer (who reported only $300 on the census) and all the rest of which were headed by artisans and unskilled workers. Perhaps because there were fewer alleys here, the one medium-width residential street, Wistar, contained a fairly even mixture of nonmanual and manual households. It should be noted, however, that most of the artisans living on Wistar Street were moderately prosperous – two jewelers and a silversmith reporting between $2,000 and $2,200, a tailor and a bricklayer reporting $1,200 each, a machinist reporting $4,800, to cite several examples – whereas most of the nonmanual householders were bookkeepers, clerks, small retailers, and schoolteachers, the teachers clustered near the school at the corner of Wistar and Eleventh. The wider east-west streets (Mt. Vernon, Green, and Spring Garden) were, as might be expected, almost uniformly nonmanual. It is interesting that this was true of Spring Garden Street, which was the busiest (but also the most fashionable) commercial street in this section of the city. The 34 householders of Spring Garden Street were nearly all prosperous businessmen and professionals, 6 of whom lived above their stores or offices.[115] It is also interesting that even the numbered north-south streets in this grid-unit were mostly nonmanual. Of the 40 households on Tenth and Eleventh streets, only 3 were headed by artisans or other workers reporting less than $1,000 on the census. Most were merchants, professionals, and clerks.

These two grid-units near the edge of dense urban settlement suggest that class segregation by frontage may have been more fully developed on and near the expanding periphery of the city than near its center. That it was significant beyond the periphery as well, in the emerging suburbs, is suggested by the West Philadelphia grid-unit (actually the developed parts of a pair of contiguous grid-units) extending from just above Market Street to just below Walnut, and centered on a new commercial street at first named Till but soon integrated into the Philadelphia gridiron system as Fortieth Street. Miller and Siry have described West Philadelphia as a rapidly developing suburb, characterized by "a planned uniformity of house style and price which attracted a relatively homogeneous social class of buyers and tenants."[116] Presumably, parts of West Philadelphia were occupied by few people other than this homogeneous social class – the "central middle class" in Miller and Siry's terminology[117] – and displayed the kind of areal homogeneity that later became common in upper- and middle-class suburbs. I have chosen to examine instead the most heterogeneous of West Philadelphia grid-units, where the presence of large numbers of urban fringe and residential service workers provides a better test of the extent and nature of class segregation in the emerging suburb.

These final grid-units cannot be mapped as precisely as the others, as addresses for the residents of West Philadelphia were listed in the city directories only in approximate terms – as Market above Thirty-ninth, for example, or Oak near Till. Nevertheless, the patterns of class segregation already observed in the less distant and more heavily populated districts of the city are visible here too. They are most evident on two quite different streets, Chestnut and Ludlow. Chestnut Street was thinly populated in 1860, partly because there were still empty building lots to be filled, but also because the houses that had been built were the large detached homes of the "central middle class." On Chestnut near Fortieth 10 households are identifiable, headed by 2 physicians, a merchant, an agent, a clerk, an "ex-alderman" reporting $50,500 on the census, a carpenter reporting $51,000, a master blacksmith reporting $4,375, and two women, one reporting $20,000 on the census, the other reporting $10,000. Residing with the last mentioned was an architect, reporting $14,000, who apparently was her son. The master blacksmith and one of the physicians also had resident adult sons, both of whom were druggists.

Of the households 3 contained resident gardeners, suggesting that at least some of these houses were surrounded by spacious and well-tended lawns and gardens.

Ludlow Street (originally named Oak), a narrow alley behind Chestnut Street, contained twice as many households on what appears to have been the same amount of frontage. One of the 20 households on Ludlow near Fortieth (or "Oak near Till") was headed by a grocer reporting $10,000 on the census, but all the rest were headed by artisans and unskilled workers (10 by the former, 9 by the latter), nearly all of whom reported little or no property. A little farther up Ludlow, near a crossing alley named Rose, were 33 more households. One of these was headed by an "old iron" merchant reporting $10,300 on the census, and another was headed by a prosperous shoemaker reporting $2,150. The other 31 household heads on Ludlow near Rose were propertyless artisans and laborers. On Rose itself were 8 households, 1 headed by a female shopkeeper reporting $400, 1 headed by a boltmaker reporting $50, and 6 headed by unskilled workers reporting $50 or less.

The commercial streets in these grid-units were more diverse, but not to the degree that might be expected. Fortieth Street was just emerging as the commercial spine of this residential area, and had only 11 households, headed by men ranging from a wealthy agent to a propertyless laborer. Market Street was more densely populated (it was the major road into the city as well as a local commercial street) but contained a sequence of fairly homogeneous clusters or rows rather than a mixture of diverse households. Those residing on Market below Fortieth Street were mostly merchants and prosperous artisans (the shoemaker who reported $25,000 on the census was surely a manufacturer or wholesaler, and the two well-to-do carpenters were almost certainly building contractors), while most of those living above Fortieth were artisans with modest amounts of wealth. Market Street was somewhat different from any of the streets we have examined, but considered as a whole these two adjoining grid-units on the metropolitan periphery were much like those closer to the more densely populated center.[118]

The pattern that emerges from all of these grid-units beyond the heart of downtown Philadelphia, from Society Hill to West Philadelphia, is a clear one and is easily summarized. In each little cluster of streets and alleys we have reconstituted for the year before the Civil War, true diversity was found mainly on the commercial, usually north-south, streets, whereas all but one or two of the residential, usually east-west, streets, and the alleys, were homogeneous and clearly associated with particular classes. In several grid-units,

medium-width residential streets contained less prosperous groupings of middle-class households and a little more diversity than was
to be found on the widest streets, which suggests a remarkably fine
calibration of wealth and status with residential frontage. Finally, in
all of the grid-units in which they were located, boardinghouses and
hotels tended to cater to either manual or nonmanual workers, and
only rarely combined both under the same roof and at the same table,
while boarders in private homes usually worked on the same side of
the manual-nonmanual divide as their landlords. The pattern varied
from one grid-unit to another, but the similarities clearly outweighed
the differences. Within the heterogeneous districts of the expanding
city (it should be recalled that I selected only heterogeneous grid-
units, and avoided the city's most homogeneous districts), antebellum
Philadelphians sorted themselves into households, streets, and alleys
that expressed the growing divergence between men and the families
of men who worked with their hands, and men and the families of
men who worked with their heads.

It is easier to describe this pattern, however, than to understand
its significance. Did it reflect only the different market capacities of
men and women in the manual and nonmanual sectors, or did it
express as well a widespread desire to live among socially compatible
neighbors? Miller and Siry write that "the arbiter of social status and
contact was the block front, and not the square block,"[119] an observation with which we can certainly agree, but did the configuration
of upper- and middle-class streets and working-class alleys *originate*
in social distinctions rather than, or in addition to, differing disposable
incomes? The tendency of clerks, bookkeepers, and small retailers to
live in proximity to merchants and professionals of greater means,
but seldom among artisans of lesser means, suggests that social affinities associated with worktype may well have operated independently of income to shape the distribution of families in urban space.
This inference of deliberate class segregation seems reasonable, but
the particular patterns we have described lead to a second question:
Could segregation within such small homogeneous spaces have *contributed* to social definitions and to the formation of exclusive social
milieux? The social symbolization of urban space was clearer and more
powerful in New York, where Fifth Avenue, Five Points, and the
Bowery were place names suggestive of districts that were in fact
larger and more homogeneous than most Philadelphia neighborhoods
of affluence and working-class life.[120]

We may be somewhat more skeptical about the *totality* of Philadelphia's homogeneous residential milieux. Pine Street and Stampers
Street were separate social worlds in most respects, but they both

adjoined the public market on Second Street, just as most residents of Spring Garden and Nectarine Streets were about equally close to the Spring Garden Street market below Tenth. Street dwellers and alley dwellers shopped in these markets, and mingled as well on the commercial streets that ran through each neighborhood.[121] To this extent Philadelphia may have preserved the heterogeneous face-to-face relations of the eighteenth century. That these relations were the same in the post-Jacksonian city, however, is doubtful – quite apart from the withering of deferential assumptions and the democratic mien of the American working class, the good clothing of some working men and women may even have made them difficult to identify as inferiors. In the public mingling of classes on the streets and in the markets and stores of Philadelphia's neighborhoods, the "plain dark democracy of broadcloth" asserted itself, to the detriment of both the old culture of rank and the emerging system of class distinctions. Perhaps this is one reason why the nonmanual middle-class focused so much of its energies during this era on defining and seeking to conform to proper social relations within the more controllable environment of the domestic interior. We must return to that controllable interior, therefore, to understand how and to what degree the domestic revolution, and the wave of consumption on which it rode, helped clarify the substance and boundaries of the emerging middle class.

Mother and Master Charley: consumption, feminization, and the middle-class family

Half a dozen times between 1857 and 1860 two back pages of *Harper's New Monthly Magazine* (just in front of the monthly fashion plates) were devoted to the misadventures of Master Charley, irrepressible scion of a prosperous city family. "Our Charlie is a nice boy," wrote his biographer (the spelling would be changed to "Charley" in subsequent episodes), "with a wonderful faculty of picking up acquaintances." For example:

> The other day he came in, dragging an ungainly, old-looking lad by the hand. "Ma," he said, "Mayn't this nice little boy stay to tea with me? His mother keeps the candy store, and he's given me his big knife, and two sticks of candy for my little knife." The "nice boy" had clearly the best of the bargain; but as Master Charlie had disposed of the candy, the "nice boy" firmly declined all propositions to "trade back." He offered, however, to give two more sticks of candy for the knife, which offer was gladly accepted by Charlie.

The nice boy didn't stay to tea.

Charlie's last acquaintance resulted disastrously. "Does your Pa live here?" asked his new friend. – "Yes." – "Has your Pa ever been in the Tombs?" – "No." – "My Pa has been there more'n a week; and he can go there just when he's a mind to. My Pa can lick your Pa; and I can lick you."

And he did "lick" him.[122]

Figure 5.10, the second half of this illustrated sketch (entitled "Charlie's Side-Walk Acquaintances"), shows Charlie as a pretty, quite feminine-looking little boy with very long blond hair, clad in the dress that most boys from respectable homes wore during their first four or five years.[123] Besides this striking femininity of appearance, Charlie displays several other characteristics in this initial episode. First, he is either unaware of or is simply indifferent to class distinctions, and is quite pleased to bring into his home "nice boys" whom his mother would most definitely prefer not to have to tea. (The fact that Charlie was able to find these boys only underscores the final observation of the previous section.) Second, he has an unerring instinct for getting into scrapes of various kinds. And third, he is a poor trader, and not much of a fighter either. Subsequent episodes would confirm all of these attributes, and add at least one other – Charley is rather hard on parlor furniture (Figure 5.11).[124] In addition to these aspects of Master Charley's character and talents, there is an interesting observation to make about his immediate circumstances. Charley is surrounded by women. His "Ma" is there to receive (and send packing) the "nice boy," to break up Charley's boxing match with Pat Dooly, "the pet of the news-boys," for which Charley trained himself into a fighting weight of thirty-nine pounds, and, more interestingly, to present him with his first pair of pantaloons. An old man, perhaps Charley's grandfather, watches this ceremony, as do a young male servant, two female servants, and Charley's little sister. But his father is not present. It is one of the female servants who dutifully admires Master Charley's heroic pose on that initial day of manhood, one hand in his pocket, one foot planted firmly on an overturned washtub, and it is "Ma" who lifts the covers to find Charley sleeping in his pantaloons that night. It is "Ma," finally (with both female servants looking on in sorrow), who changes Master Charley back into his dress and who inspects the pantaloons that have been shredded by Charley's fall from the chair, boxes, and books he had piled up and climbed in order to get a look at himself in the dresser-top mirror. Master Charley does have a "Pa" – who lives at home, not in the municipal prison – but he is nowhere to be found in any of these sketches.[125]

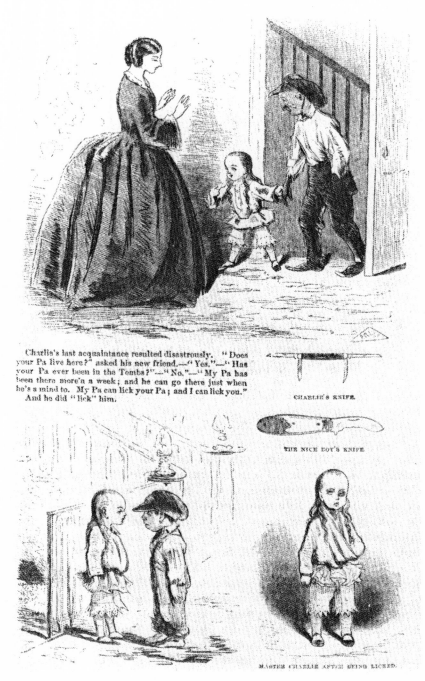

Charlie's last acquaintance resulted disastrously. "Does your Pa live here?" asked his new friend.—"Yes."—"Has your Pa ever been in the Tombs?"—"No."—"My Pa has been there more'n a week; and he can go there just when he's a mind to. My Pa can lick your Pa; and I can lick you."
And he did "lick" him.

CHARLIE'S KNIFE.

THE NICE BOY'S KNIFE.

MASTER CHARLIE AFTER BEING LICKED.

Figure 5.10. Master Charlie's sidewalk acquaintances, 1857 (courtesy of Cornell University Libraries)

Figure 5.11. Master Charley in the parlor, 1860 (courtesy of Cornell University Libraries)

Charley's biographer understood very well the tensions that lay within the canon of domesticity that so many historians, and so many contemporary documents, tell us was successfully enshrined in middle-class homes during these years. His little sketches, written to provide a moment's amusement for the middle-class readers of *Harper's*, did so by playing upon the perplexities and anxieties of real householders and parents who struggled each day to keep children in line, parlors intact, and all things in conformity with the new domestic religion. If domesticity was a religion, and Sarah Josepha Hale, Horace Bushnell, Catharine Beecher, Andrew Jackson Downing, and John Howard Payne its prophets and scribes, then Master Charley was its mischievous choirboy, slingshot tucked beneath his robes. The tensions he reveals are those of gender and class, which are, and were in reality, closely related. It is Charley's mother who constructs and presides over the middle-class domestic world, and it is in the guise of a well-groomed little girl that Charley is forced to venture out from that world into the dangerous streets. Is Charley so ill-equipped for the struggles of the streets because of his feminization and his subjection to female authority? It may or may not be his mother's fault that Charley loses in trade and in battle. She is, to use Ann Douglas's term, a "champion of sensibility," not of commerce or warfare.[126] Charley's father may yet intervene to instruct his son in bourgeois values and business practices.[127] In the meantime, Charley revenges himself upon his doting mother by bringing unwanted working-class guests into her middle-class sanctuary, and by smashing the sanctuary's relics.

Charley's father would have been less indifferent to class distinctions, no doubt, but if there had been a series of sketches called "Master Charley's Pa," it too would certainly have been based on differences between male and female sensibilities, focusing this time on the tensions between husband and wife. In numerous other pages, including some quite serious ones, Harper's articulated these differing sensibilities in the context of the evolution of a more refined middle-class culture revolving around the well-furnished, female-directed middle-class home. "Are we a polite people?" the editors asked in 1857, before detailing the ways in which American men were not. Well-dressed "gentlemen by self-appointment" put their French boots on top of the furniture, wore their five-dollar hats indoors, shoveled dinner into their mouths with their knives, slapped each other on the back, bawled "ribaldry and noisy impertinence" into each other's ears, and, as Fanny Trollope never tired of pointing out, spat tobacco juice everywhere and anywhere, even at times on the Brussels carpet.[128] It was the function of women to combat this rude male behavior, to refine and, more specifically, to domesticate personal habits formed in less elegant surroundings, including the rustic ones in which many city men had been born and bred. "No civilized man is so helpless and dependent in certain respects as an American gentleman," wrote Harper's in a long article on "Domestic Society in Our Country," "and the reason is obvious: our wives do our thinking in these matters, and we are perfectly content to follow their lead. A large part of our social system is under their control, and they legislate for our dress, etiquette, and manners without the fear of a veto. . . . It is indeed, the subtlest, and most pervasive influence in our land."[129]

The domestic influence of middle-class American women is by now a familiar theme in the historical literature of the nineteenth-century family. According to this literature, perhaps best exemplified by Nancy Cott's excellent study of the diaries and letters of one hundred "middle-class" and "upper-middle-class" New England women, the home, the traditional domestic tasks of women, and the particular task of childrearing over which women were acquiring nearly complete control, were increasingly sanctified during the early years of the nineteenth century and served increasingly as the foundation for the assertion of the moral superiority of women over men. Some historians have stressed the gains in personal esteem that finally accrued to the "separate sphere" of womanhood in the nineteenth century, including those that resulted from a more genuinely companionate marriage.[130] Others, including Cott, contend that these gains were bought at the price of increasing confinement and continuing subjugation to male authority in all things other than those pertaining to childrearing, manners, and other matters of sensibility.[131] All these contradictions and nuances within the canon of domesticity have been examined at length; yet at least three relatively neglected aspects of the reorganization of gender roles and influence deserve emphasis here. One concerns the nature and extent of male acquiescence. *Harper's* blithely noted that men were "perfectly content" to follow the female lead in domestic manners, but as late as 1857, a year after the article just cited, the same magazine could list a whole catalogue of continuing male abuses against decent social behavior. Some men no doubt did freely acquiesce in their wives' urgings to behave in a more genteel fashion, and surely there were large numbers who gave up spitting and took their feet off the furniture in response to their own desire for self-esteem and social status. But obviously there were others who did not choose to change their rough habits, just as some men did not defer to their wives in the raising of children.[132] In some middle-class homes, in other words, the domestication of males – both Charley and his Pa – was a battle to be won, not a smooth and painless process of acquiescence to superior feminine sensibility.[133]

A second facet of the emerging domestic canon, and one more closely connected to the central argument of this chapter, is the role of the specific *setting* of domestic relations, and of consumption and consumer goods, in shaping both the middle-class home and the reorganization of gender roles within it. As Karen Halttunen points out, it was the parlor, the most carefully and elaborately furnished room in every middle-class home and the space within the home where the family socialized with other people of its own choosing, that served as "the arena within which the aspiring middle classes worked to establish their claims to social status, to that elusive quality of 'gentility'."[134] Halttunen's fascinating discussion of parlor etiquette, and of the elaborate theatrical performances that took place within the parlors of the 1850s and beyond, pertains most forcefully to the

wealthiest and most socially ambitious middle-class families.[135] But
more ordinary middling folk also found that the parlor made demands
on their deportment. "It is impossible to say," confesses Russell
Lynes, "whether the stuffiness of the room dictated the increasing
stiffness of manners or if the determination to behave genteelly made
the room more uncomfortable, more formal, and more forbidding."[136]
Put another way, some men either found it more difficult, or found
themselves less inclined, to spit on the Brussels carpet than on the
sanded floors of earlier middling homes, to drape their legs over the
new parlor sofa, or to tell loud stories while their daughters (or their
hosts' daughters) were at the piano. The carpet, the sofa, and the
piano, therefore, all artifacts of the new middle-class way of life,
exerted their influence over middle-class modes of behavior, especially the behavior of men.

And it was partly through these consumer goods that women
exerted their influence. Increasingly, as women assumed responsibility for the management of the home, the purchase of those
goods that helped define the middle-class household (and refine
male behavior) became a female function and prerogative.[137] The
point applies not only to durable goods but to food as well. Faye
Dudden observes that during the 1850s the responsibility for marketing in middling homes shifted from the husband to the wife,
and offers the interesting suggestion that this shift reflected in part
the increasing desire and ability of the wife to exert control over
the production of more refined and elaborate meals.[138] (These were
meals, one might add, that the wife might have compelled her
husband to eat more slowly, and with a fork rather than a knife.)
It is not clear that women gained complete ascendancy over the
furnishing of the home – men's names dominate the list of piano
purchasers in the 1855 city directory advertisement of J. E. Gould's
Great Piano and Melodeon Emporium of Philadelphia[139] – but contemporary discussions of shopping focused mainly on women, and
almost certainly the woman's role in the selection and acquisition
of goods was expanding along with the pace of acquisition itself.
The retailer and the tradesman succeeded, according to *Harper's*,
"by pleasing women."[140] There can be little doubt that women
played a significant role in the shaping of the middle-class home.
In most cases it was probably a decisive one.

Woman's moral superiority, proclaimed so often by men as well as
women, could be squandered, however, if she played the role of
consumer too aggressively and in service to the wrong ambitions.
The fear of extravagance was expressed often in this age of expanding
consumption and social aspiration, and was often dramatized in tales

of free-spending wives who ruined their hardworking husbands, and of unhappy young women who married only for money and lived unhappy (and usually unhealthy) lives of artificial display.[141] These were women who violated the canon of domesticity by creating too lavish homes, by spending too much money on clothing and jewelry that added nothing to the home environment, and by delegating or even neglecting the crucial tasks of childrearing and household supervision so that they could be free to shop, make calls on other fashionable or aspiring women, and attend fashionable affairs. Lydia Maria Child complained in her *Letters from New York* that "of those duties which are feminine by universal consent, few are considered genteel by the upper classes. It is not genteel for mothers to wash and dress their own children, or make their clothing, or teach them, or romp with them in the open air." To Child it was "one of the saddest sights to see a young girl, born of wealthy and worldly parents, full of heart and soul, her kindly impulses continually checked by etiquette, her noble energies repressed by genteel limitations."[142] Focusing on consumption rather than the neglect of maternal duty, *Frank Leslie's Illustrated Newspaper* noted that "the middling classes (if we have a middling class where all strive to be 'first families') are virtually banished" from the opera, social affairs, and even certain churches, by their inability or unwillingness to compete with the dress of extravagant women (males are explicitly exculpated here).[143] Both of these complaints, and many others like them, associate excesses of consumption and neglect of domestic duty with exaggerated social ambition; that is, with the quest for an upper-class rather than a middle-class identity. Robert McGlone has pointed out (correctly, I believe) that those women who aspired to the middle class rather than the "upper ten thousand" lived according to a very different ideal, one that combined refinement of manners and surroundings with domestic duty.[144] These women (Master Charley's Ma was clearly one of them) were active managers of the home, to whom domestic servants and elegant parlors provided the necessary assistance and the proper environment (and to some extent the reward) for the effective performance of the duties of wife and mother.[145] Extravagant women attracted attention through their display; those conforming to the domestic canon attract ours through their numbers, for *Leslie's* clearly exaggerated the extent of extreme social climbing. "Fashion lives on exclusiveness," concluded *Harper's*. "The great mass of our women are in the middle classes, and the preponderating portion of them are true to womanly instincts in their genuine appreciation of goodness."[146]

By now it should be clear that the final aspect of the nineteenth-century domestic revolution that I wish to emphasize is its relationship to the formation of the American urban middle class. Virtually every historian of the emerging canon of domesticity (and as we have just seen, some contemporary commentators as well) has recognized its middle-class character, or at the very least the middling social condition of those who left behind the documents on which our understanding is based. "The canon of domesticity," writes Cott, "expressed the dominance of what may be designated a middle-class ideal, a cultural preference for domestic retirement and conjugal-family intimacy over both the 'vain' and fashionable sociability of the rich and the promiscuous sociability of the poor."[147] Mary Ryan has gone further than this by arguing that the *emergence* of a distinct middle class was closely connected with, and largely dependent upon, the development of the domestic ideal. "Early in the nineteenth century," she writes, "the American middle class molded its distinctive identity around domestic values and family practices."[148] By midcentury these values and practices, particularly those concerning the rearing and education of children, had evolved into a set of specific strategies for securing the family's foothold in the developing middle class. First, "prescient native-born couples" began to limit the size of their families, "thereby concentrating scarce financial and emotional resources on the care and education of fewer children." Second, these same couples "initiated methods of socialization designed to inculcate values and traits of character deemed essential to middle-class achievement and respectability," values and traits not of the aggressive entrepreneur but of the "cautious, prudent small-business man" (thereby helping to define "the upper as well as the lower boundaries of the middle class"). Third, children were kept within their parents' household for longer periods, prolonging parental surveillance and material support. Fourth, these resident children were given greater amounts of formal schooling, a crucial tactic intended to help them secure positions in the expanding nonmanual work force. And finally, the young men who emerged from this middle-class "cradle" were encouraged to delay their marriages until they had secured their own middle-class positions, a tactic that also contributed to the perpetuation of the tactical sequence, because it encouraged the reproduction of small families.[149] The implication of all this (and not merely the final tactic) is that the sequence was self-perpetuating – that, once implemented, these strategies would succeed in gaining or securing each family's position in the middle class, and established middle-class families would be the ones most likely to pursue the same strategies in subsequent generations.

I would add to Ryan's argument that consumption too was a family strategy, a more or less deliberate attempt to shape the domestic environment in ways that signified social respectability, and that facilitated the acquisition of habits of personal deportment that could set a family apart from both the rough world of the mechanics and the artificial world of fashion. Were these strategies in fact confined to the middle class? Susan Hirsch, in her study of industrial workers in Newark, argues that "while the Victorian family ideal found its most perfect embodiment in bourgeois homes, craftsmen patterned their households on the same lines as their employers." Women and children seldom worked outside of the home, men married late, families were controlled in size, and teenage boys remained more frequently in their parents' homes.[150] "Consumption became an important family activity," writes Hirsch, although she quickly concedes that the practice of keeping wives and children out of the work force limited workers' families "to a modest level of consumption."[151] To some extent these working-class family patterns reflect local conditions – Newark's industries offered few jobs to women, apprenticeships that required boys to move out of their parents' homes were rapidly declining in number, and wages for skilled male mechanics were relatively high.[152] But even in other cities, where married women did work more frequently to supplement their husbands' wages, there is evidence that the domestic ideal influenced life within working-class homes. In Lynn, the widespread employment of married women as shoebinders was, according to Mary Blewett, "a carefully controlled assignment of work designed to fit the role of women and to maintain gender relationships in the family.... Female family members adapted their traditional needle skills to hand sew the leather uppers in their kitchens, without disrupting their domestic duties or their child care tasks."[153] In New York's sixth ward, most Irish workers' wives who contributed to family income did so by taking in boarders, a practice that even middle-class women did not perceive as a violation of their domestic responsibilities.[154] The middle-class domestic ideal, finally, was central to the reformist strategy of female participants in the Washingtonian temperance movement of the early 1840s. Whereas Washingtonian men integrated teetotalism with working-class recreational customs, Washingtonian women, according to Ruth Alexander, emphasized "women's maternal and moral responsibilities" in ways that "paralleled values and behaviors of the nineteenth century's new middle class." Female Washingtonianism, concludes Alexander, attested to the wider appeal of nineteenth-century domesticity, and in particular to "the viability of a domestic model for women who had little material security."[155]

On the other hand, the domestic ideal that shaped working-class family life was not quite the same as the middle-class ideal, and, for most, the day-to-day realities were certainly very different. Blewett observes that female shoebinders did bring nondomestic work into their homes and experienced a growing gender-consciousness "defined not only by domesticity but also by their work for wages" in the "separate sphere" of shoebinding.[156] She also describes two interesting stories printed in the *Awl* (the male shoemakers' newspaper in Lynn) that promote a female ideal quite different from the one found in middle-class magazines and advice books – the *Awl*'s ideal woman was a wage-earning wife who spurned false notions of gentility (and destructive ambitions for a finely furnished house) and contributed her wages to the family's income and her support to the workingman's movement.[157] Christine Stansell's account of working-class domestic life in New York City distances workers even farther from the middle-class ideal of peaceful, privatized, domestic sanctuaries. Privacy and peace were impossible in the crowded tenements of New York, and the boundaries between public and private spaces were "fluid and permeable" as neighbors regularly assisted in crises that might soon be their own, intervened in quarrels they could not help overhearing, socialized through open windows and doors, looked upon each other's drying laundry, and in many other ways participated in "shifting communities of cooperation and contention [that] had none of the counterbalancing elements of the female domestic sphere of calm and affection that bourgeois men and women prized."[158] New York's working-class districts were the most crowded and extensive of any of the major cities, and Stansell's analysis probably obscures important differences between the domestic lives of better-paid mechanics and poor laborers; but it is clear – in Lynn as well as in New York – that even where the middle-class ideal of domesticity did penetrate into the working-class home, it neither reflected nor produced familial experiences identical with those of the middle class. The setting of domestic life, which I have argued was associated with the elevation of manners and the forming of new social identities, was distinctly different for workers and for non-manual businessmen, if not by intention then at least because one group but not the other was able to buy the domestic interiors and household locations that permitted the fulfillment of the domestic ideal.

Childrearing strategies differed as well, at least insofar as these were manifested in school attendance. Historians of education working in several different cities have pointed out that children from working-class families attended school less regularly and for fewer years than did children from middle-class families,[159] and census data

Table 5.1. *School attendance by age of child and occupational category of father, American-born white children, Philadelphia, 1860 (in percentages of children attending school within the year)*

| | Occupational category of father | | | |
Age of child	High nonmanual	Low nonmanual	High manual	Low manual
3	0	2	4	0
4	8	9	11	9
5	6	11	18	26
6	29	46	52	61
7	35	67	76	57
8	100	75	76	60
9	81	73	81	83
10	73	85	86	78
11	85	74	76	58
12	70	86	91	71
13	86	82	73	47
14	71	75	59	50
15	78	67	49	28
16	30	41	23	6
17	29	28	8	7
18	33	11	3	0
19	0	8	0	0
n	(224)	(889)	(1,575)	(229)

Source: U.S. Census of Population, 1860, manuscript schedules (Philadelphia Social History Project family file).

pertaining to Philadelphia suggest that workers' children tended to leave school one, two, or even three years earlier than children from nonmanual homes (Table 5.1).[160] In Philadelphia in 1860, most children of nonmanual proprietors and workers were still attending school at fifteen, while the fifteen-year-olds from manual workers' homes were not. School attendance declined for all groups after fifteen, but remaining in school was significantly more characteristic of middle-class than of working-class children. Large numbers of workers, it would seem, in Philadelphia and in other cities, either did not attempt to implement what Ryan has defined as middle-class child-rearing strategies, or found that their attempts to do so broke down at the crucial stage where status-enhancing values were to be joined to status-enhancing skills.

Middling families, then, reasonably perceived their homes and their domestic strategies and habits to be distinct from those of manual workers, as well as from those of the fashionables who did not even aspire to the domestic ideal. If this was an achievement – and it was often described that way by contemporary writers – it was one that should be attributed largely to the women who shaped the middle-class home, sometimes with and sometimes without the cooperation of the men who provided the financial means. At least partly in response to the new ways in which middling women performed the roles of wife, mother, household manager, and consumer, the American urban middle class "molded its distinct identity." In this respect we may say that middle-class formation was a phenomenon that went beyond the realignment of work, workplace relations, incomes, and opportunities. Events on the other side of the retail sales counter, and in the "separate sphere" of domestic womanhood, were influential, perhaps even crucial, in generating new social identities. To this extent, middle-class formation was woman's work.

6 Coming to order: voluntary associations and the organization of social life and consciousness

Work and family life are the principal preoccupations of most men and women, and the workplace and the home are the immediate milieux of the most crucial social relations in most societies. To these essential relations and places, however, antebellum Americans added something new and quite notable – a greatly expanded associational life within formally organized, specialized, voluntary institutions, whose multiplication in this era was indeed one of its outstanding characteristics. Voluntary organizations had existed before – historians have probably underestimated their significance in the eighteenth century – but it was in the three decades preceding the Civil War that formal associations became so numerous, so elaborately organized, so appealing to so many people, so various in purpose, and in many instances so powerful, that this may fairly be called an era of voluntary institutional innovation without parallel in American history. As arenas of class-relevant social life, moreover, the new voluntary societies were especially important, for all of them were formed and driven forward by choice rather than necessity, and in some of them the kinds of choices made by their members were impelled above all by judgments of the social worth of other existing or prospective members. More than in the workplace, the marketplace, and the home, decisions as to whether and how to be involved were voluntary expressions of social preference.

It is a relatively straightforward matter to examine the overall pattern of associational preference by identifying the members of specific organizations, and to some extent it will be the task of this chapter to answer the simple but significant question, Who joined what? It hardly needs stating, however, that answers to this question, gained from existing studies and the membership lists and other records of a wide variety of organizations, lead to more complicated issues concerning the social meanings of voluntary participation of various types. In what ways, beyond the development of more or less exclusive organizational rosters, did voluntary associations help mold

192

and maintain social identities? Can we identify specific institutional styles and purposes with organizations that recruited members from one or another social class? Did any institutions succeed in *mitigating* class distinctions through the recruitment of members from all classes, and the pursuit of a specifically interclass fellowship? These questions differ from those informing the large number of studies that contest whether certain kinds of organizations – societies devoted to social reform and the dispensation of Christian benevolence – were agencies for controlling and asserting authority over inferior classes.[1] They enunciate a rather different strategy, one that focuses inward on the experience of organizational participation and the formation of social identities but at the same time looks outward to a wider array of organizations, including those that offered fellowship, intellectual stimulation, amusement, or physical exercise, no less than those that promised the triumph of evangelical Christianity and the quiescence of the working class. The point of this strategy is not to conflate Bible societies and baseball clubs (nor is it to gloss over their primary purpose of winning souls and baseball games) but to understand both as institutions through which individuals expressed and to some extent shaped themselves as members of society. Put another way, it is to respect their differences while searching for the common thread of class-defining experience.

The evangelical united front

Let us begin with the Bible societies and other organizations that quickly coalesced into an "evangelical united front" during and immediately after the Second Great Awakening.[2] Scholars who differ widely over the motives that underlay benevolent and moral reform – whether reformers were impelled by altruism or by status anxiety and a need to reassert control over inferior classes – are in much closer agreement as to the social backgrounds of reform leaders, particularly in the earlier years of revival-inspired institutional development. "The leaders of the benevolent groups," wrote Clifford S. Griffin nearly thirty years ago, were mostly "wealthy men and men becoming wealthy through business, finance, and the law."[3] This view has since been subjected to only modest correction, primarily by those who would *extend* it to the wives and daughters of such men, and by those who point to a somewhat more inclusive pattern of leadership in certain kinds of reform societies, especially those founded slightly later and with more radical goals. Nancy A. Hewitt's recent study of activist women in Rochester encapsulates most of these corrections. Nearly all of the women (172 of 185) who held office in Rochester's various benevolent organizations – the Orphan Asylum, the Home for the Friendless, and others – had fathers or husbands who were professionals, bankers, merchants, or manufacturers, and the 47 women who served these organizations for twenty or more years were *all* from this class.[4] Antislavery and women's rights activists, however, were drawn from a broader base – only 40% were the wives and daughters of professionals and large-scale businessmen, while nearly 20% were the wives and daughters of artisans.[5] To be sure, the apparent democratization of female participation suggested by the last figure seems to have been confined to more militant reform organizations. In Providence, Rhode Island, according to Susan Porter Benson, nearly all of the women who sat on the board of the Employment Society between 1837 and 1852 were the wives and daughters of professionals, merchants, and manufacturers "of great wealth and prominence."[6] And as Edward Pessen, Frederic Cople Jaher, and Carroll Smith-Rosenberg have shown, the men and women who led the benevolent and reform societies of the nation's larger cities continued to be recruited from the upper reaches of urban society.[7]

It may be significant, however, that many of these urban reformers had only recently attained – and in some cases would only later attain – social prominence. Jaher notes that in New York, and even in Boston, reformers often were men of rising or recently established wealth and influence, who were more likely than older patricians to espouse the values of more ordinary people, and less likely to interpret social change in terms of a crisis in personal social status and influence.[8] Men such as Nathan Appleton in Boston, and Arthur and Lewis Tappan in New York, had made their own fortunes, adhered to the bourgeois virtues that they believed were essential to their success in the business world, and regarded benevolent and reform societies as opportunities not for the reassertion of patrician influence but for the exercise of the kind of public responsibility that their wealth and evangelical beliefs required.[9] There may have been a significant social distance, and a corresponding difference of outlook, between long-established and newly emerging elites. An even greater social distance separated the old urban elite from the "vast second tier of volunteers" identified by Paul Boyer. These "urban-morality foot soldiers," according to Boyer, "were often first-generation urbanites active in evangelical churches and holding what would later be called white-collar jobs – clerks, accountants, bank tellers – on the lower rungs of the business or professional ladders."[10] What is most interesting about this distinction between wealthy and prominent leaders and less exalted staffers is that it directs attention away from the issues of social

control and altruism among elites (old or new) and toward the issue
of self-definition among middling folk:

> From this perspective, [writes Boyer,] the decision to participate in
> an urban moral-reform society might reflect less the wish to con-
> trol others than an impulse toward self-definition, a need to avow
> publicly one's own class aspirations. The Bible, tract, and Sunday
> school societies enabled members of this still inchoate middle class
> to seek each other out, join together in purposeful common effort,
> and submit to the oversight of others who shared their
> aspirations.[11]

These are important refinements of the traditional view of antebellum reformers. They posit a more complex community of activists
and a more complex array of motives, including, for nonleaders and
perhaps some leaders as well, finding a place within a "still inchoate
middle class." In truth, antebellum reform societies have left little
documentation of the men and women who staffed their middle and
lower ranks, and the connection Boyer proposes between voluntary
institutional participation and middle-class self-definition must be
pursued in other ways through the records that survive. I shall attempt to do so through some of the records left behind by one reform
movement – perhaps the most important of the era – the temperance
crusade. How did the participation of various kinds of Americans in
this crusade transcend the immediate issues of drink and drunkenness
and speak to deeper issues of social identity and definition?

The earliest temperance organizations were small and exclusive
associations, and the movement they directed against excessive drinking relied heavily and quite explicitly upon the influence of traditional
elites within their communities. This, however, was before temperance became a crusade on a national level. Inspired by the revivals,
by attacks on drinking that issued from increasing numbers of evangelical pulpits, and by the newly formed American Temperance Society (originally the American Society for the Promotion of
Temperance), local reformers formed numerous societies in the late
1820s and early 1830s that broadened the temperance movement by
bringing into the organizational nexus – as participants as well as
recipients – all those who could be convinced to forswear drink and
join the cold-water army. In smaller cities, the leadership also could
be broadened, and even relocated among non-elites. In Providence,
for example, an informal temperance movement based entirely upon
the example and influence of local men of rank gave way to several
formal organizations that enrolled large numbers of artisans along
with smaller numbers of professionals, merchants, and clerks. More

importantly, these organizations, according to John S. Gilkeson's tabulations, were led mainly by shopkeepers, clerks, and small manufacturers, rather than by the wealthy merchants and gentlemen who
had led previous local reform movements. This relocation of leadership helped change social perceptions and interclass relations in Providence. As Gilkeson argues, the organized temperance movement
there evolved into a "program for middle-class respectability and a
sharp critique of fashionable taste."[12] More specifically, the intensification of the temperance crusade, and the division of the community
into "warring camps" over drink and related issues, served to underscore the middling status of the temperate, for the enemies of the
"stable, industrious, sober middle classes" (as the teetotalers of Providence began to see themselves) were both above and below, and "in
their eyes, the rich appeared to be just as intemperate, idle, and self-
indulgent as the vice-ridden poor."[13] This emerging association between temperance and middling status seems to have been occurring
in Worcester, Massachusetts, as well. Ian Tyrrell's account of the
licensing controversy of the 1830s locates the proponents of a no-
license law among the rising manufacturers of that city, and their
opponents among workers and the existing social elite.[14]

In larger cities, however, the leadership of the temperance movement remained in the hands of wealthy professionals and merchants,
although, as already suggested, many of these men were newcomers
to wealth, leadership, and in some cases even the city itself. The
organizations they founded were, not suprisingly, more complex than
those of the smaller cities, and the social implications of their structure
and activities may well have been quite different. The New York City
Temperance Society, for example, was both more inclusive and more
hierarchical than the temperance societies of smaller cities. Founded
in 1829 at a public meeting held at the Masonic Hall, the NYCTS was
from the start aggressive in its recruitment of members. One of its
first acts was to print three thousand copies of a temperance and
membership appeal, and its constitution specifically provided that
membership would be open to all who could pay annual dues.[15] By
early 1833 subsidiary societies had been created in each ward of the
city, and by 1835 there were forty-five additional subsidiaries attached
to individual churches, several youth societies, and, reflecting the
parent society's eagerness to reach the city's workingmen, societies
organized among sailors, stonecutters, and gold- and silversmiths.[16]
In that year the NYCTS reported 50,284 members, a number that
would grow to 166,879 by 1842.[17] The leaders of this huge organization
were a different breed from those who directed the smaller societies
in Providence and Worcester, and the very structure of the NYCTS

suggests how much more hierarchical the temperance movement was in the larger cities. The parent body consisted of a small number of officers, a large board of managers, and a small executive committee that was formally responsible to the board of managers but was effectively in control of the organization.[18] In 1830 the society was nominally led by Smith Thompson, a United States district judge, and by John T. Irving, First County Judge, who were president and vice-president, respectively. The executive committee consisted of three physicians, two wealthy merchants (one of whom was Arthur Tappan), the Reverend Joshua Leavitt, and Eleazar Lord, president of the Manhattan Insurance Company. Interestingly, three of these seven men were neighbors at 16, 18, and 20 Beach Street, and two were near neighbors on Charlton Street (the other two lived on Broadway and on Park Place). The board of managers was a much larger group, and was slightly more inclusive. Most of its members were easily identified in the city directory, and these consisted of 34 professionals, 19 merchants and other apparently large-scale businessmen, 4 retailers, and 9 men listing artisanal occupations. Whether the last were handworking artisans is impossible to say, but several listed business addresses on Broadway, Pearl Street, and other major downtown streets.[19]

Leadership and membership in the New York City Temperance Society were entirely different matters, and it would be a mistake to view this organization as a classless community of reformers and reformed drunkards. Minutes of the executive committee strongly suggest that the officers, board, and executive committee had no contact of any kind with the membership at large. Agents appointed by the executive committee addressed audiences in churches, consulted with individuals in various wards, churches, and trades, and did whatever mingling was necessary to start up subsidiary societies. After 1832, presidents of the ward societies did sit on the executive committee, which met in the homes or the Wall Street offices of its principal members. A list of the ward society officers for 1837, however, reveals the ward presidents to be surprisingly similar to the other executive committee members – mostly merchants, doctors, and lawyers. This was true even in working-class wards. The temperance society of the heavily working-class sixth ward, for example, was led by a merchant, Samuel Rathbone, while the president of the eleventh ward society was Samuel Sargent, M.D. Only the society of the thirteenth ward, in one of the most remote and homogeneously working-class districts of the city, was led by an artisan, a printer named William G. Boggs. Other ward society officers also consisted mainly of professionals and nonmanual businessmen, although some of these may have been rather less exalted than the leaders of the parent society.[20] It is clear, in sum, that the leaders of the New York City Temperance Society were, to use Clifford Griffin's phrase, "wealthy men and men becoming wealthy" through business and the professions, and that these leaders had no real association with the very large numbers of humbler folk who joined the society at the grass-roots level. This, indeed, would have been modified only slightly if the presidents or other officers of the several trades' temperance societies been allowed to sit on the executive committee. The president of the Marine Temperance Society was Edward Richardson, a commission merchant, while three other identifiable officers consisted of a merchant, a shipmaster, and the minister of the Mariners' Church. The Gold and Silver Smiths' Temperance Society was led by William J. Mullen, a Broadway manufacturer of gold watch dials. Other officers were master silversmiths, jewelers, and watchcase makers with shops or stores on major business streets. John D. Norris, who owned a stone yard, was president of the Stone Cutters' Temperance Society, and the only other identifiable officer was a tract missionary named Nathaniel Gray. Only the House Carpenters' Temperance Society was led by men listed in the city directory with the simple artisanal title of carpenter.[21]

The mere expansion of leadership roles in the NYCTS, at both the central and the subsidiary society levels, did involve in the movement a number of professionals and businessmen, and even a few artisans, who were not even recent arrivals into the city's elite. Thus, even without being able to identify a secondary tier of "urban-morality foot soldiers" drawn from the city's clerical workers, and without attempting to specify further the social position of *arrivistes* such as Arthur Tappan, we can posit an increased role in the temperance crusade by men of middling rank, and a degree of cooperation among professionals and businessmen of great and modest wealth and standing. Whether the NYCTS tended to clarify or obscure the boundary between the upper and middle classes of the city is difficult to assess, but this question should not obscure the pattern that stands out most clearly in the organization's records – New York's businessmen and professionals undertook the task of eliminating alcoholic drink from the city by associating with each other in an organization designed to reach downward, in a distinctly hierarchical fashion, into the various neighborhoods and trades. Nominally, businessmen and manual workers were members of the same organization, but the structure of that organization emphasized the differences between them rather than their common commitment to the temperance movement. A circular addressed to "Manufacturers and Mechanics" by the executive committee in 1837 is suggestive of the leadership's perceptions of and relations with their fellow teetotalers in the working class. The circular begins with a discussion of the greater exposure of mechanics to alcohol, the interests of employers in having sober workers, and, at greater length, each employer's responsibility to influence his workers to avoid drink. This discussion is followed by a series of questions addressed to employers concerning the amount and pattern of drinking in their factories and workshops. The circular might have been sent out to small, handworking master artisans, but the published answers to its questions all came from employers or supervisors of from seven to forty men.[22] No circular was ever sent to wage-earning workers. In sum, if the NYCTS had any influence at all in shaping the social contours of New York, it was to sharpen the growing divide between the business and working classes.

This divide also informed the more widely circulated temperance literature of the 1830s. For example, in the *Temperance Recorder*, an important monthly newspaper published by the New York State Temperance Society (and purchased in very large numbers by the NYCTS for distribution in New York City),[23] it underlay nearly all of the central arguments and rhetorical motifs. One of the most important of these was the doctrine of influence inherited from the more elite organizations of previous decades. In the 1830s this doctrine was largely recast in occupational terms, and was addressed exclusively to professionals and nonmanual businessmen – doctors, clergymen, merchants, and manufacturers.[24] The manufacturers were invariably described as or assumed to be large-scale managers rather than handworking masters, as in one article imploring supervisors in shipyards to influence their workers to give up drink, or in another citing with approval a sandpaper manufacturer's idea of printing temperance messages on the back of each sheet of sandpaper (thereby influencing not only his own workers but all those handworking masters and workers who used the sandpaper later on).[25] Only rarely were workers addressed directly in the *Temperance Recorder*, and then the appeal took a quite different form. An article entitled "Mechanics and laboring men – would you be independent?" describes the "neat, new, well-painted, two-story dwellings" the workers of the Matteawan Manufacturing Company were able to afford after the company's agent excluded drink from company premises.[26] Unlike those addressed to businessmen, this article appealed to workers to reap the benefits of submitting to the influence (or even the authority) of their superiors.

A second motif, closely related to the first, was the corruption of the businessman's proper influence by those who were engaged in the production and sale of intoxicating drink. The *Temperance Recorder* is filled with diatribes against distillers, wine and liquor merchants, and tavernkeepers, as the producers of intemperance and even as *traitors* to a class otherwise made up of men who worked hard, performed useful functions for society, served rather than disrupted the family, and appealed to rationality rather than to animal appetites. With more than a hint of smugness, the *Recorder* frequently predicted that liquor dealers and others in the infernal trade would disqualify themselves from even the outward appearance of respectability, as the business of selling liquor almost always led to laziness and dissipation, to drink itself, and to financial ruin.[27] One might expect that the principal villains identified in this temperance newspaper would be drunkards, and that a major preoccupation of its upper- and middle-class editors would be the creation of a more docile and productive work force through the exertion of proper controls over the drinking habits of workers by men such as the agent of the Matteawan Manufacturing Company. Actually, the problem of working-class drinking was discussed in the *Recorder* with considerable restraint, while the deepest contempt and most passionate denunciations were aimed not at drunkards but at these class traitors – manufacturers and dealers of alcoholic drink – who confounded the association between nonmanual enterprise and social worth.

Drunkards, of course, did receive a good deal of attention in the *Temperance Recorder*, and the manner in which they were described subtly reinforced the nonmanual-manual divide. The disastrous effects of drink and drunkenness were conveyed most often through purportedly true stories of individual drunkards, nearly all of whom were identified as wealthy, educated, or respectable, or by specific nonmanual occupations, before they took to drink. Moderate drinking invariably led to heavy drinking and drunkenness, and drunkenness to financial ruin and the destruction of family life. Often it led to the death of the drinker, his impoverished wife (the drunkard in these tales was almost always male), or his children.[28] The loss of respectability, of the ability to pursue a respectable occupation, of wealth, and of family life in a well-appointed home (the forced sale of furniture is a common motif) was crucial to these tales, and spoke clearly and powerfully to the major preoccupations of the upper and middle classes. It could have spoken to the concerns of mechanics as well, but the latter were hardly ever mentioned, except to provide contrast to the poignant story of a drunkard fallen from higher ranks. In one issue, for example, a woodcut portrays two men, one drunk and slovenly dressed, the other neatly dressed and sober. The first is described as once a "very respectable, useful, and wealthy man" made poor by drink, the other as "once a poor man, a day laborer," now a "quite independent" farmer who drinks only cold water.[29] It is interesting that the two men do not quite trade places – the latter becomes "independent" but not wealthy. The sober laborer's elevation to the yeomanry rather than to great wealth may have been calculated to accord with middle-class ideas as to the proper channels and limits of his ambition.

The *Temperance Recorder* was intended for a general audience. Other publications, such as the temperance almanacs issued from the same editorial offices as the *Recorder*, seem to have been aimed at small farmers and workers, and in fact the characteristic temperance tale in these almanacs is of the mechanic or small farmer who comes to grief because of drink. In the *American Temperance Almanac* for 1835, for example, are six moral tales told by a mother to her impressionable "Henry" and "Harriet." One describes how a small farmer drank and was reduced to day labor, and the other five describe the misfortunes of artisans and other manual workers. The children ask why they themselves are poor while Mr. Johnson, a merchant, is rich. The answer is that their father squanders his $4 or $5 in weekly pay on drink.[30] The uniformity of these tales is as striking in the almanacs as it is in the *Temperance Recorder*, and contributes to our understanding of the editors' sense of the most fundamental divisions in the larger society. So, too, does the *Temperance Almanac* for 1836, which replaced these moral tales with essays addressed to specific groups, including mechanics, farmers, young men, and temperate drinkers. Mechanics and farmers are isolated as occupational groups (the address to mechanics asks why so few of this group ever prosper), while the "young men" are told that successful public leaders, clergymen, physicians, and lawyers cannot be intemperate. Here, and in other contemporary publications as well, the phrase "young men" was used to address or describe only those who aspired to the prestige and wealth of the nonmanual sector. Young mechanics and farmers, or perhaps more accurately those young tradesmen and husbandmen who did not expect to cross the nonmanual-manual divide, were counseled not as "young men" but as mechanics and farmers.[31] The address to temperate drinkers is also instructive, for the three examples provided of drunkards who began as temperate (hence, as apparently respectable) drinkers are a clergyman, a major public official, and a merchant.[32] This compartmentalization of occupations in the *Temperance Recorder* and the almanacs was not accidental. It gave substance to a social order that temperance leaders perceived as endangered, not merely by the spread of misery and the loss of worker productivity, but by the confusing social anomalies created by the alcohol-induced downfall of once respected professionals and businessmen. This theme is encountered over and over again in the temperance literature of the day. When, for example, George W. Bethune delivered a temperance sermon in 1833, he could think of no more compelling a story than that of his encounter on a steamboat with the lawyer who had once defended Aaron Burr, and who, now inebriated, was saved only by Bethune's intervention "from being classed with the lowest of passengers."[33]

All of these tales and exhortations date from the period before the economic crisis of 1837, when the temperance movement was in the hands of wealthy and middling professionals and businessmen. What was the effect of the increasing role of workingmen after that date, and especially after 1840, with the advent and spread of the Washingtonian movement? Washingtonianism differed from the temperance movement of the early 1830s, not only in its much greater success in recruiting workingmen but also in its structure and style. Washingtonian societies lacked the elaborate hierarchy of organizations such as the New York City Temperance Society, and altered as well the content and tone of the temperance meeting. Under the auspices of the evangelical leaders who had founded the American Temperance Society and its affiliates, the temperance meeting had been a decorous affair, devoted to organizational matters and to addresses from clergymen, doctors, and other learned and influential men who could combine evangelical moralizing with statistical and anatomical evidence of the evil effects of drink. Washingtonians, on the other hand, purportedly members of an egalitarian community of reformed drunkards, based their meetings on the confessional relation of personal experience by any and all of its members, and on frequent and rousing group singing. The Washingtonian meeting, according to Aaron B. Grosh's *Washingtonian Pocket Companion*, should always open with singing (the bulk of Grosh's manual is devoted to the words and music of 112 songs), and should then dispense quickly with whatever business matters were at hand, referring as many as possible to committees. "Then call for speakers," instructs Grosh, and let there be "as many 'experiences' as possible." Whenever the gathered get restless, Grosh advises, get a lively speaker or introduce a song. Pledges should be called for "when the audience feel in the right spirit."[34] This was obviously a far livelier type of meeting than the older temperance reformers were used to, and if it was the most important of the Washingtonian innovations, it was not the only one. *The Crystal Fount*, a Washingtonian newspaper published in New York City, details a large number of steamboat excursions, picnics, dances, concerts, and other social events designed to offer young people of both sexes an attractive and alcohol-free alternative to the more customary and dangerous pleasures of the city. These were not quiet or staid affairs; indeed, every effort was made to make them as much fun as possible. Typical of the events described in *The Crystal Fount* was the Lady Marian Society picnic of August 1842. This female auxiliary sponsored a steamboat excursion and picnic, which was attended by several temperance fire companies and a brass band. There were speeches at the picnic, but there was also a great deal of singing and dancing, and the emphasis in *The Crystal Fount*'s description is on the good time had by all.[35] Occasionally, the fun could go too far, even for *The Crystal Fount*. Earlier in the same month the paper chided Hose Company No. 13 for including in their temperance concert the bawdy song "Pretty, Pretty, Polly Hawkins," which kept the audience roaring.[36]

"Experience meetings" and raucous temperance galas did not sit well with temperance reformers who had built their movement on more respectable foundations. As Sean Wilentz notes, "Washingtonianism, for all its good will, soon proved anathema to the city's older temperance advocates; their differences exposed abiding social and ideological tensions within the cold-water army."[37] Ian Tyrrell's persuasive account of the movement locates these tensions along class lines. In its early days, Washingtonianism was welcomed by most upper- and middle-class temperance reformers, and a number of them joined Washingtonian societies and forged links to existing associations of the older type. As Washingtonianism had begun as a more or less plebeian movement of mainly working-class former drunkards, and as it lacked the elaborate hierarchy of organizations such as the NYCTS, its embrace by wealthier and more respectable reformers would seem to have created a nearly unique opportunity for the creation of a genuinely classless community among temperance reformers. Instead, according to Tyrrell, upper- and middle-class members devoted themselves to reforming the Washingtonian societies to conform to older patterns, purging them of experience meetings and "vulgar entertainments."[38] *The Crystal Fount*, now under management somewhat less sympathetic to these entertainments, observed with regret the reaction of many of the original Washingtonians, drawn from "among the lowest portion of the community," to the efforts of the more respectable reformers: "Among many of the pioneers of this work, there is a jealousy of these men, who have never been drunkards; and the moment any person of wealth and standing in the community, comes forward, and is willing to take part in the cause, instantly a cry is raised by these jealous spirits – *the rich against the poor*."[39]

Where the upper- and middle-class reformers succeeded, working-
class Washingtonians withdrew, and *The Crystal Fount* soon recognized "societies composed mainly of men who move in a higher class
of society than others" and "societies composed of an entirely opposite class of men," who distanced themselves from those they were
increasingly apt to call "the silk stocking gentry."[40] Washingtonianism, in other words, had become compartmentalized by class. By
1845, in New York City, Worcester, and no doubt in other places as
well, the old-line respectable reformers had succeeded in taking over
most of the Washingtonian societies, and most artisans and other
workers had withdrawn – some back to the barroom, others to invest
their energies in a revitalized trades union and labor reform movement, still others to form new societies such as the Rechabites, Good
Samaritans, and Sons of Temperance.[41] The separation of classes during this plebeian phase of temperance reform was never complete.
Some artisans remained in the Washingtonian movement until it died
out, and some of those who joined the new organizations were small
nonmanual businessmen and clerical workers. The 16 founders of the
New York City Sons of Temperance, for example, all former Washingtonians, consisted of the publisher of *The Organ* (the city's Sons
of Temperance newspaper), a paper dealer, a clerk, 4 printers, 2
bookbinders, an engraver, 2 painters, a ship painter, a paperhanger,
a carpenter, and a tailor. Of the thirteen artisans in this group, 7 (or
8 of 14 if the publisher of the society's newspaper is classified as a
printer) worked in closely related trades, and closely related to these
was the paper store of Daniel H. Sands. It is interesting, though
perhaps not as significant as the larger pattern of class separation
within the temperance movement as a whole, that this one unambiguously nonmanual businessman among the founding Sons was
the Patriarch of the organization.[42]

Temperance reformers brought to the movement, through all of its
phases and local variations, presumptions grounded in the experience
of class. Well situated to help fulfill the promise of a classless republic,
temperance activists instead perpetuated old social affinities and,
through their organizations, created new experiences that reinforced
the boundary between well-off professionals and businessmen on the
one hand, and poorer artisans and laborers on the other. Some of the
less wealthy professionals and businessmen in the movement may
also have helped give substance to the moral boundary between the
very rich and the respectable middle class, but this theme seems to
have been more clearly articulated, or in any case remains more visible, in smaller cities such as Providence than in larger cities such as
New York.

Not every reform movement or benevolent society was as complex as the temperance crusade, or functioned in the same fashion. Philanthropic institutions led by wealthy elites and staffed, as Boyer suggests, by "foot soldiers" recruited from the ranks of clerical workers, did not offer memberships to the recipients of their benevolence, and neither did the interregional Bible, tract, missionary, and Sunday school societies designed to preserve traditional forms of authority over a population that was migrating far beyond the boundaries of established communities.[43] Antislavery societies, on the other hand, gathered individuals from a fairly wide range of social backgrounds into organizations that, as Lawrence J. Friedman has shown, could function as intense subcommunities of true believers. The members of the abolitionist cliques that Friedman examined, and most abolitionist leaders, were generally of the same sort as those who led the temperance societies (many, indeed, were the same people), but opposition to slavery could create local organizations that were more genuinely inclusive than any type of temperance society.[44] The Philadelphia City Anti-Slavery Society, for example, was an auxiliary society to the larger Anti-Slavery Society of the City and County of Philadelphia. In 1838, those of its members identifiable in the city directory included a gentleman, a clergyman, 14 merchants and retailers, 2 agents, a stove manufacturer, 5 teachers, the superintendent of the Philadelphia Orphan Asylum, a dentist, 2 artists, 19 artisans listing a variety of trades, and one porter.[45] The presence on this list of 2 hairdressers and a porter (occupations in which blacks predominated) suggests this may have been a biracial society as well as an occupationally inclusive one. Antislavery societies in Worcester, Lynn, and other smaller cities were also diverse in their memberships, while antislavery petitions were signed in New York City and elsewhere by large numbers of artisans and other workers.[46] Those who signed petitions did not necessarily join societies, and there was probably more diversity among the antislavery constituency than there was among the organized community of antislavery activists. But the patterns of membership in Philadelphia, Worcester, and Lynn suggest that the antislavery crusade, unlike the temperance crusade, was carried forward by organizations in which class distinctions were of little consequence.

The agenda of the antislavery societies helps explain why they were different from the temperance societies, and, more specifically, why they were more inclusive. The issue that united northern abolitionists was not their own behavior, nor the effects of slavery on local social relations, but the evils of an institution that functioned in a region remote from their daily lives. It was also an issue that more consistently focused reformist energies on the political system. The Philadelphia City Anti-Slavery Society, and others like it, were essentially political institutions – indeed, they may well have been little more than instruments for mobilizing general support among the voting population of a given area (most of the members of the Philadelphia society were in fact from a small area within the northeastern quadrant of the city) for the specific purpose of promoting antislavery in the national and state legislatures. Of course, once formed, an organization of this type *could* have functioned as a class-mitigating social institution for the activists it recruited from different walks of life, but it is impossible to tell from membership lists alone whether it actually did. In any case, the much larger numbers of less radical benevolent and reform societies of the antebellum era tended to reinforce rather than to blur the boundaries of class. The effects of the evangelical united front on the social experiences and feelings of the many different Americans who became involved in its various crusades cannot be summarized in a single statement. But it is fair to say that it did more to articulate social boundaries, and to give substance to them through organized group life, than to institutionalize a class-free Christian republic.

Books, banks, and baseball

The benevolent and reform societies inspired by the evangelical awakening have received a disproportionate amount of attention from historians of antebellum voluntarism. Also important were countless other organizations – lyceums and literary societies, music societies and dancing assemblies, militia and fire companies, baseball and cricket clubs, brass bands and lodges – that expressed the specific interests of very large numbers of Americans, especially those who lived in cities and towns. Many of these organizations also expressed in a more or less overt way the social preferences of their members, and some seem to have been designed at least in part for that very purpose. This is especially evident in certain associations created by the urban upper class. The Boston Athenaeum, for example, was founded in 1807 by a small group of wealthy professionals, who restricted membership in the organization by issuing shares at the very high price of $300. The original intention may have been to attract only bibliophiles, but soon nearly all of Boston's wealthiest professionals and businessmen had purchased shares. "The Boston elite was not coterminus with the Athenaeum subscription list," concludes Ronald Story, but the correspondence was "extremely close." More important, the Athenaeum quickly came to play an important role in defining and maintaining the upper class in Boston. Its "principal function," according to Story, was "to socialize the young, acculturate the arriviste, [and] consolidate the disparate" into an upper class that was even more self-conscious and distinct than it had been in previous generations.[47]

Elite organizations had existed for many years, but in the antebellum era they became more numerous and varied. Library companies, and literary, philosophical, historical, and scientific societies multiplied in cities that already had them, and were founded in cities that did not. All were headed by each city's leading families.[48] Voluntary militia companies (the First City Troop in Philadelphia, for example) sometimes became elite preserves,[49] and in the larger cities there appeared, as early as the 1830s, the forerunners of the exclusive clubs that flourished after the Civil War. Several of these were formed by older elites and may well have been responses to the assertiveness of parvenu businessmen and evangelical reformers. The Union Club of New York City, for example, was founded in 1836 by wealthy Knickerbockers as a purely social organization. According to a nearly contemporary account, its purpose was not to socialize the *arriviste* into the upper class but to assert an older form of exclusiveness:

> From its inception it was the representative organization of the old families. Livingstons, Clasons, Dunhams, Griswolds, Van Cortlandts, Paines, Centers, Vandervoorts, Van Rensselaers, Irelands, Stuyvesants, Suydams, and other names of Knickerbocker fame, filled its list of membership with a sort of aristocratic monotony of that Knickerbockerism which has since . . . earned the epithet of the Bourbons of New York. Hence, sprang up that contest of the old magnates of New York society with the new Napoleons of wealth by trade, which for years agitated the club, and has occasionally threatened to rent it asunder; for these Vans, of whatever final syllables, have always made a sort of grand fetish of pedigree, insisting that a man, like a horse, ought always to be blooded.[50]

Organizations such as the Union Club could be described in a tone of gentle ridicule, for they appeared to be based on prestige and power that was in decline, and served to isolate the old elite rather than to perpetuate its active influence. Other new clubs that associated old and new men of wealth with the city's intellectual and literary leaders – the Century Club and Sketch Club in New York, and the Saturday Club in Boston, for example – were taken more seriously, as were such organizations as the New York Yacht Club and the Philadelphia Cricket Club, in which wealthy men combined to pursue a fashionable interest in a specific sport.[51] The latter are particularly interesting where they were organized around activities in which non-elites engaged. Cricket, for example, was played for some years in America by English immigrants of all classes, and when the St. George Cricket Club was founded in New York in 1839 it included significant numbers of artisans.[52] Large numbers of white- and blue-collar Americans began to play the game in the 1840s, and by the end of the 1850s, according to George B. Kirsch's recent estimate, there were as many as ten thousand cricket players in the United States, organized into four hundred clubs. There were probably more than one hundred junior and senior clubs in and around Philadelphia, the acknowledged capital of American cricket.[53] Yet, when the Philadelphia Cricket Club was organized in William Rotch Wister's law office in 1854, the original and proposed members represented a very narrow range of the city's cricket-playing population – the 28 identified in the city directory included 17 attorneys, 2 doctors, a gentleman, 4 merchants, an auctioneer, an accountant, a brass molder, and a painter and glazier.[54] Some of these men may have been tapped for their ability on the field, and the preponderance of attorneys may suggest little more than the existence of a network of friendship and acquaintance within a given trade. But in fact the Philadelphia Cricket Club quickly became and long remained an institution clearly associated with the city's upper class.[55]

Elite clubs of this sort often justified themselves as promoters of the game, and of healthful, manly exercise. The Franklin Barge Club, which consisted almost entirely of merchants, was for a few years part of the "Schuylkill Navy" of prestigious rowing clubs. Its constitution addresses the "rational enjoyment" and "health" to be gained from "the manly exercise of rowing," and goes on to stipulate an elaborate set of rules governing members' behavior in the meeting room and on the water.[56] But the minutes of the Philadelphia Quoit Club reveal how important exclusive socializing could be in some of these organizations. Founded in 1829, the Quoit Club was restricted to twenty members, all drawn from the loftiest regions of Proper Philadelphia. In 1842, for example, those of its members listed in the city directory included 6 gentlemen, 4 merchants, a broker, and a doctor. Of these men, 7 lived on Chestnut Street (2 in Boston Row, an expensive block of homes above Twelfth), while 4 lived on Walnut. The rules of the club focused not on quoits but on the dinner that each member was to offer in turn as Caterer of the Day. Dinner was to begin at two-thirty and end at four, with "Wine and Segars upon the Green." The club president was entitled to bring three guests, and each other member one, but only from outside of Philadelphia. Any transgression of club rules was to result in a fine of either $12 or a case of claret. Meetings were held at various members' country seats.[57] This club was never very important, and was disbanded in 1855. But for about a quarter of a century it did provide a small number of Cadwaladers, Kuhns, and Ingersolls with "manly exercise" in a setting that, more than anything else, emphasized their membership in Philadelphia's upper class.

Clubs and other associations that were distinctly upper class are not difficult to identify, and neither are networks of organizations led by locally prominent families. Lee L. Schreiber has traced upper-class leaders of the Pennsylvania Academy of Fine Arts to leadership roles in the Library Company of Philadelphia, the Philadelphia Atheneum, the Apprentices' Library, the board of trustees of the University of Pennsylvania, the American Philosophical Society, the Philadelphia Society for the Promotion of Agriculture, the Linnean Society, the Franklin Institute, the Historical Society of Pennsylvania, the Free and Accepted Order of Masons, the Welsh Society, the St. Andrew's Society, the Hibernian Society (which was open to those not of Irish birth or descent), the Society of the Sons of St. George, the Philadelphia Dancing Assembly, the Schuylkill Fishing Company, the Philadelphia Club, the First City Troop, the Wistar Party, the Tuesday Club, and the Musical Fund Society.[58] Some of these organizations – the Masons, for example – were not exclusive, but leadership was ordinarily an upper-class prerogative, and only wealthy and prominent individuals could serve as leaders of several organizations at one time. Prominence in local society, indeed, was both a qualification and a result of multiple leadership. Put another way, the interlocking directorate of local elites enhanced the social standing of wealthy organizational leaders, and helped set these leaders apart from lesser folk who might have qualified for important positions in one or two societies, and might belong to several more, but could not claim a more general organizational leadership.

Upper-class multiple leadership did not necessarily link all types of local organizations into a single network. It is more likely that if all the interconnections among associational leaders could be sketched out within a single city, the result would be a small number of fairly distinct clusters of leadership groups, each with its own social implications, and each connected to the others by a small number of individuals. The leaders of the "evangelical united front" seem to have constituted one such cluster, and in Philadelphia the leaders traced by Schreiber through various cultural and social organizations may have been another. Yet a third may have been the men who sat on the boards of the city's major banks, savings institutions, and insurance companies. These profit-producing companies were not voluntary associations in the usual sense, but service on their boards was similar to service on the boards of philanthropic or cultural organizations, particularly in these early years, when local financial institutions were perceived as critical catalysts of a particular city's economic growth, and savings societies were formed specifically to promote ambition, sobriety, and thrift among the working classes. Philadelphia had a number of such institutions, and their leadership was drawn almost entirely from among the city's major businessmen. The board of the Bank of the United States in 1840, for example, consisted of 7 merchants, 3 gentlemen, an attorney, and 2 men not clearly identifiable in the city directory. They all lived on the most prestigious streets in the city, and some bore instantly recognizable Proper Philadelphia names such as Waln and Ingersoll. Taken together, the boards of all nine of the large downtown banks (capitalized at a million dollars or more) included 56 merchants, 9 gentlemen, 4 attorneys, a judge, a doctor, the president of a railroad, a broker, 3 grocers, 3 druggists (all wealthy manufacturers and wholesalers of drugs and other products), 3 other manufacturers, and 3 men who appear to have been retailers. One small downtown bank added a sea captain to 6 merchants, an attorney, and a doctor. On the board of the Philadelphia Savings Fund Society, the oldest such institution in the country, sat 10 merchants, 5 gentlemen, 2 attorneys, the agent of the Holland Land Company, and Condy Raguet, the founder of the society, who was also president of the Atlantic Insurance Company. Nineteen downtown insurance companies were led by the same mixture of big businessmen, gentlemen, and professionals. It little mattered if the name of the institution suggested a humble clientele. The board of the Farmers' and Mechanics' Bank consisted entirely of merchants, while the Mechanics' Bank was ruled by 7 merchants, 2 gentlemen, and a High Street stationer.[59]

A number of these men sat on two or more boards of major financial institutions. P. L. Laguerenne, a merchant who lived and worked on Chestnut Street, was a director of the Bank of Pennsylvania, the Spring Garden Fire Insurance Company, and the Atlantic Insurance Company. Robert Toland, a High Street merchant who lived on Walnut Street, sat on the boards of the Girard Bank and three insurance companies. Lewis Waln represented one of Philadelphia's most exalted families on the boards of three especially prestigious institutions: the Bank of the United States, the Philadelphia Savings Fund Society, and the Philadelphia Contributorship for the Insurance of Houses from Loss by Fire. There was also at least some connection between this cluster of institutions and others. Joseph R. Ingersoll, for example, was a director of the Bank of the United States, a trustee of the

University of Pennsylvania, and an officer of the Historical Society of Pennsylvania and the House of Refuge. He was also president of the Pennsylvania Academy of Fine Arts.[60]

Whether these interconnected clusters of organized activity by wealthy and prominent urbanites contributed to the cohesiveness and common awareness of the upper class or whether, as Lee Benson has suggested, it produced a set of "increasingly differentiated and competitive elites,"[61] is discussed in the next chapter. Here I turn instead to the question of whether distinct patterns of association are visible at lower levels of the social structure, and in particular whether middling folk created organizations that helped give substance to an emerging middle class. Perhaps it is most useful to note first that some financial institutions of the sort just described were led by men who occupied distinctly lower positions within the business community. On the same list of Philadelphia institutions in 1840, for example, were six small banks located outside the Chestnut Street financial center, mostly on the border between the city and adjoining districts, and generally identifying themselves with the districts, as did the Bank of Penn Township on the corner of Sixth and Vine, or the Southwark Bank just below Cedar on Second Street. The men who sat on the boards of these banks were, for the most part, merchants, retailers, and manufacturers in the districts, men who worked and lived at addresses that were not central or fashionable. Four men (out of fifty identified by occupation) were listed in the directory with artisanal titles, but it is impossible to say whether they were handworking craftsmen, manufacturers, or retailers. Three savings institutions and a loan company, two in the city and two in the districts, were led by a mixture of merchants, retailers, and artisans. Among the artisans was the hatter Charles Oakford, by this time a manufacturer and retailer of some importance. These ten financial institutions, in addition to three insurance companies led by a similar group of men, can be said to have had a middle-class leadership. What is notable is how distinct this leadership was from that of the Bank of the United States or the Philadelphia Savings Fund Society. Not one Chestnut Street or Walnut Street merchant or professional sat on any of these thirteen boards.

Middling people did not create or lead citywide philanthropic or cultural organizations of the sort that displayed and magnified the importance of the upper class, and that were likely to leave abundant records for future historians to read. But they did form themselves into small societies or clubs for the pursuit of literary discussion, music, sport, or sociability, and the records of a few of these organizations survive. For example, the Amphion was an amateur music society that met once a month in Philadelphia, first in a fourth-story room above the College of Pharmacy, then in a third-story room above the forwarding house of Freed, Ward, and Freed, and still later, from 1854, in a fourth-story room in a building on Sansom Street owned by Charles Oakford. Dues of $2 per month maintained a small treasury. Members mentioned in the society's minutes between 1849 and 1854 included two druggists, a merchant (from well outside the business center), a music store proprietor, a broker, a leather dealer, a jeweler, a conveyancer, and an accountant. Three members mentioned in 1849 were located five years later in the city directory as a merchant, a broker, and a clerk.[62] Several other Philadelphia societies were of a similar character. The Franklin Literary Union was founded in 1859 by twenty-seven young men, who stipulated that future members must be over eighteen years of age and "of good moral character," and who declared in the preamble to their constitution that "the improvement of the mental faculties is of the highest importance to our success in life." The society met monthly according to a detailed set of rules and resolved to publish a *Magazine of the Franklin Literary Union*. Dues were set at a very low 25¢ per month, but if this was an invitation for workingmen to join, there is no evidence that any did. Only 6 of the 27 charter members could be located in the city directory, apparently because most were as young as the preamble and constitution suggest. These 6 were a merchant, a conveyancer, 2 clerks, an accountant, and a law student.[63] The Round Table, founded in 1839 for "literary improvement of the members, and the encouragement of single blessedness," also appears to have been designed for youthful socializing, in this instance between kindred spirits of both sexes. Meetings were held Monday evenings in the homes of female members, and the mandated half past nine termination of "the regular business of the society" left time for informal socializing afterward. The identifiable male members were 2 doctors, a manufacturer, a grocer, a dry goods storekeeper, and a watchmaker. Another was listed four years later in the directory as a commission merchant.[64]

Associations of this sort are difficult to locate and reconstruct, as they played virtually no public role and generated documentary records that seldom found their way into historical collections. Diaries help uncover a few, and also help us understand what role they played in their members' lives. The diary of Henry Pierce, a clerk in a Boston hat store in the 1840s, is one such record. Pierce led an active social life while boarding with his employer in Brookline, and his diary is filled mainly with references to evenings spent calling on young ladies and attending the meetings, practices, and performances of two music societies to which he belonged: the well-known Handel and Haydn Society (led by the piano manufacturer Jonas Chickering),[65] and an unnamed glee club that had only twelve members. These associations took up a fairly large amount of Pierce's time and obviously were important to him, as they gave him a chance to indulge two major interests, music and socializing among his peers of both sexes. Pierce also belonged to a Bachelors Club and to an Odd Fellows lodge, but these organizations took much less of his time. Pierce's social life within and beyond these various organizations was passed largely, though not entirely, in the presence of other young clerks and nonmanual retailers of hats, dry goods, and stationery. (However, on one occasion his glee club met at the home of a Miss Hill, whose father was listed in the city directory as a harness maker, and on another he, a friend, and two ladies called at the house of a sash maker named Willard Clough.) What is perhaps most notable about this active social life is that organizations played an important role in it only while Pierce was young and single. Later in his life, as a married man, a partner in the hat store, and a homeowner in the suburb of Dorchester, Pierce (now in his forties) recorded an evening routine of euchre played at home with his wife and friends, interrupted by an occasional visit to the theater, or to Brookline to call on the widow of his old employer. Apparently the only organization to which Pierce belonged at this stage of his life was his church.[66]

While Henry Pierce was singing and socializing in his music societies in the 1840s, other young men were playing cricket and baseball. The clubs they formed were more visible than glee clubs or small literary societies, and historians have been able to analyze the social patterns of club membership and activity. What they have found is that both the clubs and the competition between them were structured largely along the manual-nonmanual fault line. George B. Kirsch observes that the most prominent cricket clubs in New York, Philadelphia, and Boston consisted of professionals, businessmen, and a few prosperous artisans, while each city had a number of clubs consisting almost entirely of artisans and workers. The three most prominent clubs in Newark, a heavily industrialized city, were all about 80% manual. In New York, the Brighton Cricket Club was white collar, while the New Brighton Mechanics' Club was blue collar. Manual workers often played on company teams alongside their fellow workers and under the leadership of their employers. According to Kirsch, white- and blue-collar teams seldom played against each other.[67] Baseball was organized along similar lines. Harold Seymour and Melvin Adelman each note that America's pioneer baseball club, the Knickerbocker Base Ball Club of New York, consisted almost entirely of businessmen and clerks.[68] The Eckford Club of Brooklyn introduced mechanics to baseball under the leadership of Henry Eckford, Brooklyn's wealthiest shipbuilder. This was a company team, made up of Eckford's shipwrights. The Excelsior Club of Brooklyn, by contrast, consisted of merchants and clerks. Nonmanual proprietors and workers dominated baseball in New York and Brooklyn during the 1840s, but by the 1850s the percentage of mechanics was increasing. This did not necessarily integrate the sport, as most new clubs appear to have been drawn from specific occupational groups – there were teams of policemen, of bartenders, of schoolteachers, of physicians, and even of clergymen.[69] Butchers' teams appear to have been led by wealthy food purveyors.[70] And if playing was occupation-specific, spectating was class-specific, at least according to Adelman, who argues that attendance at baseball games extended down no farther than "the more prosperous members of the middle class."[71]

Most of Adelman's and Seymour's discoveries are paralleled in Stephen Freedman's analysis of baseball in Chicago just before and after the Civil War. Chicago had a large number of company teams (fifty by 1870), which played other teams from the same industry. Hence, dry goods teams, consisting of white-collar players, played other dry goods teams, while blue-collar metals manufacturing teams played other blue-collar teams in their industry. Private teams were mostly white-collar. Freedman notes also that journalists in Chicago wrote of baseball as a middle-class sport, and contrasted it with more brutal working-class sports such as boxing. Baseball, to its early Chicago promoters, was a source of healthful exercise for desk-bound businessmen and clerical workers, and gave middle-class women a chance to enjoy countrylike outdoor air.[72] Sports of this type, organized into clubs along class lines, played outdoors in a relatively rustic setting and in a nonviolent manner, were in fact easily interpreted in terms of middle-class values and experiences. As Peter Levine notes, the "promise of sport" to antebellum cultural reformers and advisors was precisely that the playing and observing of it was bound up with middle-class notions of "character," health, and the release of pressures built up in the world of nonphysical work.[73]

All these organizations expressed the social affinities of their members, and it is significant that they followed so closely the manual-nonmanual divide. Other organizations followed it exactly by basing themselves on the occupations of their members – medical and bar associations, merchants' clubs, mercantile library associations, and, on the other side of the divide, trades associations and workingmen's cooperatives. Among nonmanual occupation-linked organizations, the mercantile library associations are the most interesting, as they helped socialize large numbers of young urban clerks into the commercial world. Their role was not to instruct clerks in business procedures but to indoctrinate them in the "commercial theory of value," to teach them the language of "character" and the bearing of the man of business, and to expand their personal contacts among merchants and other clerks.[74] Founded first in Boston and New York in 1820, mercantile library associations gradually spread to virtually all of the nation's major cities, and attracted large numbers of members in most places. By 1853 the New York association had more than 4,000 members, while those in Boston and Cincinnati each had more than 2,200. Most accumulated large libraries (the New York Mercantile Library Association's 37,000 volumes constituted the second largest collection in the city and the fifth largest in the nation),[75] and all offered numerous lectures by important figures in business, the professions, and public life. "The cultivated taste of most of the clerks," wrote *Hunt's Merchants' Magazine*, "demands a high order of intellectual repast."[76] This may or may not have been wishful thinking, but *Hunt's* was close to the truth when it evaluated the consequences of the clerks' management of the association in New York and other cities: "The management of the society's affairs by the clerks is a means of teaching them order, dignity, self-respect, business tact, and some aptitude even for political and other office."[77]

Hunt's identifies here an organizational didactic that applies as well to many of the other middle-class associations, and may have been especially important when it applied to young people. Don Harrison Doyle describes this same didactic in the context of the emerging towns of the Midwest, where most voluntary associations were led by merchants and professionals who were trying to establish themselves within a new and still fluid social order.[78] Organizations helped identify certain men as moral and dependable members of the community, and, more important, imparted to them skills valuable for the community's development. In Doyle's terms, these organizations were:

> ... schools to teach a variety of new skills, values, and a new social discipline demanded by modern society. ... The very process of creating new lodges, literary clubs, reform societies, or fire companies gave dozens of men within the community first-hand experience in drafting constitutions, recruiting members, presiding over meetings, public speaking, and resolving conflicts.[79]

Most of the middle-class organizations in the larger cities were in fact of the sort that generated constitutions and bylaws, and that operated according to rules that emphasized order and dignity. Most met indoors, in parlors or in meeting rooms, and those that carried their activities outdoors did so in the controlled and respectable environment of the cricket or baseball field, usually outside the city. These "orderly assemblies" contrasted with organizations that were most clearly linked to the working class. Trades associations and fire companies had constitutions, rules of conduct, and indoor meetings, but their most important and prominent activities occurred outdoors, and often were occasions of actual or implied conflict of a fundamental type. In both form and content the strike emphasized class divisions within society, and so, too, did orderly parades in support of strikers, although one purpose of the parades was to integrate labor agitation with more traditional and consensual forms of outdoor collective activity.[80]

The street brawls of fire companies and their associated gangs were more notorious in this era, and even more clearly associated with working-class violence. The fire companies of Philadelphia, as Bruce Laurie and others have observed, had once been led and staffed by wealthy and middling men, but after 1830 many were falling increasingly into the hands of workingmen. In the predominantly working-class district of Southwark, according to Laurie, firemen were nearly all journeymen by the 1840s, and each fire company in the district served as the principal means for organizing and carrying into the streets the community's most important political and cultural battles. The Weccacoe Engine Company, for example, was pro-temperance and Nativist, and often did battle with the Weccacoe Hose Company, which was anti-temperance and Democratic. Fighting was a way of life for the firemen of Southwark, and it is clear that young workers in the district joined fire companies with the prospect, and even for the purpose, of getting involved in organized street conflict.[81] It is less clear whether companies in more prosperous sections of the city were so violent, but it is suggestive that in the city proper, and in the inner portion of the Northern Liberties, several companies that had earlier been heterogeneous in their membership were becoming more clearly linked to a specific class. The Pennsylvania Fire Company, for example, which had been evenly divided between manual and nonmanual members through at least the mid-1830s, had become almost entirely nonmanual by 1847. Its identifiable members in the latter year consisted of six merchants, an attorney, two clerks, a bookseller, an ice dealer, a brewer, and a tailor.[82] The Philadelphia Hose Company, which appears to have been mixed in membership before 1837, had only two artisans among twelve merchants and clerks after 1853.[83] And the Delaware Fire Company, which was originally located near the business center and had maintained a heterogeneous membership of merchants and artisans through at least 1824, had moved by 1858 to the western edge of the city, and was made up almost entirely of workingmen.[84]

Urban workingmen also developed institutions that were not as formally organized as trades associations and fire companies. Susan G. Davis describes how young male workers in Philadelphia used traditional forms of collective action – masking, masquerading in fantastic dress, performing "rough music" – to stage parodic "street Christmases" on Chestnut and other fashionable streets. Elaborate parodies of militia uniforms, here and in various counterparades staged by working-class militia units, not only poked fun at the expensive uniforms of upper-class militia units but expressed the resentment of workers at their own forced service in poorly equipped and poorly dressed public units. This street theater relied little if at all on orderly indoor meetings of formal associations.[85] No written constitution or bylaws governed the operation of the working-class saloon, either, and the organization of boxing matches was accomplished entirely without a supporting structure of clubs or other formal associations. Yet the saloon and the ring were significant institutions among working men, the former functioning as a more or less private club for its regular customers, whose attendance, as Richard Stott notes, was assured in part by the small size and dreariness of working-class boardinghouses. Stott also points out that workers were not confined to a single saloon, but during the course of an evening made a customary round among several saloons, all of which catered specifically to a working-class clientele.[86] This was partially a matter of proximity, and it is possible that saloons were less thoroughly segregated by class in cities such as Philadelphia, where residential districts were less homogeneous than they were in cities such as New York. The single young workingmen who frequented the saloons did have their counterpart in the large numbers of single clerks, many of them country boys living in equally cramped boardinghouses. But clerks, unlike manual workers, had access to respectable homes, and the few diaries that survive suggest that at least some of them spent their evenings in domestic visits (and at literary and music society meetings) rather than in saloons. The ethos of the workers' saloons may have been a further impediment to their integration across class lines. Elliott Gorn's recent account of the development of prize fighting in the United States connects this violent sport with the culture of the saloon, and describes both as plebeian inversions of the emerging ethos of middle-class manliness. Where the middle-class ethos was based on "character" and was embodied in the Victorian ideals of self-control, morality, and steady productivity, the ethos of the saloon was based on "honor" among one's peers (particularly important, Gorn argues, among men in the "dishonored" trades) and was embodied in a rough masculine conviviality in which bravery amid bloodshed played no small part. "In the saloon," writes Gorn, as well as in the firehouse and the gang, "many working-class males found their deepest sense of companionship and human connectedness."[87] The working-class saloon, in short, was no place for a dry goods clerk.

Churches, lodges, and the classless ideal

There were, of course, institutions in antebellum America in which workers, clerks, businessmen, and professionals gathered in a fellowship that to a greater or lesser extent modified, ignored, or even repudiated the boundaries of class. The churches of the evangelized republic were as variable as they were plentiful; yet they were all organized in some fashion around doctrines of social inclusiveness and Christian brotherhood, derived largely from Scripture but based also on inherited notions of the individual church as a unified and unifying institution within the local community, where the rich, the middling, and the poor were expected to worship in a single communion. These doctrines were, in truth, more communitarian than they were egalitarian. Indeed, local churches most often supported social hierarchies through means that ranged from theological interpretation to the rental and assignment of pews, although the reconciliation between God's family of souls and Caesar's world of greater and lesser mortals was never an easy matter. Nor was the ideal of social inclusiveness easily maintained in an age of proliferating denominations and growing cities. By the middle of the nineteenth century even very small American communities ordinarily contained several churches of different denominations, while in the larger cities each of the major denominations was represented by as many as two or three dozen individual churches, located in neighborhoods of varying wealth and prestige. The already considerable tensions betweeen hierarchy and communion in Christian thought and practice were necessarily affected by these developments, which raise obvious questions concerning the church as a social institution. Did churches, by bringing people of varying means and circumstances into a common worship, ameliorate the effects of social disparities originating in the secular life of the city? Or was this common worship compartmentalized or trivial, suspending for a few Sunday hours if at all the divergence of experience and feeling that obtained during the rest of the week? Worse still, was the traditional common worship of rich,

middling, and poor itself breaking down under the pressures of con-
gregational multiplication in differentiated urban neighborhoods?
These questions are best approached not through the doctrines or
social composition of denominations or other broad movements, but
through the congregations of individual churches, where the inclusive
ideal met the realities of social affinity and urban space.

How did practicing Christians sort themselves out within the
churches of antebellum American cities? It is relatively easy to identify
a significant number of distinctly working-class churches within some
of the more homogeneously working-class districts of the city, and
still easier to identify a smaller number of well-known churches that
catered to the fashionably well-to-do (New York's Grace Church, for
example, whose sexton, Isaac Brown, played approximately the same
role in mid-nineteenth-century New York that Beau Nash played for
the fashionable society of eighteenth-century Bath).[88] A more balanced
view of the overall array of individual congregations can be gained
from the registers of Presbyterian churches in Philadelphia. Presbyterians were well represented among all classes in the city, and their
churches were found in all of the city's districts. The churches I selected were in neighborhoods ranging from fashionable Washington
Square and Walnut Street to heterogeneous Society Hill (adjacent to
the areal grid-unit examined in the preceding chapter), to plebeian
Southwark and Kensington. The memberships of these churches provide a suggestive if not a definitive view of the degree and direction
of change in the specific communities of the larger city's practicing
Christians.

Two facts stand out from the analysis of these church registers.
One is the quite different roles played by the churches of the plebeian
periphery and those of wealthier or more heterogeneous central
neighborhoods. The former, represented here by the First Presbyterian churches of Kensington and Southwark, were distinctly tied to
their immediate neighborhoods, drawing members from the few
blocks surrounding the church. Nearly every male member of the
Kensington church in the 1810s and again in the 1850s resided on the
half-dozen or so short streets surrounding Palmer Street, where the
church was located.[89] Southwark Presbyterians were only slightly
more dispersed around their church on German Street.[90] However,
the members of these two churches were not quite inclusive of all
Presbyterians in their neighborhoods. At least some of the few local
professionals and businessmen joined more prestigious churches outside the neighborhood, leaving the nearby churches with even more
consistently plebeian memberships than they would have had if these
men had worshiped locally. During the 1850s, for example, Captain

Josiah Homewood, who lived on Christian Street near the Delaware River, and Dr. Wilson H. Pile, who lived on Catherine Street near Sixth, walked or rode quite close to the Southwark church on their way to the Third Presbyterian Church on Pine Street ("Old Pine") in the city proper. In both Southwark and Kensington, a mere handful of nonmanual businessmen and clerks remained within congregations that otherwise consisted of artisans and unskilled workers. "Old Pine," meanwhile, and even more strikingly the First Presbyterian Church on Washington Square, consisted of professionals, business-men, and a smaller number of artisans, drawn not only from their own neighborhoods but, as the sabbath journeys of Captain Home-wood and Dr. Pile suggest, from less prestigious neighborhoods else-where in the city.[91] In transcending their neighborhoods in this way, these churches developed a Christian fellowship based more on class than on community.

A second pattern evident in the church registers is the increasing social homogenization of individual congregations over time. The Kensington church, already quite homogeneous during the early years of the century, merely remained so, but others, including the First Presbyterian Church of Philadelphia, became more clearly as-sociated with one or another social class. In 1830, fifty of sixty iden-tifiable male members of the First Presbyterian were professionals, nonmanual businessmen, and clerical workers (the other ten were artisans); by 1855 the proportion had risen to seventy-four of eighty-five.[92] The Third and Fourth churches, each of which had an even mixture of nonmanual and manual members at the beginning of the century, moved in opposite directions. By the 1850s, "Old Pine," still located in the midst of a quite heterogeneous neighborhood (it re-mains today at the same site on the corner of Fourth Street and Pine), was at least three-quarters nonmanual, while the Fourth Presbyterian, which had moved toward the southeastern corner of the city from its old site a few blocks from "Old Pine," appears to have become a congregation of unskilled workers. Actually, only five members of the Fourth Presbyterian Church can be identified with confidence in the city directories, a poor result that seems to derive from the un-derrepresentation in the directories of less skilled workers, in partic-ular those of the newer peripheral areas of the city.[93] These five were a plasterer, a drayman, a gardener, a laborer, and a worker in the "front office" of the Pennsylvania Railroad. The latter, one Charles Lombard, became a member in 1858 while he was living about one block from the church on Thirteenth Street. He remained a commu-nicant of this church for no more than a year. By 1859, Lombard, who still lived about a block from the Fourth Presbyterian, is listed among the members of "Old Pine," eight blocks away. Finally, there is the still more interesting history of the Tenth Presbyterian Church, a new congregation founded in 1830 at the corner of Twelfth and Walnut, four blocks north of the Fourth Presbyterian. Between 1830 and 1848 sixty-seven identifiable males were admitted to membership in this church, forty-seven of whom worked in the nonmanual sector. Eighteen artisans and two watchmen accounted for the other twenty. After 1848, however, this mixture was decisively shifted toward the already dominant professionals and businessmen. Between 1849 and 1863, not one identifiable artisan or other manual worker was admitted to the Tenth Presbyterian Church.[94] Church membership was shaped by many things, including proximity, old habits and loyalties, the effectiveness of individual pastors, and doctrinal disputes over such issues as freedom of the will, temperance, and slavery. What these few church registers strongly suggest, however, is that in the big cities it was also (and increasingly) shaped by class.

Churchmen did not always address the issues raised by this sorting of congregations by social class, and when they did it was not necessarily in a tone of regret. "The moment you enter a city," wrote the renowned New School pastor Albert Barnes in 1841, "you are struck with the almost entire exclusion of the extremes of the population from all access to the Gospel and the means of grace."[95] Was Barnes attacking or defending the middle-class character of his own congregation at the First Presbyterian Church of Philadelphia? These ambiguities disappear when we turn from churchmen to the spokesmen of another set of institutions, the fraternal lodges of the Free and Accepted Order of Masons and the International Order of Odd Fellows. Both of these organizations, which developed rapidly in size and significance from about the 1840s (the Masons rebounding from the nearly disastrous anti-Masonic assaults of the late 1820s and 1830s, the American IOOF growing along lines no longer dictated by its English parent after the separation of the two bodies in 1843), extended membership and all of their various honors and degrees to manual workers as well as to professionals, nonmanual businessmen, and clerks. Both pointed to this social inclusiveness (though in interestingly different ways) as one of their central virtues. In these and in other respects – the use of elaborately symbolic ritual and ceremony, the shrouding of purpose and procedure in secrecy, the insistent exclusion of women, to name the most important – the fraternal orders were quite different from the other organizations discussed here, including the churches, and at first view they suggest a very different answer to the question of how voluntary associations affected social networks and identities in antebellum America. How did they, in fact, relate to other aspects of the organizational revolution of these decades, and to larger patterns in American social development? Did the fraternal orders succeed where the churches did not in ameliorating widening social divisions within the cities of the republic?

Georg Simmel, in an essay written in the early years of this century, provides two very important clues to the interpretation of Freemasonry, Odd Fellowship, and other forms of fraternalism.[96] The first is his simple observation that the ritualization of structure and ceremony retards and even prevents change within these organizations, which we may take as a warning against seeking too close a correspondence between the specific symbols and rituals of the fraternity and the beliefs and practices of the less ritualized, more rapidly changing society within which the fraternity continues to exist in the generations after it was originally formed.[97] Can the hierarchies, ceremonies, and mystic symbols of nineteenth-century American Freemasonry, for example, be interpreted as aspects of nineteenth-century American culture when they were developed and essentially frozen in form in early-eighteenth-century England? A specific configuration of cultural and institutional circumstances, quite alien to the American nineteenth century, led a number of mainly aristocratic Englishmen to develop a mystical brotherhood within the form (but, importantly, not the substance) of a construction workers' guild – a spreading interest in science and more specifically in architecture as the queen of sciences, an older but still compelling association between science, magic, and brotherhood (shaped in turn by Rosicrucianism and latitudinarianism, both fashionable among literate aristocrats), the available precedent of the tradesmen's guild as an institution of secular fraternalism.[98] That all of the elaborate symbols, ceremonies, and rationales of Freemasonry were phrased in the language of a manual trade suggests little if anything about the early Freemasons' attitudes toward social inclusiveness, and in fact the early English lodges of "Accepted" (as opposed to "Practical" or real working) Masons contained very few workingmen.[99] Still less should this language have spoken to the social concerns of nineteenth-century American Freemasons, the mere inheritors of a frozen ritual whose origins most would have been hard-pressed to explain, except in terms prescribed by the ritual itself.

And yet this seemingly accidental configuration (from a nineteenth-century standpoint) of lofty purpose and manual work did reveal itself in a set of pronouncements by nineteenth-century Masonic spokesmen that went beyond ritual and the necessities of mere fraternalism. Over and over again Freemasons, and Odd Fellows too, contrasted the "artificial" distinctions of contemporary society with the more "rational" inclusiveness and hierarchy of merit that obtained within the fraternal order, and offered the latter as the ultimate reform society for an age of social reform.[100] This unambiguously contemporary reformism brings us, however, to Simmel's second observation, that the hierarchies of merit within fraternal societies, as well as their rituals and symbols, represent carefully constructed antitheses to the larger society, that "nevertheless repeat in themselves the forms of the greater structures." The secret society, writes Simmel, "borrows the sort of organic completeness . . . from the greater whole to which its individual members were already adapted, and to which it can most easily offer a parallel by means of this very imitation."[101] Hence, the antithetical hierarchy of merit apes the artificial social hierarchy it purports to reject, the effect being not to attack through ridicule and parody (as in the case of the counterparades of the public militia companies, or the dress and behavior of the Bowery b'hoys and g'hals), but to acquiesce in and even reinforce the existing social structure. The very secrecy of the lodge's affairs, I would add, the permanent shroudedness of the results of merit, gives the lie to pronouncements of the fraternal society's role in reforming society as a whole. The alternative order of Freemasonry or Odd Fellowship, in sum, was just that – a precisely and securely bounded alternative that acquired meaning and appeal only within the continuing social order it was certain not to threaten.

It should be noted that there were differences between the way Freemasons and Odd Fellows addressed these matters, and that these differences reflect their respective histories. Odd Fellowship, unlike Freemasonry, was at first a distinctly working-class movement, the first English lodges of the late eighteenth and early nineteenth centuries serving mainly as convivial societies for tramping workingmen.[102] Not surprisingly, the first permanent American lodge was founded by a handful of immigrant English artisans, who, under the leadership of a coach spring maker (later a porter cellar proprietor) named Thomas Wildey, held their first meeting in Baltimore's Seven Star Tavern in 1819.[103] For the first few years American Odd Fellowship was much like its English counterpart, conducting meetings whose purpose appears to have been confined to the provision of good fellowship and cheer to English workers who had made the long tramp beyond the sea. Here is a description of one such meeting, stumbled upon one night by two young men at The Three Loggerheads Tavern near the Baltimore docks in 1821:

> We found a large room in the second story; it was well lighted, and pretty well filled with people. At the moment a noisy com-

motion seemed to be prevailing; but by three vigorous blows of a
mallet, an orderly silence was produced. . . . All at once the silence
was broken, a deep tenor voice rendered "Old King Cole" with all
the original variations; the vocal imitations of the four-and-twenty
fiddlers, fifers, drummers, etc., were loudly given, amid thunders
of applause. This was followed by a soliloquy from Richard III, in
imitation of a great actor of that day. This was well received.
There was then a hubbub of internal commotion, which lasted until stopped again by the loud-sounding mallet. A sweet, delicate
voice then executed "The Poor Little Sweep." This was rendered
with a pathos that not only had the loud applause of the inside
audience, but also of the delighted listeners on the outside. At
this stage, my friend and myself concluded to obtain a more favorable position for the enjoyment of the treat. Accordingly, we
entered the bar-room and inquired, "What is the charge to the
'Free and Easy'?" The barkeeper indignantly replied, "There is no
free and heasy here, it's Hodd Fellows' lodge that is above."[104]

The character of Odd Fellowship began to change, however, after
American workers began to join and form lodges, and as numerous
businessmen and professionals who abandoned Freemasonry after
the Morgan affair sought less controversial avenues to fraternalism.
Meetings were transferred from taverns to halls, drinking disappeared, rules, rituals, and degrees of membership were introduced,
and conviviality was supplemented if not supplanted by a didactic of
self-improvement and organizational decorum. Aaron B. Grosh's *Odd-
Fellow's Manual*, which first appeared in 1852 (recall that Grosh had
earlier written a *Washingtonian Pocket Companion*), made all of these
changes quite explicit:

In the transaction of our business we pursue strict parliamentary
rules, that our members may be qualified for any public stations
to which they may be called by their fellow-citizens. And when
business has beeen performed, we indulge in social intercourse,
and even in cheerful and innocent hilarity and amusement. But all
in strict order and decorum, goodfellowship and prudence are
constantly to be kept in view. . . . [105]

Exercise yourself in the discussions of your Lodge [advised
Grosh, some pages later]; not for the purpose of mere debate,
contention, or "love of opposition," but to improve yourself in
suitably expressing your sentiments, and to render yourself useful
to the Order. For this purpose, make yourself well acquainted
with the rules of order and debate, that you may not violate
them. Note what is peculiarly easy and correct in the style and

manner of others, that you may engraft it on your own. . . . Be
sure to be always "in order."[106]

The Odd Fellow, once "a jolly, roystering blade," must now, according to Grosh, behave as a gentleman of "courteous speech and
easy manners."[107] However, this dramatic transformation of form and
purpose in the order as a whole, and of the ideal Odd Fellow as an
individual, was not accompanied by a complete transformation of
membership. Manual workers were neither driven from nor repelled
by Grosh's "bourgeoisified" Odd Fellowship, and as Brian Greenberg
has demonstrated in his study of Albany, New York, artisanal Odd
Fellows were to be found in numbers at each degree of membership
within each local lodge.[108] Greenberg points to the lodge as an "agency
whereby the worker was imbued with the viewpoints of other
groups," and, more specifically, where he was socialized into an ethic
of "diligence, sobriety, honesty, industriousness, and frugality."[109]
This suggests that Odd Fellowship attracted those mainly skilled
workers (were some of them actually nonmanual proprietors?) who
were most ambitious to rise in the world, most comfortable with
middle-class values, and least interested in maintaining plebeian loyalties, codes of honor, and life-styles. It suggests also that Odd Fellowship reached downward into the working class primarily as a
means of expanding the influence and imposing the values of the
middle class, rather than to replace the artificial distinctions of society
with a class-free fraternalism and a hierarchy of merit.

This interpretation is compelling, but risks losing sight of the cross-
class sociability that did occur in Odd Fellows lodges, and probably
misrepresents somewhat the elan of an organization that did originate
as a working-class social club. Nowhere in the literature that either
attacks or defends Odd Fellowship is it stated that bourgeois values
were brought to the order by businessmen and taught to workers,
and it is possible to find within the repeated assertion of a class-free
brotherhood and hierarchy of merit a hint of the old working-class
radicalism, if not of the Ricardian then at least of the "Jack's as good
as his master" variety. The same should not be said of the Freemasons'
fraternalism, however, which is conveyed in a somewhat different
tone. Albert G. Mackey, an important Masonic spokesman during
this era, began his extensive description and defense of the older
fraternity this way: "Without altogether abandoning those artificial
distinctions of rank and social position, *which the good order and well-
being of society require at all times to be observed*, the Mason meets his
brother Mason in the lodge upon one common level of brotherhood
and equality."[110] Here the antithetical brotherhood of the fraternal

society is so carefully bounded that one wonders whether Brother Mackey was more devoted to equality within the Masonic order or to the "artificial distinctions of rank and social position" beyond it. He was, indeed, explicit in his admiration of both. The latter were never so explicitly praised by a spokesman for the Odd Fellows.

The Masons, too, reveal a somewhat more discriminate fellowship than the Odd Fellows in many of their individual lodges. Masonic lodges were generally associated with the more prosperous and influential sectors of the community by those outside the fraternity (they were antirepublican, even aristocratic, cabals, in the minds of the anti-Masons), and in smaller cities such as Kingston, New York, surviving membership rolls indicate that the brotherhood was in fact less inclusive than Masonic spokesmen claimed it was. In Kingston during the 1850s, the one Masonic lodge contained 38 members who can be identified clearly on the manuscript schedules of the New York State and federal censuses. Of these men 11 were professionals (8 were lawyers), 5 were public officials (including a judge and all 3 of the men who served as sheriff of Ulster County during the decade), 17 were merchants and manufacturers, and 1 was a clerk. In addition, there was a wealthy farmer, a wagon maker who reported $5,900 in real and personal property on the 1860 census, and 2 artisans (a painter reporting $200 on the census, and a printer listing $100) who were the only identifiable members of the lodge who could have been considered workers. A handful of other members, less easily identified on the censuses, may have been handworking artisans, but the Kingston lodge was clearly an institution of the local professional and business class. Interestingly, it was also an institution of political activists. No fewer than 23 of its identifiable members were candidates for, or holders of, elected public offices (ranging from town collector to congressman), or activists in one or another political party. Some were among the most active and influential politicians in the town. (Brother Jacob B. Hardenbergh, for example, was the "Whig Warwick of Kingston," according to one local paper.) Membership in the Masonic lodge seems, indeed, to have been an important stepping-stone to political influence and public office in Kingston, and this, rather than the bonds of socially inclusive fraternalism, may have been the source of its appeal to so many local lawyers and businessmen. The term "inclusive" applies to the Masonic lodge of antebellum Kingston, but only to describe its nearly equal mixture of Democrats and Whig-Republicans.[111]

The Masonic order in the larger cities does appear to have been more socially inclusive, but here too it is necessary to qualify the idea of "one common level of brotherhood." At the level of the individual lodges, where Masonic fellowship was actually experienced, the social range was often much smaller than it was across the city as a whole. In Philadelphia, for example, the membership of three of six Masonic lodges that I sampled (from the two-dozen lodges that functioned during the 1840s), was restricted almost entirely to professionals, businessmen, and clerical workers who lived in or near the center of the city, many at fashionable addresses or in the hotels that catered to the business class. Joining Lodge 51 during the 1840s were 30 merchants; 11 retailers, brokers, and other nonmanual businessmen; 5 gentlemen; 10 professionals; a sculptor; 15 clerks, accountants, book-keepers, and salesmen; and only 4 men listed in the membership records with artisanal titles (2 tailors, an engraver, and a cake baker). Of these artisans, 2 lived on major streets in the heart of the down-town, and another shared an address with a fellow lodge member who is listed as a merchant. In Lodge 121, 79 nonmanual proprietors and workers (including 17 professionals, 35 merchants, and 12 clerical employees) shared Masonic fellowship with only 3 artisans. Slightly less exclusive was Lodge 91, where 8 artisans joined with 36 profes-sionals, businessmen, and clerks. It is important to note that a sig-nificant number of the members of these downtown lodges were clerical workers, and that most of the clerks in my sample belonged to these lodges. Here is another instance of how nonmanual busi-nessmen associated more freely with nonmanual workers than they did with manual proprietors, and another indication of where the most fundamental lines were being drawn in antebellum American society.

The other three sampled lodges were significantly more inclusive, but these, too, fell rather short of the kind of social mixing that Ma-sonic spokesmen claimed for the order as a whole. Lodge 2 combined 24 artisans, 3 sailors, and an oysterman with 61 men of the nonmanual sector. Many of the last were listed in occupations that were often lucrative, but, in striking contrast to the members of the lodges already described, few were residents of the central business district, and none lived at a fashionable address. This interesting omission of downtown businessmen did not derive from the location of the lodge itself, for Lodge 2 met at the central Masonic Hall on Chestnut Street, and its members were drawn in nearly equal numbers from both the northern and southern portions of the city. The pattern was even more pronounced in Lodge 158, which had an impressive mixture of 40 professionals, nonmanual businessmen, and clerks; 28 artisans; 7 harbor pilots; and 13 seamen and unskilled workers. Nearly all mem-bers of this lodge, including the professionals and businessmen, were drawn from the northern and southern peripheries of Philadelphia.

Lodge 211, finally, was somewhat different in that it attracted its membership almost entirely from Kensington on the northern periphery. Its 38 artisans and 6 unskilled workers met with 44 of Kensington's nonmanual proprietors and workers, most of whom appear to have been small neighborhood retailers (there was only 1 professional, an attorney, and only 2 men who were listed as merchants). Interestingly, no fewer than 14 were innkeepers – former artisans, perhaps, and quite possibly political activists within this clearly bounded and intensely political section of the city, where taverns were often the centers of political organization. The Kensington lodge may well have been a more plebeian version of the Freemasons of Kingston.[112]

In any case, the Masons of Philadelphia met within lodges that reflect to various degrees the social affinities expressed in the membership records and practices of the other, less explicitly egalitarian organizations discussed in this chapter. Yet it must be recognized that the pattern of class separation in the lodges was less clearly etched than it was in most other voluntary societies. Lawyers, merchants, retailers, and clerks did mingle with artisans, and even a few unskilled workers, to a greater exent in the lodges than they did in temperance societies, library and literary associations, baseball clubs, or even churches. If the fraternal spokesmen are to be believed, the difference was deliberate – those Masons and Odd Fellows who did belong to genuinely inclusive lodges sought an interclass fellowship that was increasingly difficult to maintain at work, in neighborhoods, at public amusements, and in other voluntary organizations, where society's "artificial" distinctions prevailed. It is more certainly the case that it was a *male* fellowship they sought, but I believe these two impulses were related – in opposition to social judgments, manners, and exclusive practices that revolved primarily around the home, and that issued increasingly from women. Despite frequent attacks, both fraternities insistently remained male during these years, resisting even the suggestion that they sanction separate auxiliary organizations for women.[113] In her interesting recent analysis of Freemasonry in Europe and America, Mary Ann Clawson notes that this gender exclusiveness was originally based on the notion, prevalent in the eighteenth century, that women were morally inferior to men, but that in the nineteenth century it acquired a new foundation as an "implicit alternative to the sentimental moral culture" that so emphatically dispelled the idea of male moral superiority.[114] The alternative did not always remain implicit, even as it related to issues of class. D. W. Bristol's *Odd Fellow's Amulet*, first published in 1848, includes a fascinating essay on "The Social Influence of Odd Fellowship," which contrasts the lodge with both the home and the workplace, both of which are described as places of disguise and deception. "The drawing room," no less than the place of business, "is a most unfit place to form an opinion of the character of men," writes Bristol. "Under such circumstances you do not see the man, you only view the drapery [an important image] which imperative circumstances have thrown around him." In the workplace these circumstances are the demands of maximizing profits; in the drawing room they are the demands of correct and socially exclusive behavior. The lodge, by contrast, is a liberating "middle region," where the disguise required by business and society falls away, and the true man emerges. Crucial is the presence of other men of different social classes:

> Here place around him men in every circumstance of life, and of every creed and profession, and before him a worthy object to enlist his feelings, and then you will have evoked the true man, and may study him at your leisure. Does he now enter into the feelings and interests of those around him? Does he act here, where all eyes except a few are shut out from him, with interest and energy? Has he forgotten the caste which the world has arbitrarily assigned to the men around him? Does he look at them with a fellow feeling, and honor them as men, not as rich or poor, but men who are acting on the same broad bases as himself, and whose hearts beat responsive to the same calls as his own?[115]

Note that this is not the rear-guard resistance of tobacco-chewing masculinity, but an alternative sentimentality that seeks a class-free fellowship uncomplicated by the "drapery" of the affluent home. Elsewhere in his *Amulet*, Bristol cultivates a still more sentimental, even morbid, but resolutely male image of fraternal benevolence, in numerous scenes where men shed tears by the deathbeds of fellow lodge members.[116] Again, as Simmel warns, antithesis was only partly oppositional, and ultimately supportive. The efforts by Bristol, Mackey, Grosh, and others to form a more decorous and sentimental fraternalism were part of a larger cultural and social transformation that was only more obvious in the parlors and parlorlike retail shops in which their wives cut such prominent figures. The lodges, in sum, were both exceptional to and characteristic of an organizational revolution that manifested, in nearly all its particulars, society's "artificial" distinctions.

7 Experience and consciousness in the antebellum city

How did antebellum Americans interpret the changes in routine social experience described in the preceding four chapters? Did the categorical boundaries we have seen taking shape in the daily lives of urban Americans manifest themselves in an awareness (and meaningful taxonomy) of class? More specifically, did those boundaries generate the perception of an emerging and ascending middle class, distinct not only from contemporary social elites and manual workers but also from the "middling sorts" who had inhabited the smaller, preindustrial, socially integrated cities of the eighteenth century? Did the term "middle class," or anything like it, come into widespread use during these years as a way of expressing a significant transformation in urban social relations, and in the meaning of intermediacy in American society?

Such questions provide the focus of this chapter. Against them, however, we must set others that refer to alternative sources of identity, in particular to what is ordinarily known as ethnicity. The same men and women I have discussed within social hierarchies can be understood as members of ethnic groups whose claims are generally assumed to have been at variance with, and even destructive of, class identity. How, in fact, did class and ethnic identities interact in antebellum America? And how did ascending class identities accommodate themselves to an equally ascending political rhetoric of classlessness? This question, raised in Chapter 4, must be raised again in the context of partisan loyalties that were shaped at least partly along ethnocultural lines. Did these ethnocultural alignments among the electorate leave room for a politics of class? Can we find any significant manifestation of middle-class consciousness in politics? If not, can we explain its absence without explaining away the middle class itself?

Experience: networks of class in urban America

Before attempting to answer these questions it should prove useful to synthesize briefly the discussions of the preceding four chapters, which point in a topically piecemeal fashion to increasingly distinctive class experiences in antebellum American cities. The concept of class, which refers first and foremost to the sources and consequences of hierarchy in productive and other social relations – to what becomes manifest in differentials of power, wealth, and prestige – provides the obvious principle of this synthesis. Yet the various experiences I have described can be synthesized not merely into social hierarchies but also into social networks, by which I mean the arrays of inter-actions characteristically experienced by the members of specific groups of people in their daily rounds – within the home, at work, on the streets and in public markets, in stores, taverns, restaurants, and theaters, at church, within the meeting rooms of voluntary so-cieties, at the homes of friends, and in whatever other public and private spaces people confront and interact with one another.[1] Clearly, these are complementary syntheses; moreover, the social network illuminates the hierarchy in a highly significant way. For what historians have called the transition from a "pre-class" to a "class" society was primarily a shift in the nature of inequality and of unequal social relations as the personalized, face-to-face hierarchies of the eighteenth century gave way to the more distant, categorical hierarchies of the nineteenth century, particularly within the larger cities. Hence, the experience of class in the nineteenth-century city can be understood in no small degree as the process by which people were brought together and kept apart, attracted to one another and repelled, and as the effect that resulting social networks had on the way people lived and perceived themselves as living in society. This is not to say, of course, that all personal encounters were of equal importance, or that class was no more than the sum of all social interactions. Nor does the delineation of social networks by itself address the issue of inequality and power within each relationship. But even simple aggregations of the daily round of people passed and met, ignored and acknowledged, smiled upon and argued with, can be suggestive of how significant the *presence* of diverging social groups were in each group's experience, and how that presence (or absence) shaped each group's identity, and, more broadly, its culture.

Understanding social experience in this fashion can tell us not only how class developed in the daily lives of city people, it can provide as well specific bridges between daily experience and the larger forces that were transforming the city. Social networks were shaped in spe-cifiable ways by industrialization and other aspects of economic de-velopment (changes in modes of production, to be sure, but also changes in retailing and other forms of economic activity), by the changing scale of the city, by the redistribution of people and institutions within increasingly specialized urban space, and by the development of greater numbers of more formalized institutions within that space. Specifying these influences is one way of reducing these large forces – industrialization, urbanization, institutionalization – to human scale, and a very good way of connecting them to the development of social classes. Hence, we can gain fundamental insights into the patterns and causes of urban social development by tracing, even in the imprecise and incomplete manner permitted by surviving sources, the ways in which city people came upon one another in daily life.

Let us begin on the familiar ground of the city's social extremes. Nearly all of the many accounts of working-class life in this era recognize that the restructuring of industrial production played a major role in physically separating workers from nonworkers in workshops, in dwellings, and on neighborhood streets. The enlargement of workshops and the expansion of outwork transferred most industrial production from the master's home or home-connected workshop, and reduced the amount of personal contact that could occur on a daily basis between the wage earner on the one hand, and the master's family (including in many instances the master himself) on the other. Removed from his employer's home, the worker now found living quarters in increasingly homogeneous working-class streets and districts, where his and his family's personal encounters were increasingly confined to other working people, and to the small shopkeepers, themselves often former manual workers, who served the neighborhood. Working-class neighborhoods never became islands, and in cities such as Philadelphia many workers remained on alleys that were at once distinct from and just behind the major streets on which more prosperous people lived. Even in New York, where hundreds of thousands of workers squeezed into the tenements of the distinctly plebeian East Side, *Harper's* Master Charley, who did not live on the East Side, could find street urchins with whom to fight, trade pocketknives, bring to tea, and in other ways distress his middle-class mother – newsboys, delivery men's assistants, the "nice boy" whose mother ran the little candy shop around the corner. Construction workers in their thousands still walked through and worked in every district of the city, and so did artisans and unskilled workers and peddlers of all sorts. But the direction of change was clear, and the extent of change, significant. Increasingly in the industrializing city, workers worked and lived among other workers.

After hours, workers were more likely to encounter each other in the commercial institutions that catered specifically to them. Particular theaters, minstrel shows, and above all saloons became working peo-

ple's preserves, and were almost certainly more frequently attended
by workers no longer beholden to their employers after the close of
the workday. Those who lived in boardinghouses must have made
quite regular use of these institutions, where, hardly less than in the
boardinghouses themselves, they met other workers. Voluntary societies provided an alternative venue but not usually a broader range
of personal associations. Workers joined fewer associations than did
middling and wealthy people, and those they did join were, with a
few exceptions, distinctly their own. Trades unions, fire companies,
public militia companies (not voluntary for most workers), many baseball and cricket clubs, Washingtonian societies, and the churches of
working-class neighborhoods, were largely and in some cases entirely
confined to working-class memberships. Again, the pattern was not
perfectly exclusive. Fancy men of the wealthier classes slummed at
workers' theaters and other disreputable places in the wrong parts
of town, and some voluntary societies – lodges, and one type not
discussed in Chapter 6, political parties – brought workers into seemingly egalitarian relations with men of the nonmanual sector. Even
here, though, first appearances can be deceiving. Political parties –
like the New York City Temperance Society – were organized by
wards, where most participants met most often with others of their
own social condition. Finally, even institutions formed by the well-
to-do to relieve misery, and to reestablish the traditional responsibilities of the rich toward the poor, relied increasingly on paid case-
workers and swept the homes and streets of the poor nearly clean of
well-meaning "visitors" from the world beyond.

Some workers, by no means all, did come to occupy a separate
social world within the antebellum city – their social networks reasonably can be described as consisting almost entirely of other workers. The culture that developed within those networks, a culture well
described by Elliott Gorn, Christine Stansell, and others, reflected the
physical isolation of workers and their families from the middle and
upper classes. "Honor" rather than "character," intervention rather
than privacy, defined the central values and domestic lives of this
separate "Sahara" within the Victorian American city. Can we specify
which workers inhabited this world? Clearly, the poorest and least
skilled were the most likely to live in the domestic milieux described
by Stansell, and the young and single (a large body, recall) were most
visible in the fire companies, theaters, saloons, and the outlandish
attire of Mose the Bowery b'hoy. Older, married, and more skilled
workers and masters can be traced through the streets and institutions
of the city with much less certainty. Butchers and other tradesmen
served middle-class customers from markets and neighborhood

shops, and small numbers of artisans (no doubt some were really manufacturers or retailers) are found on the membership rolls of organizations dominated by nonmanual businessmen and professionals. But my analyses of incomes and rents, households and organizations, suggest a significant degree of closure in these networks as well. Large numbers of skilled workers and handworking master craftsmen no doubt lived largely within the working-class world.

The social networks of wealthy and "old family" city dwellers were less powerfully affected by the transformation of urban work, institutions, and space, if only because these networks were already fairly clearly delineated by the end of the eighteenth century. Still, the very removal of most manual workers from nearby workshops and streets, along with the establishment or expansion of fashionably expensive residential streets and districts, the growing practice among the elite of summering in spas and other fashionable resorts, and the founding of new exclusive institutions such as the Philadelphia Cricket Club, made these networks clearer than they were in the days when they relied principally on exclusive dancing assemblies and private dinner parties. The main questions with respect to these networks, indeed, are whether they tended to divide within the upper class – replacing a unified patriciate with a series of functionally distinct elites – and whether any or all such networks were altered with respect to the exclusion or inclusion of new wealth, and of new, evangelically inspired values.

The issue of old and new wealth is one of long standing and dates from the antebellum era itself, when the social claims of the newly rich were frequently satirized in newspaper columns, magazine articles, and books by social critics ranging in their own social standing from city reporter George G. Foster, through *Harper's* editor George William Curtis, to Charles Astor Bristed, the Cambridge-educated grandson of John Jacob Astor.[2] Not surprisingly, the satirical edge of most of these contemporary accounts was sharpened by the success of social climbing in blurring, if not quite erasing, the distinction between the parvenu "shopkeeper aristocracy" and the "true, well bred, and unpretending aristocracy" of older elite families.[3] Social climbing was ridiculed, in other words, in part because it was not obviously ridiculous, and there are episodes in Curtis's and Bristed's fictional accounts that convey how established patricians accommodated to the aspirations of the *arrivistes*.[4] The most recent large-scale historical study of the urban upper class attaches considerable importance to this accommodation. Frederic Cople Jaher, in *The Urban Establishment*, strikes a convincing middle ground between those who have argued that the larger antebellum cities contained relatively closed and self-perpetuating upper classes that easily and quickly absorbed the very few who made genuinely new fortunes, and those who have argued that a formerly unified urban upper class was breaking down into separate functional elites.[5] Jaher's view is that the urban upper class became *more* coherent and distinct during these years, in part because it did remain open to new claimants who might have formed alternative elite clusters had they been excluded, and that this upper class retained and even extended its influence by continuing to espouse bourgeois values that other less wealthy members of the business community could admire. These processes occurred in New York, despite the difficulties of grafting aggressive and dour Yankee entrepreneurs onto a more retiring Knickerbocker stock, but they were more successful and complete in Boston, which attracted fewer wealthy or upwardly mobile newcomers from other regions, and in which the years 1820 to 1860 witnessed the amalgamation and nearly unchallenged ascendancy of a distinct, multifunctional upper class almost deserving the caste-name Brahmin.[6] Within its board rooms and its subscription libraries, on the streets of Beacon Hill and in the parlors and dining rooms of its exclusive homes, this Brahmin class (it was not, after all, a caste) established what was very nearly a single and precisely bounded upper-class social network. Jaher's discussion of this network accords almost perfectly with that of Ronald Story, who would add only that it extended to the classrooms, offices, and grounds of Harvard College. After 1825, argues Story, Boston's upper class increasingly monopolized Harvard and used its facilities "to engender elegance, self-discipline, and solidarity and to channel student contacts away from the masses and toward the broader elite community."[7]

We must not imagine that Boston's Brahmins lived entirely apart from middling folk, or from working people who were not their own personal servants. Nor can we gloss over the differences between Boston, New York, and other cities, for each had its own configuration of upper-class competition and accommodation. Jaher's argument succeeds so well in Boston because old-stock Yankees of established wealth retained something of the Puritan guardedness against idle pleasures, and because the city's new men of wealth, most of whom were also old-stock Yankees, were even more insistent that wealth carried with it obligations as well as privileges. The two sets spoke the same language of duty and restraint; hence, there was less occasion for disagreement over fundamental matters, including those raised by evangelical reform. New York, however, was a different matter, and here we may suspect that Jaher understates somewhat the cleavages caused by disagreements over such questions as the proper use of wealth and the propriety of embracing European aristocratic manners and values. The distinction that Foster, Curtis, Bristed, and others made between genuine and would-be aristocrats of old and new wealth may not have been as significant, after all, as the distinction between wealthy evangelicals and other serious-minded Yankees such as Arthur Tappan and James Harper on the one hand, and fashionable and pleasure-seeking aristocrats of either old or new wealth on the other. Bristed's Knickerbocker hero, Harry Masters, can talk to an English lord and a New York City *arriviste* with considerable ease and, even in the latter instance, not much displeasure. But could he have tolerated Arthur Tappan's or Joshua Leavitt's insistence that alcoholic drink was evil and that it was the prominent man's obligation to influence his inferiors, by example as well as by intrusion, to take the cold-water pledge? Harry is a Whig who professes a serious interest in political and social questions, but he is also an enthusiast for fine wines and sherry cobblers. He is also quite fond of fast horses, expensive cigars, and stylish (even foppish) clothes, and lives the life of an independently wealthy gentleman without a hint of guilt or self-deprecation. Harry's more serious-minded and socially retiring brother, Carl, is, at the same time, a "gentleman of the world" who "did not think 'teetotalism' necessary to prevent gentlemen from becoming drunkards," and who "took his regular exercise on Sundays as well as on other days."[8] Bristed's insider's account of the New York upper class, at once satirical and affectionate, amounts to a defense of this decidedly nonevangelical patrician life-style, and what is probably most significant about it is that no wealthy evangelical appears in its pages. Arthur Tappan, it seems, was as welcome in Bristed's "first set" as a clerk in a workingman's saloon.

Wealthy evangelicals may not have been "gentlemen of the world" in Bristed's sense, but they did assert claims to both leadership and gentility that were if anything more visible and compelling than those of any real-life Carl or Harry Masters. To them we might add an unknown number of other wealthy and serious-minded men of business – men such as the plain-living Philadelphia Quaker merchant Nathan Trotter – who had neither time for nor interest in the cultivation of society or its manners.[9] Outside Boston, such men may have constituted both a separate elite and a separate social network, one based on the exclusiveness of the board room rather than the ball-room. The structure of the New York City Temperance Society (and the large-scale businesses that some of these men ran) suggests that this was a powerful enough means of confining their associations primarily to other rich and prominent men, and to the families of such men. Yet we should recognize the likelihood that these elites did mingle somewhat more freely with like-minded people who lacked their wealth and institutional leadership, if only because they did not insist on translating their money into the "first set's" form of social exclusiveness. Arthur Tappan and Nathan Trotter were by no means middling men, but in their values, their behavior, and perhaps too in their network of associations, they may have confused somewhat the otherwise clear boundary between the city's upper and middle classes.

Although much less has been written by historians or by contemporaries about the middle-class daily round, the social networks of middling folk are less elusive than might be expected. The observations already made about the increasing articulation of working-class and upper-class worlds are alone suggestive of a more distinctive middle-class social milieu. But much can be added by synthesizing my more direct observations of changes that contributed most significantly to a new middle-class way of life. One of the most important, certainly, was the expansion and alteration of nonmanual work and work environments, and in particular the increasing differentiation of those environments within individual firms and within larger sections of the city devoted to retailing, wholesaling, banking, insurance, and other services. What needs emphasis here is not that nonmanual work became more distinctive but that increasing numbers of the men who performed it did so in each other's presence, and in the absence of men who worked with their hands. Those "white-collar" men who worked in the growing downtown were also more likely to encounter each other on the streets outside their stores and offices, in downtown restaurants, and in the omnibuses, horsecars, and commuter trains that brought many businessmen but very few manual workers to work each day.[10] By no means all of the city's nonmanual businessmen, professionals, and clerks worked in the heart of the downtown, and not all the manual workers were banished to other districts. Large-scale printing, light manufacturing, custom craftsmanship, and outwork remained centralized, and although much of it was performed in specialized subdistricts set apart from the centers of commerce and finance, there were workshops of various kinds on and quite near even the most fashionable retail streets. Charles Oakford, for example, maintained an upstairs hat-finishing shop close to his retail store on Chestnut Street. His sales and office clerks seldom if ever interacted with the workers in this shop during the hours of work, but we can be less certain they did not meet on Chestnut Street itself. What one can suggest is that Oakford's clerks were much less likely to encounter these or any other manual workers on the Chestnut Street of the 1850s than they would have been on the Chestnut Street of the 1790s, for this part of the city was now quite clearly dominated by businessmen, clerks, and their upper- and middle-class customers.

Oakford's customers were men, but many if not most of the new retailers catered to women, who, therefore, were present in large numbers in the stores and on the streets of the downtown shopping districts. Contemporary illustrations of these stores and streets are filled with well-dressed women, some of them accompanied by men and children, others alone or with other women. We can be sure that these were upper- and middle-class women, for not only does their dress suggest it, but the prices in the downtown stores were set to cultivate their patronage and not that of the working class. Shopping as well as work, then, and the networks of women as well as men, were affected by the transformation of economic activity and urban space. In this connection I would emphasize the interesting stylistic convergence between middle-class parlors and the interiors of retail stores that was occurring in these years. Middle-class women were taking charge of the important business of designing and furnishing homes that had grown much larger (more than doubling in size since the turn of the century), and that had become central to the new canons of domesticity and true womanhood. Women expressed their social identities and aspirations in part by placing themselves and their families within these larger and more expensively furnished homes, and especially within the elaborately decorated parlors where guests were received and entertained. As the parlor became the emblem of the respectable woman, and her characteristic environment – one might say her "office" – it is easy to understand why retailers who sold the furnishings of the parlor and the clothing to be worn there would design their store interiors to look like well-decorated parlors. The effect, in any case, was to create an axis of respectability, stretching from the parlors of upper- and middle-class homes to the interiors of downtown retail stores, a more or less unified environment designed in the several styles of Victorian elegance. Women who traveled along this axis remained within that environment, which served as a backdrop to significant and casual interactions between them and other similarly situated women, the men and children who accompanied them, and the retail merchants and salesclerks who served them. It is difficult to imagine many working people participating in these interactions. More likely cross-class interactions were between shoppers of the "upper ten thousand" and middle-class shoppers, retailers, and clerks. How frequently the former utilized the wide variety of well-understood forms of address and avoidance to keep a proper distance remains impossible to say.

The question of social distance – again so difficult to answer – arises in the context of other public spaces, and at other social boundaries, for when middle-class women left their homes they did not always go to fashionable downtown shops. Neighborhood shops were more varied in character, and so, too, were the people who bought and sold food and other goods in the public markets. (It is interesting that George Foster added humor to his accounts of the perils of urban life by depicting well-dressed ladies and gentlemen in crowded markets, where, according to Foster, they were increasingly anomalous.)[11] The question does not arise within certain other spaces, such as the theaters and restaurants that were becoming increasingly oriented to one or another social class, or in the context of the many new middle-class voluntary associations. Many of these groups met in the homes of their members, and it is clear that the home – more precisely the parlor within the home – was becoming the most characteristic and significant meeting place for middling folk, not only in their organizational capacities but even more commonly as evening or Sunday visitors. The home was, of course, the social environment from which undesirable associations were most easily excluded, and the desire to contain social relations within certain bounds was probably one of the wellsprings of the ascending canon of domesticity. In any case, middle-class social visiting does appear to have been growing more frequent. Contemporary diaries and other records are filled with accounts of such visiting, and we may reasonably regard the elaboration of parlors within the growing homes of the middle class as both a response to and a catalyst of an increased desire for extrafamilial (but intraclass) domestic socializing. Nathan Webb, who taught school in Boston in the late 1780s, spent most of his evenings alone. Henry Pierce, who clerked in the same city more than half a century later, spent most of his evenings in parlors, talking and singing with his fellow clerks, members of his employer's family, and other middling folk.

Pierce's diary chronicles these social evenings and permits as well the reconstruction of much of the ordinary daily round of a typical clerk in a big-city retail store. Pierce lived in the suburban Brookline home of his employer, Robert Bacon, along with at least three other young men who worked in the same store, two of whom were Bacon's sons. Up at seven, Pierce and his fellow clerks breakfasted at home and commuted, probably by rail, to the store in the heart of Boston's downtown. Bacon's store sold hats, caps, trunks, umbrellas, gloves, and hatters' materials, such materials suggesting that at least a few of its customers were artisans, but Pierce himself seems to have worked only on journals and ledgers, not at the sales counter. His diary includes no mention of the midday meal, but this must have been taken in town, either at the store with the other clerks, or at a downtown restaurant. After commuting home and dining with the family (Pierce makes no mention of this meal either, but resident clerks' pay generally included board as well as lodging), Pierce spent most of his evenings in middle-class parlors, either rehearsing for his music societies' concerts, playing whist, Old Maid, or Simon's Slipper, or calling on young ladies. Accompanying him on the latter excursions were one or two of his fellow clerks, or friends such as a Dr. Wheat (whose first name is not mentioned) or Joseph G. Oakes, a stationer. Occasionally, Pierce attended lectures and, presumably, the meetings of the Bachelors' Club and Odd Fellows lodge that are mentioned in passing in his diary. Pierce does not seem to have attended church every Sunday, and when he did his mind was not entirely distracted from the social preoccupations of a young bachelor. "Attended School St. Church," he recorded one Sunday in March, "& heard Mr. Soule & saw several other attractions!" Two such attractions, encountered not at church but in their own homes, appear to have been the daughters of artisans, but with these possible exceptions Pierce's associations, at work, at home, and during his evening and Sunday excursions, appear to have been confined to middling people whose incomes were derived from the nonmanual sector.[12] Pierce's was a middle-class world of ledgers and desks, finished goods and downtown streets, white collars and broadcloth coats, railway cars, music societies, and suburban parlors. It was a daily social milieu – a network of significant and trivial interactions – that overlapped but little with the upper-class and working-class worlds that were not so very far away.

Experience and consciousness: the evolving language of class

The diverging networks of the antebellum city were shaped by the kinds of changes that were difficult to perceive as they occurred, and by social affinities that did not require much thought or discussion. That these were matters of daily experience rather than of momentous choice, and of feeling more than of deliberation and discourse, is captured by the occasional comments of those who undertook to describe and explain American society as something different from that of aristocratic Europe, where classes were more tangible, more significant, and more frequently formalized in law and institutions. The Hungarian visitors Francis and Theresa Pulszky, for example, wrote quite typically that America differed from England in having no classes, at least in the sense that they understood the term. What it had instead, the Pulszkys added, was "coteries," in which "the family of the wealthy naturally associate with their equals in wealth, the poor with the poor"[13] – not classes, but networks of affiliation that are clearly grounded in differences of wealth. James Fenimore Cooper's native perspective also emphasized how naturally the "silent laws of usage" created patterns of attraction and avoidance, although to Cooper these were more purely matters of style rather than of wealth. Cooper's subject was the American gentleman, but his comments, only slightly amended, could apply to any of the city's emerging social networks:

> In all civilized communities, there is a class of men, who silently and quietly recognize each other, as gentlemen; who associate together freely and without reserve, and who admit each other's claims without scruple or distrust. This class may be limited by prejudice and arbitrary enactments, as in Europe, or it may have no other rules than those of taste, sentiment and the silent laws of usage, as in America.[14]

Yet Americans were not entirely silent about the changing character of social affiliation. During these years, social commentators would probe beneath observations such as these to discover an urban social order that seemed fundamentally different from what it had been a generation or two earlier. Several would grope, though often unconsciously, for a new social taxonomy that would describe more accurately a society in which older forms of affiliation and sympathy were being replaced by new ones (or, in the minds of the more pessimistic, by none at all).[15] And finally, writers on subjects only marginally related to the redefinition of urban society would make their own contributions to this new taxonomy, sometimes in the offhanded manner that implies the closest connection to common speech.[16] Do these experiments and "accidents" of social taxonomy suggest new forms of consciousness (or, to use Anthony Giddens's less demanding term, "awareness") that accord with and seem to grow out of the daily experience of diverging social networks? Was this divergence expressed in terms stronger than those offered by the Pulszkys and James Fenimore Cooper? Did there emerge a language of class, and if so, did this language address *all* the diverging social networks of the city, including the intermediate ones I have called a "middle class"?

Much earlier I observed that this term was rarely used in eighteenth-century America, and that the term "class," when it was applied to society, was as likely to refer to differences of gender, race, or age as to hierarchical social distinctions. The more customary language of "ranks," "sorts," or "stations" (there were other terms as well, including "estates," which had a connotation all its own) reflects a society where interactions between those of high, middling, and low rank (alternatively, "better sorts," "middling sorts," and "lower sorts") were common, and occurred in situations structured not by institutionalized hierarchies, settings, and rules but by perceived differences of status and traditionally understood rules of patronage and clientage or, lacking these specific ties, of privilege and deference. A deferential society requires personal, face-to-face relations of this sort and tends to dissolve where these relations are mediated through institutions or are attenuated across urban space. The eighteenth-century American city preserved the conditions where deference, and a "culture of rank," could continue to thrive. Its spaces and physical structures were small, and so were its institutions. Merchants' wharves, craft shops, public markets, street vendors, churches, fire companies, and public meetings brought people of all ranks into frequent contact, sometimes casually, sometimes in the context of specific vertical relations. If it is accepted that terms such as "ranks" and "sorts" imply a personal, deferential order, it can be further claimed that there was in the eighteenth-century city a congruence of language and social experience.

That congruence was preserved during the nineteenth century, for as social relations changed in the big city, so did the terms used to describe them. But the process was far from neat, and the result by no means clear, even at the end of the antebellum period. The sequence and timing of taxonomic development, moreover, suggests no simple relation between language and social experience. The earliest appearances of class terminology in American publications, for example, seem to have occurred shortly after the Revolution, in the context of the reassertion of traditional political prerogatives by merchants and other wealthy men. These innovations appear to have responded more to political events than to changes in the structure of daily experience. And if they were somewhat isolated usages, the more sustained use of at least some aspects of a class terminology – in particular the recognition of "working classes" or even a "working class" – began at an early stage in the reorganization of urban social relations. As early as the 1820s, *The Mechanic's Free Press* regularly identified its constituency not only as "producers" and "working-men," but also with such terms as "the producing class," "the working classes," and "the working class." It also printed, in 1828, the articles of association of the Philadelphia Mechanic's Union of Trade Associations, which included in its preamble a remarkable tripartite division of modern society, clearly distinguishing the "mechanic and productive classes" from the "middling classes" along the manual-nonmanual fault line, middling classes being defined as the "venders of the products of human industry." The highest class is identified in the preamble as "capitalists," and it is noteworthy that only they are accused of "ill gotten abundance," even though the associating mechanics made it clear in the preamble and elsewhere that producers stood apart from all those who did not work with their hands.[17] The effect was to establish two quite clear social boundaries, and three quite distinctive classes.

The Mechanic's Free Press did not settle the issue of how Americans caught up in the industrial and urban revolutions would refer to themselves and each other within society. Terms such as "working class" and "working classes" spread beyond the pages of the radical newspapers and were printed frequently throughout the antebellum period, often in a manner that implied widespread familiarity and usage in daily speech. But "middling classes," as we shall see, had a more difficult journey, and even "class" itself was forced to share the road with other travelers, including some very old ones. Note the variety of terms of differentiation in William Ellery Channing's 1841 analysis of the consequences of urban growth:

> It is the unhappiness of most large cities that, instead of inspiring union and sympathy among different "conditions of men," they consist of different ranks, so widely separated indeed as to form different communities. In most large cities there may be said to be two nations, understanding as little of one another, having as little intercourse, as if they lived in different lands. . . . This estrangement of men from men, of class from class, is one of the saddest features of a great city.[18]

"Conditions of men," "ranks," "communities," "nations," and finally "classes" – all in a few lines that underscore not only the separation of social networks in day-to-day urban experience, but also the continuing uncertainty as to how that separation should be defined. "Class" would eventually prevail (it was probably prevalent even when Channing wrote), but not without ambiguities and lingering rivals. Frederick Grimké's long volume celebrating American institutions, published in 1848, contains a somewhat troubled chapter on "The Classes of Society," in which Grimké posits a number of dichotomous "orders of men," including the young and the old, the rural and the urban, the parties of majority and minority, and "the most general division of society," namely, "the superior and inferior classes." Grimké's reference here is primarily to distinctions of wealth, but he quickly notes the connection between these distinctions and those originating in the industrializing workplace: "Capital and labor give rise to another division of society, not materially different from the classification into the higher and lower orders, but pointing more directly to the causes which . . . lead to their distribution."[19] Grimké, however, was no proto-Marxist, for it was his prediction that these worrisome divisions would be mitigated by the "communication of freedom to all" and by the continuing numerical dominance of "the middle class."[20] I will turn to Grimke's "middle class" shortly. Here all I suggest is that his use of "class" as the primary but not exclusive term for describing the most fundamental hierarchical divisions in American society was becoming quite typical. Channing's linguistic disarray was increasingly resolved in the direction suggested by Grimké's "Classes of Society."

The "working," "producing," "laboring," or "lower" classes were the most frequently evoked in this fashion, but after 1840 or so there appeared a variety of terms to describe, criticize, and defend the urban upper class. We have already encountered some of these terms – Brahmins and Knickerbockers in specific cities, and, more generally (though with primary reference to New York), "shopkeeper aristocracy," "first set," and "upper ten thousand," the last sometimes abbreviated to "upper ten." There were others that, like some of the above, betrayed their origins in satirical popular journalism – "codfish aristocracy," for example, and "shoddy aristocracy" (the term "shoddy" referring not to the appearance of those so designated, but to the fact that some of them made their fortunes making "shoddy" cloth or clothing out of a mixture of new fiber and reprocessed rags). Still other terms – "aristocracy," "society," "best society," "higher classes," "upper classes," and "upper class" – were more likely to appear in more sober books and journals.[21] The wide variety of terms does not suggest that American writers had difficulty deciding whether wealthy and exclusive urbanites constituted a class. On the contrary, all these terms emphasized the conscious exclusiveness of the rich and well-born, and their frequent repetition in widely circulating newspapers, magazines, and books only reinforced the separateness of the "upper ten," or "higher classes," or "codfish aristocracy" from the rest of urban society. It hardly needs stating that "aristocracy" and its variations were not used to suggest that the urban upper class maintained reciprocal ties of patronage and clientage with those beneath it in the social order.

Terms of social intermediacy appear less frequently in the surviving written record, and it is more difficult to assess either the currency or the meaning of such terms as "middle class," "middle classes," "middling class," and "middle class of men." To be sure, the Me-

chanic's Union of Trade Associations and Walt Whitman clearly identified their "middling classes" and "middle class" as retailers and
salaried (that is, nonmanual) workers within the urban economy,
meanings that fit quite well the emerging experiential patterns I have
been describing. But other usages can be found that do not fit so well,
including one or two that locate the middle class outside the city and,
by implication, identify it with a traditional rather than an emerging
social order. Frederick Grimké, influenced perhaps by sensationalist
critiques of the city as an increasingly attenuated noncommunity of
the very rich and the very poor, resolved the impending battle between the social extremes by assuring his readers that "the middle
class will forever outnumber both the others." Grimké was thinking
in national rather than local terms, however, and his "middle class"
is not a mediating urban presence but merely a vast rural counter-
weight to the socially and economically polarized city.[22] This connection between the middle class and the countryside could be made,
moreover, even before urban polarization became a popular literary
theme. A brief article entitled "The Middle Classes," published in
the *Journal of Health* in 1830, argues that both luxury and poverty
endanger good health, while "the greatest average amount of health
and vigour" is enjoyed by "those in the medium conditions of life,"
who are defined as: "The rural classes – the decent citizens – people
possessed of education and employment, but neither over-refined,
nor overworked – the farmer and moderate proprietor – the man of
action and enterprise."[23] The various phrases within this definition
are not necessarily mere elaborations of "rural classes," and one or
two – "moderate proprietor," "men of action and enterprise" – are
perhaps suggestive of urban rather than rural middling folk. It is
possible that the anonymous author was a city dweller. (The journal
was published in Philadelphia, and who but a city dweller could
believe that farmers were not overworked?) It is possible, too, that
the title "The Middle Classes" was an urban phrase shaped by urban
experience. Against these possibilities, however, we must set what
is most manifest – that this author applied the phrase first and foremost to country people.

Most writers did set their middle class within the city, but they did
not always agree as to the boundaries that distinguished that class
from others within the urban social structure. They did agree, as I
suggested earlier, that the middle class had risen to a position distinctly superior to that of the working class and could no longer be
spoken of in the same breath with the poor and "inferior" inhabitants
of the city. Only a few instances of the traditional linkage of the
"middling and poor" remain, the last, perhaps, in Walt Whitman's

Democratic Vistas, which calls for a democratic "programme of culture, drawn out, not for a single class alone, or for the parlors or lecture rooms, but with an eye to practical life, the west, the workingmen, the facts of farms and jackplanes and engineers, and of the broad range of women also of the middle and working strata."[24] This was, however, the cosmic Walt, who characteristically expressed his inclusive ideals in long lists of contrasting aspects of the American social and physical landscape. Could "middle" and "working" be intended here as contrasts? It would appear not, but Whitman knew to place middling folk in parlors and lecture rooms, just as he placed his salaried "middle class" in suburban homes. Less ambiguous were one or two earlier statements by more ordinary writers, who updated the conventional usages of the eighteenth century only by substituting "classes" for "sorts." Commenting on the recent financial panic and the continuing deterioration of the American economy, the introduction to an 1837 New York City directory advised: "Let the poor and middling classes of society, return to industrious and frugal habits, and learn wisdom from sad experience."[25] And four years earlier the author of a report to the New York City Temperance Society from its sixth ward auxiliary remarked that a tavern selling nonalcoholic beverages in the ward "might soon draw a necessary line between the temperate and intemperate, among the middle and lower classes, which has not yet been effectively drawn."[26] The context of the latter statement, in particular, helps explain the linkage of "middle" and "lower." The sixth ward, one of the poorest in the city, was an area where nonmanual proprietors would have been little better off than manual workers. In any case, these were unusual statements for their time. More characteristic of the era were expressions of social intermediacy that stood alone, or that made connections with the upper rather than the lower class. In a brief article on the "Philosophy of Advertising," for example, *Hunt's Merchants' Magazine* noted that "Fifty thousand papers circulated among the lower classes is worth less to the advertiser than five thousand which go among the middle and upper classes."[27]

The "middle class" or "middle classes" of nineteenth-century usage unquestionably were more exalted than the "middling sorts" of the eighteenth century. But this does not mean that everyone who used the more modern terms intended to exclude from the middle class all those who performed manual labor. *Hunt's*, we can be sure, did so, but others clearly did not. In its *Third Annual Report*, published in 1836, the American Anti-Slavery Society contrasted the "honest, hard-handed, clear-headed, free laborers, and mechanics of the North," which it called "the middle ground of society" (not quite "the middle class"), with the "purse-proud aristocrats and penniless profligates" that constituted society's "head and tail."[28] This was, to be sure, a highly political statement, and we can accuse the abolitionists of exaggerating the social standing of whoever they thought might be persuaded to join the antislavery crusade. More suggestive of common perceptions are descriptions of the middle class that can be separated from political rhetoric or arise in contexts that are not political or otherwise argumentative. A letter to the editor of the *New York Tribune*, published in 1855, is a good example. Arguing only that the Yorkville section of Manhattan's upper East Side receives too little attention in the press, it then sets out to describe the area, noting first that "we have the dwellings of millionaires and the cabins of day laborers."

> But, [it continues,] our population is mostly made up of the middle class, (if there be any classes in democratic America). We have a large sprinkling of builders, master-masons, carpenters, &c.; we have merchants and brokers, who do business "down-town;" printers, bookbinders, book keepers, clerks, journeymen of every trade, whose daily work is performed "down-town," have their abodes here.[29]

Similar to this description is one offered ten years later by Dr. James L. Brown, sanitary inspector of the eleventh sanitary district in New York's ninth ward. This was a West Side district with a predominantly native-born population. Dr. Brown found very few wealthy families there, "and *comparatively* few of the very poor or vicious." Instead, the bulk of the inhabitants consisted of "what may be called the middle class of people, composed mainly of trades-people, clerks, mechanics of the better class, cartmen, etc."[30] And a year after the publication of this report (we go only slightly beyond our period here), an article in the *New York Times* urged the construction of apartment houses in the city for those members of "the 'middle class,' if we may so call it," who are being driven from the city by high rents. By "middle class" this author meant "the class of professional men, clergymen, artists, college professors, shop-keepers, and upper mechanics – persons with an income, say, of $2,500 or $3,000 a year."[31]

These few items suggest that the tendency to perceive mechanics as members of the middle class may have been widespread, and to them we can add the very direct statement by the Providence Association of Mechanics and Manufacturers, noted earlier: "It is to this class to which, as mechanics, we belong."[32] The departure of this usage from the developing patterns of social experience should be neither denied nor exaggerated. It is probably significant that Dr. Brown's report and the *New York Times* article refer to "mechanics of the better class" and "upper mechanics," the latter referring also to an income level that would exclude mechanics who were not actually manufacturers, retailers, or nonmanual businessmen of some sort. The author of the *Times* article, if not Dr. Brown, may well have been thinking after all of a distinctly nonmanual middle class. The Yorkville correspondent to the *Tribune* clearly was not, but leaves us with a different puzzle by including in the "middle class" those "journeymen of every trade" who commuted from the upper East Side to the downtown, thereby attributing to them a daily journey that historians have established as beyond the means of wage earners during the 1850s. Accepting his terms (which is what the present analysis is all about), we are left with what appears to be an older view of urban society, more in accord with the preindustrial world of middling master and journeymen artisans than with contemporary social relations. (Note that all three writers employ the modern term "middle class" with some reluctance: "if there be any classes in democratic America," "what may be called the middle class of people," "the 'middle class,' if we may so call it.") The Providence mechanics certainly used the term with reference to the middling status of the preindustrial artisan, but it is essential to recall that these men were large- and medium-scale manufacturers, and that they identified themselves as "middling class" not to avoid a degrading association with inferior classes but to deny their journeymen's contention that they had become self-aggrandizing capitalists, insensitive to their workers' well-being and the traditions of their trades. In their confrontations with militant journeymen it served these manufacturers well to resume the guise of "mechanics," and to emphasize their middling status as well as their industrial role in traditional terms, distancing themselves from the merchant class in terms of wealth, power, and social position. The posture was not entirely insincere. These were men who had been trained as mechanics, and who had risen through their trades before rising above them. As Gary Kornblith has observed, they were "proud that they had once worked with their hands and that they no longer did so."[33]

I do not wish to argue away these descriptions of a middle class that does not follow the manual-nonmanual fault line, for they suggest a wider perception, not all of it originating in confusion over (or self-serving use of) the term "mechanic." Indeed, I would summarize this discussion by pointing not only to the emerging categorical language of class but also to the limits and ambiguities of linguistic change, and its imperfect relationship to changing social experience. Americans did shift decisively during these years from a social taxonomy that referred primarily to each individual's position within a hierarchical relation (a taxonomy of "rank"), to one that referred primarily to the existence of broadly homogeneous social categories (a taxonomy of "class"). Included in this process was the emergence and gradual refinement of the term "middle class," applied to a significant stratum within the urban population in meaningful contradiction to more or less sensationalized accounts of the polarization of the city into ever more inclusive upper and lower classes. Yet the process was imperfect and incomplete, especially in the evolution of terms for expressing social intermediacy. The first edition of John Russell Bartlett's *Dictionary of Americanisms*, published in 1848, contains no entry entitled "middle class." Neither does the second edition, published eleven years later, although the percolation of new usage is suggested by an entry entitled "Middling Interest," a political term, as we shall see, but defined in the dictionary as "the middle class of people."[34] The various usages I have described here and in earlier chapters indicate that Americans were indeed using the term "middle class" and its near equivalents, but that some of them were doing so apologetically ("the 'middle class,' if we may so call it"), and that even among those who used it forcefully there was less than full agreement as to what the term should mean. One of the most forceful social taxonomers of the era, George Foster, contradicted all the usages we have examined, and himself to boot. At one point Foster collects "the substantial tradesmen, mechanics and artizans of the city" into a "great middle class," and at other points adds to this class (also called the "respectable middle class") less substantial artisans and even wage-earning workers. These poorer artisans and workers, however, are also counted among the "working class," and, to add further to his readers' confusion, among the "great middle working class."[35] Foster's contributions were idiosyncratic. But they are symptomatic of the ambiguities that no doubt remained in common perceptions of the emerging middle class. On the eve of the Civil War these perceptions reflected, but also refracted through very old lenses, the daily networks of urban social life.

Alternative identities: class, ethnicity, and the classless republic

George Foster's inability to resolve the placement of mechanics within the social structure is traceable to his concern over the effects of large-scale Irish and German immigration on the fabric of city life. Foster blamed the immigrants for much of the squalor in Five Points and other poor areas of New York, and it was clearly the native-born workers – Mose and Lize among them – whom he elevated to the "great middle working class" and, on occasion, to the "great middle class."[36] This serves to remind us that class was by no means the only source of social identity in the antebellum city, that ethnic attachments were capable of exerting particularly strong claims on the identities and loyalties of at least some portions of the population, and that native workers' self-perceptions and perceptions by others were shaped in part by the dramatic increase in the numbers of foreign-born workers in American cities. It reminds us also that class awareness must be set within the larger array of alternative, competing, perhaps even class-defeating social identities.

There are at least four reasons for attributing greater power to ethnic than to class identity. One, certainly, is that ethnic identity is usually unambiguous, being derived from one's place of birth or the place of birth of one's parents or ancestors, and is especially clear when the ethnic group is insulated from ethnically mixed marriages and the prospect of rapid assimilation into other cultures. Another is the association of ethnic identity with, and its implementation through, particular symbols, rituals, myths, and other traditions, including some that are reflected in such everyday matters as dress and cuisine. These in turn can be (and in this era were) reinforced by two historically specific phenomena – the rise of territorial states, which for many people enlarged ethnic group membership and loyalty into citizenship and patriotism, and mass migration, which made the collision and defense of ethnic cultures more significant among both migrating and host populations.[37]

None of these aspects or sources of ethnicity underlies class identities. What the latter draw upon are the less precisely defined, less easily sanctified, and more diverse phenomena of daily experience, objectified to some extent through hierarchies of power and subordination in the workplace, through the material and social rewards associated with specific occupations and types of work, through styles of living and manifest values that come to be recognized as indicative of one or another class, and through more or less clearly bounded social networks. These class-shaping experiences do not always create and command group loyalties of an intense kind, and are particularly unlikely to do so among intermediate classes. Indeed, it is mainly among the upper and subordinate classes that we can find class-shaping experiences that resemble the sources of ethnic identity in their explicitness and power. Like ethnic groups, upper classes tend to be ascriptive; more accurately, their members try, within the constraints of prevailing ideologies and rates of mobility, to add distinctions of birth to those of wealth and style. To the extent that they succeed, upper-class identity becomes something like ethnic identity, an unshakable inheritance from one's ancestors and a source of great pride. Working classes, again like ethnic groups, sometimes succeed in mobilizing group loyalty by evoking well-understood symbols and myths in response to the hostility of other classes. The solidarities that result can be as compelling and even as enduring as those nurtured in the soil and symbolism of the old country. Middle classes, on the other hand, generally lack these sources of cohesion. They take shape, as I have suggested, through experiences that less frequently include such explicit evocations of the boundaries and character of the group, and of the consequences of belonging to it. In America, it is often claimed, even the highest and lowest classes do not usually succeed in these evocations, whereas ethnic groups generally do. But if this view accords greater power to ethnic than to class identity in a general way, it should be modified to emphasize the ways that ethnic solidarity contrasts most strikingly with class solidarity in the middle of the social structure.

Yet I would argue that the social identity of middling folk in antebellum American cities was in fact shaped more decisively by class than by ethnicity. Class identity, growing as it does out of the entire round of daily experiences and associations, is at the very least more continuous than ethnic identity, and if it made fewer explicit claims on the consciousness of middling folk, it was more fundamental as an expression of the presence or absence of those things through which individuals located themselves within society. Here it may be useful to recall not only Anthony Giddens's distinction between consciousness and awareness, but also Samuel Gompers's notion of "class feeling." Gompers, remember, regarded class consciousness as an intellectual construct that appeals mainly to theoretical socialists, whereas class feeling is a "primitive force that had its origin in experience only," and remains "one of the strongest cohesive forces in the labor movement."[38] To Gompers, this "feeling" of class, though seldom articulated as class consciousness, is nonetheless fundamental to the way working people identify with and respond to one another, and, more generally, to the way they perceive themselves as members of society. His insight can be extended upward in the social structure with no great difficulty, for if middling folk have less need for solidarity, they have no less foundation for feeling the commonality of their experience. Against the explicit identification with an ethnic group, therefore, we must set the often implicit but continuously significant "feeling" of the commonalities of class, grounded in daily experience and in the most fundamental circumstances of social life.

Moreover, the specific historical configuration of class and ethnicity in antebellum American cities makes the contest between these sources of identity, particularly for middling folk, less significant than

I have thus far made it seem. Several generations of scholars have demonstrated that most Irish and German immigrants of the period 1830 to 1860 entered into and remained within the manual sector of the urban economy, the Irish in particular concentrating in (and often numerically dominating) the less skilled jobs. In Boston in 1850, for example, fewer than 7% of the immigrant men and women listed in the work force were identified in manifestly nonmanual jobs and proprietorships, and many of these appear to have been peddlers, tavernkeepers, and petty proprietors of various kinds. If some of the artisans among these immigrants were actually manufacturers or retailers, a much larger number who worked in menial domestic jobs were omitted entirely from the occupational listings, so the true percentage of nonmanual immigrants was undoubtedly even lower. In contrast, fully 46% of the native-born work force was listed in manifestly nonmanual occupations, a figure that would surely exceed 50% if the proper number of "upper mechanics" were switched to the nonmanual sector. And with reference to the shape of the immediate future beyond 1850, we should observe that there were 3,392 clerks listed on the 1850 census for Boston, 3,241 of whom were native-born.[39] In other cities, the proportion of immigrants working in nonmanual occupations was higher than it was in Boston, but not by a great deal. In New York, among both sexes, it may have approached 15%, and it was nearly 14% among adult male immigrants in Philadelphia.[40] In the smaller city of Kingston, New York, it was 5% among Irish males and 11% among Germans. Only 1% of the immigrant work force in Kingston were listed in clerical occupations, while at least 64% of its Irish, and 36.5% of its Germans, worked in unskilled manual jobs.[41]

What these figures and others like them tell us is that ethnicity rarely created cross-pressures of competing identity for antebellum middling folk. The overwhelming majority of immigrants were manual workers, and the overwhelming majority of professionals, nonmanual businessmen, and clerical workers were native-born (and, we can safely say, of native-born parentage). This would change in subsequent generations, as the children and grandchildren of Irish and German immigrants would rise into the middle class while retaining ethnic identities, but there was not a significant amount of such movement before the Civil War. To an extent that was unique in American history – for there can be only one initial mass migration of alien workers – the intensification of ethnic differentiation and identification reinforced class boundaries. But did it also reinforce class awareness (or "class feeling") among middling folk? There were, after all, large numbers of American-born manual workers, and we have already described one American journalist's attempts to elevate these fellow Americans into something approaching the middle class. But it is clear that middle-class Americans were more disposed to distance themselves from native-born workers than to embrace them. George Foster himself, even while elevating native white workers over immigrants (and native blacks) in terms occasionally suggestive of a very broad native-born middle class, wrote most often of Mose and other native workers as occupants of a quite separate, even exotic, social world, a "Sahara of the East," where they lived "somehow – from day to day and week to week – upon the labor of their hands," pursuing the energetic amusements, defiant styles, and distinctive codes of honor that made them so different from middle-class people who spent their days in stores and their evenings in parlors.[42] The East Side, inhabited by both native and immigrant workers, constituted to Foster "the unknown regions of Proletaireism" in New York,[43] and little we have seen in other writings of the period, or in the behavior of middling folk, suggests that the latter identified themselves in any significant way with the native-born members of that socially distant and unknown world. Rather than elevating native workers into a larger and more amorphous middle class, or mitigating class boundaries by creating a cross-class community of native-born Americans, the massive migrations of the antebellum era – so closely linked with industrial development, changes in work, and the changing scale and structure of the big city – contributed to the distinctiveness of classes and the power of class identity.[44]

The class identity of middling folk may have been affected by a different sort of ethnic divergence, however, one defined by those fundamental differences of religious orientation – evangelical or pietistic on the one hand, liturgical or ritualistic on the other – that political historians have found to have been so powerful in creating and maintaining partisan alignments within the American electorate. Many of the "ethnocultural" analyses of political behavior reveal not merely a split between pietistic native Americans and ritualistic immigrant Catholics and Lutherans over such issues as temperance, public schooling, and, most obviously, immigration itself, but similar divisions, over a wider range of issues, among native American Protestants. These divisions were not closely correlated with class, which would seem to justify Paul Kleppner's conclusion that partisan affiliations "were not rooted in economic class distinctions" but were "political expressions of shared values derived from the voter's membership in, and commitment to, ethnic and religious groups."[45] Perhaps, too, they justify Lee Benson's broader statement that "ethnocultural and religious attributes, not economic attributes, mainly functioned as the concrete bases of group cohesion and social and ideological conflict," not merely in politics but in American society as a whole.[46]

Actually, both Kleppner and Benson may have claimed too much. Quite apart from technical difficulties involved in defining religious orientation and conflict within variable local contexts, in translating religious groups into blocs of votes within election districts, and in controlling for the effects of other variables, ethnocultural analyses of voting behavior have not proved uniformly persuasive in explaining political alignments in the antebellum period.[47] At different times and in various places, economic correlates of voting behavior appear to have been stronger than ethnocultural ones, and it is not always clear how or whether class and ethnoreligious identities can be separated for analysis.[48] The ethnocultural historians, in other words, have ruled out explanations of American political behavior based on simple class categories, but they have not demonstrated that class was irrelevant to politics.

Nor have they demonstrated that the "concrete bases of group cohesion" inevitably manifest themselves in a straightforward way in politics. Several historians of the working class, indeed, have described a tendency for class and ethnic identities among American workingmen to bifurcate, each identity expressing itself most forcefully in its "own" institutional and social setting – class at work and in the labor unions, ethnicity in the neighborhoods and in politics. The workingmen of Newark, according to Susan Hirsch, "rarely aired their economic grievances in the political arena; they did not perceive the political structure as amenable to working-class action."[49] But those grievances did exist, and created a class identity no less powerful than the ethnic identity that did find expression through politics. The "counterclaims of class and ethnic groups," to use Hirsch's terms, were resolved institutionally through "craft unionism and ethnic politics."[50] To examine only one of these institutions, therefore, in Newark and in other places where workers struggled against other classes and each other, is to gain a quite incomplete and fundamentally misleading view of workers' social preoccupations.[51]

The preoccupations of other groups, too, can be misrepresented by even very astute analyses of politics and politically relevant behavior. As Amy Bridges has shown in her recent study of politics in antebellum New York City, social identities and antagonisms may be excluded from politics for a variety of reasons; indeed, they are routinely excluded, for political institutions ordinarily "work to promote some solidarities and undermine others."[52] Partisan divisions, moreover, "are not simply the epiphenomena of 'natural' divisions" that do manifest themselves politically, for parties become phenomena in their own right, representing the interests and values of many different groups (and, therefore, representing no group perfectly), and acquiring styles and exerting pressures that derive from their own development as institutions. In Bridges's terms, they assume "an existence that is relatively autonomous from the social forces they organize. [In] the long run politics produces its own, *partisan* identities and solidarities."[53]

It is not difficult to understand why class identities, and in particular middle-class identities, should have been among those social phenomena excluded by developing political parties. One of the most distinctive features of American political history is the early date at which white workingmen were made part of the electorate by the abolition of property restrictions on the suffrage.[54] Another is the extent to which political parties responded to this expanded political community as they developed the purpose and means of electoral mobilization. There were many parties in antebellum America, but the enduring ones were those that built the broadest base of partisan loyalty, and they did so by mobilizing voters from all classes in as many election districts as possible, partly through the elaboration and extension of institutional machinery, and partly through the articulation of a rhetoric of classless democracy. Both of these strategies for the creation of mass parties left little room for the expression of class solidarities, which appeared with diminishing frequency, and in an increasingly localized fashion, as the parties developed within the peculiarly American context of a multiclass electorate.[55]

But if middle-class identity was suppressed in the parties on behalf of the "respectable worker" and victory in the sixth ward, it was accomplished with little sense of loss on the part of middling folk. Both the standing of the middle class within the nineteenth-century political system and the particular values and life-styles of the middle class made the political assertion of class unnecessary and unlikely. This is not to say politics was unimportant to middle-class citizens – quite the contrary was true in this era of intense political debate and extremely high voter turnout. Rather, it is to point out that the post-Jacksonian political system, nationally and locally, worked rather well with respect to public policies that touched specifically upon the class interests of urban middling folk – toleration and support of business enterprise, low taxation, improvement of urban services ranging from mass transit to sidewalks in downtowns and in emerging suburbs – while the rise of a more participatory electoral system and a more democratic ideology removed most of the deferential elements that had traditionally confined middling folk to a role distinctly subordinate to that of the rich.[56]

The one explicitly middle-class political movement of this era occurred before this favorable configuration of policy and process had taken form, and at a moment when political institutions were in a state of flux. The self-named Middling Interest in Boston arose at that unsettled moment when the New England metropolis was undergoing the transition from a town to a city form of government, and when traditional relations between the better and middling sorts were under stress from several sources, only one of which was the question of how voting in the new city would be conducted. The issue of the city charter had itself arisen in the context of disputes over the taxation of auction sales, the equity of local property assessments, the cost of local government, and the relationship between the courts and treasuries of the town and the county, all of which tended to place large numbers of middling Bostonians in opposition to the merchant-dominated, Federalist elite. The first of these issues had resulted in the ouster of the Federalist board of selectmen in the spring of 1820, and the rest brought to a head the old dispute over whether Boston, now a city of more than 40,000 inhabitants, should not finally surrender the town-meeting form of government. By January 1822 the voters of Boston had approved a proposed city charter and a further proposal to vote for city officials within individual wards rather than at Faneuil Hall, where, it was feared, established elites could most easily perpetuate their influence over voters. The resolution of these issues did not resolve the tensions that underlay them, and the first election contested under the new charter was fought at least partly over the issue of the enforcement of an 1803 law prohibiting the construction in Boston of wooden (hence, cheaper) buildings over ten feet tall. Around this issue cohered an electoral coalition of Republicans and dissident Federalists (supporters of Josiah Quincy, who had narrowly lost the mayoral nomination to Harrison Gray Otis in the Federalist caucus), who called themselves the "Middling Interest." Drawing support from the same less wealthy businessmen and master craftsmen who had fought against the taxing of auction sales and for the city charter and ward voting, this coalition succeeded in preventing the election of Otis and in forcing a compromise that gave the mayoralty to John Phillips.

The Middling Interest seems to have accomplished little else of a concrete nature, and to have disappeared from Boston's politics within a year or two. When Quincy was elected to the mayoralty in 1823, he was supported by what one historian has called "the already disintegrating Middling Interest."[57] It is in the disintegration of Boston's Middling Interest, however, that we may perceive the real political triumph of middle-class values and interests. The Middling Interest has been called a "vehicle of political and ideological transition" from the deferential polity of the eighteenth-century town to the more competitive nineteenth-century city of individual interests. Andrew Cayton's discussion of Josiah Quincy's mayoralty is cast entirely in these terms. Quincy, according to Cayton, "did not impose values or regulations from above," as might have been expected from a man of his social position operating in the traditions of Boston politics. Rather, he "accepted profit oriented individualism, greater political participation, and the legitimacy of decisions made in the political and social marketplace."[58] Whether or not this Boston patrician accepted the economic and political claims of middling folk, it is clear that in Boston and in other American cities there was an emerging political environment that made the appearance of dissident middle-class movements increasingly unlikely. Only partly was this a matter of satisfying middle-class interests, or of deflecting middle-class political participation into channels defined by mass-based parties. The individualistic, competitive values for which the Middling Interest had argued were those most at odds with sustained, explicitly class-based organization. Moreover, the social values, styles, and networks that gave the middle class its greatest coherence were not those that required expression through politics. The most important ones, indeed, were shaped into a canon of domestic privatism and intraclass sociability by the most influential large category of Americans remaining outside the electorate, middle-class women. Middle-class identity, in sum, should not be thought insignificant because it did not usually manifest itself in explicit ways in politics, however important the latter may have been in this first era of mass partisanship. Its significance was expressed in other ways, in the physical milieux and social round of daily life, in new styles and manners, and in a changing though not yet clarified and still half-apologetic taxonomy of social class. If "middle class" meant very little in the political arena, and meant somewhat different things in writing and speech, its meaning was clear enough, and important enough, in the parlors of middling folk.

8 White-collar worlds: the postbellum middle class

The most clearly defined social structure in American history, and the deepest awareness among Americans of the classes that divided them, emerged in the years following the Civil War. Yet, continuing industrialization, institutionalization, and other such phenomena would eventually confuse and erode class boundaries and alter the meanings of class. These contrary developments should occasion neither puzzlement nor surprise. Classes are not crystals in a laboratory jar, and class formation, unlike crystallization, is not a process that continues along one progressive path until all of its constituent elements have been recombined into a perfect (and, to the knowing scientist, predictable) form. Human affairs are less tidy than that. A term such as "class formation," therefore, is most accurately used not to invoke the progress of classes toward their ultimate and perfect form but to describe a society in which those forces that cause classes to take shape are relatively (and perhaps temporarily) more powerful than those contrary or differing forces that cause them to dissolve, or that create alternative experiences and identities. America before and after the Civil War was just such a society, but it would not remain so. By the last years of the nineteenth century the mostly formed crystals of class would alter in form and partly dissolve, in violation of the laws of chemistry but not those of history.

Industrialization, work, and class

In the final section of this chapter, I shall briefly discuss some of the ways in which industrialization and other aspects of economic development became forces of class dissolution rather than of class formation. I shall not venture far into this complex subject, however, or past the latter decades of the nineteenth century. Nor shall I discuss the immediate post–Civil War decades at great length in the earlier sections, for much of what happened to the social structure of the larger American cities during these decades was prefigured by developments of the antebellum era. It will suffice to focus here on a small number of new departures – on several differences of kind and degree that are essential elements of the history of the developing middle class. Among them are differences in the way the middle class of nonmanual proprietors and salaried prospective proprietors and managers was set apart from the working class of manual wage earners.

The post–Civil War decades are well known as an era of massive industrialization, of increasingly bitter conflict between capital and labor in railroading, mining, and heavy industry, and of escalating public debate over the consequences of industrial development and conflict. Focused on such issues as capital concentration, the role of unions in a free labor market, the morality and efficacy of strikes, and the mutual obligations of employer and employee, this debate was partly based on (and further promoted) the observation that the American work force had become profoundly bifurcated between the office and the workshop, and that manual work was an activity now performed mainly by factory hands and other wage earners in large-scale settings. This observation was at once well founded and exaggerated. Industrial concentration was occurring everywhere, most visibly in the larger cities and in specialized industrial centers. In Philadelphia, the number of industrial firms employing more than fifty hands nearly doubled between 1860 and 1880, and the proportion of the city's industrial work force accounted for by these firms rose from half to two-thirds. The proportion working in small artisan shops declined from 10% to only 7%.[1] The largest industrial firms, moreover, were growing to sizes never before seen, and in industrial centers such as Paterson, New Jersey, a dozen factories and mills employing a thousand and more manual workers could dominate the local economy and townscape.[2] On the other hand, the "disappearing artisan" appears to have reached a stable plateau during these years. In Philadelphia, the proportion of artisan shops within the array of industrial firms actually increased slightly between 1860 and 1880, as custom producers of expensive goods, small subcontractors to large shops and factories, and various construction and neighborhood service tradesmen resisted consolidation.[3] Not surprisingly, social critics who debated the industrial future tended to ignore custom shoemakers, neighborhood bakers, independent paperhangers, and other such artisanal survivors. Understandably preoccupied with factory workers and great capitalists, and assuming the continuing relocation of production from the small shop to the factory, their descriptions of the postbellum industrial workplace belie a more complex reality.

This bias suggests we look to other sources not quite so caught up in the polemics of contemporary social debate – sources that reveal in less obvious but perhaps more profound ways how far fundamental realignments had proceeded, both in the workplace and in common perceptions of urban-industrial society. One of the more interesting sources of this type is the United States Census and the new methods developed by Francis Amasa Walker and later census superintendents to represent the occupational structure in a more meaningful way. Walker was the first superintendent to address the identification and classification of occupations as a problem in modern economic and social taxonomy. Raising this issue of practical social science in a general way (Walker described his task as one of preventing "the use on the returns of those general and unmeaning terms which have hitherto embarrassed the work of compilation"),[4] his new methods nonetheless echo the concerns of contemporary social critics in their preoccupation with the ascendancy of factory production and the gulf between white-collar and blue-collar work. For the 1870 census, for example, Walker first divided occupations into four functional categories and then refined the taxonomy of those within the category he called "Manufactures and Mining." "Factory hands" and "mill operatives" were identified within specific types of factories and mills, while the term "mechanic" was abandoned wherever possible in favor of more accurate descriptions. More important, terms suggesting artisanal production – many of those ending in "maker" – gave way to those suggesting mechanized factory production: "operative," "operator," and "worker." Many of the "makers" that did remain in the revised taxonomy, moreover, were clearly industrial rather than artisanal: artificial flower makers; bag makers; blind, door, and sash makers – to name three of the first five.[5] Finally, in his instructions to census enumerators Walker specifically addressed the confusion between factory workers, artisans, and nonmanual proprietors within specific industries. "Do not apply the word 'jeweler' to those who make watches, watch chains, or jewelry in large manufacturing establishments," he ordered.[6] These were to be described as "gold and silver workers." And if this term clearly expresses the transition from artisanal to factory production in the precious metals industry, so, too, in only a slightly less obvious way, does Walker's treatment of those who continued to work in smaller shops, which Walker perceived primarily as places of retail sales rather than of production. In a striking departure from previous practice, no watchmaker, jeweler, or silversmith is listed in the 1870 census. All these former artisans are listed in the Trade and Transportation sector, as "traders and dealers in gold and silver ware and jewelry."[7] There are, indeed, at least a dozen types of "traders and dealers" who in earlier censuses would have been listed as artisans rather than as nonmanual businessmen.

Walker's efforts to separate and more effectively describe the non-manual and manual sectors in the population census were paralleled by a small but telling innovation introduced twenty years later to the manufacturing census by Carroll D. Wright. Earlier manufacturing censuses had compiled employment and payroll data from individual industrial firms, permitting crude calculations of average wages for male and female workers. Recognizing the growth of the managerial and clerical work force within manufacturing firms, Wright initiated the collection of data pertaining to salaries and white-collar employment, which he tabulated separately from data pertaining to manual wages earned according to time or piecework. The simplicity of the resulting categories in the published census underscores the distinction that was uppermost in Wright's mind. Proprietors and managers of industrial firms obviously earned a good deal more than office clerks, but Wright listed them in a single category. Skilled and un-skilled operatives were lumped together as well.[8] In the following census S. N. D. North refined this system somewhat by eliminating proprietors (as earners of profits rather than salaries) and by sepa-rating the salaries of corporate officers from those of general super-intendents, managers, and clerks. Clerks remained identified with management, however, and the manufacturing census continued to emphasize the distinction between those who earned salaries and those who earned wages – the worlds of the office and the workshop.[9]

The census was not the only document that was changing to suit the times. "Books of trades" had for some generations offered career advice to young readers, usually in the form of quite traditional de-scriptions of individual trades. As these books grew more and more anachronistic they seem to have fallen out of favor, and the genre may even have disappeared for a time. It reappeared, however, in quite different form during the last decade of the century with the publication in 1892 of Henry L. Everett's *What Shall I Learn?*, a full-sized and detailed survey of some sixty occupations. Everett's book includes a number of traditional trades but emphasizes newer occu-pations and work within large, modern workplaces. Where Edward Hazen and other earlier writers had focused on tailors and shoe-makers, Everett changes shoemakers to boot and shoe manufacturers and adds analytical chemists, mechanical engineers, designers, machine-tool makers, and a variety of other occupations found mainly within modern industrial enterprises. In each essay the author de-scribes the amount and kind of training required of young aspirants, the chances and speed of promotion from one level to another, the salary or wage to be expected at each level, and the amount of capital (ranging from very little to $100,000) required to open a firm of one's own. The newer scientific occupations are clearly the preferred ones, but Everett is careful to note that even the traditional trades "are now conducted upon scientific principles," so that "no person need feel that he has derogated his dignity by following them as a business."[10] Everett observes that in several of these modernizing trades (shoe-making and cutlering, for example) boys are first given an overview of the trade by working first in the company's *store* before they are given more specific manual training in the factory.[11] This may or may not have been common practice, but it is significant that Everett could quite offhandedly describe industries where the store was a better place from which to view the whole productive process than was the workshop floor itself.

The subdivision of productive tasks in modern industry made the various trades more difficult to illustrate, and Everett's is perhaps the first book of trades to be published without pictures of people at work. Illustrations of a particular trade or industry were feasible only in longer texts, such as the series of nine long articles on American industry that *Harper's Monthly* published between 1885 and 1890. Sensing the problem of comprehending the whole made up of so many parts, *Harper's* titled each article with the finished product rather than the industry or work process – the first in the series is "A Pair of Shoes"; the third, "A Glass of Beer"; the last, "A Suit of Clothes."[12] Here too, it seems, the best vantage point (and one particularly suited to the magazine's consumption-oriented readers) was the store, not the workshop. The latter is described in detail, of course, and is illustrated with a sequence of views, most of which depict very large, mechanized factory rooms occupied by large numbers of workers (Figure 8.1). What is conveyed most clearly is the large-scale industrial character of modern manual work, the fascinating fact of modern life that so much is required from so many men, women, and machines to produce "a pair of shoes" or "a glass of beer." Also evident in most of these illustrations, however, are the unfortunate consequences of industrial concentration. The factories are grim, ugly, poorly lighted places, where roughly dressed workers toil at heavy jobs. A reformist message may be implicit in these illustrations, but the articles themselves matter-of-factly convey the details of each industry's productive processes and employment trends. The illustrations were probably intended and interpreted in a similar way – as facts of industrial life that were accepted because they were more or less expected. Factory work, after all, *was* rough, hard, and dirty. The same kinds of images, indeed, can be found in publications that cel-

Figure 8.1. Factory production in the 1880s: sugar making (courtesy of Cornell University Libraries)

ebrated the triumphs of mechanization. The illustrations of mechanized hat making that accompanied a *Scientific American* article in 1876, for example, depict the somber surroundings in which the new machines were operated – unfinished factory floors, dark brick and block walls, a grimy, utterly blank window through which three felt makers standing over their machine have neither time nor reason to look (Figure 8.2).[13] These were, quite simply, the facts of industrial life and were understood as such by the middle-class readers of illustrated magazines.

All these descriptions and images focused upon work in trades and occupations that were being transformed, or were created, by the factory and the machine. One document of this era stands out in its depiction of small, nonmechanized workshops and work sites. In 1874, the Boston lithographer Louis Prang brought out a series of views for use in public schools, entitled "Aids for Object Teaching: Trades & Occupations." These lithographs constitute a kind of book of trades without text, a careful delineation of the tools and work processes associated with twelve occupations ranging from farming and housekeeping to shoemaking, carpentry, and lithography itself.

Figure 8.2. Felt makers, 1876 (courtesy of Cornell University Libraries)

Other than the first two and gardening, the setting and work of these occupations are clearly artisanal, and like the books of trades that preceded them the views themselves are in many respects anachronistic. But they are not entirely so, for in one important respect Prang departs from a tradition that stretches back to at least the seventeenth century. Books of trades and other early series of illustrations invariably depict artisanal trades in a single room, and the master, where he is clearly present, is always depicted as a manual worker.[14] Prang's views are very different. His apron-clad shoemaker (Figure 8.3) sits at the bench, next to a window (the tree beyond suggesting a more pleasant scene than the one that lay beyond the felt makers' window in Figure 8.2). His work, his tools, and the random clutter of the workshop are all quite traditional. What is new, and startlingly so, is the retail shoe store just beyond the open doorway, an uncluttered space in which a fully suited man, obviously the master of the store and the workshop, waits upon a well-dressed female customer. The shoe dealer is not emphasized, as the trade Prang wishes to depict is that of the maker of shoes. But that shoemaker is clearly a journeyman, and the proprietor of this quaint little shop is a quite modern nineteenth-century retailer.

Prang's tinsmiths are portrayed in exactly the same fashion – two aproned smiths in a cluttered foreground workshop, a suited proprietor waiting upon a lady in the background retail store – and his

Figure 8.3. Prang's Aids for Object Teaching: Trades & Occupations – Shoemaker (courtesy of the Library of Congress)

tailors add the further dimension of hierarchy among the shop workers (Figure 8.4). The foreground workshop is here clearly divided into two spaces, and the premises as a whole into three. On the left, facing left, is the skilled cutter, working in shirtsleeves but otherwise quite well dressed. Beyond the very lightly shaded doorway, this time in a background retail store that occupies the center of the illustration, stands the master tailor (or clothier), who wears his jacket while he measures a customer. The master's back is turned to the cutter in the foreground shop. On the right side of the workshop, visually separated from the master, the customer, and the cutter by a large, prominent stove, stovepipe, and coal scuttle, crowd four less skilled workers, two male sewers who sit cross-legged by the window, a female sewing-machine operator, and a male presser. All appear to be younger than the cutter and the master, none is as well dressed, and all face the light of the window and hence away from their superiors. In at least three ways – dress, placement within the premises, and orientation (age is perhaps a fourth) – Prang establishes the hierarchy of relations within this not-so-traditional tailor's shop. It is in part a hierarchy of manual skill, but here and in the other views it is above all a hierarchy that sets the storekeeping businessman above his handworking, artisanal employees.[15]

These are all incidental, though highly suggestive, clues to the changing realities and perceptions of manual work in the years fol-

Figure 8.4. Prang's Aids for Object Teaching: Trades & Occupations – Tailor
(courtesy of the Library of Congress)

lowing the Civil War. No doubt they take on more meaning when
set beside Washington Gladden's *Working People and Their Employers*,
William Graham Sumner's *What Social Classes Owe to Each Other*, Edward Bellamy's *Looking Backward*, and other items that form the familiar catalogue of contemporary debate over the consequences of
industrialization. No such debate raged over the changing character
of nonmanual work; yet similar clues suggest that Americans were
aware of significant developments in stores and offices that in some
respects resembled and were closely associated with those affecting
the manual worker. In his efforts to modernize the presentation of
occupational data in the United States census, for example, Francis
Walker devoted much attention to differentiating between types and
levels of nonmanual employment and to recording the presence and
growth of such employment in different sectors of the economy. The
1860 census had listed many different types of merchants, dealers,
and other proprietors but made very few distinctions between types
or places of salaried employment. Clerks in stores and offices were
combined in one entry, and the only office task recognized with a
separate occupational title was bookkeeping. Bank officers, who were
listed separately from bankers, were the only middle-level business
officials recognized in the census.[16] Walker understood how poorly
these few titles represented the developing worlds of white-collar

work. His 1870 census identified clerical workers and officials of various kinds, and tabulated their numbers within every sector of the economy except agriculture. Under Professionals and Personal Services, for example, Walker distinguished between clerks and copyists in private offices, clerks in government offices, and clerks in hotels and restaurants. In addition, there was a separate entry for shorthand writers (most of whom were still independent contractors rather than salaried office workers) and separate listings for public and private officials. Trade and Transportation included an even wider array of distinctions of the same sort. Bookkeepers and accountants in stores were distinguished from clerks in stores, who themselves were distinguished, for the first time, from clerks and bookkeepers in banks, express companies, insurance offices, railroad offices, and telegraph offices, all of which were listed separately. Commercial travelers (that is, traveling salesmen) were also listed separately, as were salesmen and saleswomen who were neither store clerks nor travelers. Middle managers, or officials, were separately listed for trading and transportation companies, banks, express companies, insurance companies, railroad companies, and telegraph companies. Finally, Walker recognized the growth of office work in the industrial sector. Under Manufactures and Mining he listed the clerks and bookkeepers of manufacturing establishments, and, on separate lines, the officials of manufacturing and mining companies.[17]

Most of these new occupational categories were justified by the numbers of people tabulated within them and, even more, by the rapid increase in these numbers between 1870 and 1880. Thus, there were more than 6,000 clerks and copyists in American professional offices in 1870, and more than 25,000 in 1880. Bookkeepers and accountants in stores increased from more than 30,000 to just under 60,000 during the decade, while those working for industrial firms increased from fewer than 6,000 to more than 10,000. Office workers in insurance companies nearly doubled, while those in banks and railroad companies increased at slightly lower rates. Commercial travelers nearly quadrupled from 7,200 in 1870 to 28,000 in 1880, and salesmen and saleswomen more than doubled from 14,000 to 32,000, while store clerks, by far the largest category of nonmanual employees, increased from 222,000 to 353,000. Those few new categories and company types that did not attract large numbers were dropped (shorthand writers and telegraph companies, for example), and, even in 1880, the surviving ones described no more than 7% of the nonagricultural work force.[18] But it is clear that Walker had identified a major growth point in the American economy, and a significant aspect of the evolution of work. Henceforth, it would be impossible to ignore the growth of managerial and clerical tasks and hierarchies within the nation's enlarging institutions.

Managers, salesmen, bookkeepers, and clerks were particularly numerous in the major cities, and constituted a higher proportion of the work force there than in smaller cities and towns.[19] It is not surprising that when New York–based national magazines approached the subject of nonmanual work they did so in the context of metropolitan institutions. During the 1870s, *Harper's* published several articles on the customhouse, the post office, the city's newspapers, and other New York institutions, focusing at least partly on the varieties and organization of office work within them. These occasional articles were prologue to a series of eight long essays written by Richard Wheatley, which ran nearly concurrently with the series on major industries. Wheatley's first contribution, "The New York Custom House," appeared in 1884 and devoted considerable attention to the organization of work in this large downtown institution, describing in detail how 1,538 mostly nonmanual employees functioned within eight separate divisions.[20] By 1891, *Harper's* had published seven more of Wheatley's articles, dealing with the stock, produce, real estate, and maritime exchanges, the chamber of commerce, the police department, and the city's banks.[21] The two series appear to have been deliberately juxtaposed by *Harper's* and represent between them a significant editorial statement concerning the course of modern institutional development. What is notable about this statement is that it required the balance-weight of essentially white-collar institutions. To these editors – who worked in the large downtown offices of a major industrial firm – one could not fully understand centralization, specialization, and other aspects of the transformation of work without looking at the office as well as the factory.

By the time the *Harper's* articles appeared, this thought was no longer new. Indeed, Wheatley's descriptions of newspaper offices, the police department, and other institutions were anticipated by sixteen years and more by Matthew Hale Smith in his widely read book *Sunshine and Shadow in New York*. The Adams Express Company, wrote Smith, was an "immense business" that required "25 to 50 distinct departments, each with an efficient head. Order, system, and despatch reign throughout the house." At the American Telegraph Company, "the headquarters smack of mystery. Everything is systematized, and order and quiet rule. The endless click of a hundred instruments sounds like a distant cotton factory."[22] Earlier generations found mystery in those cotton factories, but Smith now found it in a new kind of factory that no less systematically manufactured messages. Here was a resonant metaphor for a new age of white-collar work – a metaphor, it must be emphasized, for neither Smith, nor Wheatley, nor anyone else argued as yet that office workers and factory workers experienced the scale and structure of post–Civil War institutions in the same way. On the contrary, to these authors modern work was driving the white- and blue-collar worlds even further apart.

It must also be emphasized that the theme of the modern office was not a large one in the popular literature of any of these decades. The rapid growth of office work in the 1860s, the 1870s, and even the 1880s proceeded from a relatively small base, and would have to continue into the 1890s and beyond before it could be widely recognized as a phenomenon shaping the working lives of large numbers of people. Industrial management and office work in particular were in their infancy, as Alfred D. Chandler emphasizes, and it is interesting to observe that the *Harper's* "white-collar" articles of the 1880s focused on relatively old institutions that had grown larger, rather than on new institutions that were introducing new kinds of office work.[23] Missing, too, in the 1880s were two related themes that would later become prominent, with no small effect on the way work was perceived in relation to social class – the feminization of office work, and the emergence of a large corps of "proletarianized" office workers (and store clerks), performing routinized and sometimes mechanized tasks, receiving low pay, and lacking realistic opportunities to advance to higher levels of management or to proprietorship.[24] It is worth dwelling for a moment on the way these themes were deflected in contemporary discussions of women and young men at work.

Some influential journals – *Scribner's Monthly*, for example – staunchly defended the doctrine of separate spheres for men and women, and rarely depicted middle-class women outside the domestic environment.[25] Others, such as *Harper's Monthly*, occasionally attacked that doctrine and defended the right of women of any class to work outside the home.[26] Yet, even as late as 1882, when *Harper's* considered the question of "Money-Making for Ladies," its review of acceptable options included virtually everything except working in an office – taking in boarders, teaching, pickling and pie and cake baking, operating a lunchroom for ladies, china and seashell painting, market gardening, beekeeping, poultry farming, and shopping on commission.[27] The last option suggests also that *Harper's* was more comfortable having women in front of sales counters than behind them. Seven years earlier it had published a fascinating "Practical Love Story" of just such a commission shopper, a strong-minded young daughter of a once wealthy but now bankrupt Wall Street broker, who turned her expertise as a shopper into a growing business, fully aware of how unacceptable this would be to the society in which she had once moved. To *Harper's*, though, this display of ingenuity and pluck was more than acceptable, and when it awarded her the prize of marriage to a sensible young gentleman from within her old circle, the enterprising commission shopper was not immediately banished to the home. Rather, her husband was taken on as a partner in the business, and only the mention of twin babies at the very end of the story suggests an end to the heroine's business career.[28] Similarly enterprising (and similarly rewarded) female storekeepers, salesclerks, or office workers are, however, missing from the pages of *Harper's*.[29]

The "proletarianization" of nonmanual work made as little impact as feminization on the major middle-class magazines in the 1880s. When *Scribner's* described "The Progress of a Clerk" in 1881, it concerned itself only with the work, salaries, and opportunities of male clerks within banks and wholesale firms. Specialization and departmentalization were new themes in this article, but everything else would have been traditional a generation earlier. Bank clerks, according to *Scribner's*, were taken on as office boys at eighteen and then promoted to the bookkeeping, correspondence, or cashier's departments, depending on their aptitudes. Wholesalers' clerks began while as young as sixteen and after four years rose to become assistant bookkeepers, entry clerks, or shipping clerks. Those who became salesmen were well on their way to independence. Also traditional were *Scribner's* observations concerning the exclusive, intraclass character of clerical recruitment. Advertisements for vacant clerkships invariably attracted a thousand applicants, but vacancies were generally filled by the protégés of older employees and by the relations of customers. *Scribner's* noted with approval the opinion of one banker that the best clerks were the sons of poor gentlemen – boys who were not spoiled by wealth but who still possessed "a sense of honor and refinement of taste."[30]

If *Harper's* and *Scribner's* had looked a little more closely, they would have found both male and female clerical workers, especially in large stores, who faced very different prospects, and who came from very different social backgrounds. Even before the Civil War the dry goods palaces in the larger cities were creating low-paying, dead-end nonmanual jobs, and as these emporiums grew even larger after the war and evolved into department stores, the numbers of such jobs multiplied. In the 1870s and 1880s, R. H. Macy & Co. (not yet one of the great department stores, but growing rapidly) employed a superintendent, several buyers, and a few others who earned respectable salaries. Most of its staff, however, consisted of young salesclerks and cashgirls, many of them Irish immigrants, who worked for very low weekly wages and were seldom if ever promoted to higher positions. When Rowland Macy took an interest in one Abiel La Forge, a young man who had been his son's officer during the war, he found La Forge a clerkship with a wholesaler and brought him back as a buyer only after he had finished the training that could not be provided behind the counter of Macy's own store.[31] But before the last ten or fifteen years of the century, the numbers of dead-end clerical jobs, and the numbers of women working in any capacity in stores and offices, were limited. Of the 353,444 store clerks recorded on the 1880 census, only 23,722, or fewer than 7%, were women, and in New York City, which had the largest collection of department stores and dry goods palaces, only one of every eight clerical store employees was female.[32] Women were an even smaller presence in offices, accounting for less than 6% of the nation's bookkeepers, cashiers, and accountants, and only half of 1% of its office clerks.[33]

It is more difficult to tabulate the numbers of poorly paid white-collar workers, male or female, who lacked the prospect of promotion or significant increases in salary. When Scribner's traced the "progress" of young male wholesale clerks, it reported significant salary increases (which brought a teenage clerk's salary from $100 in his first year to $780 in his fourth) that did not involve promotion beyond clerical ranks.[34] It is likely that increases of this magnitude were typical for male clerical workers, just as they had been twenty or thirty years earlier. It is also likely that many such workers would continue to rise, if not to proprietorships then at least to higher salaried positions within the store or office. In the closest analysis of this issue, Carole Srole has found that one-quarter of a large cohort of young male clerical workers in Boston in 1870 had become professionals and independent businessmen by 1885, while a slightly smaller proportion had gone into (mostly skilled) manual jobs. The half that remained in salaried office work, however, were not necessarily static; indeed, Srole recognizes that a large number who did not become proprietors, as many would have done some years earlier, "found new opportunities as accountants, commercial travellers, managers, and head bookkeepers."[35]

The incomes that attached to those opportunities, as to the professions and business proprietorships that did remain open to aspiring young clerks, remained distinctly higher than those gained by manual workers. In this respect, too, there are only limited indications of convergence between the nonmanual and manual sectors, a fact that further underscores the sharp distinctions between nonmanual and manual work experiences that characterize the interpretations of Francis Walker, Louis Prang, Richard Wheatley, and others. Manual incomes did rise during this period, but only slowly and sporadically until after 1880, when rising annual incomes joined with falling prices to give wage earners their first significant gains since the Civil War. The rising nominal incomes of the Civil War decade had been more than offset by rapid inflation, while the long-term price decline that began shortly after the war was nearly offset by the declining annual incomes that characterized the economically depressed 1870s. In 1880, according to Clarence Long's thorough analysis of contemporary wage surveys, the average annual earnings of industrial wage earners were only $345, some 16% higher than they had been in 1860, but only 6% higher in real terms, and still well below what contemporary and later analysts regarded as the poverty line.[36]

These are crude averages, which do not reflect the wide differences of manual incomes earned in jobs of higher and lower skill, in larger and smaller cities, and in industries that provided more or less regular work. Nor do they reflect the profits of manual proprietorships or the total incomes of those working-class families who drew upon the earning capacities of wives and children. Most of these refinements can be found in Michael Haines's analysis of family income strategies among Philadelphia industrial workers in 1880. Haines finds a range of industrial incomes in Philadelphia, from the $1,255 earned by highly skilled and steadily employed iron rollers down to the $336 earned by ordinary factory laborers. (Eudice Glassberg, analyzing very similar data, reports an average annual income of $374.27 for unskilled workers, a figure close to Haines's factory laborers, and an average skilled workers' annual income of $578.67.)[37] Haines divides his sample into quartiles, the lowest of which averaged $304 in 1880, and the highest of which averaged $873. In each quartile approximately one in eight of these two-parent families supplemented its income by taking in boarders, while a wage-earning wife was found in only one in fifty. A much higher proportion, ranging from 77% among the lowest quartile to 50% among the highest, lived partly upon the wages of children. Haines does not estimate how large the contribution of these various sources was, but he makes it clear that the income of wives and children was in most families a matter of necessity, the product of a working-class life cycle that typically combined the declining wages of the older male worker with the increasing expenses of his growing family. Thus, to Haines, the supplementation of the primary worker's income was the customary means of averting the "'built-in' path toward poverty," not a vehicle for traveling the road to middle-class comfort.[38]

All the surveys of manual incomes in this era focus on wages – yet another indication of how well established in the minds of nonworkers was the equation between manual work and wage employment. But as we have seen, there were still independent artisans in the work force, manual proprietors who lived on profits rather than wages. Unfortunately, there is no reliable way to tabulate these profits, or even to separate handworking masters either from small manufacturers or from those proprietors the census had learned to identify as "traders and dealers" of particular types of goods. The closest anyone has come to this goal is Bruce Laurie, Theodore Hershberg, and George Alter's tabulation of the *gross* profits of the smallest industrial shops listed in the manufacturing census for Philadelphia in 1850 and 1880. At the earlier date these profits appeared to be little higher than the wage levels of skilled work, but by 1880 they had improved in a few trades to levels that were distinctly higher than skilled wages. Small boot- and shoemakers earned only $520 in 1880 (slightly *below* Glassberg's average for skilled wage earners in the same city and year), but butchers earned an average of $1,665, printers earned $1,058, and bakers averaged $914.[39] On the other hand, when we consider the rents, wages, and other expenses that had to come out of these gross profits, we must conclude that even the butchers enjoyed no more than a modest net income from their trade. In many other trades there were probably few independent handworkers who made significantly higher incomes than the skilled wage earners of related industries.

Even less systematic information survives concerning the profits of nonmanual businessmen, or the salaries of officials or clerical workers.[40] The scattered references to salary levels in business firms, and the somewhat more extensive lists of salaries in government offices, do, however, provide telling contrasts to the wage and profit data from the manual sector. They tell us, for example, that officials, and even clerks in government offices, were well paid. In 1871, the collector of customs in New York City was paid a salary of $6,000, while deputy collectors earned $3,000.[41] These were fairly high-ranking offices, but as Cindy Sondik Aron's careful study reveals, ordinary clerical workers in the federal government also received relatively attractive salaries in the years following the Civil War. In the Treasury Department, the vast majority of male clerks (83%) earned more than $1,200 in 1881, while a small number (8%) were paid more than $2,000. The Interior Department was slightly less generous, paying 70% of its male clerks more than $1,200, and 6% more than $2,000. Female clerical salaries had been set at $900 in 1865, but a few of the women who worked in these departments earned less (7% and 16%, respectively), while a larger number (21% and 23%) were paid more.[42] All these salaries, except the very lowest on the federal pay scales, were comfortably above the average earnings of skilled manual workers.

Also better paid were the officials and clerks of the private sector. Bank cashiers, according to *Harper's*, earned between $2,000 and $15,000, depending on the size of the bank, while in 1871 the male and female buyers in Macy's store were paid salaries of from $1,300 to $1,500, to which commissions on their departments' sales were probably added. Eighteen years later, Macy paid at least one of his buyers $1,820 plus 1.5% of his department's sales, with a guaranteed total remuneration of $4,000.[43] Clerical salaries were lower, of course, but senior clerks were paid significantly more than skilled workers. In Chicago, for example, Bessie Pierce has found references to salaries of $2,000 for accountants, and $1,000 to $2,000 for bookkeepers just after the Civil War, while Gwendolyn Wright reports $1,500 as the salary for a clerk in a Chicago insurance firm in 1880.[44]

Examples of this sort could be multiplied, as could those of significantly lower salaries paid to very junior clerks. I shall supply only one more example, which would seem to summarize this discussion better than any other. In 1887, a few years beyond the period I am attempting to describe here, *Harper's* printed an excellent article on workers' living standards in Europe and America. Among the several specific illustrations of American workers of greater or lesser means is a description of a master carpenter living in Brooklyn in a pleasant two-story house, with a personal and family income well above the norm for an American mechanic. The carpenter himself earns $900, while two daughters who work in a straw-hat factory contribute $712 between them. (One of these daughters, encountered by the author at a hotel on the New Jersey shore, begs not to be revealed as a factory girl to her friends, a bookkeeper, a medical student, and the son of a judge. She explains that they think she is a teacher, and that "they would be unpleasant if they knew that I am a factory girl.") The largest contributor to the family income, however, is a son who earns $1,092 as a clerk in a wholesale house.[45] At twenty-two, this clerical son already earns more than his artisanal father, and, more significant, the disparity is likely to grow. The income of the father, assuming that he remains a craftsman and does not become a contractor of other people's labor, has almost surely peaked – the work of his own hands will bring him no more than the $900 he makes now. Indeed, it will bring him less as age slows him down. The son's income, on the other hand, is likely to rise well beyond its present level, even if he becomes no more than a salesman, a bookkeeper, or even a senior clerk. If he becomes a businessman in his own right, it could climb much higher. No master artisan who remained at his bench, and certainly no operative who toiled each day in a factory, could match these prospects.

Middle-class suburbs

One of the most notable developments of the post–Civil War era was the manner in which the continuing disparity between nonmanual and manual incomes was expressed in the relocation of homes within an increasingly class-segregated metropolis. Two or three decades of accelerating suburbanization by wealthy city dwellers had by this time redefined the character of the urban periphery and had added the suburban home to the list of desirable consumer goods for the non-manual middle class. This was by no means a sudden process, and actual suburbanization by the nonwealthy before the Civil War appears to have been limited both by the availability of the right kinds of housing and transportation, and by a widespread desire to remain in the city, close to one's place of employment. The latter should not be underestimated. When New York journalists, writing both before and after the war, observed that large numbers of middling people were relocating their homes outside of lower and middle Manhattan, they invariably stressed the push of high city prices rather than the pull of suburban homes, lawns, and neighborhoods. "We have now in New York only the rich and the poor," wrote *Scribner's* in 1873, in language of the sort we will have to return to later. "The middle class, who cannot live among the rich, and will not live among the poor, . . . go out of the city to find their houses."[46] This was flight, not the eager pursuit of the suburban dream. Yet by the time those lines were published, that dream was reshaping middle-class conceptions of the good life and was contributing, even in less expensive cities, to a dramatic upsurge of middle-class suburbanization.

After 1873, according to Sam Bass Warner, new home construction by Boston's "central middle class" was located exclusively in the sub-urbs, and the number of dwellings in the three emerging suburbs of Dorchester, Roxbury, and West Roxbury increased during the decade from 8,545 to 13,448, despite the adverse effects of the depression that lasted nearly to the decade's end. Prosperity, streetcar electrifi-cation, and other factors increased the pace of middle-class subur-banization after 1880 (Warner's three "streetcar suburbs" contained 31,059 dwellings in 1900), but the pattern was established during the 1870s.[47] Impelling this impressive migration, according to Warner, were not only reactions to the expensive, congested, and hostile city, but the increasingly compelling attractions of suburban life, expressed through a "rural ideal" that was more in accord with middle-class values than with the values of earlier, more affluent suburbanites. "In this new land," writes Warner, "the rural ideal, by its emphasis on the pleasures of private family life, on the security of a small community setting, and on the enjoyment of natural surroundings, encouraged the middle class to build a wholly new residential environment: the modern suburb."[48] Others have stressed the domestic rather than the rural aspects of this ideal, but there is little dissent from Warner's observation that middling folk were now moving out from the city because they wanted to.[49]

The new middle-class suburbs greatly increased areal class segregation in the metropolis. As Warner explains, only families who enjoyed the higher incomes of the nonmanual sector could support a comfortable way of life on one income; hence, only they could locate their homes four, five, or six miles out from the city center along the arterial streetcar lines, well beyond the outer limits of the crosstown lines that most multiple-earner families required for the daily commutation of all of its working members.[50] In these more distant parts of the new suburbs, physical reality best conformed to the rural ideal and permitted the larger lawns, detached houses, and architectural styles that had been laid down on a larger individual scale by wealthier suburban predecessors.[51] It also permitted the most distinct physical separation from the urban working classes, a generally unstated motive that nonetheless may have significantly increased the appeal of the "rural ideal." By the end of the century the attractive detached suburban house, set within a homogeneous neighborhood of commuting businessmen, professionals, officials, and senior clerical workers, had become one of the principal molders of middle-class life, and one of its most powerful symbols.

In the earlier stages of post–Civil War suburbanization, however, middle-class families did not always move so far or to areas that were so rural, and when they built new homes they did not necessarily abandon urban forms. Theodore Hershberg and several of his colleagues have shown that in Philadelphia, which was expanding as rapidly as Boston (the authors estimate that one-third of the buildings extant in Philadelphia in 1880 had been built since 1870), a large majority of the white-collar workers of several selected industries traveled less than one mile to and from work. These officials and clerks did commute greater distances than did manual workers in the same industries, but it is clear that most of them either continued to live in relatively centralized neighborhoods or found homes within a less distant urban periphery.[52] Significant new areas of middle-class settlement were in fact opening up on the immediate periphery of the city, conforming only in part to the type of suburb that later became so closely associated with the middle class. Were they neighborhoods of a new type, or did they merely extend the spatial and physical patterns of the inner city? To what extent, and in what ways, did they physically separate the middle and working classes? These new areas of the expanding metropolis require a closer look if we are to understand fully the ways in which middling folk searched for and defined acceptable living space.

Before examining one such area, it will be useful to look once more at the central, semiperipheral, and suburban neighborhoods of Philadelphia that have been described in some detail through the manuscript schedules of the 1860 census. Had these neighborhoods changed in character by 1880, and do any changes we find help illuminate the process of middle-class movement to and beyond the urban periphery? The most central area in our earlier analysis, the grid-unit lying between Chestnut and Walnut Streets below Seventh, had certainly changed, for by 1880 the expansion of business and the erection of new business structures such as the large *Public Ledger* Building at Sixth and Chestnut left it nearly empty of residents. Only 31 households remained in this downtown grid-unit, 7 of them headed by janitors who probably lived in quarters within commercial buildings. Even the residential hotels had gone, although there were at least two nearby that continued to serve an exclusively business clientele.[53] This was, of course, merely the latest phase of a long process of downtown depopulation that in every city transformed the old urban core, once full of both businesses and homes, into a Central Business District (or CBD, as the geographers say) that was workplace to many and home to none.

Outside the immediate downtown, however, neighborhoods became more rather than less heavily populated, and some were changing in character. In nearby Society Hill, the grid-unit centering on Pine Street from above Second to Fourth contained many more households on each of its streets and alleys, and within these households were larger numbers of boarders and resident sons who were members of the work force.[54] The greater density of the grid-unit is clearly associated with a downward shift in its class composition, although many nonmanual businessmen and employees remained, and there was still a hierarchy of streets. Pine Street was still dominated by nonmanual businessmen, professionals, and office workers, although it may be significant that many of the merchants and professionals were older men who had retired or were approaching retirement age. Stampers Street, the narrow alley behind Pine, was still filled with laborers and other manual workers (as was Cypress, the other alley in this grid-unit), in striking contrast to the residents of the broader and more handsome street a few yards away. As in 1860, the commercial north-south streets, Third and Fourth, contained a mixture of nonmanual and manual households, many of whom were engaged in storekeeping and in neighborhood service trades. The other east-west streets in the grid-unit, however, were now distinctly more plebeian than they had been in 1860. Artisans, factory workers, laborers, petty proprietors, and policemen (a police station had been opened on Union Street between Third and Fourth) crowded into the brick row houses on Lombard and Union streets, many of which had been converted from single-family dwellings into flats. Clerks and salesmen were there too – as boarders, rarely as heads of household – but they were now greatly outnumbered by manual workers on every street except Pine. The area was by no means a slum, but it clearly was no longer attracting middle-class families. Indeed, it is reasonable to assume that for some years it had been exporting these families to other neighborhoods. In 1880 only 13% of the male heads of household in this grid-unit were professionals, businessmen, officials, or clerical workers under the age of forty.

A little farther from the business center changes were less dramatic, and some of the neighborhoods and streets that had formerly attracted middle-class residents continued to do so. In the grid-unit east of Logan Square, the 1500 block of Race and Cherry streets, once almost entirely nonmanual, now contained many more households headed by manual workers, while Summer and Winter streets east of Sixteenth had become almost entirely manual. The streets closest to Logan Square, however (Seventeenth, and the 1600 blocks of Race, Cherry, and Summer), retained their middle-class character. Similarly, the grid-unit stretching south of Mt. Vernon and west of Tenth contained streets that were shifting toward manual workers (Spring Garden and Wistar), streets that remained almost entirely nonmanual (Mt. Vernon and Green), and a narrow street (Nectarine) that continued to be dominated by skilled and unskilled manual workers. In both of these grid-units there were indications of a shift away from the old street-alley pattern of class segregation, and toward the areal segregation that would be more common in the years to come. In the grid-unit east of Logan Square, the 1500 block contained the working-class alleys (Gebhard, Graydon, and Path). Hence, the downward shift of the major streets surrounding those alleys gave the block as a whole a more uniformly working-class character, while the block immediately to the west (closer, recall, to Logan Square) was uniformly middle class. And in the second of these two grid-units beyond the downtown, the two streets closest to Nectarine Street (and to the downtown itself) were the ones becoming most like this working-class alley in the composition of its households, while the streets farthest away remained distinctly more prosperous.

In the rapidly developing "streetcar suburb" of West Philadelphia, evidence of a new form of areal segregation was a good deal stronger. In its earliest phase of development, as we have seen, West Philadelphia had preserved the street-alley form of segregation that characterized the old city center and its surrounding neighborhoods. By 1880, however, this was changing in a number of places. Ludlow Street (formerly Oak), the narrow alley that ran between and parallel to Chestnut Street and the major commercial thoroughfare of Market Street, retained the traditional array of skilled and unskilled workers' households. Sansom Street, on the other hand, which ran between Chestnut and Walnut (two streets of expensive homes), departed from this pattern. Below Fortieth, Sansom contained only three dwellings, home to five working-class households, the rest of the street consisting of the unbuilt rear portions of the properties fronting on Chestnut and Walnut. (Not even carriage houses appear on a contemporary map of these streets, which would seem an unlikely omission were it not for the horsecar tracks that ran down Chestnut Street and Locust, one block south of Walnut.)[55] Sansom above Fortieth did have rows of dwellings, but at least 16 of the 19 households that lived in them were headed by nonmanual proprietors and workers, among them a commission grain merchant, a retired dry goods merchant, a teacher of German, a bank clerk, and a bookkeeper who worked at Baldwin's locomotive works. Sansom Street, in other words, was in part a street of less imposing but still middle-class homes within a solidly middle-class neighborhood, and in part an essentially uninhabited lane running behind the backyards of the neighborhood's larger suburban houses. A close look at the map of this portion of West Philadelphia reveals more streets of this type over a broader area south of Walnut Street, and suggests that a relatively homogeneous middle-class suburb was in fact emerging a block and more away from the Market Street thoroughfare.

Roger Miller and Joseph Siry have analyzed West Philadelphia in just these terms, pointing to areas where the old street-alley pattern of segregation remained, and to areas where the "central middle class" (their term, as well as Warner's) lived in homogeneous neighborhoods. They provide as well interesting and detailed examples of commuting middle-class suburbanites, such as Robert D. Work, a hat and cap retailer who bought his house at 3803 Locust Street in 1865 for $5,500, and for years afterward commuted from there to his store on Third Street near the downtown terminus of the original West

Philadelphia horsecar line – a distance of nearly four miles.[56] Work lived on a major street, but others like him are described by Miller and Siry as the residents of smaller streets that, in older sections of Philadelphia, would have contained manual workers. Woodland Terrace, for example, a short, narrow street running between Baltimore and Kingsessing (now Woodland) avenues, was home in 1870 to 14 families who occupied large, comfortable, semidetached houses. Most of these families were headed by moderately prosperous downtown merchants between the ages of thirty and fifty. All but 2 had moved by 1880, but their replacements differed from them only in age, the average householder of Woodland Terrace in 1880 being a businessman or professional of fifty-one.[57]

In nearly every respect these sections of West Philadelphia conform to the well-defined image of the middle-class commuter suburb. The one significant departure is the advanced age of many of West Philadelphia's householders. The 1880 residents of Woodland Terrace were, in fact, typical of the suburb as a whole. In the grid-unit extending from Market to Walnut above Thirty-ninth Street, the average male householder's age was forty-six, while on Chestnut and Walnut streets it was more than fifty-one. Women householders, most of whom were widows (women headed nearly one in five of the households in the grid-unit), averaged sixty years in age. The proportion of male householders who were nonmanual proprietors and workers under the age of forty (17.4%) was, indeed, only moderately higher than it was in the crowded grid-unit around Third and Pine, and was no higher than in the other grid-units we have examined in the old city. It does rise to 25% when we exclude Market and Ludlow streets to focus on the more purely suburban parts of the grid-unit, but even this higher proportion does not suggest a neighborhood of young families.

The surprisingly middle-aged character of the streetcar suburb in 1880 reflects, I believe, two conditions that contrast with later eras of rapid suburban development. One, discussed at length by Warner, is the prevailing form of home financing – the short-term, nonamortizing mortgage loan, generally extending to no more than half the value of the property – that made the purchase of a home quite difficult for young people who had not yet accumulated much capital.[58] The second, which would have affected prospective tenants as well as purchasers, was the recency of the economic depression. In 1880, numerous young clerks and businessmen continued to lodge in other people's households, hostages of hard times that still prevented their becoming secure householders on their own. No fewer than 15 clerks, salesmen, retailers, and other young office and store workers, ranging in age from eighteen to thirty-five, lived with their parents or grand-parents in 9 of the 19 households that occupied the 1600 block of Cherry Street. It is likely that all of these young men, and others like them from all over the city, left their parental homes in the following few years to become householders in their own right, in the suburbs or elsewhere. The rapid suburbanization of the 1880s surely reflects the resulting upsurge in middle-class family formation no less than it does the movement of existing families from the center to the periphery.

But did these young middle-class householders, and older ones too, all seek suburban homes and neighborhoods that fulfilled the rural ideal? I suggested earlier that developing neighborhoods on the immediate periphery of the old city were neither as distant nor as rustic as the streetcar suburbs. In the northwest corner of the city, for example, the settled population had by 1880 pushed outward along Philadelphia's endlessly repeating gridiron of streets to a distance of perhaps two miles from the heart of the downtown. Horsecar service was vital to this expansion, but the neighborhoods that developed even at the ends of the horsecar lines in this direction were as much extensions of the city as they were "streetcar suburbs" in the density, style, and placement of their houses, and in their overall character (Figure 8.5).[59] Yet, these were neighborhoods that were even more homogeneously middle-class, and that pointed even more clearly to the class-segregated metropolis. Fully 80% of the male householders of a selected three-block segment of the northwestern periphery pursued nonmanual occupations in 1880, a proportion that compares favorably with the most homogeneous sections of West Philadelphia. Moreover, as Table 8.1 indicates, this urban periphery was more attractive to younger middle-class householders than was the rustic suburb beyond the Schuylkill River. Three of every eight male household heads there were under the age of forty, and the proportions of nonmanual proprietors and workers among these younger householders was even higher, a remarkable 91%, than it was among older heads. More than a third of the male householders were professionals, businessmen, officials, and clerks under forty, a proportion twice that of the West Philadelphia grid-unit.

What is most notable about this small slice of a much larger neighborhood, however, is how decisively it broke the Philadelphia tradition of segregation by frontage within integrated areas. Each of the three blocks, which together extend from Broad Street to Seventeenth between Oxford Street and Columbia Avenue, was bisected by a narrower street. One of these streets, Carlisle, was apparently empty of households, much in the manner of Sansom Street below Fortieth

Figure 8.5. Houses on the Philadelphia nonsuburban periphery (photo by George Thomas, Photographer)

in West Philadelphia. The other two, Sydenham and Willington, contained approximately half of the area's manual workers (in only 22% of its households), but in each case these workers were outnumbered by white-collar neighbors. Sydenham Street contained twenty-three households, thirteen headed by clerical workers and nonmanual proprietors (a book publisher, a grocer, a perfume manufacturer, to name a few), and ten headed by skilled manual workers. Of Willington's 15 male householders reporting occupations, only 3 performed manual work – a steel frame maker, a hairdresser, and a housepainter. These blocks, it should be noted, were fairly close to a number of large factories and mills and quite accessible to a large number of relatively well-paid workers in machine shops and metal-processing plants. A few of these workers, almost all of them older men, did find their way to this neighborhood, but what is most striking is that its narrow back streets did not fill up with them, as they surely would have in older sections of the city. In the three sampled blocks there were nearly as many manufacturers as there were industrial workers, and the area as a whole – the narrow streets almost as decisively as

Table 8.1. *Male householders in a three-block portion of the northwestern periphery of Philadelphia, 1880, by age and occupational category*

	Age 20–39		Age 40+		Total	
	n	%	n	%	n	%
Occupation:						
Professionals, nonmanual proprietors, officials	49	74.2	76	69.1	125	71.0
Clerical workers	11	16.7	5	4.5	16	9.1
Skilled proprietors and workers	4	6.1	23	20.9	27	15.3
Unskilled workers	—	—	—	—	—	—
No occupation	2	3.0	6	5.5	8	4.6
Total	66	100.0	110	100.0	176	100.0
% of total households		(37.5)		(62.5)		(100.0)

Source: U.S. census manuscripts, 1880.

the wide streets – was dominated by its commuting middle class. Here was a district, not quite suburb and not quite city, that contributed no less than the suburbs to the separation of classes in urban space.[60]

As the old street-alley system began to give way in Philadelphia to an emerging pattern of areal segregation, contemporaries there and elsewhere expressed their awareness of the separation of classes in the metropolis. In New York, a city longer accustomed to areal segregation, several writers described this phenomenon in temporal as well as spatial terms – even the daily ebb and flow of the population across the city's segregated spaces was structured in class terms. In two separate accounts of life in the American metropolis, James Dabney McCabe and Junius Henri Browne describe the sequence of ferry commuters between Brooklyn and New York. Beginning at five A.M., writes McCabe, "vast swarms of workingmen pour over the river." These are succeeded, after six, by factory and shop girls, then by retail clerks and salesmen, then by wholesale clerks, and finally by ascending categories of businessmen, culminating in "the great capitalists" who arrive in New York after ten.[61] Browne's account is quite similar, except that it includes what must be one of the first attempts to represent the difference between manual and nonmanual workers by the color of their shirts: When the mechanics and factory workers, "with their flannel and check shirts," are succeeded on the ferry after seven by salesmen, accountants, and clerks, "the shirts of the passengers begin to whiten and raiment to improve."[62]

In a lighthearted piece entitled "Bowery, Saturday Night," *Harper's* combines the spatial and temporal aspects of class segregation in New York. After observing how the process of attraction and repulsion has created a city of class and ethnic "quarters," *Harper's* describes the sequence of Madison Avenue and Fourth Avenue horsecar passengers who travel each afternoon through and to the working-class Bowery. These cars

> . . . hardly belong to the Bowery; they get their loads nearer the
> City Hall, and carry them through, not taking up or putting down
> many hereabouts. . . . Their cargoes are largely made up of spruce
> Wall Street men and down-town clerks and merchants, with here
> and there an economical lady from "above Fourteenth," who has
> been shopping at low prices in the Bowery. . . . Thanks to the
> early-closing movement, the hard-working attaches of the whole-
> sale and shipping houses in the lower wards begin, a trifle later,
> to furnish their quota; but they, too, are for the most part through
> passengers. . . . Then, at various intervals, from four until six, with
> belated exceptions, lingering along till six or seven, or even after,
> come swarms of weary and grimy mechanics and other workmen,
> with bevies of laughing shop-girls and factory operatives.[63]

Only the latter actually stop at the Bowery. It is their "quarter," and it is theirs "almost as distinctively as if assigned to them by despotic edicts of the Middle Ages."[64] All the others merely pass through, segregated on the horsecars, to their own segregated "quarters."

Each of these descriptions was written around 1870. Accelerating middle-class suburbanization after that date would exacerbate the separation of classes these passages describe and would increase the already well-established sense of the metropolis as an aggregation of separate social worlds, occasionally passing each other but rarely touching. George Foster had described such a class-divided metropolis years earlier, but always with a note of regret, and often accompanied by the stated hope of a reintegrated urban community sometime in the future.[65] The postwar writers, by contrast, freely accepted an urban present and future in which class segregation was pervasive and irremediable, and not especially to be brooded over. It seemed, indeed, inherent in the very structure of the "great metropolis," which Browne describes as "a little world in itself" and as "an intensification of the country," in which all the contrasting elements of society are concentrated and juxtaposed.[66]

But if there could be no community between the city's classes and districts, what of community within them, and in particular the social networks and identities that we might expect to find among the suburbanizing middle class? Warner has written of a consensus of values in Boston's streetcar suburbs that greatly facilitated the process by which land was platted and sold, houses designed and built, neighborhoods settled and defined. But it was a consensus built around the values of individual and family privacy rather than of community, and the neighborhoods that Warner found in Boston's suburbs were fragmented and weak, not communities at all but merely spatially proximate families of similar means who kept largely to themselves.[67] Middle-class suburbanization was not, in fact, associated with any new burst of associational activity, and Warner is correct to point to the physical design of suburbs that provided endless streets of private housing and very few public spaces or structures where communal action and feeling could be nurtured. And yet these houses and streets in the suburbs and on the less distant urban periphery still contributed significantly both to middle-class awareness and to the refinement of middle-class social networks. Warner's objection is to the absence of community, not to the broader and less demanding identification of individuals and families with the middle class. The very withdrawal he describes, into the distinctively middle-class suburban home, was of the sort most likely to increase this broader social identity. Moreover, Warner probably overstates the isolation of suburban middle-class families from one another. The absence of new forms of associational activity can be explained as much by the preponderance of older householders – men such as Henry Pierce, who moved to Dorchester after the days of his active club life had ended – as by the withdrawal of socially active young men into their suburban domestic shells. Informal domestic visiting among like-minded people continued in the suburbs, and may even have been enhanced, although it changed somewhat in character as the merchant householder's clerks were increasingly replaced in the parlor by neighbors.[68] Finally, formal organizations did survive, some remaining downtown in accessible locations, others – most notably churches – following their members to, or being created anew in, the suburbs, where they were even more homogeneously middle-class than they had been in the city.[69] Unquestionably, post–Civil War suburbanization further separated the social networks of larger American cities, and sharpened the already clearly visible boundaries of the middle class.

The awareness of class

The continuing process of sorting out classes at the workplace and in metropolitan space made the denial of class more difficult in post–Civil War America. Not surprisingly, many continued to make this denial, but as William Graham Sumner pointed out, their loyalty to the classless republic was increasingly out of phase with common perceptions of social reality. "It is commonly asserted that there are in the United States no classes, and any allusion to classes is resented," wrote Sumner in 1883. "On the other hand, we constantly read and hear discussions of social topics in which the existence of social classes is assumed as a simple fact."[70] Similarly, Francis Amasa Walker, who had worked so hard to make sense of an emerging industrial society, bristled at the suggestion that a term such as "the working classes" had no meaning in America, or that there could be significant questions about what sorts of people were designated by it: "There are large and important bodies of producers who are clearly enough pointed out thereby, and who well enough understand themselves to be meant. It is not an inexact expression, for no one not intended by it would deem himself, or be deemed by others, to be included." The latter was a particularly sharp point, intended to deflate the egalitarian hypocrisies of those "professional men and employers of labor, shopkeepers and clerks, artists and teachers" who knew very well the real boundaries of their own social worlds.[71]

Industrialization and the removal of large numbers of middling folk from the cities to the suburbs were, however, events that focused attention on the dualities of capital and labor and of the urban rich and poor, dualities that obscured or denied the existence of a middle class. Analysts of large cities, in particular, emphasized – one might even say reveled in – the polarities of urban life, the "sunshine" of great wealth and fashionable society, the "shadow" of widespread poverty. "Whoever writes of New York truly, will do so in lines of light and gloom," asserted Matthew Hale Smith. "A portion of New York is Paradise: a large part is Pandemonium."[72] On the other hand, I earlier observed how statements of this sort were indebted to a European-bred style of urban sensationalism that depended on the shocking juxtaposition of the very rich and the very poor, and that focused attention away from the large part of the metropolitan population that lived somewhere between Paradise and Pandemonium. Those writing in other genres had little difficulty in recognizing the presence of a large urban middle class. James Richardson, for example, who contributed a long article to *Scribner's* on the apartment house as a solution to the problem of middle-income housing in New York, divided the city's population into three parts: first, "people with incomes sufficient to enable them to live as they choose"; second, "a broader and more numerous class, . . . embracing the well-to-do, from those who may live handsomely with economy, down to those whose income does not exceed twenty-five hundred to three thousand a year"; and third, "the very poor," a group in which Richardson meant to include "the better sorts of New York laboring men."[73] There are gaps and inconsistencies here, and the language is more cumbersome than it needs to be, but Richardson clearly conveys a tripartite urban social structure, even in this most famously polarized of cities.

The sensationalist writers, too, could find the middle class intruding on their depictions of urban polarization. As noted in Chapter 1, James Dabney McCabe felt the need to justify his view of the polarized city by referring to the suburbanization of the "middle class," just as *Scribner's* would do a few years later using exactly the same terminology.[74] If New York was a city of two classes in McCabe's account, it was only because its middle class had migrated to the suburbs. McCabe no less than *Scribner's*, in other words, recognized the middle class as an important component of the metropolitan social structure; indeed, he had much less difficulty than Richardson in finding the proper term to describe it. This, I believe, is more important than his attempt to get the middle class out of his way by exaggerating the extent to which it had deserted the city for the suburbs. The entire literature of urban social polarization, I would further argue, must be understood in this way. Those who wrote of "the beauty and deformity, the good and evil, the happiness and misery" of the city of contrasts did not really believe that the city consisted only of the rich and the poor.[75] Most of them were, in fact, members of that urban middle class their art required them to deny.

Writers more concerned with industrial questions also referred occasionally but easily to the middle class as a specific and important part of a society torn by conflicts between capital and labor. Francis Walker, who believed "working classes" an unambiguous term, used "middle class" and "the great middle class" with equal certainty, contrasting them to "the Upper Ten Thousand" as clearly as he contrasted "working classes" to a specified array of nonmanual occupations.[76] Walker, it may be objected, was a man who was atypically concerned about questions of social taxonomy. More indicative of common language, perhaps, are the terms with which a sympathetic Committee of the Senate upon the Relations Between Labor and Capital elicited the testimony of John Morrison, a machinist, concerning the declining social status of men who worked in what had been one of the best paid and most highly skilled of trades. During hearings held in 1883, Morrison was asked: "Dividing the public, as is commonly done, into the upper, middle, and lower classes, to which class would you assign the average workingman of your trade at the time when you entered it, and to which class would you assign him now?" Morrison accepted the premise of a widely understood three-class social structure, and described the decline of "upper mechanics" within it: "I would now assign them to the lower class. At the time I entered the trade I should assign them as merely hanging on to the middle class, ready to drop out at any time."[77]

"Middle class" was still not a term that appeared frequently in public discourse, but these few examples suggest it was rather more familiar, and more acceptable, to the post–Civil War than to the pre–Civil War generation. It appeared more often in its simplest forms, "middle class" and "middle classes" (rather than, say, "the middling class of people"), and no longer required apologetic accompaniments (e.g., "if there be any classes in democratic America"). Had its meaning become clearer as well? The machinist's testimony suggests a more general revision of the meaning of "middle class" that would have brought it into closer agreement with the everyday experiences of city people – a somewhat overdue demotion of the "upper mechanic" by those who had not previously recognized the separation of nonmanual from manual social worlds. How many other machinists, or schoolteachers, or lawyers, responding to less leading questions, would have contradicted Morrison's assessment of the social worth of the skilled worker? A personal letter written in 1877 by Lydia Maria Child to Sarah Blake Shaw, a Boston acquaintance, helps explain why it is so difficult to accumulate large numbers of contemporary statements concerning the meanings and boundaries of class:

> No observing person can help being aware of an increasing tendency toward a strong *demarcation of classes* in this country. The genteel classes do not inter-marry with the middle classes; the middle classes do not intermarry with the laboring class; nothing is *said* about it, but there is a systematic avoidance of it. Moreover, they don't mix socially; they are as much strangers to each other, as if they live in different countries.[78]

The "systematic avoidance" of the subject of social demarcation, first cousin to the outright denial that classes existed in America, did not obscure to Child the increasingly distinctive three-class structure of daily social life. Writing again to Mrs. Shaw a month later, Child herself helped fill the void by defining the boundaries of class, but with results that were strikingly different from those that emerge from the testimony of John Morrison:

> As for *classes*, the Vanderbilts and Stewarts, they do not constitute a *class*; there are too few of them. By the genteel class, I mean those who live in mansions of their own, with incomes ranging from $5000 to $20,000, or more. By the middle class, I mean farmers and mechanics, who work with their *hands*, own a house, with or without some acres of land, with incomes, from their own la-

bor, varying from $300 a year to $1,500. By the laboring class, I mean those who own no dwelling, and subsist upon the proceeds of their labor upon the premises of other people.[79]

What shall we make of this "middle class" consisting entirely of farmers and mechanics, and of this social structure that simply omits a large number of nonmanual proprietors and employees who earned between $1,500 and $5,000 per annum? Child preserves, even emphasizes, the distinction between nonmanual and manual work. Later in the same letter she writes at length (but critically) of how "all want to crawl into employments deemed genteel; employments that do not soil the clothes, or the hands." But why, having established the significance of the boundary between nonmanual and manual work, should she place the middle class below that boundary? In the epilogue to this book I consider Child's social categories as a rural analogue to the social structures that had emerged in the nation's cities. But it is too simple a matter to regard Child merely as a spokeswoman for the rural point of view. Aspects of her own background and experience enter her classifications in ways that were obvious even to Child herself. Most obvious is that Child was, or considered herself to be, the daughter of a mechanic – indeed, this was a favorite topic of hers, and she appears to have had a reputation in polite society for being rather too proud of her humble background. In her first letter to Mrs. Shaw she observes, "how often it has been hinted to me that I should stand a great deal better with the upper classes, if I would avoid mentioning that my father was a mechanic," and in the second she retorts to Mrs. Shaw's own accusation of misplaced pride. This emphasis on what was ordinarily obscured was closely linked to Child's political life as an antislavery reformer, to her generally radical political disposition, and to the fact that she perceived herself as something of a conscience to the New England upper class, to which her books and political activities gave her access. It was also exaggerated. Child's father was in fact a prosperous baker and real estate investor who was able to sell his bakery while still a relatively young man and live for many years on his investments, despite parting with $3,000 on one occasion to buy his daughter and her husband a farm.[80] Child, in sum, could have done more than obscure her father's early career as a "mechanic" – she could have claimed him a gentleman. That she did not do so was as unusual as her definition of the middle class. Both, I would argue, reflected this old reformer's preference for a society somewhat different from the one she saw around her.

Immediately following her definitions of the genteel, middle, and laboring classes, Lydia Child rebuked Mrs. Shaw and her circle for considering themselves middle class. They were not aristocratic, she conceded, but lived too well, "and are unaccustomed to wait upon yourselves." This self-classification by a small group of Boston acquaintances was the occasion for Child's detailed discussion of class, and in the final analysis is probably more important than Child's response. Mrs. Shaw and her friends were pleased to think of themselves as middle class, and so, I believe, did many more Americans who fell either within Child's "genteel class" or through the very large fissure between it and her "middle class." Businessmen, professionals, officials, and clerical workers, living well but lacking great wealth and the access that great wealth sooner or later provided to the city's most exclusive social circles – this was the urban and suburban middle class. They were increasingly aware of themselves as such and, as Lydia Child herself suggested, were aware that they lived in a "different country" from those above and below them in the well-understood social structure of the Gilded Age.

Toward the twentieth century

The boundaries of the "different country" that was the urban middle class were drawn on the unstable ground of modern experience. By the last years of the nineteenth century a new combination of forces would affect the social landscape of American cities in ways that made some of these boundaries less firm and less clear, ironically, just as the term "middle class" was achieving a quite stable form and a widely understood meaning within the American language.[81] Particularly important were several developments that began to confuse and ultimately would weaken the distinction between nonmanual and manual work, and with it the lower boundary of the middle class. The expansion of permanently low-paying nonmanual jobs in offices and stores, for example, which occurred during a period of modest improvement in manual workers' annual incomes, produced for the first time in industrial America a degree of income overlap between the nonmanual and manual sectors that could not be accounted for by the temporarily low incomes of very young clerks. Not many manual workers were pushed into or close to middle-class income levels, and it would be easy to exaggerate the effect on this overlap of the 25% improvement in average industrial workers' incomes between 1880 and 1900.[82] At the end of the century and beyond, most workers' families still required incomes from more than one source to sustain even a very modest style of living.[83] Rather, the significant developments were those that were restructuring the incomes and opportunities associated with the lower levels of salaried nonmanual work.

The enormous expansion of clerical work in offices and large retail stores during the last two decades of the nineteenth century engulfed the old world of business apprenticeship. The half-million store clerks and clerical office workers of 1880 had tripled by the end of the century, and by far the greatest numbers of additions were in the lowest-paying jobs that offered the least chance of promotion or salary improvement. To be sure, a large number of the new store and office "proletarians" were women, many of them young working-class daughters who were pleased to accept their $6 or $8 a week as department store salesclerks or typists rather than as seamstresses or factory operatives.[84] Women working in clerical jobs increased more than tenfold between 1880 and 1900, and by the latter date constituted nearly one-quarter of the clerical work force.[85] Several recent studies have shown that all but a few of these women were at the bottom of the white-collar hierarchy, and that offices in particular were clearly stratified by gender.[86] However, this does not mean that all white-collar males were pushed up to higher levels. On the contrary, nearly a million men are tabulated in the 1900 census as store or office clerks, and the average weekly salaries of male clerical workers revealed by contemporary surveys – $10 or $11 – suggest that the bottom of the broadening white-collar pyramid was still occupied by greater numbers of men than women.[87]

The poorly paid *young* male clerk was, of course, nothing new, and the real question is whether the rapid expansion of low-level clerical work, the increasing scale of specific nonmanual workplaces – department stores, corporate offices, and the like – and the reorganization of work and work roles within these workplaces had changed the opportunity for young male clerks to rise within the business world. This is not an easy question to answer. Carole Srole's analysis of Boston clerks reveals a gradual but steady increase in the numbers of young men who remained in salaried employment for at least fifteen years, and a corresponding decline in the numbers who became independent businessmen or professionals.[88] But of their salary increases and promotions she can say little. The range of weekly clerical salaries reported in contemporary surveys suggests that the traditional pattern of very low starting salaries coupled with substantial annual raises was largely preserved among male employees. The 1902 Boston survey, for example, reports a range of from $4 to $28 among male clerks averaging just under $10 per week, and a range of from $9 to $38.50 among male bookkeepers averaging nearly $20 per week. Salesmen, who averaged $15 per week, varied even more widely, from as little as $3 to as much as $60.[89] There is nothing in this survey that says that salary differences were correlated with years of experience, but it is reasonable to believe that they were. There must also have been considerable scope for significant promotion within emerging business bureaucracies, for the middle levels of management were expanding even more rapidly than the lower levels of routine clerical work, albeit from a smaller base. Thus, while clerical workers were tripling in number, officials in trade, transportation, manufacturing, and mining were increasing nearly fivefold, from fewer than 68,000 in 1880 to more than 318,000 in 1900. Nearly all of these officials were men, as were all but a few of the 93,000 commercial travelers who also represented a significant step up the ladder from clerical work. At the end of the century, there were approximately three upper- or middle-level officials, one traveling salesman, and two bookkeepers, cashiers, and accountants, for every ten office or store clerks in the male white-collar work force – a set of ratios that need not have been too discouraging for the ambitious young clerk who lacked the prospect of setting up as an independent businessman.[90]

Yet the circumstances of clerking were surely changing for many young men whose predecessors had entered into menial jobs in stores and offices expecting to be trained for the business world. Clerical ascent was undoubtedly slower and less certain in the larger bureaucracies, and with increasing numbers of managers being trained in colleges and universities rather than through clerkships – not yet a widespread development, but a portentous one – the possibility of a significant bifurcation of rewards, opportunities, and identities within the male white-collar world was significantly enhanced. The partial feminization of the lower levels of the nonmanual hierarchy, and the working-class origins of many male and female workers at these levels, may also have deepened the divide between management and routine clerical work, while weakening the divide between clerks and skilled workers. Children from blue-collar homes were still less likely than white-collar children to complete or even enter high school, and, having left school, were still less likely to enter white-collar jobs. But as Reed Ueda's and Joel Perlmann's recent studies have shown, these gaps were steadily closing.[91] Ileen DeVault has argued, moreover, that the skilled working-class parents of clerical workers in turn-of-the-century Pittsburgh viewed their children's achievement "as a continuation of their own social status within the working-class community" rather than as upward mobility into the middle class. "For these labor aristocrats," DeVault continues, "the collar line did not loom as the fundamental social divide. The new clerical positions occupied instead a social position equivalent to their own."[92] That some of their children may have shared this view is suggested by the organization during these years of the Retail Clerks' National (later

International) Protective Association (RCIPA) as an affiliate of the American Federation of Labor, which brought a portion of the clerical work force into the mainstream of the American labor movement. As Jürgen Kocka points out, the leaders of this white-collar union promoted the idea that retail clerks were part of the working class – one indicator of many to Kocka that "the collar line in America remained less distinct and socially less significant than it was in Germany."[93]

Germany, whose corporate and bureaucratic traditions made of its *Angestellten* very nearly a legal class or estate, sets too extreme a standard of comparison, and Kocka is careful to moderate his dismissal of the social power of the "collar line" in America.[94] We, too, should be careful not to exaggerate the effects of changing circumstances on the social identification of nonmanual workers. The RCIPA never organized more than a small minority of retail clerks (apparently no more than fifty thousand during the first decade of the twentieth century, and far fewer during the preceding and succeeding decades), and its campaign to create bonds of identity between clerks and the manual working class does not appear to have been very successful. Neither, according to Kocka, were the union's efforts to convince retail clerks that they were no longer being trained to become businessmen. In 1905 the RCIPA estimated that about half of America's salesclerks did expect to rise in the business world, and Kocka concludes that salesclerks generally continued to identify with management rather than with labor.[95] The middle-class status of clerks in other settings, moreover, was more secure than it was in retail stores. In manufacturing firms, where the office and the workshop were most strikingly juxtaposed, white-collar workers retained a clear sense of superiority over blue-collar workers, and in government offices, as Cindy Sondik Aron has shown, male and female clerical workers continued to be recruited from the established middle class.[96] In the latter setting, feminization did not proletarianize office work but, rather, enhanced it as middle-class women "helped to transfer some of the norms of the Victorian parlor into the workplace."[97] Only a small portion of the clerical work force was employed in public offices of the sort Aron has analyzed, but I believe her observations pertain in some measure to private sector offices as well, despite the working-class backgrounds of many male and female clerks. The office, indeed, was increasingly articulated, as downtown retail stores earlier had been, as a status-conferring workplace, and it is interesting to observe in this connection how Aron's "norms of the Victorian parlor" shaped the idealized representations of offices in the illustrated advertising of firms that sold office furniture and equipment. The cover of the 1886 catalogue of the Schlicht & Field Co., a typical example, portrays

Figure 8.6. Schlicht & Field Co. catalogue, 1886 (courtesy of the Collection of Advertising History, Archives Center, National Museum of American History, Smithsonian Institution)

a dignified office interior with a carpet on the floor, framed pictures on the walls, and a well-dressed young "couple" (one easily overlooks the improbability of their being married) performing routine office tasks (Figure 8.6). The scene is very nearly that of the middle-class parlor, enhanced as such by the surrounding sprig of flowers and berries. The distance between such idealizations and the actual circumstances of office work may often have been great, but the form of the idealization is telling. It suggests, along with other evidence considered by Kocka and others, that the "proletarianization" of clerical work and reward had not as yet significantly affected the social identity of white-collar workers, or the perception of these workers as members of the middle class.

The middle-class standing of those workers had been based primarily on their work and on their economic prospects, but through the middle decades of the nineteenth century it was reinforced by the broader patterns of immigration and ethnicity. At the end of the century, too, nonmanual proprietors and workers consisted mainly of native-born Americans, but by this time there was a potentially unsettling complication. The children of Irish, German, and other immigrant groups of the mid-nineteenth century – native-born Americans who were at the same time distinguishable ethnics – had moved in significant numbers into the nonmanual sector. In Poughkeepsie, for example, the proportions of second-generation ethnics in the clerical work force rose steadily from 10% in 1860, to 17% in 1870, and to 22% in 1880.[98] In Philadelphia ten years later it was 31%, with a nearly identical representation of second-generation ethnics among salesmen, and smaller but significant representations among a variety of other nonmanual occupations.[99] Differences remained, but the penetration of the nonmanual sector by the children of immigrants increased the likelihood that class and ethnicity would become separate rather than reinforcing identities, or, as Kocka has suggested, that ethnicity would reinforce rather different social boundaries, setting second-generation skilled and white-collar workers apart from "new immigrants" from Eastern and Southern Europe who worked in unskilled and semiskilled jobs in factories and sweatshops.[100] The upsurge and shifting pattern of immigration surely increased the significance of ethnic identity, just as the growing distinction between old and new ethnic groups and the penetration of the former into nonmanual occupations made its influence more complicated. Daniel Walkowitz observes a mixing of white-collar and blue-collar Irish and French Canadians in the ethnic organizations of Troy and Cohoes, New York, during the 1880s, and tentatively suggests "that the rise of the new ethnic middle class within these organizations began to shift the members' loyalties from social class to ethnicity."[101] Walkowitz (and Kocka too) may well be right, but at the same time his caution seems well advised. It is difficult to infer the balance of competing social identities among the middle-class members of the Fenians or the French-Canadian Political Club, and still more difficult to weigh the appeais of class and ethnicity among those white-collar ethnics who did not join these or other ethnic organizations. Some of the latter no doubt emphasized their American birth while staking a claim within the respectable middle class. Still, we should recognize that for a small but growing number of white-collar Americans – the children and to some extent even the grandchildren of the old immigrants – class identity was not nourished by membership in the majority ethnic group. For the first time, middle-class identity and ethnic identity pulled in different directions.

The pressures that began to build against the boundaries and meanings of class in the late nineteenth century increased and multiplied during the twentieth. The urban upper class, once so evident a part of the social landscape, began to lose visibility and force, receding from public view especially rapidly after Americans turned to more specialized celebrities in aviators, film stars, and athletes. The question "Who killed society?" was already a fairly trivial one when Cleveland Amory asked it in 1960, except perhaps to historians and to displaced patricians, and with the withdrawal of the upper class (for it is not dead, but carries on many of its ancient rituals largely outside the public eye), the boundary between the upper and middle classes became much more difficult to locate.[102] In the twentieth century, too, large numbers of manual workers finally began receiving incomes that could purchase the comforts that had long been associated with, and in fact had helped define, the nonmanual middle class. Steven Ross has made the intriguing suggestion that the more striking income overlap that developed during the early decades of the twentieth century may not only have confused class boundaries, but may also have created a dual social identity among well-paid manual workers. The latter, Ross proposes, continued to see themselves as members of the working class with reference to the relations of the workplace, but also came to see themselves as middle class with reference to consumption and their lives away from work.[103] That many American workers now identify themselves as middle class is well established; indeed, if one of these two identities in Ross's formulation has since faded, it is surely the older identification with the working class, if only because the expansion of the service sector (and so many hard-to-classify jobs within it) has made the meaning of "working class" ambiguous even with respect to work itself.

To be sure, Americans continue in their everyday speech to distinguish between white-collar and blue-collar work and workers;[104] indeed, the very simplicity and ubiquity of these symbols in contemporary society attest to the continuing power of the ancient value judgment that in preindustrial society limited the social and political aspirations of even quite prosperous master craftsmen, and in the age of early and maturing industrialization helped create and perpetuate the distinction between the middle and working classes. But the distinction between white-collar and blue-collar work is socially less significant than it once was, in large part because it no longer symbolizes the consistent set of differences in income, living standards, and social experience that, along with work-type itself, gave shape to the class structure of the nineteenth century. Perhaps these contemporary inconsistencies, and the resulting attenuation of class symbolization, ought to be taken as evidence of a national consensus of identities and values. And perhaps because we describe ourselves often and so freely as "middle class" we ought to recognize the existence of a specifically middle-class consensus that incorporates most of the American population. As others continue to grapple with this question with respect to twentieth-century American society, I can only hope they will recognize the historical limits of this meaning of "middle class." During the nineteenth century many Americans came to experience class not as part of a national consensus of values but in daily routines and social networks that made their lives visibly similar to those of some people and visibly different from those of others. And when they came to speak of class it was to express those similarities and differences in a manner that was significant and reasonably precise. In nineteenth-century America, "middle class" represented a specific set of experiences, a specific style of living, and a specific social identity – a social world, in sum, that was distinct from others above and below it in the tangible hierarchy that was society.

Epilogue: City, town, village, farm – the geography of class in nineteenth-century America

This book is based on evidence drawn almost entirely from the largest cities in America from the age of the Revolution to the end of the nineteenth century – a nation and an era in which most of the population lived on farms and in small villages and towns. Urbanization was one of the major forces of the nineteenth century, and in the United States it was a process that included the appearance, proliferation, and continuing growth of the first large cities. At the beginning of the nineteenth century, a handful of major towns in America, none of which exceeded 60,000 inhabitants, accounted for less than 4% of the nation's population. At the century's end, several of these towns, along with others that had not even existed in 1800, were metropolises containing 300,000, 500,000, or a million or more inhabitants, and it may be noted that there were more people living in New York and Philadelphia in 1900 than had lived in the entire nation at the time of the first census in 1790. Yet even the 38 cities with more than 100,000 inhabitants in 1900 constituted less than 20% of the American population, while a nearly equal proportion lived in the 1,659 small cities and towns that had fewer than 50,000 residents. More important, fully 60% of the population continued to live in villages and on farms.[1] We have focused, in sum, upon a minority – the most interesting and appropriate minority, I would argue, and one of increasing weight, but a minority all the same – which raises obvious questions concerning the relations between the patterns we have observed in the larger cities and those that developed during the same years in smaller cities and towns, in villages, and across the countryside of scattered farms. What was the nature and extent of the differences between urban and rural social milieux with respect to the experience and awareness of class, and with particular reference to the emergence of the middle class? Were big-city social patterns and identities replicated in any way in smaller communities? Can we speak of class, and more specifically of the middle class, in small-town and rural America? If so, does this to some extent reflect the

298

influence of major cities and their institutions over those who lived in the small communities of an urbanizing nation? Did small communities, on the other hand, resist or temper categorical relations and identities of any kind by retaining a personalized society of specific hierarchical and equal relations – a society of "ranks," perhaps, that had in the cities evolved into a society of "classes" by the middle of the nineteenth century?

These are difficult questions that would, if approached as problems of historical research, require at least another book to answer. It is possible, however, to venture some preliminary answers in this brief epilogue by considering what others have already written about smaller nineteenth-century American communities, bearing in mind that existing studies reflect their authors' own interests and agendas, and cannot always be made to answer questions that we put to them after the fact. This limitation, indeed, has suggested to me a particular strategy. Rather than attempt a comprehensive review of what has been written about rural and small-town America, I shall draw on those few studies that have been framed at least partly along lines similar to those that shaped this volume, or that for any reason promise the best answers to the questions just raised.

Paul Faler's *Mechanics and Manufacturers in the Early Industrial Revolution* is one such study and a logical place to begin if we imagine our task as one of venturing outward from the major urban center. Lynn, Massachusetts, the focus of Faler's inquiry into the evolving social relations of early industrial capitalism, is representative of a particular type of smaller city that appeared and proliferated during the nineteenth century – the industrial satellite of a major city, located only a few miles from that city, and maintaining close relations of one or more sorts with it. Lynn was actually less of a satellite than Lowell, Lawrence, or any of the other nearby textile towns whose factories were built, financed, and operated by the wealthy merchants of Boston. Its shoe manufactories and shops were largely homegrown, and some of its closest economic ties were to the more distant cities of Philadelphia and Baltimore, which served as conduits to the southern market in which the majority of Lynn's shoes were sold.[2] Nevertheless, Lynn's proximity to Boston and to the smaller port of Salem (both of which mediated to some extent the shoe town's relation with cities outside the region), shaped its economic and social development in crucial ways. Most important, Lynn's location within an emerging metropolitan region permitted the town's development as a specialized industrial center that could focus most of its resources and population on the production of shoes while drawing on the commercial, financial, and other services of the larger and more complex central city. Without Boston, Lynn would have required a wider array of local wholesalers, brokers, shippers, bankers, and insurers to help export its production, and a larger number of importers of food and other products, and of retailers of various types, to sustain and supply its more varied population. Put another way, Lynn would have been more like Boston and most other cities, its industrial sector set within a much wider range of urban activities.

This specialization or "imbalance" of the industrial satellite imparted a distinct character to its local society. In Lynn, as in Newark, Paterson, and other similar places, local life reflected the size, circumstances, and values of its industrial working class, as well as the relative absence of the wealthy merchants, bankers, and professionals who were so visible in larger cities. Both conditions sharpened class awareness among workers and gave prominence to the assertion of the various strains of the mechanics' ideology – the first because these were workers who were experiencing in concentrated numbers and in the most significant way the reorganization of production and productive relations, and the second because the countervailing voice of the merchant capitalist either was not articulated locally or was easily ignored. This is not to say that Lynn and the other industrial satellites were one-class towns, or that class conflict occurred only across wider, metropolitan spaces. Local capitalists existed, and if local class conflict was muted initially, as it was in Lynn, by the artisanal origins of many emerging manufacturers, and by remnants of traditional craft relations, it would soon emerge more clearly as the interests of manufacturers and workers were clarified.[3] What made the Lynn of 1860 fundamentally different from the Lynn of 1800, Faler concludes, was the formation of class among both manufacturers and workers: "Lynn was a town but no longer a community: a people growing apart, two parts with two bodies of shared experiences, each part creating traditions, values, and institutions that answered to their distinctive needs."[4]

In significant ways, the evolution of class experience in Lynn resembled that of the larger cities. Faler describes the emergence of separate neighborhoods of manufacturers and workers, and the development of institutions that further divided Lynn's proprietors and wage earners into separate social networks. Shoe manufacturers, professionals, and other proprietors founded and joined the Social Library, the Silsbee Street Debating Club, the Franklin Club, the Natural History Society, the Social Union, the Exploring Club, the Gnomologian Society, and other exclusive organizations, and sent their children to the Lynn Academy and, when the academy closed, to the Lynn High School. No fee was required at the latter institution, but of fifty boys enrolled in 1854, only two were the sons of shoemakers. Wage-earning shoemakers, meanwhile, founded unions and cooperatives, and joined volunteer fire companies that operated separately from two private fire clubs made up of manufacturers and other businessmen.[5] All of this was based on the changing relations of the industrializing workplace where, Faler emphasizes, employers were withdrawing from the productive process, removing themselves from the shop floor to "carpeted counting rooms and shoe rooms with beautifully painted and grained counters and doors," and dressing in the clothes of the businessman rather than those of the producing artisan.[6] This physical and social withdrawal, finally, at the workplace and in the larger community, fed upon and nurtured further the withdrawal of sympathies between manufacturer and worker that transformed the personalized hierarchies of the small community of producing mechanics into the categorical class identities of the industrial city. The process was clear in Lynn, a city that at the end of the antebellum era numbered fewer than 20,000 inhabitants.[7]

But if the particulars of that process were similar in Lynn and in larger cities, the outcome was somewhat different. Faler frequently refers to Lynn's dominant manufacturers as "middle class" and to the development of distinct neighborhoods and institutions among them as "the maturing of the middle class" in the industrial city.[8] The term appears to have been carefully chosen, as Faler contrasts Lynn's emerging manufacturers to the merchant aristocrats of nearby North Shore ports, and emphasizes the absence from Lynn of a distinct upper class. As the manufacturers prospered, they did "become in wealth and life style much like the aristocrats and capitalists of Salem" and were accused of behaving as aristocrats by their increasingly alienated employees.[9] But Faler does not trace the development of a three-class system in Lynn, and I believe that his focus on the bifurcation of experience and identity within the industrial satellite city reflects more than a Marxist predisposition to find only two classes. Lynn's manufacturers, along with its professionals and other businessmen, do not seem to have divided into separate, hierarchical social networks, even though some of the wealthiest among them may have longed to be recognized as a class apart from the rest of the local bourgeoisie. Lynn developed two classes, and at most the embryo of a third, and this appears to have been typical of the industrial satellite city, where the "old" and wealthy families of the metropolis did not reside.[10] In a purely local sense, therefore, Lynn's "middle class" was really an upper class, the dominant group of a simple pair. Yet Faler is right to call it a middle class, for Lynn's society is best understood in a larger, metropolitan perspective. Not only the merchant princes of Salem, but the even loftier Brahmins of Boston, were known as a class to the manufacturers and the workers of Lynn, and helped define their own social identities. The distinction may have meant little to Lynn's workers, but it could hardly have failed to set limits on the pretensions of its manufacturers. The system of social experiences and identities in the industrial satellite cities was not, in sum, entirely different from that of the metropolitan center – it was, indeed, the same system in a truncated form.

The majority of smaller American cities were not industrial satellites but more "balanced" communities outside the immediate orbit of a metropolitan center. Utica, New York, for example, the subject of Mary P. Ryan's *Cradle of the Middle Class*, was a small commercial and industrial city in the center of New York State, 175 miles from New York City, and more than 60 miles from the closest city of any size. No single economic activity dominated Utica in the manner that shoe manufacturing dominated Lynn; hence, its workers and proprietors were significantly more diverse, and its public discourse was less frequently devoted to the social issues generated by industrialization. Yet, according to Ryan, class formation was a discernible and significant aspect of Utica's early development – underpinning the history of family and gender that is the primary focus of her study was "a major historical process" that Ryan forthrightly calls "the emergence of a definable middle class."[11] The details of that process need not be recited again here; suffice it to say that Utica's emerging middle class, like its counterpart in the larger cities, made significant use of fairly exclusive voluntary associations and focused its energies on the solidification of status within an increasingly distinct white-collar sector.[12]

On the other hand, the broader array of class relations that these middle-class strategies imply is not entirely clear, and it is difficult to determine from Ryan's analysis whether upper and lower classes similar to those of larger cities were also taking shape in nineteenth-century Utica. Ryan devotes little attention to the changing circumstances (or family strategies) of manual workers, or to establishing the exclusiveness of local "elite commercial families" that included several offshoots of the Van Rensselaers, one of the most aristocratic families in the state.[13] One larger contextual issue she does address may be reasonably taken as an important *limit* to the extent and significance of class formation in the smaller city. Utica's size – in 1840, at least, when the local population was fewer than 13,000 – seemed to preclude a significant separation of class networks in the daily routine of city life. "The men and women of Utica were in easy reach of one another in 1840 when the entire city was only ten blocks square," writes Ryan.[14] So too were people of different social condition. Ryan points to an 1838 lithograph depicting the casual, interclass street life of the small city to support this view: "Men and women stopped beside a crude farm wagon to chat. Workers and businessmen paused in the street for leisurely conversation. Children used the same streets as their playground."[15] The contrast between this scene and, say, *Harper's* description of rush-hour omnibuses passing through the Bowery could hardly be greater and supports the idea that the smaller city was not an environment that could easily sustain the categorical class distinctions that flourished in the metropolis.

My own study of Kingston, New York, a town slightly smaller than Utica, partly contradicts this view and suggests that the lithograph Ryan describes is an excessively bucolic representation of the small-city environment during the antebellum era. Kingston (and Utica, too, I am sure) was a busy place, and its streets, stores, workshops, and homes were distributed into fairly distinct districts of retailing, industrial production, and class-based residence. In and near the center of the two adjoining villages that constituted the emerging city were retail stores, fashionable churches, and the homes of Kingston's nonmanual businessmen and professionals. Farther from the center were large and small workshops and the homes of most skilled and some unskilled manual workers, while larger numbers of workers, not all of them unskilled, lived on the periphery, many of them in the vicinity of a large limestone quarry and cement plant.[16] This was a pattern characteristic of larger cities (save only for suburbanization, which had barely begun in Kingston before the Civil War), and it did physically separate Kingston's different social strata during and after the workday. The scale of separation was smaller, of course, but it may have been sufficiently large to nourish separate class identities. Kingstonians themselves clearly sensed a significant change in the scale of the community. This was the era when directories and maps of Kingston first appeared, when houses began to be numbered on many streets, and when local newspapers pointed out the need for street signs. It was also a time when local growth had made an anachronism of the traditional practice of attending to matters of personal honor through the pages of the town's newspapers. In 1849, the local diarist Nathaniel Booth observed in the paper a friend's intention to publish his side of a domestic argument. Booth dismissed the gesture in a manner that suggests something of the distance that Kingston, a town of only some 10,000 inhabitants, had traveled toward the separate networks of the developed city: "What do the public care about him or his affairs. . . . I doubt if any beyond his immediate neighborhood has even heard of him."[17]

The separation of classes in the small city was not purely, nor even primarily, a function of city growth. Kingston and Utica, after all, were smaller than Philadelphia and New York had been in the late eighteenth century, when people of various sorts intermingled on the streets and in the markets and shops of the craft-dominated city. The scale of the city, large and small, must be understood in conjunction with the structure and distribution of existing institutions, and by the middle of the nineteenth century the most important urban institutions – including industrial workshops, retail stores, and others that distributed work and workers into specific spaces – were increasing the segmentation of cities of all sizes, including those as small as Kingston and Utica. The physical separation of classes in these smaller nineteenth-century cities was, as I have already suggested, less dramatic than it was in larger cities of the same era, and contributed less powerfully to the creation of distinct social networks. But it was sufficiently advanced to contradict the socially integrating effects of a still small urban scale, and to contribute to the class identities of those already disposed to locate themselves and others within a hierarchical "map" of the community.

This disposition toward class awareness in the small city was no doubt enhanced by the close cultural connections between the large and small cities of developing urban regions. This is a subject about which much more could be known, but it is clear that big-city ways and ideas were by no means foreign to the residents of the small city. In Kingston, which is some ninety miles from New York, local businessmen and others traveled regularly to the metropolis to purchase goods, attend the theater, visit relatives and friends, or simply tour the city. Numerous local institutions maintained formal relations with analogous institutions in the big city, and Kingston supplied its share of members to New York–based organizations such as the American Art Union. Local newspaper editors culled many items from the big-city press, and, perhaps most important of all, Kingstonians subscribed to those magazines, *Harper's*, *Godey's*, *Frank Leslie's*, and others, that so frequently depicted and analyzed modern city life.[18] New York–based writers commonly represented their city as the "brain" of a far-flung nervous system, and if this conceit overstates the intellectual dependence of the residents of smaller communities on the thinkers and style setters of the metropolis, it does not seriously misrepresent the commonalities of experience and culture within the urban region as a whole.[19] Kingstonians and Uticans were certainly well aware of the developing class distinctions of the metropolis, and Ryan's analysis strongly suggests that similar distinctions were being made by Utica's white-collar middle class. Should we say that this small-city middle class was modeled on big-city lines, or simply point to the similarities as aspects of a shared culture?

At the *upper* levels of provincial urban society this close connection to the metropolis seems to have had a very different result. Kingston and Utica, unlike Lynn, contained old and fairly wealthy families, some of whom maintained social connections with a cosmopolitan elite that included the "upper ten" of New York City.[20] But it is difficult to identify these families as a local upper class, set apart from the rest of the community through exclusive formal and informal associations and a distinctively sumptuous style of living. The smaller fortunes of most provincial notables may have been a factor, while surely another was the small number of such people in any one community. Of equal importance, however, was their very orientation to the larger and more imposing social world beyond the small city, a cosmopolitanism that made local social standing less worth striving for, and left the mechanisms of upper-class exclusiveness less developed. This underdevelopment of the local upper class, incidentally, was not incompatible with the maintenance of more traditional, personal relations of patronage and deference, but it is difficult to find evidence of such "pre-class" relations in the surviving records of, or commentary on, communal affairs in the small city.

It is reasonable to assume that these various resemblances and connections to the large city were inversely related to both community size and the distance of the locality from a major urban center. Presumably, there were thresholds of distance and size beyond and beneath which the urban pattern of social organization was of little relevance, or was relevant only as an easily resisted alien influence. Presumably, too, the vast majority of nineteenth-century Americans lived in communities that had not gained those thresholds, that were organized into local networks and hierarchies that differed fundamentally from those of the city, and that imparted social identities far different from those generated within urban social worlds. These are sound assumptions, but it is important to recognize how thresholds of size were affected by time and the dynamics of communal development – the age of a community, the rate and prospects of its growth, the process and rate of local population turnover, and the external forces that influence the community's continuing growth, stabilization, or decline. Communities differed, in other words, not only according to size and location but also according to what might be called their stage of development. Not just the first two, but all three, were crucial to the shape of local social relations. This is the fundamental finding of Don Harrison Doyle's *Social Order of a Frontier Community*, a study of the founding and early development of Jacksonville, Illinois.

Doyle's Jacksonville was founded in 1825, grew slowly at first, and then grew more rapidly as the countryside around it filled up and the town acquired rail links to larger urban centers. By 1850, Jacksonville had 2,745 residents, a number that doubled during the ensuing decade to more than 5,500. Still a third to a fourth the size of Kingston and Utica (which had grown to 16,000 and 22,000, respectively), it was nonetheless a growing, economically diverse, and socially heterogeneous center, whose history confirmed most of the more sober expectations of local boosters. Growth brought profits to those boosters, but it also exacerbated the problem of constructing a coherent social order, as did the high rate of population turnover – the doubling of Jacksonville's population during the 1850s was achieved despite the persistence of only 27% of those who had been living in the community at the start of the decade. Doyle's analysis of the task of community building proceeds, therefore, from the fundamental fact that at any given moment during this era of rapid population growth and turnover, most of Jacksonville's residents were strangers to one another.[21]

As in larger places, where size as well as flux limited the scope of purely personal relations, a stable social order was achieved in Jacksonville through formal voluntary institutions, through rules of conduct that these organizations helped to promulgate, and through the fitting of new individuals into the ongoing roles and statuses that the "voluntary community" and the community as a whole had come to provide. This last process was influenced by judgments and aspirations of a personal nature – strangers were no doubt quickly judged as friendly or reserved, coarse or refined, by those they met face-to-face – but Doyle demonstrates the essentially categorical nature of local society and the crucial interrelations among persistence, associational participation, occupation, and social status. Put most simply, professionals and business proprietors were much more likely than skilled and unskilled manual workers to remain in Jacksonville and gain local respectability.[22] The stable and activist core of the community was essentially white collar, and was recognized as such. Hence, white-collar people entered the community in a different way and at a different level than blue-collar people, and this categorical reception and assumption of communal roles outweighed the effects of personality in most instances. Doyle does not hesitate to identify Jacksonville's white-collar activists as a middle class, and emphasizes the middle-class values that took shape within the voluntary community.[23] It should be noted that Doyle does include artisanal proprietors in the white-collar category in his statistical tables, a technical decision that might suggest an important difference in the social meaning of work in larger and smaller places, and a different boundary between the middle and working classes. However, in his analysis of occupational transitions among the stable population, Doyle suggests that many of these artisans expressed their aspirations, and their recognition of the social value of white-collar status, by calling themselves merchants, agents, or dealers rather than assuming the titles of their trades.[24]

The frenetic population turnover that shaped the social relations of Jacksonville and other frontier communities gradually abated, and the stable core of residents gradually grew in relation to the number of recent arrivals. In Jacksonville, as local growth began to slow, and as rival towns won most of the contests for growth-inducing institutions (such as the University of Illinois, lost to Champaign in 1867), local residents began to revise their expectations for the town, and reinterpreted Jacksonville as "a small, intimate, self-consciously genteel community" rather than as an emerging city.[25] Did the character of local social relations also change as the town's population stabilized in this manner? This question is not raised in Doyle's study, which terminates in 1870, and it is in any case better asked of other frontier communities that remained smaller than Jacksonville. Let us imagine prairie towns that stabilized at smaller sizes, those of the sort described in Lewis Atherton's classic work *Main Street on the Middle Border*. Atherton deals with the founding and early growth of small midwestern towns, but his focus is on town life during the phase that Jacksonville was just entering as Doyle's narrative ends. In Bosworth, Missouri (population 401 in 1900), and other small towns of Atherton's research and personal memory, we find a rather different, more personalized society, in which the stable core of known residents is enlarged, and where local life is organized according to a moral order preserved through personal as well as institutional means.[26] Viewing Doyle's and Atherton's books together, therefore, leads us to posit a history of class formation in the small towns of midwestern America that, from the customary point of view, looks like a film run in reverse. First, there was a phase of rapid local development, where social life paralleled that of the city in the categorical and institutional character of social judgment, and where membership in a categorically defined (that is, white-collar) middle class powerfully influenced one's role within the community. This phase gradually gave way to another, the development of a more personalized social order, where class distinctions were more often qualified by collective judgments of each individual's personality, character, and willingness to conform to community norms, and where the lengthening bonds of local kinship and long-term personal acquaintance to a large extent superseded institutional and categorical means of structuring personal relations. The transition would have been particularly evident in smaller towns that stabilized at a size below which the conditions of class were largely preserved, and less evident in those that grew into small cities.

It may be objected that this curious sequence could not have occurred in the thousands of agricultural communities – villages and small stretches of open farmland – in which most Americans lived, for these were highly personal societies from the very start. John Mack Faragher found evidence of a fairly active communal life in Sugar Creek, Illinois, an open-country settlement of some two hundred dispersed farming households not far from Jacksonville. Distinctions existed in Sugar Creek between larger and smaller landowning farmers, and, more crucially, between owner-operators and tenant farmers (there were few farm laborers), but these distinctions do not appear to have shaped the life of frontier cooperation and exchange in the same way that categorical occupational distinctions shaped people's lives in cities and towns.[27] On the other hand, Hal S. Barron's *Those Who Stayed Behind*, a study of the persistently rural (if nonfrontier) community of Chelsea, Vermont, traces a history much like the one just sketched for new urban settlements. Barron, indeed, insists on a view of rural development that contrasts older agricultural settlements with both newer rural settlements and cities, as economic systems and as communities, and that appreciates the older, more stable rural community as a particular form of equilibrium within a system generally characterized by growth and flux.[28] As a young and growing community, Chelsea developed a stratified society in which village-dwelling professionals and merchants, and the wealthier farmers, were recognized as a superior class. Carriages and chaises symbolized this superiority, which was also embodied in membership in the local Masonic lodge.[29] Barron does not dwell on the nature of local social distinctions but does emphasize both their significance in a fundamentally divided community and their connection with the rapid population turnover associated with early development.[30]

As Chelsea matured, a quite different society evolved there. Migration into the community slowed significantly as undeveloped land disappeared, as the enormous expansion of western agriculture confined existing farms in Chelsea to sheep raising and to other activities that required few hands beyond those provided by the farm family, and as distant industrialization reduced demand for the products of local artisans. Migration out of the community continued, however, halving the local population over the second half of the nineteenth century. Barron correctly insists that this out-migration be understood as part of the process of stabilization rather than as abandonment. Few if any farms were actually abandoned, and few people left Chelsea as entire family groups. Rather, farms were passed down to a single son, while other children settled, often with parental assistance, on farms in nearby towns (the most common pattern), on more distant farms, or in cities. Under these conditions the "stable core" of the community gradually became nearly the entire community, a development reinforced by the very common practice of finding a wife or husband within the borders of the town.[31]

Endogamy, family continuity, and reduced in-migration, within a setting of relatively limited and uniform economic opportunity, all operated in the same direction. Chelsea became a community organized by kinship, propinquity, and friendship – by personal ties that had little or nothing to do with class distinctions. Barron describes the community as having resolved earlier distinctions and conflicts into a stable consensus of values and beliefs, and an inclusive local society in which voluntary associations and casual socializing cut across remaining hierarchies of occupation and economic well-being.[32] He argues, moreover, that Chelsea's history was in these respects typical of those of older rural communities in many parts of the country, including Atherton's Middle Border. Stabilization and its attendant changes in local social relations were not "simply another Yankee peculiarity." Rather, the patterns of change in Chelsea were "indications of the more general characteristics that distinguished settled rural society from the rest of nineteenth-century America."[33]

The film run in reverse – depicting initial class distinctions gradually mitigated by community stabilization and expanding kinship relations – would appear to apply to rural as well as to small-town America. Yet the social assumptions, ambitions, and active prejudices that both Doyle and Barron associate with the early phases of communal development in nineteenth-century America were not easily erased from the cultures of the stabilizing small town and countryside. Some of the children who left the family farm in a brother's hands did go to the city – some reluctantly, some eagerly. Defenders of country ways worried about the latter group, and about the meaning of their apparent rejection of rural life. The terms used by one such spokesman, quoted by Barron, are interesting. Addressing the would-be migrant, he wrote, "You are tempted to exchange the hard work of the farm, to become a clerk in a city shop, to put off your heavy boots and frock, and be a gentleman, behind the counter!"[34] There is more than a hint here of those cultural commonalities discussed earlier in this epilogue. Country people, too, understood the terms and means of social ascendancy in the city, and it is particularly interesting to see the stream of country lads migrating to city clerkships explained in terms of social rather than economic aspiration. Moreover, the specific prejudices that this passage addressed were not confined to the restless young men of the stable countryside. I return, finally, to the letter written to Mrs. Shaw by Lydia Maria Child from her Massachusetts farm in August 1877:

> I do not know of a farmer in this rustic town, who would not object to his daughter's marrying the son of a day laborer; and the daughters themselves will put up with any deprivations at home, rather than go to help a neighbor in any emergency, for a dollar, or two dollars a day. All want to crowd into employments deemed genteel; employments that do not soil the clothes, or the hands. Hence, the supply of teachers and artists is much greater than the demand, and a good deal of it not above mediocrity; while there is absolute suffering for services not deemed genteel, but which are absolutely necessary. There is no use in being blind to the fact; an unwillingness to be *known* to labor with the hands *does* pervade all classes of the community. Moreover, each class draws a line between itself and the class below it.[35]

The issue of how and whether social distinctions developed, functioned, and abated in rural America is by no means resolved. Indeed, it has hardly been raised, and it awaits further research in a wide variety of other local and regional contexts – dispersed farm communities of the Midwest and West, for example, or subregions of the plantation and upcountry South.[36] Lydia Child's frank description of class distinctions in a Gilded Age Massachusetts rural community obviously does not settle the issue, but it does underscore how mistaken it would be to see the city and the country in simple, antithetical terms – to assume that what was true of the city was necessarily *untrue* of the country. On the contrary, within particular regions the various connections between cities, towns, villages, and farms imparted common understandings that to some extent contradicted obvious differences in their purely local social relations. These differences deserve further exploration – but so, too, do the similarities that took the experience and awareness of class beyond the borders of the big city.

Notes

Chapter 1. The elusive middle class

1 Walt Whitman, *I Sit and Look Out: Editorials from the Brooklyn Daily Times, by Walt Whitman*, selected and edited by Emory Holloway and Vernolian Schwarz (New York, 1932), p. 145.

2 Walt Whitman, *Leaves of Grass: Comprehensive Reader's Edition*, Harold W. Blodgett and Sculley Bradley, eds. (New York, 1965), pp. 39, 41, 94.

3 The shifting social taxonomy of serious writers on politics and political economy is ably discussed in Martin J. Burke, "The Conundrum of Class: Public Discourse on the Social Order in America" (Ph.D. dissertation, University of Michigan, 1987).

4 Louis Hartz, *The Liberal Tradition in America: An Interpretation of American Political Thought Since the Revolution* (New York, 1955), pp. 51–2. The recognition of deep political conflicts that revolve primarily around "ethnocultural" differences stems mainly from Lee Benson, *The Concept of Jacksonian Democracy: New York as a Test Case* (Princeton, 1961). For a succinct discussion of the basic tenets of the "ethnocultural school," see Benson, "Group Cohesion and Social and Ideological Conflict: A Critique of Some Marxian and Tocquevillian Theories," *American Behavioral Scientist* 16 (1973): 741–67. It is instructive to contrast Hartz's and Benson's discussions of American society and politics with Harold Perkin, *The Origins of Modern English Society, 1780–1880* (London, 1969).

5 On Tocqueville as a source for the middle-class consensus, see Seymour Drescher, *Dilemmas of Democracy: Tocqueville and Modernization* (Pittsburgh, 1968). Drescher notes that Tocqueville "chose to use the independent middle class as his ideal type, and to systematically exclude or quarantine all dissonant data" (p. 278).

6 Paul G. Faler, "Cultural Aspects of the Industrial Revolution: Lynn, Massachusetts, Shoemakers and Industrial Morality, 1826–1860," *Labor History* 15 (1974): 367–94; Bruce Laurie, *Working People of Philadelphia, 1800–1850* (Philadelphia, 1980). See also Herbert G. Gutman, *Work, Culture, and Society in Industrializing America: Essays in American Working-Class and Social History* (New York, 1976); Sean Wilentz, *Chants Democratic: New York City and the Rise of the American Working Class, 1788–1850* (New York, 1984); Faler, *Mechanics and Manufacturers in the Early Industrial Revolution: Lynn,*

Massachusetts, 1780–1860 (Albany, N.Y., 1981); Alan Dawley, *Class and Community: The Industrial Revolution in Lynn* (Cambridge, Mass., 1976); Susan E. Hirsch, *Roots of the American Working Class: The Industrialization of Crafts in Newark, 1800–1860* (Philadelphia, 1978); Daniel J. Walkowitz, *Worker City, Company Town: Iron and Cotton-Worker Protest in Troy and Co-hoes, New York, 1855–84* (Urbana, Ill., 1978); Francis G. Couvares, *The Remaking of Pittsburgh: Class and Culture in an Industrializing City, 1877–1919* (Albany, N.Y., 1984); Roy Rosenzweig, *Eight Hours for What We Will: Workers and Leisure in an Industrial City, 1870–1920* (Cambridge, 1983); Steven J. Ross, *Workers on the Edge: Work, Leisure, and Politics in Industrializing Cincinnati, 1788–1890* (New York, 1985); Brian Greenberg, *Worker and Community: Response to Industrialization in a Nineteenth-Century American City, Albany, New York, 1850–1884* (Albany, N.Y., 1985); John T. Cumbler, *Working-Class Community in Industrial America: Work, Leisure and Struggle in Two Industrial Cities, 1880–1930* (Westport, Conn., 1979); Michael H. Frisch and Daniel J. Walkowitz, eds., *Working-Class America: Essays on Labor, Community and American Society* (Urbana, Ill., 1983); Milton Cantor, ed., *American Working-Class Culture: Explorations in American Labor and Social History* (Westport, Conn., 1979).

7   Edward Pessen, *Riches, Class, and Power Before the Civil War* (Lexington, Mass., 1973); Frederic Cople Jaher, *The Urban Establishment: Upper Strata in Boston, New York, Charleston, Chicago, and Los Angeles* (Urbana, Ill., 1982); Ronald Story, *The Forging of an Aristocracy: Harvard and the Boston Upper Class, 1800–1870* (Middletown, Conn., 1980); Story, "Class and Culture in Boston: The Athenaeum, 1807–1860," *American Quarterly* 27 (1975): 178–99; and three historical works by the sociologist E. Digby Baltzell: *Philadelphia Gentlemen: The Making of a National Upper Class* (Glencoe, Ill., 1958); *The Protestant Establishment: Aristocracy and Caste in America* (New York, 1964); *Puritan Boston and Quaker Philadelphia: Two Protestant Ethics and the Spirit of Class Authority and Leadership* (New York, 1977).

8   See Lee Soltow, *Men and Wealth in the United States: 1850–1870* (New Haven, 1975); Soltow, "Economic Inequality in the United States in the Period from 1790 to 1860," *Journal of Economic History* 31 (1971): 822–39; Soltow, "The Wealth, Income, and Social Class of Men in Large Northern Cities of the United States in 1860," in James D. Smith, ed., *The Personal Distribution of Income and Wealth* (New York, 1975), pp. 233–76; Pessen, *Riches, Class, and Power Before the Civil War*; Stuart M. Blumin, "Mobility and Change in Ante-Bellum Philadelphia," in Stephan Thernstrom and Richard Sennett, eds., *Nineteenth-Century Cities: Essays in the New Urban History* (New Haven, 1969), esp. pp. 204–5; Michael B. Katz, *The People of Hamilton, Canada West: Family and Class in a Mid-Nineteenth-Century City* (Cambridge, Mass., 1975), pp. 44–93; Robert E. Gallman, "Trends in the Size Distribution of Wealth in the Nineteenth Century: Some Speculations," in Soltow, ed., *Six Papers on the Size Distribution of Wealth and Income* (New York, 1969), pp. 1–25; and Craig Buettinger, "Economic Inequality in Early Chicago, 1849–1850," *Journal of Social History* 11 (1978):

413–18. For the most recent and comprehensive account, see Jeffrey G. Williamson and Peter H. Lindert, *American Inequality: A Macroeconomic History* (New York, 1980).

9   It should be noted that the terms "bourgeoisie" and "middle class" are by no means interchangeable. For two valuable essays, see Peter Stearns, "The Middle Class: Toward a Precise Definition," *Comparative Studies in Society and History* 21 (1979): 377–96; and Arno J. Mayer, "The Lower Middle Class as Historical Problem," *Journal of Modern History* 47 (1975): 409–36.

10 C. Wright Mills, *White Collar: The American Middle Classes* (New York, 1951), p. 3.

11 E. P. Thompson, *The Making of the English Working Class* (London, 1963); Thompson, "Eighteenth-Century English Society: Class Struggle Without Class?" *Social History* 3 (1978): 133–65.

12 Mills, *White Collar*, p. 7.

13 Sam Bass Warner, Jr., *Streetcar Suburbs: The Process of Growth in Boston, 1870–1900* (Cambridge, Mass., 1962), pp. 8–9, 55–6, 162–3.

14 Burton Bledstein, *The Culture of Professionalism: The Middle Class and the Development of Higher Education in America* (New York, 1976), p. ix.

15 Paul E. Johnson, *A Shopkeeper's Millennium: Society and Revivals in Rochester, New York, 1815–1837* (New York, 1978), p. 8. The emphasis is mine.

16 Paul Boyer, *Urban Masses and Moral Order in America: 1820–1920* (Cambridge, Mass., 1978), pp. 61, 179.

17 Mary P. Ryan, *Cradle of the Middle Class: The Family in Oneida County, New York, 1790–1865* (Cambridge, 1981), xiii, 13.

18 Karen Halttunen, in *Confidence Men and Painted Women: A Study of Middle-Class Culture in America, 1830–1870* (New Haven, 1982), writes of antebellum sentimentalism as "central to the self-conscious self-definition of middle-class culture during the most critical period of its development" (p. xvii). In *The New Metropolis: New York City, 1840–1857* (New York, 1981), Edward K. Spann notes, almost in passing, an "emerging middle class" (p. 243). John S. Gilkeson, Jr., *Middle-Class Providence, 1820–1940* (Princeton, 1986), is an attempt to trace the role of a developing middle-class culture in one American city. See also Sean Wilentz, "Artisan Origins of the American Working Class," *International Labor and Working Class History*, no. 19 (1981): 4; Wilentz, "Artisan Republican Festivals and the Rise of Class Conflict in New York City, 1788–1837," in Frisch and Walkowitz, eds., *Working-Class America*, esp. p. 62; Gary John Kornblith, "From Artisans to Businessmen: Master Mechanics in New England, 1789–1850" (Ph.D. dissertation, Princeton University, 1983).

19 For an excellent and relatively recent discussion of this aspect of Marxist theory, see Anthony Giddens, *The Class Structure of the Advanced Societies* (New York, 1975), pp. 23–40.

20 See, for example, Marx's discussion of the politics of the French "petty bourgeoisie" in *The Eighteenth Brumaire of Louis Napoleon*, in Karl Marx and Friedrich Engels, *Collected Works* (New York, 1979), vol. 11, pp. 103–97.

21　Nicos Poulantzas, *Classes in Contemporary Capitalism* (London, 1975), pp. 205, 287; Erik Olin Wright, *Class, Crisis, and the State* (London, 1978), pp. 61–87; and Dale L. Johnson, *Class and Social Development: A New Theory of the Middle Class* (Beverly Hills, 1982), pp. 24, 106.

22　Johnson, *Class and Social Development*, p. 10.

23　For an excellent discussion of Marxism as a theory of capitalist development, see Isaiah Berlin, *Karl Marx: His Life and Environment*, 4th ed. (New York, 1978), esp. pp. 89–116. On the more successful application of Marxism to "epochal" rather than more specific "historical" questions, see Raymond Williams, "Base and Superstructure in Marxist Cultural Theory," *New Left Review*, no. 82 (1973): 3–16.

24　Johnson, *Class and Social Development*, p. 22; Michael B. Katz, Michael J. Doucet, and Mark J. Stern, *The Social Organization of Early Industrial Capitalism* (Cambridge, Mass., 1982), p. 39.

25　Johnson, *Class and Social Development*, pp. 106, 105, 200.

26　J. H. Hexter, "A New Framework for Social History," in Hexter, *Reappraisals in History: New Views on History and Society in Early Modern Europe*, 2d ed. (Chicago, 1979), pp. 15–16.

27　Ibid., p. 16. In a similar spirit Sean Wilentz writes of his abandonment of "the familiar, essentialist concept of class consciousness" (one part of the Marxian "package deal"), on grounds that "historians who have stuck to this particular concept have usually allowed it to tyrannize them, so that they try to see how closely the past approximated the ideal – thereby using a concept to account for why something that presumably *should* have happened, did not, before coming to terms with what *did* happen" (*Chants Democratic*, p. 15).

28　Poulantzas, *Classes in Contemporary Capitalism*, esp. pp. 193–208, 285–90; and Mills, *White Collar*, esp. pp. 3, 6.

29　Stanislaw Ossowski, *Class Structure in the Social Consciousness* (London, 1963), pp. 32–3.

30　Dale Johnson, as an orthodox Marxist, has complained about Giddens's "Marxized Weberian perspective . . . . A rather indiscriminate eclecticism in his theoretical position leads to some provocative critiques but does not lend itself to the construction of a coherent theory" (*Class and Social Development*, pp. 24–5n).

31　Giddens, *Class Structure of the Advanced Societies*, pp. 132, 105, 107–9, 111, and esp. pp. 177–97. Emphases are in the original. See Ralf Dahrendorf, *Class and Class Conflict in Industrial Society* (Stanford, 1959).

32　See Gerard DeGré, "Ideology and Class Consciousness in the Middle Class," *Social Forces* 29 (1950–1): 173–9.

33　One exception is the early nineteenth-century "Middling Interest" in Boston. See Robert A. McCaughey, "From Town to City: Boston in the 1820s," *Political Science Quarterly* 88 (1973): 191–213; and Andrew R. L. Cayton, "The Fragmentation of 'A Great Family': The Panic of 1819 and the Rise of a Middling Interest in Boston, 1818–1822," *Journal of the Early Republic* 2 (1982): 143–67.

34 Giddens, *Class Structure of the Advanced Societies*, p. 111. The emphasis is in the original.

35 Samuel Gompers captured this distinction, or something quite like it, in his memoir of a life spent forging the principles and institutions of practical unionism. Gompers recalls arguing with socialists that "the *Klassen Bewustzein* (class consciousness) of which they made so much" was the property of intellectuals ("all who had imagination"), while "that primitive force that had its origin in experience only was *Klassengefühl* (class feeling)." This "class feeling," rooted in the experience of working-class life rather than in the theory of capitalist development and inevitable class conflict, was "one of the strongest cohesive forces in the labor movement." Samuel Gompers, *Seventy Years of Life and Labor: An Autobiography* (New York, 1925), vol. 1, p. 383. I am grateful to Gerd Korman for directing me to this passage.

36 Stuart M. Blumin, "The Hypothesis of Middle-Class Formation in Nineteenth-Century America: A Critique and Some Proposals," *American Historical Review* 90 (1985): 299–338.

37 On the millenarian Marx, see Robert C. Tucker, *The Marxian Revolutionary Idea* (New York, 1969).

38 Thompson, *Making of the English Working Class*, p. 9.

39 Ryan, in the closest analysis to date, suggests the same, even though her study ends in 1865. She makes only moderate claims for the period she examines, and at one point notes that the "making of the middle class in the industrial age" (following 1865) was "conditioned by" developments in the antebellum era. See Ryan, *Cradle of the Middle Class*, pp. 239, 155.

40 Edward Countryman, *A People in Revolution: The American Revolution and Political Society in New York, 1760–1790* (Baltimore, 1981), p. 12. See also Eric Foner, *Tom Paine and Revolutionary America* (New York, 1976), which contends that the phrase "middle-class objectives" is anachronistic to the eighteenth century (p. 272). Joyce Appleby, in her review of Foner's book, writes of Paine: "To the extent that he helped undermine the rationale for group solidarity and thereby liberated men from traditional restraints, it seems more appropriate to register his contribution – at least on this side of the Atlantic – to the making of the American middle class" (*American Historical Review* 85 [1980]: 716). Other eighteenth-century historians who do use the term "middle class" include Carl Bridenbaugh, *Cities in Revolt: Urban Life in America, 1743–1776* (New York, 1955), e.g., p. 332; Carl and Jessica Bridenbaugh, *Rebels and Gentlemen: Philadelphia in the Age of Franklin* (New York, 1942), pp. 361–4 (but note their hesitation to use the term on pp. 14–15); Charles S. Olton, *Artisans for Independence: Philadelphia Mechanics and the American Revolution* (Syracuse, 1975), p. x; Richard Alan Ryerson, *The Revolution Is Now Begun: The Radical Committees of Philadelphia, 1765–1776* (Philadelphia, 1976), p. 254 (for "middle classes," see pp. 189–90); Bernard Friedman, "The Shaping of Radical Consciousness in Provincial New York," *Journal of American History* 56

(1970): 796; Robert Gough, "Notes on the Pennsylvania Revolutionaries of 1776," *Pennsylvania Magazine of History and Biography* 96 (1972): 90 (but note that "middle class" is enclosed in quotation marks).

41   Gary B. Nash, *The Urban Crucible: Social Change, Political Consciousness, and the Origins of the American Revolution* (Cambridge, Mass., 1979), p. x. Nash draws here on a Marxian taxonomy that recognizes "ranks," "estates," or "orders" under precapitalist modes of production, and "classes" as the products of maturing industrial capitalism. Even Marxists who would use "class" to describe precapitalist society retain the idea that classes are different under capitalism. As E. J. Hobsbawm explains, "under capitalism class is an immediate and in some sense directly *experienced* historical reality, whereas in pre-capitalist epochs it may merely be an analytical construct which makes sense of a complex of facts otherwise inexplicable." Hobsbawm, "Class Consciousness in History," in István Mészáros, ed., *Aspects of History and Class Consciousness* (London, 1971), p. 8. On the historical evolution of the middle class and its taxonomy (but more relevant to Europe than to the United States), see G. D. H. Cole, "The Conception of the Middle Classes," in Cole, *Studies in Class Structure* (London, 1955); and Asa Briggs, "The Language of 'Class' in Early Nineteenth-Century England," in Briggs and John Saville, eds., *Essays in Labour History* (London, 1960).

42   J. H. Hexter refers to "the general myth of the ever-rising middle class," in "The Myth of the Middle Class in Tudor England," Hexter, *Reappraisals in History*, p. 71. My own friends will recognize here a possible application of Blumin's Law, most simply stated as: It happened in my period. This is in effect a complaint that historians are often tempted to exaggerate the significance of events that occur in the time periods in which they are most interested, and sometimes apply to these periods concepts that are appropriate only to others. Hexter complains that the concept of the rising middle class is inappropriate to the sixteenth century. Interestingly, he suggests that it does apply to the nineteenth century. So, after all, it happened in *my* period.

43   Louis Wirth, "Urbanism as a Way of Life," *American Journal of Sociology* 44 (1938): 14. Note the differences between labor-capital relations in large textile towns, as described, for example, in Thomas Dublin, *Women at Work: The Transformation of Work and Community in Lowell, Massachusetts, 1826–1860* (New York, 1979), and in small textile hamlets and villages, as described in Anthony F. C. Wallace, *Rockdale: The Growth of an American Village in the Early Industrial Revolution* (New York, 1978), and in Jonathan Prude, *The Coming of Industrial Order: Town and Factory Life in Rural Massachusetts, 1810–1860* (Cambridge, 1983).

44   Nash, *Urban Crucible*; Fernand Braudel, *Capitalism and Material Life: 1400–1800* (New York, 1974), p. 373.

45   Gary John Kornblith's recent dissertation "Artisans to Businessmen," which examines the mechanics' associations of Providence, Salem, and Boston, does introduce one big city into the list.

46 Local variations of social structure and culture have emerged as an interesting theme in recent scholarship on the American city. Studies such as Baltzell, *Puritan Boston and Quaker Philadelphia*, Jaher, *The Urban Establishment*, and William H. Pease and Jane H. Pease, *The Web of Progess: Private Values and Public Styles in Boston and Charleston, 1828–1843* (New York, 1985), demonstrate how carefully we must consider the particularities of place when crafting generalizations about the city.

47 Junius Henri Browne, *The Great Metropolis: A Mirror of New York* (Hartford, 1869), p. 23.

48 Edward Winslow Martin [James Dabney McCabe], *The Secrets of the Great City: A Work Descriptive of the Virtues and Vices, the Mysteries, Miseries, and Crimes of New York City* (Philadelphia, 1868), p. 38. For a fuller discussion of Browne's and McCabe's descriptions of New York, see Stuart M. Blumin, "Explaining the New Metropolis: Perception, Depiction, and Analysis in Mid-Nineteenth-Century New York City," *Journal of Urban History* 11 (1984): 9–38.

49 Peter George Buckley, "To the Opera House: Culture and Society in New York City, 1820–1860" (Ph.D. dissertation, State University of New York at Stony Brook, 1984), p. 31. See also Christine Stansell, *City of Women: Sex and Class in New York, 1789–1860* (New York, 1986).

50 Katz et al., *Social Organization of Early Industrial Capitalism*, p. 25. The "objective relations" to which this statement refers consist of allegedly strong relationships between class and wealth, as demonstrated by the extent to which a two-class occupational model explains variation in assessed property in Hamilton and in the value of dwellings in Buffalo. But the authors' analysis of these relationships is seriously flawed. Their own calculations reveal that a two-class model explains only 13%, 3%, and 18% of the variation in assessed wealth in Hamilton in 1851, 1861, and 1871 respectively, and only 9% of the variation in dwelling values in Buffalo in 1855. The fact that a sixteen-category occupational model explains only a small amount of additional variation in two of the four instances leads them to conclude that "the majority of the variation in economic rank attributable to occupation was in fact accounted for by class." This statement may be challenged on at least three grounds. First, the fact that the two-class model explains most of the variation "attributable to occupation" means very little, except that "class" explains *even less* than the modest amounts of variation explained by the sixteen-category model. Second, in two of the four calculations (Hamilton, 1851 and 1861), it explains significantly less, in one case even falling short of the "majority" the authors claim. And third, the data used for measuring wealth do not reflect the actual distribution of wealth with sufficient accuracy. See ibid., pp. 47–9.

51 Adrienne Siegel, *The Image of the American City in Popular Literature: 1820–1870* (Port Washington, N.Y., 1981), p. 6. See also Janis P. Stout, *Sodoms in Eden: The City in American Fiction Before 1860* (Westport, Conn., 1976); Dan Schiller, *Objectivity and the News: The Public and the Rise of Commercial*

Journalism (Philadelphia, 1981); Eugene Arden, "The Evil City in American Fiction," *New York History* 35 (1954): 259–79; Blumin, "Explaining the New Metropolis"; Spann, *The New Metropolis*, pp. 19, 426.

52   George G. Foster, *New York by Gas-Light: With Here and There a Streak of Sunshine* (New York, 1850), p. 5.

53   McCabe, *Secrets of the Great City*, p. 38.

54   In Chapter 7, I briefly examine the efforts of one of these writers, George Foster, to define and describe what he called "the great American middle class."

Chapter 2. "Middling sorts" in the eighteenth-century city

1   E. B. O'Callaghan, ed., *Documents Relative to the Colonial History of the State of New-York* (Albany, N.Y., 1856), vol. 7, p. 795. The same letter is printed in *Collections of the New-York Historical Society for the Year 1877* (New York, 1878), pp. 68–9, with slightly different capitalization and punctuation.

2   *Collections of the New-York Historical Society for the Year 1919* (New York, 1920), pp. 327–8. The context of these designations was the Assembly election of 1746.

3   See, for example, J. C. D. Clark, *English Society, 1688–1832: Ideology, Social Structure and Political Practice During the Ancien Regime* (Cambridge, 1985); John Cannon, *Aristocratic Century: The Peerage of Eighteenth-Century England* (Cambridge, 1984); Roland Mousnier, *The Institutions of France Under the Absolute Monarchy, 1598–1789: Society and the State* (Chicago, 1979); Mousnier, *Social Hierarchies: 1450 to the Present* (London, 1973); and many of the works cited in notes 40 and 41 of Chapter 1 above.

4   Gary B. Nash, *The Urban Crucible: Social Change, Political Consciousness, and the Origins of the American Revolution* (Cambridge, Mass., 1979), is the study of eighteenth-century "laboring classes" that were only beginning "to behave in class-specific ways," and of "the emergence of new modes of thought based on horizontal rather than vertical divisions in society" (see esp. p. xi). Nash draws here on E. P. Thompson's influential article, "Eighteenth-Century English Society: Class Struggle Without Class?" *Social History* 3 (1978): 133–65.

5   On the corporate organization of European cities and towns, see Mousnier, *Institutions of France*, and Mack Walker's splendid *German Home Towns: Community, State and General Estate* (Ithaca, N.Y., 1971). The attenuation of corporate forms in colonial America is discussed in a number of works, including Richard B. Morris, *Government and Labor in Early America* (New York, 1946); and Jon C. Teaford, *The Municipal Revolution in America: Origins of Modern Urban Government, 1650–1825* (Chicago, 1975).

6   For a general discussion of incomes and living standards, see Jackson Turner Main, *The Social Structure of Revolutionary America* (Princeton, 1965), pp. 77–8, 88, 132–3, 158–9. Liberalism as a Revolutionary ideology

is discussed in Joyce Appleby, "The Social Origins of American Revolutionary Ideology," *Journal of American History* 64 (1978): 935–58.

7 Richard L. Bushman, "Freedom and Prosperity in the American Revolution," in Larry R. Gerlach, ed., *Legacies of the American Revolution* (Logan, Utah, 1978), pp. 61–83; Bushman, "'This New Man': Dependence and Independence, 1776," in Bushman et al., eds., *Uprooted Americans: Essays to Honor Oscar Handlin* (Boston, 1979), pp. 79–93; Edmund S. Morgan, "The Puritan Ethic and the American Revolution," *William and Mary Quarterly*, 3d ser., 24 (1967): 3–43; Rowland Berthoff, "Peasants and Artisans, Puritans and Republicans: Personal Liberty and Communal Equality in American History," *Journal of American History* 69 (1982): 579–98; David E. Shi, *The Simple Life: Plain Living and High Thinking in American Culture* (New York, 1985).

8 Jack P. Greene, "Social Structure and Political Behavior in Revolutionary America: John Day's *Remarks on American Affairs*," *William and Mary Quarterly*, 3d ser., 32 (1975): 481–94.

9 Philadelphia *Aurora*, February 15, 1796. Emphases are in the original.

10 See the examples of "class" in Charles G. Steffen, *The Mechanics of Baltimore: Workers and Politics in the Age of Revolution* (Urbana, Ill., 1984), pp. 131, 135, 193, and the more general discussion in Martin J. Burke, "The Conundrum of Class: Public Discourse on the Social Order in America," (Ph.D. dissertation, University of Michigan, 1987).

11 Cannon, *Aristocratic Century*, p. 169.

12 For examples of several of these usages, see *Pennsylvania Packet*, January 15, July 6, October 1, 1782.

13 Nash carries his argument beyond the Revolutionary era in "The Social Evolution of Preindustrial American Cities, 1700–1820: Reflections and New Directions," *Journal of Urban History* 13 (1987): 115–45. In *The Urban Crucible*, Nash emphasizes that "class" has "a different meaning for the preindustrial period than for a later epoch" (p. xi), and we can observe that the *Aurora's* use of "middle class" is imbedded in a quite traditional invocation of one of the tenets of the "moral economy."

14 John Lambert, *Travels Through Canada and the United States of North America in the Years 1806, 1807, & 1808*, 2d ed. (London, 1813), vol. 2, pp. 63–4.

15 Abraham Ritter, *Philadelphia and Her Merchants . . .* (Philadelphia, 1860), p. 33.

16 Ibid., pp. 31, 34, 79.

17 *Claypoole's American Daily Advertiser*, January 2, 1798.

18 Ritter, *Philadelphia and Her Merchants*, pp. 72–3.

19 Arthur H. Cole, "The Tempo of Mercantile Life in Colonial America," *Business History Review* 33 (1959): 277–99.

20 The Duke de la Rochefoucault Liancourt, *Travels Through the United States of North America . . . in the Years 1795, 1796, and 1797 . . .* (London, 1799), vol. 1, p. 558.

21 Louis B. Wright and Marion Tinling, eds., *Quebec to Carolina in 1785–1786: Being the Travel Diary and Observations of Robert Hunter, Jr., a Young Merchant of London* (San Marino, Calif., 1943), pp. 168–73.

22 Carl Bridenbaugh, *The Colonial Craftsman* (New York, 1950), p. ix. See especially the illustrations facing pp. 5, 101, and 116.

23 This is a common view that is further substantiated by the numerous nonbusiness transactions and other personal items that artisans recorded in their daybooks and journals. See the discussion in the third section of this chapter.

24 Deborah Dependahl Waters, " 'The Workmanship of an American Artist': Philadelphia's Precious Metals Trades and Craftsmen, 1788–1832," (Ph.D. dissertation, University of Delaware, 1981), pp. 113–16.

25 Ibid., p. 114; Anthony N. B. Garvan et al., eds., *The Mutual Assurance Company Papers*, vol. 1: *The Architectural Surveys, 1784–1794* (Philadelphia, 1976), pp. 252–3.

26 Federal Direct Tax of 1798, manuscript assessment lists, Pennsylvania, microfilm reel 1, Philadelphia, High Street Ward; Edmund Hogan, *The Prospect of Philadelphia* . . . (Philadelphia, 1795), p. 26.

27 See the illustrations in Elizabeth Gray Kogen Spera, "Building for Business: The Impact of Commerce on the City Plan and Architecture of the City of Philadelphia, 1750–1800" (Ph.D. dissertation, University of Pennsylvania, 1980), p. 169.

28 Ibid., p. 167.

29 Philadelphia *General Advertiser*, March 27, 1794.

30 Spera, "Building for Business," p. 171.

31 Amos Pope, *An Astronomical Diary: or Almanack, for . . . 1794* (Boston, 1793).

32 Waters, " 'Workmanship of an American Artist,' " pp. 117–18.

33 Ritter, *Philadelphia and Her Merchants*, p. 154.

34 It is interesting to note that William Birch was himself an Englishman quite familiar with the shops of London and that this particular scene is the one he chose to convey the variety and density of outdoor peddling. Even his depictions of the central markets are empty of such activities. Could Birch have been making his own comment here on "Cooke's Folly"? Birch's views are published in Martin P. Snyder, *City of Independence: Views of Philadelphia Before 1800* (New York, 1975), and in S. Robert Teitelman, ed., *Birch's Views of Philadelphia: A Reduced Facsimile of "The City of Philadelphia . . . As It Appeared in the Year 1800"* (Philadelphia, 1982).

35 Minutes of the Transactions of the Taylors Company of Philadelphia, Historical Society of Pennsylvania.

36 Nash uses the term "face-to-face relationships" to describe the late-seventeenth-century cities, which were still smaller, but I believe he would agree that it is appropriate to the eighteenth-century city as well. See Nash, *Urban Crucible*, pp. 4–5. For a similar discussion, see Sam Bass Warner, Jr., *The Private City: Philadelphia in Three Periods of Its Growth* (Philadelphia, 1968), pp. 3–21.

37 Nash, *Urban Crucible*, p. 7.

38 *Pennsylvania Packet*, July 18, 1782.

39 Churches did, of course, vary in status. William Strickland, an English

visitor to New York in the 1790s, contrasts fashionable Trinity Church with the Presbyterian Church on Wall Street, attended by "the middling class, no Aristocrats but good plain republicans." William Strickland, *Journal of a Tour in the United States of America, 1794–1795. Collections of the New-York Historical Society for the Year 1950* (New York, 1971), pp. 47n, 65. Churches within denominations also varied in the status of their communicants. In Philadelphia, wealthy Presbyterians seem to have worshiped at the First and Second Presbyterian Churches, while the Third and Fourth were congregations of middling and poorer folk. The Third, on Pine Street quite close to a number of expensive homes, admitted 41 new male communicants in the 1790s. Of these, 1 was a physician, another was a professor of mathematics, 3 were sea captains, 9 were innkeepers and storekeepers of various kinds, and 3 were clerks. There were also a schoolteacher, a sexton, 18 artisans, and 4 unskilled workers. The Fourth admitted 43 male communicants between 1800 and 1805. These included 3 physicians and a merchant, 6 grocers, 4 tavernkeepers, 3 teachers, 9 artisans, and 8 unskilled workers. (Third Presbyterian Church of Philadelphia, Communicants, 1771–1823; Fourth Presbyterian Church of Philadelphia, Register, 1800–1835. Both of these manuscript volumes are at the Presbyterian Historical Society in Philadelphia.)

40 The Rev. Andrew Burnaby, *Travels Through the Middle Settlements in North America in the Years 1759 and 1760; with Observations upon the State of the Colonies*, 3d ed. (London, 1798), pp. 67–8.

41 This subject requires much more research, but certain kinds of organizations – craft societies for example – were obviously restricted to members of a given social level. Some were more restricted than their purpose and structure would suggest. The American Society Held at Philadelphia for Promoting Useful Knowledge was apparently open to all who had an interest in science and technology, offered premiums to inventive "merchants, artisans, manufacturers and others" who made worthwhile discoveries and improvements, and levied a small admission fee and annual dues. Yet its identifiable members were almost all men of wealth and prominence, and the few who were directly involved in the production of goods were wealthy manufacturers rather than simple artisans. The Delaware Fire Company of Philadelphia was not so exalted, but most of its members were merchants, while only four can be identified as artisans – two tailors, a watchmaker, and a cabinetmaker. The New-York Society Library was managed by a board of trustees made up entirely of rich and prominent men, while fully 75–80% of the 444 identifiable members were merchants, professionals, and high-ranking public officials – a high proportion indeed for so large an organization. The membership records of the first two of these organizations may be found at the Historical Society of Pennsylvania. The members of the third are listed in *The Charter, Bye-Laws, and Names of the Members of the New-York Society Library* . . . (New York, 1793). For a recent discussion of late-eighteenth-century urban institutions as contributors to separate communities within the stratified city, see Nash, "Social Evolution."

42   The occupations and property assessments of the members and officers of several Philadelphia Masonic lodges can be found in Wayne Andrew Huss, "Pennsylvania Freemasonry: An Intellectual and Social Analysis, 1727–1826" (Ph.D. dissertation, Temple University, 1985).

43   Judith M. Diamondstone, "Philadelphia's Municipal Corporation, 1701–1776," *Pennsylvania Magazine of History and Biography* 90 (1966): 183–201. Diamondstone observes that "The Corporation . . . thought of itself as a public agency in the same sense in which Eton is a public school" (p. 193). For a more complete discussion of this and other municipal governments in this era, see Teaford, *Municipal Revolution.*

44   James A. Henretta, "Economic Development and Social Structure in Colonial Boston," *William and Mary Quarterly,* 3d ser., 22 (1965): 90.

45   Roger J. Champagne, "Liberty Boys and Mechanics of New York City, 1764–1774," *Labor History* 8 (1967): 129–30. Bruce M. Wilkenfeld, in "The New York City Common Council, 1689–1800," *New York History* 52 (1971), notes that artisanal representation on the Common Council declined somewhat during the years preceding the Revolution (pp. 256–65).

46   Edward Countryman, *A People in Revolution: The American Revolution and Political Society in New York, 1760–1790* (Baltimore, 1981), pp. 58–9, 76, 85. See also Richard Buel, Jr., "Democracy and the American Revolution: A Frame of Reference," *William and Mary Quarterly,* 3d ser., 21 (1964): 178–9. An almanac of 1779 continued to distinguish between power "derived from the people" and power "seated in the people," the latter being a source of disorder and tyranny: John Anderson, *Anderson Revised: The North-American Calendar . . .* (Providence, 1779).

47   *New-York Journal,* April 12, 1770, supplement.

48   Nash, *Urban Crucible.* In a slightly earlier discussion Nash had referred to these challenges as "radical": Gary Nash, "The Transformation of Urban Politics, 1700–1765," *Journal of American History* 60 (1974): 605–32, but he changed "radical" to "popular" in *The Urban Crucible.*

49   Gary B. Nash, "Artisans and Politics in Eighteenth-Century Philadelphia," in Ian M. G. Quimby, ed., *The Craftsman in Early America* (New York, 1984), pp. 63, 68.

50   I am using the term "deference" here in the way that J. G. A. Pocock claims it was used in the eighteenth century: "the voluntary acceptance of a leadership elite by persons not belonging to that elite, but sufficiently free as political actors to render deference not only a voluntary but also a political act." See Pocock, "The Classical Theory of Deference," *American Historical Review* 81 (1976): 517. The freedom of the non-elite to accept or reject leadership as a prerogative of the elite is crucial in distinguishing between deference and coercion. This, of course, does not settle the question of *why* the non-elite would defer. Howard Newby, in "The Deferential Dialectic," *Comparative Studies in Society and History* 17 (1975): 139–64, explains this acquiescence in terms of both reciprocity and tradition. According to Newby, subordinates in a deferential relation are "vociferous in the defence of their own self-respect. Their relationship to those above them in the social hierarchy . . . is perceived more as one

of partnership than servility" (p. 145). At the same time, the origins of deference "lie in the processes of legitimization by tradition of the hierarchical nature of the social structure by those in superordinate positions" (p. 146). In a widely cited essay, E. P. Thompson questions the depth of deferential acquiescence in eighteenth-century England: "Deference could be very brittle indeed, and made up of one part of self-interest, one part of dissimulation, and only one part of the awe of authority." See Thompson, "Patrician Society, Plebeian Culture," *Journal of Social History* 7 (1974): 399–400. Dissimulation obviously is nondeferential behavior, but self-interest could easily be framed in deferential terms. The very core of the concept, indeed, is the belief of non-elites that their acquiescence to elite authority was in their own self-interest.

51 *Pennsylvania Packet*, July 6, 1782.

52 This judgment is based on my reading of more than five hundred issues, selected through systematic sampling, of four major newspapers in New York and Philadelphia, ranging in political sentiment from James Rivington's *Royal Gazette* to the radical Philadelphia *Aurora*. I also read less systematically in other papers, following up leads provided by other historians.

53 The few quotations that follow represent my reading of approximately one hundred almanacs published between 1772 and 1793.

54 *The Pennsylvania Town and Country-man's Almanack, for . . . 1773* (Wilmington, 1772).

55 *The Federal Almanack, for . . . 1794* (New Brunswick, N.J., 1793).

56 See, for example, the adages printed in David Rittenhouse's *Father Abraham's Almanack, for . . . 1780* (Philadelphia, 1779).

57 [Benjamin West], *Bickerstaff's New-England Almanack, for . . . 1787* (Norwich, Conn., 1786).

58 Tabulating occupations in eighteenth-century American cities is extremely difficult, owing to the incompleteness and frequent ambiguity of local tax assessment lists and other records. Most tabulations have yielded fairly consistent results with respect to major occupational categories, however, and there is a particularly broad agreement that artisans constituted approximately half of the male urban work force. Retailers range from 10% to 15% in most tabulations, to which I would add a nearly equal number of nonwealthy merchants and professionals, and minor officials, as nonmanual "middling sorts." For specific tabulations and some of their difficulties, see: Jacob M. Price, "Economic Function and the Growth of American Port Towns in the Eighteenth Century," *Perspectives in American History* 8 (1974): 177–83; Warner, *Private City*, pp. 226–7; Nash, *Urban Crucible*, pp. 387–91; Sharon V. Salinger, "Artisans, Journeymen, and the Transformation of Labor in Late Eighteenth-Century Philadelphia," *William and Mary Quarterly*, 3d ser.; 40 (1983): 67; Allan Kulikoff, "The Progress of Inequality in Revolutionary Boston," *William and Mary Quarterly*, 3d ser., 28 (1971): 377; Gary B. Nash, Billy G. Smith, and Dirk Hoerder, "Laboring Americans and the American Revolution," *Labor History* 24 (1983): 414–39; Hermann Wellenreuther,

"Labor in the Era of the American Revolution: A Discussion of Recent Concepts and Theories," *Labor History* 22 (1981): 573–600. One tabulation that differs substantially from the general pattern is Edward C. Papenfuse, *In Pursuit of Profit: The Annapolis Merchants in the Era of the American Revolution, 1763–1805* (Baltimore, 1975), p. 136. But the difference is easily accounted for by the exclusion of slaves (who were twice as numerous as taxable inhabitants) from the Annapolis tax assessment list.

59 Stephen Botein, "'Meer Mechanics' and an Open Press: The Business and Political Strategies of Colonial American Printers," *Perspectives in American History* 9 (1975): 157, 160.

60 *New-York Journal*, January 18, 1770. This phrase actually occurs in the letter of a defender of nonimportation, who cites the attitude of two opponents from South Carolina. What is most interesting here is that the correspondent lets the remark pass with no objection or other comment, even though he has much to say about other aspects of the Carolinians' argument.

61 See John K. Alexander, *Render Them Submissive: Responses to Poverty in Philadelphia, 1760–1800* (Amherst, Mass., 1980), p. 154.

62 Philadelphia *Aurora*, February 17, 1796.

63 *The Miraculous Power of Clothes, and the Dignity of the Taylors: Being an Essay on the Words, Clothes Make Men* (Philadelphia, 1772). This was a German pamphlet translated for William Mentz, who may have been a tailor. As a postscript he proposes a law that would require people to pay for their clothes and carry with them their tailor's receipt. See also the inversion (to become very popular in the Romantic era) in which rich men, fat from feasting at sumptuous tables, become in death the sumptuous feast of worms and insects: e.g., "The Tomb," in *Weatherman's Almanack, for . . . 1787* (Portland, Maine, 1786).

64 Nathan Webb diary, November 11, 1788, Massachusetts Historical Society.

65 Ibid., November 12, 1788.

66 Alexander Graydon, *Memoirs of a Life, Chiefly Passed in Pennsylvania* (Harrisburg, 1811), p. 40.

67 Ibid., p. 80.

68 The historian Carl Bridenbaugh complains about this practice among the "gentry" in *Cities in Revolt: Urban Life in America, 1743–1776* (New York, 1955), p. 284, but then commits the same offense himself in several places; e.g., pp. 305, 312, 352.

69 "Memorial of the First Company of Philadelphia Militia Artillery, 1779," *Pennsylvania Archives*, 1st ser., 7 (Philadelphia, 1853), pp. 392–5.

70 *New-York Journal*, April 30, 1768, supplement.

71 *Pennsylvania Evening Post*, April 27, 1776. This letter has been discussed by Nash in "Artisans and Politics" and by J. R. Pole in *The Pursuit of Equality in American History* (Berkeley, 1978), p. 20.

72 Quoted in Steffen, *Mechanics of Baltimore*, p. 131.

73 *New-York Journal*, December 17, 1767.

74 See Foner, *Tom Paine*, pp. 45–56. Foner, I believe, somewhat overstates this argument.

75 Roland M. Baumann, in "Philadelphia's Manufacturers and the Excise Taxes of 1794: The Forging of the Jeffersonian Coalition," *Pennsylvania Magazine of History and Biography* 106 (1982): 3–39, discusses sugar refiners and tobacconists as men who remained a step or two below the merchant elite, despite accumulating impressive fortunes. Peter J. Parker, in "The Philadelphia Printer: A Study of an Eighteenth-Century Businessman," *Business History Review* 40 (1966): 24–46, counts thirteen printers in Philadelphia who were also booksellers. He also notes, however, that there was a very rapid turnover in this business.

76 Waters, "'The Workmanship of an American Artist,'" is an excellent recent discussion of Philadelphia's precious metals craftsmen.

77 In Philadelphia, the leading hatters seem to have been particularly successful. See my discussion of High Street Ward in the next section of this chapter.

78 Foner, *Tom Paine*, p. 40.

79 [Nathan Daboll], *Freebetter's New-England Almanack for . . . 1773* (New London, Conn., 1772).

80 [Benjamin Workman], *Father Tammany's Almanac, for . . . 1787* (Philadelphia, 1786). This phrase recurs in a number of almanacs.

81 *To the Inhabitants of Pennsylvania in General, and Particularly Those of the City and Neighbourhood of Philadelphia* (Philadelphia, 1779). See a similar broadside issued by soap boilers: *To the Inhabitants of the City of Philadelphia, and Parts Adjacent* (Philadelphia, 1772).

82 *To the Inhabitants of Pennsylvania*. On merchants' opposition to price controls during the inflationary crisis of 1779, see Foner, *Tom Paine*, pp. 170–1.

83 Lambert, *Travels*, vol. 2, p. 90.

84 See Shi, *The Simple Life*; Bushman, "Freedom and Prosperity"; Berthoff, "Peasants and Artisans"; Foner, *Tom Paine*.

85 The most recent analysis of the Philadelphia data is Billy G. Smith, "Inequality in Late Colonial Philadelphia: A Note on Its Nature and Growth," *William and Mary Quarterly*, 3d ser., 41 (1984): 629–45. See also Nash, *Urban Crucible*, pp. 395–6; Henretta, "Economic Development and Social Structure," p. 82. Papenfuse, *In Pursuit of Profit*, p. 263, finds less concentration (24% of assessed wealth owned by the richest 5%) in the smaller city of Annapolis in 1783, but Smith's figures for Philadelphia are roughly consonant with Alice Hanson Jones's tabulations for five Mid-Atlantic counties, weighted to represent the region as a whole. See Jones, *Wealth of a Nation to Be: The American Colonies on the Eve of the Revolution* (New York, 1980), pp. 162–7, 190–1. Gloria L. Main, in "Inequality in Early America: The Evidence from Probate Records of Massachusetts and Maryland," *Journal of Interdisciplinary History* 7 (1977): 567, derives wealth distributions from the probate records of Boston that are similar to those found in local tax records by Nash and Henretta. Sharon

V. Salinger and Charles Wetherell, in "Wealth and Renting in Prerevolutionary Philadelphia," *Journal of American History* 71 (1985): 826–40, suggest on the basis of rents and the imputed rental value of owner-occupied dwellings that incomes were significantly less skewed than wealth.

86 G. B. Warden, in "Inequality and Instability in Eighteenth-Century Boston: A Reappraisal," *Journal of Interdisciplinary History* 6 (1976): 585–620, criticizes Henretta's interpretation of the Boston tax lists, but his own interpretation fails to resolve deeper problems. Tax assessors not only rated real and personal property at different proportions of their real value, but underassessed property in a curvilinear, not a linear, fashion. Assessments were not made for all types of property and, most important, excluded property that each taxpayer may have owned beyond the boundaries of the taxing authority. Probate records overcome many of these difficulties but introduce some of their own, most notably the exclusion of many decedents. For a recent, brief discussion of these deficiencies, see Thomas M. Doerflinger, *A Vigorous Spirit of Enterprise: Merchants and Economic Development in Revolutionary Philadelphia* (Chapel Hill, 1986), pp. 64–5.

87 Bridenbaugh, *Cities in Revolt*, p. 139. Bridenbaugh describes the life-style of the urban elite in greater detail on pp. 336–48.

88 Alice Hanson Jones, "Wealth Estimates for the American Middle Colonies, 1774," *Economic Development and Cultural Change* 18 (1970): 131.

89 Rochefoucault, *Travels*, vol 2, p. 385.

90 Lambert, *Travels*, vol. 2, pp. 99–100.

91 Isaac Weld, Jun., *Travels Through the States of North America . . . During the Years 1795, 1796, and 1797*, 4th ed. (London, 1807), vol. 1, p. 21.

92 Rochefoucault, *Travels*, vol. 2, p. 383.

93 This was true to a large extent even among Philadelphia's Quakers. See Frederick B. Tolles, *Meeting House and Counting House: Quaker Merchants of Colonial Philadelphia* (Chapel Hill, 1948), for a classic account of how some Quaker merchants capitulated to the world and its goods, and how even the "dry" Quakers who did not still found ways of displaying their wealth.

94 Henretta, "Economic Development and Social Structure," pp. 80, 82, 87; Smith, "Inequality," p. 633.

95 Rochefoucault, for example, observes that "the shopkeeper and the artizan live much better here than in Europe, and the table of a family, in easy circumstances, living upon their income, is not better served in England and France, than a great many of those of tailors, hair-dressers, &c. of Philadelphia, or New York, or of all other large towns in America." Rochefoucault, *Travels*, vol. 2, p. 672. This was an exaggeration, as were so many of the comments of wealthy and well-placed visitors. Still, American artisans *were* better off than the artisans of Europe, who were often poor.

96 Gary B. Nash, "Urban Wealth and Poverty in Pre-Revolutionary Amer-

ica," in Jack P. Greene and Pauline Maier, eds., *Interdisciplinary Studies of the American Revolution* (Beverly Hills, 1976), p. 28.
97 Main, *Social Structure*, pp. 133, 274, 78.
98 Charles S. Olton, *Artisans for Independence: Philadelphia Mechanics and the American Revolution* (Syracuse, 1975), p. 25.
99 Billy G. Smith, "The Material Lives of Laboring Philadelphians, 1750 to 1800," *William and Mary Quarterly*, 3d ser., 38 (1981): 180, 194–7. I calculated these percentages from Smith's estimate of bare subsistence costs of £60.82 (Pennsylvania currency), and master shoemakers' earnings of £74.10 on his own labor and £15.60 on the labor of each journeyman. Smith does not say whether the journeymen's wages he cites were "found" or "not found," although he implies the latter. The 3s. 9d. he cites for journeymen shoemakers, and the 4s. he cites for tailors, coincide with those noted in the leatherworking artisans' broadside and the Taylors Company minutes, cited in the first section of this chapter, but both documents are silent on the question of room and board. Sharon V. Salinger claims, I believe correctly, that most journeymen did *not* live with their masters, or did so only occasionally; hence, it is likely that the wages indicated in the documents were "not found." See Salinger, "Artisans, Journeymen, and the Transformation of Labor," p. 74.
100 Smith, "Material Lives," p. 200.
101 Amos Pope, *An Astronomical Diary: or Almanack for . . . 1794* (Boston, 1793).
102 Joshua Haines account book, 1796; William Forbes account book, 1768–80; David Evans daybook, 1774–1812; William Lawrence daybook, 1769–98, and account book, 1804–12; A. Howell account book, 1791–99; Joseph Graisbury ledger, 1763–73; at Historical Society of Pennsylvania. Garret Abeel daybook, 1774–76, at New-York Historical Society.
103 Federal Direct Tax of 1798, manuscript assessment lists, Pennsylvania, microfilm reels 1–4, Philadelphia. Another excellent feature of these tax lists is their separation of residential from purely business properties into separate lists. No local assessment list that I am aware of does this; hence, the federal list for dwellings may be the only one in which each occupant's listing clearly refers to a structure that included his home.

With reference to the representativeness of my sample, I assume the three central wards (High Street, Walnut, South) to be representative also of Middle, North, Upper Delaware, Lower Delaware, Chestnut, and Dock (including Locust, set off from Dock in 1800). These core wards had a total population in 1800 of 25,896, which constituted 39.9% of the total metropolitan population (the City, plus Southwark, Northern Liberties East, and the inner part of Northern Liberties West). My file includes 465 cases from the three central wards, constituting 37.1% of the file, and 1.87% of the total population of all the core wards. The inner part of Northern Liberties East I take to be representative of a "semiperiphery" that includes also North Mulberry, South Mulberry, and New Market (including Cedar, set off from New Market in 1800). These wards and districts had a population in 1800 of 20,141, or 31.0% of the metropolis. My file contains 421 cases from the semiperiphery, or 33.5% of the whole file, and 2.1% of the total population of these wards and districts. Northern Liberties West (inner) represents, I believe, a periphery that includes also the outer portion of Northern Liberties East, and East and West Southwark. These contained 29.1% of the metropolitan population, while my 370 cases represent 29.4% of the total file and 1.95% of the total peripheral population. These figures are summarized in the accompanying table.

	Core	Semiperiphery	Periphery
% of total population	39.9	31.0	29.1
% of file	37.1	33.5	29.4
File size/population	1.87	2.10	1.95

The mean assessment values for wards other than those represented in the sample are derived from summary lists pertaining to those wards ("General Lists," as opposed to the "Particular Lists" from which the sample was drawn). The three wards for which even summary data are not available (Chestnut, Dock, and New Market) were assigned to zones according to their location. For discussions of the Federal Direct Tax of 1798, see Lee Soltow, "America's First Progressive Tax," *National Tax Journal* 30 (1977): 53–8; and Soltow, "Egalitarian America and Its Inegalitarian Housing in the Federal Period," *Social Science History* 9 (1985): 199–213.

104 Missing from both files were occupants of dwellings valued at less than $100, as the federal law excluded these from taxation. Soltow, working from summary data, notes that fourteen states, including Pennsylvania, did list assessments lower than $100, and that in these states 46.5% of all listings were in fact under that amount. In my Philadelphia file, only one house was assessed below $100 (at $80), and only seven were assessed at $100. It is possible that the Philadelphia assessors excluded a number of houses worth less than $100, but the very small number assessed at $100, or even at slightly higher values (only 2.6% of the sampled houses were assessed at $200 or less), suggests that housing values were simply higher in the big city, and that even the cheapest houses were worth more than $100. On the other hand, a number of alleys and peripheral streets seem to have had fewer listings than the 1796 map suggests they should have had. Perhaps there were very cheap houses on these alleys and streets that were excluded from the assessment lists. If so, this would constitute a second source of bias in the file toward more prosperous householders. The mean assessment in the nation as a whole, according to Soltow, was $262. In my Philadelphia file it is $1,500. See Soltow, "Egalitarian America," pp. 202, 212n.

105 Floor space was calculated by multiplying the frontage of the dwelling

by its depth and the number of its stories. This produces a slightly inflated figure in each case, as it makes no allowance for the thickness of exterior and interior walls. On the other hand, it is not clear that a garret was regarded as an additional story. The assessments appear to have been done with great care, but it is possible that dimensions were only estimated. Hence, refinements of the figures for walls and other factors would serve only to introduce a spurious accuracy. All of these figures should be regarded as good estimates, not as perfectly accurate specifications.

106 Warner, *Private City*, p. 17.
107 I include here the city, the eastern and western portions of Southwark, and all but the outer portion of Northern Liberties West, which consisted mainly of farms. Five workshops, not included in the 124, were identified on the list of nonresidential buildings in the outer portion of Northern Liberties West.
108 *Claypoole's American Daily Advertiser*, November 8, 1798.
109 For a recent discussion of this and other aspects of Philadelphia architecture in this period, see Spera, "Building for Business."
110 Kitchens could also be located in cellars, which were not recorded on the 1798 assessment lists. But cellar kitchens were again probably more characteristic of larger houses (the third that lacked exterior kitchens, perhaps) than smaller ones. Dwellings above workshops and stores were more than a story removed from the cellar; hence, the convenience of a kitchen removed from living spaces was negated by the extra vertical distance. Several artisanal estate inventories of 1774, to be discussed shortly, indicate that cellars were ordinarily used as storage spaces for workshops rather than as kitchens. Many householders carried loaves, meat pies, and other items to bakers for baking, but there was still much work left to be done in the home kitchen or hearth.
111 See the descriptions in Rochefoucault, *Travels*, vol. 2, pp. 457–8, and in Lambert, *Travels*, vol. 2, p. 56.
112 Thomas M. Doerflinger, in "Commercial Specialization in Philadelphia's Merchant Community, 1750–1791," *Business History Review* 57 (1983): 20–49, notes that there were dozens of merchants in Philadelphia, including a number of young men, who were not wealthy. In *A Vigorous Spirit of Enterprise*, Doerflinger expands upon this point to argue that most of Philadelphia's merchants were not among the urban elite, and that only half of the members of that elite were merchants (see esp. pp. 16, 32). Doerflinger probably underestimates the number of wealthy *rentiers* and professionals whose family fortunes originated in commerce, and does concede that "the functional and symbolic core of the merchant community . . . were not the dozens of minor merchants who lived in the style of successful mechanics, but the great men of commerce" (p. 38). But his excellent portrait of a quite varied merchant community reminds us that occupational categories of the sort employed in these tables correspond only roughly with the distribution of wealth and prestige in urban society.

113 It should be recalled that there is a bias in this directory-linked subfile because only some 56% of the cases in the peripheral zone (Northern Liberties West), as compared with 76% in the other zones, could be located in the directories. If this bias were erased, Table 2.2 would reveal even higher concentrations of artisans and unskilled workers, and perhaps storekeepers as well, on the periphery.

114 See, for example, an item in *Dunlap and Claypoole's American Daily Advertiser*, February 25, 1796, calling for the draining of stagnant pools on the urban periphery, and in more centrally located alleys.

115 This pattern of segregation by frontage within small, heterogeneous areas of the city was carried to a greater extreme in London. See John Summerson, *Georgian London*, rev. ed. (London, 1970), pp. 55–9. Whether Philadelphians patterned their city on the emerging London West End or arrived independently at a similar solution to similar problems of urban development is difficult to say. Of course, the street-alley system goes back to Thomas Holmes's attempt to adapt William Penn's plan for Philadelphia to the realities of city life, at the very outset of Philadelphia's history.

116 Joseph Jackson, *Market Street, Philadelphia: The Most Historic Highway in America, Its Merchants and Its Story* (Philadelphia, 1918), p. 21.

117 Ritter, *Philadelphia and Her Merchants*, p. 156.

118 Hogan, *Prospect of Philadelphia*, pp. 3–4, 28–9.

119 Soltow argues, in "Egalitarian America," that the steeply progressive nature of the Federal Direct Tax of 1798 insured a very careful assessment. This is a reasonable point, but it also seems likely that this very feature of the tax would reinforce the tendency to undervalue the most expensive houses.

120 In New England, the figures were slightly different: Merchants (£89.1) and shopkeepers (£36.4) averaged more, and artisans (£13.6) averaged less. See Jones, *Wealth of a Nation to Be*, pp. 224, 226, 229, 232, 234, 236. All of Jones's inventories are drawn from probate records of 1774.

121 The inventories are printed in Alice Hanson Jones, *American Colonial Wealth: Documents and Methods* (New York, 1977), vol. 1, pp. 117–329. There are several other inventories (for example, those associated with the estates of "mariners") where the occupational designations are ambiguous. I have excluded them. Tobacconists and brewers were "mechanics" in the minds of many wealthy merchants, but I treat them here as being among the very small number of eighteenth-century manufacturers, men who supervised production rather than performing it themselves. Actually, it is likely that brewers did take a hand in their highly technical productive process, though their work probably was primarily managerial. In this sample of Philadelphia decedents, the one brewer was among the wealthiest of the "low nonmanuals."

122 Ibid., pp. 190–8. All of the values listed in these and the other inventories are in Pennsylvania currency. I have converted the figures I cite to sterling.

123 Ibid., pp. 135–7.

124 Ibid., pp. 285–7.
125 Ibid., pp. 269–72.
126 Ibid., pp. 277–8.
127 Ibid., pp. 273–6.
128 Ibid., pp. 307–8.
129 Ibid., pp. 200–2.
130 Ibid., pp. 141–2.
131 Ibid., p. 222.
132 Ibid., pp. 311–12.
133 Rochefoucault, *Travels*, vol. 2, p. 672.
134 Jones, *American Colonial Wealth*, vol. 1., p. 288.
135 Ibid., pp. 262–3, 266–8.
136 John Fanning Watson, *Annals of Philadelphia and Pennsylvania, in the Olden Time* . . . (Philadelphia, 1845), vol. 1, pp. 175–6, 191.
137 Peter F. Copeland, *Working Dress in Colonial and Revolutionary America* (Westport, Conn., 1977), p. 56.
138 *Poor Richard Revived: Being the Farmer's Diary . . . or . . . Almanack, for . . . 1794* (Albany, 1793).
139 Workman, *Father Tammany's Almanac, for . . . 1787*.
140 Nathaniel Ames, *An Astronomical Diary; or, an Almanack for . . . 1773* (Boston, 1772).
141 Jones, *American Colonial Wealth*, vol. 1, pp. 132–3.
142 Robert F. Oaks, "Big Wheels in Philadelphia: Du Simitière's List of Carriage Owners," *Pennsylvania Magazine of History and Biography* 95 (1971): 360–2.
143 Two other studies of eighteenth-century living standards, based on estate inventories, disclose patterns similar to those I have suggested here, although both emphasize also the consumption gains experienced by ordinary people during the century. Carole Shammas, "The Domestic Environment in Early Modern England and America," *Journal of Social History* 14 (1980): 3–24, is based on Jones's inventory sample for Massachusetts, a portion of which was drawn from Boston. Lois Green Carr and Lorena S. Walsh, "Changing Life Styles in Colonial St. Mary's County," *Working Papers from the Regional Economic History Research Center* 1 (1978): 73–118, is based on no fewer than 2,613 inventories recorded between 1658 and 1776 in a rural county in Maryland. In a novel study of claims to the Boston Overseers of the Poor following the disastrous fire of 1760, William Pencak finds that nearly 60% (126 of 214) of those who lost *all* their goods submitted very small claims of £20 or less (Massachusetts currency) for public compensation. And the fire occurred in a central section of the city. See William Pencak, "The Social Structure of Revolutionary Boston: Evidence from the Great Fire of 1760," *Journal of Interdisciplinary History* 10 (1979): 267–78.
144 Studies of these forms of Revolutionary activity include: Nash, *Urban Crucible*; Pauline Maier, *From Resistance to Revolution: Colonial Radicals and the Development of American Opposition to Britain, 1765–1776* (New York, 1972); Edmund S. Morgan and Helen M. Morgan, *The Stamp Act*

Crisis: Prologue to Revolution (Chapel Hill, 1953); Dirk Hoerder, *Crowd Action in Revolutionary Massachusetts, 1765–1780* (New York, 1977); Hoerder, "Boston Leaders and Boston Crowds, 1765–1776," in Alfred F. Young, ed., *The American Revolution: Explorations in the History of American Radicalism* (DeKalb, Ill., 1976), pp. 233–71; Gordon S. Wood, "A Note on Mobs in the American Revolution," *William and Mary Quarterly*, 3d ser., 23 (1966): 635–42; Jesse Lemisch, "Jack Tar in the Streets: Merchant Seamen in the Politics of Revolutionary America," *William and Mary Quarterly*, 3d ser., 25 (1968): 371–407; Lemisch, "The American Revolution Seen from the Bottom Up," in Barton J. Bernstein, ed., *Towards a New Past: Dissenting Essays in American History* (New York, 1968), pp. 3–45; Steffen, *Mechanics of Baltimore*; Steven Rosswurm, "The Philadelphia Militia, 1775–1783: Active Duty and Active Radicalism," in Ronald Hoffman and Peter J. Albert, eds., *Arms and Independence: The Military Character of the American Revolution* (Charlottesville, Va., 1984).

145 Crowds in particular were traditional forms of plebeian political action. In Boston, according to Hoerder, Revolutionary crowds drew on the customs of nonpolitical crowds associated with Pope's Day and other celebrations. See Hoerder, "Boston Leaders and Boston Crowds," p. 239.

146 Richard Alan Ryerson, *The Revolution Is Now Begun: The Radical Committees of Philadelphia, 1765–1776* (Philadelphia, 1976), pp. 185, 254.

147 Ibid., pp. 25–69, 95–156, 181, 254.

148 Staughton Lynd, "The Mechanics in New York Politics, 1774–1788," *Labor History* 5 (1964): 225; Countryman, *A People in Revolution*, pp. 124–5, 200–1.

149 Richard Walsh, *Charleston's Sons of Liberty: A Study of the Artisans, 1763–1789* (Columbia, S.C., 1959); Maier, *From Resistance to Revolution*, pp. 298–300, 307; Alan and Katherine Day, "Another Look at the Boston 'Caucus,' " *Journal of American Studies* 5 (1971): 19–42; G. B. Warden, "The Caucus and Democracy in Colonial Boston," *New England Quarterly* 43 (1970): 19–45.

150 Steffen, *Mechanics of Baltimore*, pp. 12–73; Ronald Hoffman, *A Spirit of Dissension: Economics, Politics, and the Revolution in Maryland* (Baltimore, 1973).

151 Patricia U. Bonomi, *A Factious People: Politics and Society in Colonial New York* (New York, 1971), p. 240.

152 Lynd, "Mechanics," p. 226; Roger J. Champagne, "New York and the Intolerable Acts, 1774," *New-York Historical Society Quarterly* 45 (1961): 196–206. This assessment of the composition of the Committee of 25 is based on my attempt to locate its members in the Roll of Freemen of New York City, 1675–1866, published in *Collections of the New-York Historical Society for the Year 1885* (New York, 1886). I identified perhaps a dozen, all of whom were merchants or gentlemen.

153 Lynd, "Mechanics," p. 228; Roger J. Champagne, "New York's Radicals and the Coming of Independence," *Journal of American History* 51 (1964):

21–40; Champagne, "Liberty Boys and Mechanics of New York City," pp. 115–35.

154 Ryerson, *The Revolution Is Now Begun*, pp. 76–7. See also p. 203.

155 Day, "Another Look," pp. 32, 39.

156 Ibid.; Ryerson, *The Revolution Is Now Begun*, pp. 275–81; Walsh, *Charleston's Sons of Liberty*; Countryman, *A People in Revolution*, p. 11.

157 Olton, *Artisans for Independence*, p. 33. Bridenbaugh calls them "an ambitious, thriving, capable group" who "found their aspirations thwarted by the refusal of the merchant aristocracy to accord them recognition – economic, social, political – commensurate with their achievements." Bridenbaugh, *Colonial Craftsman*, p. 171.

158 Charles S. Olton, "Philadelphia's Mechanics in the First Decade of Revolution, 1765–1775," *Journal of American History* 59 (1972): 325. See also Bernard Friedman, "The Shaping of Radical Consciousness in Provincial New York," *Journal of American History* 56 (1970): 781–801; Bernard Bailyn, "The Index and Commentaries of Harbottle Dorr," *Proceedings of the Massachusetts Historical Society* 85 (1973): 21–35.

159 Steffen, *Mechanics of Baltimore*, pp. 82–3, 90.

160 Ibid., p. 184.

161 Ibid., p. 207.

162 Robert F. Oaks, "Philadelphia Merchants and the Origins of American Independence," *Proceedings of the American Philosophical Society* 121 (1977): 436. A more general history of this "counterrevolution" is Robert L. Brunhouse, *The Counter-Revolution in Pennsylvania, 1776–1790* (Harrisburg, 1942). In his essay "The Social Evolution of Preindustrial American Cities," Nash points to the conservative reaction of the 1790s but argues that the "popularization of politics" nonetheless continued after the Revolution (p. 135).

163 *Aurora*, October 7, 1796.

164 Mathew Carey, *A Short Account of the Malignant Fever, Lately Prevalent in Philadelphia* . . . (Philadelphia, 1793), p. 57.

165 Ibid., pp. 98–9. Occupations were obtained from contemporary city directories. John H. Powell, in *Bring Out Your Dead: The Great Plague of Yellow Fever in Philadelphia in 1793* (Philadelphia, 1949), identifies several of these middling folk, the tavernkeeper Israel Israel, for example, as men who were wealthier than they appeared.

166 Philadelphia *General Advertiser*, October 6, 1794. Again, occupations were obtained from the city directory.

Chapter 3. Toward white collar

1 See Sean Wilentz, *Chants Democratic: New York City and the Rise of the American Working Class, 1788–1850* (New York, 1984); Bruce Laurie, *Working People of Philadelphia, 1800–1850* (Philadelphia, 1980); Paul G. Faler, *Mechanics and Manufacturers in the Early Industrial Revolution: Lynn, Massachusetts, 1780–1860* (Albany, N.Y., 1981); Daniel J. Walkowitz, *Worker*

City, Company Town: Iron and Cotton-Worker Protest in Troy and Cohoes, New York, 1855–84 (Urbana, Ill., 1978); Susan E. Hirsch, *Roots of the American Working Class: The Industrialization of Crafts in Newark, 1800–1860* (Philadelphia, 1978); and Alan Dawley, *Class and Community: The Industrial Revolution in Lynn* (Cambridge, Mass., 1976).

2　Mary P. Ryan, *Cradle of the Middle Class: The Family in Oneida County, New York, 1790–1865* (Cambridge, 1981), p. xiii.

3　Wilentz, *Chants Democratic*, pp. 11–12. Wilentz briefly discusses the issue of middle-class formation with much less stress on the "terms of confrontation" in "Artisan Origins of the American Working Class," *International Labor and Working Class History*, no. 19 (1981): 1–22.

4　The work of the recent historians of the working class is in this respect indebted to a much older historical literature, including John R. Commons, "American Shoemakers, 1648–1895," *Quarterly Journal of Economics* 24 (1909): 39–84; Commons et al., *History of Labour in the United States*, vol. 1 (New York, 1918); George Rogers Taylor, *The Transportation Revolution, 1815–1860* (New York, 1951), and others.

5　Alfred D. Chandler, Jr., *The Visible Hand: The Managerial Revolution in American Business* (Cambridge, Mass., 1977), esp. pp. 36–40.

6　Sam Bass Warner, Jr., *The Private City: Philadelphia in Three Periods of Its Growth* (Philadelphia, 1968), pp. 57–8.

7　Edwin T. Freedley, *Philadelphia and its Manufactures . . .* (Philadelphia, 1858), pp. 271–5; George J. Henkels, *Household Economy* (Philadelphia, 1867), pp. 36–7; Kathleen M. Catalano, "Furniture Making in Philadelphia, 1820–1840," *American Art and Antiques* 2 (1979): 116–23; Jan M. Seidler, "A Tradition in Transition: The Boston Furniture Industry, 1840–1880," in Kenneth L. Ames, ed., *Victorian Furniture: Essays from a Victorian Society Autumn Symposium* (Philadelphia, 1983), pp. 65–83; Page Talbott, "Philadelphia Furniture Makers and Manufacturers, 1850–1880," in Ames, ed., *Victorian Furniture*, pp. 85–101; Wilentz, *Chants Democratic*, pp. 127–8.

8　Elizabeth A. Ingerman, ed., "Personal Experiences of an Old New York Cabinetmaker," *Antiques* 84 (1963): 576–80; *Doggett's New York City Directory, for 1850–51* (New York, 1850). Hagen himself is not listed in the directory.

9　*McElroy's Philadelphia Directory for 1860* (Philadelphia, 1860).

10　Gotlieb Vollmer ledger, 1860–1, Historical Society of Pennsylvania.

11　Brewster & Co., Invoices and Sales, 1856–62, New-York Historical Society.

12　The best brief discussion is Wilentz, *Chants Democratic*, pp. 119–24.

13　*The New York City Directory, for 1851–52* (New York, 1851); *Doggett's New York City Directory, for 1850–51*. Partnerships of the type formed between Booth and Foster were not uncommon. In 1829 the piano maker Jonas Chickering became the partner of John Mackay, a merchant. Mackay handled the sales of the firm's pianos, while Chickering supervised their manufacture. See Gary J. Kornblith, "The Craftsman as Industrialist:

Jonas Chickering and the Transformation of American Piano Making," *Business History Review* 59 (1985): 354–5.

14 See *The Directory of the City of Boston* (Boston, 1850), for both the individual listing and the advertisement. A very long obituary by Thomas C. Simonds, reprinted by the author in his *History of South Boston* (Boston, 1857), pp. 251–60, notes that Alger entered the foundry business with his father upon leaving school, and indicates that he was a foundry owner (and real estate investor) throughout his life. Alger is one of five major American industrialists whose portraits form the frontispiece of the first volume of J. Leander Bishop's *A History of Manufactures from 1608 to 1860* . . . (Philadelphia, 1864). He is also listed (at $200,000) in *"Our First Men:" A Calendar of Wealth, Fashion and Gentility* . . . (Boston, 1846), p. 10.

15 *Longworth's American Almanac, New York Register, and City Directory* . . . (New York, 1842).

16 See Sean Wilentz, "Artisan Republican Festivals and the Rise of Class Conflict in New York City, 1788–1837," in Michael H. Frisch and Daniel J. Walkowitz, eds., *Working-Class America: Essays on Labor, Community, and American Society* (Urbana, Ill., 1983), pp. 37–77; Wilentz, *Chants Democratic*, pp. 271–86; John S. Gilkeson, Jr., *Middle-Class Providence, 1820–1940* (Princeton, 1986); Gary John Kornblith, "From Artisans to Businessmen: Master Mechanics in New England, 1789–1850" (Ph.D. dissertation, Princeton University, 1983), and my discussion of these works in Chapter 4.

17 Ian M. G. Quimby, "Introduction: Some Observations on the Craftsman in Early America," in Quimby, ed., *The Craftsman in Early America* (New York, 1984), p. 13.

18 These calculations are based on two data files, the very large enumeration of adult males born in the United States, Ireland, and Germany collected and coded by the Philadelphia Social History Project, and my own sample of 2,252 heads of household.

19 Philadelphia Social History Project file, 1860.

20 Kathleen Neils Conzen, *Immigrant Milwaukee, 1836–1860: Accommodation and Community in a Frontier City* (Cambridge, Mass., 1976), p. 71; Peter R. Knights, *The Plain People of Boston, 1830–1860: A Study in City Growth* (New York, 1971), pp. 82, 149–56.

21 Stuart M. Blumin, "Mobility and Change in Ante-Bellum Philadelphia," in Stephan Thernstrom and Richard Sennett, eds., *Nineteenth-Century Cities: Essays in the New Urban History* (New Haven, 1969), p. 198.

22 Peter R. Decker, *Fortunes and Failures: White-Collar Mobility in Nineteenth-Century San Francisco* (Cambridge, Mass., 1978), p. 70; Ryan, *Cradle of the Middle Class*, p. 253; Clyde Griffen and Sally Griffen, *Natives and Newcomers: The Ordering of Opportunity in Mid-Nineteenth-Century Poughkeepsie* (Cambridge, Mass., 1978), p. 5. There are as yet no comparable tabulations for New York City. Robert Ernst's tabulations from the New York State census of 1855 combines male and female workers, of whom only 23% worked in explicitly nonmanual jobs. Removing the very large num-

ber of dressmakers, seamstresses, domestic servants, and laundresses brings the nonmanual sector up to 29%. This is probably closer to the true proportion. See Robert Ernst, *Immigrant Life in New York City, 1825–1863* (New York, 1949), pp. 214–17.

23 Commons, in "American Shoemakers," esp. 59–72, and David J. Saposs in Commons, et al., *History of Labour*, vol. 1, pp. 100–4, state this position most clearly and succinctly.

24 See Herbert G. Gutman, "The Reality of the Rags-to-Riches 'Myth': The Case of the Paterson, New Jersey, Locomotive, Iron, and Machinery Manufacturers, 1830–1880," in Thernstrom and Sennett, eds., *Nineteenth-Century Cities*, pp. 98–124; Susan E. Hirsch, "From Artisan to Manufacturer: Industrialization and the Small Producer in Newark, 1830–60," in Stuart W. Bruchey, *Small Business in American Life* (New York, 1980), pp. 80–99; Faler, *Mechanics and Manufacturers*, pp. 8–27, 58–76; Wilentz, *Chants Democratic*, p. 116. A spectacular instance of the artisan-turned-manufacturer was Matthias Baldwin, a machinest and former apprentice jeweler, who built his first full-sized locomotive in a small shop in a Philadelphia alley in 1832. By 1836 he was supervising 240 workers in his new four-block locomotive works in the same city. See Freedley, *Philadelphia and Its Manufactures*, pp. 306–9; Malcolm C. Clark, "The Birth of an Enterprise: Baldwin Locomotive, 1831–1842," *Pennsylvania Magazine of History and Biography* 90 (1966): 423–44.

25 [Stephen Noyes Winslow], *Biographies of Successful Philadelphia Merchants* (Philadelphia, 1864), pp. 152–8.

26 Bruce Laurie and Mark Schmitz, "Manufacture and Productivity: The Making of an Industrial Base, Philadelphia, 1850–1880," in Theodore Hershberg, ed., *Philadelphia: Work, Space, Family, and Group Experience in the 19th Century: Essays Toward an Interdisciplinary History of the City* (New York, 1981), p. 52.

27 Freedley, *Philadelphia and its Manufactures*, p. 62.

28 *Census of the State of New York for 1855 . . .* (Albany, 1857), p. 479. The ratio of retail stores to population in New York City (15.2 per thousand) is very similar to Freedley's figure as a proportion of Philadelphia's population in 1860 (13.1 per thousand). They would be even more alike if a population total for Philadelphia in 1858 could be substituted for the 1860 figure. This suggests that Freedley's tabulation refers only to retail stores.

29 My estimates are based on the following calculations: If Freedley's figure of 7,400 stores is added to the 6,330 manufacturing firms tabulated in the 1860 census of manufactures, and these 13,730 businesses are divided into the 3,678 artisan shops employing fewer than six hands, the resulting proportion is 26.8%. If the larger denominator of 23,330 firms is used (17,000 commercial firms plus 6,330 industrial firms), the proportion of manual artisan shops is reduced to 15.8%. No doubt the numerator and both denominators should be adjusted upward, the former to include larger shops in which the proprietor performed manual work, the latter to include banks, insurance companies, shipping companies, private schools, professional practices, and other nonmanual proprietorships

that are excluded even from the larger denominator. The city's street peddlers, self-employed carters, and similar folk are probably best excluded from both sides of the calculation. I deliberately report the results of these calculations, and others like them, in approximate terms, so as not to overstate the precision of our knowledge of such matters.

30 Wilentz, *Chants Democratic*, p. 141.

31 Clive Behagg, in "Secrecy, Ritual and Folk Violence: The Opacity of the Workplace in the First Half of the Nineteenth Century," Robert D. Storch, ed., *Popular Culture and Custom in Nineteenth-Century England* (London, 1982), pp. 154–79, notes that in England middle-class people entered the manual workplace "only with great trepidation" in this era (p. 155). American views of factories and workshops often include well-dressed men, women, and even children, whose only function in the scene is that of observing visitors. This was a convention common to illustrations of all sorts, and may have been no more than that, but it may suggest that American manual workplaces were more accessible to non-workers than were the shops and factories of Britain. On the other hand, the small, out-of-the-way workshops I describe here were not the subjects of these illustrations, and it is almost certainly the case that fewer Americans outside the working class entered manual workplaces of any kind in the nineteenth century than had done so in the eighteenth century.

32 Seidler, "A Tradition in Transition," p. 67.

33 Ryan, *Cradle of the Middle Class*, p. 253.

34 William Hoffman diary, pp. 102–8, New-York Historical Society.

35 Diary and correspondence of Samuel G. Damon, David Damon papers, Massachusetts Historical Society.

36 Journal of C. A. Grinnell, Baltimore, 1837, Massachusetts Historical Society.

37 *The Baltimore Directory, for 1845* (Baltimore, 1845).

38 *Hunt's Merchants' Magazine* 33 (1855): 394. *Hunt's* is an excellent source for inquiring into the values and attitudes, as well as some of the practices, of nineteenth-century merchants. I draw extensively on it in this and the following chapter.

39 Thomas C. Cochran, "The Business Revolution," *American Historical Review* 79 (1974): 1449–66; Glenn Porter and Harold C. Livesay, *Merchants and Manufacturers: Studies in the Changing Structure of Nineteenth-Century Marketing* (Baltimore, 1971), pp. 5–10.

40 Chandler, *Visible Hand*, p. 15.

41 This is described most effectively in Porter and Livesay, *Merchants and Manufacturers*, pp. 5n, 17–20, and in Chandler, *Visible Hand*, pp. 15–28. See also the older work of Robert Greenhalgh Albion, *The Rise of New York Port [1815–1860]* (New York, 1939), esp. pp. 275–6; and Fred Mitchell Jones, *Middlemen in the Domestic Trade of the United States, 1800–1860*, *Illinois Studies in the Social Sciences* vol. 21, no. 3 (Urbana, Ill., 1937).

42 Ray Bert Westerfield, "Early History of American Auctions: A Chapter in Commercial History," *Transactions of the Connecticut Academy of Arts and Sciences* 23 (1920): 159–210; Ira Cohen, "The Auction System in the

Port of New York, 1817–1837," *Business History Review* 45 (1971): 488–510; and Albion, *Rise of New York Port*, pp. 276–82.

43 Porter and Livesay, *Merchants and Manufacturers*, p. 27.

44 Cochran, "The Business Revolution," pp. 1460, 1462–3.

45 Edward Hazen, *The Panorama of Professions and Trades; or Every Man's Book* (Philadelphia, 1836), p. 110.

46 Charles Edwards, "What Constitutes a Merchant," *Hunt's* 1 (1839): 289–303.

47 *Hunt's* 3 (1840): 11.

48 Ibid., 5 (1841): 48.

49 See, for example, ibid., 6 (1842): 153; 11 (1844): 577; 14 (1846): 435; 17 (1847): 219; 18 (1848): 119–20, 452.

50 Ibid., 17 (1847): 441–2; 19 (1848): 569–70; 20 (1849): 116, 118–20, 232–3, 347–8; 21 (1849): 473.

51 Harry E. Resseguie, "A. T. Stewart's Marble Palace: The Cradle of the Department Store," *New-York Historical Society Quarterly* 48 (1964): 133. My discussion of Stewart is based primarily on this essay, and on Resseguie, "Alexander Turney Stewart and the Development of the Department Store," *Business History Review* 39 (1965): 301–22. For a nineteenth-century description of Stewart's career before the building of the Marble Palace, see Matthew Hale Smith, *Sunshine and Shadow in New York* (Hartford, 1868), p. 53.

52 On this aspect of book publishing and retailing, see W. S. Tryon, "Ticknor and Fields' Publications in the Old Northwest, 1840–1860," *Mississippi Valley Historical Review* 34 (1947–8): 589–610; and William Chervat, "James T. Fields and the Beginnings of Book Promotion, 1840–1855," *Huntington Library Quarterly* 8 (1944–45): 75–94.

53 These figures are based on an analysis of newspaper advertising in these four cities during eight years of relatively normal economic conditions: 1772, 1792, 1805, 1815, 1825, 1835, 1845, and 1855. All the advertisements from the first issues appearing in January, April, July, and October of these years were recorded for analysis. A list of the newspapers I used, and a more complete discussion of my methods and results, can be found in Stuart M. Blumin, "Black Coats to White Collars: Economic Change, Nonmanual Work, and the Social Structure of Industrializing America," in Bruchey, ed., *Small Business in American Life*, pp. 100–21. The figures I report here repeat those found in note 15, p. 121, of that essay.

54 Ibid., table 4.1, p. 111.

55 Ralph M. Hower, in *History of Macy's of New York, 1858–1919: Chapters in the Evolution of the Department Store* (Cambridge, Mass., 1943), overstates the case somewhat by claiming: "It is practically impossible to find a specialized retail store in America around 1800 . . . , but by 1850 the cities were full of them" (pp. 82–3). For a brief discussion of increasing retail specialization in a small nineteenth-century city, see Stuart M. Blumin, *The Urban Threshold: Growth and Change in a Nineteenth-Century American Community* (Chicago, 1976), pp. 60–1.

56 Examples indicative of each attitude can be found in *Hunt's* 17 (1847):

441–2; 18 (1848): 452; 32 (1855): 776–7. See also Hower, *History of Macy's*, pp. 82–8.
57 Porter and Livesay, *Merchants and Manufacturers*, p. 21; Chandler, *Visible Hand*, p. 36.
58 *Hunt's* 17 (1847): 441.
59 See, for example, the Sharpless Brothers advertisement in *The Philadelphia Shopping Guide & Housekeeper's Companion* (Philadelphia, 1859).
60 Porter and Livesay, *Merchants and Manufacturers*, p. 17.
61 Henkels, *Household Economy*, pp. 14–15.
62 Freedley, *Philadelphia and Its Manufactures*, pp. 273–4; and the 1867 edition, pp. 293–4.
63 This is the claim of Jonathan Fairbanks in "Craft Processes and Images: Visual Sources for the Study of the Craftsman," in Quimby, ed., *The Craftsman in Early America*, p. 323. I have been unable to find earlier ones, although several earlier "books of trades" written and published in England were issued in the United States as well, including the richly illustrated *The Book of Trades, or Library of the Useful Arts* (London, 1806; Philadelphia, 1807). The illustrations that appear in Carl Bridenbaugh, *The Colonial Craftsman* (New York, 1950), are taken from Diderot's *Encyclopédie*, a decision that Bridenbaugh rather lamely justifies on grounds that "M. Diderot's engravers drew heavily from English examples for illustrations of the work of the several crafts, and thus they are much nearer to colonial practice, which closely imitated the English, than might at first appear" (p. ix). Diderot's view of a tailor's shop, which appears opposite page 116 in Bridenbaugh's book, is structurally quite similar to Hazen's 1836 illustration, but in most of its details is absurdly inappropriate to a discussion of American workshops.
64 In addition to the item just noted, see *The Book of Trades* (New York, 1836); *A Book of Trades for Ingenious Boys* (Providence, 1845); and *The Book of Trades and Professions: or, Familiar Objects Described* (Philadelphia and New York, 1851). The reasons for this antiquarianism, in what were intended to be practical schoolbooks, are worth exploring.
65 The best discussion of this spatial resorting of industrial firms within the metropolitan region is Richard Stott, "Hinterland Development and Differences in Work Setting: The New York City Region, 1820–1870," in William Pencak and Conrad Edick Wright, eds., *New York and the Rise of American Capitalism: Economic Development and the Social and Political History of an American State, 1780–1870* (New York, 1989), pp. 45–71.
66 Edwin Williams, ed., *New York as It Is in 1833 . . .* (New York, 1833), pp. 12–13.
67 Ibid., p. 12.
68 George G. Foster, *New York in Slices: By an Experienced Carver . . .* (New York, 1849), p. 12. For a good recent discussion of the development of Broadway, see Edward K. Spann, *The New Metropolis: New York City, 1840–1857* (New York, 1981), esp. p. 100.
69 *Sheldon & Co.'s Business or Advertising Directory . . .* (New York, 1845); *The New York City Directory for 1854–55* (New York, 1854).

70 Collection of Business Americana, Archives Center, National Museum of American History, Smithsonian Institution. This is an advertisement removed from an unidentified city directory. It is undated but appears to be from the 1850s. (This collection will be cited hereafter as "Smithsonian.")

71 Ibid. Another advertisement removed from an unidentified directory. The date 1853 is penciled in on one corner.

72 Lithograph by Sarony, Major and Knapp, ca. 1858, Division of Prints and Photographs, Library of Congress.

73 *The Boston Directory* (Boston, 1848); *The Boston Directory, for 1851* (Boston, 1851).

74 *The Boston Directory, for 1854* (Boston, 1854); *The Boston Directory* (Boston, 1849); *The Boston Directory* (Boston, 1860).

75 Lithograph by W. H. Rease, ca. 1856, Division of Prints and Photographs, Library of Congress.

76 *O'Brien's Philadelphia Wholesale Business Directory* . . . (Philadelphia, 1844).

77 My source here is not a city directory advertisement but Freedley, *Philadelphia and Its Manufactures* (1857 ed.), pp. 443–7.

78 *Boyd's Pictorial Directory of Broadway* (New York, 1859). The advertisement quotes a *New York Times* article of November 19, 1858.

79 *Gleason's Pictorial Drawing-Room Companion* 3 (1852): 244. This store was somewhat unusual in that nearly all of its sales clerks were women.

80 *The Boston Directory, for 1852* (Boston, 1852).

81 *Mercein's City Directory, New-York Register, and Almanac* . . . (New York, 1820).

82 An interesting hint of this change in taxonomy is provided by the Boston furniture retailer Stephen Smith, whose billhead in 1848 identified his product line as "Counting House Furniture," but whose city directory advertisement in 1854 (and billheads used after that date) used the phrase "Bank and Office Furniture" instead (Smithsonian). Was this the precise period in which the "countinghouse" became the "office"?

83 Jacob Abbott, "The Novelty Works," *Harper's New Monthly Magazine* 2 (1851): 721–34.

84 Stephen Pike, the bookseller and stationer, first appears at this location in the city directory of 1809. It is not clear whether this building and storefront predated his occupancy. In 1795 the site was occupied by a merchant, Henry McPherson. See *The Philadelphia Directory for 1809* (Philadelphia, 1809); Edmund Hogan, *The Prospect of Philadelphia* . . . (Philadelphia, 1795). Booksellers had been the leaders in creating distinctive retail storefronts in the eighteenth century.

85 John Adams Paxton, *The Philadelphia Directory and Register, for 1818* (Philadelphia, 1818).

86 See also Daniel D. Smith's advertisement in *Longworth's New-York Almanac* . . . (New York, 1817), an 1814 drawing of Beekman Street by John Rubens Smith (particularly the shop at the extreme right), and an 1809 water color of Warren and Greenwich Streets by the Baroness Hyde de Neuville.

The latter two are included in John A. Kouwenhoven, *The Columbia Historical Portrait of New York* (New York, 1972), pp. 116, 113.

87 See Walter Muir Whitehill, *Boston: A Topographical History* (Cambridge, Mass., 1968), pp. 96–8; Nicholas B. Wainwright, *Philadelphia in the Romantic Age of Lithography* (Philadelphia, 1958), pp. 23, 279; Donald Martin Reynolds, *The Architecture of New York City: Histories and Views of Important Structures, Sites, and Symbols* (New York, 1984), p. 100; Talbot Hamlin, *Greek Revival Architecture in America: Being an Account of Important Trends in American Architecture and American Life Prior to the War Between the States* (New York, 1944), pp. 148–50.

88 There is some disagreement as to the date and place (but not the architect and client) of the first Greek Revival warehouse in New York City. Hamlin, in his classic study of the Greek Revival, claims that it was on Wall Street in 1831. Reynolds, in a more recent work, asserts that it was built on Pearl Street in 1829 (see note 87). As far as I know, no one has discussed the application of the Greek Revival to retail stores.

89 Minard Lafever, *The Modern Builder's Guide* (New York, 1969; 1st ed., 1833).

90 Ibid., intro.; see also Hamlin, *Greek Revival*, pp. 146–8. Calvin Pollard, a New York City builder who was just turning to the practice of architecture, mentions six commissions for store designs in a professional diary he maintained in 1841 and 1842. Calvin Pollard diary, 1841–1842, New-York Historical Society. It is not clear whether these were wholesale or retail stores. Within a decade, as we will see, more established architects were beginning to undertake commissions for the design of retail stores.

91 See James Truslow Adams, ed., *Album of American History*, vol. 2, *1783–1853* (New York, 1945), pp. 216, 258, 260, for several New York City street scenes drawn or painted by J. W. Hill and others around 1830.

92 See, for example, *Roe's Philadelphia Pictorial Directory and Panoramic Advertiser* (Philadelphia, 1851); *Baxter's Panoramic Business Directory of Philadelphia for 1859* (Philadelphia, 1859); *Boyd's Pictorial Directory of Broadway* (New York, 1859). Kouwenhoven, in *The Columbia Historical Portrait of New York*, p. 149, claims that the first of these panoramic directories for New York was published in 1848, and presents a panoramic view of Liberty Street that was published in 1836 or 1837.

93 See *Sketches and Business Directory of Boston and Vicinity . . .* (Boston, 1860), for illustrations of four such blocks of stores on Franklin Street.

94 Illustrated city directory advertisements, removed from directories and dated 1853 and 1854 in pencil (Smithsonian).

95 Ada Louise Huxtable, "Progressive Architecture in America: Jayne Building – 1849–50," *Progressive Architecture* 37, no. 11 (1956): 133–4. See also George B. Tatum, *Penn's Great Town: 250 Years of Philadelphia Architecture Illustrated in Prints and Drawings* (Philadelphia, 1961), p. 84; and Charles E. Peterson, "Ante-Bellum Skyscraper," *Journal of the Society of Architectural Historians* 9 (1950): 27–8.

96 Margot Gayle, "Cast-Iron Architecture U.S.A.," *Historic Preservation* 27 (1975): 14–19.

97 See also various issues of *Frank Leslie's Illustrated Newspaper*. These two phenomena seem to have been connected to some extent. In several instances, illustrations appearing in magazines later appeared in the firm's city directory advertisement.

98 *Gleason's* 7 (1854): 64.

99 In one of the few studies that recognize the emergence of specialized retailing in this era, Michael and Kathleen Conzen examine both the shops of the sort I discuss here – centrally located and serving middle- and upper-class customers from various neighborhoods – and those more humble, dispersed neighborhood-based shops (groceries and others) to which I refer in the following chapter. The Conzens trace the development of secondary centers and other forms of dispersed retailing in the latter part of the nineteenth century, but in the antebellum period it is the emergence of the central retail district that impresses them as the most notable development. See Michael P. Conzen and Kathleen Neils Conzen, "Geographical Structure in Nineteenth-Century Urban Retailing: Milwaukee, 1836–90," *Journal of Historical Geography* 5 (1979): 45–66.

100 *Hunt's* 22 (1850): 420.

101 Ibid., 32 (1855): 136.

102 *Harper's New Monthly Magazine* 7 (1853): 130.

103 For a detailed European reaction, see H. Reid, *Sketches in North America* . . . (London, 1861), pp. 223–8.

Chapter 4. Republican prejudice

1 Nathan Appleton, *Labor, Its Relations in Europe and the United States Compared* (Boston, 1844), pp. 8, 13.

2 Carl Siracusa, *A Mechanical People: Perceptions of the Industrial Order in Massachusetts, 1815–1880* (Middletown, Conn., 1979), pp. 79–80.

3 Edwin T. Freedley, *Philadelphia and Its Manufactures* . . . (Philadelphia, 1858), p. 65.

4 Siracusa, *A Mechanical People*, pp. 108–11.

5 Sean Wilentz, *Chants Democratic: New York City and the Rise of the American Working Class, 1788–1850* (New York, 1984), pp. 117, 405.

6 Bruce Laurie, Theodore Hershberg, and George Alter, "Immigrants and Industry: The Philadelphia Experience, 1850–1880," in Hershberg, ed., *Philadelphia: Work, Space, Family, and Group Experience in the Nineteenth Century: Essays Toward an Interdisciplinary History of the City* (New York, 1981), p. 105. See also Laurie, *Working People of Philadelphia, 1800–1850* (Philadelphia, 1980), p. 12. One well-known "workingman's budget" for a family of five living in Philadelphia in 1851 (published as a letter to the editor in the *New York Tribune* on May 27, 1851), amounted to $538.44. This is a little lower than the $582 obtained for 1855 by deflating Eudice Glassberg's "estimated minimum adequate standard of living" for a Philadelphia family of five in 1880, by Jeffrey G. Williamson and Peter H. Lindert's cost of living index for skilled workers in Mid-Atlantic

cities, 1855–80. See Glassberg, "Work, Wages, and the Cost of Living: Ethnic Differences and the Poverty Line, Philadelphia, 1880," *Pennsylvania History* 66 (1979): 39; Williamson and Lindert, *American Inequality: A Macroeconomic History* (New York, 1980), p. 107. A less-well-known workingman's budget of $648 was published in a trades union journal in 1835, and was compared to journeymen shoemakers' wages of $416 for a full year's work. See Christine Stansell, *City of Women: Sex and Class in New York, 1789–1860* (New York, 1986), p. 243. For a contemporary discussion of wages and living costs in the big city around the same time as this earlier budget see M[athew] Carey, *Appeal to the Wealthy of the Land* (Philadelphia, 1833). Clarence D. Long, *Wages and Earnings in the United States, 1860–1890* (Princeton, 1960), specifies $297 as the average annual earnings of industrial workers in the nation as a whole in 1860 (p. 68).

7 *The British Mechanic's and Labourer's Handbook and True Guide to the United States* (London, 1840), p. 21. On changing nominal and real wage rates, see Donald R. Adams, Jr., "Wage Rates in the Early National Period: Philadelphia, 1785–1830," *Journal of Economic History* 28 (1968): 404–26; Adams, "Earnings and Savings in the Early 19th Century," *Explorations in Economic History* 17 (1980): 118–34; Adams, "The Standard of Living During American Industrialization: Evidence From the Brandywine Region, 1800–1860," *Journal of Economic History* 42 (1982): 903–17; Williamson and Lindert, *American Inequality*, esp. pp. 307, 319; Robert A. Margo and Georgia C. Villaflor, "The Growth of Wages in Antebellum America: New Evidence," *Journal of Economic History* 47 (1987): 873–95. The new evidence to which Margo and Villaflor refer consists of records of wages paid by the U.S. Army to civilian workers in different regions of the country. Their analysis of such wages in the Northeast suggests there was no sustained rise or fall in real wages between 1820 and 1840, a very steep rise between 1840 and 1846, and a fairly steep but erratic decline between 1846 and 1855, during which northeastern workers gave back about half the gains they experienced in 1840–6. The overall rise in real wages in this region from 1820 to 1856 was, according to their calculations, about 32%, which is somewhat lower than some of the earlier estimates. Most of the gains in real wages derived from falling prices rather than rising nominal wages.

8 I refer to the *New York Tribune* budget of 1851. The *New York Times* workingman's budget on which Wilentz bases his subsistence estimates includes a still higher allocation for food. Interestingly, it also includes a small sum for charitable donations. See *New York Times*, November 8, 1853.

9 See Alexander Keyssar, *Out of Work: The First Century of Unemployment in Massachusetts* (Cambridge, 1986), esp. chap. 2. Margo and Villaflor, "The Growth of Wages," observe with respect to the increasing real wage rates of the depression era: "For workers who were unemployed or underemployed (a significant percentage) the increase in real wages overstates the true gains in purchasing power" (p. 890). Indeed, it may assert

gains where there were really losses. The absence of unemployment as a variable in wage *rate* series constitutes their most serious deficiency. What we are trying to learn, after all, is how actual incomes changed. Rates of pay are only part of the story.

10   Laurie, et al., "Immigrants and Industry," p. 106.

11   *The British Mechanic's and Labourer's Handbook*, p. 21.

12   Ibid., p. 60. On the abundant workers' diet and its relationship to the fast pace of work in American shops, see Richard Stott, "British Immigrants and the American 'Work Ethic' in the Mid-Nineteenth Century," *Labor History* 26 (1985): 99–107.

13   Richard Stott, "Workers in the Metropolis: New York City, 1820–1860" (Ph.D. dissertation, Cornell University, 1983), esp. pp. 307–8. See the revision of this dissertation, forthcoming from Cornell University Press.

14   On workers' consumption patterns, see the excellent and extensive discussion in Stott, "Workers in the Metropolis," pp. 281–328. See also Dorothy S. Brady, "Consumption and the Style of Life," in Lance E. Davis, Richard A. Easterlin, and William N. Parker, eds., *American Economic Growth: An Economist's History of the United States* (New York, 1972), p. 79. Stott also establishes the youthfulness of the New York City work force (pp. 45–96). In Philadelphia in 1860, 42.5% of those listed on the census in skilled occupations were under thirty, and, as the property columns of the census suggest, a significant number of those older than thirty were well-to-do nonmanual businessmen rather than workers or small masters.

15   George G. Foster, *New York by Gas-Light: With Here and There a Streak of Sunshine* (New York, 1850), p. 107. On Foster's treatment of Mose and Lize see Stuart M. Blumin, "Explaining the New Metropolis: Perception, Depiction, and Analysis in Mid-Nineteenth-Century New York City," *Journal of Urban History* 11 (1984): 20–3. On Mose himself, see Richard M. Dorson, *America in Legend: Folklore from the Colonial Period to the Present* (New York, 1973), pp. 99–107; James Boyd Jones, Jr., "Mose the Bowery B'hoy and the Nashville Volunteer Fire Department, 1849–1860," *Tennessee Historical Quarterly* 40 (1981): 170–81; Adrienne Siegel, *The Image of the American City in Popular Literature: 1820–1870* (Port Washington, N.Y., 1981), p. 32. Peter George Buckley breaks new ground in understanding the Bowery b'hoy both in popular literature and on the streets in "To the Opera House: Culture and Society in New York City, 1820–1860" (Ph.D. dissertation, State University of New York at Stony Brook, 1984), chap. 4.

16   William Hoffman diary, 1847–50, New-York Historical Society, p.98.

17   Allan Stanley Horlick, *Country Boys and Merchant Princes: The Social Control of Young Men in New York* (Lewisburg, Pa., 1975), pp. 121–43. Horlick also discusses William Hoffman. *Hunt's Merchants' Magazine* 2 (1840): 160–1 describes a salesman's contract, specifying $600 per annum salary, drawn up during the depression year of 1839. Also of interest is a brief article in *Hunt's* 20 (1849): 570, which mentions a hypothetical starting salary of $600 for a clerk of twenty-one. The purpose of this item, written

by the editor of another magazine, is to cool the ambition of clerks too eager to exceed their salaries by going into business for themselves.

18 Robert McCoskry Graham diary, New-York Historical Society, December 6, 1848.

19 See Ralph M. Hower, *History of Macy's of New York, 1858–1919: Chapters in the Evolution of the Department Store* (Cambridge, Mass., 1943), pp. 194–200, on the compensation levels of different kinds of department store workers after the Civil War.

20 The Philadelphia mercantile firm of Nathan Trotter & Co., for example, earned between $7,000 and $60,000 per year, on sales that ranged from $50,000 to $375,000, between 1815 and 1849. The median net profit during this period was $20,000. Nathan Trotter shared these profits during most of these years with only one partner, his brother Joseph. Nathan was a plain-living Quaker, who reinvested most of his income. His annual living expenses ranged from approximately $1,000 to approximately $4,000 while his wealth accumulated to more than $800,000. See Elva Tooker, *Nathan Trotter, Philadelphia Merchant: 1787–1853* (Cambridge, Mass., 1955), pp. 54, 219–20, 224–5.

21 William Gowans letters and miscellaneous papers, 1826–70, New-York Historical Society, letter of June 21, 1832.

22 Ibid., manuscript obituary, manuscript memorial.

23 R. G. Dun & Co. Collection, Baker Library, Harvard Graduate School of Business Administration: New York City, vol. 191, p. 415; vol. 192, p. 567; vol. 189, p. 239.

24 Ibid., Boston, vol. 69, pp. 469, 420.

25 Ibid., New York City, vol. 189, pp. 210, 213; vol. 191, pp. 424, 511, 516.

26 Ibid., Boston, vol. 69, p. 468.

27 Ibid., New York City, vol. 192, p. 566.

28 Rowe himself did "very well" for at least a year after his failure, before failing again and closing his business in 1860.

29 R. G. Dun & Co. Collection, New York City, vol. 191, p. 429.

30 Ibid., New York City, vol. 189, p. 203.

31 Ibid., New York City, vol. 191, p. 426.

32 *Hunt's* 38 (1858): 772.

33 For a number of reasons the federal income tax implemented in 1863 did not produce records of individual income useful to this study. The tax law exempted various kinds of income from taxation, permitted a deduction for rent, and set the minimum taxable income at $600. More importantly, there appears to have been a great deal of misrepresentation of income in response to the tax – a privately published tabulation for New York City contains some 18,000 taxpayers, while New York's households numbered approximately 160,000. A speech in Congress noted that only 9,464 persons in the entire nation reported incomes in excess of $5,000. See Rufus S. Tucker, "The Distribution of Income Among Income Taxpayers in the United States, 1863–1935," *Quarterly Journal of Economics* 52 (1938): 547–87; Joseph A. Hill, "The Civil War Income Tax," *Quarterly Journal of Economics* 8 (1894): 416–52, 491–8.

34   Philadelphia Social History Project file. Even some 23% of older and presumably well-established merchants, attorneys, and bankers (specifically, those aged forty to fifty-nine) reported no property. It appears that the census enumerators were much less diligent in collecting information concerning the property holdings of boarders, wives, and resident children than they were in recording the property of heads of household. According to my sample, approximately one-third of Philadelphia's heads of household reported no property. This is considerably smaller than the 61% of "propertyless" adult males, and may have been close to the true proportion. On the other hand, to analyze only household heads is to eliminate the large numbers of clerks, manual workers, and others who lived in boardinghouses and in other people's houses.

35   We cannot expect the property entries to be perfectly accurate. I did find a reassuringly close correspondence between the census entries and the wealth estimates contained in the credit reports of the Mercantile Agency for a small sample of males living in Kingston, New York.

36   Property, as defined in the instructions to the census enumerators, included all forms of real property and all forms of personal property ("bonds, stocks, mortgages, notes, live stock, plate, jewels, or furniture") except for clothing. Real or personal property totals of less than $100 were to be excluded. Some enumerators did report totals of less than $100, but others did not. Hence, the absence of an entry could mean that the respondent owned clothing and small amounts of other goods. See Carroll D. Wright, *The History and Growth of the United States Census* . . . (Washington, 1900), p. 157. Wright presents the instructions to census enumerators for 1870, but it is apparent that these instructions were the same as those used in 1860.

37   These categories conform to coding decisions made by the Philadelphia Social History Project, and to the project's vertical classification scheme (VERT). My first category is the same as VERT 1, the second combines VERT 2 and 7, the third is identical with VERT 3, and the fourth combines VERT 4, 5, and 6. I would have coded some occupations differently (for example, I would have placed merchant tailors in the second rather than the first category, sea captains in the second rather than the third, and peddlers in the fourth rather than the second), but most involve only a few cases, and recoding them would alter Table 4.1 only slightly. For this reason, and also to maintain comparability with other studies based on the same files, I have not recoded specific occupations.

38   Very similar patterns to those in Table 4.1 are obtained by examining the relationship between occupational category and reported wealth within specific age and ethnic groups. Wealth shifts upward somewhat for native Americans and for older cohorts, but the differences between the occupational categories within each group remain much the same.

39   The term is Algie M. Simons's. See his *Social Forces in American History* (New York, 1911), p. 210. On the question of the extent to which workers embraced the success ethic, see Laurie, *Working People of Philadelphia*, pp. 32–49; Paul Faler, "Cultural Aspects of the Industrial Revolution: Lynn, Massachusetts, Shoemakers and Industrial Morality, 1826–1860,"

Labor History 15 (1974): 367–94; James A. Henretta, "The Study of Social Mobility: Ideological Assumptions and Conceptual Bias," *Labor History* 18 (1977): 166–78.

40 On the study of vertical mobility and some of its pitfalls, see Clyde Griffen, "The Study of Occupational Mobility in Nineteenth-Century America: Problems and Possibilities," *Journal of Social History* 5 (1972): 310–30; Stuart M. Blumin, "The Historical Study of Vertical Mobility," *Historical Methods Newsletter* 1 (1968): 1–13; Michael B. Katz, "Occupational Classification in History," *Journal of Interdisciplinary History* 3 (1972): 63–88; Henretta, "The Study of Social Mobility."

41 For an interesting discussion of "shipboard mobility," see Peter R. Decker, *Fortunes and Failures: White-Collar Mobility in Nineteenth-Century San Francisco* (Cambridge, Mass., 1978), pp. 66–9.

42 Clyde Griffen and Sally Griffen, *Natives and Newcomers: The Ordering of Opportunity in Mid-Nineteenth-Century Poughkeepsie* (Cambridge, Mass., 1978), p. 55.

43 Ibid., p. 60.

44 Ibid., p. 70. The figure of 30% was calculated by me from other figures in this table. Many of the skilled German immigrants may have been former masters who took jobs as journeymen for a short time before resuming business in the new world.

45 Ibid., p. 67.

46 Ibid., p. 60.

47 Ibid., p. 165.

48 Peter R. Knights, *The Plain People of Boston, 1830–1860: A Study in City Growth* (New York, 1971), pp. 98–9. It is not clear how Knights sorted tradesmen into workers and large and small proprietors before 1860. Censuses before that date did not list real and personal property, while tax records would have proved an unreliable and troublesome source. As for his small sample sizes, Knights notes: "Researchers with limited time, patience, or resources should make sail conformable with the weather" (p. 6). An apt metaphor for a study of Boston.

49 Stuart M. Blumin, "Mobility in a Nineteenth-Century City: Philadelphia, 1820–1860" (Ph.D. dissertation, University of Pennsylvania, 1968), p. 105. These figures are based on city directory samples ranging in size from 950 to 1,835.

50 Louis H. Arky, "The Mechanics' Union of Trade Associations and the Formation of the Philadelphia Workingmen's Movement," *Pennsylvania Magazine of History and Biography* 76 (1952): 163. See also Edward Pessen, *Most Uncommon Jacksonians: The Radical Leaders of the Early Labor Movement* (Albany, N.Y., 1967), p. 12.

51 Most historians who have studied *The Mechanic's Free Press* have failed to focus on this pervasive motif. One exception is Rex Burns, *Success in America : The Yeoman Dream and the Industrial Revolution* (Amherst, Mass., 1976), p. 116.

52 [Philadelphia] *Mechanic's Free Press: A Journal of Practical and Useful Knowledge*, April 19, 1828.

53 Ibid., April 4, 1829. These and most other editorial remarks were probably

written by William Heighton. But as the editorials were not signed, and as there seem to have been other editors besides Heighton, I will generally refer to "the editors" rather than to Heighton.

54 Ibid., August 9, 1828.
55 Ibid., July 26, 1828.
56 Ibid., May 17, 1828.
57 Ibid., September 13, 1828.
58 Ibid., July 19, 1828.
59 Ibid., August 16, 1828. For a tale written in a similar tone, see ibid., May 5, 1831.
60 Ibid., June 28, 1828. See also ibid., August 30, 1828, and September 6, 1828, for articles and letters identifying masters as nonproducing enemies of the producing mechanic.
61 Ibid., May 3, 1828.
62 Walter Hugins, *Jacksonian Democracy and the Working Class: A Study of the New York Workingmen's Movement, 1829–1837* (Stanford, 1960), pp. 85–8, for a good brief account of Evans's career as an editor and reformer.
63 See Wilentz's account in *Chants Democratic*, pp. 335–43, which stresses the wide appeal of this idea among radicals in the 1840s, but admits that it did not penetrate as deeply into the trades unions or the working masses.
64 See, for example, *The Working Man's Advocate*, April 6, 1844. Evans's reform was in fact realized in a small portion of the federal lands with the enactment of the Homestead Act of 1862, six years after Evans's death.
65 Ibid., March 30, 1844, April 6, 1844.
66 Ibid., May 18, 1844.
67 Ibid., November 2, 1844.
68 Ibid., April 27, 1844.
69 Ibid., May 11, 1844. Emphases are in the original.
70 Ibid., January 25, 1845.
71 "The Editor's Table," *Harper's New Monthly Magazine* 12 (1856): 261.
72 Ibid., 17 (1858): 839. See also ibid., 15 (1857): 389: "Labor has a right, undoubtedly, if it pays for them, to drape its brawny form in broadcloth and silk. Protests are uttered, we know, even in this land of equality, against 'the uppishness of the lower classes.' "
73 "The Editor's Easy Chair," ibid., 7 (1853): 129.
74 Charles Edwards, "What Constitutes a Merchant," *Hunt's* 1 (1839): 289.
75 For examples of each of these, see ibid., 1 (1839): 381; 34 (1856): 133; 1 (1839): 21–7.
76 Edward Everett, "Accumulation, Property, Capital, and Credit," ibid., 1 (1839): 22.
77 Jonathan F. Stearns, "Men of Business: Their Intellectual Culture," in *The Man of Business, Considered in His Various Relations* (New York, 1857), p. 6.
78 Philip Hone, "Commerce and Commercial Character," *Hunt's* 4 (1841): 143.

79 Nathan Appleton, ibid., 11 (1844): 219.
80 Theodore Parker, ibid., 16 (1847): 396.
81 *Hunt's* 20 (1849): 570. The author also notes that few clerks, determined on the dry goods trade, would take a position in a bookstore, or a music store, or a manufacturing firm. But this was a matter of calculated opportunity rather than pride. See also ibid., 17 (1847): 442; 18 (1848): 119–20; 7 (1843): 153; 26 (1852): 648.
82 J. M. Bellows, "Mercantile Education," ibid. 10 (1844): 145.
83 Burns, *Success in America*, pp. 22, 29–31.
84 Ibid., p. 31
85 [John Frost], *The Young Merchant* (Philadelphia, 1839), pp. 101, 223–4, 269.
86 Ibid., p. 279.
87 [John Frost], *The Young Mechanic*, 2d. ed. (New York, 1843), pp. 11–15, 25–6, 44, 61.
88 Ibid., p. 11. See also pp. iii, 10.
89 Ibid., p. 199.
90 Ibid., e.g., pp. 189–200.
91 James W. Alexander, *The American Mechanic and Working-Man*, 2 vols. (New York and Philadelphia, 1847), II, p. 215.
92 Ibid., p. 219.
93 Ibid., I, p. 2.
94 Ibid., pp. 7, 161.
95 Ibid., p. 53.
96 James W. Alexander, "The Merchant's Clerk Cheered and Counselled," in *The Man of Business . . . His Various Relations.*
97 Alexander, *American Mechanic*, II, p. 215.
98 Ibid., p. 236. See also I, pp. 16–19, 24–8, 105–12, 146–7; II, pp. 188–96, 200, 202–14.
99 Ibid., II, pp. 203–4.
100 On unions and equal rights, see ibid., I, pp. 134–5, 285; II, pp. 115, 123. On reading, see I, pp. 161–274; II, pp. 55–107.
101 On gardening and other domestic pleasures, see ibid., I, pp. 8–10, 28–34; II, pp. 9–44, 224–37. One can easily imagine how workers living in congested urban working-class neighborhoods must have responded to Alexander's advice that they work in their cottage gardens.
102 Ibid., I, pp. 105, 80. The childlike tone of Alexander's sketches is very striking. I could not help noticing the similarity of construction and tone in the following sentences: "I regret to say that Sammy is sadly destitute of thrift"; ibid., I, p. 105. "I am sorry to say that Peter was not very well during the evening"; Beatrix Potter, *The Tale of Peter Rabbit* (New York, n.d.), p. 56.
103 Alexander, "Merchant's Clerk," pp. 15–20, 26–7, 35–45, 42–3.
104 James W. Alexander, "The Young Man of Business Cheered and Counselled," in *The Man of Business, Considered in Six Aspects: A Book For Young Men* (Edinburgh, 1864), p. 13. Note the change of title in Alexander's essay in the Scottish edition.

105 Griffen and Griffen, *Natives and Newcomers*, pp. 36, 147–8. The Griffens refer mostly to the post–Civil War period, but I believe their observations are relevant to the antebellum period as well.

106 John S. Gilkeson, Jr., *Middle-Class Providence, 1820–1940* (Princeton, 1986), pp. 53–5.

107 Gary J. Kornblith, "From Artisans to Businessmen: Master Mechanics in New England, 1789–1850" (Ph.D. dissertation, Princeton University, 1983), esp. pp. 497–501.

108 Ibid., p. 497; Gilkeson, *Middle-Class Providence*, p. 95.

109 See Edward K. Spann, *The New Metropolis: New York City, 1840–1857* (New York, 1981), pp. 94–116; Blumin, "Explaining the New Metropolis," pp. 23–4.

110 Kornblith, "Artisans to Businessmen," pp. 219, 224–5, 230.

111 Sean Wilentz, "Artisan Republican Festivals and the Rise of Class Conflict in New York City, 1788–1837," in Michael H. Frisch and Daniel K. Walkowitz, eds., *Working-Class America: Essays on Labor, Community, and American Society* (Urbana, Ill., 1983), pp. 48–9, 61–3; Wilentz, *Chants Democratic*, pp. 271–86. See also Howard B. Rock, *Artisans of the New Republic: The Tradesmen of New York City in the Age of Jefferson* (New York, 1979), pp. 129–32.

112 See Bruce Sinclair, *Philadelphia's Philosopher Mechanics: A History of the Franklin Institute, 1824–1865* (Baltimore, 1974); Kornblith, "Artisans to Businessmen," pp. 460–8.

113 See the letter from "Brutus," *Mechanic's Free Press*, October 11, 1828. See also Kornblith, "Artisans to Businessmen," pp. 455–6.

114 Stearns, "Men of Business," pp. 4–5.

115 John Todd, "Men of Business: Their Position, Influence, and Duties," in *The Man of Business . . . His Various Relations*, pp. 5, 28.

Chapter 5. "Things are in the saddle"

1 Edward K. Spann, *The New Metropolis: New York City, 1840–1857* (New York, 1981), p. 96. Not everyone recognizes the significance of the consumer revolution of the antebellum era. Michael E. Sobel, for example, begins his historical sketch of consumption in the United States in 1860. See Sobel, *Lifestyle and Social Structure: Concepts, Definitions, Analyses* (New York, 1981), p. 32. Daniel Horowitz's more recent and more effective account, *The Morality of Spending: Attitudes Toward the Consumer Society in America, 1875–1940* (Baltimore, 1985), focuses on the post–Civil War period but recognizes the significance of changes before the war.

2 David E. Shi, *The Simple Life: Plain Living and High Thinking in American Culture* (New York, 1985), p. 101.

3 Isaac Ferris, "Men of Business: Their Home Responsibilities," in *The Man of Business, Considered in His Various Relations* (New York, 1857), pp. 24–5.

4 Mary P. Ryan, *Cradle of the Middle Class: The Family in Oneida County, New York, 1790–1865* (Cambridge, 1981). Virtually every study of the

nineteenth-century domestic revolution locates it specifically among the middle class. See, for example, Nancy F. Cott, *The Bonds of Womanhood: "Woman's Sphere" in New England, 1780–1835* (New Haven, 1977); Ann Douglas, *The Feminization of American Culture* (New York, 1976); Kathryn Kish Sklar, *Catharine Beecher: A Study in American Domesticity* (New Haven, 1973); David P. Handlin, *The American Home: Architecture and Society, 1815–1915* (Boston, 1979); Barbara Welter, "The Cult of True Womanhood: 1820–1860," *American Quarterly* 18 (1966): 151–74; Gerda Lerner, "The Lady and the Mill Girl: Changes in the Status of Women in the Age of Jackson," *Midcontinent American Studies Journal* 10 (1969): 5–14; Kirk Jeffrey, "The Family as Utopian Retreat from the City," *Soundings* 55 (1972): 21–41.

5   Frederick B. Perkins, "Social and Domestic Life," in *Eighty Years' Progress of the United States* . . . (New York, 1861), vol. 1, p. 250.

6   Ibid., p. 254; *The British Mechanic's and Labourer's Handbook and True Guide to the United States* (London, 1840), p. 60. See also *Harper's New Monthly Magazine* 15 (1857): 389; John Fanning Watson, *Annals of Philadelphia and Pennsylvania, in the Olden Time* . . . (Philadelphia, 1845), vol. 1, p. 175.

7   *Manufactures of the United States in 1860* . . . (Washington, D.C., 1865), p. cxlvii.

8   The advertisement of J. E. Gould's Great Piano and Melodeon Emporium in *McElroy's Philadelphia City Directory* of 1855 suggests the actual pattern of piano ownership. Gould's listed the purchasers, by name and address, of four different brands of pianos. Of the 111 Philadelphia purchasers of the pianos of Hallet, Davis & Co., Nunns & Clark, and Bacon & Raven, 52 were merchants, brokers, and other commercial proprietors and executives, 24 were professionals (a figure that includes 5 teachers), 7 were listed in the directory as gentlewomen, 13 were manufacturers, 2 were public officials, 6 were clerical employees, and 7 were artisans. Some of the last, undoubtedly, were manufacturers or retailers: the "tailor" F. Sarmiento, for example, was a wealthy clothier. The few who purchased Haines, Bro. & Cummings pianos, a cheaper brand, included 1 merchant, 1 woman who operated a seminary, and 3 artisans (2 tailors and a copperplate printer). Artisans and other manual workers could, of course, buy pianos secondhand. Newspaper advertisements placed by piano stores and private parties in 1860 indicate that the prices of new pianos ordinarily ranged upward from around $175, while used pianos ranged from $25 to $150. Pianos could be purchased on installment, or rented. See, for example, the advertisements in the Philadelphia *Public Ledger*, January 2, 1860, February 4, 1860, and March 7, 1860. We shall see in a survey of estate inventories probated in Philadelphia in 1861, 3 artisanal inventories that included a piano, and 26 that did not. Of the 3 who owned pianos, moreover, 2 were almost certainly nonmanual businessmen, while the third, a hatter, was one of the most prosperous of those who probably were handworking artisans.

9   [Isabella Lucy Bird Bishop], *The Englishwoman in America* (London, 1856), pp. 122–3.

10   *Manufactures of the United States in 1860*, pp. li–lviii.
11   Philadelphia *Public Ledger*, January 2, 1860, March 7, 1860.
12   Edgar W. Martin, *The Standard of Living in 1860* (Chicago, 1942), p. 102.
13   George L. Miller, "Classification and Economic Scaling of 19th Century Ceramics," *Historical Archaeology* 14 (1980): 1–40.
14   Philadelphia *Public Ledger*, February 4, 1860.
15   Ibid., February 4, 1860, April 13, 1860. An 1853 advertisement in *The Illustrated News* suggests that prices started at $4 in Genin's fashionable Broadway hat store.
16   Martin, *The Standard of Living*, p. 195.
17   For examples of such views, see the advertisement for the Columbian Foundry and Burr Mill Stone Factory in *Doggett's New York City Directory, for 1849–1850* (New York, 1849); the advertisement for Wagner & McGuigan, lithographers, in *McElroy's Philadelphia Directory, for 1856* (Philadelphia, 1856); and the *Harper's New Monthly Magazine* article on the Novelty Works, cited in Chapter 3.
18   *The American Penny Magazine* 1 (1845): 181.
19   Ibid., p. 217.
20   *The Illustrated News*, May 21, 1853.
21   George G. Foster, *New York by Gas-Light: With Here and There a Streak of Sunshine* (New York, 1850), p. 107.
22   Christine Stansell, in *City of Women: Sex and Class in New York, 1789–1860* (New York, 1986), argues that young workingwomen cultivated "a style of dress and manner which was a studied departure from ladyhood, an implicit rejection of bourgeois female decorum" (p. 93). On the "Republic of the Bowery," see Sean Wilentz, *Chants Democratic: New York City and the Rise of the American Working Class, 1788–1850* (New York, 1984), pp. 257–71, 300–1, 329–30. Charles H. Haswell's reminiscence dates the distinctive Bowery style to the early 1830s, well before Benjamin Baker's play and Francis Chanfrau's stage portrayal made Mose a national figure. See Haswell, *Reminiscences of an Octogenarian of the City of New York (1816 to 1860)* (New York, 1896), pp. 270–1.
23   [James Dawson Burn], *Three Years Among the Working-Classes in the United States During the War* (London, 1865), pp. 21, 80–1, 107; *British Mechanic's and Labourer's Handbook*, p. 61.
24   See the tabulations of published workingmen's budgets in Martin, *Standard of Living*, p. 397, and in Dorothy S. Brady, "Consumption and the Style of Life," in Lance E. Davis, Richard A. Easterlin, and William N. Parker, eds., *American Economic Growth: An Economist's History of the United States* (New York, 1972), p. 79. Richard Stott, in "Workers in the Metropolis: New York City, 1820–1860" (Ph.D. dissertation, Cornell University, 1983), estimates a slightly higher proportion for food, and a lower proportion (15.7%) for clothing (p. 291). He also notes that the proportions of their incomes that workers spent on food was lower in the United States than it was in Europe (pp. 290–2). It was still much above the proportion expended by American middle-class families, however. Stott discusses workingmen's diet in detail on pp. 306–14.

25 Peter George Buckley writes at length of diverging bourgeois and working-class "theater cultures" in "To the Opera House: Culture and Society in New York City, 1820–1860" (Ph.D. dissertation, State University of New York at Stony Brook, 1984).

26 Foster, *New York by Gas-Light*, p. 87. See also David Grimsted, *Melodrama Unveiled: American Theater and Culture, 1800–1850* (Chicago, 1968), pp. 52–6; Wilentz, *Chants Democratic*, pp. 257–9; Stott, "Workers in the Metropolis," pp. 382–5. For a fascinating description of an evening on the Bowery and at the Bowery Theater in 1840, see Haswell, *Reminiscences*, pp. 355–65.

27 Wilentz, *Chants Democratic*, p. 30.

28 Haswell, *Reminiscences*, pp. 438–40. Another reminiscence revealing the fashion for opera is N. T. Hubbard, *Autobiography of N. T. Hubbard, With Personal Reminiscences of New York City from 1798 to 1875* (New York, 1875), pp. 93–129.

29 Haswell, *Reminiscences*, pp. 452–5. See also Wilentz, *Chants Democratic*, pp. 358–9, Spann, *The New Metropolis*, pp. 235–9, and Richard Moody, *The Astor Place Riot* (Bloomington, Ind., 1958).

30 Wilentz, *Chants Democratic*, p. 359; Buckley, "To the Opera House."

31 Wilentz, *Chants Democratic*, pp. 258–9; Stott, "Workers in the Metropolis," pp. 384–5.

32 See, for example, the advertisement in the Philadelphia *Public Ledger*, April 30, 1858.

33 Foster, *New York by Gas-Light*, pp. 44–51, 64–71. See also Foster, *New York in Slices: By an Experienced Carver* . . . (New York, 1849), pp. 66–75. Foster is also a good source for Philadelphia. See George Rogers Taylor, " 'Philadelphia in Slices' by George G. Foster," *Pennsylvania Magazine of History and Biography* 93 (1969): 23–72.

34 *British Mechanic's and Labourer's Handbook*, p. 97. See also Martin, *Standard of Living*, pp. 394–5.

35 Robert Ernst, *Immigrant Life in New York City, 1825–1863* (New York, 1949), pp. 48–9; Spann, *The New Metropolis*, pp. 146–50, 430.

36 See Stott, "Workers in the Metropolis," pp. 372–5, on workingmen's boardinghouses. The various kinds of tenements are succinctly described in Margaret Elizabeth Woods, "The Establishment of a Metropolitan Board of Health in New York City in 1866: A Study of the Process of Social Reform" (M.S. thesis, Cornell University, 1981), pp. 21–8.

37 *Report of the Council of Hygiene and Public Health of the Citizens Association of New York upon the Sanitary Condition of the City* (New York, 1865), p. 349. This publication is usually cited as *Report on the Sanitary Condition of the City*.

38 Writing not long after the Civil War, James Dabney McCabe claimed that most of "the most skilled mechanics" of New York City lived in tenements. See McCabe, *Lights and Shadows of New York City; or, the Sights and Sensations of the Great City* . . . (Philadelphia, 1872), p. 686.

39 *Report on the Sanitary Condition of the City*, p. 166. See also pp. 94, 121–2, 149, 197.

40 Lemuel Shattuck, *Report to the Committee of the City Council Appointed to Obtain the Census of Boston for the Year 1845* . . . (Boston, 1846), p. 55. On Boston housing after 1845, concentrating on poor Irish immigrants, see Oscar Handlin, *Boston's Immigrants: A Study in Acculturation*, rev. ed. (New York, 1968), pp. 88–123.

41 On Baltimore, see Sherry H. Olson, *Baltimore: The Building of an American City* (Baltimore, 1980), pp. 117–18, and Gary Lawson Browne, *Baltimore in the Nation: 1789–1861* (Chapel Hill, 1980), pp. 187–90. On Philadelphia, see Sam Bass Warner, Jr., *The Private City: Philadelphia in Three Periods of Its Growth* (Philadelphia, 1968), p. 52.

42 *A Compendium of the Ninth Census* . . . (Washington, D.C., 1872), p. 543. Families per dwelling was computed from the census data.

43 Elizabeth B. McCall, *Old Philadelphia Houses on Society Hill, 1750–1840* (New York, 1966), p. 46; Louis H. Arky, "The Mechanics' Union of Trade Associations and the Formation of the Philadelphia Workingmen's Movement," *Pennsylvania Magazine of History and Biography* 76 (1952): 165. Many of Philadelphia's alley dwellings had been built before 1798, when the city's houses were surveyed pursuant to the Federal Direct Tax of that year (see Chapter 2). On the 1798 assessment list, more than 80% of the alley dwellings were two stories tall, and 85% contained fewer than nine hundred square feet of floor space.

44 Gary Browne, in *Baltimore in the Nation*, notes that most Baltimore row houses were two stories tall, but that "several blocks of the more cheaply constructed row houses," three stories tall, had been built for skilled workers by 1850 (p. 190). He does not indicate how many rooms were in these houses, or whether any were occupied by more than one family.

45 Burn, *Three Years Among the Working-Classes*, pp. 102–3. For other contemporary references, see Stott, "Workers in the Metropolis," pp. 298–304.

46 Stott, "Workers in the Metropolis," pp. 299–300.

47 Samuel Gompers, *Seventy Years of Life and Labor: An Autobiography* (New York, 1925), vol. 1, p. 24.

48 Historians have made it quite clear that most workers could not afford to commute, except by foot (and in New York, by ferry) during this era. See George Rogers Taylor, "The Beginnings of Mass Transportation in Urban America: Part I," *Smithsonian Journal of History* 1(1966): 39–40, 48; Kenneth T. Jackson, *Crabgrass Frontier: The Suburbanization of the United States* (New York, 1985), pp. 20–44; Henry C. Binford, *The First Suburbs: Residential Communities on the Boston Periphery, 1815–1860* (Chicago, 1985), pp. 126–39; Spann, *The New Metropolis*, pp. 187, 190.

49 Walt Whitman, *I Sit and Look Out: Editorials from the Brooklyn Daily Times, by Walt Whitman*, selected and edited by Emory Holloway and Vernolian Schwarz (New York, 1932), p. 145.

50 *Frank Leslie's Illustrated Newspaper*, September 26, 1857.

51 Spann, *The New Metropolis*, pp. 108–9, 190, 201.

52 Ibid., p. 108; *Hunt's Merchants' Magazine* 33 (1858): 772.

53 Michael Batterberry and Ariane Batterberry, *On the Town in New York: A*

History of Eating, Drinking and Entertainments from 1776 to the Present (New York, 1973), p. 58.

54 Leslie Dorsey and Janice Devine, *Fare Thee Well: A Backward Look at Two Centuries of Historic American Hostelries, Fashionable Spas, and Seaside Resorts* (New York, 1964), esp. pp. 31–46.

55 Spann, *The New Metropolis*, p. 98.

56 William Gowans letters and miscellaneous papers, 1826–70, New-York Historical Society, letter of June 21, 1832.

57 Thomas Butler Gunn, *The Physiology of New York Boarding-Houses* (New York, 1857), p. 17.

58 [James Fenimore Cooper], *Notions of the Americans: Picked up by a Travelling Bachelor* (London, 1828), vol. 1, p. 192. See also Montgomery Schuyler, "The Small City House in New York," *The Architectural Record* 8 (1899): 357–61.

59 See John Tauranac, *Essential New York: A Guide to the History and Architecture of Manhattan's Important Buildings, Parks, and Bridges* (New York, 1979), p. 15.

60 Cooper, *Notions of the Americans*, vol 1, p. 192. Cooper goes on to describe New York houses "of pretensions altogether superior to those just named" (p. 193); i.e., the houses of the rich.

61 These specifications were obtained by scanning *Longworth's American Almanac, New-York Register, and City Directory* (New York, 1835). Alfred Thomas was traced through a number of other city directories as well.

62 Ibid.

63 McCall, *Old Philadelphia Houses*, p. 177.

64 Ibid., p. 179; manuscript population schedules, U.S. Census of 1860; *Cohen's Philadelphia City Directory, City Guide and Business Register, for 1860* (Philadelphia, 1860); *McElroy's Philadelphia Directory for 1860* (Philadelphia, 1860). One difficulty with this interpretation is that Stiles too reported only personal property. Possibly he thought of the house on Third Street as a personal investment, more like stocks and bonds than like real estate. Possibly he simply did not tell the census enumerator about his real estate. McCall, in *Old Philadelphia Houses*, notes the sale of the property in 1853 to the grocer Edward Styles, not Stiles. There is no Edward Styles listed in the city directories for any of these years. I believe the most reasonable interpretation is that Stiles did own the Third Street house.

65 This portrait of the west side of Third above Pine is based on the sources just cited, along with *The Philadelphia Shopping Guide & Housekeeper's Companion for 1859* (Philadelphia, 1859). Galbraith, the gilder, is listed in McElroy's directory as residing in Dove Place, a narrow street in the working-class district of Southwark, not far from Third and Pine. Perhaps he did, but moved into his workshop before the census enumerator made his rounds. In either case, his dwelling space must have been fairly restricted. A third artisan, a tailor named Joseph Monks, seems to have lived between Galbraith and Stratton, but as I could not determine whether he worked at home or elsewhere, I do not discuss him in the

text. Dr. Kinkelein, who appears in all three directories, does not appear at Third and Union in the census. Perhaps he was moving out as Galbraith was moving in. Three addresses are unaccounted for in the sources.

66 Gervase Wheeler, *Homes for the People, in Suburb and Country* . . . (New York, 1867), p. 300. Although this book appeared in 1867, a "first edition," which was not published, was written in 1855. The publisher's preface clearly indicates that the construction costs listed in the body of the book are those that prevailed at the time of the first edition.

67 Ibid., pp. 308–10.

68 Ibid., pp. 315–21.

69 Ibid., pp. 43–7, 50–4, 321–7.

70 Warner, *The Private City*, p. 66. For similar summaries see Martin, *Standard of Living*, p. 116; Spann, *The New Metropolis*, p. 120.

71 Warner, *The Private City*, p. 65n.

72 Spann, *The New Metropolis*, pp. 118–19. For a detailed history of the building of the Croton system, see Nelson Manfred Blake, *Water for the Cities: A History of the Urban Water Supply Problem in the United States* (Syracuse, 1956), pp. 121–71.

73 Warner, *The Private City*, p. 108; Blake, *Water for the Cities*, p. 269.

74 Faye E. Dudden, *Serving Women: Household Service in Nineteenth-Century America* (Middletown, Conn., 1983), p. 138.

75 *The Seventh Census of the United States: 1850* . . . (Washington, D.C., 1853), tabulates 93,608 families in New York City and 72,392 families in the County of Philadelphia (a small number living in areas not yet incorporated into the City of Philadelphia). See pp. 112, 186. If the proportion of middle-class families is assumed to fall somewhere within the range of 35% to 40%, then the total numbers of such families ranged from approximately 25,000 to approximately 37,500. In Boston in 1845, 31% of the city's houses were supplied with aqueduct water. See Shattuck, *Report*, p. 57.

76 According to age-specific mortality rates (1859–61) and population counts (1860) published by the U.S. census, 4,912 Philadelphians aged twenty and older died in 1860. See *Statistics of the United States . . . in 1860 . . .* (Washington, D.C., 1866), p. 522, and *Population of the United States in 1860 . . .* (Washington, D.C., 1864), pp. 406–11. Probate records for Philadelphia are located in the Register of Wills, Philadelphia County, at the Philadelphia City Hall.

77 I selected the records for 1861 because I had hoped to link each inventory to an entry in the manuscript population schedules of the 1860 census. Unfortunately, the census index that would have made that feasible was not published in time for my analysis. I was, however, able to associate inventories with occupations for many decedents and husbands of decedents by tracing decedents' names through the city directories. McElroy's 1860 directory was particularly helpful, as it lists the first names of the late husbands of many widows. These names could then be traced back to earlier directories until the husbands' occupations could be found.

Of the 109 decedents (or decedents' husbands) 13 were identified only as "gentlemen" or "gentlewomen," even in directories published years before their deaths. Some of these "gentry" were wealthy, but others were not. I have excluded them from the following analysis, as they add nothing to our understanding of the relationship between occupation and consumption.

78 Register of Wills, 1861, wills nos. 167, 218, 383, 408, 445.
79 Ibid., will no. 239.
80 Ibid., will no. 313.
81 Ibid., will no. 387.
82 Ibid., will no. 320.
83 Ibid., will no. 122.
84 Ibid., wills nos. 354, 146, 99.
85 Ibid., will no. 241. Edwards's estate was valued at $76,233.49. The wealthiest of the thirteen was George Thomas, an auctioneer, whose estate was valued at $329,837.09 (will no. 254).
86 Ibid., will no. 281.
87 Ibid., will no. 318.
88 R. G. Dun & Co. Collection, Baker Library, Harvard Graduate School of Business Administration: Philadelphia, vol. 1, p. 543.
89 *The Philadelphia Shopping Guide.* The explanation of capitalized entries is on p. 54.
90 Register of Wills, wills nos. 47, 104, 141, 216, 273, 342, 415.
91 Ibid., will no. 133.
92 Ibid., wills nos. 67, 264.
93 Ibid., wills nos. 198, 319.
94 Ibid., will no. 260.
95 Ibid., will no. 96.
96 Stott, "Workers in the Metropolis." Stott develops this argument in greater detail in the forthcoming revision of this dissertation.
97 George G. Foster, *Celio: or, New York Above-Ground and Under-Ground* (New York, 1850), p. 115.
98 Binford, *The First Suburbs*, pp. 129–42, 154–86.
99 For a general account of suburbanization in this era, see Jackson, *Crabgrass Frontier*, pp. 20–72.
100 On the "shared symbolization" of urban "social worlds," see Anselm L. Strauss, *Images of the American City* (Glencoe, Ill., 1961), p. 67.
101 The most notable proponent of this point of view is Sam Bass Warner, Jr.: See *The Urban Wilderness: A History of the American City* (New York, 1972), pp. 82–3, and *The Private City*, p. 50. See also Theodore Hershberg et al., "The 'Journey-to-Work': An Empirical Investigation of Work, Residence and Transportation, Philadelphia, 1850 and 1880," in Hershberg, ed., *Philadelphia: Work, Space, Family, and Group Experience in the 19th Century: Essays Toward an Interdisciplinary History of the City* (New York, 1981), pp. 128–73; Kathleen Neils Conzen, "Patterns of Residence in Early Milwaukee," in Leo F. Schnore and Eric E. Lampard, eds., *The New Urban History: Quantitative Explorations by American Historians*

(Princeton, 1975), pp. 145–83; David Ward, *Cities and Immigrants: A Geography of Change in Nineteenth-Century America* (New York, 1971); Peter R. Knights, *The Plain People of Boston, 1830–1860: A Study in City Growth* (New York, 1971). Betsy Blackmar, in "Re-walking the 'Walking City': Housing and Property Relations in New York City, 1780–1840," *Radical History Review*, no. 21 (1979): 131–48, argues, correctly I believe, that areal class-segregation was developing rapidly in New York City during this era. But New York was probably in advance of other cities in this respect.

102   Janet Rothenberg Pack, "Urban Spatial Transformation: Philadelphia, 1850 to 1880, Heterogeneity to Homogeneity?" *Social Science History* 8 (1984): 437. David Ward makes a similar argument for the English city of Leeds during the period from 1841 to 1871. Ward recognizes, however, the significance of small, non-areal patterns of the sort I describe later in the chapter. See Ward, "Environs and Neighbours in the 'Two Nations': Residential Differentiation in Mid-Nineteenth-Century Leeds," *Journal of Historical Geography* 6 (1980): 141, 158–62.

103   Pack, "Urban Spatial Transformation," p. 437.

104   Ibid., pp. 440–5.

105   Ibid.

106   It should be noted that the Philadelphia Social History Project also collected smaller, supplemental files from the census that do specify household and family relationships. I utilize these files in later paragraphs, but they cannot be used for a grid-unit analysis of residential segregation.

107   Homogeneity, moreover, is defined in terms of four occupational categories: high nonmanual, low nonmanual, high manual (skilled), and low manual (unskilled). For present purposes, a more telling index would combine the last two and recognize as homogeneous a grid-unit that consisted almost entirely of the homes of skilled *and* unskilled workers. In Pack's analysis, a grid-unit evenly divided between such workers is identified as heterogeneous.

108   Alan N. Burstein, "Immigrants and Residential Mobility: The Irish and Germans in Philadelphia, 1850–1880," in Hershberg, ed.,*Philadelphia*, p. 183. Oscar Handlin made essentially the same point in *Boston's Immigrants*, pp. 91–100. See William S. Hastings, "Philadelphia Microcosm," *Pennsylvania Magazine of History and Biography* 91 (1967): 164–80, for a detailed but rather discursive analysis of the streets and alleys of the center of Philadelphia between 1820 and 1840.

109   Roger Miller and Joseph Siry, "The Emerging Suburb: West Philadelphia, 1850–1880," *Pennsylvania History* 47 (1980): 143. See also pp. 103–4.

110   The proper census entries were located by referring to the manuscript census schedule page numbers that the Philadelphia Social History Project incorporated as a variable in each of its cases. The project file includes all Irish, German, and native-born black adult males, but only a one-in-six sample of native-born white males and no women. I recorded,

instead, every adult male irrespective of birthplace or race, and every female household head (other adult women, except servants, rarely had occupations listed, and servants were aggregated in my file as a variable pertaining to each head of household), from all the manuscript pages associated with my selected grid-units within the project file. This procedure resulted in the selection of some cases that were not really in the grid-unit (most of which were eliminated later) and, no doubt, the overlooking of some cases that really were. Household relations were imputed by examining placement within the household, age, sex, race, and in some cases occupation (e.g., for servants). Most relations were easy to specify, and in the following analysis the principal distinction, between household heads and others, is reinforced by the fact that census enumerators were instructed explicitly to list heads of household first. The project-defined grid-units, in order of their discussion in the text, are numbers 057594, 059596, 050591, 054588, and 035593/594, the last being a combination of two contiguous units. On the difficulty of using census data for the analysis of spatial segregation, see Kathleen Neils Conzen, "Mapping Manuscript Census Data for Nineteenth Century Cities," *Historical Geography Newsletter* 4 (1974): 1–7.

111   The occupational title "mariner" is difficult to interpret. Most who were mariners were ordinary seamen, but others were ship's officers, and some sea captains were also merchants. In his will, Simeon Tobey identified himself as a "mariner." (See Register of Wills, 1861, will no. 70.) His city directory listing in the few years before his death uses the term "gentleman" instead. Before that he was listed as president of the Pennsylvania Insurance Company and, still earlier, as a sea captain.

112   There were also a few identifiable private homes in this grid-unit, mostly on Walnut and Sixth Streets. The Walnut Street homes, and the Sixth Street homes facing Washington Square, were headed in nearly every instance by attorneys, physicians, and wealthy women. Two narrow streets, Sansom and Swanwick, were either nearly empty of homes or contained the houses of people who were not listed in the directory. Only three householders on Sansom Street (the deputy superintendent of the port, a lumber dealer, and a tavernkeeper) could be identified. No residents could be identified on Swanwick Street.

113   The configuration of residences and offices and stores was obtained by comparing my census–directory file with the listings in *The Philadelphia Shopping Guide* for Fourth Street. Only two residents combined dwellings and workplaces at the same address.

114   Edwin T. Freedley, *Philadelphia and Its Manufactures . . .* (Philadelphia, 1858), p. 274.

115   Again, the configuration of residences, offices, and stores was obtained by referring to *The Philadelphia Shopping Guide*. Beyond the downtown, only the most important commercial streets were listed in the *Guide*.

116   Miller and Siry, "The Emerging Suburb," pp. 102–3, 115.

117   Ibid., pp. 102–3.

118   There were three other streets in these grid-units: Walnut, Sansom

(originally York), and Filbert. In 1860 only one household (a merchant's family living on Walnut near Fortieth) could be identified on these three streets. By 1880, Walnut and Sansom had acquired sufficient numbers of households to allow their incorporation into the analysis of residential patterns. Filbert seems to have developed as a purely commercial or industrial street and contained no identifiable residents in either 1860 or 1880.

119 Miller and Siry, "The Emerging Suburb," p. 143.

120 I state here an opinion that might be disputed by specialists in Philadelphia history, who would point to Rittenhouse Square, Kensington, Southwark, and perhaps a few other place names powerfully suggestive of Philadelphia's upper and lower classes. It might also be argued that New York's distinct districts were better known (and remain better known to those of us who try to recapture such things) because *all* of New York's doings were better publicized than were those of the Quaker City. I do believe, however, that the New York districts mentioned in the text were homogeneous over larger areas than any equivalent districts of Philadelphia, and that their names did convey more powerful images to contemporaries. Greater publicity by New York's more aggressive publishing industry only assisted the process.

121 Faye Dudden, in *Serving Women*, pp. 136–7, claims that middle-class women, not their servants, began to take over food-shopping responsibilities from their husbands during this period.

122 "Charlie's Side-Walk Acquaintances," *Harper's* 15 (1857): 861–2.

123 Citing evidence obtained from *Godey's Lady's Book*, Robert Elno McGlone claims that dresses were worn to age four or five, but that some mothers tried to prolong the period and in various ways "betrayed a wish to dress their little boys as girls." See McGlone, "Suffer the Children: The Emergence of Modern Middle-Class Family Life in America, 1820–1870" (Ph.D. dissertation, University of California at Los Angeles, 1971), p. 139.

124 "Master Charley in the Snow," *Harper's* 20 (1860): 430.

125 The other four sketches are: "Scenes from Master Charley's Love Life," *Harper's* 19 (1859): 141–2; "Master Charley's Fourth of July," *Harper's* 19 (1859): 429–30; "Master Charley's First Pantaloons, *Harper's* 20 (1860): 717–18; and "Master Charley's Prize Fight," *Harper's* 20 (1860): 861–2.

126 Douglas, *The Feminization of American Culture*, p. 12. According to Douglas, though, she and her liberal ministerial allies were in a "fixed fight: they had agreed to put on a convincing show and lose" (p. 12). That is, the tensions identified years ago by William E. Bridges between the nurturance of Christian sensibilities and the development of capitalist ambitions and abilities, were resolved in favor of the latter. See Bridges, "Family Patterns and Social Values in America, 1825–1875," *American Quarterly* 17 (1965): 3–11.

127 William H. Pease and Jane H. Pease, "Paternal Dilemmas: Education, Property, and Patrician Persistence in Jacksonian Boston," *New England Quarterly* 53 (1980): 150–2. See also Carl N. Degler, *At Odds: Women and*

the Family in America from the Revolution to the Present (New York, 1980), p. 74.

128 *Harper's* 15 (1857): 388–91; Frances Trollope, *Domestic Manners of the Americans* (New York, 1949). See, for example, pp. 133, 184, 226, 234, 340, and, in this edition, pp. 58n–59n, 340n.

129 *Harper's* 12 (1856): 557.

130 See especially Carl Degler's summary of this point of view in *At Odds*, pp. 27–51.

131 See especially Cott, *The Bonds of Womanhood*, and Douglas, *The Feminization of American Culture*. Douglas goes to great pains to differentiate between women's influence and men's authority, and to argue that the doctrine of "influence" was at bottom a way of flattering middle-class women into subjugation. The literature on nineteenth-century domesticity does not contradict Mary Beth Norton's argument, in *Liberty's Daughters: The Revolutionary Experience of American Women, 1750–1800* (Boston, 1980), that eighteenth-century American women were no less confined to the domestic sphere. It was the more or less sincere sanctification of domesticity – the emergence of the canon – not increasing confinement to the home, that the historians of the nineteenth century describe.

132 See the interesting (if extreme) instance of paternal engagement discussed in William G. McLoughlin, "Evangelical Childrearing in the Age of Jackson: Francis Wayland's Views on When and How to Subdue the Willfulness of Children," *Journal of Social History* 9 (1975): 20–39. A contemporary document asserting patriarchal claims that most historians would regard as anachronistic is Ferris, "Men of Business."

133 For a discussion of tensions between men and women, associated with the redefinition of gender roles in the antebellum era, see Ronald Preston Byars, "The Making of the Self-Made Man: The Development of Masculine Roles and Images in Ante-Bellum America" (Ph.D. dissertation, Michigan State University, 1979), esp. pp. 113–51.

134 Karen Halttunen, *Confidence Men and Painted Women: A Study of Middle-Class Culture in America, 1830–1870* (New Haven, 1982), pp. 59–60.

135 Ibid., esp. pp. 92–123, and pp. 153–90. Throughout her book Halttunen uses the term "middle class," and her conclusion relates the "new theatricality of middle-class culture" to the consolidation of the middle class "as a class with social borders clearly defined by detailed criteria of social expertise" (p. 197). However, her middle class was clearly a wealthy group with aspirations to membership in the urban upper class. As we will see in Chapter 7, when contemporary Americans began to use the term "middle class," they almost invariably did so to define a much broader, and generally less wealthy group, inclusive of Halttunen's families, perhaps, but also of retailers, clerks, and more modest middling folk who did not put on elaborate parlor theatricals. I argue in the ensuing paragraphs that many found alternative aspirations as well. Halttunen's middle class, in sum, is probably best described as an "upper middle class."

136 Russell Lynes, *The Domesticated Americans* (New York, 1957), p. 149. Lynes's book, written for a general audience, is a quite detailed and useful analysis of the urban middle-class home.

137 Gunther Barth, in *City People: The Rise of Modern City Culture in Nineteenth-Century America* (New York, 1980), notes that female shopping became one aspect of the "separation of spheres": "Shopping also reinforced the separation between the two spheres of life, leaving the acquisition of the funds for shopping to man while making the task itself a woman's affair" (p. 146).

138 Dudden, *Serving Women*, pp. 136–7.

139 See *McElroy's Philadelphia City Directory* of 1855, and note 8, above.

140 *Harper's* 15 (1857): 557.

141 Men could be criticized in this way too, as in a brief article in *Hunt's* 6 (1842): 25, attacking the "large speculator" for trying to gain the confidence of others in his projects by giving the appearance of great wealth. But this was much less common than the indictment of female extravagance. *Hunt's*, recall, was a magazine written for, and almost entirely about, men.

142 L[ydia] Maria Child, *Letters From New York: Second Series* (London, 1845), pp. 280–1. Anthony F. C. Wallace, in *Rockdale: The Growth of an American Village in the Early Industrial Revolution* (New York, 1978), notes the reluctance of daughters of local textile mill owners to settle into domestic roles, and their ambivalence toward motherhood (see p. 24). For a more extended discussion, see McGlone, "Suffer the Children," pp. 19–78.

143 *Frank Leslie's Illustrated Newspaper*, October 10, 1857.

144 McGlone, "Suffer the Children," esp. pp. 76–8.

145 Faye Dudden, Nancy Cott, and Mary Ryan all make the interesting point that the managerial aspects of women's "separate sphere" drew upon business models, and that in this sense the middle-class home resembled the business world to which it was supposed to offer a complete contrast. See Dudden, *Serving Women*, pp. 163–6; Cott, *Bonds of Womanhood*, p. 73; Ryan, *Cradle of the Middle Class*, p. 73.

146 *Harper's* 12 (1856): 558.

147 Cott, *Bonds of Womanhood*, p. 92.

148 Ryan, *Cradle of the Middle Class*, p. 15.

149 Ibid., pp. 161, 184–5.

150 Susan E. Hirsch, *Roots of the American Working Class: The Industrialization of Crafts in Newark, 1800–1860* (Philadelphia, 1978), pp. 54, 71. Hirsch's use of "Victorian" here should occasion no surprise. The new domestic canon was one aspect of a larger set of values that is often called "Victorian," most often in describing England (and in particular the English middle class) but also with reference to the United States. See Daniel Walker Howe, "Victorian Culture in America," in Howe, ed., *Victorian America* (Philadelphia, 1976), pp. 3–28. The adjective "Romantic" is perhaps even more apt. See, for example, Degler, *At Odds*, pp. 66–8.

151 Hirsch, *Roots of the American Working Class*, p. 65. James W. Alexander,

whose advice to workingmen we have already examined, described the ideal workingman's home in modest terms: "The walls should be white, the floors and wood-work should be scoured, the movables should be in their places, and no unsightly utensil should be more conspicuous than necessity requires." See Alexander, *The American Mechanic and Working-Man* (New York and Philadelphia, 1847), vol. 2, p. 11.

152 Hirsch, *Roots of the American Working Class*, pp. 26, 38–41, 71–4.

153 Mary H. Blewett, "Work, Gender, and the Artisan Tradition in New England Shoemaking, 1780–1860," *Journal of Social History* 17 (1983): 224.

154 Carol Groneman, " 'She Earns as a Child: She Pays as a Man': Women Workers in a Mid-Nineteenth-Century New York City Community," in Milton Cantor and Bruce Laurie, eds., *Class, Sex, and the Woman Worker* (Westport, Conn., 1977), p. 89. In Philadelphia, as late as 1860, there was only the slightest relationship between class and the presence of boarders in white native-American households. Approximately 60% of the city's households headed by native-born white unskilled workers contained one or more boarders, but so, too, did more than half of those headed by artisans and by "low nonmanual" proprietors and workers, and 45% of those headed by "high nonmanual" businessmen and professionals. These calculations are based on a sample of 2,525 households drawn from census manuscripts by the Philadelphia Social History Project as a supplement to its larger file of adult male workers. In this supplemental file, household relationships are imputed.

155 Ruth M. Alexander, " 'We Are Engaged as a Band of Sisters': Class and Domesticity in the Washingtonian Temperance Movement, 1840–1850," *Journal of American History* 75 (1988): 775, 785.

156 Blewett, "Work, Gender, and the Artisan Tradition," pp. 224, 228.

157 Ibid., pp. 230–3. It is difficult to say, however, whether these stories were written to defend the values of Lynn's working-class wives or to convince those wives not to pursue the middle-class domestic ideal.

158 Stansell, *City of Women*, chap. 3. The quoted passages are on pp. 52 and 62. See also pp. 77–83. Alexander, in " 'We Are Engaged as a Band of Sisters,' " writes of a female Washingtonian domestic ideal shaped "not by domestic privacy and comfort, but by familiarity with poverty, insecurity, and violence" (p. 775).

159 Michael B. Katz, *The Irony of Early School Reform: Educational Innovation in Mid-Nineteenth-Century Massachusetts* (Cambridge, Mass., 1968), esp. pp. 39, 90–3, 270–1; Selwyn Troen, "Popular Education in Nineteenth-Century St. Louis," *History of Education Quarterly* 13 (1973): 23–40; Stanley K. Schultz, *The Culture Factory: Boston Public Schools, 1789–1860* (New York, 1973), pp. 278–309; David B. Tyack, *The One Best System: A History of American Urban Education* (Cambridge, Mass., 1974), p. 67; Carl F. Kaestle, *The Evolution of an Urban School System: New York City, 1750–1850* (Cambridge, Mass., 1973), pp. 88–100; and Carl F. Kaestle and Maris A. Vinovskis, *Education and Social Change in Nineteenth-Century Massachusetts* (Cambridge, Mass., 1980), pp. 9–45, and esp. pp. 87–90.

One interesting but neglected issue is whether children from different social classes attended the same schools. Selma Berrol's analysis of the registers of one New York City grammar school in 1855 suggests there was significant mixing of middle-class and working-class (but not upper-class) children in public schools located in neighborhoods that were themselves socially heterogeneous. But her research only scratches the surface of this issue. See Selma Berrol, "Who Went to School in Mid-Nineteenth Century New York? An Essay in the New Urban History," in Irwin Yellowitz, ed., *Essays in the History of New York City: A Memorial to Sidney Pomerantz* (Port Washington, N.Y., 1978), pp. 43–60.

160   Table 5.1 is restricted to American-born whites in order to eliminate the effect of ethnic and racial differences in attitudes toward schooling. Separate tabulations for boys and for girls yielded remarkably similar results; hence, there was nothing to be lost, and a simpler table to be gained, by combining them.

Chapter 6. Coming to order

1   The argument that reformers were motivated by an increasingly compelling desire to exert control over subordinate social classes can be found in: Clifford S. Griffin, *Their Brothers' Keepers: Moral Stewardship in the United States, 1800–1865* (New Brunswick, N.J., 1960); Charles I. Foster, *An Errand of Mercy: The Evangelical United Front, 1790–1837* (Chapel Hill, 1960); John R. Bodo, *The Protestant Clergy and Public Issues, 1812–1848* (Princeton, 1954); Peter Dobkin Hall, *The Organization of American Culture, 1700–1900: Private Institutions, Elites, and the Origins of American Nationality* (New York, 1982); Charles C. Cole, Jr., *The Social Ideas of the Northern Evangelists, 1826–1860* (New York, 1954); Michael B. Katz, *The Irony of Early School Reform: Educational Innovation in Mid-Nineteenth-Century Massachusetts* (Cambridge, Mass., 1968); Paul E. Johnson, *A Shopkeeper's Millennium: Society and Revivals in Rochester, New York, 1815–1837* (New York, 1978); David J. Rothman, *The Discovery of the Asylum: Social Order and Disorder in the New Republic* (Boston, 1971). Joseph R. Gusfield, in *Symbolic Crusade: Status Politics and the American Temperance Movement* (Urbana, Ill., 1963), argues most explicitly that this desire was impelled by increasing status anxiety among elites who saw their social authority endangered by democratization and rapid social change. Challenges to the social-control thesis include: Lois W. Banner, "Religious Benevolence as Social Control: A Critique of an Interpretation," *Journal of American History* 60 (1973): 23–41; William A. Muraskin, "The Social-Control Theory in American History: A Critique," *Journal of Social History* 9 (1976): 559–69; William W. Cutler, III, "Status, Values and the Education of the Poor: The Trustees of the New York Public School Society, 1805–1853," *American Quarterly* 24 (1972): 69–85; Lawrence Frederick Kohl, "The Concept of Social Control and the History of Jacksonian America," *Journal of the Early Republic* 5 (1985): 21–34. W. David Lewis, in "The Reformer as Conservative: Protestant Counter-Subversion in

the Early Republic," in Stanley Coben and Lorman Ratner, eds., *The Development of American Culture* (Englewood Cliffs, N.J., 1970), pp. 64–91, sees social control and status anxiety as important motives before 1830, but not after, as reform entered a new phase. James L. McElroy, too, differentiates between elite-controlled, conservative moral reform movements before 1830 or so, and, drawing upon John L. Thomas, more radical, "Romantic" reform movements after 1830. See McElroy, "Social Control and Romantic Reform in Antebellum America: The Case of Rochester, New York," *New York History* 58 (1977): 17–46, and Thomas, "Romantic Reform in America, 1815–1865," *American Quarterly* 17 (1965): 658–81. Lewis and McElroy's arguments are mirrored in Ann M. Boylan's recent study of Boston and New York reformers: "Women in Groups: An Analysis of Women's Benevolent Organizations in New York and Boston, 1797–1840," *Journal of American History* 71 (1984): 497–523. Finally, Priscilla Ferguson Clement, in *Welfare and the Poor in the Nineteenth-Century City: Philadelphia, 1800–1854* (Cranbury, N.J., 1985), has attempted to find a balance of motives – social control, altruism, and economy – among Philadelphia reformers concerned with poor relief.

2 The term "evangelical united front" was coined by Foster, in *Errand of Mercy*.

3 Griffin, *Their Brothers' Keepers*, p. xii.

4 Nancy A. Hewitt, *Women's Activism and Social Change: Rochester, New York, 1822–1872* (Ithaca, N.Y., 1984), pp. 262–3. These tabulations exclude those Hewitt lists as "unknown."

5 Ibid., pp. 268–9, 272. A similar argument is made by Boylan, in "Women in Groups." But Boylan's data from New York City and Boston suggest a more consistently upper-class female organizational leadership.

6 Susan Porter Benson, "Business Heads and Sympathizing Hearts: The Women of the Providence Employment Society, 1837–1858," *Journal of Social History* 12 (1978): 303.

7 Edward Pessen, *Riches, Class, and Power Before the Civil War* (Lexington, Mass., 1973); Frederic Cople Jaher, *The Urban Establishment: Upper Strata in Boston, New York, Charleston, Chicago, and Los Angeles* (Urbana, Ill., 1982); Carroll Smith Rosenberg, *Religion and the Rise of the American City: The New York City Mission Movement, 1812–1870* (Ithaca, N.Y., 1971). Raymond Mohl, in *Poverty in New York: 1783–1825* (New York, 1971), extends this pattern back into the late eighteenth century.

8 Jaher, *Urban Establishment*, pp. 239, 62.

9 Lois Banner's term for these societies, with reference to the motives of their leadership, is "workshops in republicanism." See Banner, "Religious Benevolence as Social Control," p. 40.

10 Paul Boyer, *Urban Masses and Moral Order in America: 1820–1920* (Cambridge, Mass., 1978), p. 15.

11 Ibid., p. 61. In a similar vein, Daniel Walker Howe has written that even well-to-do Whig reformers were as concerned with "self-control" as they were with "social control" – in other words, that reformers of both the upper and the middle class used reform movements to define their own

social identities as well as those of subordinate classes. See Howe, *The Political Culture of the American Whigs* (Chicago, 1979), p. 300.

12 John S. Gilkeson, Jr., *Middle-Class Providence, 1820–1940* (Princeton, 1986), p. 28. Gilkeson's tabulations of temperance society members and officers are on p. 29.

13 Ibid., p. 32.

14 Ian R. Tyrrell, *Sobering Up: From Temperance to Prohibition in Antebellum America, 1800–1860* (Westport, Conn.), pp. 87–115.

15 *First Annual Report of the New York City Temperance Society* . . . (New York, 1830), pp. 3–4, 48.

16 *Fourth Annual Report of the New-York City Temperance Society* (New York, 1833), pp. 6–7; *Sixth Annual Report of the New-York City Temperance Society* (New York, 1835), pp. 6, 12–18.

17 *Sixth Annual Report*, pp. 17–18; New York City Temperance Society, executive committee minutes, 1829–42, p. 270, New York Public Library.

18 *First Annual Report*, p. 48. The executive committee originally consisted of 7 members. It was expanded to 11 and then to 30 in 1832, as presidents of the several ward societies were made *ex officio* members. The minutes of the executive committee clearly reveal the committee's broad mandate to control the affairs of the society.

19 Ibid., p. 52. The names listed in the report were traced to the city directory of 1830.

20 *Eighth Annual Report of the New-York City Temperance Society* (New York, 1837), p. 4. The names listed here were traced to *Longworth's American Almanac* . . . (New York, 1837).

21 *Eighth Annual Report*, p. 5.

22 Ibid., pp. 47–58.

23 NYCTS executive committee minutes, pp. 70, 78.

24 See, for example, *Temperance Recorder*, October, 1833, July, 1834, and September, 1834.

25 Ibid., October, 1833, March, 1833.

26 Ibid., December, 1835.

27 For example, ibid., November, 1834.

28 See, for example, ibid., March, 1833, April, 1833. The underlying question of the extent of alcoholic consumption in antebellum America is taken up in W. J. Rorabaugh, *The Alcoholic Republic: An American Tradition* (New York, 1979).

29 *Temperance Recorder*, August, 1833.

30 *American Temperance Almanac, for* . . . *1835* (Albany, N.Y., 1835), pp. 9, 11, 19, 21, 23, 25.

31 *The Temperance Almanac, for* . . . *1836* (Albany, N.Y., 1836), pp. 6–9. See also my discussion of John Frost's *The Young Mechanic* in Chapter 4.

32 Ibid., p. 13.

33 George W. Bethune, *The Substance of an Address in Favor of Temperance Societies* (Utica, N.Y., 1833).

34 The Reverend Aaron B. Grosh, *The Washingtonian Pocket Companion* . . . (Utica, N.Y., 1845), pp. 8–9.

35 *The Crystal Fount*, August 24, 1842. A few months later, the various events of this sort would be collected in this paper into a regular column headed "Temperance Amusements."

36 Ibid., August 10, 1842.

37 Sean Wilentz, *Chants Democratic: New York City and the Rise of the American Working Class* (New York, 1984), p. 312.

38 Tyrrell, *Sobering Up*, pp. 191–206. Tyrrell's interpretive study largely supplants John Allen Krout's standard narrative, *The Origins of Prohibition* (New York, 1925).

39 *The Crystal Fount*, March 1, 1843.

40 Ibid., March 15, 1843.

41 Tyrrell, *Sobering Up*, pp. 209–17.

42 The list of founders is from George Faber Clark, *History of the Temperance Reform in Massachusetts: 1813–1883* (Boston, 1888), p. 57. Occupations are from *Longworth's American Almanac* . . . (New York, 1842), and from B. H. Mills, *The Temperance Manual: Containing a History of the Various Temperance Orders* . . . (Upper Alton, Ill., and Boston, 1864), p. 230.

43 Peter Dobkin Hall, in *The Organization of American Culture*, interprets these societies as adaptations by the "Standing Order" to national expansion, the growth of cities in the East, and new transportation and organization technologies. See also Foster, *Errand of Mercy*.

44 Lawrence J. Friedman, *Gregarious Saints: Self and Community in American Abolitionism, 1830–1870* (Cambridge, 1982). On the social backgrounds of antislavery leaders, see Gerald Sorin, *The New York Abolitionists: A Case Study of Political Radicalism* (Westport, Conn., 1971).

45 Philadelphia City Anti-Slavery Society, constitution and list of members, 1838, Historical Society of Pennsylvania. The membership list was traced to city directories.

46 Edward Magdol, *The Antislavery Rank and File: A Social Profile of the Abolitionists' Constituency* (Westport, Conn., 1986), esp. p. 47; John B. Jentz, "The Anti-Slavery Constituency in Jacksonian New York City," *Civil War History* 27 (1981): 101–22.

47 Ronald Story, "Class and Culture in Boston: The Athenaeum, 1807–1860," *American Quarterly* 27 (1975): 196, 198.

48 See Jaher, *The Urban Establishment*; Pessen, *Riches, Class and Power*; E. Digby Baltzell, *Philadelphia Gentlemen: The Making of a National Upper Class* (Glencoe, Ill., 1958).

49 See Susan G. Davis, *Parades and Power: Street Theatre in Nineteenth-Century Philadelphia* (Philadelphia, 1986), pp. 51–2, 70–1, 99.

50 Francis Gerry Fairfield, *The Clubs of New York* (New York, 1873), p. 60.

51 Compare, for example, Fairfield's discussion of the Union Club with his discussion of the Century Club and New York Yacht Club, ibid., pp. 29–105. Stow Persons, in *The Decline of American Gentility* (New York, 1973), pp. 103–9, emphasizes the genteel quality of the Century, Sketch, and Saturday clubs.

52 Melvin L. Adelman, *A Sporting Time: New York City and the Rise of Modern Athletics, 1820–70* (Chicago, 1986), pp. 101–12.

53 George B. Kirsch, "American Cricket: Players and Clubs Before the Civil War," *Journal of Sport History* 11 (1984): 29n.
54 Philadelphia Cricket Club, minutes, 1854–64, Historical Society of Pennsylvania.
55 Baltzell, *Philadelphia Gentlemen*, pp. 397–9; John A. Lester, ed., *A Century of Philadelphia Cricket* (Philadelphia, 1951).
56 Falcon Barge Club of Philadelphia, constitution and membership list, 1834–9, Historical Society of Pennsylvania. Members located in city directories included 24 merchants, a broker, a gentleman, a doctor, an attorney, a druggist, a quill manufacturer, a clerk, a master tailor, the proprietor of a paperhangings store, and the first teller of the Girard Bank.
57 Philadelphia Quoit Club, minute book, 1829–55, Historical Society of Pennsylvania.
58 Lee L. Schreiber, "Bluebloods and Local Societies: A Philadelphia Microcosm," *Pennsylvania History* 48 (1981): 251–66.
59 The institutions and their directors are listed in *McElroy's Philadelphia Directory for 1840* (Philadelphia, 1840). Occupations were identified by tracing the directors' names to the body of the directory.
60 Pessen, *Riches, Class and Power*, pp. 256, 273.
61 Lee Benson, "Philadelphia Elites and Economic Development: Quasi-Public Innovation During the First American Organizational Revolution, 1825–1861," *Working Papers from the Regional Economic History Research Center* 2 (1978): 30.
62 The Amphion, minute book, 1849–68, Historical Society of Pennsylvania.
63 Franklin Literary Union of Philadelphia, minute book, 1859–62, Historical Society of Pennsylvania.
64 The Round Table, constitution and minutes, 1839–41, Historical Society of Pennsylvania.
65 Pessen, *Riches, Class and Power*, p. 272.
66 Henry Pierce diary, Massachusetts Historical Society. See esp. the entries of January 5, January 8, January 30, February 4, February 11, August 4, and August 9, 1845, and daily entries from 1870.
67 Kirsch, "American Cricket," pp. 42–6.
68 Adelman, *A Sporting Time*, p. 123. Harold Seymour, in *Baseball: The Early Years* (New York, 1960), provides the details: Between 1845 and 1860 the Knickerbocker included 17 merchants, 12 clerks, 5 brokers, 4 professionals, 2 insurance men, a bank teller, a cigar dealer, a hatter, a cooperage owner, a stationer, a U.S. marshal, and several gentlemen (p. 16).
69 Seymour, *Baseball*, p. 24.
70 Adelman, *A Sporting Time*, pp. 138–41.
71 Ibid., p. 149.
72 Stephen Freedman, "The Baseball Fad in Chicago, 1865–1870: An Exploration of the Role of Sport in the Nineteenth-Century City," *Journal of Sport History* 5 (1978): 43–9, 54–7.

73 Peter Levine, "The Promise of Sport in Antebellum America," *Journal of American Culture* 2 (1980): 623–34.

74 See Allan Stanley Horlick, *Country Boys and Merchant Princes: The Social Control of Young Men in New York* (Lewisburg, Pa., 1975), pp. 252–9.

75 *Hunt's Merchants' Magazine* 29 (1853): 443, 446.

76 Ibid., p. 444.

77 Ibid., p. 445.

78 Don Harrison Doyle, "The Social Functions of Voluntary Associations in a Nineteenth-Century American Town," *Social Science History* 1 (1977): 333–55. Approximately one-third of the voluntary association officers in Jacksonville, Illinois, were artisans, but Doyle argues that most of these were actually retailers, and observes that most had shed their artisanal titles within ten years. See pp. 336, 342.

79 Ibid., pp. 348–9.

80 Davis, *Parades and Power*, pp. 159ff. See also Alan Dawley, *Class and Community: The Industrial Revolution in Lynn* (Cambridge, Mass., 1976).

81 Bruce Laurie, "Fire Companies and Gangs in Southwark: The 1840s," in Allen F. Davis and Mark H. Haller, eds., *The Peoples of Philadelphia: A History of Ethnic Groups and Lower-Class Life, 1790–1940* (Philadelphia, 1973), pp. 71–87.

82 Pennsylvania Fire Company, fire and meeting roll, 1806–47, Historical Society of Pennsylvania.

83 Philadelphia Hose Company, constitution and membership roll, 1834–70, Historical Society of Pennsylvania.

84 Delaware Fire Company, membership roll, 1824, 1858–71. Other companies near the center of the city that had become almost entirely manual in membership include the United States Hose Company and the Reliance Fire Company. See United States Hose Company, membership roll, 1848; Reliance Fire Company, roll book, 1820–71. The Washington Fire Company, located in the city just above Southwark, had an evenly divided membership in 1828, but its surviving records do not include later membership rolls. See Washington Fire Company, constitution, by-laws, and membership roll, 1828. All of these records are at the Historical Society of Pennsylvania.

85 Susan G. Davis, " 'Making Night Hideous': Christmas Revelry and Public Order in Nineteenth-Century Philadelphia," *American Quarterly* 34 (1982): 185–99; and Davis, *Parades and Power*.

86 Richard Stott, "Workers in the Metropolis: New York City, 1820–1860" (Ph.D. dissertation, Cornell University, 1983). See also Jon M. Kingsdale, "The 'Poor Man's Club': Social Functions of the Urban Working-Class Saloon," *American Quarterly* 25 (1973): 472–89.

87 Elliott J. Gorn, *The Manly Art: Bare-Knuckle Prize Fighting in America* (Ithaca, N.Y., 1986), esp. pp. 133–44. The quotation is from p. 142.

88 On Grace Church and Isaac Brown, see Jaher, *Urban Establishment*, pp. 230–1. Bruce Laurie discusses working-class churches and religious life in *Working People of Philadelphia, 1800–1850*.

89 First Presbyterian Church of Kensington, Roll of Members, 1814–1948, Presbyterian Historical Society. My statement is based on the identification of male members in city directories. Approximately half of the listed members were identified in the directories. This is a fairly high proportion, considering the peripheral location of the neighborhood and that the register entries refer to new members, many of whom were young men and boys.

90 First Presbyterian Church of Southwark, Records of Communicants, Baptisms, and Marriages, 1827–48, Presbyterian Historical Society. This list consists of males admitted to membership from 1827 to 1831, and fathers of infants baptized during these same years. Only a third of the list was located in city directories.

91 Third Presbyterian Church of Philadelphia, Register of Communicants, 1831–68; First Presbyterian Church of Philadelphia, List of Communicants, 1830; *List of Communicants in the First Presbyterian Church, Philadelphia* (Philadelphia, 1855); Presbyterian Historical Society. That members of the First Presbyterian sometimes passed other Presbyterian churches on their way to Philadelphia's most prestigious New Light church was observed some years ago by Robert W. Doherty in "Social Bases for the Presbyterian Schism of 1837–1838: The Philadelphia Case," *Journal of Social History* 2 (1968): 69–79.

92 First Presbyterian Church, List of Communicants, 1830; *List of Communicants* (1855).

93 Third Presbyterian Church, Register; Fourth Presbyterian Church of Philadelphia, Register, 1843–78, vol. 3, Presbyterian Historical Society. I am certain that the very low representation of Fourth Church members in the directories does not result entirely from the youthfulness of new male members, as I searched for each member in the directories of at least the five years succeeding his admission to membership.

94 Tenth Presbyterian Church of Philadelphia, Register, 1830–80, vol. 1, Presbyterian Historical Society.

95 Quoted in Doherty, "Social Basis," p. 77.

96 There were a number of fraternal movements in this era besides the Masons and Odd Fellows, including several large ones growing out of the temperance crusade. In this closing section I examine only these two large and explicitly inclusive organizations.

97 Georg Simmel, "The Sociology of Secrecy and of Secret Societies," *American Journal of Sociology* 11 (1906): 484.

98 Mary Ann Clawson, "Brotherhood, Class and Patriarchy: Fraternalism in Europe and America" (Ph.D. dissertation, State University of New York at Stony Brook, 1980), esp. pp. 124–43 on the founding of Freemasonry in England, pp. 221–43 on its exportation to continental Europe, pp. 272–7 on the early years of Freemasonry in America, and pp. 123, 151, 153, 177–80, and 189–221 on the specific cultural and institutional influences mentioned here.

99 Ibid., pp. 232–3.

100 Examples from each order would include Albert G. Mackey, *The Mystic Tie; or, Facts and Opinions, Illustrative of the Character and Tendency of Freemasonry* (New York, 1856); and the Reverend D. W. Bristol, *The Odd Fellow's Amulet* (Auburn, N.Y., 1851).

101 Simmel, "The Sociology of Secrecy," p. 482.

102 The Reverend Aaron B. Grosh, *The Odd-Fellow's Manual . . .* (Philadelphia, 1868), pp. 20–6.

103 Ibid., p. 28; Thomas Irons, *A Brief History of Odd Fellowship, Briefly Told* (Philadelphia, 1925), pp. 19–20. Wildey's occupation, and those of the other founders, were confirmed in C. Keenan, *The Baltimore Directory, for 1822 & 23 . . .* (Baltimore, 1822), and in *Matchett's Baltimore Director, Collected Up to May 1833 . . .* (Baltimore, 1833). The other founders were a printer, a currier, a painter, a cabinetmaker, and a sawyer.

104 Quoted in Irons, *A Brief History*, pp. 71–2.

105 Grosh, *Odd-Fellow's Manual*, p. 84.

106 Ibid., pp. 199–200.

107 Ibid., p. 200.

108 Brian Greenberg, "Worker and Community: Fraternal Orders in Albany, New York, 1845–1885," *Maryland Historian* 8 (1977): 41. This essay is incorporated into Greenberg's larger study, *Worker and Community: Response to Industrialization in a Nineteenth-Century American City, Albany, New York, 1850–1884* (Albany, N.Y., 1985), chap. 5.

109 Greenberg, "Worker and Community," pp. 38–9.

110 Mackey, *The Mystic Tie*, p. 3. The emphasis is mine.

111 This analysis of Masonic membership in Kingston is based on data described in my book *The Urban Threshold: Growth and Change in a Nineteenth-Century American Community* (Chicago, 1976). Briefly stated, these data consist of a list of members of the Mt. Horeb Lodge, Royal Arch Masons, the manuscript schedules of the New York State census of 1855 and the United States census of 1860, local newspapers, and other sources in which local political activists are identified. Lynn Dumenil, in *Freemasonry and American Culture, 1880–1930* (Princeton, 1984), pp. 12–13, observes the same disjuncture between the professed classlessness of Freemasonry and the predominantly white-collar membership of the Live Oak Lodge of Oakland, California, later in the century.

112 The above analysis is based on the Register of Members, vols. 2–1 and 2–2, at the Grand Lodge of the Free and Accepted Masons of Pennsylvania. A rather different analysis, based on what I believe are inadequate categories, can be found in Wayne A. Huss, *The Master Builders: A History of the Grand Lodge of Free and Accepted Masons of Pennsylvania, Vol 1: 1731–1873* (Philadelphia, 1986).

113 See Mackey, *Mystic Tie*, pp. 70–2; Bristol, *Odd Fellow's Amulet*, pp. 92–102, 238–43. For a characteristic attack on fraternalism, based in part of the exclusion of women, see Joseph T. Cooper, *Odd-Fellowship Examined in the Light of Scripture and Reason* (Philadelphia, 1854).

114   Clawson, "Brotherhood, Class and Patriarchy," p. 331.
115   Bristol, *Odd Fellow's Amulet*, pp. 177–9.
116   For example, ibid., pp. 213–16.

Chapter 7. Experience and consciousness in the antebellum city

1   This definition of social networks is broader than most, as it includes the casual and anonymous interactions of the street and other public places – interactions that were recurring and patterned in a categorical rather than a personal sense. My concern is to trace the growing physical separation of social classes in urban space, and not merely the changing character of significant personal relationships. On networks in social theory and research, see Claude S. Fischer, *Networks and Places: Social Relations in the Urban Setting* (New York, 1977), and the essays in Samuel Leinhardt, ed., *Social Networks: A Developing Paradigm* (New York, 1977). Fischer recognizes this broader definition: "We are each the center of a web of social bonds that radiates outward to the people we know intimately, those whom we know well, those whom we know casually, and to the wider society beyond. These are our personal *social networks*" (p. vii).

2   George William Curtis, *The Potiphar Papers* (New York, 1856); C[harles] Astor Bristed, *The Upper Ten Thousand: Sketches of American Society* (New York, 1852); and any of the books by George G. Foster cited earlier – social climbing by the newly rich is an important theme in all of them.

3   Foster, *New York Naked* (New York, n.d.), pp. 71, 75.

4   In Curtis's story of a lavish ball thrown by the social climbing Mrs. Potiphar, for example, one young aristocrat permits himself to attend by resolving not to be introduced to the host. But he does attend, and in the process helps Mrs. Potiphar accomplish her purpose. See Curtis, *Potiphar Papers*, p. 20.

5   Frederic Cople Jaher, *The Urban Establishment: Upper Strata in Boston, New York, Charleston, Chicago, and Los Angeles* (Urbana, Ill., 1982). The argument for a closed upper class is made most forcefully in Edward Pessen, *Riches, Class, and Power Before the Civil War* (Lexington, Mass., 1973). On the perception of functionally divided elites, see Lee Benson, "Philadelphia's Elites and Economic Development: Quasi-Public Innovation During the First American Organizational Revolution, 1825–1861," *Working Papers from the Regional Economic History Research Center* 2 (1978): 25–53; and Stow Persons, *The Decline of American Gentility* (New York, 1973).

6   Jaher, *Urban Establishment*, esp. pp. 44–87, 173–250. Charleston, in Jaher's account, was very much closer to Boston than it was to New York (see pp. 336–99). E. Digby Baltzell distinguishes between Boston Brahmins and Philadelphia Gentlemen on grounds of the character of their local leadership, but sees both groups as integrated, multifunctional upper classes. See Baltzell, *Puritan Boston and Quaker Philadelphia:*

Two Protestant Ethics and the Spirit of Class Authority and Leadership (New York, 1979).

7   Ronald Story, *The Forging of an Aristocracy: Harvard and the Boston Upper Class, 1800–1870* (Middletown, Conn., 1980), p. 164.

8   Bristed, *Upper Ten Thousand,* p. 255.

9   Elva Tooker, *Nathan Trotter: Philadelphia Merchant, 1787–1853* (Cambridge, Mass., 1955).

10 Several scholars, most notably George Rogers Taylor, have demonstrated that the fares for these transportation facilities were beyond the range of workingmen. See Taylor, "The Beginnings of Mass Transportation in Urban America: Parts I and II," *Smithsonian Journal of History* 1 (Summer and Autumn, 1966): 35–52, 31–54; Kenneth T. Jackson, *Crabgrass Frontier: The Suburbanization of the United States* (New York, 1985); Henry C. Binford, *The First Suburbs: Residential Communities on the Boston Periphery, 1815–1860* (Chicago, 1985).

11 George G. Foster, *Fifteen Minutes Around New York* (New York, 1854), pp. 110–11.

12 Henry Pierce diary, Massachusetts Historical Society. The quotation is from the entry of March 16, 1845.

13 Francis Pulszky and Theresa Pulszky, *White, Red, Black: Sketches of Society in the United States . . .* (London, 1853), vol. 3, p. 179.

14 James Fenimore Cooper, *The American Democrat* (1838; New York, 1931), p. 114.

15 The perception of the big city as a place where older forms of social affiliation were being replaced only by selfishness and alienation may be seen in Samuel I. Prime, *Life in New York* (New York, 1851); and in Lydia Maria Child, *Letters from New York* (New York and Boston, 1843). Mrs. Child, however, revised her view, and presents a distinctly more optimistic view of urban society in her *Letters from New York: Second Series* (London, 1845).

16 Charles Astor Bristed, in an interesting essay on the American language, warns his readers that the written language sometimes differs in important respects from the spoken language, even among the higher classes. See Bristed, "The English Language in America," *Cambridge Essays, Contributed by Members of the University* (London, 1855), p. 63. We are, of course, forced to rely upon the written record, and to infer its relationship to possibly quite different and variable patterns of daily speech. On the other hand, parts of the written record are more clearly reflective of common speech than others.

17 *Mechanic's Free Press,* October 25, 1828.

18 William Ellery Channing, *A Discourse on the Life and Character of Rev. Joseph Tuckerman* (Boston, 1841), pp. 7–8. Quoted in Asa Briggs, "The Language of 'Class' in Early Nineteenth-Century England," in Briggs and John Saville, eds., *Essays in Labour History* (London, 1960), p. 48.

19 Frederick Grimké, *Considerations upon the Nature and Tendency of Free Institutions* (Cincinnati, 1848), pp. 455, 458, 468.

20 Ibid., pp. 455, 473.

21 George Foster, not surprisingly, is an excellent source for the most acerbic terminology. See his *New York in Slices: By an Experienced Carver . . .* (New York, 1849), p. 71, *New York by Gas-Light: With Here and There a Streak of Sunshine* (New York, 1850), pp. 38, 83, 95–6, 106, and *New York Naked*, pp. 39–40, 43–5, 53–5. *Harper's New Monthly Magazine* can be consulted almost at random for "higher classes," "society," and other more sober expressions, as well as for quite frequent discussions of "classes" in general.

22 Grimké, *Considerations*, p. 473.

23 *Journal of Health* 1 (1830): 358. I was led to this fairly obscure reference by Burton Bledstein's discussion of it in *The Culture of Professionalism: The Middle Class and the Development of Higher Education in America* (New York, 1976).

24 Walt Whitman, *Complete Poetry and Selected Prose* (Boston, 1859), p. 479.

25 *New York As It Is* (New York, 1837), p. iv.

26 *Fourth Annual Report of the New-York City Temperance Society* (New York, 1833), p. 14.

27 *Hunt's Merchants' Magazine* 33 (1855): 765.

28 *Third Annual Report of the American Anti-Slavery Society . . .* (New York, 1836), pp. 81–2.

29 *New York Tribune*, March 10, 1855.

30 *Report of the Council of Hygiene and Public Health of the Citizens Association of New York upon the Sanitary Condition of the City* (New York, 1865), p. 120.

31 *New York Times*, October 19, 1866.

32 See Chapter 4, above.

33 Gary J. Kornblith, personal communication, December 6, 1985. There are other indications that manufacturers could be referred to as "mechanics" without a loss of status. The *Sixth Annual Report of the New-York City Temperance Society* (New York, 1835), for example, cites the contribution to the cause of "a very respectable mechanic of this city" who employed twenty-five hands (p. 19).

34 John Russell Bartlett, *Dictionary of Americanisms: A Glossary of Words and Phrases Usually Regarded as Peculiar to the United States* (New York, 1848; 2d ed., Boston, 1859), p. 270. Burton Bledstein claims, in *The Culture of Professionalism* (p. 13), that the first appearance of "middle class" in an American dictionary occurred only in 1889.

35 Foster, *New York by Gas-Light*, pp. 69, 101, 109; *New York Naked*, pp. 115, 146, 150; *New York in Slices*, p. 72.

36 Foster's unsympathetic attitude toward immigrants led to a brief assistant editorship of a nativist magazine in 1853. See George Rogers Taylor, "Gaslight Foster: A New York 'Journeyman Journalist' at Mid-Century," *New York History* 58 (1977): 310.

37 As Eric Hobsbawm has so brilliantly demonstrated in *Primitive Rebels: Studies in Archaic Forms of Social Movement in the 19th and 20th Centuries* (Manchester, U.K., 1959), state formation could sharpen ethnic identities in *opposition* to national citizenship, among those peripheral groups who

were forced into legal amalgamation with the dominant groups within centralizing states. Mass migration, however, often could accomplish what states could not, as the collision with alien host populations and institutions tended to enlarge parochial identities. Hence, in the new world County Kerry men tended to become Irishmen, and Palatines tended to become Germans. Mass migration (and the response to it) also at least temporarily preserved endogamy and cultural defensiveness. In both respects it contributed to the clarity of ethnic identity.

38 See Chapter 1, note 35.
39 Oscar Handlin, *Boston's Immigrants: A Study in Acculturation*, rev. ed. (New York, 1968), pp. 250–1. German immigrants had a significantly higher proportion of nonmanual workers than the Irish, 18.2% as compared to 6.2%. But there were far fewer Germans in Boston than there were Irish.
40 Robert Ernst, *Immigrant Life in New York City, 1825–1863* (New York, 1949), p. 218; Theodore Hershberg, Alan N. Burstein, Eugene P. Ericksen, Stephanie W. Greenberg, and William L. Yancey, "A Tale of Three Cities: Blacks, Immigrants, and Opportunity in Philadelphia, 1850–1880, 1930, 1970," in Hershberg, ed., *Philadelphia: Work, Space, Family, and Group Experience in the 19th Century: Essays Toward an Interdisciplinary History of the City* (New York, 1981), p. 471. These figures pertain to 1850.
41 Stuart M. Blumin, *The Urban Threshold: Growth and Change in a Nineteenth-Century American Community* (Chicago, 1976), p. 88. These figures pertain to 1860. In Milwaukee in 1860, 13% of Irish immigrants and 17% of German immigrants were listed in nonmanual occupations. These proportions drop to 6% and 7% if petty proprietors are excluded. See Kathleen Neils Conzen, *Immigrant Milwaukee, 1836–1860: Accommodation and Community in a Frontier City* (Cambridge, Mass., 1976), p. 66.
42 Foster, *New York by Gas-Light*, p. 87.
43 Ibid., p. 107.
44 Douglas T. Miller, in "Immigration and Social Stratification in Pre–Civil War New York," *New York History* 49 (1968), concludes in a similar vein: "A close examination of New York's society in the pre–Civil War period indicates that heavy immigration widened the gulf between classes and increased class consciousness" (p. 157).
45 Paul Kleppner, *The Cross of Culture: A Social Analysis of Midwestern Politics, 1850–1900* (New York, 1970), p. 35.
46 Lee Benson, "Group Cohesion and Social and Ideological Conflict: A Critique of Some Marxian and Tocquevillian Theories," *American Behavioral Scientist* 16 (1973), p. 748.
47 On the technical problems involved in ethnocultural political analysis, see James E. Wright, "The Ethnocultural Model of Voting: A Behavioral and Historical Critique," *American Behavioral Scientist* 16 (1972–3): 653–74. Ronald P. Formisano has noted: "An embarrassing fact of life for historians of nineteenth-century politics is that while they have discovered that religion counted for very much in politics, it is almost impossible to

measure precisely religious affiliation among the electorate." See Formisano, *The Transformation of Political Culture: Massachusetts Parties, 1790s–
1840s* (New York, 1983), p. 289.

48 Examples of recent studies qualifying a straightforward ethnocultural
interpretation include Amy Bridges, *A City in the Republic: Antebellum New
York and the Origins of Machine Politics* (New York, 1984); Paul Goodman,
"The Social Basis of New England Politics in Jacksonian America," *Journal
of the Early Republic* 6 (1986): 23–58; Donald J. Ratcliffe, "Politics in Jack-
sonian Ohio: Reflections on the Ethnocultural Interpretation," *Ohio History* 88 (1979): 5–35; Michael F. Holt, "The Election of 1840, Voter
Mobilization, and the Emergence of the Second American Party System:
A Reappraisal of Jacksonian Voting Behavior," in William J. Cooper, Jr.,
Michael F. Holt, and John McCardell, eds., *A Master's Due: Essays in
Honor of David Herbert Donald* (Baton Rouge, 1985), pp. 16–58, esp. pp. 24–
7. Goodman stresses the importance of local contexts and offers results
that illustrate the difficulty of separating religion from class. On the
second issue, see also Ronald P. Formisano, "Toward a Reorientation of
Jacksonian Politics: A Review of the Literature, 1959–1975," *Journal of
American History*, 63 (1976): 62.

49 Susan E. Hirsch, *Roots of the American Working Class: The Industrialization
of Crafts in Newark, 1800–1860* (Philadelphia, 1978), p. xiii.

50 Ibid., p. 116.

51 David Montgomery makes essentially the same argument with reference
to native-born and Irish workers in the Kensington district of Philadelphia
in "The Shuttle and the Cross: Weavers and Artisans in the Kensington
Riots of 1844," *Journal of Social History* 5 (1972): 411–46. That this bifurcation of consciousness has been a unique and general feature of American working-class culture is argued in Ira Katznelson, *City Trenches:
Urban Politics and the Patterning of Class in the United States* (Chicago, 1981).

52 Bridges, *A City in the Republic*, p. 12.

53 Ibid., p. 13. This point of view is effectively expressed in the title and
in much of the contents of Joel H. Silbey's recent collected essays, *The
Partisan Imperative: The Dynamics of American Politics Before the Civil War*
(New York, 1985).

54 See Bridges, *A City in the Republic*, p. 6, and Katznelson, *City Trenches*,
pp. 61–4.

55 See Sean Wilentz, *Chants Democratic: New York City and the Rise of the
American Working Class, 1788–1850* (New York, 1984), one attempt to
interpret the Democratic party in New York City as an institution that
promoted working-class solidarity. But Wilentz's own evidence shows
how difficult this was after the mid-1830s. An interesting question is why
class solidarities, but not ethnocultural ones, were excluded. To answer
this, one must understand that ethnocultural groups were not perceived
as such at the time, and that the issues around which they cohered were
more likely than class-based issues to be regarded as matters of persua-
sion rather than of specific group interest. It made sense to appeal to all

classes on ethnocultural grounds. It made less sense to appeal to all ethnic or religious groups on class grounds.

56 On the latter, see Ronald P. Formisano, "Deferential-Participant Politics: The Early Republic's Political Culture, 1789–1840," *American Political Science Review* 68 (1974): 473–87. The *local* support of middle-class interests can be seen in Blumin, *The Urban Threshold*, chap. 7, and especially in Michael H. Frisch, *Town into City: Springfield, Massachusetts, and the Meaning of Community, 1840–1880* (Cambridge, Mass., 1972).

57 Robert A. McCaughey, "From Town to City: Boston in the 1820s," *Political Science Quarterly* 88 (1973): 202.

58 Andrew R. L. Cayton, "The Fragmentation of 'A Great Family': The Panic of 1819 and the Rise of the Middling Interest in Boston, 1818–1822," *Journal of the Early Republic* 2 (1982): 166–7. The Middling Interest is discussed in similar terms in Formisano, *The Transformation of Political Culture*, pp. 181–7.

Chapter 8. White-collar worlds

1 Bruce Laurie and Mark Schmitz, "Manufacture and Productivity: The Making of an Industrial Base, Philadelphia, 1850–1880," in Theodore Hershberg, ed., *Philadelphia: Work, Space, Family, and Group Experience in the 19th Century: Essays Toward an Interdisciplinary History of the City* (New York, 1981), p. 52.

2 Herbert G. Gutman, "Class, Status, and Community Power in Nineteenth-Century American Industrial Cities: Paterson, New Jersey: A Case Study," in Gutman, *Work, Culture, and Society in Industrializing America: Essays in Working-Class and Social History* (New York, 1976), pp. 238–9.

3 Laurie and Schmitz, "Manufacture and Productivity," p. 52. Stephan Thernstrom, in *The Other Bostonians: Poverty and Progress in the American Metropolis, 1880–1970* (Cambridge, Mass., 1973), claims that self-employed artisans "largely disappeared from Boston by 1880" (p. 292n). If by "largely disappeared" Thernstrom means the confinement of masters to the limited roles and presence just indicated, he is quite correct. However, he could have made the same claim for 1860.

4 *Ninth Census – Volume I. The Statistics of Population of the United States . . .* (Washington, D.C., 1872), p. xxxiii.

5 Walker identified twenty different types of "operatives" where the 1860 census, with more than twice the total number of occupational listings in this sector, identified only two (sewing-machine operatives and silk operatives). Margo Anderson Conk, in *The United States Census and Labor Force Change: A History of Occupation Statistics, 1870–1940* (Ann Arbor, 1978), labels Walker's new classification scheme "artisanal," to contrast his continuing use of simple alphabetization within each sector to Alba M. Edwards's "industrial" subdivisions of the manufacturing sector on the 1910 census (p. 28). This is the only point at which I would take issue

with Conk's excellent discussion of evolving census taxonomies. Walker, it seems to me, was clearly searching for a taxonomy that would accurately represent an industrial rather than an artisanal work force.

6 *Ninth Census – Volume I*, p. xxxiii.

7 *Ninth Census – Volume I*, p. 708.

8 *Report on Manufacturing Industries in the United States at the Eleventh Census: 1890. Part I. Totals for States and Industries* (Washington, D.C., 1895), p. 20.

9 *Census Reports. Volume VII. Manufactures: Part I: United States by Industries* (Washington, D.C., 1902), pp. civ, 3, 59.

10 Henry L. Everett, *What Shall I Learn? or, The Young Men's Business Guide* (Philadelphia, 1892), p. 3.

11 Ibid., pp. 40–3, 77–80.

12 The whole series is, *Harper's New Monthly Magazine*: "A Pair of Shoes," 70 (1885): 273–89; "A Glass of Beer," 71 (1885): 666–83; "A Silk Dress," 71 (1885): 240–61; "A Lampful of Oil," 72 (1886): 235–57; "A Lump of Sugar," 73 (1886): 72–95; "A Printed Book," 75 (1887): 165–88; "A Sheet of Paper," 75 (1887): 113–30; "A Piece of Glass," 79 (1889): 245–64; "A Suit of Clothes," 80 (1890): 685–708.

13 *Scientific American* 34 (1876): 50.

14 See the books of trades noted in Chapter 3, above. An interesting discussion of earlier depictions of trades (by French artists) is William H. Sewell, Jr., "Visions of Labor: Illustrations of the Mechanical Arts Before, In, and After Diderot's *Encyclopédie*," in Steven L. Kaplan and Cynthia J. Koepp, eds., *Work in France: Representations, Meaning, Organization, and Practice* (Ithaca, N.Y., 1986), pp. 258–86.

15 Prang's views may be seen in Katherine Morrison McClinton, *The Chromolithographs of Louis Prang* (New York, 1973), pp. 120–26.

16 *Population of the United States in 1860* ... (Washington, D.C., 1864), pp. 656–79.

17 *Ninth Census – Volume I*, pp. 674–85.

18 Ibid.; *Statistics of the Population of the United States at the Tenth Census* (Washington, D.C., 1883), pp. 744–51. Other officials and office workers were included in the census but were merged with nonoffice employees in ways that prevent their separate tabulation.

19 It is difficult to tabulate these proportions in the published census, as the occupational tables for individual cities collapse a number of the relevant occupational categories and exclude others. In New York City in 1880, identifiable salesmen, accountants, bookkeepers, office clerks, and store clerks constituted 9.6% of the total work force and 11.5% of the total male work force (ibid., p. 892). The actual percentage of salaried employees was somewhat higher, as several types of office workers and all salaried officials are excluded from the table or cannot be isolated.

20 Richard Wheatley, "The New York Custom House," *Harper's* 69 (1884): 38–61.

21 The remaining seven are as follows: "The New York Stock Exchange," 71 (1885): 829–53; "The New York Produce Exchange," 73 (1886): 189–218; "The New York Police Department," 74 (1887): 495–518; "The New

York Real Estate Exchange," 77 (1888): 928–44; "The New York Banks," 80 (1890): 457–73; "The New York Maritime Exchange," 80 (1890): 756–66; "The New York Chamber of Commerce," 83 (1891): 502–17.

22   Matthew Hale Smith, *Sunshine and Shadow in New York* (Hartford, 1868), pp. 259, 417. As to the popularity of Smith's book, Frank Luther Mott classifies it, in *Golden Multitudes: The Story of Best Sellers in the United States* (New York, 1947), as a "better seller," implying sales approaching 300,000 copies. A. Austin Allibone estimates that Smith sold 25,000 copies within a month of publication. See Allibone, *Critical Dictionary of English Literature and British and American Authors* (Philadelphia and London, 1877), vol. II, p. 2151.

23   Alfred D. Chandler, Jr., *The Visible Hand: The Managerial Revolution in American Business* (Cambridge, Mass., 1977).

24   Margery W. Davies, in *Woman's Place Is at the Typewriter: Office Work and Office Workers, 1870–1930* (Philadelphia, 1982), observes that public debate over the propriety of women's working in offices began in earnest only in the 1890s (p. 79).

25   See, for example, *Scribner's Monthly, an Illustrated Magazine for the People* 1 (1871): 107–8, 452–3. My statement is based on a review of all the issues of *Scribner's Monthly* from 1871 through 1881, and all the issues of its successor, *The Century*, from 1881 through 1890.

26   See, for example, *Harper's* 70 (1885): 484.

27   Ibid., 65 (1882): 112–16.

28   "A Shopper By Proxy: A Practical Love Story," ibid. 51 (1875): 579–82.

29   Again, my review of this magazine included every issue between 1870 and 1890.

30   *Scribner's* 22 (1881): 789–91. The quotation is on page 789.

31   Ralph M. Hower, *History of Macy's of New York, 1858–1919: Chapters in the Evolution of the Department Store* (Cambridge, Mass., 1943), pp. 114–15, 194–9, 124–7.

32   *Tenth Census*, pp. 760, 776, 792, 892.

33   The most accessible tabulation of office workers by gender is Davies, *Woman's Place*, appendix, table 1. Women constituted a majority of stenographers and typists, but there were only 5,000 men and women in these occupations in 1880.

34   *Scribner's* 22 (1881): 790.

35   Carole Srole, " 'A Position That God Has Not Particularly Assigned to Men': The Feminization of Clerical Work, Boston 1860–1915" (Ph.D. dissertation, University of California at Los Angeles, 1984), pp. 120, 148. I have excluded office boys from Srole's tabulations, as I have from all of the above calculations and discussion. The U.S. census, too, listed office boys separately from clerks. Clyde and Sally Griffen, in *Natives and Newcomers: The Ordering of Opportunity in Mid-Nineteenth-Century Poughkeepsie* (Cambridge, Mass., 1978), find an overall pattern of clerical mobility similar to Srole's, but with slightly higher upward and slightly lower downward mobility rates over the ten-year period 1870–80 (p. 60). Isolating a young clerical cohort in the previous decade (1860–70) reveals,

however, a significantly higher and more traditional 61% rate of clerical mobility into professional and proprietary positions (p. 62).

36   These figures are from Clarence D. Long, *Wages and Earnings in the United States, 1860–1890* (Princeton, 1960), p. 68. On wage and price series, see also Jeffrey G. Williamson and Peter H. Lindert, *American Inequality: A Macroeconomic History* (New York, 1980), pp. 107, 307, 319, and Paul A. David and Peter Solar, "A Bicentenary Contribution to the History of the Cost of Living in America," in Paul Uselding, ed., *Research in Economic History: An Annual Compilation of Research*, vol. 2 (Greenwich, Conn., 1977), pp. 16–17. On the poverty line in 1880, see Eudice Glassberg, "Work, Wages, and the Cost of Living: Ethnic Differences and the Poverty Line, Philadelphia, 1880," *Pennsylvania History* 66 (1979): 17–58, and Michael R. Haines, "Poverty, Economic Stress, and the Family in a Late Nineteenth-Century American City: Whites in Philadelphia, 1880," in Theodore Hershberg, ed., *Philadelphia*, pp. 240–76. But see also the criticism of this kind of poverty-line analysis in John F. McClymer, "The Historian and the Poverty Line," *Historical Methods* 18 (1985): 105–10.

37   Glassberg, "Work, Wages, and the Cost of Living," p. 48. In Massachusetts in 1875, Carroll D. Wright had found average annual incomes among skilled metal workers of $745.11, among skilled shop workers of $794.87, and among carpenters of $723.86. These are cited in Jeffrey G. Williamson, "Consumer Behavior in the Nineteenth Century: Carroll D. Wright's Massachusetts Workers in 1875," *Explorations in Entrepreneurial History*, 2d ser., 4 (1967): 108. John F. McClymer has analyzed the details of Wright's survey and reports that some 58% of the workers whose wages and household budgets were examined in 1875 (all were employees of large factories and mills in major towns) were able to maintain adequate levels in at least two of the three basic categories of necessary consumption – food, shelter, and clothing. Some of these ordinary workers made trade-offs, dressing well, say, at the expense of eating well. More than 23% of Wright's sample fell below standard in at least two categories of necessary consumption, while 19% rose sufficiently above the ordinary workers' standard of living to afford a piano, carpeting, a sewing machine, or other such possessions. See McClymer, "Late Nineteenth-Century American Working-Class Living Standards," *Journal of Interdisciplinary History* 17 (1986): 379–98.

38   Haines, "Poverty, Economic Stress, and the Family," pp. 246–7, 260, 262.

39   Bruce Laurie, Theodore Hershberg, and George Alter, "Immigrants and Industry: The Philadelphia Experience, 1850–1880," in Hershberg, ed., *Philadelphia*, p. 106.

40   The Massachusetts Bureau of Statistics of Labor, *Seventh Annual Report* (Boston, 1876), includes the results of a survey of 1,616 white-collar and 5,921 blue-collar employees in Suffolk County (Boston) in 1875. Average white-collar earnings were $1,054, while skilled workers' earnings averaged $603. These results are cited in Thernstrom, *Other Bostonians,*

p. 298. The ratio between average white-collar and blue-collar incomes on this survey is almost precisely the same as the ratio between a somewhat different mix of nonmanual and manual incomes revealed on the U.S. manufacturing census fifteen years later. Average incomes tabulated on the 1890 manufacturing census are as follows: officers, firm members and clerks = $890; skilled and unskilled operatives = $498; pieceworkers = $500. See *Report on Manufacturing Industries*, p. 20.

41 "The New-York Custom House," *Harper's* 43 (1871): 13–14.

42 Cindy Sondik Aron, *Ladies and Gentlemen of the Civil Service: Middle-Class Workers in Victorian America* (New York, 1987), pp. 84–5.

43 *Harper's* 80 (1890): 466; Hower, *History of Macy's*, pp. 194–5.

44 Bessie Louise Pierce, *A History of Chicago*, vol. 2: *From Town to City, 1848–1871* (Chicago, 1940), p. 155; Gwendolyn Wright, *Moralism and the Model Home: Domestic Architecture and Cultural Conflict in Chicago, 1873–1913* (Chicago, 1980), p. 83. Pierce's sources are local newspapers and reminiscences. Wright's source is less clear.

45 "How Working-Men Live in Europe and America," *Harper's* 74 (1887): 787.

46 *Scribner's* 6 (1873): 748.

47 Sam Bass Warner, Jr., *Streetcar Suburbs: The Process of Growth in Boston, 1870–1900* (Cambridge, Mass., 1962), pp. 61, 183.

48 Ibid., p. 14.

49 Kenneth T. Jackson, in *Crabgrass Frontier: The Suburbanization of the United States* (New York, 1985), writes of the domestic ideal as an influence in previous decades, and as a "movement" by the 1880s (p. 91).

50 Warner, *Streetcar Suburbs*, pp. 56, 63. The outer limits of both arterial and crosstown streetcar service expanded during this era, so the boundaries of class-based settlement were far from fixed.

51 Ibid., p. 131. Roger Miller and Joseph Siry, in "The Emerging Suburb: West Philadelphia, 1850–1880," *Pennsylvania History* 47 (1980): 99–145, also note that the West Philadelphia homes of the "central middle class" were designed in imitation of the costlier suburban houses of the wealthy.

52 Theodore Hershberg, Harold E. Cox, Dale B. Light, Jr., and Richard R. Greenfield, "The 'Journey-to-Work': An Empirical Investigation of Work, Residence and Transportation, Philadelphia, 1850 and 1880," in Hershberg, ed., *Philadelphia*, pp. 154, 134–40.

53 My descriptions of this and other grid-units in Philadelphia is based on a complete enumeration of the residents listed on the manuscript schedules of the 1880 U.S. census. The two hotels were located at 517 Chestnut Street and 44 North Fourth Street, and contained as residents 4 professionals, 37 nonmanual businessmen, 4 public officials, 4 clerks, a journalist, 2 machinists, and a patrolman.

54 I will not supply quantitative comparisons with 1860 households in these neighborhoods, as an unknown portion of the increase in density is attributable to the greater inclusiveness of the 1880 file. As the 1880 census includes residential addresses for each entry, no search for addresses in

the city directory was required; hence, no cases had to be eliminated because of difficulties in establishing a positive link between the two sources.

55 See Miller and Siry, "The Emerging Suburb," plates 2 and 5, which reproduce portions of J. D. Scott's 1878 *Atlas of West Philadelphia*.
56 Ibid., pp. 114–15.
57 Ibid., p. 120. I cannot resist claiming an element of "participant observation" here, as I was myself a resident of a portion of one of these houses (it is pictured in Miller and Siry's article) while a student at the University of Pennsylvania. This was not, however, quite as long ago as 1880.
58 Warner, *Streetcar Suburbs*, pp. 119–20. Philadelphia was notable during this era for its large numbers of building societies, which were cooperative home loan organizations that created significant pools of mortgage loan capital. These societies appear to have been particularly important to manual workers, and helped Philadelphia preserve its character as a "city of homes" by providing loans that allowed a large number of workers to purchase their own houses. For contemporary discussions of the Philadelphia building societies, see R. R. Bowker, "Working-Men's Homes," *Harper's* 68 (1884): 783–4, and especially Charles Barnard, "A Hundred Thousand Homes: How They Were Paid For," *Scribner's* 11 (1876): 477–87. It is not clear whether young businessmen, looking toward the suburbs, utilized these societies. A close study of home financing in late-nineteenth-century Philadelphia would have to take this question into account.
59 George E. Thomas alludes to the development of this section of Philadelphia in "Architectural Patronage and Social Stratification in Philadelphia Between 1840 and 1920," in William W. Cutler III and Howard Gillette, Jr., eds., *The Divided Metropolis: Social and Spatial Dimensions of Philadelphia, 1800–1975* (Westport, Conn., 1980), pp. 85–123.
60 To ascertain the representativeness of this three-block area of the northwest periphery, I collected census data from two other nearby streets, Master and Jefferson. The households on these streets were virtually identical to those within the sample area.
61 James Dabney McCabe, Jr., *Lights and Shadows of New York Life; or, the Sights and Sensations of the Great City* . . . (Philadelphia, 1872), p. 300.
62 Junius Henri Browne, *The Great Metropolis: A Mirror of New York* (Hartford, 1869), pp. 103–4.
63 "Bowery, Saturday Night," *Harper's* 42 (1871): 671–2.
64 Ibid., p. 670.
65 George G. Foster, *New York in Slices: By an Experienced Carver* . . . (New York, 1849), p. 3; Foster, *New York By Gas-Light: With Here and There a Streak of Sunshine* (New York, 1850), p. 5; Foster, *New York Naked* (New York, n.d.), pp. 16–17.
66 Browne, *Great Metropolis*, pp. 697, 28.
67 Warner, *Streetcar Suburbs*, pp. 153–60.

68 Henry Pierce and his fellow clerks had visited regularly in their em-
    ployer's parlor, in the Brookline house they all shared. But when Pierce
    later moved to Dorchester, his own clerks seem not to have lived with
    him or visited his home. Rather, his domestic visitors, who called nearly
    every evening, appear to have been neighbors of approximately the same
    age as Pierce and his wife. See Henry Pierce diary, Massachusetts His-
    torical Society. Clyde and Sally Griffen, in *Natives and Newcomers*, agree
    that clerks in this era were less likely to visit with their employers (p. 136).
    Scribner's, in its monthly "Home and Society" column, frequently offered
    advice to householders concerning the reception and entertainment of
    visitors.

69 Kenneth Alan Scherzer, in "The Unbounded Community: Neighborhood
    Life and Social Structure in New York City, 1830–1875" (Ph.D. disser-
    tation, Harvard University, 1982), observes the increased homogeneity
    of New York City churches that relocated uptown. Jürgen Kocka, in *White
    Collar Workers in America, 1890–1940: A Social-Political History in Interna-
    tional Perspective* (Beverly Hills, 1980), p. 129, briefly describes the lively
    social life, in formal and informal (and homogeneously middle-class)
    associations, of suburban Bostonians around the turn of the century.

70 William Graham Sumner, *What Social Classes Owe to Each Other* (New
    York, 1883), p. 13.

71 Francis Amasa Walker, "What Shall We Tell the Working Classes?" *Scrib-
    ner's Magazine* 2 (1887): 619. This is a different magazine from *Scribner's
    Monthly*, which by this time had changed its title to *The Century*.

72 Smith, *Sunshine and Shadow*, pp. 706, 708.

73 James Richardson, "The New Homes of New York: A Study of Flats,"
    Scribner's 8 (1874): 70.

74 Edward Winslow Martin [James Dabney McCabe], *The Secrets of the Great
    City: A Work Descriptive of the Virtues and Vices, the Mysteries, Miseries, and
    Crimes of New York City* (Philadelphia, 1868), p. 38. This book was re-
    published four years later under McCabe's name as *Lights and Shadows
    of New York Life*. See note 61, above.

75 Browne, *Great Metropolis*, preface.

76 Francis Amasa Walker, "Our Domestic Service," *Scribner's* 11 (1875): 274.

77 U.S. Congress, *Report of the Committee of the Senate upon the Relations
    Between Labor and Capital* (Washington, D.C., 1885), quoted from Leon
    Litwack, ed., *The American Labor Movement* (Englewood Cliffs, N.J., 1962),
    p. 13.

78 Lydia Maria Child to Sarah Blake (Sturgis) Shaw, July 31, 1877, microfilm
    (Millwood, N.Y., 1979). Emphases are in the original. The manuscript is
    in the Houghton Library, Harvard University. I am very grateful to Jane
    Pease for bringing this letter, and the one that follows, to my attention.

79 Ibid., August 25, 1977. Emphases are in the original.

80 Helene G. Baer, *The Heart Is Like Heaven: The Life of Lydia Maria Child*
    (Philadelphia, 1964), pp. 19–26, 98.

81 Burton Bledstein, in *The Culture of Professionalism: The Middle Class and the*

Development of Higher Education in America (New York, 1976), p. 13, claims that the first American dictionary definition of "middle class" appeared in *The Century Dictionary* in 1889.

82 This figure was calculated from the generally consistent tabulations of average annual incomes in Long, *Wages and Earnings in the United States* p. 68, and Albert Rees, *Real Wages in Manufacturing, 1890–1914* (Princeton, 1961), p. 33. Weekly wage rates in a number of trades were actually significantly higher than the weekly compensation rates for low-paying clerical jobs, but manual workers suffered from significantly longer periods of unemployment. See Thernstrom, *Other Bostonians*, p. 300, and, for a more general discussion, Alexander Keyssar, *Out of Work: The First Century of Unemployment in Massachusetts* (Cambridge, 1986), esp. pp. 75, 308–11. Long's and Rees's tabulations of annual incomes are adjusted for unemployment patterns.

83 Keyssar, *Out of Work*, p. 45. The most revealing near-contemporary survey of workers' incomes, budgets, and life-styles, Margaret F. Byington's *Homestead: The Households of a Mill Town* (Pittsburgh, 1910), establishes this point even for steadily employed steelworkers of the next decade.

84 Kocka, *White Collar Workers*, p. 85. An excellent recent study emphasizing the working-class backgrounds of many clerical workers in this period is Ileen A. DeVault, "Sons and Daughters of Labor: Class and Clerical Work in Pittsburgh, 1870s–1910s" (Ph.D. dissertation, Yale University, 1985).

85 On the numbers of male and female office workers, see the tabulations in Davies, *Woman's Place*, table 1. Salesclerks of both sexes are tabulated in Kocka, *White Collar Workers*, p. 67.

86 DeVault, "Sons and Daughters of Labor," pp. 46–8, 75–6, and Davies, *Woman's Place*, pp. 55–9, make this point most directly.

87 A 1902 survey in Boston revealed an average male clerical salary of $9.76 per week, while a Pittsburgh survey in 1900 reported the slightly higher figure of $11. See Kocka, *White Collar Workers*, p. 77, and DeVault, "Sons and Daughters of Labor," p. 122. Curiously, the disparity between average nonmanual and manual incomes for males is somewhat *greater* in the manufacturing census of 1900 than it is in the manufacturing census of 1880, despite the elimination of proprietors from the nonmanual category in the later census. In 1900, corporate officers averaged $2,035; general superintendents, managers, and clerks averaged $957; and wage earners averaged $491. Among women who worked in manufacturing firms, the ratio between nonmanual incomes ($415) and manual incomes ($273) was somewhat smaller than it was among men. See *Census Reports*, pp. civ, cxv, 3, 59.

88 Srole, "A Position That God Has Not Particularly Assigned to Men," p. 148.

89 Kocka, *White Collar Workers*, p. 77. Very similar ranges were reported in Pittsburgh, according to DeVault, who notes: "Beginning their careers at fairly low wages, men planned on eventually earning $30 to $40 a week" ("Sons and Daughters of Labor," pp. 122–3).

90 *Report on the Population of the United States at the Eleventh Census: 1890*
(Washington, D.C., 1897), part 2, p. ci; *Twelfth Census of the United States,
Taken in the Year 1900: Population* (Washington, D.C., 1902), part 2,
pp. 505–7; Kocka, *White Collar Workers*, p. 67; Davies, *Woman's Place*, table
1. Middle-level nonmanual employees were not necessarily promoted
from the ranks of clerical workers but could be recruited from a large
pool of independent businessmen. Hence, clerical opportunities may not
have been as great as these ratios suggest.

91 Reed Ueda, *Avenues to Adulthood: The Origins of the High School and Social
Mobility in an American Suburb* (Cambridge, 1987); Joel Perlmann, "Cur-
riculum and Tracking in the Transformation of the American High School:
Providence, Rhode Island, 1880–1930," *Journal of Social History* 19 (1985):
29–55; Perlmann, "Who Stayed in School? Social Structure and Academic
Achievement in the Determination of Enrollment Patterns, Providence,
Rhode Island, 1880–1925," *Journal of American History* 72 (1985): 588–614;
Perlmann, "After Leaving School: The Jobs of Young People in Providence, R.I., 1880–1915," in Ronald K. Goodenow and Diane Ravitch,
eds., *Schools in Cities: Consensus and Conflict in American Educational History*
(New York, 1983), pp. 3–43. Ueda's data (pertaining to high school students in Somerville, Massachusetts) suggest a somewhat slower convergence than do Perlmann's. Ueda concludes that the expanding system
of secondary education in America continued to provide only a "small
window of opportunity" for children born into the working class, and
that the turn-of-the-century high school still did more to define than to
confuse "the experiential boundaries separating the middle class from
the industrial working class" (pp. 221, 117). Similarly, Mark J. Stern, in
Society and Family Strategy: Erie County, New York, 1850–1920 (Albany,
N.Y., 1987), finds that in and around Buffalo, school attendance among
fifteen- to nineteen-year-old boys from working-class families began to
rise significantly only after the turn of the century (p. 101). Stern concludes that "in 1900, high school remained a business-class phenomenon" (p. 112). All these recent studies qualify in differing degrees Joseph
F. Kett's argument, in *Rites of Passage: Adolescence in America, 1790 to the
Present* (New York, 1977), that "the closing decades of the 19th century
saw the emergence of a sharp difference between the opportunities available to middle-class and working-class youth" (p. 151), but they do not
contradict Kett's sense that this difference was significant at the turn of
the century.

92 DeVault, "Sons and Daughters of Labor," p. 341.

93 Kocka, *White Collar Workers*, p. 133. On the founding and functioning of
the RCIPA, see pp. 55–63, 68–76.

94 Ibid., pp. 84–92.

95 Ibid., pp. 86–8. DeVault also observes that male clerks of all types (but
not female clerks) identified with management and looked forward to
promotion (DeVault, "Sons and Daughters of Labor," p. 78). Susan Porter Benson has argued that female department store clerks accepted training programs that gave them "a veneer of middle-class or elite culture,"

and were attracted to jobs that commanded more respect from supervisors than did most forms of blue-collar work, but that they maintained a strong sense of the class difference that separated them from management. See Benson, "'The Customers Ain't God': The Work Culture of Department-Store Saleswomen, 1890–1940," in Michael H. Frisch and Daniel J. Walkowitz, eds., *Working-Class America: Essays on Labor, Community, and American Society* (Urbana, Ill., 1983), pp. 188–91.

96   Kocka, *White Collar Workers*, pp. 131–3; Aron, *Ladies and Gentlemen of the Civil Service*.

97   Aron, *Ladies and Gentlemen of the Civil Service*, p. 187.

98   Griffen and Griffen, *Natives and Newcomers*, p. 132.

99   *Report on Population of the United States at the Eleventh Census*, p. 710. See also Glassberg, "Work, Wages, and the Cost of Living," p. 51.

100   Kocka, *White Collar Workers*, pp. 136–7.

101   Daniel J. Walkowitz, *Worker City, Company Town: Iron and Cotton-Worker Protest in Troy and Cohoes, New York, 1855–84* (Urbana, Ill., 1978), p. 164.

102   Cleveland Amory, *Who Killed Society?* (New York, 1960).

103   Steven Ross, personal communication, March 28, 1986.

104   It may be thought peculiar that I have not analyzed these terms as I did "middle class" and its variations. I did not do so because "white collar" and "blue collar" did not appear in any of the sources I examined from the period that represents the focus of my study. These were late-nineteenth- and twentieth-century terms, which appeared (should we be surprised?) just as the social distinctions between nonmanual and manual workers were becoming subject to forces that would later cause them to erode.

Epilogue. City, town, village, farm

1   U.S. Bureau of the Census, *Historical Statistics of the United States: Colonial Times to 1970, Bicentennial Edition, Part 2* (Washington, D.C., 1975), pp. 11–2; *Twelfth Census of the United States, Taken in the Year 1900: Population* (Washington, D.C., 1902), p. 432. The most complete and satisfying statistical analysis of nineteenth-century urbanization, in the United States and elsewhere, remains Adna Ferrin Weber, *The Growth of Cities in the Nineteenth Century: A Study in Statistics* (New York, 1899).

2   Paul G. Faler, *Mechanics and Manufacturers in the Early Industrial Revolution: Lynn, Massachusetts, 1780–1860* (Albany, N.Y., 1981), p. 17.

3   Faler's discussion of the origins of Lynn's shoe manufacturers, and of the evolution of separate class identities among manufacturers and workers, differs in important respects from Alan Dawley's discussion in *Class and Community: The Industrial Revolution in Lynn* (Cambridge, Mass., 1976). Faler's, in my opinion, is the more convincing.

4   Faler, *Mechanics and Manufacturers*, p. 233.

5   On residential segregation by class in Lynn, see ibid., pp. 168, 189; on institutions, see pp. 195–203.

6   Ibid., pp. 76, 166–7.

7 On the transformation of deferential into class relations between workers
   and manufacturers, see ibid., pp. 177–80; on the population of Lynn, see
   p. 148.
8 Ibid., p. 196.
9 Ibid., p. 76.
10 See Susan E. Hirsch, *Roots of the American Working Class: The Industrialization of Crafts in Newark, 1800–1860* (Philadelphia, 1978), p. 10.
11 Mary P. Ryan, *Cradle of the Middle Class: The Family in Oneida County, New
   York, 1790–1865* (Cambridge, 1981), p. xiii.
12 Ibid., pp. 105–45, 165–85. Ryan's analysis is unique in stressing the *temporary* significance of voluntary association as a class-forming phenomenon, the period of significant association among the middle class in
   Utica being confined to the 1830s and 1840s, and forming one phase of
   a cycle of development from the patriarchal family, to the extrafamilial
   organizational experience, and back again to the now privatized and
   romanticized family. This sequence appears overly schematic to me, and
   the idea of a "return" from voluntary associations to the family is contradicted by other studies that show no abatement in organizational
   participation. Ryan's focus is on particular associations, especially reform
   societies, that rose and fell with political and other tides. Had she studied
   the whole range of associations in Utica – lodges, fire companies, baseball
   clubs, and the like – she too might have found a longer-lasting associational experience. In casting doubt on this cyclical interpretation, however, I do not question the fundamental relation between voluntary
   participation, the specific family strategies that Ryan describes, and
   middle-class formation. Ryan's analysis stands without the notion of a
   "return" to the family.
13 Ibid., p. 82.
14 Ibid., p. 143.
15 Ibid., pp. 106–7.
16 Stuart M. Blumin, *The Urban Threshold: Growth and Change in a Nineteenth-
   Century American Community* (Chicago, 1976), pp. 112–14. This description overstates somewhat the simplicity, but not the extent, of residential
   differentiation in Kingston. Near the center of Rondout, the younger of
   the two adjoining villages, was a neighborhood of unskilled workers on
   the nearby Delaware & Hudson Canal Company dock.
17 Ibid., pp. 117–18.
18 See the summary of these connections, ibid., pp. 3–5, and various details
   throughout the book. *Godey's Lady's Book* was published in Philadelphia,
   not New York, and it should be recognized that the residents of one
   urban region were not foreclosed from interacting with the metropolis
   of another. Nor, as Allan R. Pred has demonstrated in *Urban Growth and
   the Circulation of Information: The United States System of Cities, 1790–1840*
   (Cambridge, Mass., 1973), were extralocal relationships always hierarchical in the way this "central place" discussion suggests. Smaller cities
   interacted with other small cities, and could give as well as take in their
   interactions with larger places. This said, it was still the case that Kingston

and other New York State communities were in a region dominated by New York City.

19   See, for example, George G. Foster, *New York in Slices: By an Experienced Carver* . . . (New York, 1849), p. 63.

20   Blumin, *Urban Threshold*, pp. 193–4, 198, briefly describes the interesting if tragic career of Kingston's Judge James C. Forsyth, whose attempts to keep up with the expensive life-style of the metropolitan upper class drove him to large-scale embezzlement, fraud, and, ultimately, flight.

21   Don Harrison Doyle, *The Social Order of a Frontier Community: Jacksonville, Illinois, 1825–70* (Urbana, Ill., 1978). On the founding and early growth of Jacksonville, and on population persistence, see pp. 19–20, 261–2. On the idea of a majority of transient strangers, see p. 92.

22   Ibid., pp. 262, 269–71.

23   See, for example, ibid., p. 178.

24   Ibid., pp. 102, 225.

25   Ibid., p. 255.

26   Lewis Atherton, *Main Street on the Middle Border* (Bloomington, Ind., 1954). Jacksonville had grown to 9,200 in 1870, a two-thirds increase over its 1860 population, and then grew much more gradually to 15,000 by the end of the century. See *Statistics of the Population of the United States at the Tenth Census* (Washington, D.C., 1883), p. 140; *Twelfth Census of the United States, Taken in the Year 1900: Population* (Washington, D.C., 1902), p. 127.

27   John Mack Faragher, "Open-Country Community: Sugar Creek, Illinois, 1820–1850," in Steven Hahn and Jonathan Prude, eds., *The Countryside in the Age of Capitalist Transformation: Essays in the Social History of Rural America* (Chapel Hill, 1985), pp. 233–58. The distinction between tenancy and land ownership did, however, affect community life through striking differentials of out-migration. Landowning farmers were much more likely than tenants to remain in the community and to develop ties of kinship and friendship there.

28   Hal S. Barron, *Those Who Stayed Behind: Rural Society in Nineteenth-Century New England* (Cambridge, 1984), e.g., pp. 134–5.

29   Ibid., pp. 22–3.

30   Ibid., pp. 23–6.

31   Ibid., chaps. 4 and 5.

32   Ibid., chap. 6.

33   Ibid., p. xii. See also pp. 11–15, 76–7, 111, 128–31.

34   Ibid., p. 33.

35   Lydia Maria Child to Sarah Blake (Sturgis) Shaw, August 25, 1877, microfilm (Millwood, N.Y., 1979).

36   An excellent economic and political analysis that suggests a different sort of social order is Steven Hahn, *The Roots of Southern Populism: Yeoman Farmers and the Transformation of the Georgia Upcountry, 1850–1890* (New York, 1983). Hahn and Prude, *The Countryside in the Age of Capitalist Transformation*, contains summary articles by both Hahn and Barron, plus several other pertinent essays.

Bibliography

The following is a nearly complete list of the primary and secondary sources on which this study is based. To conserve space, however, I have excluded approximately one hundred eighteenth-century almanacs and several hundred city directories. Some of these excluded items are cited in the notes.

Primary sources

Unpublished

Baker Library, Harvard University Graduate School of Business Administration, Boston
    R. G. Dun & Co. Collection, credit ledgers for Boston, New York City, and Philadelphia
Grand Lodge, Free and Accepted Masons of Pennsylvania, Philadelphia
    Register of Members, vols. 2–1, 2–2, 1818–1855
Historical Society of Pennsylvania, Philadelphia
    American Society Held at Philadelphia for Promoting Useful Knowledge, rules and statutes, ca. 1790
    The Amphion, minute book, 1849–1868
    Delaware Fire Company, minutes, 1782–1785, membership roll, 1824, 1858–1871
    Dohan and Taitt letter book, 1859–1860
    David Evans daybook, 3 vols., 1774–1812
    Falcon Barge Club of Philadelphia, constitution and membership list, 1834–1839
    William Forbes account book, 1768–1780
    Fourth Ward Spring Garden American Association, constitution and by-laws, 1844
    Franklin Literary Union of Philadelphia, minute book, 1859–1862
    Joseph Graisbury ledger, 1763–1773
    Joshua Haines account book, 1796
    A. Howell account book, 1791–1799
    Irving Literary Institute, minute book, 1843–1845

William Lawrence daybook, 1769–1798, account book, 1804–1812

Abraham Mitchell & Co. daybook, 1844–1858

Minutes of the Transactions of the Taylors Company of Philadelphia Instituted and Begun the 20th day of August, 1771

Thomas Morgan ledger, 1771–1803

George Morrison account book, 1767–1779

Pennsylvania Fire Company, fire and meeting roll, 1806–1847

Philadelphia City Anti-Slavery Society, constitution and list of members, 1838

Philadelphia Cricket Club, minutes, 1854–64

Philadelphia Hose Company, constitution and membership roll, 1834–1870

Philadelphia Literary and Billiard Association, constitution and membership list, ca. 1857

Philadelphia Quoit Club, minute book, 1829–1855

Reliance Fire Company, roll book, 1820–1871

The Round Table, constitution and minutes, 1839–1841

United States Hose Company, membership roll, 1848

Gotlieb Vollmer ledger, 1860–1861

Washington Fire Company, constitution, by-laws, and membership roll, 1828

Massachusetts Historical Society, Boston

Samuel G. Damon diary, 1840

Ambrose Davenport diary, 1839–1862

C. A. Grinnell journal, 1837

Henry Pierce diary, 1845, 1870

Nathan Webb diary, 1788–1791

National Museum of American History, Smithsonian Institution, Washington

Warshaw Collection of Business Americana

New-York Historical Society, New York City

Garret Abeel daybook, 1774–1776

Charles D. Bliven daybook, 1834–1842

Elisha Blossom, Jr., daybook, 1811–1818

Brewster & Co., Invoices and Sales, 1856–1862

Matthias Bruen account book, 1834–1844

Abner Gilbert & Co. daybook, 1845–1846

William Gowans letters and miscellaneous papers, 1826–1870

Robert McCoskry Graham diary, 1843–1849

William Hoffman diary, 1847–1850

Samuel Lyman Munson diary, 1861–1862

Calvin Pollard diary, 1841–1842

George Stevens Schermerhorn daybook, 1835–1839

John Andrew Wolfer account book, 1844

New York Public Library, New York City

New York City Temperance Society, executive committee minutes, 1829–1842

Presbyterian Historical Society, Philadelphia
  First Presbyterian Church of Kensington [Philadelphia], roll of members,
    1814–1948
  First Presbyterian Church of Philadelphia, list of communicants, 1830
  First Presbyterian Church of Southwark [Philadelphia], records of com-
    municants, baptisms, and marriages, 1827–1848
  Fourth Presbyterian Church of Philadelphia, register, 1800–1835; 1843–
    1878, vol. 3
  Tenth Presbyterian Church of Philadelphia, register, 1830–1880, vol. 1
  Third Presbyterian Church of Philadelphia, communicants, 1771–1823
    register of communicants, 1831–1868
Microfilm
  The Collected Correspondence of Lydia Maria Child. Millwood,
    N.Y.,1979
  Eighth U.S. Census, manuscript population schedules, Philadelphia
  Federal Direct Tax of 1798, manuscript assessment lists, Philadelphia
  Register of Wills, Philadelphia County, 1861
  Tenth U.S. Census, manuscript population schedules, Philadelphia

Published

Newspapers

Aurora General Advertiser, Philadelphia, 1796
Claypoole's American Daily Advertiser, Philadelphia, 1798
The Crystal Fount, New York, 1842–1843
Dunlap and Claypoole's American Daily Advertiser, Philadelphia, 1794–1796
General Advertiser, Philadelphia, 1792, 1794
The Mechanic's Free Press. A Journal of Practical and Useful Knowledge, Phila-
    delphia, 1828–1831
New-York Journal; or the General Advertiser, New York, 1767–1768, 1770, 1774
New York Times, New York, 1853, 1866, 1878
New York Tribune, New York, 1851, 1855
Pennsylvania Evening Post, Philadelphia, 1776
Pennsylvania Packet, Philadelphia, 1770–1790
Public Ledger, Philadelphia, 1858, 1860
Rivington's New-York Gazetteer, New York, 1774
Royal Gazette, New York, 1778, 1782
Temperance Recorder, Albany, 1833–1836
The Working Man's Advocate, New York, 1844–1845

Magazines

The American Penny Magazine and Family Newspaper, 1845–1846
Ballou's Pictorial Drawing Room Companion, 1855
The Century, 1881–1890
Frank Leslie's Illustrated Newspaper, 1857

Gleason's Pictorial Drawing Room Companion, 1852–1854
Harper's New Monthly Magazine, 1850–1890
Hunt's Merchants' Magazine and Commercial Review, 1839–1870
The Illustrated News, 1853
Scientific American, 1876
Scribner's Magazine, 1887
Scribner's Monthly, an Illustrated Magazine for the People, 1871–1881

U.S. census publications

Census Reports. Volume VII. Manufactures: Part I: United States by Industries.
     Washington, D.C., 1902.
A Compendium of the Ninth Census. . . . Washington, D.C., 1872.
Historical Statistics of the United States: Colonial Times to 1970, Bicentennial Edi-
     tion. Washington, D.C., 1975.
Manufactures of the United States in 1860. . . . Washington, D.C., 1865.
Ninth Census – Volume I: Statistics of the Population of the United States. . . .
     Washington, D.C., 1872.
Population of the United States in 1860. . . . Washington, D.C., 1864.
Report on Manufacturing Industries in the United States at the Eleventh Census:
     1890. Part I. Totals for States and Industries. Washington, D.C., 1895.
Report on Population of the United States at the Eleventh Census: 1890. Wash-
     ington, D.C., 1897.
The Seventh Census of the United States: 1850. . . . Washington, D.C., 1853.
Statistics of the Population of the United States at the Tenth Census. Washing-
     ton, D.C., 1883.
Statistics of the United States . . . in 1860. . . . Washington, D.C., 1866.
Twelfth Census of the United States, Taken in the Year 1900: Population. Wash-
     ington, D.C., 1902.

Other publications

Alexander, James W. *The American Mechanic and Working-Man*, 2 vols. New
     York and Philadelphia, 1847.
  "The Merchant's Clerk Cheered and Counselled," in *The Man of Business,*
     Considered in His Various Relations. New York, 1857.
The American Temperance Almanac, for . . . 1835. Albany, N.Y., 1835.
Appleton, Nathan. *Labor, Its Relations in Europe and the United States Com-*
     pared. Boston, 1844.
Bartlett, John Russell. *Dictionary of Americanisms: A Glossary of Words and*
     Phrases Usually Regarded as Peculiar to the United States. New York, 1848.
     2d ed., Boston, 1859.
Beharrell, the Reverend Thomas G. *The Brotherhood; Being a Presentation of*
     the Principles, of Odd-Fellowship. . . . Cincinnati, 1861.
Bethune, George W. *The Substance of an Address in Favor of Temperance Socie-*
     ties. Utica, N.Y., 1833.
[Bishop, Isabella Lucy Bird]. *The Englishwoman in America.* London, 1856.

Bishop, J. Leander. *A History of Manufactures from 1608 to 1860....* Philadelphia, 1864.

The Book of Trades. New York, 1836.

The Book of Trades, or Library of the Useful Arts. 3 vols. London, 1806; Philadelphia, 1807.

The Book of Trades and Professions: or, Familiar Objects Described. Philadelphia and New York, 1851.

A Book of Trades for Ingenious Boys. Providence, 1845.

Brissot de Warville, J. P. *New Travels in the United States of America.* Edited by Durand Echeverria. Cambridge, Mass., 1964.

Bristed, Charles Astor, "The English Language in America," in *Cambridge Essays, Contributed by Members of the University*, pp. 57–78. London, 1855.

The Upper Ten Thousand: Sketches of American Society. New York, 1852.

Bristol, the Reverend D. W. *The Odd Fellow's Amulet....* Auburn, N.Y., 1851.

The British Mechanic's and Labourer's Handbook and True Guide to the United States. London, 1840.

Browne, Junius Henri. *The Great Metropolis: A Mirror of New York.* Hartford, 1869.

"The Burghers of New Amsterdam and the Freemen of New York, 1675–1866," in *Collections of the New-York Historical Society for the Year 1885*. New York, 1886.

[Burn, James Dawson]. *Three Years Among the Working-Classes in the United States During the War.* London, 1865.

Burnaby, the Reverend Andrew. *Travels Through the Middle Settlements in North America in the Years 1759 and 1760; with Observations upon the State of the Colonies.* 3d ed. London, 1798.

Carey, M[athew]. *Appeal to the Wealthy of the Land.* Philadelphia, 1833.

A Short Account of the Malignant Fever, Lately Prevalent in Philadelphia.... Philadelphia, 1793.

Census of the State of New York for 1855.... Albany, N.Y., 1857.

The Charter, Bye-Laws, and Names of the Members of the New-York Society Library.... New York, 1793.

Chastellux, Marquis de. *Travels in North America in the Years 1780, 1781, and 1782.* 2 vols. Translated by Howard C. Rice, Jr. Chapel Hill, 1963.

Child, L[ydia] Maria. *Letters from New York.* New York and Boston, 1843.

Letters from New York: Second Series. London, 1845.

"The Colden Papers," in *Collections of the New-York Historical Society for the Year 1877*. New York, 1878.

"The Colden Papers," in *Collections of the New-York Historical Society for the Year 1919*. New York, 1920.

Constitution and By-Laws of Geneva Division No. 29, of the Sons of Temperance, of the State of New York. Geneva, N.Y., 1845.

Constitution and By-Laws of the Washington Division, No. 1, of the Sons of Temperance, of the State of Massachusetts. Boston, 1844.

Cooper, James Fenimore. *The American Democrat.* Cooperstown, N.Y., 1838; New York, 1931.

Notions of the Americans: Picked up by a Travelling Bachelor. 2 vols. London, 1828.

Cooper, Joseph T. *Odd-Fellowship Examined in the Light of Scripture and Reason.* Philadelphia, 1854.

Curtis, George William. *The Potiphar Papers.* New York, 1856.

Degree Book of the Independent Order of Good Templars. . . . Ithaca, N.Y., 1854.

Digest of the Laws of the Independent Order of Odd-Fellows. . . . n.p., 1864.

Eighth Annual Report of the New-York City Temperance Society. New York, 1837.

Everett, Henry L. *What Shall I Learn? or, The Young Men's Business Guide.* Philadelphia, 1892.

Fairfield, Francis Gerry. *The Clubs of New York.* . . . New York, 1873.

Ferris, Isaac. "Men of Business: Their Home Responsibilities," in *The Man of Business, Considered in His Various Relations.* New York, 1857.

Field, M. *City Architecture; or, Designs for Dwelling Houses, Stores, Hotels, etc.* . . . New York, 1853.

Fifth Report of the American Temperance Society. . . . Boston, 1832.

First Annual Report of the Executive Committee of the American Society for the Promotion of Temperance. Andover, Mass., 1828.

First Annual Report of the New York City Temperance Society. . . . New York, 1830.

Foster, George G. *Celio: or, New York Above-Ground and Under-Ground.* New York, 1850.

Fifteen Minutes Around New York. New York, 1854.

New York by Gas-Light: With Here and There a Streak of Sunshine. New York, 1850.

New York in Slices: By an Experienced Carver. . . . New York, 1849.

New York Naked. New York, n.d.

Fourth Annual Report of the New-York City Temperance Society. New York, 1833.

Freedley, Edwin T. *Philadelphia and Its Manufactures.* . . . Philadelphia, 1858; 2d ed., Philadelphia, 1867.

[Frost, John]. *The Young Mechanic.* 2d ed., New York, 1843.

The Young Merchant. Philadelphia, 1839.

Garvan, Anthony N. B., et al., eds. *The Mutual Assurance Company Papers.* Vol. 1: *The Architectural Surveys, 1784–1794.* Philadelphia, 1976.

Gompers, Samuel. *Seventy Years of Life and Labor: An Autobiography.* 2 vols. New York, 1925.

Graydon, Alexander. *Memoirs of a Life, Chiefly Passed in Pennsylvania.* Harrisburg, 1811.

Grimké, Frederick. *Considerations upon the Nature and Tendency of Free Institutions.* Cincinnati, 1848.

Grosh, the Reverend Aaron B. *The Odd-Fellow's Manual.* . . . Philadelphia, 1868.

The Washingtonian Pocket Companion. . . . Utica, N.Y., 1845.

Gunn, Thomas Butler. *The Physiology of New York Boarding-Houses.* New York, 1857.

Haswell, Charles H. *Reminiscences of an Octogenarian of the City of New York (1816 to 1860)*. New York, 1896.

Hazen, Edward. *The Panorama of Professions and Trades; or Every Man's Book*. Philadelphia, 1836. 2d ed., *Popular Technology; or Professions and Trades*. 2 vols. New York, 1844.

Henkels, George J. *Household Economy*. Philadelphia, 1867.

Hubbard, N. T. *Autobiography of N. T. Hubbard, with Personal Reminiscences of New York City from 1798 to 1875*. New York, 1875.

Ingerman, Elizabeth A., ed. "Personal Experiences of an Old New York Cabinetmaker." *Antiques* 84 (1963): 576–80.

Jones, Alice Hanson. *American Colonial Wealth: Documents and Methods*. 3 vols. New York, 1977.

Lafever, Minard. *The Modern Builder's Guide*. New York, 1833; 1969.

Lambert, John. *Travels Through Canada and the United States of North America in the Years 1806, 1807, & 1808*. 2 vols. 2d ed., London, 1813.

List of Communicants in the First Presbyterian Church, Philadelphia. Philadelphia, 1855.

McCabe, James Dabney, Jr. [Edward Winslow Martin, pseud.]. *The Secrets of the Great City: A Work Descriptive of the Virtues and Vices, the Mysteries, Miseries, and Crimes of New York City*. Philadelphia, 1868. Reissued as: James Dabney McCabe, Jr. *Lights and Shadows of New York City; or the Sights and Sensations of the Great City*. . . . Philadelphia, 1872.

Mackey, Albert G., M.D. *The Book of the Chapter*. . . . New York, 1858.
  The Mystic Tie; or, Facts and Opinions, Illustrative of the Character and Tendency of Freemasonry. New York, 1856.

Mease, James, M.D. *The Picture of Philadelphia*. . . . Philadelphia, 1811.

"Memorial of the First Company of Philadelphia Militia Artillery, 1779," in *Pennsylvania Archives*, 1st ser., vol. 7, pp. 392–5. Philadelphia, 1853.

"The Middle Classes." *Journal of Health* 1 (1830): 357–8.

Mills, B. H. *The Temperance Manual: Containing a History of the Various Temperance Orders*. . . . Upper Alton, Ill., and Boston, 1864.

The Miraculous Power of Clothes, and Dignity of the Taylors: Being an Essay on the Words, Clothes Make Men. Philadelphia, 1772.

O'Callaghan, E. B., ed. *Documents Relative to the Colonial History of the State of New-York*. . . . Vol. 7. Albany, N.Y., 1856.

"Our First Men": A Calendar of Wealth, Fashion and Gentility. . . . Boston, 1846.

Perkins, Frederick B. "Social and Domestic Life," in *Eighty Years' Progress of the United States* . . . vol. 1. New York, 1861.

[Prime, Samuel I]. *Life in New York*. New York, 1851.

Pulszky, Francis, and Pulszky, Theresa. *White, Red, Black: Sketches of Society in the United States* . . . 3 vols. London, 1853.

Reid, H[ugo]. *Sketches in North America*. . . . London, 1861.

Report of the Council of Hygiene and Public Health of the Citizens Association of New York upon the Sanitary Condition of the City. New York, 1865.

Ritter, Abraham. *Philadelphia and Her Merchants*. . . . Philadelphia, 1860.

Rochefoucault, Duke de la. *Travels through the United States of North America
. . . in the Years 1795, 1796, and 1797 . . .* 2 vols. London, 1799.

Shattuck, Lemuel. *Report to the Committee of the City Council Appointed to Obtain the Census of Boston for the Year 1845.* . . . Boston, 1846.

Simonds, Thomas C. *History of South Boston.* Boston, 1857.

Sixth Annual Report of the New-York City Temperance Society. New York, 1835.

Smith, Matthew Hale. *Sunshine and Shadow in New York.* Hartford, 1868.

Smyth, J.F.D. *A Tour in the United States of America . . .* 2 vols. London,
1784.

*Statistics of Philadelphia: Comprehending a Concise View of all the Public Institu-
tions and Fire Engine and Hose Companies of the City and County of Philadelphia on the First of January, 1842.* Philadelphia, 1842.

Stearns, Jonathan F. "Men of Business: Their Intellectual Culture," in *The
Man of Business, Considered in His Various Relations.* New York, 1857.

Strickland, William. *Journal of a Tour in the United States of America, 1794–
1795. Collections of the New-York Historical Society for the Year 1950.* New
York, 1971.

Sumner, William Graham. *What Social Classes Owe to Each Other.* New York,
1883.

Teitelman, S. Robert, ed. *Birch's Views of Philadelphia: A Reduced Facsimile of
"The City of Philadelphia . . . As it Appeared in the Year 1800."* Philadelphia, 1982.

The Temperance Almanac, for . . . 1836. Albany, N.Y., 1836.

Third Annual Report of the American Anti-Slavery Society. . . . New York, 1836.

*To the Inhabitants of Pennsylvania in General, and Particularly Those of the City
and Neighbourhood of Philadelphia.* Philadelphia, 1779.

To the Inhabitants of the City of Philadelphia, and Parts Adjacent. Philadelphia,
1772.

Tocqueville, Alexis de. *Democracy in America.* Edited by J. P. Mayer. Garden City, N.Y., 1969.

Todd, John. "Men of Business: Their Position, Influence, and Duties," in
The Man of Business, Considered in His Various Relations. New York,
1857.

Trollope, Frances. *Domestic Manners of the Americans.* London, 1832; New
York, 1949.

U.S. Department of Labor, Bureau of Labor Statistics. *History of Wages in
the United States From Colonial Times to 1928.* Washington, D.C., 1929.

Watson, John Fanning. *Annals of Philadelphia and Pennsylvania, in the Olden
Time . . .* 2 vols. Philadelphia, 1845.

Weld, Isaac, Jun. *Travels Through the States of North America . . . During the
Years 1795, 1796, and 1797.* 2 vols. 4th ed., London, 1807.

Wheeler, Gervase. *Homes for the People, in Suburb and Country.* . . . New
York, 1867.

Whitman, Walt. *Complete Poetry and Selected Prose.* Boston, 1959.

  *I Sit and Look Out: Editorials from the Brooklyn Daily Times, by Walt Whit-
man.* Selected and edited by Emory Holloway and Vernolian Schwarz.
New York, 1932.

Wilson, Thomas. *Picture of Philadelphia, for 1824.* . . . Philadelphia,1823.

[Winslow, Stephen Noyes]. *Biographies of Successful Philadelphia Merchants.* Philadelphia, 1864.

Wright, Louis B., and Tinling, Marion, eds. *Quebec to Carolina in 1785–1786: Being the Travel Diary and Observations of Robert Hunter, Jr., a Young Merchant of London.* San Marino, Calif., 1943.

Yates, the Reverend John A. *The Temperance Society, A National Institution for Decision of Character: An Address.* Schenectady, N.Y., 1834.

Secondary sources

Adams, Donald R., Jr. "Earnings and Savings in the Early 19th Century." *Explorations in Economic History* 17 (1980): 118–34.

"The Standard of Living During American Industrialization: Evidence From the Brandywine Region, 1800–1860." *Journal of Economic History* 42 (1982): 903–17.

"Wage Rates in the Early National Period: Philadelphia, 1785–1830." *Journal of Economic History* 28 (1968): 404–26.

Adelman, Melvin L. *A Sporting Time: New York City and the Rise of Modern Athletics, 1820–70.* Chicago, 1986.

Albion, Robert Greenhalgh. *The Rise of New York Port: [1815–1860].* New York, 1939.

Alexander, John K. *Render Them Submissive: Responses to Poverty in Philadelphia, 1760–1800.* Amherst, Mass., 1980.

Alexander, Robert L. "Baltimore Row Houses of the Early Nineteenth Century." *American Studies* 16 (1975): 65–76.

Alexander, Ruth M. " 'We Are Engaged as a Band of Sisters': The Meaning of Domesticity in the Washingtonian Temperance Movement, 1840–1850." *Journal of American History* 75 (1988): 763–85.

Appleby, Joyce. "The Social Origins of American Revolutionary Ideology." *Journal of American History* 64 (1978): 935–58.

Arden, Eugene. "The Evil City in American Fiction." *New York History* 35 (1954): 259–79.

Arky, Louis H. "The Mechanics' Union of Trade Associations and the Formation of the Philadelphia Workingmen's Movement." *Pennsylvania Magazine of History and Biography* 76 (1952): 142–76.

Aron, Cindy Sondik. *Ladies and Gentlemen of the Civil Service: Middle-Class Workers in Victorian America.* New York, 1987.

Atherton, Lewis. *Main Street on the Middle Border.* Bloomington, Ind., 1954.

Baer, Helene G. *The Heart Is Like Heaven: The Life of Lydia Maria Child.* Philadelphia, 1964.

Bailyn, Bernard. "The Index and Commentaries of Harbottle Dorr." *Proceedings of the Massachusetts Historical Society* 85 (1973): 21–35.

Baltzell, E. Digby. *Philadelphia Gentlemen: The Making of a National Upper Class.* Glencoe, Ill., 1958.

The Protestant Establishment: Aristocracy and Caste in America. New York, 1964.

Puritan Boston and Quaker Philadelphia: Two Protestant Ethics and the Spirit of Class Authority and Leadership. New York, 1979.

Banner, Lois W. "Religious Benevolence as Social Control: A Critique of an Interpretation." *Journal of American History* 60 (1973): 23–41.

Barron, Hal S. *Those Who Stayed Behind: Rural Society in Nineteenth-Century New England.* Cambridge, 1984.

Barth, Gunther. *City People: The Rise of Modern City Culture in Nineteenth-Century America.* New York, 1980.

Batterberry, Michael, and Batterberry, Ariane. *On the Town in New York: A History of Eating, Drinking and Entertainments from 1776 to the Present.* New York, 1973.

Baumann, Roland M. "Philadelphia's Manufacturers and the Excise Taxes of 1794: The Forging of the Jeffersonian Coalition." *Pennsylvania Magazine of History and Biography* 106 (1982): 3–39.

Behagg, Clive. "Secrecy, Ritual and Folk Violence: The Opacity of the Workplace in the First Half of the Nineteenth Century," in Robert D. Storch, ed., *Popular Culture and Custom in Nineteenth-Century England,* pp. 154–79. London, 1982.

Bell, Whitfield J. "Some Aspects of the Social History of Pennsylvania, 1760–1790." *Pennsylvania Magazine of History and Biography* 62 (1938): 281–308.

Benson, Lee. *The Concept of Jacksonian Democracy: New York as a Test Case.* Princeton, 1961.

    "Group Cohesion and Social and Ideological Conflict: A Critique of Some Marxian and Tocquevillian Theories." *American Behavioral Scientist* 16 (1973): 741–67.

    "Philadelphia's Elites and Economic Development: Quasi-Public Innovation During the First American Organizational Revolution, 1825–1861." *Working Papers from the Regional Economic History Research Center* 2 (1978): 25–53.

Benson, Susan Porter. "Business Heads and Sympathizing Hearts: The Women of the Providence Employment Society, 1837–1858." *Journal of Social History* 12 (1978): 302–12.

    " 'The Customers Ain't God': The Work Culture of Department-Store Saleswomen, 1890–1940," in Michael H. Frisch and Daniel J. Walkowitz, eds., *Working-Class America: Essays on Labor, Community, and American Society,* pp. 185–211. Urbana, Ill., 1983.

Berg, Harry D. "The Organization of Business in Colonial Philadelphia." *Pennsylvania History* 10 (1943): 157–77.

Berlin, Isaiah. *Karl Marx: His Life and Environment.* 4th ed., New York, 1978.

Bernard, Richard M. "A Portrait of Baltimore in 1800: Economic and Occupational Patterns in an Early American City." *Maryland Historical Magazine* 69 (1974): 341–60.

Bernstein, Leonard. "The Working People of Philadelphia From Colonial Times to the General Strike of 1835." *Pennsylvania Magazine of History and Biography* 74 (1950): 322–39.

Berrol, Selma. "Who Went to School in Mid-Nineteenth Century New York? An Essay in the New Urban History," in Irwin Yellowitz, ed., *Essays in the History of New York City: A Memorial to Sidney Pomerantz,* pp. 43–60. Port Washington, N.Y., 1978.

Berthoff, Rowland. "Independence and Enterprise: Small Business in the American Dream," in Stuart W. Bruchey, ed., *Small Business in American Life,* pp. 28–48. New York, 1980.

"Peasants and Artisans, Puritans and Republicans: Personal Liberty and Communal Equality in American History." *Journal of American History* 69 (1982): 579–98.

Binford, Henry C. *The First Suburbs: Residential Communities on the Boston Periphery, 1815–1860.* Chicago, 1985.

Blackbourn, David. "The *Mittelstand* in German Society and Politics, 1871– 1914." *Social History* 4 (1977): 409–39.

Blackmar, Betsy, "Re-walking the 'Walking City': Housing and Property Relations in New York City, 1780–1840." *Radical History Review,* no. 21 (1979): 131–48.

Blake, Nelson Manfred. *Water for the Cities: A History of the Urban Water Supply Problem in the United States.* Syracuse, 1956.

Bledstein, Burton. *The Culture of Professionalism: The Middle Class and the Development of Higher Education in America.* New York, 1976.

Blewett, Mary H. "Work, Gender, and the Artisan Tradition in New England Shoemaking, 1780–1860." *Journal of Social History* 17 (1983): 221–48.

Blumin, Stuart M. "Black Coats to White Collars: Economic Change, Nonmanual Work, and the Social Structure of Industrializing America," in Stuart W. Bruchey, ed., *Small Business in American Life,* pp. 100–21. New York, 1980.

"Explaining the New Metropolis: Perception, Depiction, and Analysis in Mid-Nineteenth-Century New York City." *Journal of Urban History* 11 (1984): 9–38.

"The Historical Study of Vertical Mobility." *Historical Methods Newsletter* 1 (1968): 1–13.

"The Hypothesis of Middle-Class Formation in Nineteenth-Century America: A Critique and Some Proposals." *American Historical Review* 90 (1985): 299–338.

"Mobility and Change in Ante-Bellum Philadelphia," in Stephan Thernstrom and Richard Sennett, eds., *Nineteenth-Century Cities: Essays in the New Urban History,* pp. 165–208. New Haven, 1969.

"Mobility in a Nineteenth-Century City: Philadelphia, 1820–1860." Ph.D. dissertation, University of Pennsylvania, 1968.

The Urban Threshold: Growth and Change in a Nineteenth-Century American Community. Chicago, 1976.

Bode, Carl. *The American Lyceum: Town Meeting of the Mind.* Carbondale, Ill., 1956.

Bodo, John R. *The Protestant Clergy and Public Issues, 1812–1848.* Princeton, 1954.

Bolton, G. C. "The Idea of a Colonial Gentry." *Historical Studies* 13 (1968): 307–28.

Bonomi, Patricia U. *A Factious People: Politics and Society in Colonial New York*. New York, 1971.

Botein, Stephen. "'Meer Mechanics' and an Open Press: The Business and Political Strategies of Colonial American Printers." *Perspectives in American History* 9 (1975): 127–225.

Boyer, Lee R. "Lobster Backs, Liberty Boys, and Laborers in the Streets: New York's Golden Hill and Nassau Street Riots." *New-York Historical Society Quarterly* 57 (1973): 281–308.

Boyer, Paul. *Urban Masses and Moral Order in America: 1820–1920*. Cambridge, Mass., 1978.

Boylan, Anne M. "Women in Groups: An Analysis of Women's Benevolent Organizations in New York and Boston, 1797–1840." *Journal of American History* 71 (1984): 497–523.

Brady, Dorothy S. "Consumption and the Style of Life," in Lance E. Davis, Richard A. Easterlin, and William M. Parker, eds., *American Economic Growth: An Economist's History of the United States*, pp. 61–89. New York, 1972.

"Relative Prices in the Nineteenth Century." *Journal of Economic History* 26 (1964): 145–203.

Branca, Patricia. *Silent Sisterhood: Middle Class Women in the Victorian Home*. London, 1975.

Bridenbaugh, Carl. *Cities in Revolt: Urban Life in America, 1743–1776*. New York, 1955.

The Colonial Craftsman. New York, 1950.

Bridenbaugh, Carl, and Bridenbaugh, Jessica. *Rebels and Gentlemen: Philadelphia in the Age of Franklin*. New York, 1942.

Bridges, Amy. *A City in the Republic: Antebellum New York and the Origins of Machine Politics*. New York, 1984.

Bridges, William E. "Family Patterns and Social Values in America, 1825–1875." *American Quarterly* 17 (1965): 3–11.

Briggs, Asa. "The Language of 'Class' in Early Nineteenth-Century England," in Asa Briggs and John Saville, eds., *Essays in Labour History*. London, 1960.

"Middle-Class Consciousness in English Politics, 1780–1846." *Past and Present* 9 (1956): 65–74.

Brobeck, Stephen. "Revolutionary Change in Colonial Philadelphia: The Brief Life of the Proprietary Gentry." *William and Mary Quarterly*, 3d ser., 33 (1976): 410–34.

Browne, Gary Lawson. *Baltimore in the Nation: 1789–1861*. Chapel Hill, 1980.

"Business Innovation and Social Change: The Career of Alexander Brown After the War of 1812." *Maryland Historical Magazine* 69 (1974): 243–55.

Brownlee, W. Elliott. "Household Values, Women's Work and Economic Growth, 1800–1930." *Journal of Economic History* 3 (1979): 199–210.

Brunhouse, Robert L. *The Counter-Revolution in Pennsylvania, 1776–1790.* Harrisburg, 1942.

Brynn, Soeren Stewart. "Some Sports in Pittsburgh During the National Period, 1775–1860." *Western Pennsylvania Historical Magazine* 51 (1968): 345–63; 52 (1969): 57–79.

Buckley, Peter George. "To the Opera House: Culture and Society in New York City, 1820–1860." Ph.D. dissertation, State University of New York at Stony Brook, 1984.

Buel, Richard, Jr. "Democracy and the American Revolution: A Frame of Reference." *William and Mary Quarterly*, 3d ser., 21 (1964): 165–90.

Buettinger, Craig. "Economic Inequality in Early Chicago, 1849–1850." *Journal of Social History* 11 (1978): 413–18.

Bunkle, Phillida. "Sentimental Womanhood and Domestic Education, 1830–1870." *History of Education Quarterly* 14 (1974): 13–30.

Burke, Martin J. "The Conundrum of Class: Public Discourse on the Social Order in America." Ph.D. dissertation, University of Michigan, 1987.

Burns, Rex. *Success in America: The Yeoman Dream and the Industrial Revolution.* Amherst, Mass., 1976.

Burstein, Alan N. "Immigrants and Residential Mobility: The Irish and Germans in Philadelphia, 1850–1880," in Theodore Hershberg, ed., *Philadelphia: Work, Space, Family, and Group Experience in the 19th Century: Essays Toward an Interdisciplinary History of the City*, pp. 174–203. New York, 1981.

Bushman, Richard L. "Freedom and Prosperity in the American Revolution," in Larry R. Gerlach, ed., *Legacies of the American Revolution*, pp. 61–83. Logan, Utah, 1978.

" 'This New Man': Dependence and Independence, 1776," in Bushman et al., eds., *Uprooted Americans: Essays to Honor Oscar Handlin*, pp. 79–93. Boston, 1979.

Byars, Ronald Preston. "The Making of the Self-Made Man: The Development of Masculine Roles and Images in Ante-Bellum America." Ph.D. dissertation, Michigan State University, 1979.

Cannon, John. *Aristocratic Century: The Peerage of Eighteenth-Century England.* Cambridge, 1984.

Carr, Lois Green, and Walsh, Lorena S. "Changing Life Styles in Colonial St. Mary's County." *Working Papers from the Regional Economic History Research Center* 1 (1978): 73–118.

Catalano, Kathleen M. "Furniture Making in Philadelphia, 1820–1840." *American Arts and Antiques* 2 (1979): 116–23.

Cayton, Andrew R. L. "The Fragmentation of 'A Great Family': The Panic of 1819 and the Rise of a Middling Interest in Boston, 1818–1822." *Journal of the Early Republic* 2 (1982): 143–67.

Champagne, Roger J. "Liberty Boys and Mechanics of New York City, 1764–1774." *Labor History* 8 (1967): 115–35.

"New York and the Intolerable Acts, 1774." *New-York Historical Society Quarterly* 45 (1961): 195–207.

"New York Politics and Independence, 1776." *New-York Historical Society Quarterly* 46 (1962): 281–303.

"New York's Radicals and the Coming of Independence." *Journal of American History* 51 (1964): 21–40.

Chandler, Alfred D., Jr. *The Visible Hand: The Managerial Revolution in American Business.* Cambridge, Mass., 1977.

Chervat, William. "James T. Fields and the Beginnings of Book Promotion, 1840–1855." *Huntington Library Quarterly* 8 (1944–5): 75–94.

Clark, Clifford E., Jr. "The Changing Nature of Protestantism in Mid-Nineteenth Century America: Henry Ward Beecher's *Seven Lectures to Young Men.*" *Journal of American History* 57 (1971): 832–46.

"Domestic Architecture as an Index to Social History: The Romantic Revival and the Cult of Domesticity in America, 1840–1870." *Journal of Interdisciplinary History* 7 (1976): 33–56.

Clark, George Faber. *History of the Temperance Reform in Massachusetts, 1813–1883.* Boston, 1888.

Clark, J. C. D. *English Society, 1688–1832: Ideology, Social Structure and Political Practice During the Ancien Regime.* Cambridge, 1985.

Clark, Malcolm C. "The Birth of an Enterprise: Baldwin Locomotive, 1831–1842." *Pennsylvania Magazine of History and Biography* 90 (1966): 423–44.

Clark, Victor S. *History of Manufactures in the United States, 1607–1860.* Washington, 1916.

Clawson, Mary Ann. "Brotherhood, Class and Patriarchy: Fraternalism in Europe and America." Ph.D. dissertation, State University of New York at Stony Brook, 1980.

Clement, Priscilla Ferguson. *Welfare and the Poor in the Nineteenth-Century City: Philadelphia, 1800–1854.* Cranbury, N.J., 1985.

Cochran, Thomas C. "The Business Revolution." *American Historical Review* 79 (1974): 1449–66.

Cohen, Ira. "The Auction System in the Port of New York, 1817–1837." *Business History Review* 45 (1971): 488–510.

Cole, Arthur H. "The Tempo of Mercantile Life in Colonial America." *Business History Review* 33 (1959): 277–99.

Cole, Charles C., Jr. *The Social Ideas of the Northern Evangelists, 1826–1860.* New York, 1954.

Cole, G. D. H. "The Conception of the Middle Classes," in G. D. H. Cole, *Studies in Class Structure,* pp. 78–100. London, 1955.

Commons, John R. "American Shoemakers, 1648–1895." *Quarterly Journal of Economics* 24 (1909): 39–84.

Commons, John R., et al. *History of Labour in the United States,* 4 vols. New York, 1918–1935.

Conk, Margo Anderson. *The United States Census and Labor Force Change: A History of Occupation Statistics, 1870–1940.* Ann Arbor, 1978.

Conzen, Kathleen Neils. *Immigrant Milwaukee, 1836–1860: Accommodation and Community in a Frontier City.* Cambridge, Mass., 1976.

"Mapping Manuscript Census Data for Nineteenth Century Cities." *Historical Geography Newsletter* 4 (1974): 1–7.

"Patterns of Residence in Early Milwaukee," in Leo F. Schnore and Eric E. Lampard, eds., *The New Urban History: Quantitative Explorations by American Historians*, pp. 145–83. Princeton, 1975.

Conzen, Michael P., and Conzen, Kathleen Neils. "Geographical Structure in Nineteenth-Century Urban Retailing: Milwaukee, 1836–90."*Journal of Historical Geography* 5 (1979): 45–66.

Copeland, Peter F. *Working Dress in Colonial and Revolutionary America*. Westport, Conn., 1977.

Cott, Nancy F. *The Bonds of Womanhood: "Woman's Sphere" in New England, 1780–1835*. New Haven, 1977.

Countryman, Edward. *A People in Revolution: The American Revolution and Political Society in New York, 1760–1790*. Baltimore, 1981.

Couvares, Francis G. *The Remaking of Pittsburgh: Class and Culture in an Industrializing City, 1877–1919*. Albany, N.Y., 1984.

Crowley, J. E. *This Sheba, Self: The Conceptualization of Economic Life in Eighteenth Century America*. Baltimore, 1974.

Crowther, Simeon J. "A Note on the Economic Position of Philadelphia's White Oaks." *William and Mary Quarterly*, 3d ser., 29 (1972): 134–6.

Cumbler, John T. *Working-Class Community in Industrial America: Work, Leisure and Struggle in Two Industrial Cities, 1880–1930*. Westport, Conn., 1979.

Cutler, William W., III. "Status, Values and the Education of the Poor: The Trustees of the New York Public School Society, 1805–1853."*American Quarterly* 24 (1972): 69–85.

Dahrendorf, Ralf. *Class and Class Conflict in Industrial Society*. Stanford, 1959.

Daniels, Bruce C. "Defining Economic Classes in Colonial Massachusetts, 1700–1776." *Proceedings of the American Antiquarian Society* 83 (1973): 251–9.

"Long Range Trends of Wealth Distribution in Eighteenth Century New England." *Explorations in Economic History* 11 (1973–4): 123–35.

David, Paul A., and Solar, Peter. "A Bicentenary Contribution to the History of the Cost of Living in America," in Paul Uselding, ed., *Research in Economic History: An Annual Compilation of Research*, vol. 2, pp. 1–80. Greenwich, Conn., 1977.

Davies, Margery W. *Woman's Place Is at the Typewriter: Office Work and Office Workers, 1870–1930*. Philadelphia, 1982.

Davis, Susan G. "'Making Night Hideous': Christmas Revelry and Public Order in Nineteenth-Century Philadelphia." *American Quarterly* 34 (1982): 185–99.

Parades and Power: Street Theatre in Nineteenth-Century Philadelphia. Philadelphia, 1986.

Dawley, Alan. *Class and Community: The Industrial Revolution in Lynn*. Cambridge, Mass., 1976.

Day, Alan, and Day, Katherine. "Another Look at the Boston 'Caucus.' " *Journal of American Studies* 5 (1971): 19–42.

Decker, Peter R. *Fortunes and Failures: White-Collar Mobility in Nineteenth-Century San Francisco*. Cambridge, Mass., 1978.

Degler, Carl N. *At Odds: Women and the Family in America from the Revolution to the Present*. New York, 1980.

DeGré, Gerard. "Ideology and Class Consciousness in the Middle Class." *Social Forces* 29 (1950–1): 173–9.

DeMotte, Charles M. "Family and Social Structure in Colonial New Haven."*Connecticut Review* 9 (1975): 82–95.

DeVault, Ileen A. "Sons and Daughters of Labor: Class and Clerical Work in Pittsburgh, 1870s–1910s." Ph.D. dissertation, Yale University, 1985.

Diamondstone, Judith M. "Philadelphia's Municipal Corporation, 1701–1776." *Pennsylvania Magazine of History and Biography* 90 (1966): 183–201.

Dodd, Jill Siegel. "The Working Classes and the Temperance Movement in Ante-bellum Boston." *Labor History* 19 (1978): 510–31.

Doerflinger, Thomas M. "Commercial Specialization in Philadelphia's Merchant Community, 1750–1791." *Business History Review* 57 (1983): 20–49.

A Vigorous Spirit of Enterprise: Merchants and Economic Development in Revolutionary Philadelphia. Chapel Hill, 1986.

Doherty, Robert W. "Social Bases for the Presbyterian Schism of 1837–1838: The Philadelphia Case." *Journal of Social History* 2 (1968): 69–79.

Dorsey, Leslie, and Devine, Janice. *Fare Thee Well: A Backward Look at Two Centuries of Historic American Hostelries, Fashionable Spas, and Seaside Resorts*. New York, 1964.

Dorson, Richard M. *America in Legend: Folklore from the Colonial Period to the Present*. New York, 1973.

Douglas, Ann. *The Feminization of American Culture*. New York, 1977.

Doyle, Don Harrison. "The Social Functions of Voluntary Associations in a Nineteenth-Century American Town." *Social Science History* 1 (1977): 333–55.

The Social Order of a Frontier Community: Jacksonville, Illinois, 1825–70. Urbana, Ill., 1978.

Drescher, Seymour. *Dilemmas of Democracy: Tocqueville and Modernization*. Pittsburgh, 1968.

Dublin, Thomas. *Women at Work: The Transformation of Work and Community in Lowell, Massachusetts, 1826–1860*. New York, 1979.

Dudden, Faye E. *Serving Women: Household Service in Nineteenth-Century America*. Middletown, Conn., 1983.

Dumenil, Lynn. *Freemasonry and American Culture, 1880–1930*. Princeton, 1984.

East, Robert A. *Business Enterprise in the American Revolutionary Era*. New York, 1938.

"The Business Entrepreneur in a Changing Colonial Economy, 1763–1795." *Journal of Economic History* 6 (1946): suppl. 20, 16–27.

Echeverria, Durand, ed. "The American Character: A Frenchman Views the New Republic from Philadelphia, 1777." *William and Mary Quarterly*, 3d ser., 16 (1959): 376–413.

Edwards, Alba M. *Comparative Occupation Statistics for the United States, 1870 to 1940.* Washington, D.C., 1943.

Egnal, Marc, and Ernst, Joseph A. "An Economic Interpretation of the American Revolution." *William and Mary Quarterly,* 3d ser., 29 (1972): 3–32.

Epstein, Amy Kallman. "Multifamily Dwellings and the Search for Respectability: Origins of the New York Apartment House." *Urbanism: Past and Present* 10 (1980): 29–39.

Ernst, Robert. *Immigrant Life in New York City, 1825–1863.* New York, 1949.

Fairbanks, Jonathan. "Craft Processes and Images: Visual Sources for the Study of the Craftsman," in Ian M. G. Quimby, ed., *The Craftsman in Early America,* pp. 299–330. New York, 1984.

Faler, Paul G. "Cultural Aspects of the Industrial Revolution: Lynn, Massachusetts, Shoemakers and Industrial Morality." *Labor History* 15 (1974): 367–94.

Mechanics and Manufacturers in the Early Industrial Revolution: Lynn, Massachusetts, 1780–1860. Albany, N.Y., 1981.

Faragher, John Mack. "Open-Country Community: Sugar Creek, Illinois, 1820–1850," in Steven Hahn and Jonathan Prude, eds., *The Countryside in the Age of Capitalist Transformation: Essays in the Social History of Rural America,* pp. 233–58. Chapel Hill, 1985.

Finkel, Kenneth. *Nineteenth-Century Photography in Philadelphia: 250 Historic Prints from the Library Company of Philadelphia.* New York, 1980.

Fischer, Claude S. *Networks and Places: Social Relations in the Urban Setting.* New York, 1977.

Foner, Eric. *Tom Paine and Revolutionary America.* New York, 1976.

Formisano, Ronald P. "Deferential-Participant Politics: The Early Republic's Political Culture, 1789–1840." *American Political Science Review* 68 (1974): 473–87.

"Toward a Reorientation of Jacksonian Politics: A Review of the Literature, 1959–1975." *Journal of American History* 63 (1976): 42–65.

The Transformation of Political Culture: Massachusetts Parties, 1790s–1840s. New York, 1983.

Foster, Charles I. *An Errand of Mercy: The Evangelical United Front, 1790–1837.* Chapel Hill, 1960.

Freedman, Stephen. "The Baseball Fad in Chicago, 1865–1870: An Exploration of the Role of Sport in the Nineteenth-Century City." *Journal of Sport History* 5 (1978): 42–64.

Friedman, Bernard. "The Shaping of Radical Consciousness in Provincial New York." *Journal of American History* 56 (1970): 781–801.

Friedman, Lawrence J. *Gregarious Saints: Self and Community in American Abolitionism, 1830–1870.* Cambridge, 1982.

Frisch, Michael H. *Town into City: Springfield, Massachusetts, and the Meaning of Community, 1840–1880.* Cambridge, Mass., 1972.

Gallman, Robert E. "Trends in the Size Distribution of Wealth in the Nineteenth Century: Some Speculations," in Lee Soltow, ed., *Six Papers on the Size Distribution of Wealth and Income,* pp. 1–25. New York, 1969.

Garrard, Rachel P. "English Probate Inventories and Their Use in Studying the Significance of the Domestic Interior, 1570–1700," in Ad Van der Woude and Anton Schuurman, eds., *Probate Inventories: A New Source for the Historical Study of Wealth, Material Culture and Agricultural Development. A. A. G. Bijdragen*, vol. 23, pp. 55–82. Wageningen, 1980.

Gayle, Margot. "Cast-Iron Architecture, U.S.A." *Historic Preservation* 27 (1975): 14–19.

Gelber, Steven M. "Working at Playing: The Culture of the Workplace and the Rise of Baseball." *Journal of Social History* 16 (1983): 3–22.

Giddens, Anthony. *The Class Structure of the Advanced Societies.* New York, 1975.

Gilkeson, John S., Jr. *Middle-Class Providence, 1820–1940.* Princeton, 1986.

Gist, Noel P. *Secret Societies: A Cultural Study of Fraternalism in the United States.* Columbia, Mo., 1940.

Glassberg, Eudice. "Work, Wages, and the Cost of Living: Ethnic Differences and the Poverty Line, Philadelphia, 1880." *Pennsylvania History* 66 (1979): 17–58.

Glazer, Walter S. "Participation and Power: Voluntary Associations and the Functional Organization of Cincinnati in 1840." *Historical Methods Newsletter* 5 (1972): 151–68.

Goodman, Paul. "Ethics and Enterprise: The Values of a Boston Elite, 1800–1860." *American Quarterly* 18 (1966): 437–51.

"The Social Basis of New England Politics in Jacksonian America." *Journal of the Early Republic* 6 (1986): 23–58.

Gorn, Elliott J. *The Manly Art: Bare-Knuckle Prize Fighting in America.* Ithaca, N.Y., 1986.

Gough, Robert. "Can a Rich Man Favor Revolution?: The Case of Philadelphia in 1776." *Pennsylvania History* 48 (1981): 235–50.

"Notes on the Pennsylvania Revolutionaries of 1776." *Pennsylvania Magazine of History and Biography* 96 (1972): 89–103.

Greenberg, Brian. "Worker and Community: Fraternal Orders in Albany, New York, 1845–1885." *Maryland Historian* 8 (1977): 38–53.

Worker and Community: Response to Industrialization in a Nineteenth-Century American City, Albany, New York, 1850–1884. Albany, N.Y., 1985.

Greenberg, Stephanie W. "Industrial Location and Ethnic Residential Patterns in an Industrializing City: Philadelphia, 1880," in Theodore Hershberg, ed., *Philadelphia: Work, Space, Family, and Group Experience in the 19th Century: Essays Toward an Interdisciplinary History of the City*, pp. 204–32. New York, 1981.

Greene, Jack P. "Search for Identity: An Interpretation of the Meaning of Selected Patterns of Social Response in Eighteenth-Century America." *Journal of Social History* 3 (1969–70): 189–220.

"The Social Origins of the American Revolution: An Evaluation and an Interpretation." *Political Science Quarterly* 88 (1973): 1–22.

"Social Structure and Political Behavior in Revolutionary America: John Day's *Remarks on American Affairs.*" *William and Mary Quarterly*, 3d ser., 32 (1975): 481–94.

Griffen, Clyde. "Small Business and Occupational Mobility in Mid-Nineteenth-Century Poughkeepsie," in Stuart W. Bruchey, ed., *Small Business in American Life*, pp.122–41. New York, 1980.

The Study of Occupational Mobility in Nineteenth-Century America: Problems and Possibilities." *Journal of Social History* 5 (1972): 310–30.

Griffen, Clyde, and Griffen, Sally. *Natives and Newcomers: The Ordering of Opportunity in Mid-Nineteenth-Century Poughkeepsie*. Cambridge, Mass., 1978.

Griffin, Clifford S. "Religious Benevolence as Social Control, 1815–1860." *Mississippi Valley Historical Review* 44 (1957): 423–44.

Their Brothers' Keepers: Moral Stewardship in the United States, 1800–1865. New Brunswick, N.J., 1960.

Grimsted, David. *Melodrama Unveiled: American Theater and Culture, 1800–1850*. Chicago, 1968.

Groneman, Carol. " 'She Earns as a Child: She Pays as a Man': Women Workers in a Mid-Nineteenth-Century New York City Community," in Milton Cantor and Bruce Laurie, eds., *Class, Sex, and the Woman Worker*, pp. 83–100. Westport, Conn., 1977.

Grubb, Farley. "Immigrant Servant Labor: Their Occupational and Geographic Distribution in the Late Eighteenth-Century Mid-Atlantic Economy." *Social Science History* 9 (1985): 249–75.

Gusfield, Joseph R. *Symbolic Crusade: Status Politics and the American Temperance Movement*. Urbana, Ill., 1963.

Gutman, Herbert G. "The Reality of the Rags-to-Riches 'Myth': The Case of the Paterson, New Jersey, Locomotive, Iron, and Machinery Manufacturers, 1830–1880," in Stephan Thernstrom and Richard Sennett, eds., *Nineteenth-Century Cities: Essays in the New Urban History*, pp. 98–124. New Haven, 1969.

Work, Culture, and Society in Industrializing America: Essays in American Working-Class and Social History. New York, 1976.

Hahn, Steven. *The Roots of Southern Populism: Yeoman Farmers and the Transformation of the Georgia Upcountry, 1850–1890*. New York, 1983.

Haines, Michael R. "Poverty, Economic Stress, and the Family in a Late Nineteenth-Century American City: Whites in Philadelphia, 1880," in Theodore Hershberg, ed., *Philadelphia: Work, Space, Family, and Group Experience in the 19th Century: Essays Toward an Interdisciplinary History of the City*, pp. 240–76. New York, 1981.

Hall, Peter Dobkin. "The Model of Boston Charity: A Theory of Charitable Benevolence and Class Development." *Science and Society* 38 (1974–5): 464–77.

The Organization of American Culture, 1700–1900: Private Institutions, Elites, and the Origins of American Nationality. New York, 1982.

Halttunen, Karen. *Confidence Men and Painted Women: A Study of Middle-Class Culture in America, 1830–1870*. New Haven, 1982.

Hamlin, Talbot. *Greek Revival Architecture in America: Being an Account of Important Trends in Architecture and American Life Prior to the War Between the States*. New York, 1944.

Hampel, Robert L. *Temperance and Prohibition in Massachusetts: 1813–1852.* Ann Arbor, 1982.

Handlin, David P. *The American Home: Architecture and Society, 1815–1915.* Boston, 1979.

Handlin, Oscar. *Boston's Immigrants: A Study in Acculturation.* Rev. ed. New York, 1968.

Harrington, Virginia D. *The New York Merchant on the Eve of the Revolution.* New York, 1935.

Hartz, Louis. *The Liberal Tradition in America: An Interpretation of American Political Thought Since the Revolution.* New York, 1955.

Hastings, William S. "Philadelphia Microcosm." *Pennsylvania Magazine of History and Biography* 91 (1967): 164–80.

Heale, M. J. "From City Fathers to Social Critics: Humanitarianism and Government in New York, 1790–1860." *Journal of American History* 63 (1976): 21–41.

   "Humanitarianism in the Early Republic: The Moral Reformers of New York, 1776–1825." *Journal of American Studies* 2 (1968): 161–75.

   "Patterns of Benevolence: Associated Philanthropy in the Cities of New York, 1830–1860." *New York History* 57 (1976): 53–79.

   "Patterns of Benevolence: Charity and Morality in Rural and Urban New York, 1783–1830." *Societas* 3 (1973): 337–59.

Henretta, James A. "Economic Development and Social Structure in Colonial Boston." *William and Mary Quarterly*, 3d ser., 22 (1965): 75–92.

   "The Study of Social Mobility: Ideological Assumptions and Conceptual Bias." *Labor History* 18 (1977): 166–78.

Hershberg, Theodore; Burstein, Alan N.; Ericksen, Eugene P.; Greenberg, Stephanie W.; and Yancey, William L. "A Tale of Three Cities: Blacks, Immigrants, and Opportunity in Philadelphia, 1850–1880, 1930, 1970," in Theodore Hershberg, ed., *Philadelphia: Work, Space, Family, and Group Experience in the 19th Century: Essays Toward an Interdisciplinary History of the City*, pp. 461–91. New York, 1981.

Hershberg, Theodore; Cox, Harold E.; Light, Dale B., Jr.; and Greenfield, Richard R. "The 'Journey-to-Work': An Empirical Investigation of Work, Residence and Transportation, Philadelphia, 1850 and 1880," in Theodore Hershberg, ed., *Philadelphia: Work, Space, Family, and Group Experience in the 19th Century: Essays Toward an Interdisciplinary History of the City*, pp. 128–73. New York, 1981.

Hewitt, Nancy A. *Women's Activism and Social Change: Rochester, New York, 1822–1872.* Ithaca, N.Y., 1984.

Hexter, J. H. "The Myth of the Middle Class in Tudor England," in J. H. Hexter, *Reappraisals in History: New Views on History and Society in Early Modern Europe*, 2d ed., pp. 71–116. Chicago, 1979.

   "A New Framework for Social History," in J. H. Hexter, *Reappraisals in History: New Views on History and Society in Early Modern Europe*, 2d ed., pp. 14–25. Chicago, 1979.

High, James. "The Origins of Maryland's Middle Class in the Colonial Aristocratic Pattern." *Maryland Historical Magazine* 57 (1962): 334–45.

Hill, Joseph A. "The Civil War Income Tax." *Quarterly Journal of Economics* 8 (1894): 416–52, 491–8.

Hirsch, Susan E. "From Artisan to Manufacturer: Industrialization and the Small Producer in Newark, 1830–60," in Stuart W. Bruchey, ed., *Small Business in American Life*, pp. 80–99. New York, 1980.

Roots of the American Working Class: The Industrialization of Crafts in Newark, 1800–1860. Philadelphia, 1978.

Hobsbawn, E. J. "Class Consciousness in History," in István Mészáros, ed., *Aspects of History and Class Consciousness.* London, 1971.

Hoerder, Dirk. "Boston Leaders and Boston Crowds, 1765–1776," in Alfred F. Young, ed., *The American Revolution: Explorations in the History of American Radicalism*, pp. 233–71. DeKalb, Ill., 1976.

Crowd Action in Revolutionary Massachusetts, 1765–1780. New York, 1977.

Hoffman, Ronald. *A Spirit of Dissension: Economics, Politics, and the Revolution in Maryland.* Baltimore, 1973.

Hogeland, Ronald W. "Charles Hodge, The Association of Gentlemen and Ornamental Womanhood, 1825–1855." *Journal of Presbyterian History* 53 (1975): 239–55.

" 'The Female Appendage': Feminine Life-Styles in America, 1820–1860." *Civil War History* 17 (1971): 101–14.

Holt, Michael F. "The Election of 1840, Voter Mobilization, and the Emergence of the Second American Party System: A Reappraisal of Jacksonian Voting Behavior," in William J. Cooper, Jr., Michael F. Holt, and John McCardell, eds., *A Master's Due: Essays in Honor of David Herbert Donald*, pp. 16–58. Baton Rouge, 1985.

Horlick, Allan Stanley. *Country Boys and Merchant Princes: The Social Control of Young Men in New York.* Lewisburg, Pa., 1975.

Horowitz, Daniel. *The Morality of Spending: Attitudes Toward the Consumer Society in America, 1875–1940.* Baltimore, 1985.

Horwitz, Richard P. *Anthropology Toward History: Culture and Work in a 19th-Century Maine Town.* Middletown, Conn., 1978.

Howe, Daniel Walker. *The Political Culture of the American Whigs.* Chicago, 1979.

"Victorian Culture in America," in Daniel Walker Howe, ed., *Victorian America*, pp. 3–28. Philadelphia, 1976.

Hower, Ralph M. *History of Macy's of New York, 1858–1919: Chapters in the Evolution of the Department Store.* Cambridge, Mass., 1943.

Hugins, Walter. *Jacksonian Democracy and the Working Class: A Study of the New York Workingmen's Movement, 1829–1837.* Stanford, 1960.

Huss, Wayne A. *The Master Builders: A History of the Grand Lodge of Free and Accepted Masons of Pennsylvania.* vol. I: 1731–1873. Philadelphia, 1986.

"Pennsylvania Freemasonry: An Intellectual and Social Analysis, 1727–1826." Ph.D. dissertation, Temple University, 1985.

Hutson, James H. "An Investigation of the Inarticulate: Philadelphia's White Oaks." *William and Mary Quarterly*, 3d ser., 28 (1971): 3–25.

Huxtable, Ada Louise. "Progressive Architecture in America: Jayne Building – 1849–50." *Progressive Architecture* 37, no. 11 (1956): 133–4.

Irons, Thomas. *A Brief History of Early Odd Fellowship, Briefly Told*. Philadelphia, 1925.

Jackle, Robert Carl. "Philadelphia Across the Schuylkill: Work, Transportation and Residence in West Philadelphia, 1860–1910." Ph.D. dissertation, Temple University, 1985.

Jackson, Joseph. *Market Street, Philadelphia: The Most Historic Highway in America, Its Merchants and Its Story*. Philadelphia, 1918.

Jackson, Kenneth T. *Crabgrass Frontier: The Suburbanization of the United States*. New York, 1985.

Jaher, Frederic Cople. "Old and New Elites and Entrepreneurial Activity in New York City from 1780 to 1850." *Working Papers from the Regional Economic History Research Center* 2 (1978): 55–78.

The *Urban Establishment: Upper Strata in Boston, New York, Charleston, Chicago, and Los Angeles*. Urbana, Ill., 1982.

Jeffrey, Kirk. "The Family as Utopian Retreat from the City." *Soundings* 55 (1972): 21–41.

Jentz, John B. "The Antislavery Constituency in Jacksonian New York City." *Civil War History* 27 (1981): 101–22.

Johnson, Dale, ed. *Class and Social Development: A New Theory of the Middle Class*. Beverly Hills, 1982.

Johnson, Michael P. "Planters and Patriarchy: Charleston, 1800–1860." *Journal of Southern History* 46 (1980): 45–72.

Johnson, Paul E. *A Shopkeeper's Millennium: Society and Revivals in Rochester, New York, 1815–1837*. New York, 1978.

Johnston, Norman J. "The Caste and Class of the Urban Form of Historic Philadelphia." *Journal of the American Institute of Planners* 32 (1966): 334–50.

Jones, Alice Hanson. "Wealth Estimates for the American Middle Colonies, 1774." *Economic Development and Cultural Change* 18 (1970): iii–x, 1–172.

Wealth of a Nation to Be: The American Colonies on the Eve of the Revolution. New York, 1980.

Jones, Fred Mitchell. *Middlemen in the Domestic Trade of the United States, 1800–1860*. Illinois Studies in the Social Sciences, vol. 21, no. 3. Urbana, Ill., 1937.

Jones, James Boyd, Jr. "Mose the Bowery B'hoy and the Nashville Volunteer Fire Department, 1849–1860." *Tennessee Historical Quarterly* 40 (1981): 170–81.

Jordan, Jean P. "Women Merchants in Colonial New York." *New York History* 58 (1977): 412–39.

Kaestle, Carl F. *The Evolution of an Urban School System: New York City, 1750–1850*. Cambridge, Mass., 1973.

Kaestle, Carl F., and Vinovskis, Maris A. *Education and Social Change in Nineteenth-Century Massachusetts*. Cambridge, Mass., 1980.

Katz, Michael B. *The Irony of Early School Reform: Educational Innovation in Mid-Nineteenth-Century Massachusetts*. Cambridge, Mass., 1968.

"Occupational Classification in History." *Journal of Interdisciplinary History* 3 (1972): 63–88.

The People of Hamilton, Canada West: Family and Class in a Mid-Nineteenth-Century City. Cambridge, Mass., 1975.

Katz, Michael B.; Doucet, Michael J.; and Stern, Mark J. *The Social Organization of Early Industrial Capitalism.* Cambridge, Mass., 1982.

Katznelson, Ira. *City Trenches: Urban Politics and the Patterning of Class in the United States.* Chicago, 1981.

"The Crisis of the Capitalist City: Urban Politics and Social Control," in Willis D. Hawley et al., *Theoretical Perspectives on Urban Politics*, pp. 214–29. Englewood Cliffs, N.J., 1976.

Kerber, Linda. "The Republican Mother: Women and the Enlightenment – An American Perspective." *American Quarterly* 28 (1976): 187–205.

Kett, Joseph F. *Rites of Passage: Adolescence in America, 1790 to the Present.* New York, 1977.

Keyssar, Alexander. *Out of Work: The First Century of Unemployment in Massachusetts.* Cambridge, 1986.

Kingsdale, Jon M. "The 'Poor Man's Club': Social Functions of the Urban Working-Class Saloon." *American Quarterly* 25 (1973): 472–89.

Kirby, John B. "Early American Politics – the Search for Ideology: An Historiographic Analysis and Critique of the Concept of 'Deference.' " *Journal of Politics* 32 (1970): 808–38.

Kirsch, George B. "American Cricket: Players and Clubs Before the Civil War." *Journal of Sport History* 11 (1984): 28–50.

Klein, Milton. "Democracy and Politics in Colonial New York." *New York History* 40 (1959): 221–46.

Kleppner, Paul. *The Cross of Culture: A Social Analysis of Midwestern Politics, 1850–1900.* New York, 1970.

Knights, Peter R. *The Plain People of Boston, 1830–1860: A Study in City Growth.* New York, 1971.

Kocka, Jürgen. *White Collar Workers in America, 1890–1940: A Social-Political History in International Perspective.* Beverly Hills, 1980.

Kohl, Lawrence Frederick. "The Concept of Social Control and the History of Jacksonian America." *Journal of the Early Republic* 5 (1985): 21–34.

Kornblith, Gary J. "The Craftsman as Industrialist: Jonas Chickering and the Transformation of American Piano Making." *Business History Review* 59 (1985): 349–68.

"From Artisans to Businessmen: Master Mechanics in New England, 1789–1850." Ph.D. dissertation, Princeton University, 1983.

Kouwenhoven, John A. *The Columbia Historical Portrait of New York.* New York, 1972.

Krout, John Allen. *The Origins of Prohibition.* New York, 1925.

Kulikoff, Allan. "The Progress of Inequality in Revolutionary Boston." *William and Mary Quarterly*, 3d ser., 28 (1971): 375–413.

Laurie, Bruce. "Fire Companies and Gangs in Southwark: The 1840s," in Allen F. Davis and Mark H. Haller, eds., *The Peoples of Philadelphia: A History of Ethnic Groups and Lower-Class Life, 1790–1940*, pp. 71–87. Philadelphia, 1973.

Working People of Philadelphia, 1800–1850. Philadelphia, 1980.

Laurie, Bruce; Hershberg, Theodore; and Alter, George. "Immigrants and Industry: The Philadelphia Experience, 1850–80," in Theodore Hershberg, ed., *Philadelphia: Work, Space, Family, and Group Experience in the 19th Century: Essays Toward an Interdisciplinary History of the City*, pp. 93–119. New York, 1981.

Laurie, Bruce, and Schmitz, Mark. "Manufacture and Productivity: The Making of an Industrial Base, Philadelphia, 1850–1880," in Theodore Hershberg, ed., *Philadelphia: Work, Space, Family, and Group Experience in the 19th Century: Essays Toward an Interdisciplinary History of the City*, pp. 43–92. New York, 1981.

Leinhardt, Samuel, ed. *Social Networks: A Developing Paradigm*. New York, 1977.

Lemisch, Jesse. "The American Revolution Seen from the Bottom Up," in Barton J. Bernstein, ed., *Towards a New Past: Dissenting Essays in American History*, pp. 3–45. New York, 1968.

——— "Jack Tar in the Streets: Merchant Seamen in the Politics of Revolutionary America." *William and Mary Quarterly*, 3d ser., 25 (1968): 371–407.

——— "Listening to the 'Inarticulate': William Widger's Dream and the Loyalties of American Revolutionary Seamen in British Prisons." *Journal of Social History* 3 (1969): 1–29.

Lemisch, Jesse, and Alexander, John K. "The White Oaks, Jack Tar, and the Concept of the 'Inarticulate.' " *William and Mary Quarterly*, 3d ser., 29 (1972): 109–34.

Lerner, Gerda. "The Lady and the Mill Girl: Changes in the Status of Women in the Age of Jackson." *Midcontinent American Studies Journal* 10 (1969): 5–14.

Lester, John A. *A Century of Philadelphia Cricket*. Philadelphia, 1951.

Levine, Peter. "The Promise of Sport in Antebellum America." *Journal of American Culture* 2 (1980): 623–34.

Lewis, W. David. "The Reformer as Conservative: Protestant Counter-Subversion in the Early Republic," in Stanley Coben and Lorman Ratner, eds., *The Development of an American Culture*, pp. 64–91. Englewood Cliffs, N.J., 1970.

Litwack, Leon, ed. *The American Labor Movement*. Englewood Cliffs, N.J., 1962.

Lockridge, Kenneth A. "Social Change and the Meaning of the American Revolution." *Journal of Social History* 6 (1972–73): 403–39.

Lockwood, Charles. "The Bond Street Area." *New-York Historical Society Quarterly* 56 (1972): 309–20.

Long, Clarence D. *Wages and Earnings in the United States, 1860–1890*. Princeton, 1960.

Lynd, Staughton. "The Mechanics in New York Politics, 1774–1788." *Labor History* 5 (1964): 225–46.

Lynd, Staughton, and Young, Alfred. "After Carl Becker: The Mechanics and New York City Politics, 1774–1801." *Labor History* 5 (1964): 215–24.

Lynes, Russell. *The Domesticated Americans*. New York, 1957.

McCall, Elizabeth B. *Old Philadelphia Houses on Society Hill, 1750–1840*. New York, 1966.

McCaughey, Robert A. "From Town to City: Boston in the 1820s." *Political Science Quarterly* 88 (1973): 191–213.

McClinton, Katharine Morrison. *The Chromolithographs of Louis Prang*. New York, 1973.

McClymer, John F. "The Historian and the Poverty Line." *Historical Methods* 18 (1985): 105–10.

"Late Nineteenth-Century American Working-Class Living Standards." *Journal of Interdisciplinary History* 17 (1986): 379–98.

McCormick, Richard L. "Ethno-Cultural Interpretations of Nineteenth-Century American Voting Behavior." *Political Science Quarterly* 89 (1974): 351–77.

McCreary, George W. *The Ancient and Honorable Mechanical Company of Baltimore*. Baltimore, 1901.

McElroy, James L. "Social Control and Romantic Reform in Antebellum America: The Case of Rochester, New York." *New York History* 58 (1977): 17–46.

McGlone, Robert Elno. "Suffer the Children: The Emergence of Modern Middle-Class Family Life in America, 1820–1870." Ph.D. dissertation, University of California at Los Angeles, 1971.

McKee, Samuel D., Jr. *Labor in Colonial New York, 1664–1776*. New York, 1935.

McLoughlin, William G. "Evangelical Childrearing in the Age of Jackson: Francis Wayland's Views on When and How to Subdue the Willfulness of Children." *Journal of Social History* 9 (1975): 20–39.

Madison, James H. "The Evolution of Commercial Credit Reporting Agencies in Nineteenth-Century America." *Business History Review* 48 (1974): 164–86.

Magdol, Edward. *The Antislavery Rank and File: A Social Profile of the Abolitionists' Constituency*. Westport, Conn., 1986.

Maier, Pauline. *From Resistance to Revolution: Colonial Radicals and the Development of American Opposition to Britain, 1765–1776*. New York, 1972.

Main, Gloria L. "Inequality in Early America: The Evidence from Probate Records of Massachusetts and Maryland." *Journal of Interdisciplinary History* 7 (1977): 559–81.

Main, Jackson Turner. *The Social Structure of Revolutionary America*. Princeton, 1965.

Margo, Robert A., and Villaflor, Georgia C. "The Growth of Wages in Antebellum America: New Evidence." *Journal of Economic History* 47 (1987): 873–95.

Martin, Edgar W. *The Standard of Living in 1860*. Chicago, 1942.

Mayer, Arno J. "The Lower Middle Class as Historical Problem." *Journal of Modern History* 47 (1975): 409–36.

Melder, Keith. "Ladies Bountiful: Organized Women's Benevolence in Early 19th-Century America." *New York History* 48 (1967): 231–54.

Miller, Douglas T. "Immigration and Social Stratification in Pre–Civil War New York." *New York History* 49 (1968): 157–68.

Miller, George L. "Classification and Economic Scaling of 19th Century Ceramics." *Historical Archaeology* 14 (1980): 1–40.

Miller, Richard G. "Gentry and Entrepreneurs: A Socioeconomic Analysis of Philadelphia in the 1790s." *Rocky Mountain Social Science Journal* 12 (1975): 71–84.

Miller, Roger, and Siry, Joseph. "The Emerging Suburb: West Philadelphia, 1850–1880." *Pennsylvania History* 47 (1980): 99–145.

Mills, C. Wright. *White Collar: The American Middle Classes.* New York, 1951.

Mintz, Steven. *A Prison of Expectations: The Family in Victorian Culture.* New York, 1983.

Modell, John, and Hareven, Tamara K. "Urbanization and the Malleable Household: An Examination of Boarding and Lodging in American Families." *Journal of Marriage and the Family* 35 (1973): 467–79.

Mohl, Raymond. *Poverty in New York, 1783–1825.* New York, 1971.

Montgomery, David. "The Shuttle and the Cross: Weavers and Artisans in the Kensington Riots of 1844." *Journal of Social History* 5 (1972): 411–46.

Moody, Richard. *The Astor Place Riot.* Bloomington, Ind., 1958.

Morantz, Regina M. "Making Women Modern: Middle Class Women and Health Reform in 19th Century America." *Journal of Social History* 10 (1977): 490–507.

Morgan, Edmund S. "The Puritan Ethic and the American Revolution." *William and Mary Quarterly,* 3d ser., 24 (1967): 3–43.

Morgan, Edmund S., and Morgan, Helen M. *The Stamp Act Crisis: Prologue to Revolution.* Chapel Hill, 1953.

Morris, Richard B. "Class Struggle and the American Revolution." *William and Mary Quarterly,* 3d ser., 19 (1962): 3–29.

Government and Labor in Early America. New York, 1946.

Mousnier, Roland. *The Institutions of France Under the Absolute Monarchy, 1598–1789: Society and the State.* Chicago, 1979.

Social Hierarchies: 1450 to the Present. London, 1973.

Muraskin, William A. "The Social-Control Theory in American History: A Critique." *Journal of Social History* 9 (1976): 559–69.

Murtagh, William John. "The Philadelphia Row House." *Journal of the Society of Architectural Historians* 16 (1957): 8–13.

Nash, Gary B. "Artisans and Politics in Eighteenth-Century Philadelphia," in Ian M. G. Quimby, ed., *The Craftsman in Early America,* pp. 62–88. New York, l984.

"Poverty and Poor Relief in Pre-Revolutionary Philadelphia." *William and Mary Quarterly,* 3d ser., 33 (1976): 3–30.

"Slaves and Slaveowners in Colonial Philadelphia." *William and Mary Quarterly,* 3d ser., 30 (1973): 223–56.

"Social Change and the Growth of Prerevolutionary Urban Radicalism," in Alfred F. Young, ed., *The American Revolution: Explorations in the History of American Radicalism,* pp. 3–36. DeKalb, Ill., 1976.

"The Social Evolution of Preindustrial American Cities, 1700–1820: Reflections and New Directions." *Journal of Urban History* 13 (1987): 115–45.

"The Transformation of Urban Politics, 1700–1765." *Journal of American History* 60 (1974): 605–32.

"Up from the Bottom in Franklin's Philadelphia." *Past and Present*, no. 77 (1977): 57–83.

The Urban Crucible: Social Change, Political Consciousness, and the Origins of the American Revolution. Cambridge, Mass., 1979.

"Urban Wealth and Poverty in Pre-Revolutionary America," in Jack P. Greene and Pauline Maier, eds., *Interdisciplinary Studies of the American Revolution*, pp. 9–48. Beverly Hills, 1976.

Nash, Gary B.; Smith, Billy G.; and Hoerder, Dirk. "Laboring Americans and the American Revolution." *Labor History* 24 (1983): 414–39.

Neale, R. S. *Class and Ideology in the Nineteenth Century.* London, 1972.

Newby, Howard. "The Deferential Dialectic." *Comparative Studies in Society and History* 17 (1975): 139–64.

Norton, Mary Beth. *Liberty's Daughters: The Revolutionary Experience of American Women, 1750–1800.* Boston, 1980.

Oaks, Robert F. "Big Wheels in Philadelphia: Du Simitière's List of Carriage Owners." *Pennsylvania Magazine of History and Biography* 95 (1971): 351–62.

"Philadelphia Merchants and the Origins of American Independence." *Proceedings of the American Philosophical Society* 121 (1977): 407–36.

O'Boyle, Lenore. "The Classless Society: Comment on Stearns." *Comparative Studies in Society and History* 21 (1979): 397–413.

"The Middle Class in Western Europe, 1815–1848." *American Historical Review* 71 (1966): 826–45.

Olson, Sherry H. *Baltimore: The Building of an American City.* Baltimore, 1980.

Olton, Charles S. *Artisans for Independence: Philadelphia Mechanics and the American Revolution.* Syracuse, 1975.

"Philadelphia's Mechanics in the First Decade of Revolution, 1765–1775." *Journal of American History* 59 (1972): 311–26.

Ossowski, Stanislaw. *Class Structure in the Social Consciousness.* London, 1963.

Pack, Janet Rothenberg. "Urban Spatial Transformation: Philadelphia, 1850 to 1880, Heterogeneity to Homogeneity?" *Social Science History* 8 (1984): 425–54.

Papenfuse, Edward C. *In Pursuit of Profit: The Annapolis Merchants in the Era of the American Revolution, 1763–1805.* Baltimore, 1975.

Parker, Peter J. "The Philadelphia Printer: A Study of an Eighteenth-Century Businessman." *Business History Review* 40 (1966): 24–46.

Pease, William H., and Pease, Jane H. "Paternal Dilemmas: Education, Prosperity, and Patrician Persistence in Jacksonian Boston." *New England Quarterly* 53 (1980): 147–67.

The Web of Progress: Private Values and Public Styles in Boston and Charleston, 1828–1843. New York, 1985.

Pencak, William. "The Social Structure of Revolutionary Boston: Evidence from the Great Fire of 1760." *Journal of Interdisciplinary History* 10 (1979): 267–78.

Perkin, Harold. *The Origins of Modern English Society, 1780–1880.* London, 1969.

Perlmann, Joel. "After Leaving School: The Jobs of Young People in Providence, R.I., 1880–1915," in Ronald K. Goodenow and Diane Ravitch, eds., *Schools in Cities: Consensus and Conflict in American Educational History,* pp. 3–43. New York, 1983.

"Curriculum and Tracking in the Transformation of the American High School: Providence, Rhode Island, 1880–1930." *Journal of Social History* 19 (1985): 29–55.

"Who Stayed in School?: Social Structure and Academic Achievement in the Determination of Enrollment Patterns, Providence, Rhode Island, 1880–1925." *Journal of American History* 72 (1985): 588–614.

Persons, Stow. *The Decline of American Gentility.* New York, 1973.

Pessen, Edward. *Most Uncommon Jacksonians: The Radical Leaders of the Early Labor Movement.* Albany, N.Y., 1967.

Riches, Class, and Power Before the Civil War. Lexington, Mass., 1973.

"Social Structure and Politics in American History." *American Historical Review* 87 (1982): 1290–1325.

Peterson, Charles E. "Ante-Bellum Skyscraper." *Journal of the Society of Architectural Historians* 9 (1950): 27–8.

"Philadelphia Society in 1804." *Pennsylvania Magazine of History and Biography* 11 (1887): 89–92.

Pierce, Bessie Louise. *A History of Chicago.* Vol. 2: *From Town to City, 1848–71.* Chicago, 1940.

Plummer, Wilbur C. "Consumer Credit in Colonial Philadelphia." *Pennsylvania Magazine of History and Biography* 66 (1942): 385–409.

Pocock, J. G. A. "The Classical Theory of Deference." *American Historical Review* 81 (1976): 516–23.

Pole, J. R. *The Pursuit of Equality in American History.* Berkeley, 1978.

Porter, Glenn, and Livesay, Harold C. *Merchants and Manufacturers: Studies in the Changing Structure of Nineteenth-Century Marketing.* Baltimore, 1971.

Poulantzas, Nicos. *Classes in Contemporary Capitalism.* London, 1975.

Powell, John H. *Bring Out Your Dead: The Great Plague of Yellow Fever in Philadelphia in 1793.* Philadelphia, 1949.

Pred, Allan R. *Urban Growth and the Circulation of Information: The United States System of Cities, 1790–1840.* Cambridge, Mass., 1973.

Price, Jacob M. "Economic Function and the Growth of American Port Towns in the Eighteenth Century." *Perspectives in American History* 8 (1974): 123–86.

Prude, Jonathan. *The Coming of Industrial Order: Town and Factory Life in Rural Massachusetts, 1810–1860.* Cambridge, 1983.

Quimby, Ian M. G. "Introduction: Some Observations on the Craftsmen in

Early America," in Ian M. G. Quimby, ed., *The Craftsman in Early America*, pp. 3–16. New York, 1984.

Rader, Benjamin C. "The Quest for Subcommunities and the Rise of American Sports." *American Quarterly* 29 (1977): 355–69.

Rasmusson, Ethel E. "Democratic Environment – Aristocratic Aspiration." *Pennsylvania Magazine of History and Biography* 90 (1966): 155–82.

Ratcliffe, Donald J. "Politics in Jacksonian Ohio: Reflections on the Ethnocultural Interpretation." *Ohio History* 88 (1979): 5–35.

Rees, Albert. *Real Wages in Manufacturing, 1890–1914.* Princeton, 1961.

Resseguie, Harry E. "A. T. Stewart's Marble Palace: The Cradle of the Department Store." *New-York Historical Society Quarterly* 48 (1964): 131–62.
"Alexander Turney Stewart and the Development of the Department Store." *Business History Review* 39 (1965): 301–22.

Reynolds, Donald Martin. *The Architecture of New York City: Histories and Views of Important Structures, Sites, and Symbols.* New York, 1984.

Rock, Howard B. "The American Revolution and the Mechanics of New York City: One Generation Later." *New York History* 57 (1976): 367–94.
Artisans of the New Republic: The Tradesmen of New York City in the Age of Jefferson. New York, 1979.

Rodgers, Daniel T. *The Work Ethic in Industrial America: 1850–1920.* Chicago, 1978.

Rorabaugh, W. J. *The Alcoholic Republic: An American Tradition.* New York, 1979.

Rosenberg, Carroll Smith. *Religion and the Rise of the American City: The New York City Mission Movement, 1812–1870.* Ithaca, N.Y., 1971.

Rosenzweig, Roy. *Eight Hours for What We Will: Workers and Leisure in an Industrial City, 1870–1920.* Cambridge, 1983.

Ross, Steven J. *Workers on the Edge: Work, Leisure, and Politics in Industrializing Cincinnati, 1788–1890.* New York, 1985.

Rosswurm, Steven. "The Philadelphia Militia, 1775–1783: Active Duty and Active Radicalism," in Ronald Hoffman and Peter J. Albert, eds., *Arms and Independence: The Military Character of the American Revolution*, pp. 75–118. Charlottesville, Va., 1984.

Rothman, David J. *The Discovery of the Asylum: Social Order and Disorder in the New Republic.* Boston, 1971.

Rotundo, E. Anthony. "Body and Soul: Changing Ideals of American Middle-Class Manhood, 1770–1920." *Journal of Social History* 16 (1983): 23–38.

Rubinstein, W. D. "The Victorian Middle Classes: Wealth, Occupation, and Geography." *Economic History Review*, 2d ser., 30 (1977): 602–23.
"Wealth, Elites and the Class Structure of Modern Britain." *Past and Present*, no. 76 (1977): 99–126.

Ryan, Mary P. *Cradle of the Middle Class: The Family in Oneida County, New York, 1790–1865.* Cambridge, 1981.

Ryerson, Richard Alan. *The Revolution Is Now Begun: The Radical Committees of Philadelphia, 1765–1776.* Philadelphia, 1976.

Salinger, Sharon V. "Artisans, Journeymen, and the Transformation of Labor in Late Eighteenth-Century Philadelphia." *William and Mary Quarterly*, 3d ser., 40 (1983): 62–84.

"Colonial Labor in Transition: The Decline of Indentured Servitude in Late Eighteenth-Century Philadelphia." *Labor History* 22 (1981): 165–91.

Salinger, Sharon V., and Wetherell, Charles. "A Note on the Population of Pre-Revolutionary Philadelphia." *Pennsylvania Magazine of History and Biography* 109 (1985): 369–86.

"Wealth and Renting in Prerevolutionary Philadelphia." *Journal of American History* 71 (1985): 826–40.

Scherzer, Kenneth Alan. "The Unbounded Community: Neighborhood Life and Social Structure in New York City, 1830–1875." Ph.D. dissertation, Harvard University, 1982.

Schiller, Dan. *Objectivity and the News: The Public and the Rise of Commercial Journalism.* Philadelphia, 1981.

Schlereth, Thomas J. "Artisans and Craftsmen: A Historical Perspective," in Ian M. G. Quimby, ed., *The Craftsman in Early America*, pp. 34–61. New York, 1984.

Schreiber, Lee L. "Bluebloods and Local Societies: A Philadelphia Microcosm." *Pennsylvania History* 48 (1981): 251–66.

Schultz, Stanley K. *The Culture Factory: Boston Public Schools, 1789–1860.* New York, 1973.

Schuurman, Anton. "Probate Inventories: Research Issues, Problems and Results," in Ad Van der Woude and Anton Schuurman, eds., *Probate Inventories: A New Source for the Historical Study of Wealth, Material Culture and Agricultural Development. A. A. G. Bijdragen*, vol. 23, pp. 19–31. Wageningen, 1980.

Schuyler, Montgomery. "The Small City House in New York." *The Architectural Record* 8 (1899): 357–88.

Scott, Donald M., "The Popular Lecture and the Creation of a Public in Mid-Nineteenth Century America." *Journal of American History* 66 (1980): 791–809.

Seidler, Jan M. "A Tradition in Transition: The Boston Furniture Industry, 1840–1880," in Kenneth L. Ames, ed., *Victorian Furniture: Essays from a Victorian Society Autumn Symposium*, pp. 65–83. Philadelphia, 1983.

Sewell, William H., Jr. "Visions of Labor: Illustrations of the Mechanical Arts Before, In, and After Diderot's *Encyclopédie*," in Steven L. Kaplan and Cynthia J. Koepp, eds., *Work in France: Representations, Meaning, Organization, and Practice*, pp. 258–86. Ithaca, N.Y., 1986.

Seymour, Harold. *Baseball: The Early Years.* New York, 1960.

Shammas, Carole. "The Domestic Environment in Early Modern England and America." *Journal of Social History* 14 (1980): 3–24.

Shi, David E. *The Simple Life: Plain Living and High Thinking in American Culture.* New York, 1985.

Siegel, Adrienne. *The Image of the American City in Popular Literature: 1820–1870.* Port Washington, N.Y., 1981.

Silbey, Joel H. *The Partisan Imperative: The Dynamics of American Politics Before the Civil War.* New York, 1985.

Simmel, Georg. "The Sociology of Secrecy and of Secret Societies." *American Journal of Sociology* 11 (1906): 441–98.

Simon, Grant Miles. "Houses and Early Life in Philadelphia." *Transactions of the American Philosophical Society*, new ser., 43 (1953): 280–8.

Sinclair, Bruce. *Philadelphia's Philosopher Mechanics: A History of the Franklin Institute, 1824–1865.* Baltimore, 1974.

Singleton, Gregory H. "Protestant Voluntary Organizations and the Shaping of Victorian America," in Daniel Walker Howe, ed., *Victorian America*, pp. 47–58. Philadelphia, 1976.

Siracusa, Carl. *A Mechanical People: Perceptions of the Industrial Order in Massachusetts, 1815–1880.* Middletown, Conn., 1979.

Sklar, Kathryn Kish. *Catharine Beecher: A Study in American Domesticity.* New Haven, 1973.

Smith, Billy G. "Death and Life in a Colonial Immigrant City: A Demographic Analysis of Philadelphia." *Journal of Economic History* 37 (1977): 863–89.

"Inequality in Late Colonial Philadelphia: A Note on Its Nature and Growth." *William and Mary Quarterly*, 3d ser., 41 (1984): 629–45.

"The Material Lives of Laboring Philadelphians, 1750 to 1800." *William and Mary Quarterly*, 3d ser., 38 (1981): 163–202.

Smith, Thomas E. V. *The City of New York in the Year of Washington's Inauguration, 1789.* New York, 1889.

Smith, W. Wayne. "Jacksonian Democracy on the Chesapeake: Class, Kinship and Politics." *Maryland Historical Magazine* 63 (1968): 55–67.

Snyder, Martin P. *City of Independence: Views of Philadelphia Before 1800.* New York, 1975.

Sobel, Michael E. *Lifestyle and Social Structure: Concepts, Definitions, Analyses.* New York, 1981.

Soltow, Lee. "America's First Progressive Tax." *National Tax Journal* 30 (1977): 53–8.

"Economic Inequality in the United States in the Period from 1790 to 1860." *Journal of Economic History* 31 (1971): 822–39.

"Egalitarian America and Its Inegalitarian Housing in the Federal Period." *Social Science History* 9 (1985): 199–213.

Men and Wealth in the United States: 1850–1870. New Haven, 1975.

"The Wealth, Income, and Social Class of Men in Large Northern Cities of the United States in 1860," in James D. Smith, ed., *The Personal Distribution of Income and Wealth.* National Bureau of Economic Research, *Studies in Income and Wealth*, vol. 39, pp. 233–76. New York, 1975.

Sorin, Gerald. *The New York Abolitionists: A Case Study of Political Radicalism.* Westport, Conn., 1971.

Spann, Edward K. *The New Metropolis: New York City, 1840–1857.* New York, 1981.

Spera, Elizabeth Gray Kogen. "Building for Business: The Impact of Commerce on the City Plan and Architecture of the City of Philadelphia, 1750–1800." Ph.D. dissertation, University of Pennsylvania, 1980.

Srole, Carole. " 'A Position That God Has Not Particularly Assigned to Men': The Feminization of Clerical Work, Boston, 1860–1915." Ph.D. dissertation, University of California at Los Angeles, 1984.

Stansell, Christine. *City of Women: Sex and Class in New York, 1789–1860*. New York, 1986.

Stearns, Peter. "The Middle Class: Toward a Precise Definition." *Comparative Studies in Society and History* 21 (1979): 377–96.

Steffen, Charles G. "Changes in the Organization of Artisan Production in Baltimore, 1790–1820." *William and Mary Quarterly*, 3d ser., 36 (1979): 101–17.

The Mechanics of Baltimore: Workers and Politics in the Age of Revolution, 1763–1812. Urbana, Ill., 1984.

Stern, Mark J. *Society and Family Strategy: Erie County, New York, 1850–1920*. Albany, N.Y., 1987.

Story, Ronald. "Class and Culture in Boston: The Athenaeum, 1807–1860." *American Quarterly* 27 (1975): 178–99.

The Forging of an Aristocracy: Harvard and the Boston Upper Class, 1800–1870. Middletown, Conn., 1980.

Stott, Richard. "British Immigrants and the American 'Work Ethic' in the Mid-Nineteenth Century." *Labor History* 26 (1985): 86–102.

"Hinterland Development and Differences in Work Setting: The New York City Region, 1820–70," in William Pencak and Conrad Edick Wright eds., *New York and the Rise of American Capitalism: Economic Development and the Social and Political History of an American State, 1780–1870*, pp. 45–71. New York, 1989.

"Workers in the Metropolis: New York City, 1820–1860." Ph.D. dissertation, Cornell University, 1983.

Stout, Janis P. *Sodoms in Eden: The City in American Fiction Before 1860*. Westport, Conn., 1976.

Strauss, Anselm L. *Images of the American City*. Glencoe, Ill., 1961.

Summerson, John. *Georgian London*, rev. ed. London, 1970.

Talbott, Page. "Philadelphia Furniture Makers and Manufacturers, 1850–1880," in Kenneth L. Ames, ed., *Victorian Furniture: Essays from a Victorian Society Autumn Symposium*, pp. 85–101. Philadelphia, 1983.

Tatum, George B. *Penn's Great Town: 250 Years of Philadelphia Architecture Illustrated in Prints and Drawings*. Philadelphia, 1961.

Philadelphia Georgian: The City House of Samuel Powel and Some of Its Eighteenth-Century Neighbors. Middletown, Conn., 1976.

Tauranac, John. *Essential New York: A Guide to the History and Architecture of Manhattan's Important Buildings, Parks, and Bridges*. New York, 1979.

Taylor, George Rogers. "The Beginnings of Mass Transportation in Urban America: Parts I and II." *Smithsonian Journal of History* 1 (Summer, 1966): 35–52; 1 (Autumn, 1966): 31–54.

"Gaslight Foster: A New York 'Journeyman Journalist' at Mid-Century." *New York History* 58 (1977): 297–312.

"'Philadelphia in Slices' by George G. Foster." *Pennsylvania Magazine of History and Biography* 93 (1969): 23–72.

The Transportation Revolution: 1815–1860. New York, 1951.

Teaford, Jon C. *The Municipal Revolution in America: Origins of Modern Urban Government, 1650–1825.* Chicago, 1975.

Thernstrom, Stephan. *The Other Bostonians: Poverty and Progress in the American Metropolis, 1880–1970.* Cambridge, Mass., 1973.

Poverty and Progress: Social Mobility in a Nineteenth Century City. Cambridge, Mass., 1964.

Thomas, George E. "Architectural Patronage and Social Stratification in Philadelphia Between 1840 and 1920," in William W. Cutler III and Howard Gillette, Jr., eds., *The Divided Metropolis: Social and Spatial Dimensions of Philadelphia, 1800–1975,* pp. 85–123. Westport, Conn., 1980.

Thomas, John L. "Romantic Reform in America, 1815–1865." *American Quarterly* 17 (1965): 658–81.

Thompson, E. P. "Eighteenth-Century English Society: Class Struggle Without Class?" *Social History* 3 (1978): 133–65.

The Making of the English Working Class. London, 1963.

"Patrician Society, Plebeian Culture." *Journal of Social History* 7 (1974): 382–405.

Tolles, Frederick B. *Meeting House and Counting House: Quaker Merchants of Colonial Philadelphia.* Chapel Hill, 1948.

Tooker, Elva. *Nathan Trotter: Philadelphia Merchant, 1787–1853.* Cambridge, Mass., 1955.

Troen, Selwyn. "Popular Education in Nineteenth-Century St. Louis." *History of Education Quarterly* 13 (1973): 23–40.

Tryon, W. S. "Ticknor and Fields' Publications in the Old Northwest, 1840–1860." *Mississippi Valley Historical Review* 34 (1947–8): 589–610.

Tucker, Robert C. *The Marxian Revolutionary Idea.* New York, 1969.

Tucker, Rufus S. "The Distribution of Income Among Income Taxpayers in the United States, 1863–1935." *Quarterly Journal of Economics* 52 (1938): 547–87.

Tyack, David B. *The One Best System: A History of American Urban Education.* Cambridge, Mass., 1974.

Tyrrell, Ian R. *Sobering Up: From Temperance to Prohibition in Antebellum America, 1800–1860.* Westport, Conn., 1979.

Ueda, Reed. *Avenues to Adulthood: The Origins of the High School and Social Mobility in an American Suburb.* Cambridge, 1987.

Wainwright, Nicholas B. *Philadelphia in the Romantic Age of Lithography.* Philadelphia, 1958.

Walker, Mack. *German Home Towns: Community, State and General Estate.* Ithaca, N.Y., 1971.

Walkowitz, Daniel J. *Worker City, Company Town: Iron and Cotton-Worker Protest in Troy and Cohoes, New York, 1855–84.* Urbana, Ill., 1978.

Wallace, Anthony F. C. *Rockdale: The Growth of an American Village in the Early Industrial Revolution.* New York, 1978.

Walsh, Margaret. "The Democratization of Fashion: The Emergence of the

Women's Dress Pattern Industry." *Journal of American History* 66 (1979): 299–313.

Walsh, Richard. *Charleston's Sons of Liberty: A Study of the Artisans, 1763–1789.* Columbia, S.C., 1959.

Ward, David. *Cities and Immigrants: A Geography of Change in Nineteenth-Century America.* New York, 1971.

"Environs and Neighbours in the 'Two Nations': Residential Differentiation in Mid-Nineteenth-Century Leeds." *Journal of Historical Geography* 6 (1980): 133–62.

Warden, G. B. "The Caucus and Democracy in Colonial Boston." *New England Quarterly* 43 (1970): 19–45.

"The Distribution of Property in Boston, 1692–1775." *Perspectives in American History* 10 (1976): 81–128.

"Inequality and Instability in Eighteenth-Century Boston: A Reappraisal." *Journal of Interdisciplinary History* 6 (1976): 585–620.

Warner, Sam Bass, Jr. *The Private City: Philadelphia in Three Periods of Its Growth.* Philadelphia, 1968.

Streetcar Suburbs: The Process of Growth in Boston, 1870–1900. Cambridge, Mass., 1962.

The Urban Wilderness: A History of the American City. New York, 1972.

Waters, Deborah Dependahl. "'The Workmanship of an American Artist': Philadelphia's Precious Metals Trades and Craftsmen, 1788–1832." Ph.D. dissertation, University of Delaware, 1981.

Weber, Adna Ferrin. *The Growth of Cities in the Nineteenth Century: A Study in Statistics.* New York, 1899.

Wellenreuther, Hermann. "Labor in the Era of the American Revolution: A Discussion of Recent Concepts and Theories." *Labor History* 22 (1981): 573–600.

"Rejoinder [to Gary B. Nash, Billy G. Smith, and Dirk Hoerder]." *Labor History* 24 (1983): 440–54.

Welter, Barbara. "The Cult of True Womanhood: 1820–1860." *American Quarterly* 18 (1966): 151–74.

Westerfield, Ray Bert. "Early History of American Auctions: A Chapter in Commercial History." *Transactions of the Connecticut Academy of Arts and Sciences* 23 (1920): 159–210.

Whitehill, Walter Muir. *Boston: A Topographical History.* Cambridge, Mass., 1968.

Wiebe, Robert. *The Search For Order, 1877–1920.* New York, 1967.

Wilentz, Sean. "Artisan Origins of the American Working Class." *International Labor and Working Class History*, no. 19 (1981): 1–22.

"Artisan Republican Festivals and the Rise of Class Conflict in New York City, 1788–1837," in Michael H. Frisch and Daniel J. Walkowitz, eds., *Working-Class America: Essays on Labor, Community, and American Society,* pp. 37–77. Urbana, Ill., 1983.

Chants Democratic: New York City and the Rise of the American Working Class, 1788–1850. New York, 1984.

Wilkenfeld, Bruce M. "The New York City Common Council, 1689–1800." *New York History* 52 (1971): 249–73.

Williams, Raymond. "Base and Superstructure in Marxist Cultural Theory." *New Left Review*, no. 82 (1973): 3–16.

Keywords: A Vocabulary of Culture and Society. New York, 1976.

Williamson, Jeffrey G. "American Prices and Urban Inequality since 1820." *Journal of Economic History* 36 (1976): 303–33.

"Consumer Behavior in the Nineteenth Century: Carroll D. Wright's Massachusetts Workers in 1875." *Explorations in Entrepreneurial History,* 2d ser., 4 (1967): 98–135.

Williamson, Jeffrey G., and Lindert, Peter H. *American Inequality: A Macroeconomic History.* New York, 1980.

Willis, J., and Wettan, R. "Social Stratification in New York City Athletic Clubs, 1865–1915." *Journal of Sport History* 3 (1976): 45–63.

Wirth, Louis. "Urbanism as a Way of Life." *American Journal of Sociology* 44 (1938): 3–24.

Wolf, Stephanie Grauman. "Documentary Sources for the Study of the Craftsman," in Ian M. G. Quimby, ed., *The Craftsman in Early America,* pp. 17–33. New York, 1984.

Wood, Gordon S. "A Note on Mobs in the American Revolution." *William and Mary Quarterly,* 3d ser., 23 (1966): 635–42.

"Rhetoric and Reality in the American Revolution." *William and Mary Quarterly,* 3d ser., 23 (1966): 3–32.

Woods, Margaret Elizabeth. "The Establishment of a Metropolitan Board of Health in New York City in 1866: A Study of the Process of Social Reform." M.S. thesis, Cornell University, 1981.

Wooster, Harvey A. "Manufacturer and Artisan, 1790–1840." *Journal of Political Economy* 34 (1926): 61–77.

Wright, Carroll D. *The History and Growth of the United States Census. . . .* Washington, D.C., 1900.

Wright, Erik Olin. *Class, Crisis, and the State.* London, 1978.

Wright, Gwendolyn. *Moralism and the Model Home: Domestic Architecture and Cultural Conflict in Chicago, 1873–1913.* Chicago, 1980.

Wright, James E. "The Ethnocultural Model of Voting: A Behavioral and Historical Critique." *American Behavioral Scientist* 16 (1972–3): 653–74.

Young, Alfred F. *The Democratic Republicans of New York: The Origins, 1763–1797.* Chapel Hill, 1967.

"George Robert Twelves Hewes (1742–1840): A Boston Shoemaker and the Memory of the American Revolution." *William and Mary Quarterly,* 3d ser., 38 (1981): 561–623.

"The Mechanics and the Jeffersonians: New York, 1789–1801." *Labor History* 5 (1964): 247–76.

Zachary, Alan M. "Social Disorder and the Philadelphia Elite Before Jackson." *Pennsylvania Magazine of History and Biography* 99 (1975): 288–308.

Index

Abeel, Garret, 41
Academy of Music, 146
Adams, John, 41
Adams Express Company, 268
Adelman, Melvin, 213–14
Alexander, James W., 130–3, 139
Alexander, Ruth, 188
Alger, Cyrus, 71, 335n14
Alter, George, 110, 273
American Anti-Slavery Society, 246
American Art Union, 304
American Federation of Labor, 293
American Hotel, 168
American Mechanic and Working-Man, 131–3
American Penny Magazine, 142
American Philosophical Society, 209
American Society for the Promotion of Temperance, 195
American Society Held at Philadelphia for Promoting Useful Knowledge, 321n41
American Telegraph Company, 268
American Temperance Almanac, 201
American Temperance Society, 195, 202
Ames, Nathaniel, 56
Amory, Cleveland, 296
Amphion, 211–12
Annals of Philadelphia and Pennsylvania in the Olden Time, 56
Anthony, Joseph, 22
Anti-Slavery Society of the City and County of Philadelphia, 205
antislavery reform
  organizational patterns, 205
  political agenda, 205–6
Appleton, D., & Co., 102

Appleton, Nathan, 108, 111, 121, 128, 194
Apprentice's Library, 209
architecture
  commercial, 22–3, 93–8, 341n88, n90
  domestic, 155–7
Aron, Cindy Sondik, 273, 293
associations, 192–3, 387n12
  athletic, 207–9, 213–14, 368n56
  benevolent and reform, 193–9, 202–6
  church, 218–21, 383n69
  economic, 209–11
  ethnic, 209
  fire company, 216, 369n84
  fraternal, 27, 209, 221–9, 371n111
  intellectual and cultural, 206–7, 209, 211–15
  middle class, 211–16
  military, 207, 217
  and multiple leadership of social elites, 209–11
  and organizational didactic, 215–16
  social, 207, 209
  upper class, 206–10
  working class, 213–14, 216–17
Astor, John Jacob, 234
Astor Place Opera House, 145
Astor Place riot, 15, 145
Astrological Diary, 56
Atherton, Lewis, 307, 309
Atlantic Insurance Company, 210
Awl, 189

Bacon, Joseph K., 159–61
Bacon, Robert, 239

Badger, D. D., & Co., 86
Baker, Benjamin, 111
Baldwin, Matthias, 336n24
Ball, Black & Co., 100
Ball, William, 48
Ballou's Pictorial Drawing-Room Companion, 100
Baltimore Association of Tradesmen and Manufacturers, 63
Baltimore Mechanical Society, 34
Baltimore republican societies, 34
Bank of Penn Township, 211
Bank of Pennsylvania, 210
Bank of the United States, 210–11
Barnes, Albert, 221
Barron, Hal S., 308–9
Bartlett, John Russell, 249
Baudouine, Charles O., 69–70
Beecher, Catharine, 182
Bellamy, Edward, 266
Benson, Lee, 211, 253–4
Benson, Susan Porter, 194
Bethune, George W., 202
Bigelow & Mead, 114
Binford, Henry, 164
Birch, Thomas, 25
Birch, William, 25, 320n34
Bishop, Isabella Lucy Bird, 140
Bledstein, Burton, 4
Blewett, Mary, 188–9
Blumin's Law, 316n42
Blunt, E. M., 93
boarders in households, by class, 363n154
Bogardus, James, 98
Boggs, William G., 197
Bonomi, Patricia U., 60
bookkeeping
  in 18th century, 40–1
  in 19th century, 70
Booth, J. C., 70
Booth, J. C., & Co., 95
Booth, Nathaniel, 303
Boston Athenaeum, 206–7
Boston Mercantile Library Association, 105
Botein, Stephen, 30
Bowery Theater, 145, 149
boxing and working-class culture, 217
Boyer, Paul, 5, 194–5, 205

Bradley, Nathan A., 98
Brady, Benjamin, 151
Brasher, Abraham, 60
Braudel, Fernand, 14
Brewster & Co., 70
Bridenbaugh, Carl, 22, 39
Bridges, Amy, 254–5
Briggs, Charles F., 15
Brighton Cricket Club (New York City), 213
Bristed, Charles Astor, 234, 236
Bristol, D. W., 228–9
British Mechanic's and Labourer's Handbook, 110–11, 139, 144, 146–7
Brooks, Edwin A., 95, 114
Brooks, James, 151
Brooks, Lorin, 71, 114
Brooks Brothers, 81, 89
Brown, Isaac, 219
Brown, James L., 247–8
Browne, Junius Henri, 14–15, 283–4
Buckley, Peter, 14
building societies, 382n58
Burn, James Dawson, 144, 149, 161
Burns, Rex, 129
Burr, Aaron, 202
Burstein, Alan, 166
Bushnell, Horace, 182
Butcher, Job, 21
Butter Cake Dick's, 146

Cadwalader family, 209
Campbell, Felix, 162
Campbell, William, 159–61
Campion, Joseph H., 170
Canfield, Brother & Co., 102–3
Carey, Mathew, 64
Cayton, Andrew, 257
Century Club, 207
Chandler, Alfred D., 68, 78–9, 82, 269
Chanfrau, Francis, 145
Channing, William Ellery, 243
Chatham Theater, 144–5
Cheesman, Oscar, 114
Chickering, Jonas, 213, 334n13
Child, Lydia Maria, 129, 186, 288–90, 310
Christ Church, 92–3
Chrystler, Jacob, 57

Clark, Lewis A., 160
class
  and class awareness, 285–90,
    315n35
  and ethnicity, 249–53, 295–6,
    375n39, n44
  and ethnocultural political pat-
    terns, 253–6, 376n55
  as experience, 11–12
  in industrial satellite cities, 299–
    302
  in language, 18–20, 240–9, 286–90,
    296–7, 374n34, 386n104
  polarization, 14–16, 286–7, 317n50
  in rural communities, 308–10
  in small cities, 302–5
  in small towns, 306–8
  see also Giddens, Anthony; mid-
    dle class; rank; upper class;
    working class
Class Structure of the Advanced Societies, 8
Classes in Contemporary Capitalism, 7
Clawson, Mary Ann, 228
Clough, Willard, 213
Cobbett, William, 50
Cochran, Thomas C., 78–9
Colden, Cadwallader, 17–18, 33
Cole, Arthur H., 21
Colonial Craftsman, 22
Columbian Foundry and Mill Stone
  Factory, 352n17
Commercial Hotel, 168
commercial theory of value, 128
Commerford, John, 125
consumption patterns
  in 18th-century cities, 39
  in 19th-century cities, 111–12,
    138–44, 146–58, 351n8, n24
  as revealed in 18th-century estate
    inventories, 52–7
  as revealed in 19th-century estate
    inventories, 158–63
  see also domestic living space
Cooke, Joseph, 23
Cooke's Folly, 23, 25
Cooper, James Fenimore, 151, 241
Cornelius & Baker, 87
Cott, Nancy, 183–4, 187
Countryman, Edward, 27
Cradle of the Middle Class, 302

Crystal Fount, 202–4
Cumming, Charles, 87
Curtis, George William, 234, 236

Dahrendorf, Ralf, 9
Damon, Samuel G., 77–8
dancing assemblies, 26
Davis, Susan G., 217
Davy, William, 21
Day, Alan, 61
Day, Katherine, 61
Decker, Peter, 74
"deference" defined, 322n50
  see also rank
DeLancey, James, 28
DeLancey family, 27–8
Delaware & Hudson Canal Com-
  pany, 387n16
Delaware Fire Company (Philadel-
  phia), 216, 321n41
Delmonico's Restaurant, 146
Democratic Vistas, 246
Dempsey, Joseph, 52
DeVault, Ileen, 292
Dickerson's hat store, 141
Dictionary of Americanisms, 249
Diderot, Denis, 22, 339n63
Dodge, Amos, 60
Dohrmann, A., 69
domestic living space
  in 18th-century Philadelphia, 42–6
  in 19th-century cities, 155–7
Doucet, Michael, 15
Douglas, Ann, 183
Douty, William, 55
Downing, Andrew Jackson, 182
Doyle, Don Harrison, 215, 306–7,
  309
Driggs, L. S., 89
Du Simitière, Pierre, 57
Dudden, Faye, 158, 185
Dun, R. G., & Co., 114, 116, 161
Dunscomb, Daniel, 60

Eckford, Henry, 214
Eckford Club (Brooklyn), 213–14
Edwards, Charles, 80, 128
Edwards, George W., 160–1, 357n85
Elsworth, Henry, 151
Emerson, Ralph Waldo, 138
Employment Society, 194

Encyclopédie, 22
evangelical united front, 193
Evans, David, 41, 70
Evans, George Henry, 125–6
Everett, Edward, 128
Everett, Henry L., 261–2
Excelsior Club, 214
Exploring Club, 300

failure in business
among master craftsmen, 115–16
among nonmanual businessmen,
115
Faler, Paul, 3, 299–302
Faragher, John Mack, 308
Farmers' and Mechanics' Bank, 210
Father Tammany's Almanac, 56
Federal Almanack, for . . . 1794, 29
federal census as historical document, 117, 346nn34–6
Federal Direct Tax of 1798, 42,
330n119, 354n43
in Philadelphia, 42, 327n103,
328nn104–5, 329n107, n110,
n119
federal income tax of 1863 as histor-
ical document, 345n33
Fenians, 295–6
First City Troop, 207, 209
First Company of Philadelphia Mili-
tia Artillery, 34
First Presbyterian Church of Ken-
sington (Philadelphia), 219
First Presbyterian Church of Phila-
delphia, 220–1, 321n39
First Presbyterian Church of South-
wark (Philadelphia), 219
Fisher, John, 55
fishing clubs, 26
Foner, Eric, 36
Forbes, William, 41
Forrest, Edwin, 145
Forsyth, James C., 388n20
Forsyth, Presley B., 161–2
Forsyth & Brother, 161
Foster, George G., 15, 111, 143,
145–6, 164, 234, 236, 239, 249,
253, 284
Foster, H. L., 70
Fourth Presbyterian Church of Phil-
adelphia, 220–1, 321n39

Fox, Edward, 70, 75
Frank Leslie's Illustrated Newspaper,
149, 186, 304
Franklin Barge Club (Philadelphia),
208
Franklin Club (Lynn, Mass.), 300
Franklin Institute, 135, 209
Franklin Literary Union, 212
Frazer, Joseph, 53–5
Freed, Ward, and Freed, 212
Freedley, Edwin T., 75, 108
Freedman, Stephen, 214
French-Canadian Political Club, 296
Friedman, Lawrence J., 205
Frost, John, 130–2

Galbraith, Andrew J., 153, 355n65
Gay, Aaron R., 114, 116
Geisler, Charles, 162
General Society of Mechanics and
Tradesmen, 135
Giddens, Anthony, 11, 241, 251
on class awareness, 9–10
on class structuration, 8–9
Gilbert, Thomas, 52
Gilkeson, John S., Jr., 134–5, 196
Ginna, Elizabeth, 13
Girard, Stephen, 21
Girard Bank, 210
Gladden, Washington, 266
Glance at New York in 1848, A, 111
Glassberg, Eudice, 272–3
*Gleason's Pictorial Drawing-Room
Companion*, 100, 102, 105
Gnomologian Society, 300
Godey's Lady's Book, 304
Goetting, William, 53–4
Gold and Silver Smiths' Temper-
ance Society, 198
Gompers, Samuel, 149, 251, 315n35
Good Samaritans, 204
Goodrich, Samuel Griswold, 129
Gorn, Elliott, 217–18, 233
Gould, Frederick, 114–15
Gould, J. E., Great Piano and Melo-
deon Emporium, 13, 185, 351n8
Gowans, William, 13, 113–14, 116,
150
Grace Church, 219
Graham, Robert McCoskry, 113–14
Graisbury, Joseph, 12, 41

Gray, A. W., & Co., 86
Gray, Nathaniel, 198
Graydon, Alexander, 32–3
Greenberg, Brian, 225
Griffen, Clyde, 120–1, 133
Griffen, Sally, 120–1, 133
Griffin, Clifford S., 193, 198
Grimké, Frederick, 243–5
Grinnell, Charles A., 77–8
Grosh, Aaron B., 202, 224–5, 229
Gunn, Thomas Butler, 151

Hagen, Ernest, 69
Haines, Joshua, 41
Haines, Michael, 272
Hale, Sarah Josepha, 182
Halttunen, Karen, 184
Handel and Haydn Society, 212–13
Hannold, Simeon, 162
Hardenbergh, Jacob B., 226
Harper, James, 236
Harper's New Monthly Magazine, 89,
    107, 127–8, 160, 179, 182–6, 232,
    234, 262, 268–70, 274, 284, 304
Harriott, Edgar, 151
Hartz, Louis, 2, 4, 16
Harvard College, 235
Hazen, Edward, 80, 84, 261
Heighton, William, 122, 125, 127,
    348n53
Henkels, George, 83
Henretta, James, 27
Hershberg, Theodore, 110, 273, 276
Hewitt, Jane, 12
Hewitt, Nancy A., 193
Hexter, J. H., 7
Hibernian Society, 209
Hinckle, Charles, 162
Hirsch, Susan, 188, 254
Historical Society of Pennsylvania,
    209, 211
Hoffman, William, 13, 77, 112, 114
Hoit, Ichabod, 151
Holland Land Company, 210
Holt's Hotel, 150
Home for the Friendless, 194
Homes for the People, 155
Homestead Act, 348n64
Homewood, Josiah, 220
Hone, Philip, 128
Horn, B. F., 114

Hose Company No. 13, 203
House Carpenters' Temperance So-
    ciety, 198
House of Refuge, 211
Howell, A., 41
Hughes, Enoch, 53–4
Hunt, Freeman, 80, 105, 128
Hunter, Robert, 21
Hunt's Merchants' Magazine, 78, 80,
    82–3, 105, 116, 128–30, 150, 215,
    246
Hyde de Neuville, Baroness, 340n86

Illustrated News, 142–3
income
    of 18th-century craftsmen, 40,
        327n99
    of 19th-century manual workers,
        109–10, 272, 274, 290, 342n6,
        343n7, n9, 380n37, n40, 384n87
    of 19th-century master craftsmen,
        116, 273–5
    of 19th-century nonmanual busi-
        nessmen, 113–16, 345n20
    of 19th-century salaried workers,
        112–13, 116, 273–5, 291, 344n17,
        380n40, 384n87
industrial concentration, 259
Ingersoll, Joseph R., 210–11
Ingersoll family, 209–10
Ingraham, Joseph Holt, 15
Insurance Company of North
    America, 23
Irving, John T., 197

Jaher, Frederic Cople, 194, 234–5
Janeway and Company, 86
Janvier, Joseph, 54
Jayne, David, 98
Johnson, Dale L., 7
Johnson, Paul E., 5
Jones, Alice Hanson, 39, 52, 55–7
Jones & Shepard, 114
Jones Hotel, 168–9
Josselyn and Churchill, 89
Journal of Health, 245
Judson, E. Z. C., 15
Juvenile Miscellany, 129

Katz, Michael, 15
Kearney, Edmund, 52

Kinkelein, Arnold, 153, 356n65
Kirsch, George B., 208, 213
Kleppner, Paul, 253–4
Knickerbocker Base Ball Club, 213
Knights, Peter, 120–1
Kocka, Jürgen, 293, 295
Kornblith, Gary John, 134–5, 248
Kuhn family, 209

La Forge, Abiel, 271
labor theory of value, 122
Lady Marian Society, 203
Lafever, Minard, 95
Laguerenne, P. L., 210
Lamb, John, 61
Lambert, John, 20, 37, 39
Laurie, Bruce, 3, 110, 273
Lawrence, William, 41
Leach, William, 32–3
Leavitt, Joshua, 197, 236
Lee, William H., 114
Lehman, James A., 160
leisure institutions, 144–6
Letters from New York, 186
Library Company of Philadelphia,
    209
Linnean Society, 209
Live Oak Lodge, 371n111
Livesay, Harold, 78, 82–3
Livingston family, 27
Lize the Bowery g'hal, 111, 143–4,
    249
Lombard, Charles, 220
Long, Clarence, 272
Looking Backward, 266
Lord, Eleazar, 197
Lord & Taylor, 81, 98
Lott, Abraham P., 60
Lukens, Isaac, 161–2
Lynes, Russell, 185
Lynn Academy, 300
Lynn High School, 300

McAllister, John, 45
McCabe, James Dabney, 14–16, 283,
    287
McDougall, Alexander, 61
McGlone, Robert, 186
McGrath, H., 116
Mackay, John, 334n13
Mackey, Albert G., 225–6, 229

McPherson, Henry, 340n84
Macready, William, 145
Macy, R. H., & Co., 270–1
Macy, Rowland, 271, 274
Magazine of the Franklin Literary
    Union, 212
Maier, J. Mathew, 69
Main, Jackson T., 40
Main Street on the Middle Border, 307
Manhattan Insurance Company, 197
manual work
    environments, 83–91, 337n31,
        339n63
    and occupational taxonomy, 260–1
    and proprietorship, 75–6, 336n29
    in relation to domestic life, 22,
        45–6
    see also working class
Marine Temperance Society, 198
Mariners' Church, 198
Martin Edgar W., 141
Marx, Karl, 5, 11–12
Masons, Free and Accepted Order
    of, 209, 221
    class patterns in, 225–8
    and relation to domesticity, 228–9
Master Charley, 179–83, 186, 232
Masters, Carl, 236
Masters, Harry, 236
Matteawan Manufacturing Com-
    pany, 199–200
Mechanics and Manufacturers in the
    Early Industrial Revolution, 299
Mechanics' Bank, 210
mechanics' committees, 58–60
Mechanic's Free Press, 122–6, 242–3
mechanics' interest, 62–3, 135–6
Mechanic's Library Company of
    Philadelphia, 122
mercantile library associations, 214
Merry's Museum, 129
middle class
    in American usage, 2
    artisan-manufacturers in, 134–6
    as defined by American histori-
        ans, 4, 5, 157, 361n135
    distinguished from business class,
        137
    and domesticity, 139, 182–8,
        360n126, 361n131, 362n145
    gender roles and tensions in,

183–5, 191, 360n121, 361n131, 362n137, nn141–2
in Marxist theory, 5–8
and social elevation of nonmanual workers, 129–30, 133
in terminology of historians of 18th-century America, 315n40
in 20th century, 297
see also class; middling rank; nonmanual work
Middling Interest, 249, 256–7
middling rank (social location in 18th-century cities), 34–8
Miller, Roger, 166, 176, 178, 279–80
Mills, C. Wright, 4, 7
Modern Builder's Guide, 95
Monks, Joseph, 355n65
Moore, Thomas H., 170
Morgan, William, 224
Morrison, John, 287–8
Mose the Bowery b'hoy, 111, 143–5, 233, 249, 253
Mott, Samuel C., 160
Mt. Horeb Lodge, 371n111
Mullen, William J., 198
Murphy, Dennis, 153
Musical Fund Society, 209

Nash, Beau, 219
Nash, Gary, 14, 19, 26, 28, 40, 63
Natural History Society (Lynn, Mass.), 300
Neave, Samuel, 52, 57
New Brighton Mechanics' Club (New York City), 213
New England Convention of Workingmen, 126
new working class history, 66
New York City Sons of Temperance, 204
New York City Temperance Society, 196–9, 202–3, 233, 236, 246
New York Common Council, 27
New-York Journal, 28, 34
New York Mercantile Library Association, 215
New-York Society Library, 321n41
New York State Temperance Society, 199
New-York Sugar Refining Company, 89

New York Times, 247
New York Tribune, 247–8
New York Yacht Club, 207
Newman, Edward H., 98
nonimportation, 62
nonmanual sector, size of, 73–4, 267–8, 335n22, 378n19
nonmanual work, 67–8
environments, 83–107, 340n84
feminization of, in late 19th century, 291–2
feminization of, in post–Civil War era, 269–71, 379n33
and occupational taxonomy, 68–71, 261, 266–7
as perceived in post–Civil War era, 268–9
proletarianization of, in late 19th century, 290–5
proletarianization of, in post–Civil War era, 270–1
and proprietorship, 74–5
in relation to domestic life, 21–2, 383n68
and salaried employment, 76–8
and specialization, 78–83
see also middle class
Norris, John D., 198
North, S. N. D., 261
North End Caucus, 61
Novelty Works, 89–91

Oakes, Joseph G., 240
Oakford, Charles, 74, 102, 211–12, 237–8
Oaks, Robert F., 63
occupational mobility, 119–21, 271, 291–2, 379n35
occupational structure in 18th-century cities, 30
Odd Fellows, International Order of, 221
history, 223–5
mixing of classes in, 225
and relation to domesticity, 228–9
Odd Fellow's Amulet, 228–9
Odd-Fellow's Manual, 224
Olton, Charles, 40, 62
Olympic Theater, 145
Organ, 204
organizations, see associations

Orphan Asylum, 194
Ossowski, Stanislaw, 8
Otis, Harrison Gray, 256

Pack, Janet Rothenberg, 165, 173, 358n107
Panorama of Professions and Trades, 84
Park Theater, 144
Parker, Theodore, 129
Parley's Magazine, 129
Parrish, Isaac, 22
Paterson Machine Company, 86
patronage, *see* rank
Payne, John Howard, 182
Peck, Charles, 114
Pennsylvania Academy of Fine Arts, 209, 211
Pennsylvania Fire Company, 216
Pennsylvania Packet, 29
Pennsylvania Town and Country-man's Almanack, for . . . 1773, 29
People's Stove Works, 86
Perkins, Frederick B., 139
Perlmann, Joel, 292
Pessen, Edward, 194
Pettes, Henry, & Company, 87
Philadelphia Atheneum, 209
Philadelphia *Aurora*, 18–19, 31, 58, 64
Philadelphia City Anti-Slavery Society, 205–6
Philadelphia Club, 209
Philadelphia Common Council, 64
Philadelphia Contributorship for the Insurance of Houses from Loss by Fire, 210
Philadelphia Corporation, 27
Philadelphia Cricket Club, 207–8, 234
Philadelphia Dancing Assembly, 209
Philadelphia Hose Company, 216
Philadelphia Mechanic's Union of Trade Associations, 242, 244–5
Philadelphia Orphan Asylum, 205
Philadelphia Public Ledger, 277
Philadelphia Quoit Club, 208
Philadelphia Savings Fund Society, 210–11
Philadelphia Social History Project,

165, 347n37, 358n106, n110, 363n154
Philadelphia Society for the Promotion of Agriculture, 209
Phillips, John, 256
Phoenix Clothing Bazaar, 141
Pierce, Bessie, 274
Pierce, Henry, 212–13, 239–40, 285, 383n68
Pike, Stephen, 340n82
Pile, Wilson H., 220
Pollard, Calvin, 341n90
Porcupine's Gazette, 50
Porter, Glenn, 78, 82–3
Potts, William B., 160
Poulantzas, Nicos, 7
Prang, Louis, 263–5, 272
Pray, John H., and Sons, 98
Private City, 43
probate records as historical documents, 158, 326n86
Providence Association of Mechanics and Manufacturers, 134–5, 247
Pulszky, Francis, 240–1
Pulszky, Theresa, 240–1

Quimby, Ian, 71
Quincy, Josiah, 256–7
Quincy Market (Boston), 93

Raguet, Condy, 210
rank
    contrasted with class, 17–20, 316n41
    and 18th-century occupational structure, 30–3
    in 18th-century politics, 27–8, 58–64
    in 18th-century social relations, 26–30
    in language, 17–20
    see also middling rank
Rankin, A., & Co., 103
Rathbone, Samuel, 197
Rechabites, 204
Reliance Fire Company, 369n84
Retail Clerks' National (International) Protective Association, 292–3
Richardson, Edward, 198

Richardson, James, 286–7
Ritter, Abraham, 20–1, 50
Rochefoucault Liancourt, Duc de la,
    21, 39, 55
Rodgers, Peter, 162
Rogers, William D., 87
Ross, Steven, 296
Round Table, 212
Rowe, William, Jr., 115
rural ideal, 276
Ryan, Mary P., 5, 11, 74, 76, 139,
    187, 190, 302–4
Ryerson, Richard Alan, 59, 63

St. Andrew's Society, 209
St. George Cricket Club, 208
saloons as working-class institu-
    tions, 217–18
Sands, Daniel H., 204
Sanford's minstrel theater, 146
Sargent, Samuel, 197
Sarmiento, John, 175
Saturday Club, 207
Schlicht & Field Company, 293
school attendance patterns
    in antebellum era, 189–90,
        364n159
    in late 19th century, 292, 385n91
Schreiber, Lee L., 209
Schuylkill Fishing Company, 209
Scientific American, 263
Scorgie, William, 116
Scribner's Monthly, 269–71, 275,
    286–7
Sears, Isaac, 61
Second Great Awakening, 193
Second Presbyterian Church of
    Philadelphia, 321n39
Seven Star Tavern, 223
Seymour, Harold, 213–14
Shaw, Sarah Blake, 288–9, 310
Sheaff, William, 162
Shi, David, 138
Silsbee Street Debating Club, 300
Silvers, William, 162
Simmel, Georg, 222–3, 229
Singer, I. M., 102
Siracusa, Carl, 108–9
Siry, Joseph, 166, 176, 178, 279–80
Sketch Club, 207
Smith, Billy G., 40

Smith, John Rubens, 340n86
Smith, Matthew Hale, 268–9, 286
Smith, Sarah, 160
Smith, Stephen, 340n82
Smith-Rosenberg, Carroll, 194
Social Library, 300
social networks
    defined, 230–2, 372n1
    in 19th-century cities, 232–40
Social Order of a Frontier Community,
    306
Social Reformer, 126
Social Structure of Revolutionary
    America, 40
Social Union, 300
Society of the Sons of St. George,
    209
Sons of Liberty, 28, 60
Sons of Temperance, 204
South Boston Iron Foundry, 71
Southwark Bank, 211
Spann, Edward, 149–50, 157
Spera, Elizabeth, 23
Spring Garden Fire Insurance Com-
    pany, 210
Srole, Carole, 271, 291
Stamp Act crisis, 17, 61
Stansell, Christine, 189, 233
Stearns, Jonathan F., 128, 136
Stein, John Philip, 54
Stern, Mark, 15
Steuart, Robert, 63
Stevenson, Christopher, 54
Stewart, A. T., 80–1, 86
Stiles, Edward, 153, 355n64
Stites, George, 162
Stone Cutters' Temperance Society,
    198
Stoops, James, 54
Story, Ronald, 206–7, 235
Stott, Richard, 111, 163, 217
Stratton, Benjamin W., 153
Strickland, William, 92
suburbanization
    in antebellum era, 149–50, 164–5,
        176–7
    in late 19th century, 383n69
    in post–Civil War era, 275–6, 279–
        80, 285
Sumner, Charles, 105
Sumner, William Graham, 266,
    286

Sunshine and Shadow in New York, 268
Sweeney's Restaurant, 146

Tack, Elizabeth, 153
Tack, John, 153, 170
Tailer, Edward, 112, 114, 116
Tappan, Arthur, 93, 194, 197–8, 236–7
Tappan, Lewis, 93, 194
tax assessment rolls as historical documents, 42, 326n86, 327n103
Taylors Company of Philadelphia, 25
Temperance Almanac (1836), 201
Temperance Recorder, 199–201
temperance reform
  and class, 204
  organizational patterns in 1830s, 195–9
  social motifs in 1830s, 199–202
  Washingtonian, 188, 202–4
Tenth Presbyterian Church of Philadelphia, 221
Third Presbyterian Church of Philadelphia, 220–1, 321n39
Thomas, Alfred, 151
Thomas, George, 357n85
Thompson, E. P., 4, 12
Thompson, Jonah, 160
Thompson, Smith, 197
Those Who Stayed Behind, 308
Three Loggerheads Tavern, 223
Tiffany, Fite & Co., 78
Tiffany, Fite, & Grinnell, 78
Tobey, Simeon, 359n111
Tocqueville, Alexis de, 2
Todd, John, 136
Toland, Robert, 210
Tomes, Francis, and Sons, 95, 98
Town, Ithiel, 93
Trinity Church, 321n39
Trollope, Frances, 183
Trotter, Joseph, 345n20
Trotter, Nathan, 236–7, 345n20
Trotter, Nathan, & Co., 345n20
Tuesday Club, 209
Tyrrell, Ian, 196, 203

Ueda, Reed, 292
Union Club, 207

United States Hose Company, 369n84
University of Illinois, 307
University of Pennsylvania board of trustees, 209, 211
upper class
  as defined by American historians, 3
  and domesticity, 185–6
  in 20th century, 296
  see also class
Urban Establishment, 234
urban spatial structure
  in antebellum era, 85–7, 134–5, 145–55, 163–79, 359n112, n118, 360n120
  in 18th century, 20–1, 24–5, 46–51, 330n115
  in post–Civil War era, 275–85
  see also suburbanization
urbanization, 298

Van Rensselaer family, 302
Vollmer, Gotlieb, 69–70

Wagner & McGuigan, 352n17
Walker, Francis Amasa, 260–1, 266–7, 272, 286–7
Walker, Robert, 54
Walkowitz, Daniel, 295
Waln, Lewis, 210
Waln family, 210
Warner, Sam Bass, Jr., 4, 43, 68, 157–8, 163, 275–6, 280, 285
Washington, George, 41
Washington Fire Company (Philadelphia), 369n84
Washingtonian Pocket Companion, 202, 224
Watson, John Fanning, 56
wealth distribution
  in 18th-century cities, 38–40
  in 19th-century Philadelphia, 117–19
Webb, Nathan, 12, 32, 239
Weber, Max, 11
Weccacoe Engine Company (Philadelphia), 216
Weccacoe Hose Company (Philadelphia), 216
Weil, Henry, 69–70, 75
Weld, Isaac, 39

Welsh Society, 209
What Shall I Learn?, 261
What Social Classes Owe to Each Other, 266
Wheat, Dr., 240
Wheatley, Richard, 268–9, 272
Wheeler, Gervase, 155
White, Solomon, 24
White Collar, 8
Whitman, Walt, 1–2, 17, 137, 149, 245–6
Wildey, Thomas, 223
Wilentz, Sean, 66–7, 76, 109–10, 135, 145, 203
Wirth, Louis, 13
Wishart, Thomas, 50
Wistar Party, 209
Wister, William Rotch, 208
Work, Robert D., 279–80
work as perceived in post–Civil War era, 260–7
    see also manual work; nonmanual work

working class
    counterimage of despised worker, 126–7
    as defined by American historians, 3
    and domesticity, 188–9, 363n151
    and image of respectable worker, 108–9, 122, 126–7
    petty proprietors in, 133–4
    and social degradation of manual workers, 121–33
    in 20th century, 296
    youthfulness of, 111, 344n14
    see also class; manual work
Working Man's Advocate, 125–6
Working People and Their Employers, 266
Wright, Carroll D., 261
Wright, Gwendolyn, 274

yellow fever committees in Philadelphia, 64
Young Mechanic, 130–1
Young Merchant, 130–1

Printed in the United States
31586LVS00003B/16-30